T0270502

CROWN, CLOAK, AND DAGGER

Georgetown Studies in Intelligence History

Series Editors: Christopher Moran, Mark Phythian, and Mark Stout

Titles in the Series
Canadian Military Intelligence: Operations and Evolution from the October Crisis to the War in Afghanistan
David A. Charters

RICHARD J. ALDRICH
AND RORY CORMAC

CROWN, CLOAK, AND DAGGER

THE BRITISH MONARCHY
AND SECRET INTELLIGENCE
FROM VICTORIA TO ELIZABETH II

GEORGETOWN UNIVERSITY PRESS / WASHINGTON, DC

The publisher is not responsible for third-party websites or their content. URL links were active at time of publication.

Library of Congress Cataloging-in-Publication Data

Names: Aldrich, Richard J. (Richard James), 1961– author. | Cormac, Rory, author.
Title: Crown, cloak, and dagger : the British monarchy and secret intelligence from Victoria to Elizabeth II / Richard J. Aldrich and Rory Cormac.
Description: Washington, DC : Georgetown University Press, [2023] | Series: Georgetown studies in intelligence history | Includes bibliographical references and index.
Identifiers: LCCN 2022049167 (print) | LCCN 2022049168 (ebook) | ISBN 9781647123710 (hardcover) | ISBN 9781647123727 (ebook)
Subjects: LCSH: Intelligence service—Great Britain—History. | Monarchy—Great Britain—History. | Queens—Great Britain—History. | Great Britain—Kings and rulers—History.
Classification: LCC UB251.G7 A52 2023 (print) | LCC UB251.G7 (ebook) | DDC 327.1241—dc23/eng/20230524
LC record available at https://lccn.loc.gov/2022049167
LC ebook record available at https://lccn.loc.gov/2022049168

♾ This paper meets the requirements of ANSI/NISO Z39.48-1992 (Permanence of Paper).

24 23   9 8 7 6 5 4 3 2 First printing

Printed in the United States of America

Cover design by Spencer Fuller, Faceout Studio
Interior design by BookComp, Inc.

Contents

Contents

The British Royal Family Tree Since Victoria

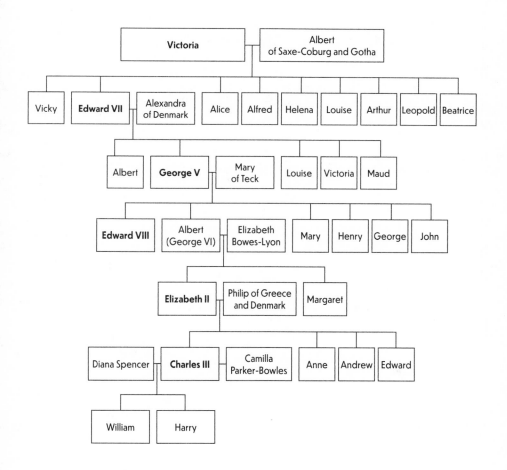

Introduction

007

On her Majesty's secret service.
—Ian Fleming

On a balmy summer evening in late July 2012, the world's most famous intelligence officer arrived at Buckingham Palace in an iconic black cab. Dressed in his trademark tuxedo, he skipped up the central red staircase and, flanked by the royal corgis, entered a gilded room. At a desk in the corner sat Queen Elizabeth II. She kept him waiting; he glanced at the clock and coughed politely.

"Good evening, Mr. Bond," she said turning to face him. "Good evening, your majesty," he quietly responded.

James Bond followed her as she made her way down the stairs and headed toward a helicopter waiting on the lawn outside. Moments later, Agent 007 and the queen jumped from the helicopter in a dramatic parachute drop down toward the Olympic Stadium in East London. The crowd gasped as they vanished from sight, before Elizabeth reappeared, wearing the same pink dress, in the royal box. The sequence formed the highlight of the Olympic Games' opening ceremony.

Organized by the Oscar-winning director Danny Boyle and partly filmed at Buckingham Palace, this masterpiece of deception involved the real queen, stunt doubles, and cameo roles for three royal corgis, Monty, Holly, and Willow. In over fifty years of Bond feature films, the paths of 007 and the Royal Family have frequently crossed. Prince Charles visited the Bond set at Pinewood Studios to the west of London in 2019. Photographs showed him inspecting and chatting with James Bond himself. More discreetly, producers borrowed some of the most striking interior designs featured in the iconic film *Goldfinger* from Princess Margaret's palace. The early 007 films were known for their conspicuous consumption, high fashion, exotic air travel, and the latest designs. Margaret's abode fitted right in.

Few realize that these momentary connections are far from fantasy and instead capture a fleeting glance of Britain's most secret partnership—the

British monarchy and its secret services. Surprisingly, the queen, like her predecessors, was no stranger to the real secret service. Shortly after ascending the throne in 1952, while discussing a troublesome Middle Eastern leader with officials, she quipped about assassinating him.

Elizabeth II knew more state secrets than any living person—and, unlike her prime ministers, she kept them. The queen was a human library of intelligence history. She knew about the British nuclear weapons program at a remarkably early stage. And she knew more about the Soviet mole, Anthony Blunt, still in her employment as surveyor of the queen's pictures, than even the prime minister did. Later, she invited the CIA's head of operations to Buckingham Palace to ask him how "my boys" were treating him. The senior CIA officer was surprised that Elizabeth knew about his real job at all.

The queen spent time in the Special Air Service (SAS) "Killing House" in Hereford, where elite special forces hone their deadly skills. She stood unflinching for the most part as operators trained with live ammunition for hostage rescue operations. Throughout her long reign, Elizabeth met many heads of Britain's intelligence agencies. When Stella Rimington, the first publicly named leader of MI5, the domestic security agency, attended lunch at Buckingham Palace, the royal household helped her to escape via an inconspicuous exit in order to avoid the assembled reporters desperate to know what a monarch might say to a spy chief.

The Royal Family and the secret services have much in common. They are two of Britain's most important institutions. They are small and secretive, seen by many as "the establishment." They feature prominently in the popular imagination. They are heavily mythologized and often misunderstood.

"M" was the code name of 007's legendary boss—the head of British intelligence— but equally it might as well have stood for "Majesty." This book not only uncovers the secret relationship between the royals and the intelligence services; it also argues that it was, above all, three royal women—Elizabeth I, Victoria, and Elizabeth II—who learned how to wield intelligence power and proved to be Britain's best spy chiefs. Elizabeth I was the pioneer and stayed on top of her intelligence community by running several rival spy empires, royal favorite against favorite. She not only took detailed interest in espionage and codebreaking but also enthused over both covert action and torture. The queen herself pursued "covert meanes" to undermine her most deadly enemy, King Philip II of Spain.

Crowned in November 1558, Elizabeth I ruled for almost half a century during a particularly turbulent era, when the need for royal spies was urgent. Europe was embroiled in what we might almost think of as a religious "Cold

War," driven by differences in ideology that potentially undermined notions of national loyalty. Plots and paranoia were rife. Elizabeth fought back with no fewer than four spy chiefs—William Cecil, Francis Walsingham, the Earl of Essex, and the Earl of Leicester—the last one also serving as her favorite and would-be lover. All four cooperated but also competed with each other to build complex intelligence operations directed largely at English Catholics either at home or plotting in Europe, together with proxy armies in the Netherlands.

The first significant covert operation under Elizabeth I was the kidnapping of John Story. An English Catholic and propagandist, he had fled to exile in the Netherlands, where he plotted against Elizabeth while working for the Spanish. Elizabeth's advisers ordered agents to kidnap Story and bring him home for questioning. The wily agents lured Story into searching their boat, then trapped him on board, and whisked him away to interrogation, punishment, and finally execution. Elizabeth's spies kidnapped others across Europe by using their targets' wives as bait, causing panic among her enemies on the continent in the process.

The main focus of plotting was Mary Queen of Scots, a Catholic who had been ejected from Scotland by Presbyterians in 1567. Mary was kept under house arrest in England and, after eighteen years of secret scheming, she was finally brought to trial. Her execution depended on evidence carefully gathered, indeed embellished, by Walsingham's army of spies, codebreakers, and agents provocateurs.

Rather as Elizabeth feared, Mary's execution did not slow European efforts to overthrow her. Increasingly complex and costly intelligence operations were still necessary, and their efforts provided early warning of the Spanish Armada in 1588 and exposed several additional covert moves against the queen. Between 1593 and 1594, agents uncovered an alleged plot by the queen's own physician, Dr. Rodrigo Lopez. Although it is unclear if he was actually guilty, Lopez had been in secret contact with the Spanish court and faced accusations of scheming to assassinate Elizabeth. After hesitating for three months, she sent Lopez and two of his friends to be hanged, drawn, and quartered in 1594.

It is hard to escape the conclusion that Elizabeth not only shaped the shadowy world of intelligence but was also somewhat degraded by it. She came to love torture and, consorting with her perverted priest hunter and notoriously zealous inquisitor Richard Topcliffe, she demanded ever more ghastly techniques and barbarous public executions to scare traitors. But her worst weak spot as a spymaster was money. She turned to alchemy to try to fund her prodigious security empire, an enterprise that predictably failed to deliver. Eventually, to save money, she disbanded her best spies after the defeat of the Armada—they died penniless and suffered royal ingratitude—and thereafter, the vast and expensive secret state she had created withered away.

Elizabeth died in March 1603, bequeathing a century of popish plots and public paranoia to her successors. Some were more interested in intelligence than others; most preferred propaganda to a more professional use of espionage. Intelligence rose and fell on the whims of the monarch. After the civil war, for example, Charles II employed more of a bounty hunter than an intelligence chief and engaged in a passionate search for those involved in the death of his father, Charles I, in 1649.

To be fair, certain later royals did play a central role in creating an early modern Bletchley Park of codebreakers and cypher experts, mostly serviced by the same devoted family of mathematics prodigies. In the seventeenth century, William III used intercepted decrypts to provoke a political crisis among England's enemies; in the early eighteenth century, George II personally authorized the recruitment of spies in France, but none displayed the talent and ambition of Queen Elizabeth.

Others were useless. George III, for example, was an especially poor user of intelligence during the American War of Independence and was outpaced by George Washington, who displayed a masterly understanding of every aspect of secret statecraft.

The relationship between monarchs and secret intelligence in the two centuries after Queen Elizabeth's death is a rather sorry story. It existed at the whims of kings, leaving intelligence power intertwined with fluctuating royal fortunes; accordingly, intelligence waxed and waned in the subsequent centuries until it was resurrected under Queen Victoria.

This book uncovers the remarkable relationship between the Royal Family and the intelligence community since the reign of Queen Victoria. Their journeys are intertwined; their histories are entangled. The monarch—even the monarchy itself—would not survive without intelligence. Meanwhile, the secret services have long been shaped by forces of the crown. This book argues that modern intelligence grew out of persistent attempts to assassinate Victoria and then operated on a private and informal basis, drawing on close personal relationships between senior spies, the aristocracy, and the monarchy.

It is a remarkable place where women rulers, rather more than men, are often playing the role of a royal "M," standing at the center of what has hitherto been assumed to be a masculine world. Since the accession of Victoria in 1837, Britain's spies have served mostly women at the top. Victoria outdid many of her male contemporaries in collecting and wielding intelligence, though she was no feminist herself (having once remarked that what are now called feminists "ought to get a good whipping"). Early in her career, Margaret Thatcher reflected on the symbolic importance of the young Queen Elizabeth II, noting that it would "help to remove the last shreds of prejudice against women aspiring to the highest places." This book reveals how both Victoria and Elizabeth II were excellent spymasters.

The mid–Victorian era was a period of political upheaval: royal intelligence channels clashed with amateur equivalents used by nation-states; royals with multiple nationalities faced increasing suspicion from politicians; and monarchs used private sources to bypass their own cabinets and protect their dynastic interests. Victoria was often at odds with her own government, for example, over issues of surveillance, and she used private royal intelligence sources to support— but also outmaneuver—government policy. She acted as an intelligence gatherer, analyst, and, in modern jargon, "consumer." Her son, King Edward VII, had restricted access to intelligence when prince, largely because of fears of blackmail and poor security practices. Despite this, he tried to continue in a similar mold as Victoria when king, drawing on private family networks across the continent.

In 1909, Mansfield Cumming, the first chief of MI6, Britain's overseas intelligence service, proclaimed himself a servant of the king, not the prime minister. His successors' royal connections often allowed them to move more easily in the royal court than in the corridors of Whitehall. This reached its apotheosis before the Russian Revolution, when MI6 intervened to try to save the Russian tsar, the king's cousin, from disaster. Afterward, fearing a similar revolt in Britain, private networks provided King George V with intelligence on the loyalty of his own subjects.

In 1936, the dramatic abdication of Edward VIII formed a dangerous turning point. What originally started as family feuding over a romantic liaison with the American divorcée Wallis Simpson escalated into a national security crisis. Fearing both the couple's Nazi sympathies and domestic instability, British spies turned their attention to Edward, creating profound dilemmas for intelligence officers who had previously been his drinking partners.

They worried about when and how to intervene. As fears grew, MI5 spied on the king himself, hiding in the bushes of Green Park near Buckingham Palace to access a telephone junction box and eavesdrop on his personal telephone calls. Even after his abdication, he remained a high-priority target as spies reported back on the less-than-salubrious company he kept, assessing him and his wife as "fifth columnists." Reading these surveillance reports on his activities, the Foreign Office complained of his "fascist sympathies." Sent away into a kind of Caribbean exile as governor of the Bahamas, the duke of Windsor was, bizarrely, both the recipient of secret service reports and under close surveillance by the same agencies.

During the Second World War, Edward's brother and successor, King George VI, gradually restored trust between the secret world and the House of

Windsor. Although initially tarnished as an enthusiastic appeaser, George eventually acquired inside knowledge of the electronic "Wizard War" that would gradually turn the tide against the Axis. The king knew all the secrets in the land, from radar research to incredibly sensitive decrypted Enigma material produced at Bletchley Park, and from secret black radio stations to the legendary D-Day deception masterminded by MI5.

He became involved in several Special Operations Executive escapades, enjoyed a personal tour of its gadgets and gizmos, and decorated numerous secret agents. The king maintained a keen interest until his death, after which the last copy of an eye-wateringly secret report on deception operations was found locked in his private dispatch box by the queen.

In the 1950s, the young Queen Elizabeth II continued her father's fastidious interest in secret statecraft, from nuclear bunkers to weekly intelligence assessments. She was much more than what the eminent constitutional historian Peter Hennessy called a "gilded sponge"; exercising her right to encourage, warn, and be consulted, she would raise her eyebrow knowingly at prime ministers and spymasters alike. On some occasions, the Foreign Office would deploy her on subtle diplomacy. On other occasions, she made suggestions of her own, often about the fate of fellow monarchs.

This close relationship lasted through four decades of the Cold War. Then, one day in the early 1990s, Queen Elizabeth's private secretary, Sir Robert Fellowes, lunched with his colleagues at MI6's crumbling headquarters, Century House. This dilapidated tower block, situated in a singularly unfashionable area south of the River Thames, seemed to symbolize the uncertain future for the agency at the end of the Cold War. With the icy conflict clearly over, Elizabeth wanted to know if MI6 still had a purpose in this new world. What should he tell her? Gerry Warner, its second in command, replied: "Please tell her it is the last penumbra of her empire."[1]

This book reveals these covert connections and argues that the relationship between spies and royals has evolved into something rather unusual. It has moved from the informal and personal to something more formal, with a real role for senior royals. The relationship remains significant even in today's era of constitutional monarchy, with monarchs and heirs taking a personal interest in the secret world. In the last century, Stewart Menzies, the chief of MI6, and himself a stepson to the king's equerry (or personal attendant), traded off rumors that he was an illegitimate son of another king. During the reign of Elizabeth II, the head of MI6 nominated its most brilliant officers for private awards from Prince Charles, who has long been fascinated by secret operations. In a dark world where life often hangs by a thread, these awards are the equivalent of a secret Victoria Cross—for acts of gallantry or ingenuity that we will never hear about. Demonstrating the close relationship, Queen Elizabeth appointed a recent head of MI5, Andrew Parker, as Lord Chamberlain in 2021, a senior member of her royal household.

Monarchy has directly shaped intelligence. Attempts to assassinate Queen Victoria stimulated the creation and growth of Special Branch, Britain's undercover police unit often dealing with national security matters. Ever since, intelligence has maintained an important function of keeping the monarch alive. In return, intelligence has shaped monarchy. Discreet protection and early warning have allowed kings and queens to remain accessible and visible in dangerous eras of war and terrorism.

Monarchy also has driven intelligence in other ways. Access to intelligence has enabled kings and queens to intervene in foreign and security policy. Royal marriages have created important dynastic intelligence networks across the continent, providing sensitive information back to the palace. The high-level attendance at royal marriages and funerals made them a forerunner of the modern Group of Twenty summit, with opportunities for diplomacy and espionage. It could even be argued that states' frustration at private royal channels and the dynastic interests they pursued have helped spur the creation of more official national intelligence services.

In return, intelligence has shaped monarchy. Tensions over secret information sat at the heart of debates about the role of the constitutional monarch in the nineteenth and twentieth centuries. Moreover, the competition between royal intelligence and that of the nation-state formed part of a broader clash between dynastic and state interests during a period of revolutionary upheaval. In this sense, the relationship between intelligence and monarchy played a part in shaping the nationalism of the nineteenth century.

Much of this took place against a backdrop of war and insecurity. European wars of the nineteenth century allowed Queen Victoria to flex her royal networks, but those farther away, in places like Russia and on the imperial frontiers, led her to demand greater intelligence coverage. The end of the First World War decimated the web of royal intelligence but, by this time, state intelligence was becoming more institutionalized. Across Europe, royals were not only decimated but also disrespected; in the 1919 election, when Lloyd George campaigned on the slogan "Hang the Kaiser," he was openly urging the lynching of the king's cousin. Even then, King George V maintained his own military intelligence network and found himself surrounded by those working for secret organizations. But the Second World War salvaged and formalized the relationship between king and intelligence.

Secret intelligence moved seamlessly from dynastic and family politics to national security politics. Yet the monarch still maintains an important role, with King Charles III now receiving the type of material once sent to his mother.

How kings and queens access and use intelligence directly affects their ability
to exercise their constitutional rights—and ultimately their power. Famously,
the Victorian essayist Walter Bagehot suggested that the crown's "mystery is
its life. We must not let in daylight upon magic." Nowhere is this mystery more
pronounced than in the relationship between the monarchy and the intelligence
services. It is now possible to let a little daylight into the most secret rooms of
the British state.

PART I

The Rise and Fall
of Royal Intelligence

1

Queen Victoria

Assassins and Revolutionaries

For a man to strike any women is most brutal, and I . . . think this
far worse than any attempt to shoot, which, wicked as it is,
is at least more comprehensible and more courageous.
—Queen Victoria, 1854

On matters of espionage, Queen Victoria was decidedly un-Victorian. In nineteenth-century Britain, "spying" was a dirty word. Victoria's subjects thought it was ungentlemanly—the kind of unscrupulous activity undertaken by despots on the continent. Yet espionage was more than un-British; it was, so the argument went, also unnecessary and counterproductive. The British population, prosperous and content, had no reason to rebel, while the foreign policy of splendid isolationism reduced the risk of war—and with it, the need for secret intelligence altogether. Espionage was counterproductive insofar as spies, saboteurs, and undercover surveillance generated mistrust; and mistrust led to rebellion.[1]

In the wake of the duke of Wellington's resounding victory in the Napoleonic Wars in 1815, Britain had few international worries for the first time in centuries. One historian has described the mid-Victorian period as a vast "chasm of spylessness."[2] The precursor to MI5 and MI6 was not created until 1909, late in the reign of Victoria's successor, Edward VII. During Victoria's reign, domestic spying was limited; and the British state lacked a formal network of human spies overseas.

Personally, the queen was far less squeamish. But then Victoria was rather continental herself; she sat at the heart of a dense network of royal relatives spanning Europe. Her uncle was king of the Belgians, whose wife was the daughter of the French king. Victoria's own daughter married the crown prince of Prussia. By the end of her long reign, Victoria had royal relatives in Bulgaria, Denmark, Germany, Greece, the Netherlands, Romania, Russia, and Spain.[3] They formed a transnational intelligence agency, and, in a world where private and public realms seamlessly blurred, the queen often knew more about foreign powers than her own ministers did. She claimed to be unimpressed when her foreign office engaged in "diplomatic intrigue, spying, &c"; but in truth, she had her own sources and did not appreciate ministerial meddling.[4]

Although she was more absorbed in foreign and dynastic affairs, Victoria did develop a personal interest in domestic intelligence. The reason was simple: her ministers might have had the luxury of seeing virtue in Britain's lack of an intelligence service, but they were not subjected to continuous threats of assassination, and neither did they have to watch revolutionaries murder their relatives across the continent. For any monarch, the stakes were dangerously high. The bearded, bomb-throwing anarchist became a dominant theme as the century wore on, and their primary target was the crowned heads of Europe.

Intelligence, for Victoria, was about survival—both physically and dynastically. It was also decidedly ad hoc, informal, and sometimes highly personal. She referred to letters from her daughter, Vicky, who was married to Prince Frederick of Prussia, about Prussian intentions as "intelligence," but they slipped seamlessly between political insight and family gossip. Victoria interpreted intelligence broadly: it ranged from secret reports sent from the Russian border to, rather bizarrely, news that her opera coach was ill and had to reschedule a lesson. To Victoria, all this was "intelligence." Like more recent connoisseurs of "open sources," she knew that intelligence was simply useful and actionable information. It did not necessarily have to come from spies.

Victoria was only eighteen years of age when she became queen in 1837. She had led a sheltered childhood, during which rigid discipline had been instilled. The young queen, diminutive and inexperienced, was not entirely innocent of politics. Her uncle Leopold, king of the Belgians, tutored her in foreign affairs as a teenager and, after she became queen, emphasized the virtues of discretion in statecraft.[5] He also offered an early lesson in deception operations and how to take advantage of nascent counterintelligence tradecraft. It was fairly standard practice, he counseled, for states to intercept, read, and reseal letters. This could be cunningly exploited by writing the letters in such a way as to send a deliberate message—accurate or otherwise—to the intercepting state.[6]

The young queen reveled in her new role, enjoying the stark contrast to her highly constrained childhood. She had a great deal to learn, and she acquired a famously intimate and trusting relationship with her first prime minister, Lord Melbourne.

Victoria was stubborn, inquisitive, and highly intelligent, with a keen eye for detail. She liked to know what was going on at home, overseas, and especially across her vast and growing empire. As she grew into the role, she rarely hesitated to advise—or berate—her ministers for failing to keep her updated or for ignoring her warnings. Throughout her reign, she remained closely involved in the affairs of successive governments. She read papers, including Foreign Office dispatches and Cabinet discussions, quickly and efficiently—and she sharply rebuked ministers if they ever dared to withhold something.

Secret information, arriving through convoluted routes to land on the government's desk, often ended up on hers, too. Early in her reign, for example, she found herself sitting alongside Melbourne in Buckingham Palace discussing the veracity of a single spy report. It concerned Russian military intentions and had come from a well-placed human source via the duke of Wellington, who continued to command the army and advise the queen as late as 1852. In the end, they thought its contents were improbable, but the image of a queen and prime minister poring over human intelligence together is a striking one.[7] She was quickly learning her craft and would go on to admonish ministers if they interpreted intelligence differently from her. More generally speaking, her red boxes, filled with official papers sent to her by the government, rarely included formalized "secret intelligence"—in the modern sense—because such agencies did not yet exist.

Victoria married Prince Albert of Saxe-Coburg and Gotha in 1840. Albert was handsome, hard-working, and, like Victoria, disciplined. Above all, he was hard-working, quickly learning about English history, law, and the constitution. Although theirs was an arranged marriage, the affection between the young couple was clear. Despite this, the queen initially froze her new husband out of statecraft, secret or otherwise—much to Albert's frustration. "I am only the husband," he once complained to a friend, "and not the master of the house!"

Things soon changed when Victoria became pregnant in 1841. The relentless red boxes of official papers continued to arrive at the palace, and the exhausted queen reluctantly resorted to reading their contents to her eager husband. His influence grew, albeit informally, thereafter. At Albert's request, Lord Melbourne advised the queen to take political guidance from her husband and, upon leaving office, told her that he had "formed the highest opinion of His Royal Highness's judgment, temper, and discretion." Victoria, he counseled, "cannot do better than have recourse to it." Melbourne's successor, Robert Peel, accordingly sent Albert nightly reports of parliamentary debates and Cabinet discussions. This was quite a turnaround; a year earlier, the queen had not allowed him a key to the red boxes, yet by 1844 he had become her informal private secretary. Eventually, he gained his own key to those boxes, which carried the most secret and sensitive affairs of state.[8]

For all the boxes' access to state secrets, however, Victoria and Albert's best intelligence did not come from them. Instead, their vast web of relations provided unrivaled sources of inside information—some of it highly sensitive—about foreign affairs. According to one senior official at Number 10, Queen Victoria selected the most intelligent member of each European royal family, and "on any question, domestic or foreign, which arose, she obtained an opinion."[9] Royal communication traveled securely through private messenger or diplomatic bags, and the queen felt confident in her sources: shared blood was more reliable than some perfidious secret agent working for money.[10] As a result, Victoria and Albert knew a great deal more about German, and broader continental, affairs than the Foreign Office did. And Albert convinced the queen that foreign policy peculiarly came within the sovereign's province.[11] Knowledge was power, and the dynastic intelligence system soon came into conflict with that of the modern nation-state both at home and abroad.

If intelligence was about survival, then Victoria's personal safety should have been the highest priority. Even in the first decade of her reign, plenty of malcontents, from Irish terrorists to loners with a grudge, wanted the young queen dead. Yet domestic intelligence, which would be necessary to unearth plots and conspiracies, barely existed. Formed in 1829, the Metropolitan Police of London was a fairly new organization at the start of Victoria's reign. It did not acquire a small detective department until 1842. By then, the queen had survived three separate assassination attempts.

The first attempt unfolded dramatically on June 10, 1840. In the early evening, Victoria and Albert left the garden gate of Buckingham Palace in a carriage. All of a sudden, as they headed toward Constitution Hill, Victoria "was deafened by the loud report of a pistol." "Our carriage," she recalled that night, "involuntarily stopped."[12]

On the path beside them, she and Albert saw "a little man," his arms "folded over his breast, a pistol in each hand." Less than 30 seconds later, the assailant aimed again. The queen ducked and "another shot," as she described it, "equally loud instantly followed."[13] He adopted the classic highwayman's pose, something he had been perfecting, steadying his left hand on his right forearm, and zoning in on his target.[14]

"My God!" Albert exclaimed as the gun fired. Catching his composure, he turned to his young wife: "Don't be alarmed." She assured him she was "not the least frightened," and, as the police eventually seized the assailant, Albert ordered the driver to carry on as if nothing had happened. In the background, onlookers chanted: "Kill him! Kill him!"[15] In the confusion, the gathering crowd first turned on the brave bystanders who had wrestled the pistols from a certain Edward Oxford. Anxious to claim responsibility, he shouted: "It was I who fired: it was me." The crowd then turned on Oxford. But it was unnecessary, because he had no wish to run away—instead, he stood with a beaming smile, taking full credit. Police constables from the A Division, who looked after royal protection, now arriving at the scene, had difficulty preventing the crowd from attacking him.[16]

The queen was morbidly fascinated by the incident. During the following days, she examined a nearby wall looking for bullet marks, spoke at length with the prime minister about the specific bullet used and the height and direction it traveled, and inspected the pistols that, in her words, "might have *finished me off* & perhaps Albert too."[17] She fiercely disputed the home secretary's assessment that the pistols were not in fact loaded.[18]

Victoria asked to be kept updated about the unfolding investigation. Melbourne soon told her that police had arrested Oxford for high treason, and intriguingly added that letters about a secret society named "Young England," with four hundred members, had been unearthed at his house. Each member was supposedly required to have a hidden "brace of pistols, a sword, a rifle and a dagger." It seemed like an elaborate conspiracy to overthrow the monarchy and the government. The French ambassador observed that these appeared to be a poor emulation of the "great secret societies" that had existed on the continent.[19]

Oxford was only eighteen, but looked several years younger. Under interrogation, he alleged that the king of Hanover, who would have assumed the throne if Victoria had died, and Lord Palmerston, the foreign secretary, were members of Young England. These wild allegations were quickly dismissed, and a jury found Oxford guilty but insane.

It was all a figment of his imagination.[20] The real driving force for Oxford had been an addiction to "penny dreadful novels." He was fascinated by the highwayman Jack Sheppard, and his favorite reading included a book titled *The Bravo of Venice*, which featured a figure who rises to prominence by becoming the so-called King of the Assassins.[21] He was fascinated by previous would-be royal assassins, now in long-term institutional confinement. Was Oxford really mad rather than malevolent? The queen was skeptical, and she talked with Melbourne "of the jury being bad."[22]

Despite press speculation to the contrary, Oxford was a lone operator. The real political significance of this assassination attempt was to trigger a vast and spontaneous outburst of popular support for the queen and her new husband. For days, huge crowds surrounded the palace, thrilled to see her going about her duties with no obvious additional protection.

Undoubtedly, Oxford was deranged. Witnesses testified to a long history of instability, characterized by maniacal fits of laughing and crying, since early childhood. When questioned by the home secretary, he again erupted in hysterical laughter, which discomforted everyone present.[23]

It was undoubtedly convenient for the authorities to find Oxford insane. Lacking intelligence capacity, the police would have struggled to uncover and penetrate such a secret society if one had existed. Besides, the state's limited surveillance capabilities were focused on the growing Chartists, a working-class male suffrage movement for political reform, and on suspicious foreign nationals who had recently arrived in Britain. Lone wolf attacks against the monarch were a more difficult proposition altogether. The queen was protected on state occasions by plainclothes officers, who had been plucked from the uniformed police to monitor suspicious characters in the crowds.[24] These arrangements were clearly insufficient. Nor were they being improved—and they needed to be.

On May 29, 1842, Albert heard "a trigger snap" as he and Victoria returned to Buckingham Palace. A short, swarthy man had stepped out from the crowd and aimed to fire. The bumbling police failed to even notice the incident. No one around him appeared to have noticed at all. Albert kept the matter highly secret, telling only the prime minister and those immediately concerned with the queen's safety.[25] Peel hurried to the palace, and the two walked in the gardens, discussing what to do next.

The next day, Albert and Victoria took matters into their own hands and launched a daring operation to flush out the assailant.[26] They repeated the same route, albeit this time traveling a little more quickly and ensuring that undercover police lurked at every corner.[27] Victoria decided that she could expose the lives of her "gentleman," but not her ladies, so she kept the ladies in waiting out of the line of fire.[28] Constantly looking over her shoulder, she unsurprisingly felt "agitated and excited."[29] Albert "looked behind every tree," she later recalled, "and I cast my eyes round in search of the rascal's face."

Constable William Trounce of the A Division had been observing a suspicious character in the same area for about 30 minutes. But as the royals approached, patriotic feelings overcame his limited undercover training. Instead of watching his suspect, he bizarrely stood smartly to attention and saluted. Meanwhile, his suspect, the same man as before, stepped forward and shot his pistol at a range of 7 yards.[30] This time, the police caught him. His name was John Francis; he was a twenty-two-year-old Londoner. He was initially detained in the same cell that Oxford had occupied two years before.[31]

Despite the mishaps, Victoria was remarkably impressed with the whole operation and the secrecy with which she had carried it out.[32] Again, she pressed ministers for details.[33] Francis was tried for high treason and sentenced to death, but this was later commuted to transportation (i.e., banishment) on the grounds that his pistol was not loaded.[34] Victoria and Albert naturally both argued for better security, and they also lobbied for a change in the law to better protect the monarch.[35]

Two days after the Francis verdict, the home secretary told Victoria of yet another assassination attempt.[36] Enough was enough. The prime minister, Robert Peel, rushed to Albert to discuss protective measures. He and the queen promoted a legislative solution, believing that such attempts would continue as long as the law allowed assailants to only be charged with high treason, a cumbersome procedure.[37] Under intense pressure from the palace, just nine days later Parliament passed the Treason Act, which introduced a new crime of intending to wound or alarm the sovereign, punishable by transportation, imprisonment, or whipping.[38]

More importantly, less than a month later, the police established the small, eight-man "Detective Department," albeit this was as much to appease public fears amid a recent murder spree as to protect the monarch. It had already existed in embryo within the A Division, which was widely considered the Metropolitan Police's elite district, but now it had an excuse to act more brazenly. Tasked by the Home Office, it cultivated ad hoc informants to gather intelligence on suspicious individuals and groups. Surveillance focused predominantly on the Chartists, while detectives consciously tried to avoid accusations of French-style authoritarian political policing with its undercover agents.[39]

Created in 1829, Peel's police force, the first "bobbies on the beat," had been regarded with suspicion as a civilian army of "bludgeon men." But the newly formed Detective Department had some unlikely allies. Charles Dickens was fascinated by this new development and wrote several press pieces praising them. Remarkably, he incorporated them into his latest novel, *Bleak House*. The first fictional detective, "Mr. Bucket," was closely modeled on a real detective-inspector, Charles Field. Some police officers worked closely with journalists to create what have been called "pseudo-autobiographies of professional men." As the century wore on, novelists, drawing on the public fascination with the science of forensics, conjured up the image of a new intelligence-driven policeman. Not all of them were men. One of the first fictional detectives was Ruth Trail of the "Secret Intelligence" series, whose office door boasted a brass plaque that read "Secret Agent."[40]

With this slowly changing public mood, the Victorian era saw the beginnings of modern state surveillance. The introduction of the penny black stamp made the postal service affordable for the average person, dramatically increasing the opportunities for state interception. Mushrooming bureaucracies, from the growth of the census to the blossoming library system, also offered a sort of indirect surveillance that earlier societies had not experienced. Public health bureaucracies began to keep comprehensive files on ordinary citizens for the first time, crime being closely associated with disease in the popular imagination.[41] Such activity might have helped the police keep order and prevent conspiracies, but not everyone was impressed. Royal fears that ordinary members of the public might obtain unseemly glimpses into the private lives of the elite formed an early counterweight against these developments.[42] Moreover, undercover police and indirect surveillance simply failed to prevent further assassination attempts.

In January 1843, Albert received "intelligence," as Victoria put it, that one of Peel's personal secretaries had been shot. The bullet, she recorded in graphic detail, "had passed through the ribs but had been extracted—no vital part had been touched, & it was hoped he would do well." She and Albert looked awkwardly across the dinner table, where, by coincidence, the victim's brother sat blissfully unaware of what had happened. Albert gently broke the news to him after dinner.[43] The next day, Peel revealed a further secret to the queen: the assassin had intended to kill Peel himself, and, in a case of mistaken identity, thought he had succeeded. Victoria was horrified.[44] Peel promised to send her all the latest intelligence, no matter how seemingly insignificant.[45]

The victim, Edward Drummond, died from his wounds five days later. Sadly, Drummond was related to Spencer Perceval, the only British prime minister to be assassinated, and they were eventually buried in the same family tomb in Charlton in Kent.[46] The queen's temperature rose further when the attacker, Daniel McNaughton, was acquitted on the grounds of insanity. "*What* security is there left now!" she thundered. "Something ought to be done," Victoria demanded of the prime minister, "to alter the law, which is indeed very defective."[47]

The very next day, debate opened in Parliament.[48] Victoria continued to keep up the pressure on the prime minister, and, three months later, the House of Lords announced new rules to change how jurors would be instructed regarding insanity. From then on, every man was to be presumed sane, leaving it for the defense to prove that, when committing the act, he, through "disease of the mind," either did not know what he was doing or did not know that it was wrong.

In the background, dramatic events abroad helped drive the change. Passions were building toward another round of momentous revolutions on the continent in 1848. In France, politics, rather than mentally disturbed assassins, fueled rising violence against royalty. Many of the assailants subscribed to an underlying anarchist philosophy, believing that by killing the king, they would unhinge the entire establishment and trigger a major change in the established social order. The most inventive was Giuseppe Fieschi, who had created a primitive form of machine gun for his formidable attack in 1835. As King Louis Philippe rode through Paris to inspect his national guard, Fieschi unleashed no fewer than twenty-five loaded guns bound together on a wooden frame. Eighteen people around the king were exterminated, while half of Freschi's own face was blown off. Yet the king survived and, emulating Victoria's famous courage under fire, he rode on to review his troops as if nothing had happened.[49]

Victoria had successfully changed the law on mental health. Despite developments on the continent, her demands for increased security did not have the same impact. The prime minister assured her that "every precaution possible" would be taken to keep her and Albert safe on state occasions but naively comforted her by saying that he had "walked home every night from the House of Commons, and, notwithstanding frequent menaces and intimations of danger, he has not met with any obstructions."[50] Prince Albert personally designed an armored parasol—made out of chain mail—to protect the queen, but it was rather heavy and she never used it.[51]

Victoria faced at least a further five assassination attempts during her reign. Another one took place in May 1849, when William Hamilton, a refugee from the Irish famine, shot at her with an unloaded home-made gun. Once again, this took place at Constitution Hill, which was rapidly becoming assassination alley for the Royal Family. The queen's escorts spotted a man with a gun and called for the coach to stop, providing him with a perfect target. There was a flash and a loud roar. A crowd fell on him rapidly, shouting "Tear him to pieces!" and "Kill him at once!" but detectives from the A Division quickly hauled him away for interrogation.[52] Under the new act, he was tried, with royal approval, for a misdemeanor, rather than high treason, and sentenced to seven years' transportation.[53]

A year later, another man stepped from a crowd and struck Victoria with his walking stick, momentarily knocking her unconscious. This was another monumental lapse of royal security, and, as the queen staggered to her feet nursing a swollen eye, the public leapt on the assailant. This attack angered Victoria more than all the others. She thought it "by far the most disgraceful & cowardly thing that has ever been done." Hitting a woman with a stick was judged "*far* worse than an attempt to shoot, which, wicked as it is, is at least more comprehensible & more courageous."[54] He faced the same punishment as the Irishman and was transported to Australia.[55]

In the spring of 1844, amid assassination attempts and the tentative growth of undercover policing and state surveillance, Britain's one long-standing and most professional intelligence success story, one that had been quietly nurtured since the English Civil War, now faced a major scandal.

The protagonist was Giuseppe Mazzini, an Italian nationalist who had taken refuge in London after being chased across Europe after a string of failed insurrections and was sentenced to death in absentia. In 1831, he had founded Young Italy, an underground movement designed to unite his country that, two years later, had 60,000 members. This was the movement that the fantasist and would-be assassin Edward Oxford had tried to emulate. After a number of failed insurrections, he was exiled to London, where he ran his movement from the British Museum. Sitting among scholars and novelists, he wrote to agents across Europe and North America agitating for a unified Italian republic.

Early in 1844, a friend called at his house in a state of distress. Two of his associates, Emilio Bandiera and his brother Attilio, had been seized shortly after arriving in Naples and executed. How had the Neapolitan police managed to find them so quickly? This increased Mazzini's existing suspicions that someone was tampering with his mail. After yet another failed uprising, this time in southern Italy, Mazzini accused the British government of intercepting his mail and tipping off the local authorities.[56] Specifically, Mazzini accused the government of "post office espionage." Setting out to prove it, he carefully placed poppy seeds, strands of hair, and grains of sand into envelopes, sealed them with wax, and mailed them to himself. Sure enough, they arrived sealed, but without their tell-tale contents.

As word spread, members of Parliament now feared that their own letters were being opened. The scandal caused outrage in Parliament and instigated a broader debate about spying. What difference, one member of Parliament asked furiously, was there between "a government breaking the seal of his letter in the Post Office, and the government employing a spy to poke his ear to the keyhole?" These underhanded practices were "singularly abhorrent to the genius of the English people."[57]

Parliamentary anger caught the national mood. Britain prided itself on being the most open of democratic powers, and the philosopher Jeremy Bentham had recently popularized the notion that secrecy was an "instrument of conspiracy" deployed by tyrants.[58] Here, in the absence of poppy seeds, surveillance and security collided with newfound ideals of liberty and privacy, driven by cheap, secure correspondence and a feeling that the home was a private space in which the state had no business.[59]

Soon, James Graham, the home secretary, was nicknamed "Fouché" by the press, after Joseph Fouché, Napoleon's notorious minister of police famous for his system of political spies. Meanwhile, Mazzini became an overnight celebrity and household name. Yet Queen Victoria was unmoved. Sympathizing with her royal relatives across Europe who faced violent republican revolutionaries, she maintained her more pragmatic attitude to security. She was also unsurprised by the exposés, having become an experienced reader of intercepted letters herself.

Before 1844, Victoria had enjoyed access to an impressive range of intercepts. She found some "most impertinent," others "curious," while some simply made her laugh.[60] They offered rich insight into the French court,[61] German politics,[62] Russian–German relations,[63] and the implications of the Spanish Carlist wars for its monarchy.[64] Victoria found them fascinating, recording how she would discuss "people *knowing things*" with her prime minister.[65] Some were particularly sensitive: one intercept was a letter written by her own uncle, King Leopold, criticizing her government;[66] another batch contained some "violent letters" by that "old foolish Sir Robert Gardiner," a former general whom she had inherited as an assistant in her own court.[67] In some cases,

Victoria not only saw the raw intercepts but also acted as an intelligence analyst. She used her encyclopedic knowledge of the intricate power structures in Europe to help her government interpret the royal material.

Therefore, when the Mazzini affair erupted, Victoria just could not understand the hysteria. She believed that the home secretary "must have, in moments of difficulty," the ability to intercept letters. She was disappointed that the government lost the subsequent debate and expressed surprise that Melbourne, with whom she was still in close touch despite his having left office, "condemned the practice."[68] And she did have some right to be surprised at his purported squeamishness: Melbourne had once forwarded reams of foreign intercepts to the palace. Admittedly, this time, with Mazzini, the state had targeted British communications—an altogether more controversial target.

Victoria's views were at odds with those of her subjects. Her dynastic sympathies, fear of revolutionaries, and loathing of republicanism help explain this. Surveillance of Mazzini was instigated at the request of Austria, which, at the time, owned large parts of Italy and was roundly repressive. This raised the thorny issue of national sovereignty and spying at the request of a foreign state. The philosopher Thomas Carlyle angrily wrote that while Englishmen had no interest in the affairs of the Austrian emperor, "it is a question vital to us that sealed letters in an English post-office be, as we all fancied they were, respected as things sacred." An editorial in *The Times* agreed that such activity "cannot be English, any more than masks, poisons, sword-sticks, secret signs and associations, and other such dark inventions."[69]

The queen had a clear interest in maintaining those monarchies that radicals like Mazzini were trying to overthrow. Surveillance mattered more to the crown than to Parliament. But Parliament won. After a lengthy inquiry, the government was forced to admit that a secret department of the Post Office had existed for two centuries. In 1655, after the English Civil War, Oliver Cromwell had appointed a postmaster general to intercept letters of monarchists suspected of plotting against his regime. With a warrant, this Secret Office and Deciphering Branch had the power to intercept mail.

Ministers tried to fudge the outcome. They kept the law the same, hoping to leave it a "mystery whether or not this power is exercised." This, the inquiry hoped, would "deter the evil-minded from applying the Post to improper use." In practice, the Peel government closed down the Deciphering Branch and the Secret Office of the Post Office altogether. Britain seemingly lost the ability to intercept and decipher letters.[70] The operatives were quietly pensioned off with money from a secret fund.[71] It was, according to the historian Christopher Andrew, a "turning point in intelligence history."[72]

The next year, the queen again discussed the issue with Robert Peel. She maintained that the power to open letters was necessary, but agreed it should not be abused. The issue of secretly resealing them was more controversial, but again the queen was in favor. She argued that if this were "not done and letters merely stopped, without being resealed before being forwarded, then hardly any information could be obtained." Intriguingly, the queen added that the Post Office was not the best institution to conduct such secret activity anyway. Instead, she thought that the Foreign Office did it "in a far more secret manner"; this was a practice she was relieved had not fallen under the recent investigation and perhaps pointed to a yet more secret office.[73]

The government did continue to watch Mazzini closely, although he wrote in code after the 1844 scandal. A few years later, the prime minister told Victoria that the authorities still hoped to "shut" him "up for a time"; but despite keeping him under surveillance, they were struggling to catch him doing anything that was actually illegal.[74] A decade after the scandal, the French king impressed Victoria with his detailed knowledge of secret societies and told her that he too had failed to "get at" Mazzini, but vented that "if I catch him, I will embalm him." Victoria listened sympathetically, knowing full well that her own ministers had been soft on the revolutionary a decade earlier.[75] A European royal club was closing in on revolutionaries, and they had found their mark.

The Mazzini affair reflected the thorny broader issue of British attitudes toward European political exiles and put the queen in a difficult position. Amid great political upheaval on the continent, dissidents fled fierce crackdowns on rebellion and insurrection. Taking advantage of Britain's liberal asylum policy, which starkly contrasted with the authoritarianism across the Channel, many found a home in London.

In nineteenth-century Britain, the position regarding refugees and exiles was remarkably liberal. Everyone was welcome, ranging from overturned monarchs and routed royalists to the leaders of failed revolutionary bands and escaped political prisoners. Between 1823 and 1900, not a single refugee was expelled. While refugees in Europe faced draconian treatment, foreigners who fled to Britain could reside in freedom. An act permitting deportation was introduced in 1848 but was scrapped five years later, never having been used. Yet behind the scenes, Victoria was pursuing a secret battle to put an end to this political openness.[76]

This was because these refugees, from Mazzini to Karl Marx, turned nineteenth-century Britain into a petri dish of radical political ideas. Often, they were at odds with each other. Mazzini declared Marx to be an authoritarian who was filled with hatred rather than love for humankind, while Marx responded that the veteran Italian nationalist was "an everlasting old ass."[77]

Nevertheless, here dissident groups could organize, plot attacks, and print material to be smuggled back to the continent. Unsurprisingly, foreign governments continuously pressured Britain to deport these subversives for trial, but Victoria's government possessed neither the means nor the inclination to place so many dissidents under surveillance.[78] Victoria, who sympathized with the European monarchs and abhorred republicanism, found herself caught between dynasty and country.

In 1844, the year of the Mazzini affair, the home secretary, James Graham, met police chiefs to discuss how to keep track of foreign nationals more effectively. At about the same time, detectives at Scotland Yard did place some refugees under surveillance.[79] The leading detective in this controversial field was Jonathan Sanders, who, fluent in French, could easily pass himself off as a refugee. Throughout the 1850s, he reported the mood among neighborhoods that had become hotbeds of radicalism and monitored meetings at political clubs popular with foreign dissidents. More often than not, his investigations concluded that these groups posed little real threat beyond drunken cries of "death to the aristocrats."[80] All the while, politicians and members of the public complained about alleged spying on political activity. Even though he sympathized with the dissidents' liberal ideals, Palmerston was forced to defend the principle of surveillance in the House of Commons.[81] The queen would have approved.

After 1848, the situation became more serious, when democratic revolutions swept across Europe, existentially challenging monarchical rule. They began in southern Europe and spread to about fifty nations, including France, Austria, the Netherlands, Denmark, and Hungary. Tens of thousands of people died in the violence that followed. British politicians were of two minds, sympathizing with those rebelling against authoritarian governments yet fearing their own radicals at home, the Chartists. Although unsettling, the overall effect was to leave Britain without a serious strategic competitor in Europe, allowing it to focus on imperial expansion. Therefore, Britain's official position was procrastination and a pragmatic neutrality, hoping no one state would gain the upper hand, and quietly admiring the chaos in the capitals of its European competitors.

Nevertheless, Victoria was understandably agitated. Reading report after report from well-placed relatives describing murder across the continent, she worried about the ease with which the revolutions were unfolding. Although it pleased the queen, Britain's initial response was small: a new law would make treasonable language a punishable felony.[82] She continued to worry, and soon found herself at odds with parts of her own government about how to intervene. Whether to place radicals under surveillance at home or even whether to launch covert actions abroad in support of them became contentious issues.

In September 1848, Palmerston, the foreign secretary, approved a covert operation to support Sicilian rebels in their uprising against the king of Naples.

Running counter to British professions of neutrality, the government allowed stocks of arms from the War Office to be sold on to the rebels via a British arms manufacturer.[83] Palmerston neglected to tell the queen, who was livid when *The Times* broke the story early the next year. Victoria was "startled" to learn that "this *was done* and *sanctioned* by Lord Palmerston!!"[84]

The queen was particularly furious because, despite the supposed neutrality, her sympathies throughout the revolutions lay with monarchs. To make matters worse, she and Albert had earlier said that *if* Sicily did become independent, they would rather it be under a monarchy than a republic. She felt that Palmerston had deliberately misrepresented this view by letting his colleagues believe that the crown supported the rebels.[85]

After the *Times* exposé, Victoria knew her government could not plausibly deny the operation; neither could they defend it. Britain would therefore need to apologize. She detested having to do so, viewing it as a humiliating affront. From her own sources, she knew that leaders across Europe assumed Britain was covertly supporting rebellion.[86] In damage limitation mode, Victoria and Albert pushed—unsuccessfully—for Palmerston's resignation.[87] Britain abandoned support for the Sicilians, after which, rather predictably, Neapolitan forces quickly regained control of the island.[88]

The Sicilian case was not a one-time occurrence. At the same time, Victoria and Palmerston had been at loggerheads about the latter's sympathy for Sardinian attempts to drive Austria out of northern Italy. Once again, Palmerston was prepared to offer secret assistance to the rebels.[89]

Meanwhile, foreign governments continued to persuade the British to spy on prominent political exiles. To achieve this, they regularly sent intelligence to monarch and ministers alike exaggerating the threat. This included intelligence from Prussia stating that Karl Marx was plotting to assassinate the queen,[90] and a stream of alarmist warnings about the terrorist threat to the 1851 Great Exhibition held in London—the most ridiculous of which involved revolutionaries disguised as trees.[91] Victoria astutely paid little notice to "absurd reports of dangers of every kind and sort," and instead lavished praise on Albert for his role in organizing the event. He had proved wrong all those "mischievous" people who up until midnight on the day the exhibition opened "maintained something dreadful would happen!"[92]

The queen was more worried about revolutionaries plotting against monarchs abroad. In October 1851, she implored Palmerston not to meet a leading Hungarian nationalist, Lajos Kossuth, who was touring the country and making inflammatory speeches.[93] She knew from her own correspondence that foreign governments, watching closely, were deeply unimpressed by Britain's lack of empathy with the public order problems they faced. Palmerston's intention to meet Kossuth encapsulated this neatly. As a result, and "disgusted" by the whole spectacle, she stretched her constitutional powers to the limit and was on the verge of demanding Palmerston's resignation.[94] Eventually, under pressure from both the cabinet and the crown, Palmerston acquiesced and resigned, but the episode left Victoria with a bitter taste.[95] The eventual breaking point had been Palmerston's support for French revolutionaries, which annoyed even his most supportive cabinet colleagues. Albert was delighted and wrote to his relatives: "Give a rogue a rope and he will hang himself."[96]

Although Kossuth only stayed in Britain for three weeks, the government kept him under surveillance afterward, hoping to catch him doing something illegal. Only eighteen months later, Queen Victoria was pleased when, after a successful intelligence operation, Albert told her that a rocket factory suspected to have been under Kossuth's direction had been seized and 800 rockets had been confiscated.[97]

The queen feared that Kossuth was only the tip of a republican iceberg. Her sources on the continent warned her of "rumours of plots directed from London" aiming for "the assassination of *all* Monarchs."[98] She learned, among other things, that European leaders believed that Britain planned to "destroy the Austrian Empire" and that London had become a menagerie of revolutionaries "kept to be let occasionally loose on the Continent to render its quiet and prosperity impossible."[99] Victoria did not believe them all, but she did sympathize with the underlying issue. Monarchs had a right to respect and loyalty; any hint of insubordination should not be encouraged.[100] After hearing of violence in Vienna, she thought of all "her dear ones" stuck in "the possession of the mob." The queen did not mince her words: "These horrible Republicans should be exterminated."[101]

In short, Britain was a reservoir of rebellious ideas in the mid–nineteenth century. Victoria's European counterparts begged her to intervene against the government's lenient policy on protecting revolutionaries.[102] Yet the queen felt powerless: Parliament would do little in terms of deportation or even surveillance.[103] This led to frequent clashes with Palmerston, who was much more sympathetic to the nationalism unfolding on the continent. She had feared Palmerston was withholding information from her about his own meddling in foreign affairs and, drawing on her royal intelligence networks, she worried that his hectoring of foreign monarchs was making Britain unpopular in Europe.[104]

Frustrated by this experience, Victoria successfully blocked the appointment of Lord Clarendon as Palmerston's successor as foreign secretary in 1851. Her rationale was instructive: she thought he was too fond of "diplomatic intrigue" and "spying."[105] When a new prime minister, Lord Derby, took office shortly afterward, she wasted little time in warning him against the dangers of "diplomatists and agents" and the harm that "intrigue" had done to Britain's international reputation as the revolutions had played out.[106] She relied on her own dynastic network to keep her updated, and she opposed secret activity conducted by her ministers that undermined European monarchism. Intelligence was fine—as long as it suited the queen's interests.

Accordingly, Victoria was pleased when Palmerston, back as home secretary, discovered "some incendiary papers" printed for Mazzini and Kossuth. They finally constituted a crime that could be prosecuted, although another minister dampened expectations by warning that the "detective Police were very inefficient." She would have been equally pleased by the new foreign secretary's suggestion that "there were many *little* services we might render" to the Austrian government giving them notice of the movements of "these dangerous Refugees."[107]

The surveillance issue climaxed in 1858. On the night of January 14, an Italian revolutionary and one-time follower of Mazzini, Felice Orsini, attempted to assassinate the French emperor, hoping to trigger a revolution that would spread to Italy. Orsini and a couple of accomplices threw three hand grenades at the emperor and his wife as they attended the Paris Opera. He missed his target but killed numerous bystanders. Such an attack was not unusual in this period, and Victoria quickly received reams of telegrams bringing her the latest intelligence from Paris and providing gory details.[108]

Orsini's London connections proved more troubling. After a dramatic and daring escape from an Austrian prison in 1855, he had fled to London and published popular accounts of his adventures. His plot to kill the emperor was hatched in London, and the bomb, which bore his name, was made in Birmingham. Unsurprisingly, the French authorities quickly accused the Foreign Office of having turned a blind eye to his activities and demanded that Britain restrict the right to asylum.[109]

Although annoyed at the criticisms of her country, Victoria accepted the point.[110] She agreed that "were similar assassins to be tolerated in France & came over to attempt to do something against us here, the whole British nation would demand instant reparation."[111] Accordingly, she supported surveillance of Orsini's former lodgings and moves to make conspiracy to murder abroad a felony. Both responses would have involved stepping up the intelligence effort against refugees.

Detectives quickly investigated Orsini's old neighborhood. The task fell to Jonathan Sanders, who specialized in the surveillance of foreign nationals. Unfortunately, witnesses saw him rummaging around without a warrant, thereby causing unwelcome publicity and criticism.[112] This inflammatory incident undermined Sanders's careful attempts not to give credence to accusations that the government was using political espionage, French-style.

The second response, a bill making conspiracy to murder abroad a felony, was even less successful. The next month, the government dramatically fell after

losing a parliamentary vote on this contentious issue. In an ironic twist, the out-
going prime minister was none other than Lord Palmerston, now trying to curb,
rather than encourage, continental rebellion.[113] This time, the queen had nothing but sympathy and tried to convince him not to resign. She was particularly
frustrated by Palmerston's opponents, writing with disdain about how Orsini
had been a regular house guest of Thomas Gibson, the member of Parliament
who had dramatically censured the government.[114] For now, Palmerston, whose
views on revolutions had so frustrated Victoria, was out of office. The queen
was relieved that his successor, Lord Derby, had "behaved remarkably well on
the Conspiracy Bill."[115] The new foreign secretary, the earl of Malmesbury, told
the queen that "letters from *private* sources" in France now indicated that criticism of Britain would subside.[116]

In the first two decades of her reign, Victoria had been an intelligence gatherer, analyst, and consumer. She learned quickly and understood intelligence
broadly, encouraging her vast dynastic network to send her insights on European attitudes and intentions. As she grew in confidence, she clashed with
her governments about sensitive issues of surveillance and covertly supporting
rebels, which placed her in a difficult position. She demanded secret material
and berated ministers if ever they kept things from her. Yet she was still fairly
inexperienced, so she often felt powerless to change things directly. Thereafter,
in the 1860s, the rise of Germany, a country with which she had a great affinity,
served only to increase the tension between monarchical and state intelligence.
And again, Victoria had all the best-placed intelligence sources. She now grew
more confident to use them to outmaneuver her governments.

2

Queen Victoria's Secrets

War and the Rise of Germany

It is evident the whole is a Prussian intrigue.
—Queen Victoria, 1866

Ruling from the very public location of Buckingham Palace, Queen Victoria sat at the pinnacle of a vast private intelligence network spanning the European continent. Victoria's network frustrated her ministers, but it proved useful on many occasions. Intelligence now became a battleground in the broader European struggle for modern nation-states. Here, Victoria's intelligence allowed her to stretch her powers to the limit, influence the cabinet, and even help prevent war.

Britain and France had a tense and complex relationship in the 1850s. The French resented Britain's provocatively welcoming attitude toward European dissidents; the British resented French despotism with all its illiberal penumbrae of shadowy police spies and political surveillance. At the same time, the two rivals joined forces to prevent Russia from exploiting the demise of the Ottoman Empire and gaining access to the strategically important Mediterranean.

The Crimean War—fought in the Balkans, Black Sea, and Baltics between 1853 and 1856—pitted Britain, France, and the Ottoman Empire against Imperial Russia. Unfortunately for Victoria, Russia was an intelligence black hole. Three factors explain this: first, Britain still had no organized intelligence service—nor even a proper military intelligence department; second, even though the invention of the telegraph drastically sped up communication, gaps in the network caused lengthy delays in information reaching London; and third, the queen's royal intelligence network proved less useful on political affairs in the Russian capital, which was so far away and where fewer European nobility circulated.

Although there was little to go on, the queen impatiently demanded updates. She tried to keep a close eye on diplomatic maneuverings in the run-up to hostilities, but much of what reached the palace was confused and contradictory. In August 1853, after the Russian tsar had sent troops to the Balkans, Victoria gratefully received what she called "very satisfactory telegraphic intelligence" from the prime minister, Lord Aberdeen, that Russia had accepted a peaceful resolution.[1] After the Ottomans scuppered this, she became increasingly alarmed at reports coming from the region.[2] Victoria's cousin, the duke of Cambridge, serving as a special emissary to the queen from Constantinople, informed her of the "wretched" state of the Turkish military. Meanwhile, her pro-Turkish ambassador in Constantinople deliberately interpreted any Russian communications he could get his hands on as evidence of Russian aggression. It took weeks for their letters to arrive at Buckingham Palace, creating much confusion.[3] The queen grew impatient.

Aberdeen promised that there was "very little chance" of a Russian attack. Accordingly, Victoria approved the dispatch of a naval fleet to Turkey that autumn on the assumption that it would not see action. This "intelligence," as Victoria called it, proved entirely wrong.[4] British commanders set sail lacking basic information about the remote region's terrain and climate, let alone secret intelligence about Russian intentions or battle plans. Staggeringly, they did not even own a proper map.[5]

Back home, newspapers claimed to have unmasked a spy of an entirely different kind. In January 1854, rumors began to circulate that Prince Albert was a Russian agent. The prince had been part of British public life for well over a decade, but remained a constitutional anomaly. As a proud German, he had never entirely fitted in. Newspapers now peddled innuendo questioning his loyalty. They accused him of orchestrating foreign relations with German princes behind ministers' backs and of thwarting any British policy that undermined his own interests. Prussia, one of the most prominent German states, supported the tsar because of intermarriage and, at a time of international tension, accusations unfairly extended to Albert being a Russian spy.[6]

Victoria was livid, and thought the attacks "abominable." In combative mood, she expressed "intense indignation" to her government.[7] Consoling her, Lord Aberdeen said that very few people shared these views and that he had received information about the origins of the attacks.[8] Although he stopped short of saying what this information was, rumors circulated that the French had covertly planted the anti-Albert articles as part of a propaganda operation to undermine British sympathies toward Germany.[9] Interestingly, the queen had heard that "Russian intrigue," as she described it, was very active in Paris, where agents were trying to prevent the French from joining the war effort.[10]

Whatever the cause, thousands of gullible Londoners assembled at the Tower of London, wildly expressing their belief that Albert was about to be imprisoned for treason. "One word more about the credulity of the public," Albert wrote to a friend on January 24, 1854. "You will scarcely believe that my being committed to the Tower was believed all over the country—nay, even 'that the Queen had been arrested!'" The prime minister was forced to publicly extoll Albert's "unimpeachable loyalty to the Crown and Country" before the attacks subsided.[11]

In truth, Albert was both busy and patriotic. He was lobbying ministers with enough letters to now fill some fifty volumes in the Royal Archives. He drew up detailed plans to raise a force of 15,000 foreigners to fight in the conflict with Russia. The government politely declined.[12] Despite her intelligence and over ten years of experience with world affairs, Victoria felt out of her depth with military matters, and the war increased Albert's influence; it now became commonplace for him to meet alone with the prime minister. Though very much in love, Victoria and Albert were also engaged in a power struggle. Albert acquired more of Victoria's government work as her pregnancies forced her to step aside. Victoria was grateful for the support, but she deeply resented being robbed of her powers as queen.[13]

As the war in Crimea intensified, improvements in the telegraph network dramatically decreased the amount of time it took for information to reach London from the theater. In the spring of 1854, it took about five days; a year later, it took only a few hours.[14] Unfortunately, there was still little intelligence to report. "If only there was more news from the front," the queen complained. "If only one knew the details." She demanded that the secretary of state for war tell her everything. But he had little to tell.[15]

Most of the reporting came from newspapers. The new position of "war correspondent," sending back detailed updates at the same speed as diplomatic reporting, infuriated senior soldiers. One effectively accused *The Times* of treason, complaining that the Russians no longer needed spies, for they could read all about British developments in the newspaper.[16] He had a point: the tsar did indeed exclaim that "we have no need of spies, we have *The Times*."[17] The royal couple, although always eager for information, prized secrecy above all else. Victoria was "much disgusted" with the journalists; Albert melodramatically expressed his fear that "soon there will not be room enough in the same country for both the Monarchy and *The Times*."[18]

Sometimes the queen did successfully beat the press to sensitive material from Crimea. In March 1854, her royal messenger brought secret intelligence from the British consul at Saint Petersburg. It was so sensitive that he had not dared put it on paper. But once safely inside Buckingham Palace, he told Victoria about Russian preparations to lay new forms of explosives, which could be detonated remotely, underneath ice sheets. The Russians, he continued, planned to entice the British fleet into icy northern waters off the coast of Saint Petersburg, which became a forgotten theater of the Crimean War, before attacking from the rear.[19] His intelligence was improbable, but it was hurriedly dispatched to the naval forces that had left for the Baltic earlier in the month.

The Crimean theater was more significant. Here, by the middle of 1854, Charles Cattley, a multilingual British diplomat with long experience of the region, began to improvise a military intelligence department. Indeed, Cattley had grown up in Russia, and his family was still there, forcing him to adopt a cover name to ensure their safety.[20] The foreign secretary, Lord Clarendon, was so impressed that he told the queen straight away about Cattley's methods, sources, and intelligence. Cattley, Clarendon eagerly recounted, had gained valuable intelligence on enemy morale, learning that Russian soldiers did not want to fight. "We curse that old tyrant and brute Nicholas," they had told him, "for dragging us from our homes." The queen listened intently. She thought it "pretty strong language."[21]

Early the next year, the duke of Newcastle, secretary of state for war, told Queen Victoria that Cattley had taken charge of a nascent "department of intelligence."[22] His sources included Polish deserters, Russian forces, and Muslim Crimean Tartars. He was willing to conduct interrogations; but so desperate were the conditions on the ground that he gained much of his intelligence by simply providing food and warm shelter. He also ran several "Tartar" spies.

As a result, Cattley tracked Russian troop movements and provided invaluable intelligence for operational planning. His main contribution was professional order-of-battle reports on the numbers and movements of the enemy; it made a considerable difference in battles across the theater.

Unfortunately, the success was short-lived; Cattley died of cholera in 1855.[23] So important was his intelligence that Queen Victoria herself described his death as "such a serious loss."[24] Shortly afterward, she grew frustrated that "with the head of the Intelligence Department dead," Britain now had "no means left" whereby "to gather information or keep up secret correspondence" with sources.[25]

Perhaps the most vexing aspect of the war for Victoria was the lack of secrecy. With the arrival of the telegraph and aggressive war reporting, it was impossible to hide the weak progress. Led by gentlemen who knew little of modern warfare, equipped only with obsolete weapons, and often short of ammunition, soldiers died mostly of dysentery and pneumonia. They were more in danger from their own side than from enemy soldiers, who were no more competent. Dissatisfaction with the running of the war increased; and in January 1855, Parliament appointed a select committee to probe this dire situation. Aberdeen resigned and was replaced by Palmerston, the royal couple's least favorite minister. It was no surprise that both Albert and Victoria had hated the frank and fearless war reporting of *The Times*.

Despite the setback, Victoria was determined to maintain as good an understanding of events in Crimea as possible. She developed an impressive grasp of allied positions, personally signed the commission of every officer, and wrote

encouraging letters to generals in the field.[26] "You never saw anyone," the secretary of state for war told the commander in the region, "so entirely taken up
with military affairs as she is."[27] On April 18, 1855, Windsor Castle hosted a
one-day war council attended by Albert.[28] A few days later, Victoria joined in a
more informal discussion, describing it as "one of the most interesting things
I ever was present at."[29] Her persistent pestering of ministers had paid off, placing her well inside the loop. In September, she received "with deep emotion,
the welcome intelligence of the fall of Sebastapol," the capital of Crimea and
perhaps the final phase of the war.[30]

British victory was achieved in early 1856, and the queen found out in the
most curious manner. Just before midnight on January 16, as she was about to
go to bed, secret news of a peace settlement arrived via the king of Prussia. It
left Victoria "astounded and indeed startled." Oddly, although the telegram was
not written in code, and the king had openly signed his name, he begged her
not to mention him as the source.[31] The deal was still a secret. She and Albert
decided that the operators along the whole line of the telegraph must have
already read the king's message and so, against his wishes, they passed on both
its content and provenance to the foreign secretary.[32]

Victoria was more skeptical than her Prussian counterpart about whether
this deal would actually result in a bone fide peace settlement; and, sure
enough, it was a slow process. The next month, Clarendon tried to update her
about various diplomatic setbacks; but, once again, Victoria had already heard
the "intelligence," as she called it, through her private channels.[33] Both sides
eventually signed a peace agreement in March 1856, denying Russia access to
a warm water port in the south and returning occupied territory to the Ottoman Empire. Victoria was unimpressed with the final deal, but begrudgingly
accepted it.[34]

Prussia had frustrated Victoria throughout the Crimean War. She accused the
king, who had oscillated between supposed neutrality and support for the tsar,
of falling victim to "Russian intrigues."[35] How she would have loved a source
close to the Prussian government, especially because Prussia would become
increasingly significant to European intrigues over the following decades. The
end of the Crimean War left France as the dominant continental land power,
sparking a chain of events leading to the unification of Germany in 1871.

Princess Victoria, known affectionately as Vicky, was Queen Victoria's eldest
child. Vicky was close to both her parents, but to her father in particular, and
she was a bright and precocious child, who, at eleven years old, had escorted
the crown prince of Prussia, nine years her senior, around the Great Exhibition.

She was fourteen when they met again at Balmoral. Victoria and Albert hoped that a marriage between the two would cement relations between London and Berlin, perhaps encouraging a more liberal Prussia in the process. Vicky married Crown Prince Frederick, known to the family as Fritz, in January 1858.

Married to the heir to the Prussian throne, the young princess had an instant place at the heart of the Prussian court. Vicky became an outstandingly well-placed source of intelligence. She sent over four thousand letters back to her mother, often full of sensitive details about state affairs. The value of this was not lost on her parents and, before his death in 1861, Albert regularly looked to her for intelligence, supplementing his own German contacts. In 1859, when Prussia mobilized against France, it was Vicky who provided the best material, including military plans.[36]

Yet Vicky was a foreigner in a strange court. Her split loyalties put her in a difficult position, and she suffered similar problems to her father's. Like Albert, she faced accusations of being a spy; unlike Albert, she actually was sending sensitive information back to her homeland. Victoria warned her eldest daughter, soon after marrying Fritz, about spies in the palace; and on one occasion, the queen berated her for sending a sensitive letter by unsecured mail rather than private messenger.[37] Otto von Bismarck, the ambitious minister president of Prussia, was under no illusions. To him, Vicky was nothing less than an English agent, and he interpreted her intimacy with Queen Victoria as potentially treasonous.[38] As his influence grew, Bismarck sought to freeze her out.

Vicky not only provided intelligence but also acted as an agent of influence. As Albert's favorite child and protégé, she promoted her father's vision of a more liberal Germany against the thoroughly autocratic style of the emperor. Highly educated and fluent in several languages, she was up to date on the latest social and political theories. She eventually read the works of Karl Marx to ensure that she had a proper understanding of socialism, but such behavior did not find favor in the Prussian court. Marx had been exiled from Germany in 1849 because of his ideas and was living in London, alongside Mazzini and other rebels.[39]

In July 1863, someone leaked letters between Fritz and his father, the king of Prussia, to the newspapers. They revealed Fritz's opposition to the king's high-handed rule. The mole was none other than Vicky herself. It was a secretive attempt to undermine the king and covertly influence Prussia in a more liberal direction.[40] *The Times* praised Vicky's liberal values and her support for the prince's protests against Prussia's slide toward tyranny.

The leaks infuriated the king; but they infuriated Bismarck even more, and he quickly accused Fritz of being too indiscreet with his wife. The king, he counseled opportunistically, should no longer trust his son.[41] Meanwhile, Vicky gave her mother the inside track on the fallout from what she "will have no doubt seen" in the newspapers.[42] A few weeks later, she wrote: "I send you *all the papers* so that you may see what Fritz has done, said, and written!"[43] Bismarck had a point.

The so-called Schleswig-Holstein question, over the status of these two small duchies in northern Europe, presented another opportunity for Vicky to provide useful intelligence to her demanding mother. The death of her father three years earlier had made her reporting from Germany even more important.

With both countries claiming rights, war broke out between Denmark and Prussia in February 1864. The causes were painfully intricate, combining Prussian nationalist aspirations, the succession of the Danish monarchy, and Danish violation of a treaty signed after the first Schleswig-Holstein war in 1852. "The Schleswig-Holstein question," Lord Palmerston, the prime minister, famously quipped, "is so complicated, only three men in Europe have ever understood it. One was Prince Albert, who is dead. The second was a German professor who became mad. I am the third and I have forgotten all about it."

After refreshing his memory, Palmerston intended to intervene in support of Denmark. Queen Victoria's natural sympathies lay with the Germans, and, desperate to avoid war with Prussia, she insisted that her ministers tone down their threats in defense of Denmark.[44] There were problems for Vicky, too. The previous year, her brother Bertie, heir to the throne, had married Princess Alexandra of Denmark instead of a German woman. Now that war had broken out between Prussia and Denmark, many suspected Vicky of supporting the Danish on behalf of her new sister-in-law, although in fact, like her mother, she supported the Germans.

At the start of February, as German troops crossed into Schleswig, the foreign secretary, John Russell, continued to agitate for intervention to help the Danes. Victoria countered that neither France nor Russia would support him. Not trusting the queen's advice, Russell double-checked via his own intelligence channels and found Saint Petersburg to be open to a naval demonstration. The queen was furious. As the Germans marched north, Palmerston and Russell pressed for naval forces to be sent to the Baltic Sea to defend Copenhagen. The queen refused—and received cabinet backing.[45] Once again, Palmerston and Victoria were at odds, and they were effectively running rival intelligence networks to promote their opposing policies.

Vicky's intelligence proved invaluable in helping the queen rebuff calls for British intervention. Throughout February 1864, she sent bundles of sensitive material on intentions, progress of battles, weather conditions, and even letters written by her husband's aide-de-camp.[46] She continually updated her mother on the animosity between Britain and Prussia, which, she thought, was "kept up by foolish trifles which could be avoided." The meddling queen used these insights to prevent a rupture of British–Prussian relations.[47]

As the war continued, Vicky warned her mother about rising tensions after "absurd, unjust, rude, and violent attacks" against Prussia in the English press.[48] A few days later, Queen Victoria again told Russell to tone down his rhetoric, which could "only be taken by Austria and Prussia as implying a threat."[49] Attempting to undercut rival channels of intelligence so as to increase her own influence, Vicky criticized information that Britain had gathered through diplomatic channels. She told Queen Victoria that the ambassador in Berlin "knows no German and understands nothing whatever of German affairs." He was, she continued, "continually misinformed" and picked "up his information from bad sources, such as other silly diplomatists who understand nothing at all."[50] In June 1864, Vicky wrote a particularly alarming letter, telling her mother that the British ambassador had "spoken of our going to war with Prussia!" This, Queen Victoria concluded sharply, "is not at all right."[51]

The queen augmented these insights from the continent with information from sources closer to home. Throughout the crisis, she used Lord Granville as a "special observer" inside the cabinet. A former foreign secretary, he now attended cabinet meetings as lord president of the council, a role that brought him into regular contact with the monarch. Granville discreetly reported individual ministers' opinions back to the palace without their knowledge, giving Victoria insights into the arguments and factions inside the government. The queen also used Granville, alongside her private secretary, to influence cabinet members against Russell and Palmerston.[52]

It is impossible to determine the decisiveness of Queen Victoria's interventions, but the outcomes matched her preferences. Rejecting the wishes of both the prime minister and the foreign secretary, her government eventually decided against military intervention. In August 1864, Denmark ceded Schleswig and Holstein to Prussia and Austria. But the queen's victory came at a price. The press criticized her for overstepping the monarch's constitutional role and being soft on Germany. After loyally defending her in Parliament, John Russell warned the queen that her relatives in Germany had "allowed rumours to go forth" that she supported the Germans over the Danes. Victoria was "most indignant" at being called out.[53] She had now been on the throne for over a quarter century. As the years had turned into decades, she had grown more confident and wilier. Not only did she berate her ministers and demand to know everything that was going on, she also intrigued against them and even tried to outmaneuver them.

Queen Victoria now received more and more intelligence from Prussia about Bismarck's growing power. The queen of Prussia told her bluntly that her husband was "under the influence of a clever, unprincipled man, who has virtually changed him."[54] As his influence grew, Bismarck tried to isolate Vicky and Fritz, even placing spies in their household to monitor their contacts and conversations. Secrets were not shared with them. While the flow of intelligence to Queen Victoria continued, its quality inevitably diminished. Vicky was playing a dangerous game; and Lady Ponsonby, wife of the queen's private secretary, worried for her safety, confiding: "I don't think the Queen realizes what an extraordinary state of things exists in Germany in the way of espionage and intrigue."[55]

In early March 1866, Princess Vicky's private secretary sent a stark warning to Buckingham Palace. Otto von Bismarck intended to provoke a war with Austria; his plan of achieving German unification through violence—or blood and iron, as he famously stated—would triumph over the hesitance of the Prussian king. Underlining the importance of royal intelligence, the British ambassador in Berlin could only confirm that a secret meeting between ministers and military officers had indeed taken place. The experienced British minister in Frankfurt confessed to being "utterly in the dark."[56]

Vicky's intelligence was accurate. Bismarck was indeed agitating for war so as to challenge Austria for leadership of the German confederation. He found pretext in a dispute over the administration of Schleswig and Holstein, which Prussia and Austria had run jointly since the war in 1864. Intelligence would be crucial in determining the outbreak and timing of the war. The future of Europe was at stake.

To determine its response, Britain needed to know, first, whether Bismarck had the ability to carry Prussia with him; and, second, whether Prussia and Austria were interpreting each other's military preparations as defensive or offensive. Britain, still without a military intelligence department, and still less an intelligence community, had yet to work out that Bismarck was deliberately misinterpreting Austrian maneuvers as offensive, and that he had enough influence to persuade the king to send troops to the southern border.[57] Victoria turned to her own trusted intelligence sources.

The queen received a flood of letters from royal houses across Germany warning that war was becoming more likely.[58] She had developed an impressive network: in addition to Vicky's access, the duke of Coburg boasted of "confidential and trustworthy" contacts in Vienna and Berlin keeping him up to date with "the most secret proceedings."[59] These royal communications soon bypassed official government channels, frustrating both Bismarck and the British foreign secretary, Lord Clarendon.[60] The Prussian court asked Victoria to mediate, but she was dissuaded by Vicky's warning that Bismarck, "the wicked man," was determined to "pin" the king to war and "paralyse any intervention from elsewhere."[61]

Vicky's position placed a great deal of pressure on her. In one letter, she hurriedly wrote: "I am not supposed to know anything contained in the Despatches, but as I did hear this I thought I would tell you." Fearful of Prussian spies and not trusting British diplomats either, she now wanted to increase the security of their communications by using coded ciphers to which even the Foreign Office would not have access.[62] The queen had first seen a new "deciphering machine," as she called it, three years earlier and thought it "very curious."[63] She now knew that this contraption was increasingly important in securing communications. Meanwhile, Clarendon grew frustrated that the queen rarely consulted him or asked him for information.[64]

Warned off mediation, Queen Victoria instead sought to drive a wedge between the Prussian king and Bismarck. She hoped not only to avoid war but also to unify Germany as a liberal ally of Britain, just as Albert had always wanted. Victoria told the king that Bismarck had betrayed his confidence by revealing their private conversations.[65] Without consulting her ministers, she warned him in strong terms of Bismarck's ambition and deception: "You are deceived, you are made to believe that you are to be attacked, and I your true friend and sister hear your honoured name attacked and abused, for the faults and recklessness of others—or rather more of *one man*.[66] She insisted that her message be hand-delivered to the king in order to avoid Bismarck's spies.[67]

Victoria assessed incoming contradictory intelligence astutely. While Vicky provided intelligence on Prussian mobilization, her mother received reports from Germany that "only Bismarck" wanted war "and was pushing the King of Prussia into it"; that Prussia would disarm if Austria disarmed first; and that Austrian defensive maneuvers had raised hopes of peace.[68] At the same time, she understood Bismarck's influence and intentions, noting that "Prussian intrigue" was coloring assessments of Austrian intentions.[69] She continued to think "the deluded" king had misread the situation in blaming Austria for imaginary offenses.[70] Fearing war, she pressed for some sort of intervention.

By contrast, diplomats in the Foreign Office clung on to the wishful assumption that Germany was heading irreversibly toward liberalism. They failed to properly understand Bismarck, pointing to his unpopularity with large sections of the population, especially in the south. As late as May 1866, Clarendon predicted that war would not break out because of a lack of domestic support.[71] Accordingly, diplomats advocated strict neutrality and refused to get involved in continental quarrels.[72]

For all her intelligence sources, the queen had little influence as the cabinet persistently blocked her requests for an intervention, including joining an alliance with Austria and France, to prevent war. She continued to push for some sort of remonstrance, but reluctantly acquiesced. All the while, she expressed strong opinions, shaped by her own intelligence sources and dynastic interests.[73] This was one battle that Victoria lost. War broke out in the middle of June 1866 and ended with a Prussian victory seven weeks later.

As the dust settled, the queen continued to press the importance of a "strong united liberal Germany" as a "most useful ally" for Britain. She used her outstanding sources to try to shape policy in her favor. Arguing against a policy of isolationism, she told the incoming foreign secretary that she would share "any private intelligence which she may receive" to shed light on the present state of feeling.[74] Or rather, she would selectively share any intelligence that backed up her stance. The delicate balance of power on the continent had been disturbed; senior diplomats in the Foreign Office now assessed that a war between Prussia and France was inevitable.[75]

Bismarck's dramatic ascendancy made Princess Vicky nervous. She was well aware of having sent piles of state secrets to Queen Victoria and, fearing they might fall into the hands of Bismarck's spies, asked her mother to burn them. The queen refused; the intelligence was too important for her personal diplomacy.[76]

The buildup to the Franco-Prussian War of 1870 was mostly about European dynasties and royal marriages. So it is all the more surprising that it was marked by a royal intelligence failure. Bismarck plotted to put a Prussian prince on the vacant Spanish throne, so as to extend his influence, humiliate France, and potentially provoke war. From Berlin, Queen Victoria's sources in the royal court informed her of wider developments—but they had no idea of Bismarck's detailed role: that he had been secretly scheming for six months.[77]

Vicky naively informed her mother merely of a Spanish invitation for a Prussian prince to take the throne. This in itself, she emphasized, was "*most profoundly secret*": the French could not find out.[78] When the initial offer was turned down, Vicky wrongly told her mother that "all thoughts about Spain are entirely given up."[79] Her husband, Crown Prince Fritz, later updated that "fresh communications were opened." He made no mention of Bismarck's insistence on them.[80]

When the news broke, the French—with some justification—were outraged by what they saw as a Prussian plot to humiliate France and provoke war. It took a great deal of diplomacy and royal letter-writing to calm tensions and convince the Prussian candidate to withdraw. Drawing on her continental sources, Victoria assumed that the matter had been settled.[81] She was wrong. Paris now demanded future guarantees from the king of Prussia that the candidature would never be renewed.[82]

The king politely refused, but in doing so presented Bismarck with another opportunity to provoke the French. Without the king's knowledge, he edited the

Prussian response to French demands. Although careful not to fabricate anything, Bismarck did deliberately give the impression that the French had been
more aggressive than was actually the case and the king brusquer in reply. He
quickly sent his edited version to the press and, posing as the injured party, sat
back to watch the fallout. Both nations began to mobilize.[83]

Victoria had an excellent network across Germany, but it lacked access to
the real center of power: Bismarck. Accordingly, the queen and her government possessed little knowledge about what was really going on. She did not
know about Bismarck's role in either the controversy over the Spanish throne
or the edited telegram. A decade later, Vicky was still telling her mother that
Bismarck, despite being "the most mischievous and dangerous person alive,"
did "*not* fan the flame" of the Franco-Prussian War.[84] This intelligence failure
exacerbated Britain's complacent response to the Spanish crisis.[85] Unaware of
Bismarck's role, and influenced by Vicky and by close relatives serving in the
German army, Queen Victoria blamed what she saw as the despotic and corrupt government in Paris: it was the "infatuated French who seem only bent
on finding a pretext to go to war."[86]

This was surprising, for the queen had been convinced, just four years earlier, that Bismarck was the "sole author" of the 1866 war.[87] So this was also an
intelligence assessment failure by Victoria. Perhaps her long-standing suspicion
of the French, alongside the lack of sources on Bismarck, affected her judgment.
Either way, Victoria prided herself on being well-enough informed to influence
European politics through her personal diplomacy. In this instance she failed
miserably, and it was not until the eventual declaration of war that the foreign
secretary started to point the finger at Bismarck.[88] Even then, however, Vicky
still insisted that France had forced Prussia into hostilities against her will.[89]

Bismarck's propaganda successfully turned British public opinion against
the French—and perpetuated his victim status. Shortly after the outbreak of
war, he told the Belgian minister in Berlin that France had previously offered
to exchange south Germany for Belgium. This alarmed King Leopold II, who
quickly fired off an angry letter to Victoria about the French desire to "dominate the world."[90] The very next day, *The Times* published a draft treaty from
1866—although Bismarck was careful not to reveal the date—between France
and Prussia, in which Paris had made similar territorial demands.[91]

The queen, lacking intelligence on Bismarck, did not know what to make of
it: "People doubted it being genuine," she wrote, or "at best some did, others,
were greatly alarmed."[92] The ambassador to Berlin verified its authenticity,
and the queen reacted with outrage toward the French, just as Bismarck
had intended.[93] Victoria then asked Vicky whether taking Belgium had been
Napoleon's idea, as Bismarck had implied, or Prussia's. Again, Vicky was unsure,
responding simply that she never trusted Bismarck.[94]

Victoria had been played, and she continued to blame the French for the war. When one British diplomat in Germany accurately reported Bismarck's role in the run-up to war, the queen's private secretary dismissed it, again preferring to blame Paris because of anti-French prejudice.[95]

Despite Victoria's sympathies for Prussia, Britain had adopted a strictly neutral position in the Franco-Prussian War. Accurate intelligence remained important for all sides, as Britain's refusal to intervene caused tension. The king of Prussia complained to Victoria about secret reports that England was supplying France with coal and artillery. This intelligence likely came from Bismarck, who was driving an anti-English campaign and, as Vicky told her mother, no one had the time to properly investigate or validate such claims.[96] Queen Victoria found it incredibly frustrating, especially because the claims directly contradicted her true sympathies.[97] She loved intrigue but hated being outmaneuvered.

Meanwhile, suspicious eyes watched Vicky constantly. Bismarck accused her of passing secrets to Queen Victoria, but Vicky insisted that she was only passing on information that "may be agreeable and useful" as a personal act. This distinction would not have appeased Bismarck, especially because he thought these secrets were making their way to the French. Vicky knew she was taking a huge risk. "England," she told Victoria, "is supposed to be on the other side."[98]

In early September 1870, the French emperor surrendered after defeat at the Battle of Sedan in northeast France. Turmoil and confusion broke out on the streets of Paris; the emperor fell, but war carried on under the new republican government. The queen quickly learned of an improvised, amateurish, but successful exfiltration of the French empress to England.

As word spread of the emperor's defeat and imperial guards abandoned their positions, a mob broke into the Tuileries Palace on the bank of the Seine. The empress, grabbing only a hat and a coat, slipped out onto the street and, as the crowd surged toward her, escaped in a horse-drawn carriage to the house of her American dentist, Thomas Evans. A famous pioneer of pain-free dentistry, Evans served the French royal court, but he also treated royal patients across the continent, including Victoria's children, the prince of Wales and Princess Vicky. In the process, he became an unofficial diplomat, delivering sensitive messages literally between the mouths of royals.[99] When the French empress arrived at his door, Evans packed all the gold he had into a bag and rode with her out of Paris. Disguised as an English doctor and an "eccentric nervous English lady," they dodged violent mobs and Prussian spies en route to the coast.[100]

Two days later, they arrived at a harbor in Normandy, where Evans met an English aristocrat, John Montagu Burgoyne, who reluctantly agreed to carry the empress across the Channel on his yacht. Under cover of darkness, she arrived

just after midnight. The weather was appalling, but, with the French authorities closing in, the empress could not wait any longer; Burgoyne had already
seen off one Parisian spy just half an hour before the empress boarded. The
boat hurriedly set sail, landing on the Isle of Wight early the next morning.[101]

News quickly reached the palace, where Victoria thought the dramatic tale of
the empress's escape from mobs and spies "too sad and shocking."[102] Underlining this ad hoc approach to intelligence, Burgoyne was at pains to point out that
his involvement was the result of pure chance.[103] It clearly made an impression
on the queen. Vicky introduced the mild, elderly dentist to her mother some
fifteen years later; neither had forgotten "that dreadful day" in Paris.[104] Another
five years after that, in 1890, Burgoyne dined with the queen at Osborne House.
She remembered him fondly as the "man who saved the Empress."[105]

The Franco-Prussian War formally ended in January 1871. Germany was
unified; the king became the German emperor, and Bismarck was made the
first chancellor of the German Empire. Fritz warned Victoria shortly afterward
that Bismarck might someday try to provoke a war against England.[106] After
unification, Bismarck stepped up his campaign against Vicky and her husband,
increasing surveillance, further isolating them, and reducing the flow of useful
information to Queen Victoria.[107]

The mid–nineteenth century pitted traditional royal intelligence channels—
indeed, even royal policies—against those of the nation-state. In a period of
great political upheaval, it formed part of a broader clash between dynastic and
state interests. Royals with split loyalties like Vicky, and Albert before her, were
a dying breed. Suspicious of Britain's liberal influence, Bismarck saw Vicky as
an English agent. In the battle between royal and state intelligence, Bismarck
was victorious.

Under constant surveillance from Bismarck's spies, Vicky, Fritz, and Queen
Victoria increasingly communicated by cipher. Victoria had once dodged spies
simply by sealing her letters with silver paper to make tampering obvious.[108]
This would no longer do. Now, only she and Vicky knew the codes, personally
decrypting each message. Vicky insisted on keeping them even from the Foreign Office, lest they fall into the wrong hands.[109] Despite the increased security, the letters contained ever less sensitive information. Bismarck had frozen
Fritz and Vicky out; whenever Fritz asked delicate questions, ministers gave a
deliberately evasive answer. Vicky simply became withdrawn.[110]

Fritz died of cancer in 1888 at just fifty-six years old. He had finally managed to become emperor but for only ninety-nine days, a tragically short length
of time. With him died Victoria's hopes of a liberal Germany, and any influence

Vicky may have had as empress. Instead, Fritz was succeeded by the pompous Kaiser Wilhelm II, whose ambitions for German power were even greater than those of Bismarck.

On the eve of Fritz's death, Vicky tried to send a stash of confidential papers, hidden in her doctor's suitcase and hat box, to Queen Victoria at Balmoral. She had already taken three crates back to Windsor during the jubilee celebrations the previous year.[111] Now, Bismarck's spies in the British Embassy found out. The new German emperor sealed Vicky's palace, threatened to open the luggage, and demanded all state papers. After a tense diplomatic standoff, he backed down, but the incident underlined that Vicky was in grave danger. The Germans could have easily interpreted her letters as evidence of a treacherous conspiracy. Fortunately, the prince of Wales used Fritz's funeral as an opportunity to remove the last of Vicky's papers out of the country.[112]

Or so he thought. Decades later, just after the Second World War, Anthony Blunt, working for British intelligence, and later exposed as a Soviet spy, warned the Royal Family that some of Vicky's papers still existed and had become "exposed to the eyes of the inquisitive and the fingers of the acquisitive." They contained not only secrets of state but also secrets of love. Blunt discreetly visited Vicky's ancestral home, then under American control, smuggling documents back to Windsor.[113]

By the end of the 1880s, Princess Vicky warned Queen Victoria that Bismarck's "creatures" had infiltrated her entourage. The system of rapportage and espionage "is so great at Berlin that they would not venture to open their lips."[114] Bismarck had begun sending his spies to her residence at Potsdam, the Neues Palais. He chose his agents carefully, then persuaded them to apply for low-grade jobs and to stay in them for a long time. His most useful spies were two menials in the accounts department, who saw much of the inner workings of the palace. Vicky and Fritz knew they were surrounded by an army of spies. When they returned for the trip, they noticed the locks had been forced and desks and filing cabinets searched. These blatant intrusions were clearly designed to intimidate, and they succeeded.[115] The British ambassador in Berlin, Sir Robert Morier, warned Vicky to write down nothing incriminating in her diary or in her letters unless it was in cypher.[116] She clearly took this to heart. The best spy in Britain's royal intelligence network had been neutralized. Victoria's ability to outmaneuver her governments dramatically declined with it.

3

Queen Victoria's Great Game

Empire and Intrigue

*It is to me inconceivable that a handful of men sitting in a room
in London, the greater part knowing little about Egypt,
should pretend to say when there is danger or not!*
—Queen Victoria, 1893

Queen Victoria developed impressive private intelligence networks in Western Europe, but when it came to imperial intrigues, she reigned in the dark—a place she did not like to be. Instead of a system of royal relatives feeding back sensitive information to London, the queen had to rely on haphazard reporting from brave adventurers traveling to distant, rugged, and poorly mapped frontiers.[1] More frustratingly, she was dependent on ministers to keep her updated on eastern matters. No longer could she use her own private sources to influence—and even outmaneuver—the government. For a demanding queen who liked to know everything first, this was quite unacceptable.

Worse still, information was patchy and took a long time to travel vast distances from the frontier. The empire quadrupled in size during Victoria's long reign and, as a result, never-ending small wars became a constant feature.[2] Imperial rivalries in Central Asia brought Russia and Britain into a protracted battle of intrigue and influence known as "the Great Game." India's northwest frontier became the key battleground for espionage, bribery, and political warfare. Here, underhanded activity triggered fewer moral concerns compared with debates about subverting the modern states of Western Europe where Victoria's friends and relatives reigned.[3]

Victoria was particularly keen for intelligence on Russia. Unfortunately, useful intelligence on Russian intrigues was hard to come by. When Victoria's second son, Alfred, married the tsar's daughter in 1874, ministers hoped for political benefits, including insight into the Russian court. In reality, their union was never likely to re-create the sort of access Vicky had in Prussia. For a start, it was a less happy marriage than Vicky's, while the queen's relationship with her new daughter-in-law was prickly. She irritated the queen's household, too; Victoria's sardonic private secretary, Henry Ponsonby, thought the young Russian was "the spoilt daughter of a semi-Eastern despot." Besides, the couple spent little time in Russia and, shortly after the wedding, the tsar dismissed a member of Alfred's entourage for being indiscreet. Although this inauspicious start left Victoria frustrated, Alfred did succeed in providing the occasional update about developments in Russia.[4]

The queen characteristically rebuked her ministers for this lack of intelligence on Russia. Before approving the appointment of a new chargé d'affaires to Saint Petersburg in 1877, she bluntly asked whether the candidate actually had any knowledge of Russia. Too many people, she moaned, left for important posts without any knowledge of either the country or the language. The foreign secretary assured her that no one who was available knew more about Russia than his man, Francis Plunkett.[5] Such knowledge was especially vital because, during this era, ambassadors doubled up as spies. Two years later, Victoria instructed the new ambassador in Romania to "make it your business to discover" Russian and Ottoman activity, the private views of other ambassadors, and information on fortifications in the region, reporting everything back to the Foreign Office in cypher.[6] She later asked the British ambassador in Russia to send back "anything of a personal nature regarding their imperial majesties the Emperor and the Empress which may come under his observation."[7]

British intelligence did become better organized in the second half of Victoria's reign. In 1873, the War Office finally created a long-overdue Intelligence Branch after a string of reviews of the poor intelligence performance during the Crimean War. Focusing mainly on India and Africa, it collected and collated military intelligence to help plan for war.[8] Over a decade later, in 1887, the navy followed suit to create its own Naval Intelligence Department. Queen Victoria kept a close eye on these developments, dining at Windsor with new intelligence chiefs. If Britain was to have an organized intelligence service, Victoria wanted to be involved.[9]

Fortunately, Britain had its own James Bond in Moscow. Lieutenant Colonel Frederick Wellesley, a relative of Wellington, owed his position to patronage from the duke of Cambridge, the queen's cousin. He was a "classic Victorian scoundrel."[10] Famous for his extravagance, for six years, and especially during the crisis of 1877–88, he produced some of the best intelligence ever obtained from the closed world of Tsarist Moscow. In Bondian fashion, when it was circulated to the Cabinet in London, it was often marked "for your eyes only." Unfortunately for Wellesley, ministers often disregarded these exhortations.[11]

Russian policy was hard to follow. The Ministry of Foreign Affairs and the Ministry of War were pursing contradictory policies, as were other individuals, often disregarding the tsar's view but claiming his authority.[12] Wellesley flourished, making the most of his meager royal connections to allow him to mingle with top Russian military leaders. His agents borrowed papers from Russian ministries, taking them just long enough for Wellesley to make copies by hand or even photograph them. He had agents in the War Office, the Russian navy, and eventually the Ministry of Foreign Affairs. Most importantly, he saw the minutes of discussion across departments and even some comments written by the prime minister and the tsar.[13]

Wellesley was not typical of the Victorian spies of empire. The majority were more like Frederick Burnaby, a traveler-cum-adventurer-cum-soldier who provided intelligence from the imperial frontier and claimed to be descended from Edward I. As a slovenly young officer, Burnaby was famed for his strength and, although later suffering ill health, his bravery never deserted him. In the autumn of 1875, he traveled across Russia and central Asia on horseback accompanied by a dwarf servant, evading Russian officers and enduring frostbite.[14] On his return, Victoria summoned him to Windsor to be regaled with tales of his adventures and hear his assessment of the Russian threat. He warned about Russian aggression and the serious threat posed to India. The queen listened avidly, agreeing with his characterization of Russia as duplicitous and dangerous. The Foreign Office was less enamored: nervous diplomats feared that his subsequent memoir, A Ride to Khiva, a bestseller that turned him into a spy celebrity, was so anti-Russian that it would spark a diplomatic incident.[15]

The next year, Burnaby traveled to Asia Minor. He was entering dangerous territory at a tumultuous time. In April 1877, while he rode through what is now eastern Turkey, news reached London that Russia had declared war on the Ottoman Empire. Fighting quickly broke out in the Balkans, but the real question was whether Russia would advance to Constantinople. Burnaby survived an attempt to poison him by Bulgarian agents and then quickly wrote another book on the subject, which the queen read with interest.[16] She was vehemently anti-Russian and, according to Henry Ponsonby, persistently saw foreign affairs as a "struggle for supremacy against Russia."[17]

Victoria liked Burnaby's intelligence reports because of their anti-Russian fervor rather than their accuracy. She broadly agreed with his outlook that Turkish rule in Asia Minor, despite its faults, was better than Russian rule. In this, he joined the "Prince of Wales set," even if Bertie found his claims of royal descent rather annoying. Burnaby was more than just a poser-cum-royal-protégé and instead was something of an intelligence visionary. Promoted to lieutenant colonel in the Blues and Royals, he became a pioneer balloonist, advocating their use for battlefield surveillance, but adding that the future of aviation lay with heavier-than-air machines.[18]

Victoria blamed Russia throughout the crisis. Turkey had brutally quashed an uprising in Bulgaria a year earlier, which sparked the war with Russia. The failed uprising had resulted in the massacre of tens of thousands of people. The queen demanded intelligence but received prevarication in response. The prime minister, Benjamin Disraeli, who cared little for oppressed minorities overseas, dismissed it as coffee house babble.[19] After consulting his "trusty agents," the Turkophile ambassador in the region agreed, warning her not to believe exaggerations of "alleged 'Bulgarian atrocities.'"[20] This suited Victoria, who was herself desperate to blame the Russians. She accused the Russians of instigating the insurrection in the first place, and of then somehow preventing the Turks from sending regular troops to quell it, thereby paving the way for ill-disciplined bands of wild men, as she put it, to commit atrocities. It was all Russia's fault.[21]

Victoria lambasted politicians, especially William Gladstone, who publicly criticized the Turkish atrocities. Gladstone had been leader of the Liberal Party, and alternated with Disraeli as prime minister, but Victoria detested him. He was, according to the queen, "half-madman," a "mischief maker and firebrand."[22] She argued that blaming Turkey for the mass killings, as Gladstone kept doing, simply emboldened Russia. Gladstone, now in the opposition, published an inflammatory pamphlet denouncing Turkish oppression and criticizing Disraeli's indifference toward the dead.

The queen was absolutely livid. Lashing out, she accused him of "consorting with a Russian female spy." Olga Novikov lost her brother in the Balkans, and had since campaigned strongly about Turkish abuses in Bulgaria. In doing so, she regularly shared the stage at public rallies with Gladstone, who saw her as a source of authentic information about Russian affairs.[23] The queen, like much of the hostile press, thought she was an agent of the tsar, sent to influence and beguile the gullible politician—and Novikov certainly requested more information from Gladstone than he was prepared to supply.[24]

Russia moved troops into the Balkans in the spring of 1877, leaving Victoria convinced that they had Constantinople firmly in their sights. Disraeli was more trusting of the tsar, initially taking the Russians at their word that they would stop short of the Ottoman capital. As was so often the case, Victoria, armed with private intelligence, thought she knew better. This time her secret source was the equerry to her son Alfred, Arthur Balfour Haig, who had married into the Russian Royal Family. Haig had secretly told her that the Russians knew it would take Britain six weeks to send troops to the theater and thus intended to get a head start on Constantinople—the real prize. Victoria passed his warning on to the prime minister but promised to keep her source secret.[25] She melodramatically warned Disraeli that if the Russians reached Constantinople, she "would be so humiliated that she thinks she would have to abdicate at once."[26]

Throughout the Turko-Russian conflict, the queen was as bellicose in her Russophobia as she was unrestrained. She scoured her intelligence to cherry-pick information, which she then used to manipulate her government into remonstrating. On one occasion, she quoted a vague report indicating that some source had supposedly heard that Russian artillery had fired on ambulances. Neither the prime minister nor the foreign secretary had noticed this report and, in the words of her private secretary, their subsequent remonstration was "entirely the Queen's doing."[27]

She urged Disraeli to "be bold," but the cabinet was split.[28] They agreed that Russian occupation of Constantinople would justify a military response, but the isolationist foreign secretary, Lord Derby, remained reluctant to take action, much to the queen's annoyance.[29] With more than a hint of bitterness, the prince of Wales told his mother: "I suppose we shall now sit with our hands folded and let the Russians do their worst, and I see nothing to prevent their taking Constantinople."[30]

Victoria was not one for sitting on her hands. On the throne for nearly half a century, her discreet meddling had grown with her confidence. She now turned to covert diplomacy. In the summer, she and Disraeli delivered an unofficial message to the tsar: Britain would intervene militarily if Russia attacked Constantinople. The messenger was Frederick Wellesley, the Bondian military attaché to the embassy in Saint Petersburg and a rare source of intelligence. He knew his mission was delicate. He told the tsar that "he was in possession of information with regard to the policy of England, which could not fail to be of the deepest interest, but that he could only communicate it on the condition of secrecy." The tsar agreed, and Wellesley delivered his message, adding that "he knew for a fact that the decision had actually been come to."[31] The extreme secrecy was necessary because Victoria had not consulted the passive Lord Derby about any of this. She and Disraeli bypassed the Foreign Office entirely.[32] Wellesley had therefore deliberately exaggerated Britain's position, in a bluff of deterrence.

In return, Victoria hoped for some intelligence that she could use. Wellesley dutifully reported Russian attitudes toward war, but he offered little insight into more tactical matters.[33] Meanwhile, the pro-Turkish ambassador in Constantinople, Henry Layard, warned that it "would be impossible to obtain the intelligence" requested by the queen regarding the amount and location of heavy weaponry on the European side of the Dardanelles—and how they could be disabled if necessary. Victoria was becoming a frustrated spymaster with high expectations. She thought this inability to get intelligence on weaponry was "unsatisfactory."[34]

The queen kept up the constant pressure on Disraeli to convince her reluctant cabinet to intervene against Russia.[35] For much of the autumn, he had managed to rebuff her so long as Turkish forces continued to hold up the Russian advance in what is now northern Bulgaria. In December, Turkish resistance finally collapsed, opening the way for Russia to march to Constantinople. Disraeli now felt the queen's breath on his collar more strongly than ever.[36] Lady Salisbury, wife of the India secretary, complained that Victoria had "lost control of herself, badgers her ministers and pushes them towards war."[37]

In her anger, the queen suspected the foreign secretary's wife, Lady Derby, of leaking secrets to the Russians. Mary Derby had grown close to the dashing Russian ambassador, who mysteriously knew all about certain sensitive matters discussed in the cabinet.[38] The queen's lack of trust in Lady Derby explains the secrecy surrounding her covert diplomacy with the tsar. With Wellesley deeply uncomfortable delivering his secret message to the tsar behind Lord Derby's back, Victoria responded that if Derby knew then, so too would his wife, closely followed by the Russian ambassador and the tsar. The entire chain would know it was a bluff and that, in reality, the cabinet was divided.[39]

Lady Derby does seem to have received secret material from her husband's private secretary, and she did meet the Russian ambassador at crucial moments during the crisis. Beyond that, it is difficult to say whether the queen was right. When questioned by Victoria's chaplain, Lady Derby angrily and resolutely denied any wrongdoing.[40] Either way, the queen did not trust the foreign secretary to make the strength of her feelings known to Russia, so she wrote to the tsar directly. When Ponsonby warned her that doing so was unconstitutional, she responded unrepentantly: It was a "miserable thing to be a constitutional Queen, and to be unable to do what is right."[41]

Wellesley had multiple security issues. He may have been peeking at Russian documents through his spies, but Tsarist codebreakers could decrypt British telegrams, something London had given up in 1844. All this worried Wellesley, who knew the Russians were reading his mail. The Russians certainly read his telegrams while he was attached to the Russian army on the campaign in 1877. He was also aware that someone in London, probably Lord Derby or his wife, was speaking too freely with the Russian ambassador—not that this mattered, given the fact that the Russians were intercepting both his and Lord Derby's telegrams anyway.[42] Wellesley urged London that it is of "the utmost importance that a Military Attaché should have no misgivings as to such information being considered secret at home." In other words, he feared that secrets he sent back to London would not remain secret for long.[43]

In 1877, as the Russian army mobilized, Wellesley was able to report that instead of having 400,000 troops, as the Russians boasted, in fact they only had just over 118,000. They were in a state of chaos, and railways could not move them. A cabinet minister showed his secret report to the French ambassador. Eventually, news made its way to the French ambassador in Moscow, and in no time at all, Wellesley was—quite rightly—regarded as a spy by the tsar and was socially snubbed.[44]

Wellesley perceived Russia as a paper tiger. Because he had a low opinion of Russian military capability, he was a constant advocate of strong actions against it all the way through the 1870s. He was also an advocate of operations to stir up rebellion among Russia's subjects on the fringes of its empire. By 1877 he was hugely influential. However, by the next year, because of multiple scandals, he had been moved to the post of military attaché in Vienna, and then he ran off with an actress who had been another gentleman's mistress, effectively ending his credibility and usefulness.[45]

The conflict—and undercurrent of intrigue—continued into 1878. Britain sent a fleet of battleships to the Dardanelles to deter Russia from entering Constantinople, but the situation remained deeply confused. In February, the queen learned that Lord Loftus, the ambassador to Russia, had "heard, from a secret source, that orders had been sent to the Russian Commander, to occupy Constantinople *with* the consent of the Sultan!"[46] Although Loftus was little respected in London, his report alarmed the queen, who was always willing to believe in Russian scheming.

Three days later, she agreed to a covert operation to buy four of the best Turkish warships and sail them on "special service with secret orders" out into the Mediterranean.[47] The idea perhaps was to feign a Turkish maneuver to lure Russia away from Constantinople. Whatever the intention, it quickly failed when the ambassador in Constantinople warned that the Russians knew all about it. He wondered if they had broken British diplomatic codes.[48] Russia, he added the next day, "had secret agents everywhere," including the German ambassador to Constantinople.[49] After the leak, one Russian mole inside the Ottoman diplomatic corps was quickly identified and dismissed.

With war between Britain and Russia looking likely, the tsar dispatched spies armed with gold to Afghanistan. Their aim was to bribe local leaders and pave the way for a 30,000-strong invasion force to strike at India. With Britain distracted by the seemingly inevitable war in the Mediterranean, Russian intelligence assumed that India was ripe for revolt. The queen, like her government, had no idea of these secret plans.[50]

The tsar ultimately backed down and, with his armies just days from Constantinople, imposed a peace treaty on the Turks in early March. This gave Russia new territory and made Bulgaria independent from the Ottoman Empire, bringing it squarely under Russian influence. Britain, alongside the other great powers, strongly objected and, after tense negotiations, reached a revised deal at the Congress of Berlin in July, giving Britain Cyprus as a naval base.[51]

Although the queen continued to be perturbed by Russian "intrigues" in Turkey, trouble was still brewing below the surface in Afghanistan.[52] The Indian government warned London about secret communications between the Russians and the Afghans, before accusing the Russians of sending a mission to

Kabul in direct contravention of their pledge not to interfere in the area.[53] The Russians initially denied all knowledge, leaving the India Office back in London skeptical of their incoming intelligence. According to one official: "I should like to know through what medium the Kabul news is received. The Intelligence I have seen for the last two years is the utmost rubbish." It was, he continued dismissively, "manufactured from bazaar gossip."[54] Ever suspicious of the Russians, the queen was inclined to believe the warnings. She and Disraeli agreed to send a firm letter to Saint Petersburg demanding an explanation.[55] The Russians were now forced to admit the mission, but insisted it was peaceful. Unsurprisingly, the queen did not believe them.[56]

Angry that the Afghans had secretly flirted with the Russians while refusing Britain's own advances, war broke out between Britain and Afghanistan in November 1878. After a string of quick military defeats, the Afghans agreed to a lengthy list of British demands, including ceding control over foreign policy, in return for peace in spring of the next year. Victoria monitored developments as closely as she could and was thrilled at outmaneuvering Tsar Alexander II, proudly knighting the officer who had led the negotiations.[57]

It proved short-lived. As Victoria herself put it, there was "always something afresh" in the region. Later that year, Afghan rebels stormed the British Embassy, killing the very same distinguished officer. Victoria was "dreadfully shocked and startled."[58] "*How* could it happen?" she demanded of the prime minister, before launching into a questionable lecture on methods of source validation: word of mouth, she thundered, was so much more reliable than written sources, which "depend on the talent of the writer."[59] The Afghan rebellion did not end for another year.

Small wars on the frontiers of empire became a way of life during Queen Victoria's long reign. Another broke out in 1882, this time with Egypt; it kicked off the scramble for Africa. In the second half of the nineteenth century, Egypt was a vassal of the decaying Ottoman Empire and had simultaneously fallen under strong Anglo-French influence after the construction of the Suez Canal in 1869. After years of nationalist agitation, a revolutionary colonel, Ahmed Arabi Pasha, seized control of the government early in 1882. Riots broke out in Alexandria, leaving about fifty Europeans dead.

From London, Queen Victoria watched with alarm. She knew that Egypt, through which the Suez Canal linked Europe with imperial Asia, was "VITAL." As turmoil spread, she impatiently insisted that any important news be ciphered directly to her.[60] She soon received intelligence outlining how Arabi was fortifying the harbor to deter the fleet of British and French warships anchored there.[61] Early on the morning of July 11, British forces launched a ten-hour bombardment of Alexandria. War followed.[62]

The queen followed developments closely. Intelligence suggested that the Ottomans were covertly encouraging Arabi's rebellion and Victoria heard that, in her words, "the Sultan had bribed a Tobacconist to poison" the previous ruler. "Monstrous!" was her verdict.[63] She quickly warned her foreign secretary to be mindful of Turkish "secret intrigues," adding that their troops could turn against British forces at any moment.[64]

Victoria was particularly concerned about the military campaign to come—and the role her third son, Prince Arthur, would play in battle. Arthur, his mother's favorite son, had been destined for a career in the army from an early age. He had already served in Ireland and Canada, and now commanded troops in Egypt. He would soon come under heavy fire from Arabi's larger and powerfully gunned army. With the worried queen's maternal instincts kicking in, the commander-in-chief of the expeditionary force, Garnet Wolseley, kept her personally updated throughout the war and made sure to praise Arthur's performance.[65]

Wolseley was a politically awkward appointment. He was an officer but not a gentleman. As his family was too poor to buy him a commission, he had only achieved his appointment through his mother's intercession with the duke of Wellington, but he proved to be a star officer and rose through the ranks by virtue of, at first his bravery, but later his intellectual mettle. Preferring the company of artists and intellectuals, he was considered a dangerous modern- izer and, once having achieved senior rank, battled it out with the queen's cousin, the duke of Cambridge, over reforms, including the expansion of the intelligence department.[66]

But now, with a crisis in Egypt, a talented upstart was required. Despite sending regular updates to Buckingham Palace, Wolseley did not tell the queen about his great deception operation. Nor did he tell the duke of Cambridge, who headed the British army. Wolseley developed elaborate plans to attack the Egyptians at Aboukir Bay, not far from Alexandria, and, after a deliberately extravagant reconnaissance mission performed with pantomime secrecy, these soon became common knowledge among the enemy. British forces deliberately kept Arabi on high alert to convince him that the advance on Cairo would come from Alexandria.[67] Prince Arthur himself was stationed in Aboukir Bay, per- haps as an elaborate—if unwitting—royal decoy.[68]

Unbeknown to the Egyptians, the real attack would come from Port Said, almost 150 miles to the east. Wolseley's deception worked masterfully; even the local war correspondents were fooled. The queen, inevitably, did know in advance. The secretary of state for war told her, in strict secrecy, that the plan was to "occupy Arabi Pasha" at Alexandria and "divert his attention from the

Canal."[69] She was delighted with the success of the deception. Her private secretary praised Wolseley's boldness in using war correspondents to spread misinformation. Doing so, Ponsonby told Wolseley, had created "some misgivings
in the press and an inclination to abuse you—but nothing is so successful as
success and the ill-humor vanished when you appeared suddenly at Ismailia
instead of Aboukir as they had announced."[70]

The army then marched inland, and the queen received a cypher marked
"very secret" informing her of an imminent, large offensive against a village not
far from the Suez Canal. Two days later, Wolseley told her of victory.[71] British troops thereafter occupied Egypt. After defeating the Egyptian forces, the
queen demanded retribution. She wanted Arabi "severely punished" to prevent
a recurrence of revolution and rebellion.[72]

The great deception and subsequent victory would not have been possible
without the brave work of Bruce Tulloch, an officer in the War Office's nascent
Intelligence Bureau. Tulloch had examined coastal defenses at Alexandria
before the bombardment and, disguised intermittently as a pen-pusher and
a hunter, ventured into enemy-controlled territory to gather intelligence on
Egyptian positions at Port Said, the Suez Canal, and the village east of Cairo
where the decisive battle would eventually be fought. He assessed the potential
for sabotage and special operations, noting in particular that bribery through
the payment of baksheesh would be rather effective.[73] He also pretended to be
a journalist to maintain the deception, telegraphing *The Standard* that rumors
of an attack on Suez were untrue. He was on a dangerous mission: the Egyptians kidnapped and slit the throat of one man accused of being a British spy.[74]
Such perilous work did not go unrecognized. On his return, Tulloch dined with
Queen Victoria at Windsor, regaling her with tales of derring-do and espionage.[75] In some ways, she liked the romance of it all. Throughout her reign, she
loved hearing about adventures and invited many an imperial spy to the castle.

Victoria continued to pay close attention to imperial intrigues during the
latter years of her reign. She enjoyed meeting those who had spent time in central Asia, listening intently to their assessments, and she continued to bemoan
the lack of intelligence coming from the frontier.[76] "All I know is from Reuter
and the newspapers," she would complain to her India secretary.[77]

She also continued to scheme and make life difficult for the Russians.
On one occasion, the queen lobbied for covert sponsorship of a new railway
through the Euphrates Valley from Aleppo to the Persian Gulf. Construction
would appear to be a private endeavor, but would secretly be backed by the
government, so as to "baffle Russian progress in the East."[78] The foreign secretary dampened the queen's enthusiastic plotting, pointing out how expensive
it would be to guarantee against loss and risk.[79]

Bribery was much simpler as a way of controlling local politics and the
emerging Arab press. Eventually, most embassies in the region had a special

fund for this purpose. The British minister in Tehran knew that there were few Persian clerics "whose religious zeal is proof against bribes." Bribes included cigars, lightbulbs, clocks, and even an artificial limb given to one particular brigand who had lost an arm. The foreign secretary admitted that he had "not hesitated to use secret service money" in Persia.[80]

But neither bribery nor deception could prevent the most visibly disastrous defeat of Victoria's reign. This was the siege of Khartoum by the local religious fighters that began in March 1884—and ended with the beheading of Major General Charles Gordon, who had been sent out to oversee the evacuation of the city, but instead stayed on to defend it, in January of the next year. This uprising determined the fortunes of two of Victoria's spies. Frederick Burnaby, now ill and tired of ballooning, wanted one last adventure. He died fighting in the Sudan, brandishing a new naval 12-gauge shotgun that his colleagues regarded as "unsporting" but he thought was an excellent technical innovation. Wolseley was luckier, leaving Egypt just before the tide turned and, after much intrigue, receiving a peerage and becoming commander of the army. His main competitors for the post had been the queen's cousin, the duke of Cambridge, and her son, the duke of Connaught.[81]

The Bulgarian coup of 1886 once more inflamed Queen Victoria's suspicions of Russian intrigue. Alexander of Battenberg had been prince of Bulgaria for almost a decade when he was overthrown by rebels acting with Russian support. Alexander was part of Victoria's network of royals: one of his brothers had married her youngest daughter, Princess Beatrice, and another married her granddaughter, Princess Victoria of Hesse and by Rhine. The children from this latter marriage included Earl Mountbatten of Burma and Princess Alice of Battenberg, the mother of Prince Philip, the duke of Edinburgh. Queen Victoria knew him affectionately as Sandro.

She noted with shock in August 1886 that "Sandro has been deposed and taken prisoner." As ever, Victoria heard the news first and, as more sources confirmed it, she quietly told Beatrice before trying to comfort Sandro's brother. Next, she characteristically demanded that the prime minister find out more details: What happened? Who was behind it?[82] For Victoria, this, as so often the case, was personal as well as political. It was indeed a royal plot, actually the work of Tsar Alexander III, who, in contrast to his father, disliked Sandro. The plan was aided and abetted by Bismarck.

From Balmoral, she fired off telegrams in every direction but received little response. Britain had few agents on the ground. Eventually, after an anxious wait, one of her sources confirmed that Sandro was "safe and thought to be in Roumania." The next day, she learned from Sofia that the revolutionary leaders had notoriously "intimate relations" with Russian agents and that Russia had spread disinformation about a fake threat coming from Serbia. This had caused Bulgaria to send troops to the border, leaving Sofia vulnerable to a coup.

The queen continued to receive conflicting reports about Sandro's safety. Some thought he was in Romania; others spotted what might have been his yacht sailing down the Danube. A few days after the coup, the queen received intelligence from Saint Petersburg that Sandro had been delivered, on board his yacht, as a "prisoner" to Russian territory. According to Victoria, this was "really, monstrous behaviour, clearly admitting, that the Russians had known and planned the whole thing."[83]

The queen anxiously demanded more intelligence on Sandro's whereabouts. Confusion reigned once again. The longer Sandro was missing, she felt, the more the situation played into the Russians' hands as they shored up their position in Sofia. She wanted him back in Bulgaria. Victoria's son, Alfred, who had married into the Russian Royal Family, was no help. Rather than providing insight into what the Russians were up to, he had to ask his mother what was going on, as "wild rumours were afloat." In fairness, the Russians allowed Sandro to proceed to Ukraine, from where he returned to Bulgaria after a successful counterrevolution. The queen was delighted, taking particular pleasure in the Russian newspapers being "very angry at the failure of their plot!"[84]

This was not the end of it. The ambassador in Saint Petersburg warned that Russia would not openly intervene but would covertly maneuver to "get rid of Sandro."[85] Not helping matters, Sandro misread the situation and offered an olive branch to the tsar, but succeeded only in antagonizing him. The tsar fired back an angry response.[86] Reuters passed a copy of both to Queen Victoria, who thought the tsar's response was "most offensive and really brutal." She asked the foreign secretary to confirm their authenticity.[87]

By now, though, Sandro's authority had been fatally undermined. The queen received a "very secret" message from the British diplomatic agent in Sofia that Sandro, facing widespread disaffection and continuing conspiracy, was determined to leave the country. She implored him not to.[88] Victoria's counter-schemes came to nothing. Sandro left Bulgaria, and the throne, on September 8, 1886. Three years later, he married an Austrian actress, settled in Graz, and became a patron of the Viennese Symphony Orchestra—and privately, he declared himself to be rather happier.[89]

Despite continued demands for intelligence from across the empire, Queen Victoria's final years were marred by accusations of naïveté in handling sensitive material. She had long developed a stubborn tendency to go rogue when it came to intelligence overseas, but now this culminated in a security scare inside the royal household. In 1877, she had declared herself empress of India and began to learn Hindustani shortly afterward, but her fondness for empire brought trouble. In particular, her trust in an Indian servant, Mohammed Abdul Karim, who became her secretary, caused ministers to worry about the security of state secrets and his ability to discreetly influence her thinking in favor of her Muslim subjects.

To mark her Golden Jubilee in the summer of 1887, Victoria appointed her first Indian servants. One of them, Karim, handsome and ingratiating, soon captured her attention. She quickly elevated him to the role of "Munshi," or teacher, before making him her secretary for India—much to the irritation of her household's members, who jealously viewed him as a pretentious interloper. This was partly racial prejudice but also indignation at his humble origins: he was a jail clerk and the son of a hospital assistant who served a cavalry regiment, the Central Indian Horse.[90]

Karim's influence quickly grew. At Balmoral Castle, Karim was allocated the room previously occupied by John Brown, a favorite servant of the queen who had died in 1883. As with Brown, the queen simply longed for human companionship; but unlike Brown, who was unassuming, Karim was keen to secure elevation, and he even requested a knighthood, one of the few things Victoria turned down. This elevation gained him regular access to the queen as she read and signed confidential documents related to India and the sensitive intrigues of the Great Game. Ministers did not trust Karim and feared that he might leak secrets into the hands of adversaries. In response, the queen sought to reassure the prime minister that "no political papers of any kind are in the Munshi's hands," even in the queen's presence. His role, she continued, was limited to helping her read words she could not understand; besides, his English was not good enough to pose a security risk anyway.[91]

This may have been true in the short term, but ministers still worried that Karim, even without access to papers, could learn about confidential matters. He became part of Victoria's inner circle, enjoying gossip with her and other European royalty. Critics worried that he had too much influence and, owing to the queen's blind affection, was untouchable.[92]

To make matters worse, Karim became close friends with a young lawyer, Rafiuddin Ahmed, who had a reputation as a Muslim political activist and was known to the Indian police as an untrustworthy "intriguer." Ahmed had helped found the Muslim Patriotic League and was linked to other, more radical groups. Through his friend Karim, he now had access to Queen Victoria herself. Nervous courtiers and twitchy ministers suspected him of sending state secrets, supplied by Karim, to the emir of Afghanistan, a key figure in the Great Game between England and Russia. Victoria certainly understood how intelligent and able Ahmed was; she used him in diplomacy with the Ottoman sultan and tried to have him appointed to the British Embassy in Constantinople.[93]

But ministers fretted about the counterintelligence risk. The secretary of state for India even warned against sending confidential papers to the queen if Karim would learn of their contents. Neither he nor Salisbury, the prime minister, thought Karim was deliberately dangerous; in fact, they saw him as a bit "stupid." But he might, they cautioned, "become a tool in the hands of other abler men."[94] He might leak intelligence or act as a covert agent of influence. One of the queen's secretaries agreed, warning the viceroy of India that Karim had access to his letters and was relaying their contents back to contacts in India. He told the viceroy how the stubborn old queen could not see the danger of letting Karim view confidential material and how Ahmed, the real brains of the operation, had been trying to exploit his simple friend. The police had apparently supplied details on Ahmed, but Victoria would simply not listen. The India Office repeated the warning and urged the viceroy to be careful about what he put in writing to the queen. More dramatically, the queen's physician, Dr. John Reid, demanded that Karim return any of Victoria's papers that he had in his possession. "If the Queen were to die and any letters of hers were found in your possession," he threatened, "no mercy will be shown you."[95]

The queen's secretary, Ponsonby, joined with Reid in a prolonged and nasty campaign against Karim. They complained to Victoria about everything they could find, ranging from Karim's multiple wives, designated "aunts," who spat on carpets, to his sexual promiscuity and venereal disease—he suffered from repeated bouts of gonorrhea. They complained mostly about his race and also his social status. Victoria was having none of it, pointing out that two of her archbishops had been the sons of a butcher and grocer. She was especially hot on racial prejudice, forbidding the use of the term "Black men" and even lecturing Lord Salisbury on the matter. Alas, Karim, as a dedicated social climber, greatly enjoyed discriminating against his fellow countrymen.[96]

Nevertheless, Karim—and Ahmed—were discreetly watched. When Karim returned on a visit to India in 1896, the viceroy put him under surveillance, asking the police to closely monitor his movements and contacts. Spying on a member of the queen's inner circle was inevitably a particularly delicate operation. The secretary of state for India approved "unobtrusive supervision" but warned that any amount of surveillance would backfire if the queen ever found out. Little was written down.[97]

Despite attempts at discretion, a deep rift developed between the queen and her household. Victoria continued to treat Karim with a level of respect that her courtiers felt was undeserved. Karim responded with an infuriating sense of entitlement: when accompanying the queen overseas, he complained about his lack of local newspaper coverage. In the spring of 1897, he traveled with the queen to the French Riviera against the explicit wishes of the royal household's members, who threatened to go on strike. The courtiers were even more incensed when Karim's friend Ahmed turned up at the hotel uninvited. Fearing that Ahmed was on the hunt for sensitive diplomatic material, the queen's private secretary brusquely dismissed him.[98]

Far from thanking her advisers for protecting her from a potential security risk, the queen was furious. She invited Ahmed to a court ball by way of apology. More significantly, she suggested that her ministers recruit him to gather intelligence on Muslims and use him in diplomacy with the Ottoman Empire. This was a quite staggering divergence from the attitude of her civil servants. The India Office thought that Ahmed's relationship with the queen—through Karim—was a breach of security.[99] Salisbury warned her that, if he were to be appointed as a diplomat, Ahmed would require "access to most important secrets." This was too much, and Salisbury tactfully rebuffed her meddling; reports on Ahmed's character were "too divergent" to make a judgment as to his fitness. "The danger of misplaced confidence," Salisbury warned, "would be very serious."[100]

In April 1897, Ponsonby complained to a friend about the ongoing Karim saga, admitting defeat in the face of the implacable queen:

> We been having a good deal of trouble lately about the Munshi here, and although we have tried our best, we cannot get the Queen to realize how very dangerous it is for her to allow this man to see every confidential paper relating to India. The Queen insists on bringing the Munshi forward as much as she can, & if it were not for our protest, I don't know where She would stop. Fortunately, he happens to be a thoroughly stupid and uneducated man, & his one idea in life seems to be to do nothing and eat as much as he can.

Despite his obvious prejudice, Ponsonby was in a sense correct: Karim represented no threat at all, and even his friends were harmless.[101]

Nevertheless, nervous ministers, high on the intrigue and paranoia of the Great Game, thought Ahmed was a "ruffian" agitator, a "Mahomedan intriguer," and perhaps even a spy. They placed him under surveillance again in 1898 but still found no conclusive proof of wrongdoing. Victoria saw him as a useful informant, providing information on the attitudes of Muslims in India. Just as she had done with European royals and the Foreign Office, she used his intelligence and insights to challenge the India Office and pursue her own instincts. She was right about Ahmed's abilities and, decades later, having served as the minister for education in Bombay, he was eventually knighted.[102]

On the prickly matter of Karim, the queen remained even more intransigent. She angrily accused her household of spying on him. "I am terribly annoyed. . . . I feel continually aggrieved at my Gentlemen wishing to spy and interfere with one of my people whom I have no personal reason of proof of doubting and I am greatly distressed about what has happened."[103] And she had a point: successive private secretaries had tried to dig up as much dirt as possible to discredit him, but the queen was ever unmoved, dismissing all their protestations as prejudice and jealousy.[104] Reid complained that "the Queen seems off her head."[105] She had become an increasingly emotional consumer of intelligence, relying more on instincts than objective analysis. Her blind hatred of Russia caused her to jump on any information that implied wrongdoing and ignore the rest. Her love of Karim blinded her to the security worries of the · royal household. This time, however, she was right.

Eventually, the secretary of state for India tried to draw a line under the affair and told the viceroy that, after being placed under surveillance, Karim had done nothing wrong and that the royal household was overreacting to his friendship with Ahmed.[106] There remains no evidence that he passed on state secrets or that he discreetly influenced her thoughts on India.[107] It made little difference. Sadly, after Victoria's death in 1901, the new king, Edward VII, sent Karim back to India and burned his correspondence with the queen. He lived quietly on the estate at Agra that the queen had given him. After Karim's death eight years later, Edward dispatched detectives to confiscate any remaining documents held at his house in India, leaving his family with few records of his loyal service. They successfully hid and preserved his diary, which only surfaced in 2011.[108] This was not the last time that the royal machine would fail to airbrush things that it did not like from the historical record.

4

Queen Victoria's Security

Fenians and Anarchists

Your Majesty is as safe as any person in your dominions.
—Lord Salisbury, 1898

In early 1881, some revolutionaries were digging beneath a cheese shop in Saint Petersburg. Part of a dedicated and violent group called the People's Will, their purpose was to mine the road above with explosives and assassinate Tsar Alexander II of Russia. As a backup plan, they would fall back on four different bomb-throwing assassins, together with further groups armed with guns, knives, and other exotic weapons stationed in the street above. This was the route that the tsar often took when returning to the Winter Palace from inspecting the troops. He traveled in a bulletproof carriage and had survived several previous assassination attempts, including dynamiting the imperial train and bombing the Winter Palace only a year before. The People's Will had been working on these preparations zealously for over a year.

The leader of the actual attack was Sophia Perovskaya, stepping in for her husband, who had been arrested two days earlier. On Sunday, March 13, 1881, the tsar traveled home after inspecting his troops. He was heavily guarded by Cossacks. His carriage was followed by three sleighs transporting his chief of security, two senior police officers, and yet more troops. The security-conscious retinue altered the route and avoided the laboriously constructed cheese-shop tunnel that had been packed with tons of dynamite. But the four bomb teams were waiting, and Perovskaya gave the signal by ostentatiously pulling out a handkerchief and blowing her nose. At 2:15, the first bomb was thrown and exploded under the tsar's carriage.[1]

There was a tremendous roar. One of the Cossacks was killed, and many nearby civilians were wounded. Yet the coach was heavily protected with steel, leaving the tsar shocked but not injured. The bomber, Nikolai Rysakov, was captured almost immediately. Despite exhortations to leave the scene, the tsar wanted to see his would-be assassin and offer sympathy to the victims. "Thank God, I'm untouched," he told those around him.

A second bomber now struck, reportedly shouting gleefully: "You spoke too soon!" There was another mighty roar. This time, the tsar was mortally injured, together with some of the assassins and many bystanders. His stomach torn open and his legs in tatters, he lay bleeding on the snow alongside his killers. Other bombers and pistoleers moved forward, but realized they were not needed. The tsar asked to be taken to the Winter Place to die. He perished within an hour.[2]

Back in Windsor, Queen Victoria's private secretary, Henry Ponsonby, received the news via a locked dispatch box that arrived as he ate dinner with his wife and children. He would usually skim its contents casually before spiriting them away from prying eyes. On this Sunday evening, he unlocked the box, glanced at the telegram inside, handed it to his wife, and immediately left the room. He hurried to tell the queen personally, leaving his startled wife waving the dramatic piece of paper and explaining the news to her family.[3]

Victoria was getting older and approaching her Golden Jubilee. She was as straight-talking as ever and took a characteristically hard line: "No punishment is bad enough for the murderers," she wrote, "hanging is too good."[4]

The assassination formed an early high point of anarchist political violence, the first wave of modern terrorism. Victoria's sources—including her son, Alfred, who had married the tsar's daughter—provided her with speedy updates about the killing and the unfolding security situation.[5] Her network of continental royals visiting Russia for the funeral provided her with regular bulletins on the political repercussions.[6]

Victoria was no fan of Russia, but she read the incoming reports with great interest and feared for the safety of the new emperor. For obvious reasons, assassination of sovereigns—however unfriendly—was an issue close to her heart. She wondered whether anarchists had infiltrated the tsar's servants or, heaven forbid, "even higher classes." No one, she continued, now "trusted his neighbour" in Saint Petersburg. She read with growing dismay about excavations around the Winter Palace as security forces hunted for unexploded bombs.[7]

Even though the conspirators had no connection to Britain, the assassination resurrected the thorny issue of London's refugee policy and disinclination to spy on political discontents. Britain's apparent softness remained a sore point for European leaders, just as it had been back in the 1850s. Russian royalty, flailing angrily after the assassination, accused Britain of protecting international criminals. Victoria's position had not changed over three decades.

Under pressure from the queen, Ponsonby sheepishly explained to Victoria that Britain had no extradition treaty with Russia. She was not impressed: "Should there not be one?" she fired at the foreign secretary.[8] Sympathizing with beleaguered sovereigns, Victoria wanted to evict all refugees from Britain, leaving the home secretary to tell her that doing so was "politically impossible." The prime minister agreed: it would go against British traditions.[9] It formed yet another issue over which Victoria, stubborn as ever, was at odds with her government.

Victoria was disappointed that Britain refused to work with European partners to determine, as she put it, "the best mode of international defence against the revolutionary attempts." For now, Britain still prided itself on a liberal asylum policy and a strong tradition of civil liberties. Ahead of her time, Victoria insisted that at the very least she should express sympathy and desire "to tolerate no murderous plots here against foreign sovereigns."[10]

Unwilling to ramp up political espionage, the British looked to other methods to counter political violence, including clamping down on public support for terrorism. Although the matter was largely unspoken—and indeed could not be spoken of—those around her knew that the anarchist threat to Victoria personally was limited because of her decision to virtually withdraw from public life after the death of Prince Albert in 1861. Secluded at Windsor, she rarely used Buckingham Palace. Her appearances were few, and so she presented only a fleeting target for even the most ambitious terrorist. Anyone digging beneath a cheese shop in London was probably wasting their time.

Some anarchists and troublemakers were present. The Foreign Office hoped that they would remain quiet and fade into the background, but some were annoyingly vocal. One, Johann Most, was a German anarchist who had settled in London having first been exiled from his homeland and then from France. From London, he advocated terrorism to bring about a revolution, popularizing the anarchist idea of the propaganda of the deed. Shortly after the assassination of the tsar, Most wrote an incendiary article glorifying the attack and was arrested after repeating his remarks at a socialist meeting. The queen thought *Freiheit*, the "shocking paper" that published Most's article, should be prosecuted.[11] Ponsonby passed on the queen's deep concerns to William Harcourt, the home secretary, who in turn forwarded them on to the commissioner of the Metropolitan Police with the note: "Tell the police to look after this."[12] Most was imprisoned for eighteen months before emigrating to America.

Victoria went further still, asking the foreign secretary to consider "the necessity of combining with other nations against the nihilists."[13] This was a step too far for politicians bent on upholding Britain's liberal traditions, and the foreign secretary was suitably dismissive: "No application has yet been made to us to combine with other nations against the nihilists. Our police give all the information they obtain to the continental governments."[14]

Most's outburst and imprisonment had coincided with the most recent attempt to kill Victoria. On March 2, 1882, the queen had just crossed the platform of Windsor Station to say goodbye to Princess Beatrice. Roderick Maclean, standing at the entrance to the station among the crowd, fired a revolver at her. A number of nearby Eton schoolboys beat him with their umbrellas before he was seized by the police. Some tried to connect him with Most and foreign anarchism, but this, the eighth and final assassination attempt on Victoria, in fact followed a rather familiar pattern. The weapon proved to be outdated and ineffective. Some reports even claimed it was a toy gun. At his trial, Maclean complained that he had sent some of his poems to the queen at Windsor Castle and had received rude replies. Once it was revealed that he had already spent time in Somerset Lunatic Asylum, he was soon dispatched to Broadmoor, where he spent the rest of his days.[15]

The authorities of course did not know that this amateur and bewildered effort would be the final attack on the queen. Meanwhile, Irish terrorism now posed a growing problem. Despite the volatile atmosphere in Ireland, the British mainland had been reasonably quiet since 1867, when Fenian rebels spectacularly failed to break an inmate out of a London jail with a bomb. The bomb, intended to blow up a prison wall, killed twelve innocent bystanders and injured many more. It caused widespread outrage, seriously undermining the Fenians' efforts to secure home rule for Ireland. A few intelligence scares followed, although Victoria remained aloof. When warned of a plot to kidnap her, the queen quipped that if the Fenians were "so silly" as to seize her, they would find her a "very inconvenient charge." When faulty intelligence suggested that eighty Fenians were traveling from Canada to murder her, she complained that the resulting security precautions made her feel like a prisoner.[16] Slightly ominously, the home secretary did tell Victoria that his detectives were "inefficient" and that their "informers were constantly false." Intelligence was weak.[17]

The Fenian terrorist threat became much more real in the early 1880s. The queen, now in her sixties, had become stoically accustomed to threats on her life. Yet this time it was different; and she did not feel safe. Although in some ways more dangerous, the aspiring assassins of the 1840s were hapless lone gunmen, some of whom were certifiably insane. Fast-forward forty years, and terrorism was part of an international conspiracy. Violent Fenians, motivated by decades of famine and oppression, emboldened by Irish home rule being debated in Parliament, found support and funding among Irish émigrés in America. With dynamite, they now had modern weaponry as lethal as it was portable. And with the assassination of the Russian tsar, Victoria had already seen the damage it could do.[18] She took the threat seriously, inquiring about what was being done to protect Buckingham Palace. Her home secretary, William Harcourt, dismissed it as "a Fenian scare of the old clumsy kind."[19]

Harcourt was wrong. Between 1881 and 1885, the Fenians carried out a series of attacks across England. Their early targets included police forces in Liverpool and military barracks in Chester. In 1883, bombs exploded in

Whitehall, at the *Times* offices, and on the London Underground. Victoria's son, Alfred, was inside the House of Commons when the Whitehall bomb detonated in March and heard the explosion clearly. The queen was 25 miles away at Windsor, but Ponsonby, who visited the scene, quickly informed her of the "wild appearance of shattered stone, glass, wood, and plaster." He told her that "there is no clue and can be no clue to the actual individuals who committed the deed."[20] The next day, Harcourt confirmed that he had no intelligence, other than the obvious assumption that the same gang was behind the string of attacks.[21]

The following year, the Fenians successfully targeted London rail stations and police headquarters at Scotland Yard. In 1885, explosions rocked the Houses of Parliament and the Tower of London. This sustained terrorism campaign had led to the creation of Special Branch in 1883—the British police force dealing with extremism, terrorism, and national security matters—to which Queen Victoria quickly offered royal patronage. She feared the Royal Family would be a target and urged for every security precaution to be taken.[22] In particular, she was scared that the royal train would be bombed as it traveled through the remote countryside to Balmoral, so detectives scoured the route for explosives, inspecting every inch of track, bridge, and tunnel. Undercover detectives inside Balmoral kept a discreet eye on all strangers.

The prince of Wales personally recommended one secret agent to Special Branch.[23] The queen knew that "detectives are all over the country."[24] Some unobtrusively followed Victoria, occasionally without her knowledge. Others followed her family. When, in 1885, detectives received intelligence about an assassination threat against one of Victoria's sons, they did not tell the prince on the grounds that he would rather not know "that anything of this unpleasant nature was in the air." Instead, detectives put him under secret surveillance. As one later recalled: "When he drove anywhere in his carriage, I followed at a discreet distance in a hansom; when he came out of any house he had been visiting of an evening, I was on the kerb hard by, carefully keeping in shadow."[25]

By 1895, Harcourt had toughened security measures, but he seldom pleased the queen. She now thought him boring, overly sensitive to criticism, and annoyingly overprotective regarding her security. He accused her of constant nagging, especially about his taking too many police precautions. On one occasion, Harcourt defended himself by saying "if anything had occurred, I should have been justly censured for want of care." Summing up the classic counterterrorism paradox, which still frustrates heads of domestic intelligence today, he added: "It is a little embarrassing to be constantly worried, first of all to do a great deal that is unnecessary and then to be blamed for doing what is prudent. . . . I must endure the reproach of having protected the Queen too much, but I shall not face the blame of having protected her too little."[26]

The terrorists enjoyed support from Fenian societies across the Atlantic in Chicago, Boston, and New York, where newspapers openly advocated the assassination of Queen Victoria. Ponsonby was shocked and concerned. "Her Majesty," he wrote to the foreign secretary on reading one particular account, "asks if this is true?"[27] Her government complained to its US counterparts about their harboring of dissidents and even their incitement to regicide, but received no response.[28] This was rather ironic, given similar European criticisms of Britain during recent decades. The nervous queen persistently summoned the home secretary for updates and reassurance.[29] He put his faith in the stretched intelligence system, telling her that "many suspected men are under observation and have been so for a long time."[30]

Despite the frequency of the bombings, British intelligence did enjoy some successes. Scotland Yard and the Home Office had developed a network of informants and agents, not just in England but also in Ireland and the United States. This was an international intelligence operation, but one which, on the surface at least, still found espionage rather squeamish. When Ponsonby congratulated the police on the arrest of a particular terrorist in 1883, he made sure to note that the success was all the more impressive, given the police's distaste for espionage. "I doubt," he wrote, "if Englishmen could ever take up the business as the French do."[31] The queen's circle was seemingly unaware of some of the more distasteful methods, including agents provocateurs, which the government employed unofficially.

Victoria took a close interest in those who were arrested. She had learned a harsh lesson the previous year, when Michael Davitt, an Irish republican politician, was released from prison. "Is it *possible* that Michael Davitt, known as one of the worst of the treasonable agitators, is also to be released?" she asked the prime minister. "I cannot believe it!"[32] Just two days later, republicans murdered the new chief secretary for Ireland, Frederick Cavendish, in Dublin. The queen was furious and rebuked her government: "This horrible event" was "the *direct result*" of releasing Davitt and other Irish prisoners. She lobbied for "such strong measures as may give her and the country security, or at least as much security as is possible."[33]

In June 1883, Harcourt told Victoria that "we have the enemy by the throat." The arrest of five members of a Fenian gang had bolstered his confidence, and he hurried straight to Windsor to tell the queen the good news.[34] The arrested Fenians—bar one, who betrayed his friends in return for deportation—were sentenced to life imprisonment for conspiracy to "depose the queen"; to levy war upon the queen; and to intimidate and overawe the Houses of Parliament."[35] Nonetheless, the dynamite campaign continued until 1885.

Two years later, the Fenians planned one more spectacular: bombing Queen Victoria's Golden Jubilee celebration at Westminster Abbey. In one of the most dramatic twists of Victoria's long, intrigue-filled reign, the mastermind of the plot was General Francis Millen, an Irish mercenary—but also a secret agent working for the British, albeit intermittently and unreliably.

Millen was born in Tyrone and was shaped by the conflicts of the mid–nineteenth century. With red hair, a beard, and a ruddy complexion, he cultivated the image of a senior commander. He served in the Crimea and leveraged this experience to secure a commission in the Mexican liberal army, rising to the rank of brigadier-general while allegedly also working for the Americans as a spy. By 1865, he had traveled to Ireland to help organize Fenian military activity, but the locals described him as a theatrical, "banana republic"–style officer. His first offer to work for the British, made the next year, was the result of this bitter factional fighting among the Irish militants, together with a desire for money.[36]

Millen thereafter had worked intermittently for the enemy. The British, keen for intelligence on his erstwhile colleagues, were receptive to his advances; and the prime minister himself, Lord Salisbury, personally sanctioned the recruitment of Millen as a British agent. Salisbury took a deep interest in the material he provided, and his red-inked monogram "S" appeared on some of Millen's most sensitive intelligence. Salisbury then approved using Millen as an agent provocateur to spearhead an assassination plot during the jubilee so as to smash the Fenian dynamite gangs once and for all and to destroy the Irish leader Charles Parnell by implicating him in the attempted murder of the queen.[37]

Edward Jenkinson was a key figure behind the plot, and was seemingly in correspondence with Millen himself during the planning phase. He acted as an unofficial spymaster working in the Home Office, building a network of Irish agents who reported to him personally and engaged in extralegal activities— much to the frustration of the police. Jenkinson used agents to provoke potential conspirators to act. One of his agents provocateurs had even used secret service money to fund bombing campaigns. Differing from Salisbury in motive, Jenkinson hoped to use the plot to frighten his own government into appeasing Irish demands.[38] The queen, whose own private secretary scorned espionage, had earlier praised the efforts of Jenkinson. "His courage and determination," she told the home secretary in 1883, "have been of the *utmost use.*" He deserved, "*the very highest praise.*"[39] But if she had known what he was up to in 1887, her opinion could well have changed.

Victoria's jubilee took place on June 20, 1887. She was a reluctant participant; she naturally disliked showy occasions and for so long had been a recluse after Albert's untimely death. Ministers had to persuade her, stubborn and grumpy as ever, to take part in the pageantry at all. She marked the occasion with a splendid royal banquet at Buckingham Palace, at which her distinguished relatives sat around a grand horseshoe table and dined off the finest golden plates. They included her private intelligence sources from across Europe, who had provided such useful insights over the past five decades. Vicky was there; so too were royals from Schleswig-Holstein and most other parts of Germany; the king of Denmark, father of the princess of Wales; and many others.

The next day, Victoria processed in an open-topped carriage from Buckingham Palace to Westminster Abbey for the ceremony, accompanied by her son-in-law, Crown Prince Fritz of Prussia, dazzling in a uniform of white and silver. Even the notoriously dowdy queen had reluctantly dressed up for the occasion.[40] Cheering crowds lined the route; the abbey was packed with British nobility and politicians. Plainclothes detectives watched anxiously for trouble.

The upper echelons of Scotland Yard had bigger worries. They knew that the Fenians, directed by Millen, had set sail from New York ten days earlier. Their mission: to detonate a bomb at Westminster Abbey. Three men, led by a tough civil war veteran, were carrying Smith & Wesson revolvers, plenty of ammunition, and more importantly a large amount of high-quality Atlas dynamite together with detonators.[41] Informants in America had quickly tipped off their handlers in Scotland Yard, although the intelligence would not have come as a surprise to Jenkinson in the Home Office. Special Branch stumbled upon the conspiracy quite independently and kept the Fenians under close surveillance. But no one was sure just how many attackers were converging on London.[42]

In the abbey, James Monro, assistant commissioner of the Metropolitan Police and head of its secret section, sat nervously through the jubilee ceremony. Fearing that an agent provocateur could well trigger a terrorist attack, let alone corrupt Britain's moral fiber, he had vehemently opposed Jenkinson's unorthodox espionage methods, and he had even arrested some of his agents. Monro won the bureaucratic battle; Jenkinson was fired earlier in the year, and his networks wound up.[43] Scotland Yard quickly confronted Millen with the details of the plot, causing him to back off. In truth, no one in Britain's rather fragmented security apparatus knew exactly what was going on.

Accordingly, Monro remained concerned enough about the event not to let his own children take up their reserved seats—just in case. There still remained a possibility that the conspirators had managed to smuggle some dynamite into the vaults. Monro received a message to that effect, but it was too late to make inquiries without causing panic among the great and good who had entered the abbey. All he could do was pray.[44]

The ceremony left the queen, in her own words, "half dead."[45] She was exhausted by the end, but it passed peacefully. There was no bomb. The terrorists docked late in Liverpool and missed the big day; but while plotting further attacks in the subsequent months, they inadvertently led the police to many of the Fenians operating on the mainland. They were given remarkable license. One of them twice visited Windsor Castle, carefully timing his possible escape by train after planting a bomb. Another managed to get inside the House of Commons.[46]

When they had gathered enough evidence, the police rounded them up—all but one. Millen unsurprisingly evaded arrest and managed to escape to New York. From across the Atlantic, he even offered to resume his role as an informant the next year. Strikingly, Prime Minister Salisbury was keen to accept this role, but the police and Home Office talked him out of it—since it would have signaled a return to Jenkinson's more dangerous agent provocateur methods.[47]

The Fenians did not realize that Millen was a British agent, but a decade later, politicians in Parliament alleged that the affair had been a "put-up job" devised by the secret service. Robert Anderson, the handler who received the intelligence about the gang's departure for Liverpool, later admitted as much: "Millen arrived in Britain to carry out his two-fold mission on behalf of Clan na Gael and the British Government."[48] In reality, no one was quite sure how the day would go.

A wave of anarchist assassinations on the continent over the next decade once more focused the attention of Special Branch on terrorism. In the space of a few short years, anarchists killed the French president and the empress of Austria-Hungary. Their ideas also gained an alarming intellectual respectability: the painters Gustave Courbet, Camille Pissarro, and Georges Seurat declared themselves to be "anarchists," as did the dramatist Oscar Wilde, even though they were more likely to be found sipping herbal tea than throwing bombs. Fearing for her own safety, Queen Victoria was horrified. Wild rumors of worldwide conspiracies to wipe out every monarch swirled across the Channel.[49]

Luckily for her, British anarchists were a lot less successful than their continental counterparts. The nascent security establishment had gained experience from the Fenian violence, the world's first modern terrorist campaign. The government had already passed anti-explosives laws in 1883, while Special Branch acquired valuable expertise countering terrorism and protecting the monarch, which now enabled it to prevent numerous anarchist bombings. The police even developed new means of disposing of recovered bombs. Neither the queen nor any visiting monarch suffered a terrorist attack on British soil; this achievement became the envy of Europe.[50]

In February 1894, a French anarchist and terrorist, Martial Bourdin, attempted to detonate a bomb outside the Royal Observatory in Greenwich Park. Although he cackhandedly succeeded only in blowing himself up, the incident showed that Britain could not be complacent. A week later, the home secretary, Herbert Asquith, updated the queen: the bomb, made from a gas pipe containing dynamite, had exploded prematurely in Bourdin's hand after he charged it with sulfuric acid too early. Detectives, he told her, thought the intended target was only a trial before a bigger attack and were still frantically trying to trace the source of a large sum of money found on Bourdin's mutilated corpse.[51] Victoria noted the discovery of "a shocking anarchist Club in London, almost entirely composed of foreigners."[52]

Shortly afterward, Lord Salisbury, now leader of the opposition, put forward an Aliens Bill designed to counter the entangled issues of anarchism and immigration. In 1894, as Parliament debated the bill over the summer, an Italian anarchist fatally stabbed the French president in Lyon. "How dreadful!" wrote the queen, the young assassin "glories in the deed."[53] She quickly lobbied the prime minister, Lord Rosebery, to pass the sections on anarchism. Britain's willingness to allow "these monstrous anarchists and assassins to live here and hatch their horrible plots in our country," she thundered, was doing the government "incalculable harm abroad." [54]

Although professing sympathy, Rosebery pointed out that the bill ran contrary to Britain's proud tradition of offering asylum. He politely reminded her that "not a single conspiracy against any foreign power or potentate has been hatched in this country" and, firing back at the queen's perceived enthusiasm for political surveillance, added that "our system of police supervision here is much more efficacious than that pursued on the continent." Despite the queen's protestations, the bill failed.[55]

Four years later, another Italian anarchist assassinated the Austrian empress on the shore of Lake Geneva, fatally stabbing her as she boarded a steamboat. Queen Victoria was horrified, again receiving gory details of the weapon—a shoemaker's awl—and the bloodstain on the dress of the empress.[56] She noted shortly afterward that Italy intended to "take stern measures to prevent these horrible murderers and anarchists from remaining in neutral Countries, and to be sent back to their own."[57]

The queen was correct. Italy proposed an international conference to counter anarchist terrorism, but her own government, having earlier helped defeat a similar initiative, was reluctant to respond to the invitation. This time, Victoria, shocked by the death of the empress, pressed the prime minister for action.[58] She was an impressively early advocate of international cooperation to fight counterterrorism. But the head of the Metropolitan Police was not an advocate—and strongly opposed the idea. Quite simply, he found it almost impossible to define what an anarchist was in the first place, to be able to declare who was an anarchist and who was not one. He added that "no English anarchist had ever been found; and that even foreign anarchists made no criminal attempts here" because popular opinion was so against anarchism. For similar reasons, he insisted that Victoria was perfectly safe.[59]

Influenced by the queen's persistent lobbying, Salisbury, now again prime minister, was more sympathetic to the Italian efforts and sent a delegation to the conference that took place late in 1898.[60] Despite pressure from Windsor, the British team abstained from many of the votes and worked behind the scenes to tone down what they saw as the more extreme continental approach. The British were the only country—of twenty-one represented at the conference— to dissent from the final agreement that encouraged governments to create surveillance agencies to monitor anarchists, share intelligence on anarchism, and introduce legislation to prohibit membership in anarchist organizations and the distribution of anarchist propaganda.[61]

The Rome Conference of 1889 did see some informal progress, although, because it was too sensitive to be committed to paper, it stayed off the record. The colorful British delegate, Howard Vincent, one of the founders of Special Branch who had since become a Conservative politician, initiated quiet meetings in the wings of the conference, where he agreed to increase intelligence sharing across borders and develop better communication between police forces. He later claimed that doing so resulted in the prevention of "anarchist outrages" for a year and a half. Vincent, also a vociferous imperialist, was knighted that year for his services.[62] Victoria saw this as a vindication of her views and was pleased.

Queen Victoria died on January 22, 1901, after sixty-three years on the throne. She had been the top "customer" for intelligence and had also directed particular operations. Not always the most objective of analysts when it came to interpreting the information, she preferred her instincts. On anarchism, her fears were correct, and she knew the threat was growing. Six months before her death, King Umberto of Italy was shot four times and killed in Monza. President McKinley of the United States suffered a similar fate only a year later. Both of the perpetrators were anarchists.

Partly at the exhortation of Victoria, intelligence had expanded. Special Branch had been created in direct response to the threat of assassination from the Fenians. Its commander also presided over a force of over six hundred specialist detectives, which had numbered just eight men at the start of her reign. Alongside them was a secretive political surveillance division called Section D, just the sort of thing that the queen had pressed for—and which figures like Palmerston had long resisted.[63] Victoria was straight-talking and constantly berated her ministers. She had pressed them to be tougher on surveillance, going against popular opinion in the process; she had demanded access to intelligence received by her ministers, while developing her own private networks, which she used to outmaneuver her governments; and she had opposed covert action in support of liberal uprisings, while thoroughly enjoying tales of deception and subversion elsewhere. She had even been used in intelligence operations as bait to lure out assassins—twice.

As her reign progressed, Victoria increasingly saw security policy, like foreign policy more broadly, as her own fiefdom. This was illustrated by a remarkable conversation the queen held with the incoming foreign secretary, Lord Rosebery, in 1886. As he nervously received his seals from the queen, she impressed upon him the importance of the Eastern question and, warning him that Russia was watching the new government closely, told him in no uncertain terms that there would be no change in foreign policy. Extraordinarily, she then "urged Lord Rosebery not to bring too many matters before the Cabinet, as nothing was decided there." It would, she continued, "be far better to discuss everything with me and Mr. Gladstone." She told him that she "frequently had intelligence of a secret nature, which it would be useful and interesting for him to hear, and which came from a reliable source."[64]

Throughout her reign, Victoria constantly and stubbornly demanded the latest intelligence. Her private sources ebbed and flowed depending on the country involved and which of her relatives were on the throne. On Germany, for example, she really did have the best sources; but on imperial matters, she was more reliant on her government. Victoria exploited the dearth of government sources to impose her own will. Knowledge, after all, is power. The problem for Victoria was that as intelligence started to become more professionalized toward the end of her reign, the scope narrowed to use her own private sources to influence or outmaneuver the government.

Her son, who succeeded her as Edward VII, was less interested in statecraft. Such was his reputation as a playboy prince that she deliberately withheld sensitive information from him for as long as possible. When he finally inherited the throne, the inexperienced king hoped to use royal sources to influence foreign policy, just as his mother had done. But secret service became more of a state activity in the early twentieth century, and ministers felt less reliant on royal networks. How Edward responded to these changes would help shape relations between crown and government for the next hundred years.

5

Edward VII and the Modernization of Intelligence

I cannot be indifferent to the assassination of a member
of my profession, or if you like, a member of my guild.
—Edward VII

In 1863, a young and rather minor princess, Alexandra of Denmark, crossed the English Channel. Her family had been relatively unknown until 1852, when her father, Prince Christian, was selected with the consent of the major European powers to succeed his second cousin as king of Denmark. She was about to become the wife of Albert Edward, the prince of Wales and the heir apparent of Queen Victoria, largely at the behest of her daughter Vicky. The subsequent wedding at Windsor was low key—albeit cheered loudly by local Eton schoolboys. In the space of just a few years, her life had been transformed. Not only had she married Prince Albert and her father become king of Denmark, but her brother had become king of Greece as George I. Alexandra further complicated the already labyrinthine connections of the British Royal Family, since her sister married the heir to the Russian throne and her nephew was the future Kaiser Wilhelm of Germany, her least favorite country. Something was bound to go wrong, and soon it did.

Edward, the prince of Wales, and his young wife, Alexandra, waited nervously as Prussian forces marched across the snowy border into Denmark in February 1864. Given that the couple had recently married and Alexandra was the daughter of the Danish king, they had a keen interest in how the war over Schleswig-Holstein had panned out. The prince, who would one day become King Edward VII, politely asked his mother for access to secret Foreign Office documents.

Queen Victoria firmly refused. A supporter of German unification, she was busily opposing ministerial plans to support the beleaguered Danes against the advancing Prussians. Bringing Edward, then in his early twenties, into the secret affairs of state would not have helped her cause. More importantly, however, she simply did not trust her own son. She admitted that he was not always "as discreet as he should be." Consequently, she agreed, as a rather poor compromise, to send him summaries of certain documents—which she herself had selected.[1]

The queen was not alone in her distrust. After the Franco-Prussian War in 1870, the foreign secretary also worried about Edward's indiscretion. He asked one of Victoria's advisers whether "really confidential matters" would remain secret if divulged to him. The prince, he explained, "asked me to keep him informed during the war. One evening I got four messages from different friends telling me to be careful. One of my first notes to him had been handed round a dinner party."[2]

Edward served the bulk of his long apprenticeship without access to secret intelligence—or even the more mundane matters of state. Worse than being indiscreet, Edward was vulnerable to blackmail. He was a playboy prince, indulging in illegal card games and extramarital relations with glamorous actresses, wealthy socialites, and high-class prostitutes. Rumor has it that a future chief of MI6, Stewart Menzies, was an illegitimate son: they certainly shared physical attributes and Menzies's mother climbed suspiciously quickly into the highest reaches of society. Either way, Menzies repeatedly used his supposed royal connection, and associated mystique, during his intelligence career.[3]

Edward tried to keep his affairs under the radar, regularly traveling semi-incognito to the continent. He tried to shake off the undercover French detectives who tailed him on frequent visits to lovers and brothels in the hopes of discovering whether any of his mistresses were in fact royalist agents of influence operating against the French Republic.[4] Meanwhile, German spies watched his movements similarly closely. They were intrigued by his dealings with French aristocrats, including the president himself.[5] Perhaps inevitably, Edward's lifestyle—so at odds with Victorian propriety—left him wide open to blackmail. On one occasion, he dispatched a trusted courier, disguised as an autograph hunter, to acquire incriminating letters he had written to a lover, the self-proclaimed "greatest whore in the world," whose brother was using them to blackmail him.[6]

In addition to Edward being indiscreet and a potential security risk, he had a reputation for idleness. It is of little surprise that Victoria continued to block his access to state secrets. Instead, she allowed his younger brother, Prince Leopold, to advise her on confidential matters. Edward was well aware of the arrangement, and of the humiliating fact that his mother thought Leopold more fit to be king than he.[7] Indeed, she seemed to prefer any of his siblings, and when she learned that Edward would be dragged into court as the result of a gambling scandal, she looked at Prince Arthur, another of her sons, and burst out: "If only you were the eldest!"[8]

Edward watched the red boxes coming and going from his mother's rooms, piling up on her desk, where they remained tantalizingly out of reach. It was not so much that he was desperate for secret material; it was more that he objected to being ignorant of important affairs, which people discussed in his hearing. The prince decided to take matters into his own hands by befriending Charles Dilke, the radical undersecretary of state for foreign affairs, whom the queen hated because his private life was even racier than that of her son. Upon meeting Dilke for the first time in March 1880, Edward quickly turned on the famed charm. They were like minds and recognized each other instantly; Dilke agreed to feed the prince information discreetly, but only after he had put his own spin on it.[9]

Toward the end of the nineteenth century, anticipating eventual succession, other ministers, including Gladstone and Disraeli, began to trust the prince with more confidential matters. Disraeli even sent him secret material behind the queen's back. More properly, Gladstone asked the queen for formal permission to, as his private secretary put it, give the prince "closer insight into State secrets." Again, she stubbornly refused.[10] When a senior diplomat in the Foreign Office insisted that the prince should see "what cards are in the hands of the players in the great European game which is going on, and how they are being played," Buckingham Palace quickly rebuffed him: "The direction of affairs is not in his hands."[11]

Edward, now portly and middle-aged, finally received a breakthrough of sorts in the early 1890s, when Gladstone returned to Number 10. The foreign secretary gave him a special golden key, once belonging to Prince Albert, for Foreign Office boxes containing secret material. Still Edward was unsatisfied, for despite now being authorized to see secret papers, he angrily accused successive ministers of just sending him "rubbish" and, in 1895, complained that their "game is not to let me see any interesting or important despatches!"[12]

As prince, Edward lacked access to official state secrets, but that did not mean he was ill informed. Like Victoria, he developed his own private system of surveillance. His frequent continental travels made him particularly cosmopolitan—he was fluent in French and German—and his strengths lay in cultivating relationships and drawing influential contacts into conversation. He maintained a network of international friends and relatives who provided him with sensitive information and he took great pride whenever entrusted with important confidences. As a result, Edward, as prince and king, possessed the best address book in Europe and had his own—often superior—sources of intelligence. Like his mother, Edward, the "Uncle of Europe," had access to a continental network of royal intelligence.[13]

The first issue that dominated Edward's agenda when he finally became king in 1901 had little to do with Europe at all. The second South African War, pitting Boer republics against British imperialism, had broken out in 1899; and Edward, long engrossed by military affairs, was watching developments as closely as he could. For all of Britain's superior might and resources, the unpopular war was dragging on and proving increasingly costly.

Edward wanted it over. He knew from friends across Europe that the war was seriously damaging Britain's reputation. Not that this was any great secret: he had already been shot at by an anarchist protester in Brussels—he carried the bullet as a souvenir for the rest of his life—and continued to be heckled by defiant renditions of the Boer national anthem whenever he travelled on the continent.

Edward took great interest in intelligence coming from the battlefield. Yet, just like Queen Victoria, he frequently complained about its inadequacy and chastised ministers accordingly. His private contacts at home and abroad occasionally furnished him with more information than the government. In late 1901, Francis Knollys, his private secretary, wrote to the prime minister about something Edward had heard. "The King hears rumours," Knollys stated, that the cabinet had received warning of an impending insurrection in South Africa and were duly worried. "Can you tell me for His information whether there is any foundation in these rumours?" Although Prime Minister Salisbury dismissed the rumors as exaggerated, the exchange pointedly reminded him of the new king's right to know. Meanwhile, Edward summoned the war secretary to the palace so often that his critics accused him of acting unconstitutionally.[14]

It was no secret that British forces committed terrible atrocities during the conflict. Facing insurgent tactics, including guerrillas hiding among civilians, they rounded up swaths of the population—including women and children—into overcrowded concentration camps. Food was scarce and disease spread; tens of thousands died in squalid conditions. Much to the horror of Whitehall, newspapers began to report on massacres, rape, and looting. The government scrambled to prosecute the most prominent journalists using the Official Secrets Act but failed on the grounds that they had simply received stolen information and therefore had not committed an offense.[15]

Frustrated ministers turned to unattributable propaganda—and used the king himself. They needed someone serious who could discredit the negative reporting and so turned to Arthur Conan Doyle. A prolific writer and spiritualist most famous for his Sherlock Holmes detective stories, Conan Doyle was also a staunch imperialist. He was perfect for the task. The government provided him with intelligence briefings, while Edward discreetly provided £500 to cover the costs of publication and marketing. The outcome—an essay called *The War in South Africa: Its Cause and Conduct*—appeared in early 1902. It was translated into many languages, and it was a huge success, refuting many of the charges laid against the British forces. Conan Doyle claimed to be writing from an "independent standpoint" without any "official authority." This was simply not true; it was covert propaganda funded by the king. Conan Doyle unsurprisingly received a knighthood shortly afterward.[16]

In early May 1902, Edward received surprising news from his nephew, Kaiser Wilhelm of Germany, who had heard, "through a private channel," that Britain was offering a generous peace deal to the Boers. This was news to Edward, who demanded an explanation from the prime minister. Salisbury, although aware of preliminary talks, denied knowledge of the precise terms and dipatched his ambassador in Berlin on a "most secret" mission to find out what Wilhelm knew. It turned out that the kaiser had an excellent—but anonymous—source inside South Africa and that his intelligence was broadly accurate. Edward was furious that his German nephew knew more than he did; and once again, he demanded to be kept better informed. From then on, Salisbury reluctantly submitted the twists and turns of each proposal to the king before the final agreement was signed at the end of the month.[17]

Britain's early humiliations and then defeat in the Boer War necessitated a thorough review. Edward was especially livid about the intelligence performance, describing the War Office's Intelligence Branch as "one of those scandals which ought to hang Lords Lansdowne and Wolseley," the secretaries of state who were responsible for it. The king quickly suggested that his friend and adviser Lord Esher should be involved in what became the Royal Commission. Esher would become a key figure in defense planning throughout Edward's reign. After every meeting, he informed the king about exactly what had been said and by whom.[18]

Esher was a dark figure who promoted the monarchy's role in politics. Edward provided him with rooms at Windsor Castle and a critically important position—superintendent of the archives, which were full of secrets. Esher artfully employed this, and his friendship with the king's private secretary, Francis Knollys, to inform and advise the king. He offered evidence from Queen Victoria's papers to show that the sovereign had been better informed in previous years, and thus suggested that ministers submit more secret business to the king. Esher was intelligent, able, and arrogant, with a gift for friendship. He possessed all the attributes for manipulation. He was a curiosity to contemporaries and has puzzled historians. A controversial *éminence grise* operating very much behind the scenes, his own work is difficult to assess. But what is clear is that Edward admired Esher. As a result, Esher provoked the suspicion traditionally felt for royal favorites. Many distrusted him as an intriguer who plotted, leaked confidential information, and interfered unconstitutionally in affairs of state.[19]

The hearings vindicated the intelligence effort. Esher told Edward that military intelligence had in fact provided "full warning" of the Boer threat as early as 1896. Frustratingly, however, requests to strengthen the Intelligence Branch had been "scoffed at by the financial authorities" inside the War Office and were never even referred to the Treasury.[20] Esher added that the blame also lay with the commander-in-chief, who, "for some unexplainable reason," did not show the intelligence to the secretary of state.[21] Although, as Esher reassured Edward, the Royal Commission caused a further strengthening of the Intelligence Branch, it had no great impact on the production of actual intelligence.[22]

Esher created a new position, inspector-general of the forces, which was filled by Edward's brother, Prince Arthur, giving the royals greater power. More importantly, Esher was using Edward and his brother to bring about cultural change. Throughout the nineteenth century, the army had scoffed at strategic intelligence and proper staff work, instead glorifying tactical intelligence gathered by the plucky amateur. In contrast, France, Austria, and Germany, and even Russia, had boasted elaborate intelligence sections within their General Staffs. Britain was now catching up.[23]

Esher's reforms also led to the creation of a special duties section in the War Office that, in 1905, worked up contingency plans for an extensive offensive intelligence system in the event of a European war. It eventually became the Secret Service Bureau, the forerunner to MI5 and MI6, in 1909.[24]

Alongside military reform and war, King Edward was most interested in foreign affairs. Over almost half a century, he had acquired great experience and knowledge of Europe, leaving politicians, at least in his mind, parochial by comparison. He had developed strong opinions on foreign policy and was keen to advise ministers as he saw fit. He read foreign dispatches carefully, highlighting any inaccuracies or inconsistencies, and remained sensitive about being kept in the dark. The shadow of his mother loomed over him as he complained time and again that ministers neither showed him as much secret material nor consulted him as often as they had Queen Victoria. He would become deeply offended at the slightest neglect, sharply rebuking ministers in protest.[25]

Frustrated at not being treated with the same courtesy or respect, Edward turned to the networks he had cultivated as prince of Wales and insisted that ambassadors abroad wrote private letters to him alongside their official dispatches. Outside royalty and officialdom, the Rothschilds and other bankers provided particularly useful foreign intelligence. He even established an informal cabinet of his own. It included Francis Knollys, his private secretary; the courtiers Lord Esher and John Fisher; Francis Bertie and Cecil Spring-Rice, both diplomats who enjoyed royal patronage; and Charles Hardinge, a diplomat who would go on to become head of the Foreign Office, and the king's inside man. Edward had breakfast with Hardinge at Buckingham Palace once a week to discuss foreign affairs. The king was not as reliant on official intelligence as ministers would have liked.[26]

Edward used his impressive black book to conduct discreet diplomacy. In the spring of 1903, he visited Paris at the culmination of a European tour. He planned it in absolute secrecy, without even telling his wife, Alix, and, when it was time to depart, he left the foreign secretary at home. He traveled instead with his friend Hardinge.[27]

Predictably, Edward's planning bypassed the British ambassador to France. Instead, he worked through the military attaché, Edward Stuart-Wortley, a friend of the French president. Edward sent secret letters directly to Stuart-Wortley's house, so as not to arouse suspicion at the embassy.[28] This channel was identical to that used by Queen Victoria when sending secret messages to Russia behind the back of her foreign secretary.

Edward had received private intelligence, including through various royal sources, on French attitudes toward England the previous year. He had learned that the president wanted closer relations with the UK, and, through Stuart-Wortley, he now knew that the president would welcome his visit.[29] Despite Edward's affection for France, this was no foregone conclusion. Anti-British sentiment was high in France in the aftermath of the Boer War and a series of disputes over colonial possessions. When ministers belatedly found out about the trip, they cautioned about negative political reactions in Germany and Russia, alongside the security risks to Edward personally. The foreign secretary warned of hostile crowds and bomb-throwing anarchists. But Edward relied on private threat assessments and predicted he would be perfectly safe.[30]

In reality, Portugal rather than Paris posed the greater security threat. As the royal yacht sailed from Britain's south coast to Lisbon, the first stop on the tour, the royal party received intelligence from British and French agents warning that a known Dutch anarchist was also en route to the Portuguese capital. The Iberian Peninsula had a poor reputation for security—especially when it came to protecting visiting dignitaries. Taking no chances, Edward stayed aboard the secure yacht while the French authorities tracked down and detained the anarchist under the pretense of problems with his papers.[31]

The visit was ultimately successful. Edward traveled on to Paris unscathed, and helped to lay the foundations for the famous Entente Cordiale between the United Kingdom and France. He was not involved in the negotiations; but his very public, if secretly planned, endorsement of better relations proved symbolically potent and helped to transform French attitudes toward England. This was a success for British and French diplomacy, for both countries had been rather isolated and focused on minor colonial disputes. The kaiser was especially frustrated by Edward's success, which pleased the king very much, since he hated the Germans almost as much as his wife did.[32]

Edward's intelligence sources remained useful for the government. Eighteen months after his visit to Paris, he received a warning that Germany intended to attack France. The king of Spain had told the French, who in turn had told Edward. Taking the intelligence seriously, Edward asked if the foreign secretary knew. He did not; Edward's sources insisted that the "communication was not intended for the British Government." "Royal confidences," they insisted, "are not to be noised abroad and we cannot give the King of Spain away."[33] Sympathetic to the privacy of royal networks, Edward instructed the French to tell the British foreign secretary—but not to divulge the royal source.[34]

To solidify the agreement with France, Edward turned to Russia. Drawing on his royal intelligence networks once again, he engaged in yet more discreet diplomacy. Suspicion between the two countries was high, having never recovered from the Crimean War in the 1850s and the competition for Central Asia that had spanned much of the nineteenth century. Like Queen Victoria before him, Edward had been an advocate of the Great Game and, toward the start of his reign, was the only one to approve of the belligerent activities of Francis Younghusband, an imperial army officer turned explorer, in Tibet. At the end of 1903, Younghusband departed on a mission to uncover Russian espionage and to settle various border disputes. Unfortunately, he exceeded his instructions and, the next year, ended up invading Tibet, killing bands of poorly armed monks, and humiliating the Chinese. When Younghusband reached his goal—the holy city of Lhasa—he found no evidence of Russian intrigue. The government swiftly dismissed him as an imperial agent, but Edward ensured he received recognition for his efforts.[35]

In 1904, amid distrust and rumors that both sides were in secret negotiations with China, Edward sent Prince Louis of Battenberg to Saint Petersburg as his representative at the christening of the son of Tsar Nicholas II.[36] It was a canny move designed to bolster relations. Demonstrating the blurring of public and private boundaries, Battenberg was personally close to the tsar while also serving as Britain's director of naval intelligence. He had used this position, alongside his royal connections, to gather information on the naval forces of various European countries.[37] On his return from the christening, Battenberg briefed the king on Russian intentions, telling him that the Russians had no aggressive plans toward India and were in a generally conciliatory mood.[38]

But the rapprochement did not last. Less than a year later, the tsar was again referring to Edward, his cousin, as "the greatest "mischief-maker" and the most deceitful and dangerous intriguer in the world."[39] The king asked the new ambassador in Russia, his old friend Charles Hardinge, on whose appointment he had insisted, to improve relations.[40]

Late the following year, revolution swept Russia. Spurred on by a recent defeat in its war against Japan, strikes and military mutinies threatened the tsar's regime. Back in London, Edward demanded to know what was going on. The answer to his request came from Donald Mackenzie Wallace, a chain-smoking journalist and well-connected Russia expert. After studying at four different universities and taking a PhD in law at Heidelberg in 1867, Wallace had become fascinated with Russia. He published a best-selling book on the subject and became a foreign correspondent for *The Times*, but he also took on secret work, typically smuggling treaties sewn into the lining of his greatcoat. Having once accompanied the young Tsar Nicholas on a tour of India, he now served as the king's private source of intelligence throughout the uprising, sending a string of long and confidential telegrams about the severity of the strikes and the prospects for the ill-fated revolution.[41] As a friend of Hardinge, he operated from the embassy in Saint Petersburg.[42] According to one royal biographer, "His Majesty's Information Service was of an exceptionally high order."[43]

There was one gap in the royal intelligence, however: a secret defense pact made between Russia and Germany earlier in the year. Much to Kaiser Wilhelm's delight, Edward failed to make any sense of the scraps of intelligence that had come his way. "I can't find out what has been going on," he ranted in frustration, bemoaning how his usual sources had all dried up. The tsar's mother (Edward's sister-in-law); the Russian ambassador, with whom he regularly played bridge; and the Danish royal family were all saying nothing. Even the Russian foreign minister, who, according to Edward, was *"such a nice man and lets me know all I want to hear,"* knew "nothing or at least won't tell! It is very disagreeable!"[44]

The man on the other end of the rant, listening intently as the loose-lipped king reeled off his list of sources, was a German aristocrat. Unfortunately for Edward, he had been sent by the kaiser to observe Anglo-French relations and swiftly reported the conversation back to Berlin. Kaiser Wilhelm then took great delight in telling Tsar Nicholas that Edward's outburst demonstrated just "how very wide is the net of secret information he has cast over Europe and you."[45]

On this occasion, Edward's net of sources simply did not know about the secret deal. When the Russian government did eventually find out what the tsar and kaiser had cooked up, it refused to ratify it on the grounds that it undermined a preexisting deal with the French.[46]

With diplomacy stalling, the British foreign secretary, Edward Grey, turned to the king, asking him to visit Russia and reprise the role he had played in 1903 in creating an atmosphere conducive to the agreement with France.[47] Politicians had been worried about his safety in France, but, in the aftermath of the failed revolution and amid a number of high-profile assassinations, the security situation in Russia was far more acute. When, in 1908, a royal trip looked likely, planning took place in the strictest secrecy. Charles Hardinge, now back in London as the most senior diplomat in the Foreign Office, explained to Arthur Nicolson, his replacement in Russia, and another rising diplomat who owed his position to royal patronage, that the prospect of the visit had to be kept as secret as possible to prevent terrorists from plotting Edward's assassination.[48] He even threatened to call off the visit entirely if it became common knowledge.[49]

As a security compromise, in June 1908, Edward eventually made the visit on board the royal yacht, meeting Tsar Nicholas off the Baltic coast. Security was tight. As Ponsonby put it, "uniform was no criterion" in spotting people who may want to harm the king.[50] Little of political or diplomatic importance occurred during the meeting, but once again direct contact between the charming king and the tsar helped solidify Anglo-Russian rapprochement.[51] This paved the way for a full state visit to Britain by Nicholas the next summer. He arrived at Cowes in the Russian royal yacht, ostentatiously flanked by naval cruisers. Less flamboyantly, he brought with him the top Russian codebreaker, who prepared the Tsar for meetings with Edward by providing him with decrypted British dispatches.[52]

British diplomatic maneuvering throughout Edward's reign was a response to the German question. The king and his nephew, Kaiser Wilhelm, had long endured a tempestuous relationship and, in a world where the political and the personal mixed, family baggage affected national security just as much.

Intelligence was paramount throughout. With both men trying to outdo each other, the battle for the latest information formed a constant backdrop to their meetings. Each accused the other of espionage, intrigue, and deception from the very start of Edward's reign. The kaiser even brought the head of his admiralty's new intelligence service with him to Queen Victoria's funeral.[53] Each sought to extract secret intelligence from their network of contacts across the continent, although Wilhelm was often less tactful than his uncle. On one occasion, he simply instructed his admirals to get British navy personnel visiting German ports "as drunk as possible."[54] He had successes, however, including the recruitment of Edward's doctor, Sir James Reid, to report on activities in the English court.[55]

In return, Wilhelm claimed that Edward ran a private intelligence network which he used to plot against Germany. When the Norwegian throne became vacant in 1905, Edward's royal sources allowed him to warn his favored candidate about German scheming and ultimately help him claim the throne. All the while, British ministers tried to rein in Edward's meddling.[56]

Edward's access to intelligence put the kaiser on the back foot—and vice versa. In 1901, Wilhelm reveled in telling Edward about the tsar's forthcoming trip to France, deliberately allowing his uncle to interpret the news as a move against England.[57] Five years later, Wilhelm sent a warship to Zanzibar, telling Edward that local disturbances necessitated the generous German gesture. Outmaneuvered again, Edward frantically scrambled for local intelligence, only to be told that nothing serious had occurred and that the Germans were lying.[58]

Nowhere was intelligence more important in the growing tension between the UK and Germany than when assessing the size and intentions of each other's navies. Empress Victoria, the kaiser's mother and Edward's older sister, had warned about the "pure madness and folly" of German naval growth as early as 1894.[59] When he became king, Edward, guided by his close friend and first sea lord John Fisher, remained deeply concerned as German naval growth not only continued but intensified. Fisher believed that Germany was "our only probable enemy" and, with Edward's personal backing, was responsible for the revolutionary Dreadnought battleship launched by the king himself in early 1906.[60]

Two years later, Fisher accurately predicted that war would break out with Germany in the summer of 1914. He held a long and secret meeting with the king to suggest launching a surprise attack on the German navy now so as to stave off the future war. Edward thought the idea was preposterous, insisting that he would not approve such an aggressive act without formerly declaring war.[61] Fisher continued to keep Edward updated on the latest intelligence but, in an attempt to keep him onside, did so slightly misleadingly. He took technical reports from the naval attaché in Berlin and dishonestly upgraded their classification, as secret or confidential, before passing them on to the king. He knew that the sensitive king, so quick to take offense, would be seduced by apparent access to secret material. The ruse worked: Edward forcefully backed Fisher in his increasingly bitter battles to build more Dreadnoughts.[62]

Throughout the summer of 1908, Edward grew increasingly concerned about German intentions. Fears spread that German spies had already sketched British harbors and studied coasts ready for an invasion. An anonymous article appeared in the respected *Quarterly Review* warning of 50,000 Germans disguised as waiters already hiding in place in Britain.[63] Novelists, such as William Le Queux, were churning out pulp fiction—supposedly based on insider accounts—about German spies and saboteurs overrunning the country. Perhaps influenced by his wife's library of Le Queux novels, Edward now spoke of the kaiser's plan to "throw a *corps d'armée* or two into England, making proclamation that he has come, not as an enemy to the king, but as the grandson of Queen Victoria, to deliver him from the Socialistic gang which is ruining the country."[64]

Meanwhile, Edward also grew wary of Austria. Wickham Steed, the Vienna correspondent for *The Times*, warned him that Emperor Franz Josef intended to annex Bosnia and Herzegovina. Edward initially refused to believe this warning. He had very recently met the emperor in person and spoken widely about European politics, yet nothing had been said about Bosnia. Steed, who had served in Vienna for over half a decade, assured Edward that his intelligence came from sources who had always proved reliable in the past. Edward remained dismissive. "I still think you are wrong," he insisted. "Surely the Emperor would have said something to me."[65]

Steed's intelligence was accurate, but the king, arrogant and touchy, placed too much confidence in his own ability to elicit information. He simply did not want to hear. The Austrian emperor had made his decision in August, had said nothing to Edward, and had then announced it in early October. One of Edward's advisers described the Austrian foreign minister as "a foxy type" who "preferred to work underground," but the king was furious at being deceived.[66] To him, the political was personal. Deception—even a lie of omission—became a personal slight.[67]

Amid this febrile, paranoid atmosphere, Edward allowed the manipulative Esher to engage in more clandestine diplomacy. In November, he secretly met the French military attaché outside Windsor and divulged that the cabinet was divided between those in favor of supporting France in a war with Germany, including Prime Minister Herbert Asquith, and those who opposed it. He added, in extreme confidence, that King Edward strongly backed the former.[68]

When Asquith told Edward shortly afterward that the German naval program might be slowing, the king was having none of it. It was thirdhand news: Asquith had heard it from the foreign secretary, who in turn had heard it hinted at by the German ambassador. The king became an intelligence analyst; increasingly wary of official German sources, he assessed any such information as worthless. He then became a royal spymaster, tasking the British naval attaché in Berlin with personally ascertaining the exact number of ships the government was building.[69] In the meantime, Edward insisted that "as long as Germany persists in her present programme of shipbuilding, we have no alternative but to build double."[70]

In early 1909, the king learned that far from tempering the shipbuilding program, Germany had in fact accelerated it. He was furious with the kaiser for not informing him; but, perhaps more tellingly, was angry with his own government for not keeping him updated. Edward was, in his own words, "very much disturbed" by the latest intelligence on German shipbuilding.

He demanded to know what type of intelligence failure had happened. Did the government lack the information in the first place, or had the cabinet willfully ignored valuable intelligence provided by the navy? If it was the latter, Edward believed that "it should come out." It would be unfair to those involved if an intelligence success remained hidden. He also wondered whether naval intelligence had failed to impress the facts strongly enough upon the cabinet. In response, Fisher reassured the king that the government was building eight Dreadnoughts and blamed any intelligence failure on a combination of German lies and an inability of the naval attaché to gain access to German ports and facilities.[71]

Edward was all the more angry, given that he had just visited Berlin and would have found the intelligence useful in his discussions with the kaiser.[72] It had ultimately proved an unsuccessful—if eventful—trip. Queen Alix, sitting next to the kaiser at dinner, had accused him of being "stupid" and "making all this commotion about nothing." When she offered him a lozenge, he showed it to his doctor, thinking that she was trying to poison him. "I should," Alix later recalled, "*like* to have!"[73]

Esher provided Edward with intelligence and an embarrassing line of questioning. Suitably armed, he could now press Asquith for the latest information on naval preparedness. Was it a fact, the king asked the prime minister, that "the Germans will have in March 1911: 17 Dreadnoughts ready for the seas, and we shall have 12 plus whatever we lay down this year?"[74]

Acquiring accurate intelligence on the future size of the German navy and its quality as a fighting force was proving difficult. The military attachés in Berlin offered little beyond generalities, not least because the Germans increasingly saw them as enemy spies and restricted their access.[75] Meanwhile, tight security around shipyards hampered early attempts by military intelligence to use commercial cover to investigate naval construction. The king knew well one of the key figures behind these operations, William Melville. He had previously overseen royal security, but Melville now focused on German espionage and warned of spies reconnoitering potential invasion routes across England. Anything of interest that he did succeed in uncovering was poorly coordinated between military intelligence, naval intelligence, and the Foreign Office. It proved ineffective.[76]

Amid war scares and spy paranoia, Asquith ordered an inquiry into foreign espionage in Britain. Richard Haldane, secretary of state for war and an old friend of the king, chaired the first meeting in March 1909. Although initially bemused by the accounts of German espionage, Haldane was ready to believe the remarkable tales coming his way. Esher sat alongside Haldane on the committee and also began skeptically. He dismissed the head of counterintelligence work in the War Office as "a silly witness." "Spy catchers," he quipped, "get espionage on the brain. Rats are everywhere—behind every arras."[77] But his initial skepticism gradually waned, especially as Haldane grew convinced.[78]

It is highly likely that Esher briefed the king on the ins and outs of the espionage hearings, just as he had done on previous occasions. Indeed, his very presence at the heart of government frustrated the Foreign Office precisely because he had a habit of repeating confidential discussions to the king.[79] He also had a strong influence over Edward on military policy.[80] At about the same time, Esher formed a secret organization called the Society of Islanders. Operating discreetly outside Parliament, Esher sought to shape defense policy by lobbying in favor of naval expansion at a rate of two to one compared with Germany. He was delighted when Edward repeated exactly his mantra that the next major war was building and argued that the British Empire floated on the strength of the navy and that "'two keels to one' is the only right and safe thing."[81]

A month later, in April, Haldane and Esher asked whether Britain could create a small secret service bureau. A further team, this time chaired by Charles Hardinge, examined the matter. Hardinge, of course, was head of the Foreign Office, highly suspicious of Germany, and a longtime friend of the king.[82] On April 28, he submitted a report that was so secret it was never printed. Only one copy existed. Hardinge created a secret service bureau and set out what the authorized MI6 historian calls "the founding charter of the modern British intelligence community."[83] The bureau would eventually split into what are now known as MI5 and MI6, with the former focused on gathering intelligence domestically and the latter operating overseas. What is striking is that three of the key individuals involved in founding the modern British intelligence system—Haldane, Esher, and Hardinge—were all favorites of King Edward.

The creation of the Secret Service Bureau by Edward's protégés was entirely fitting. The king enjoyed subterfuge and secret missions; indeed, he had used this persistently to push back against a decline in the political importance of the crown. He did maintain influence, largely through the veneration in which the monarchy was still held, but never as much as he hoped.[84] As one of his assistant private secretaries recalled, "the King always prided himself on being entirely a constitutional monarch, but at heart he was a born autocrat."[85] Royal prerogative in appointments was one of the last formal powers of the crown, and the king was obsessive about them.[86]

Courtiers, such as Esher and Knollys, tried to bolster Edward's direct input into decision-making but failed. After all, Edward was never as experienced, as respected—or as discreet—as Queen Victoria. His greatest skills lay in

cultivating strong relationships with people and helping to create an atmosphere conducive to political agreement, so often he worked indirectly.[87]

Edward's achievements were considerable. Historians have praised his diplomatic efforts in establishing the necessary conditions for alliances with France
and Russia. To be an effective diplomat, the king needed intelligence. He had
excellent private sources but was a flawed intelligence consumer. For all his
experience and traveling, he remained naive and was quick to be hurt when his
contacts lied to him. Rather arrogant, he often either thought he knew best or
thought his charm was sufficient to elicit intelligence from his friends and relatives. To make matters worse, his networks were not omniscient. Sometimes,
as with the stillborn Russo-German Treaty of 1905, they simply did not know.

Diplomacy and dynastic politics were often the same thing. When an uprising erupted in Athens during the summer of 1909, Edward's updates came via
his wife's family. He then used his own "purely private" channels to offer support for King George I, his wife's brother, and strongly urge him not to abdicate. Many of these messages were not shown to the foreign secretary, who,
upon learning of Edward's activities, had to remind the king not to interfere
in Greek affairs. Edward sent a prickly reply: "I never for a moment dreamt of
my government in any way interfering in the internal affairs of Greece. I only
wished to point out the importance of the safety of King George, my brother-
in-law, and therefore thought that the fleet should not be too far off."[88]

Edward died on May 6, 1910. His funeral was the largest gathering of European royalty in history. It offered the kaiser, who turned up with a dozen armed
bodyguards, the perfect opportunity for a final intelligence mission against
his uncle.[89] His large entourage included a German officer believed to be the
acting head of naval intelligence. While in Britain, the German discreetly visited an anonymous barbershop on Caledonian Road in north London. He was
followed by a Special Branch officer, who soon realized that the barbershop
was actually a secret post office distributing communications across a major
German spy ring. By intercepting and opening the mail, the British were able
to track down most German agents and monitor their activity before eventually rounding them up at the outbreak of war in 1914, depriving Germany of
its undercover network.[90] King Edward's death therefore marked a significant
counterespionage victory, but the intelligence battle was only just beginning.

PART II

Royal Relations
and Intrigues

6

King George V and the First World War

Our spies are the worst and clumsiest in the world.
—King George V, September 2, 1910

In late May 1906, Edward VII's eldest surviving son and heir, George, the duke of York, visited Spain. He was forty years of age, and was accompanied by his wife Mary. He was there to represent his family at the marriage of his cousin to the king of Spain. Immediately after the wedding ceremony, they rode in a regal procession of carriages from the cathedral to the reception. As they approached the palace, a loud explosion rang out. George assumed it was an artillery gun firing the first salute.

He was wrong. An anarchist had thrown a bomb, disguised as a bouquet of flowers, at the newlyweds from an upper window as the procession passed beneath. It killed about twenty people, including their driver, and injured another fifty. Miraculously, the royal bride and groom were not badly hurt, but the bride's wedding dress was drenched in blood.[1] George recorded in his diary that the couple were "covered with glass from the broken windows" and "broke down" as soon as they escaped the public gaze. Stoically, the wedding feast continued inside the palace, but George's toast wishing them a long and happy life rang rather hollow.[2]

These were dangerous times for royals. The king of Spain had already been injured in an almost identical attack a year before. The king of Portugal and his son were shot and killed by republican assassins less than two years later. As we have seen, the king of Italy and America's president, William McKinley, had been dispatched by the revolvers of deadly assassins earlier in the decade. The Russian royals had suffered numerous attacks, one of which had just killed Grand Duke Sergei Romanov, the tsar's uncle.

These deadly events were symptoms of social turbulence. King George V's reign would go on to witness the rise of anarchism, socialism, communism, fascism, Irish republicanism, and the Indian independence movement, many of which would challenge the established order and threaten the monarchies of Europe. As George's perilous visit to Spain had also illustrated, these royals were remarkably interrelated because of an obsession with lineage and royal pedigree. Therefore, as the First World War approached, royal relations, and indeed royal intrigue, especially between George and his two cousins, the tsar and the kaiser, took on great importance.

George was the second son of Edward VII and had not expected to be king, until his elder brother Albert died of pneumonia in 1892. George had been seriously ill himself with typhoid, and, sharing the family's grief, he married his brother's fiancée, Mary of Teck, shortly afterward. The two brothers had been close, and because their father had decided that time in the navy provided ideal training for princes, they both served on the cadet training ship HMS *Britannia* at Dartmouth when George was just twelve years old. Later, George commanded ships and traveled extensively, visiting many countries in the Mediterranean and the Caribbean, together with South Africa, Australia, and the United States. In 1881, the two brothers had visited the emperor of Japan, presenting him with two wallabies from Australia. But Albert's death ended what George had expected to be a long naval career. He acceded to the throne in 1910.[3]

History has rather underrated George. Famously, he has been dismissed as someone obsessed with collecting stamps and shooting animals, preferring the quiet life of a country squire to public service.[4] His first prime minister, Herbert Asquith, held a fairly condescending view of the king's mental capabilities, likening his knowledge of current affairs to "the average opinion of the man on the tube."[5]

He worked dutifully to follow the mounting complexities of European foreign policy but found lengthy Foreign Office telegrams a bit of a bore. To spice them up, his officials would mix in secret service reports. The ones he loved best contained gossip about misbehavior by the members of the royal families of Europe, who were often his relatives.[6]

Most importantly, the king was anxious to avoid war. He was unimpressed by the rampant Germanophobia of his parents, which had contributed to the spy fever of the previous decade, and indeed to the creation of a modern British secret service. He instinctively realized that war might reverberate badly on his own family, with its German ancestry advertised by a baroque collection of German titles.

When George ascended the throne, his old classmate from Greenwich Naval Academy back in 1884, Mansfield Cumming, was into his first hectic year as head of the overseas intelligence branch, which would eventually become

MI6.[7] Diary entries record their familiarity: they played billiards, and Cumming told the future king some "interesting things"—but what these were exactly is not recorded.[8]

Partly because of such close personal contacts, George had a good assessment of the elementary state of Britain's secret activities and of the general spy mania that had seized Europe. In 1910, he told a friend that the "Germans suspect that there are English spies everywhere." "Yet," he admitted, "we have no secret service funds, or at least they are much smaller than any other State, and our spies are the worst and clumsiest in the world."

By contrast, George thought that "German espionage" was "magnificently organized and lavishly financed." He believed there to be a "certain number of German spies" constantly stationed in Portsmouth and Southampton: "We have no protection against them, and so far as I am concerned German officers can examine all our ships."[9]

Perhaps for this reason, his early use of the secret service was rather peripheral. In May 1911, he decided to send a lion to Dublin Zoo that had been presented to him by the king of Abyssinia. A specialist lion keeper had traveled with the animal on its long journey from Africa. All the complex arrangements and indeed the costs of transportation of this tribute were taken care of by the British secret service.[10] This continued the royal tradition of using the secret service for eccentric personal missions and would not be the last manifestation.

As war loomed over Europe, George's opinion of the British secret service did not improve. On one occasion, because of repeated failed missions, he found himself having to intervene personally to rescue three spies from imprisonment.

The Agadir crisis of July 1911, a minor confrontation involving a German gunboat off the coast of French Morocco, had caused a major panic, which left Cumming under pressure for intelligence about the German fleet. Prompted by the wave of jingoism that accompanied the crisis, he received an offer from Bertrand Stewart, a junior officer and "intelligence enthusiast," to find out more. Cumming agreed reluctantly, warning Stewart that he was running his head into a noose. But the happy-go-lucky Stewart headed for the Netherlands and then Germany to scout out the ports.

Seven days later, Stewart was arrested in a public lavatory in Bremen. The German authorities had caught him red-handed trying to flush away an incriminating codebook passed to him by an agent. Unfortunately for Stewart, he had been double crossed: his agent had secretly defected to the Germans, insisting that they paid better. By February 1912, he was locked up in Glatz, a fortress prison used mainly to house Germans who had been convicted of dueling.

There, he joined two other luckless spies, Captain Bernard Frederick Trench and Lieutenant Vivian R. Brandon, who had been arrested for similarly amateurish activities.

The next May, George used his royal connections to secure their release. He appealed to his cousin, Kaiser Wilhelm, who agreed to set them free in honor of George's visit to Germany to attend the wedding of the kaiser's daughter.[11] The failed British spies were thrilled to receive their royal release and skipped home to freedom, although Cumming wisely decided to keep none of them on in MI6.

Meanwhile, the wedding was a huge affair. As a diplomatic gesture, Kaiser Wilhelm invited almost his entire extended family, including Tsar Nicholas II of Russia. The wedding was one of the last great social events of European royalty before the First World War began fourteen months later. Alongside this magnanimous gesture, the Germans had hoped—and British officials had feared—that George might be coaxed into discussions on naval arms control. But he deftly avoided foreign policy issues, and instead asked endless questions about shooting and the management of the Prussian royal stables.[12]

Eccentric and status-conscious, Wilhelm was delighted to have both George and Nicholas, the heads of two of the most important royal families in Europe, present at the wedding. Yet he also worried about being the odd one out, since George and Nicholas enjoyed each other's company but found Wilhelm annoying and neurotic. He therefore did everything possible to ensure that his two cousins were never alone together, convinced that if they met, they would soon be plotting against Germany. George later recalled that when they did finally manage to converse privately, he was sure that the kaiser's ear "was glued to the keyhole."[13]

Wilhelm was right to be suspicious. George and Nicholas were not only close but also looked like twin brothers. George addressed his cousin as "my dear Nicky, your ever devoted cousin and friend." They corresponded frequently, sometimes touching on dynastic problems across Europe, including the future of the Greek monarchy.[14] George had assured his cousin that "there may be difficulties with Germany, but I think they can be overcome. If only England, Russia and France stick together the peace of Europe is assured."[15] On the intriguing subject of German plots, he added, "I like to tell you everything."[16]

In November 1913, Archduke Franz Ferdinand of Austria and his wife visited Britain. They were obsessed with hunting and enjoyed a spectacular shoot on the edge of Windsor led by the king and the prince of Wales. Thereafter, they spent their time in Britain happily moving from county to county, blasting at everything that moved. Franz's wife, Sophie, the duchess of Hohenberg, was the better shot. Days later, shooting with the duke of Portland on the outskirts of Sherwood Forest, there was an accident with a gun. Portland recounted that "one of the loaders fell down. This caused both barrels of the gun he was carrying to be discharged, the shot passing within a few feet of the archduke and myself." Portland subsequently pondered "whether the Great War might not have been averted, or at least postponed, had the archduke met his death then and not at Sarajevo the following year."[17]

The next June, Franz and Sophie were not so lucky. They were killed on a visit to Sarajevo, the capital of Bosnia-Herzegovina, which was occupied by Austria-Hungary.

It is hard to understand why such an intelligent man as Ferdinand would have embarked on such a foolhardy visit. The moment he had chosen to visit Sarajevo, Serbian National Day, June 28, was itself provocative. Terrorism there was notorious, and they had faced an earlier bomb scare themselves; yet they still climbed into an open vehicle and drove down a street known as "Assassins' Alley" before being shot by associates of the Black Hand, a Serbian terrorist group. Ferdinand's death was personally distressing for George, who was almost exactly the same age and knew him well after repeated visits to Britain. George instructed the court to wear mourning for a week.

History had already shouted its warnings. Only a few years before, King Alexander of Serbia and his queen had been horribly murdered by a gang of army officers, again including members of the Black Hand. Infiltrating the palace, they hid in a cupboard inside the queen's bedroom before leaping out and shooting the young royal couple. Afterward, their bodies, mutilated and disemboweled, were reportedly thrown from a second-floor window of the palace onto piles of manure.[18]

The death of the archduke was a double tragedy, for Franz Ferdinand was a man of peace. He understood that war between Austria and Russia would mean the end of one of their royal houses—perhaps even both—and had urged a "concord of the emperors" to avoid confrontation.[19] Now, Austria demanded recompense from Serbia for the assassination and, when this was not fully met, it invaded. Europe's complex web of interlocking treaties, designed to ensure peace, now dragged each country into war. Russia had already mobilized to help its Serbian ally, and Germany warned Britain that it would have to respond with serious countermeasures. The kaiser—pompous, posturing, an ardent lover of exotic military uniforms, and above all thin-skinned—did not want to be seen backing down. The slide toward war began.

Realization dawned in Downing Street that only monarchical diplomacy could now offer a slim chance of peace. George himself would have to persuade the tsar to suspend mobilization. On the evening of July 31, the prime minister, Herbert Asquith, and his private secretary sat down to draft a personal appeal from the king to the tsar, "from Georgie to Nicky." With the ink barely dry, they then ran out of Number 10 and, with some difficulty in the gathering darkness, located a taxi and sped round to Buckingham Palace. It was 12:45 a.m., and the king had already gone to bed. Asquith deemed the matter so urgent that he sent an equerry to wake George, who surfaced in his dressing gown to approve the message.[20] It warned about the dangers of misunderstanding as a cause of war, the classic intelligence failure of being unable to read an adversary's true intentions.

Royal diplomacy failed. George's royal connections and informal intelligence networks offered nothing but negativity. Across Europe, princes and prime ministers alike felt propelled along by uncontrolled events. Gloomily, by August 1, the king concluded that there was practically "no chance of peace"—and he was right.[21]

The next day, Tsar Nicholas wrote to him expressing shock at the German declaration of war. He had expected a period of talks instead.[22] Everyone knew that Russia was like a ponderous dinosaur and would take weeks to mobilize, so the kaiser's claim to need to rush was transparent rubbish: George and Nicholas knew that he simply wished to avoid any conciliation.[23]

Two days later, German troops crossed into Belgium. Their forlorn king, Albert, appealed personally to George for help. Again, royal diplomacy and interdynastic intelligence amounted to little; the British ambassador in Berlin fled for the Channel ports with his staff in a fleet of cars and buses. He brought with him a message from Wilhelm to George renouncing his appointments as a British admiral and a field marshal.[24] For the crowned heads of Europe, the declaration of war was both personal and a prelude to disaster.

August 1914 also marked an upturn in espionage. Gustav Steinhauer was the man in charge of the German spy ring in Britain. As George had lamented, since the operation after his father's funeral, German spies had been left free to roam about in peacetime. Just a week before the declaration of war, Steinhauer had toured Britain to refresh his remaining networks. MI5 now finally swooped to arrest those left on its "watch list." The kaiser was furious at the apparent obliteration of German surveillance. He screamed: "Am I surrounded by dolts? Who is responsible? Why was I not told!?"[25]

Still, Wilhelm could always turn to royal intelligence networks of his own. A month earlier, in July, Prince Henry, Wilhelm's younger brother, was enjoying the sailing races of Cowes Week on the Isle of Wight when he heard about the Austrian ultimatum delivered to Serbia in the wake of Ferdinand's assassination. He decided to undertake a bit of amateur reconnaissance to discover what George thought about all this.

On July 26, on the way home to Germany, he dropped in at Buckingham Palace for a private conversation, cousin to cousin. He asked the king exactly how Britain would respond. The Royal Archives suggest that George was robust and said that if Germany went to war against Russia and France, it would be impossible for Britain not to be dragged into it.

Curiously, this is the opposite of what Henry reported. He told Wilhelm that George was determined to remain neutral and would try to stay out of war. This may have been George's personal sentiment, but it was not the policy of his government. Either way, the news delighted Wilhelm, who now assumed that George was neutral and used this royal intelligence to reassure his generals as they marched to war. Henry's report was doubly odd, since having told the kaiser that Britain was neutral, he nonetheless scooted back to Germany quickly, advising his sisters to do the same, suggesting that privately he expected war soon. This puzzling mission by a minor royal at a critical moment was clearly important to German decision-making.[26]

As the realities of war sunk in, George found himself in a difficult position. He had family on both sides and, while this could have provided useful intelligence channels, it put him on the defensive. Suddenly, critics accused his German relatives fighting on the British side of being hostile undercover agents. In particular, Prince Louis of Battenberg, the first sea lord, was denounced as "a damned German spy."[27] Much to George's mortification, the prince resigned his position in short order, but the press simply turned its fire on other minor royals with British connections who by accident of family found themselves fighting for the enemy.

In private, George spent much time with Asquith justifying the roles of his many relatives fighting on the other side.[28] Perhaps the most problematic was the duke of Albany, the king's cousin, who also bore the title duke of Saxe-Coburg and Gotha, the same name as the British royal family. Although educated at Eton, he had joined a German infantry regiment in 1914.[29] Even the chancellor of the exchequer, David Lloyd George, joined in, referring to the king as "my little German friend."[30] The feeling was mutual. The king would be remarkably indiscreet, making little secret of his dislike of Lloyd George, whom he referred to as "that man!"[31]

George was a military enthusiast who enjoyed military company. When he became king, he replaced many of his father's advisers with his own circle of military and naval officers whom he trusted. Once war broke out, this was transformed into his own informal intelligence network, providing him with the latest material from the front line.

Rather like Queen Victoria's informal royal intelligence network, George's personal channels of military intelligence often bypassed the government's own official machinery. Much of this sensitive material came through his close adviser, Clive Wigram. Technically, he was only assistant to Lord Stamfordham, the king's private secretary. In reality, he played a role not dissimilar from that fulfilled by Lord Esher for his father—a secret fixer and quiet modernizer. Sensing the growing tide of social unease, he secured the appointment of the first permanent palace press secretary to conduct "propaganda" and also worked with intelligence to monitor the rise of republicanism and communism. He deemed his opponents the "Palace Troglodytes."[32]

Wigram was also incredibly well connected in military circles. His network included myriad officers and generals, as well as the likes of Lord Kitchener, the war secretary, and even Maurice Hankey. A former naval intelligence officer and now the influential secretary to the committee of imperial defense, Hankey operated as a tactful go-between among the military and civilians. He managed the Whitehall machine, had access to top-secret planning material, and, perhaps most important, coordinated the record keeping at the heart of government. Hankey, at the palace's requests, had sent the king summaries of papers on the German invasion threat and continued to be a great source of defense information. George's network provided unfiltered intelligence on the conduct of the war, including some material that the government might have wanted to keep secret, directly to him.[33]

George received a steady flow of detailed and uncensored information from the front line. It came from relatives, cabinet ministers, generals, newspaper magnates, businessmen, bishops, and consular officials worldwide. Wigram wrote at least weekly, if not daily, to all the main generals—and received private letters in return.[34] The king's military intelligence was, according to some historians, "as good as, maybe better than, that on which the Cabinet had to base its conduct of military affairs."[35] His own son, the future Edward VIII, was stationed with the Intelligence Branch of General Headquarters in France and would report back to his father—although he was not the greatest of sources, being constantly bored and, as heir to the throne, frustrated by not being allowed "out of my f****** glass case."[36]

Importantly, George's network also allowed generals on the front line to circumvent formal channels and complain about things such as a shortage of munitions straight to the king himself. He even asked one field commander to deliberately go behind the back of his superior, the commander-in-chief of British forces in France, Sir John French, to feed back information. Wigram asked another commander, Douglas Haig, to send his diaries direct to the palace. The king would read them and then return them to his wife.[37]

All this activity inevitably frustrated the politicians but, like Victoria before him, it put George in a stronger position when dealing with his prime minister, service ministries, and military leaders.[38] Secret letters from his sources and the king's subsequent machinations contributed to the removal of John French as commander-in-chief in late 1915.[39]

George had a broad awareness of classified material, and not just through his own intelligence network. After complaining about the lack of warning procedures, he visited the general headquarters of the home forces to be briefed on air defense operations, including the signals intelligence underpinning warnings of Zeppelin raids. Inside what one intelligence officer called "the plotting room," he learned about "the mystery of the zeps," including how they were identified and tracked, in a "straightforward, clear manner." The intelligence officers noted that the king was "very intelligent" and grasped "things with quickness," even though "his appearance is against him and his accent is German."[40]

Royal residences, especially Sandringham on the east coast, quickly became targets of Zeppelin raids. An aerial defense detachment, armed with searchlights and guns, moved nearby to protect the king and queen whenever they were in residence—although both thought it a noisy overreaction. When Zeppelins attacked London, George and Mary would rush onto the palace balcony for a look. His mother, Queen Alexandra, refused to be frightened either. She asked the admiralty: "Please let me have a lot of rockets with spikes or hooks on to defend our Norfolk coast."[41]

The king also visited the Western Front, the focus of much of the fighting. His first visit, in 1914, was surrounded by strict secrecy and press censorship. Three plain clothes Special Branch officers provided personal security. In France, George attended a meeting between the commander-in-chief and his intelligence officers, hearing about the latest secret material. He came away satisfied.[42]

Drawing on his own networks, George concluded that the war would be won or lost on the Western Front. Others, notably Winston Churchill, disagreed and wanted to open up new campaigns, including using the Dardanelles to target Constantinople. The king unsuccessfully opposed this, but he monitored events very carefully, recording them in his diary. He also objected to opening yet another front in the Balkans, seeing it as an unnecessary risk and fearing its impact on some of the royal families there. Informed by his various sources, he asked a series of pointed questions of the government—to which he already knew the answers—in an attempt to dissuade them.[43]

For all of George's narrow focus on the Western Front, British intelligence now operated on a global scale. Indeed, the First World War is increasingly recognized as foundational for Western intelligence culture and was perhaps the moment when the secret services of states began to overtake the dynastic networks of royal spies.[44]

Across the Atlantic, human spies and codebreakers anxiously watched America's search for a compromise. It seems highly unlikely that the king would not have seen some of the secret material underpinning the Zimmerman telegram that later brought the US into the war. This was a secret German offer to Mexico to recover its lost territories, including California, if it sided with Germany. Decrypting this message was perhaps the greatest British codebreaking achievement of the war.

In the Middle East, spies secretly battled the remnants of the Turkish Empire. Around the globe, they confronted a vast conspiracy, supported by Germany, that sought to promote imperial insurrection as far afield as Canada and the northwest frontier. It was a huge relief for the overstretched spy agencies that Russia, now an ally, had ceased competing with Britain in the Great Game in central Asia.

Imperial Russia remained a focus of both intrigue and royal worries. The king's obsession with the Western Front made Russia particularly important, since Germany was currently fighting in two directions, stretching its resources. Thousands of German troops were deployed beyond Kiev and even reached the Don River. But George knew that the tsar was weak and suggestible; moreover, his regime was unstable and unlikely to survive the supreme test of total war. This presented a major dynastic problem for George and a strategic problem for the cabinet, since Russia formed an essential part of the grand alliance. Without its ally in the East, Britain might lose the war.

One of the biggest questions for intelligence networks—both formal and royal—was whether Russia would switch sides and join the Germans. George and his government knew that inside the imperial palace, pro-Allied politicians battled with an inner circle that sought a separate peace with Germany. This prospect horrified London. Desperate for manpower to feed the bloody battles at Ypres and the Somme, the cabinet had fought over the introduction of conscription and even considered improbable schemes like conscription in rebellious southern Ireland. The success of the so-called Russian peace party would have freed over a million Germans to fight on the Western Front.

By mid-1915, the Russian army was suffering defeat after defeat, and it was clear that the Romanovs were in trouble. George wrote frequently to his cousin assuring him of assistance and pleading with him to stay and fight alongside his allies. "My dear Nicky," he wrote on August 8, "I feel most deeply for you in the very anxious day through which you are now passing, when your army has been compelled to retire on account of lack of ammunition and rifles." He insisted that Britain would "fight out this awful war to the end" and noted that he was pleased Nicky's most recent letter showed that "Russia also means to fight to the end."[45]

Privately, George feared this was not the case. In September, encouraged by his wife, Nicholas fired his uncle as commander of the armed forces and took over command himself. George, who knew his kindly but ineffectual cousin better than anyone else, appreciated how disastrous this step was. He drew on all his intelligence sources to follow developments in the tsar's inner circle with increasing anxiety.[46]

By 1916, the British ambassador in Moscow, George Buchanan, repeatedly asked for permission to warn Nicholas about his deteriorating position. His superiors refused, on the grounds that it might be seen as meddling by the king. The situation was delicate, and Buchanan was unaware that some in the inner circles of the court believed that he too "was personally aiding the Grand Dukes to overthrow Nicholas II and replace him by his cousin." The tsarina even pressed her husband to banish Buchanan, but Nicholas decided against it.[47] Although Buchanan finally secured permission to speak with Nicholas privately, it was hopeless because he blindly refused to entertain the idea that his rule might be in jeopardy. Buchanan warned London of impending disaster, a warning that reached the king.[48]

In the late summer, with the Russian armies retreating in disarray, George feared that his dearest relative might sell out to the Germans. On August 23, he shared some intelligence with his cousin. "Information," he wrote, "has reached me from more than one source, including one undoubtedly well-placed neutral source, that German agents in Russia have recently been making great efforts to sow division between your country and mine by exciting distrust and spreading false reports of the intentions of my government." He urged: "Do not allow your people to be misled by the evil workings of our enemies."[49]

George did not explicitly refer to the circle around the tsarina or to "Dark Forces," but the language was blunt, and there could be no doubt what was on his mind. He wrote again in October, returning to his worries about Germany making "a separate peace with Russia."[50]

The king's information derived not only from Buchanan's embassy. There was also a growing group of MI6 personnel, mostly hidden inside the large military mission, whose reports reached him directly. The king was anxious about what MI6 officers were telling him.

On November 15, 1916, Grand Duke Michael Mikhailovich, a grandson of Nicholas I, who had long resided in London, visited Buckingham Palace. There, he had found that "Georgy" was "very much upset over the political situation in Russia." This was because "the usually well-informed agents of the British Secret Service predict a revolution in the very near future." Michael asked for the MI6 warning to be passed to the tsar by his brother Alex, who was the tsar's brother-in-law. This was a tricky mission, and for his pains the tsarina urged that he be immediately banished into exile in Siberia.[51]

The same MI6 reports clearly reached Lloyd George, the king's new prime minister. Although they disagreed on most things, they shared a view of what was going on in Russia. Lloyd George told his secretary that "the pro-Germans in the Russian government" were manipulating the leadership of the army, adding that "they are one by one getting rid of all the good men in Russia and are putting in rotters or Pro-Germans."[52] Anxiety was turning to panic, and there was a gathering mood for action.

The most eminent MI6 officer on the spot was Sam Hoare, a brilliant but mercurial figure who went on to become foreign secretary and then home secretary in the 1930s. Already a rising star, he now served as the MI6 liaison officer with the Russian secret service in Saint Petersburg.[53] Hoare eventually left the scene in March 1917, a month after the tsar's abdication. Posted to Rome, he recruited a former socialist leader named Benito Mussolini and helped to finance his first escapades as a right-wing politician. Much later, as ambassador to Spain, he presided over the bribery of Franco and his generals to keep them out of the Second World War. In other words, Hoare enjoyed a lifetime of racy covert actions and was not just a mere gatherer of intelligence.[54]

In late 1916, Hoare assessed the situation astutely. He estimated that the growing food crisis alone in Saint Petersburg was likely to lead to a revolution. He added that the war effort was badly mismanaged and that, unless something was done to change things radically, "Russia will never fight through another winter." Although he understood Russia's problems to be complex, he noted that the Parliament had focused its criticism on two particular figures, the tsarina and her adviser Rasputin, whom many believed nurtured pacifist, if not pro-German, sympathies.[55] The British, likely including the king, knew that something urgently needed to be done to prevent Russia from siding with the Germans—a move that would have devastated the war effort. By the end of the year, Hoare learnt of a plot to "liquidate" Rasputin; indeed, he might even have presided over it.[56]

Grigori Rasputin was a bearded mystic who gained considerable influence over the Russian Royal Family. The tsarina believed he was able to use his holy powers to abate the effects of haemophilia on her son, and thus regarded him as simply indispensable. He also had innumerable enemies. The Russian secret service, the Okhrana, began surveillance of him as early as 1908 at the suggestion of the commandant of the imperial court. Reports about his unsavory behavior quickly reached the Russian prime minister, Peter Stolypin. A year later, Stolypin, thoroughly alarmed, attempted to persuade Nicholas to banish him from court but found it impossible. Nicholas said he broadly agreed with his prime minister, but he preferred a quiet life and said that Rasputin's calming influence on the tsarina was invaluable. "It is better to have ten Rasputins," he quipped, "than one hysterical Empress." Stolypin then planned a secret operation to remove Rasputin from Saint Petersburg, but Rasputin found out and vanished for a while. Stolypin was assassinated the next year.[57] The tsar's sister, Xenia, an intelligent and careful observer, noted in her diary that newspapers "are forbidden to write about him" but everyone in the inner circles was talking about him, adding that "it's terrible the things they say about him."[58]

As early as May 1914, even before the outbreak of war, British diplomats were anxious about Rasputin. George Buchanan officially confirmed some of the wildest rumors, including the "fact" that Rasputin was indeed a member of the Khlysty, an orgiastic cult, and was also a genuine priest. (Neither of these facts was true.) Rumors that the tsarina kept Nicholas in a drug-induced stupor also enjoyed common currency.[59] Again, there was no evidence, but historians have noted that this did not really matter: the ubiquitous gossip that Rasputin slept with both the tsarina and her closest friends, and had defiled the tsar's daughters, "was kind of a metaphor for the degradation of the regime itself."[60]

When the Germans declared war on Russia, Nicholas had ordered the Okhrana to keep a protective watch on Rasputin. Allocating him a code name, "The Dark One," the Okhrana co-opted the servants in Rasputin's house to spy on him and recruited an agent to stake out his hometown. They gathered ample evidence of his misdeeds, but further efforts to remove him simply resulted in the tsarina switching the head of the secret police to make the problem go way.[61]

When Nicholas assumed personal control of the armed forces, he spent long periods away from the capital, and this created a dangerous political vacuum. This void was filled, with the encouragement of her husband, by the tsarina—and her close adviser Rasputin. Britain, and presumably George himself, grew increasingly worried. Although the accusations of pro-German sympathies were misdirected, both the tsarina and Rasputin favored peace with Germany. This made them a direct threat to the British Empire.

Having already survived numerous assassination attempts, Rasputin's luck finally ran out on December 30, 1916. He was killed at the home of Prince Yusupov, one of the richest men in Russia. Nearly a century after his death, the dramatic circumstances of his murder—the poisoned cakes, the gunshots, the icy grave, and rumors of British connivance in his fate—continue to fascinate. Astonishingly, there is now persuasive evidence of British involvement in his killing, which was designed to save the Russian war effort, that has been patiently unearthed by determined historians.[62]

One of the conspirators, Prince Felix Yusupov, was a Romanov but had always been a wild child. Tutors came and left with rapidity; one ended up in a mental asylum. "I still remember my music teacher," he recalled, "whose finger I bit so savagely that the poor woman was unable to play the piano for a year."[63] He had been a student at Oxford, where he made many English friends. Returning to Russia in 1909, he was initially fascinated by Rasputin, but by 1916 became convinced that the monarchy had to be saved from Rasputin and the tsarina because of the chaos they created. His coconspirator was another relative of the tsar, Grand Duke Dmitri Pavlovich. Their team also included a medical doctor, Stanilaus Lazovert, and a member of the Parliament, Vladmir Purishkevich.[64]

Predictably, they lured Rasputin to the Yusupov Palace with the promise of women. Although there is no evidence to support the widespread assertions that Rasputin belonged to a sadomasochistic religious cult that used momentary debauchery as a way of suppressing desire, police reports do show that he frequently consorted with prostitutes, sometimes many in a single evening.[65] His strongest preference was for women of a higher social order. On this particular evening, he had hoped to meet Prince Yusopov's wife, Irina, a woman of fabled beauty. His ambitions were not altogether unrealistic, given that marital infidelity was not unusual in Yusupov's aristocratic social circle. However, though Yusupov asserted that his wife would be present, she was in fact safely ensconced 2,000 miles away in Crimea.[66] The tsarina herself later confirmed that the prince had indeed "asked him to come over at night" and that "he would see Irina."[67]

Prince Yusupov's own widely publicized account involves failed poison and fatal gunshots. Yusupov insists he had laced cakes with enough potassium cyanide "to kill several men instantly," but despite Rasputin eating two of them, the poison had no effect. Yusupov was forced to watch "horror-stricken" as he partied on into the night unaffected. At three in the morning, Rasputin was drowsy with drink. Yusupov claims he rushed upstairs, borrowed a friend's revolver, and tried to dispatch Rasputin with a volley of shots. Rasputin nevertheless rose up, and only a second volley of shots from his friend, Vladimir Purishkevich, finally killed him. Purishkevich claims that he fired at Rasputin from behind at a range of about 20 yards, hitting him in the back of the head.

This torrid story has been repeated a thousand times. There is just one problem: Rasputin did not ingest a drop of poison that night. An eagle-eyed policeman spotted the corpse, wrapped in a fur coat beneath a sheet of thick ice, two days later. A detailed autopsy conducted at a nearby hospital found no trace of poison but did find bullet wounds from multiple revolvers, including a close quarter shot to the forehead (unmentioned in the royal Russian accounts).[68] Something did not add up. Fascinatingly, shortly before his departure from

Russia, Sam Hoare, the lead MI6 man on the ground, was the only foreigner to be offered the sight of Rasputin's decomposing body.[69]

The notorious poison narrative was an artistic fiction; more than that, it was an information deception operation executed by another MI6 man. Perhaps the most remarkable intelligence officer serving under Hoare was Oswald Rayner. He hailed from humble origins, having been born in the Smethwick district of Birmingham to Thomas Rayner, a draper, and his wife Florence. He was highly intelligent and won scholarships to study modern languages at Oriel College, Oxford. Here he made influential friends, including Prince Felix Yusupov, who was already living an exotic existence and styled himself after his literary hero, Oscar Wilde. Rayner later translated and copyedited Yusupov's famous memoirs. In late 1915, because of his fantastic language ability, Rayner began espionage work and was soon sent to work under Hoare in Russia.

One of the reasons that this was the perfect assassination was because it was followed up by a discreet and diligent MI6 information operation. Rayner could not have picked more perfect partners, because Purishkevich and Yusupov wished to take full credit and quickly became regarded as national heroes for what they had done.[70]

More remarkable still, many now believe that Yusupov did not fire the deadly shot—that it was in fact fired by none other than Oswald Rayner, using his Webley .455 revolver. Rayner was serving in the MI6 station in Saint Petersburg and had visited the nearby Yusupov Palace half a dozen times in the month before the assassination. He then visited several times on the day of the murder itself. Recounting these visits, his driver, William Compton, later cryptically added that "it is a little-known fact that Rasputin was shot not by a Russian but by an Englishman." He dropped a final clue: the culprit was from the same part of the country as Compton himself. Compton and Rayner both came from the Birmingham area.[71]

Two other MI6 officers in Russia, Stephen Alley and John Scale, were also friendly with Yusupov. Alley wrote to Scale afterward, triumphantly talking of the "demise of dark forces."

"Although matters here have not proceeded entirely to plan," he conceded, "our objective has clearly been achieved." He warned that "a few awkward questions have already been asked about wider involvement," but reassured Scale that "Rayner is attending to loose ends."[72] The sizeable MI6 station was determined to keep Russia in the war against Germany and had assessed the Rasputin–tsarina nexus as its biggest impediment.

The tsar's brother-in-law suspected "encouragement given to the plotters by the British ambassador." He fully understood the wartime context and British motive, accusing ambassador Buchanan of "protecting the interests of the Allies" in trying to nudge Russia toward a more liberal, effective, and anti-German government.[73] Even Tsar Nicholas, not exactly the brightest monarch in Europe, pointed to Rayner, telling the British ambassador that he suspected "a young Englishman who had been a college friend of Prince Felix Yusupof, of having been concerned in Rasputin's murder." Buchanan predictably assumed the pretense of British propriety, assuring the tsar that his suspicions were "absolutely groundless." In fact, even the ambassador, who did not enjoy the best of relations with either the MI6 station or his masters in London, had known about the assassination in advance. Buchanan also knew of the impending March revolution some three months ahead.[74]

Skeptics have made much of the fact that MI6's authorized historian, Keith Jeffery, found nothing about Rasputin in the archives of the service. Indeed, he insisted that the archives do not hold a single document linking Rayner, Hoare, or any other British officer, agent, or diplomat to the murder.[75]

But this is to misunderstand the nature of different types of secret service archives. MI6 did most of its work abroad, and very little documentary material came home from its overseas stations. In any case, MI6 had little operational rationale for curating it well. What remains in the MI6 archives is sometimes quite simply misleading. Alan Judd, the leading expert on Cumming, notes that a 1924 internal MI6 report claims that little was happening by way of operations in Russia before the Bolshevik Revolution, but he observes that other evidence now contradicts this.[76] Indeed, the material in Hoare's private papers shows a great deal of MI6 activity in Russia. In short, historians are much more dependent on family archives and papers in private hands to reconstruct the operations of MI6. By contrast, the files of Britain's domestic security service, MI5, are voluminous and well kept, partly because most of its work was done at home and also because finding spies often requires combing through the files of past cases to which they are connected.

Scores of historians have examined the Rasputin case. The recent work of Richard Cullen, former commander in the Metropolitan Police and for a while director of forensic training, has provided the breakthrough. After reviewing the documentary and forensic evidence, including the distinctive marks left by a British .455 service-issue revolver, his conclusion is compelling. Though many preferred to cling to the romantic heroics of Purishkevich and Yusupov, the truth was different. He concludes: "Rasputin's death was calculated, brutal, violent and slow and it was orchestrated by John Scale, Stephen Alley, and Oswald Rayner through the close personal relationship that existed between Rayner and Yusupov."[77]

Among the British community in Russia, the death of Rasputin triggered an exhalation of relief. Buchanan had believed that Rasputin was not only planning a separate peace with Germany but was also plotting against him personally. Francis Lindley, one of the senior diplomats at the embassy, explained that "no one is shocked by it." For the Russians, the scandalous stories about Rasputin and the tsarina were "an intolerable humiliation" to their national pride. Moreover, he added, both the tsar and tsarina were unpopular, "and their assassination is quite openly discussed." Buchanan expected more assassinations to follow and noted that a list had been drawn up of intended targets, including members of "the empress's so-called clique."[78]

King George had worried about the direction of Russia—about the influence of dark forces close to the tsar. Seventy-two hours after the assassination, Hoare sent a ten-page report to MI6 headquarters and suggested that Cumming show it to the king himself. He apologized for its sensational nature, wondering if it was more in the style of the *Daily Mail* than MI6, but presciently added that it was an event that "might well change the history of a generation." It was a colorful, if far from accurate, account of Rasputin's death, dwelling on his "unquenchable appetite" for debauchery, and insisting that "it was at an orgie that he met his death."[79] Hoare was rewarded with multiple royal decorations and ended the war appointed Commander of the Order of Saint Michael and Saint George. He received the Orders of Saint Anne and Saint Stanislas of Russia, and of Saint Maurice and Saint Lazarus.

Another local officer, assuming that the king had received "verbal news of the 'removal' of Rasputin," happily told George's private secretary that many Russians thought the assassination had checked German influence. He told the palace that Rasputin's "disappearance from the scene has given much relief to those who knew what a mischievous game he played here."[80] The whole Royal Family breathed a sigh of relief, thinking the Romanovs were now rescued. Queen Alexandra, the king's mother, told George that she was delighted by "the death of that wretched monk," adding that he "might have ruined the whole future of Russia through his influence." She remained anxious about the tsarina, whom she compared to Catherine the Great.[81]

Queen Alexandra was right to remain anxious. The assassins had hoped that Rasputin's death would be a warning shot across the bows of the tsar. They also hoped that Nicholas would send the tsarina away, perhaps to a convent, and assume a more rational course. But in fact, Nicholas and Alex retreated into isolation. Buchanan, who simultaneously welcomed the covert action but worried about its unintended consequences, reported that if "it was thought that Rasputin was dead: this was a mistake, Rasputin was killed and even buried after a funeral service attended by the imperial family but he is not dead." He was now "daily invoked in the secret councils" at the palace, and the tsar and tsarina "are isolated and appear like a besieged fortress."[82]

Meanwhile, rumors continued to spread about the pro-German tsarina. The pulp fiction writer William Le Queux wove stories about Rasputin and the tsarina doing German bidding into his bestselling books, claiming to have inside information.[83] In Moscow, Buchanan's daughter reported that the tsarina was widely considered to be communicating with the kaiser by radio from her palace rooftop.[84] These stories were clearly false. She probably favored a separate peace, but even Yusupov, who had arranged Rasputin's assassination, was clear that "neither the Tsar nor the Tsarina like the Kaiser."[85] Facts barely mattered any more. Despite Britain's best efforts, the tsar was sleepwalking toward disaster.

7

King George V and the Bolsheviks

Heard from Lockhart (our Agent in Moscow) that dear Nicky was shot.
—George V, diary, July 28, 1918

"Bad news from Russia," noted King George in his diary on February 28, 1917. Mass protests had erupted in Saint Petersburg. Large demonstrations and strikes culminated in violent clashes on the streets. Many soldiers switched sides and joined the workers. The tsar's days were numbered.

George struggled to recognize this. He added hopefully that although the "rising" was "practically a revolution," it was against the government and not the tsar and, most importantly of all, was "not against the war."[1] Nevertheless, the first Russian Revolution in the spring of 1917 soon forced the tsar's abdication and a moderate Russian government came to power. Would Russia stay in the war? And what would become of the tsar's family? George's diary also revealed that he understood the problems, noting pithily: "I fear Alicky is the cause of it all and Nicky has been weak."[2]

Although Nicholas was soon under house arrest in the Alexander Palace south of Saint Petersburg, the provisional government was keen for the whole imperial family to leave Russia altogether. The new minister of foreign affairs repeatedly asked the British to send a naval vessel to carry them off into exile. Indeed, they were not only willing but *anxious* that the tsar depart for Britain, warning that extremists were "exciting opinion against His Majesty." Britain's ambassador, George Buchanan, also took it for granted that a British ship would appear on the horizon at any moment.[3] Unfortunately for Nicholas, the newly renamed "Windsors" secretly wished him to go anywhere else.

George wrote a fulsome letter of support to his cousin quickly after the abdication. Privately, he blamed the peculiar dynamic between the Russian royal couple for their misfortune, pointing to Alexandra's eccentricities and obstinacy, together with Nicholas's stupidity and weakness. The new British wartime government, led by David Lloyd George, and dominated by the Liberals and Labour, was divided over the provisional government in Russia but, with Britain being bled by a war of attrition on the Western Front, Lloyd George simply wanted Russia to stay in the war. Also hoping for a new trade treaty, he did not want to damage relations with the new regime.

The new Russian government feared, even expected, violence. As early as March 2, it concluded that while the wider Royal Family could stay, indeed many minor royals had been complicit in the revolution, hoping it would deliver a constitutional government and improve the war effort, it was "absolutely essential and urgent" that the tsar and his immediate family leave Russia.[4] On March 19, the British ambassador warned the provisional government that "any violence done to the emperor or his family would have a mostly deplorable effect"; they responded by repeating their desire that they leave quickly, even speaking of their "deportation."[5]

On the same day, Major General Hanbury-Williams, one of the Allied commanders in Russia, met the tsar's mother, who was also King George's aunt. They both agreed that Nicholas should leave Russia immediately, while accepting that he would not leave for anywhere without his family. She worried about German U-boats and so preferred Denmark as a destination, but Hanbury-Williams was happy to take full responsibility for their safety. On balance, after a long discussion, an exit to Britain seemed the most sensible option, even though the tsar still fantasized about living out his days as a figurehead constitutional monarch, secluded in Crimea.[6]

Shortly afterward, the provisional government agreed that the whole family could travel up to Murmansk on Russia's icy Arctic coast. This was the golden moment. Hanbury-Williams, as the self-styled "doyen of the Allied mission," rightly urged that time was "of the essence" and offered to escort Nicholas personally to the port.[7] All that was required was approval from London, but there was only silence. Hanbury-Williams and Buchanan sent urgent telegrams to London. No reply came.[8]

Anxious discussions had broken out in Downing Street. On March 22, Lloyd George met the king's private secretary, Lord Stamfordham, along with senior ministers. They pondered many possibilities, even including "a plot to reinstate the emperor." Lloyd George thought that while Nicholas might not be interested, the feisty tsarina could well be enthusiastic. Money was a major stumbling block in any potential exile to Britain. The war had depleted the Treasury terribly, and Lloyd George wanted to know how the deposed family would be supported.[9] Remarkably, Buchanan was asked "can you possibly ascertain what are the private resources of the emperor?" The extravagance of the Russian Royal Family was notorious—Lloyd George did not want to foot the bill.[10]

The question of where they would live posed another problem. Windsor, Buckingham Palace, and Sandringham were already in use by George's Royal Family. Osborne House on the Isle of Wight had become a wartime hospital;

Balmoral was supposedly too chilly. These were preposterous reasons for procrastinating, and actually Balmoral, far from the public eye, would have been ideal.[11]

They turned to possible alternatives. Lloyd George strongly opposed letting the tsar go to Denmark. It was "too near Germany, and there would be a serious danger of His Imperial Majesty becoming a focus of intrigue of Germany." Despite the emotional family connections, the hard realities of war dominated the debate. Desperate to keep the Russians on their side, Lloyd George had just sent a letter to the new government stating that "the revolution is the greatest service which the Russian people have yet made to the cause for which the allies are fighting." The king thought this was "a little strong," and Stamfordham explained that the word "revolution" "had a disagreeable sound coming from an old monarchical government." Lloyd George smiled and countered: "no, an old constitutional government," adding, "our present monarchy was founded on a revolution." Stamfordham admitted that he stood corrected.[12]

Lloyd George and his colleagues confronted the classic problem of hosting eminent exiles. They feared that the Romanovs would become the center of plots for restoration, or even simply rumors of plots. The Romanov presence would reverberate on future relations with a more constitutional Russia. At the same time, they needed to keep the provisional government on their side for the sake of the war.

Tensions were high. Ultimately, the politicians agreed that, given their pledge to support the new Russian government, they could hardly refuse the request to take the tsar. Stamfordham insisted that George be consulted before the government reached any final decision.

The tsar certainly thought Britain was a likely option. In late March, he noted in his personal diary: "I looked through my books and things, and started to put aside everything that I want to take with me, if we have to go to England."[13] But back in Buckingham Palace, George grew more concerned.

Having endured the slings and arrows of public distrust at the start of the war on account of his German relatives, he now feared public reactions to receiving a fellow monarch, who was a decadent and failed ally, and his German-born wife. In the third year of a grueling war, long-standing concerns about pacifism in Britain now bled into fear of a social revolution.

The king began to receive more and more warnings against hosting the Russians. Stamfordham showed him an alarming file—called "Unrest in the Country"—of newspaper clippings and letters.[14] Lloyd George was lax in formally showing intelligence to the king, and so Stamfordham's skills and networks, drawing on sources from outside mainstream politics, became crucial. In return, Stamfordham rated George as an open-minded consumer of intelligence, being receptive even to material that was highly critical of him. In truth, the king was sensitive to criticism, but Stamfordham, rather impressively, insisted on presenting the world "unvarnished."[15]

When the War Cabinet eventually made its hesitant offer to Nicholas, George was "panic stricken." He feared that bringing his cousin to Windsor, together with the reportedly pro-German tsarina, would be unpatriotic—even dangerous.[16] Stamfordham reminded the foreign secretary, Arthur Balfour, that while the king had "a strong personal friendship for the emperor, and therefore would be glad to do anything to help him in this crisis," he had growing concerns. "His Majesty," he continued, "cannot help doubting, not only on account of the dangers of the voyage, but on general grounds of expediency, whether it is advisable that the Imperial Family should take up their residence in this country." George hoped that Balfour would talk again with Lloyd George, on the misassumption that "no definite decision has yet been come to on the subject by the Russian government."[17]

As George waited anxiously for a reply, he received more intelligence. Republicans had held a meeting at the Royal Albert Hall to celebrate recent events in Russia. A friend of a palace official wrote up an eye-witness report for the king himself; it reassured him only slightly on the grounds that no one had specifically expressed hostility to the crown. Another source, consulted by George and Stamfordham, was a London bishop. Well connected with the working classes, he warned that the public suspected royal backing of the disgraced tsar. Another contact, a colonel who worked with the poor in Essex, reported something similar the very same day. Stamfordham also showed George private intelligence, received via the editor of the *Spectator*, suggesting people assumed that some sort of "trade union" existed among kings.[18] Earlier, a member of Parliament had warned George that "if the emperor and empress and their family come here now or during the war they will be surrounded by a vast system of intrigue and espionage."[19]

When Balfour insisted that the government could hardly withdraw the offer now that it had been made, the king's panic intensified.[20] Stamfordham sternly warned that "every day the King is becoming more and more concerned about the question of the Emperor and Empress of Russia coming to this country." He received piles of information, from his own informal network as well as letters from random subjects, "saying how much the matter is being discussed, not only in Clubs but by working men, and that Labour Members in the House of Commons are expressing adverse opinions to the proposal." "As you know," Stamfordham continued, hardening the palace line, "from the first the King has thought the presence of the Imperial Family (especially of the Empress) in this country would raise all sorts of difficulties, and I feel sure that you appreciate how awkward it will be for our Royal Family who are closely connected both with the Emperor and Empress."[21]

George was so agitated that he instructed Stamfordham to send a second missive to Balfour later the same day: "He must beg you to represent to the Prime Minister that from all he hears and reads in the press, the residence in this country of the ex-Emperor and Empress would be strongly resented by the public, and would undoubtedly compromise the position of the King and Queen from whom it is already generally supposed the invitation has emanated."[22]

George had assessed the open source intelligence in the press and heeded warnings from his own networks. He came to believe that there were more Bolsheviks—or at least sympathizers—in the country than he could tolerate. Alarmed, he clearly linked the invitation to his own position. He was genuinely worried, having long thought that, with the aristocracy in retreat and the proletariat on the march, the crown was now less secure than it had been under Queen Victoria.[23] George loved his cousin, but not enough to sacrifice his own throne.

Four days later, the palace again lobbied the prime minister to revoke the invitation. Lloyd George now admitted that "evidently the matter was more serious than he was aware."[24] A strange alliance emerged, since neither Lloyd George nor the king liked each other's company. The king regarded his prime minister as dangerously radical and too sympathetic to Russia, while the prime minister regarded the king, unfairly perhaps, as someone with a small brain. There were also social tensions; Lloyd George was uncomfortable in the royal presence and did his very best to avoid royal functions, while George abhorred the leader's "rude and uncultivated manners."[25] Yet, on this single issue, they eventually agreed.

The Foreign Office warned Buchanan, Britain's man on the spot, that receiving the tsar risked bolstering the domestic antimonarchical movement. Buchanan found himself in an awkward position because the new Russian government was still under the impression that the tsar would leave. However, he accepted that "were we to do so extreme Left Parties, which are not at all well-disposed to us, as well as German agents, would be sure to make capital of his presence in England to stir up public opinion against us."[26] And so, "with tears in his eyes," Buchanan withdrew the offer of asylum.[27] Balfour further warned him that even minor members of the family, including mere dukes, of which there were many, would not be welcome.[28]

George remained resolute in his opposition. The next month, Charles Hardinge, the senior official in the Foreign Office, confirmed that, regarding the tsar, the king "was most anxious he should not come here."[29] And so, for five months after his abdication, through the spring and early summer of 1917, Nicholas lived under house arrest with his family on the edge of Saint Petersburg. He passed his days teaching his children Russian history, reading popular novels, and planting a vegetable garden. Secretly, he still hoped to live out his days quietly in the sun at his vacation home in Crimea. King George has been repeatedly blamed for this saga, but Tsar Nicholas was the architect of his own fate.[30]

Unbeknownst to London, amateur British agents still hoped to rescue the tsar. MI6, with its influential network on the ground, did not receive any instructions to exfiltrate the Russian Royal Family—but that did not stop others.

The best plot was concocted by Oliver Locker-Lampson, an eccentric figure who commanded an armored car squadron in Russia while simultaneously serving as member of Parliament for Huntingdonshire. Locker-Lampson was a superb linguist, having achieved a first in languages at Cambridge, and soon became embroiled in Russian politics. He claimed that he had been asked to participate in the rather crowded British plot to assassinate Rasputin. He also periodically corresponded privately with King George.

Perhaps unaware of the king's wishes and worries, Locker-Lampson came up with the best—and simplest—rescue plot. He had recruited a servant at the Alexander Palace who would arrive to cut the tsar's hair. Once there, he would shave off Nicholas's beard, don a false one himself, and then quickly swap clothes. The tsar would simply walk out unchallenged. Outside, he would meet Locker-Lampson in a truck and, joining up with the British military, move out to Archangel on the north coast and back to Britain by sea.

Tellingly, Locker-Lampson received no green light from Britain. In any case, most of these ideas focused on getting the tsar out alone—and the tsar was unwilling to leave without his family.[31] Locker-Lampson would have been a good bet for an attempt to rescue the tsar. He later rescued the physicist Albert Einstein from the Nazis in Europe, and then helped Ethiopia's Emperor Haile Selassie find sanctuary in Sussex to evade the clutches of Mussolini. He also assisted scores of ordinary Jewish families fleeing Germany.

There were reasons for hesitation. In the spring and summer of 1917, some optimism was in the air. Although Nicholas had abdicated, Russia was still in the war, and the provisional government might yet prove more effective than the pantomime presided over by the Romanovs. Moreover, America had finally joined the war effort on March 21.

Meanwhile, in London, the summer of 1917 marked the sum of all fears for the British Royal Family. Against the background of a Bolshevik ascendancy in Russia, the famous author H. G. Wells encouraged an active discussion of the possibility of republicanism. Pacifism, strikes, resistance to conscription, and general anti-institutionalist feeling unsettled the monarchy and contributed to a sense of an impending end to the old order. Some two hundred thousand workers were on strike in Lancashire alone. The security apparatus began to turn inward, examining defeatism, working-class organizations, and suspicious persons. Even Lloyd George urged the king to visit industrial centers in an attempt to bolster his flagging popularity with the people.[32]

In August 1917, possibilities for rescuing the Romanovs narrowed dramatically. The tsar and his family were suddenly relocated, with a reduced retinue of forty staff, to the Siberian town of Tobolsk, a thousand miles to the east. Ironically, the Russian authorities moved them for their own safety, fearing that a revolutionary crowd might try to seize and kill them in Saint Petersburg. Now, east of the Urals, they lived behind a high fence in the ramshackle governor's mansion, guarded by respectful soldiers. The local population were also deferential, and the family was able to see the villagers bowing and crossing themselves as they passed by. Even here, in August 1917, something might have been done; a deal could have been struck for their release.

Instead, disaster ensued. In the absence of organized rescue activity by MI6, more enterprising amateurs filled the vacuum and made the situation worse. Rita Khitrovo, a young friend of the Russian Royal Family, traveled to Tobolsk on her own initiative with a supply of personal letters and small presents, hoping simply to improve the morale of the incarcerated Romanovs. Suspicious local authorities viewed this as a royalist rescue mission and quickly apprehended her. The letters she carried were innocent and she went free, but the ill-advised visit triggered an urgent review of security procedures. A new hard-line commissar arrived from Moscow to guard the Royal Family. Escape from this remote location was always difficult due to distance, but this innocent blunder only served to lengthen the odds.[33]

The clock was winding down. Various adventurers and fantasists continued to hatch plots, but once the Bolsheviks took power in October 1917, the Royal Family became more likely to face revolutionary justice. Vladimir Lenin considered a public show trial, but he had other things to worry about, and so put the problem off, leaving them incarcerated for almost a year. Eventually, Allied plots and a loose army of anticommunist rebels and Czech prisoners of war advancing on the Romanov's place of imprisonment would force the hand of the Bolsheviks.

Lenin and the Bolsheviks quickly proved tough customers. The British cabinet was divided over how to deal with them. The hawks, including Winston Churchill, feared the spread of Bolshevik ideas in London, noting that two of Leon Trotsky's comrades, Georgy Chicherin and Peter Petrov, were arrested there for spreading propaganda. Trotsky, in charge of Russian foreign affairs, immediately threatened to take Buchanan and other British diplomats in Russia hostage unless they were released. The king successfully urged the cabinet to accede to his demands.[34]

Shortly afterward, Britain began the evacuation of many of its embassy staff, including Buchanan, leaving a few diplomats, but mostly military personnel and intelligence officers, on the ground. Trotsky strung along the remaining representatives, but in March 1918, Chicherin and Petrov, recently released from London, negotiated a long-feared peace treaty with Germany known as Brest-Litovsk. Some fifty German divisions were released for the Western Front.[35]

After Brest-Litovsk, there was little to lose, so Mansfield Cumming, an old friend from the king's days at the Naval College, finally considered a rescue plot. In the spring of 1918, new plans to rescue the Romanovs from their remote location focused on the Norwegians. A Norwegian businessman named Jonas Lied arrived in London from Norway for discussions with MI6. Lied had been Norwegian consul in Siberia and held timber and mining interests in the area. Working alongside Fridtjof Nansen, Norway's greatest explorer, Lied had developed new routes into Russia's interior via the Yenisei River.[36] The MI6 plan seems to have been to use these routes to extricate the tsar. There followed dinners at which he met Reginald Blinker Hall, head of Naval Intelligence, and even the prince of Wales. But although Nansen later worked with Hoare to rescue others from Russia, for now Cumming turned elsewhere.[37]

In April 1918, just as the tsar and his family were moved to the town of Ekaterinburg, some 400 miles further west, MI6 drafted the dashing Major Stephen Alley, a fluent Russian speaker whose family had worked in Russia since the 1870s. He had worked for MI6 since the start of the war and, as we have seen, was implicated alongside Oswald Rayner and his boss, Sam Hoare, in the assassination of Rasputin. Viewing him as valuable but "too hot," or perhaps because of an argument with Cumming, MI6 had withdrawn Alley when the Bolsheviks took over, but his local knowledge was irresistibly excellent. Because he was able to pass as a native Russian, he returned to Murmansk in the spring of 1918 and remained there as a secret service officer under naval cover until August. Remarkably, in 2006, Alley's personal notebook surfaced. It contained within it a sketch map of Ekaterinburg, showing details of the house where the family was being held. Most likely a reconnaissance tool from one of his extensive networks of agents, the map indicated a review of the potential for rescue.

On May 24, 1918, all this was confirmed in the most coded language. Alley informed MI6 headquarters of a possible mission in which seven "valuables" would be secured and delivered to Murmansk. To pull this off, he required £1,000 and four top intelligence officers who, like him, were native speakers and could pass as local Russians.

There is no evidence that MI6 ever implemented the plan, and depressingly little detail as to how it might have worked has since emerged. Even if the Romanovs could be spirited past four hundred fervent revolutionary guards, possibly against their own will, it is unclear how they would have made it to Murmansk.[38] Indeed, even now, the tsar still insisted on being rescued under two improbable conditions: "He will not hear of the family being separated or leaving Russian territory." Nicholas had effectively signed their death warrants.[39]

The early summer formed the last possible moment for MI6 to move the Romanovs, perhaps along the Yenisei River, given the hideous travel problems that existed due to the underdeveloped roads and terrible weather that persisted for nine months of the year,[40] but they aborted the rescue most likely because the house seemed impregnable—and because of the reluctant tsar.[41]

MI6's eleventh-hour reconnaissance of a very hard target is puzzling. It is highly unlikely that Mansfield Cumming would have acted without royal approval. Perhaps it reflected a dawning anxiety on the part of the king that the worst was now possible. Equally likely, it was perhaps a response to fears of a German plot to rescue the tsar by forcible kidnapping, overcoming the main problem of his stubborn reluctance to leave Russia. The route to Ekaterinburg through German-occupied Russia was more navigable. Karina Urbach, the distinguished historian of European royal families, confirms that there was a German plan to rescue the tsar in 1918, and British diplomats across Europe were certainly aware of it.[42] Although he had been something of an outcast during royal gatherings before the war, the kaiser was godfather to the tsar's son and heir, the weak and ailing Alexei, and genuinely wanted them to be rescued. Realistically, once the Bolsheviks had taken power in October 1917 and then imprisoned the Romanovs securely at Ekaterinburg, the kaiser had the best chance to free them. Germany had already enforced a difficult treaty upon Russia from a position of strength and had the leverage to extricate them. In other words, there were rival plots to secure the seven "valuables" at this last critical moment.

On May 28, 1918, cautious British diplomats considered whether to approach Trotsky to at least save the tsar's children. Even if he agreed, they faced a difficult dilemma. A Bolshevik escort would be "unsafe," yet a British escort would be "suspected of some Czarist conspiracy." The logical conclusion was that any attempt to rescue them would most likely endanger the lives of the very people it was designed to save.[43]

On the ground, British operatives displayed much less caution—resulting in dangerous unintended consequences. The torch now passed to Sidney Reilly, a legendary figure in MI6. An adventurous secret agent, he was busy in Moscow organizing nothing less than a counterrevolution. Working with colleagues in the French secret service, he did his best to covertly unify and fund the fragmented opposition groups. Lenin, as he well knew, had been receiving subsidies from the Germans; a veritable secret service war was now under way.

On July 6, 1918, two men claiming to be from the Cheka, Lenin's secret police, turned up at the German Embassy demanding to see the ambassador, Count Wilhelm von Mirbach. When he eventually appeared, they produced revolvers, fired repeatedly, and then threw a bomb. Mirbach survived for a few hours but died of his wounds.[44]

In the chaotic hours after this assassination, the Socialist Revolutionary opposition group seized the Cheka headquarters and held its head hostage. They failed to press their advantage, and the Bolsheviks counterattacked the next day, retook the Cheka headquarters, and arrested many opposition leaders. The next month, the head of the Saint Petersburg Cheka was assassinated, and a young Socialist Revolutionary member attempted to kill Lenin by firing at point-blank range. One bullet penetrated Lenin's lung, and another entered his body above the heart. He was not expected to live.[45]

It remains unclear whether MI6 had a hand in these intrigues. The British had a motive: the assassination of the German ambassador would have damaged relations between Russia and Berlin. Meanwhile, Reilly was trying to kill Lenin at this very moment, but there were many plots and the MI6 effort seems to have been aborted at the last minute.[46] Keith Jeffery, the official MI6 historian, insists that the shooting of Lenin was not directed by MI6 in London.[47] Perhaps Reilly, the so-called Ace of Spies, was acting off his own bat. Robert Bruce Lockhart, one of the last remaining diplomats in Russia, certainly recalls his Napoleonic addiction to "playing a lone hand."[48]

The Bolsheviks responded with ferocity. They killed alleged conspirators in their thousands—and one of the suspects they wanted particularly badly was Sidney Reilly. Only dimly aware that something had gone wrong with his own plot, Reilly waited in the street for his friend Captain Francis Crombie from the British Embassy, but he did not come. "Not like Crombie to be unpunctual," he noted. Uneasily, at midday, he decided to risk a visit to the embassy himself. Even before he arrived, it was clear that the Cheka were sweeping the streets and he "met some men and women running." A line of bodies—"the dead bodies of Bolshevik soldiers"—greeted him outside.[49]

Suspicious of British involvement in a coup, the Cheka had raided the embassy hoping to catch Reilly. Some staff members had dashed upstairs to the chancellery to destroy sensitive papers as fast as they could. "Meanwhile the gallant Crombie, a Browning automatic in each hand, had held the stairs against the red guards, and had emptied both magazines into them before he had fallen, literally riddled with bullets."[50]

The high drama continued. Most British diplomats had evacuated months ago but the remaining British representative, Bruce Lockhart, was arrested and marked for execution. The Cheka demanded to know where Reilly was—and whether Bruce Lockhart knew the terrorist who had tried to assassinate Lenin.[51] He was only saved by the counterarrest of Maxim Litvinov, the Russian diplomat in London, on yet more charges of spreading propaganda. It had become an extraordinary battle of body politics. Reilly and others working for MI6 fled to Sweden.

It was during this purge, triggered by the wake of the attempt on Lenin's life, that the Romanovs were executed.[52] This, together with the fact that the strongest allies of the anticommunist White Russians, the Czech Legions, supported by the British, were gradually advancing toward the royal captives at Ekaterinburg, almost certainly sealed their fate.[53]

So often, the eventual execution of the Romanov Royal Family is reported in isolation. The focus is on their final days and hours, with documents mined for every last grisly detail. But the lack of context clouds our understanding. The Romanovs died in a wave of panic retribution in response to a failed coup, a veritable secret service war in Saint Petersburg pursued by MI6 and the secret services of several allied countries. It is important to remember that in the wake of these assassination attempts—there was yet another attack on Lenin, in August 1918—paranoia and spy mania had broken out. During this brief period of madness, nobles, aristocrats, and White officers were rounded up and "shot like dogs" all over Russia.[54]

The executions of the Romanovs were ghastly. At about midnight on July 17, the sleeping family was woken and asked to put on their clothes, under the pretext that they would be moved to a safer location due to the advancing Czech forces. The Romanovs were then taken to a small semibasement room no more than 20 feet across. Pandemonium broke out, leading to waves of shooting with revolvers and then the use of bayonets.[55] The Czech Legion arrived a week later and sifted through the ghostly remains of the house, but there were no bodies to be found. The only survivor was the young Alexei's spaniel, who was adopted by a British officer and, ironically, lived out his last days in the shadow of Windsor Castle.[56]

For over a month, MI6 could tell the king little about the fate of the imperial family. Most assumed that the tsarina and children remained alive. In a gesture that was perhaps more show than substance, George now asked Spain for help to "rescue the family from their pitiable position." The Spanish king and queen were related to the tsarina, and George still hoped that, in the unlikely event of a rescue, she would be better off in neutral Spain than in Britain, where she had been vilified in the press for years as a pro-German traitor. On August 28, 1918, news arrived that she and all her children had most probably died with the tsar.[57]

In September 1918, George received confirmation. The intelligence officer at Murmansk had learned "from a source that he has no reason to doubt" that the whole family had been murdered.[58] According to Stamfordham, George was "deeply grieved at the ghastly fate which has befallen his relatives." He found it "almost incredible that the innocent children should not have been spared."[59] George wrote to his mother, Queen Alexandra, a few days later that he feared that "these disgusting brutes in Russia" had killed everyone.[60]

But the so-called intelligence was patchy and filled with rumor. The king forwarded a disturbing report to his younger sister, Princess Victoria, that suggested the family might all have been burned alive. Victoria's son, Lord Mountbatten, recalled that some months afterward "King George V showed me secret service reports that they had all been raped," but then asked him not to tell Victoria. Thankfully, neither of these things were true, but they must have strongly framed the king's outlook on the new Bolshevik regime.[61] Eventually, Sir Basil Thomson, director of intelligence, conducted an extensive and more accurate inquiry on the last days of the Romanovs that was given to the king.[62]

With the British Army still fighting on the Western Front, George commanded his court to wear mourning clothes for a whole month. He did so not out of respect for the millions who had died on the battlefields of Europe, but for Nicholas and his family, whose execution had now been confirmed. George and his wife Mary quietly attended a memorial service at London's only Russian Orthodox chapel.[63] Afterward, the king noted in his diary: "I was devoted to Nicky, who was the kindest of men."[64] As the war drew to a close, the final years of this dramatic decade seemed to promise social turbulence threatening the future of royal families everywhere. A real sense of fear pervaded the secret emissaries that continued to move backward and forward between London, Saint Petersburg, and Moscow, battling against the rise of Bolshevism.

Despite the overthrow of the monarchy, the tsar's mother initially refused to leave Russia. In 1918, there was a rescue attempt by a distinguished British intelligence officer, George Hill, who was recently awarded the Military Cross, together with Reilly. The queen of Romania, who was Queen Victoria's granddaughter and who had been brought up in Britain, offered support. Taking a Romanian ship and an escort of two hundred soldiers, and even the Romanian prime minister's limousine as a getaway car, they finally reached her. But the stubborn dowager refused to leave and even denied that her son was dead.

Only in 1919, at the urging of her sister in Britain, the mother of King George V, did she begrudgingly depart, fleeing Crimea over the Black Sea to London. George sent the warship HMS *Marlborough* to retrieve his aunt. The party of seventeen Romanovs included her daughter, the Grand Duchess Xenia, and five of Xenia's sons, plus six dogs and a canary. After a brief stop in the British base in Malta, they traveled to England, where she stayed with her sister. Queen Alexandra treated her well enough, and they spent time together at Marlborough House in London and at Sandringham, but Maria Feodorovna, as a deposed empress dowager, always felt that she was now "number two" in contrast to her popular sister. She eventually elected to return to her native Denmark. Here, rather as the British had feared, she lived at the huge expense of the Danish Royal Family and ran up "mountains of unpaid bills."[65]

The wily dowager had persuaded George to grant her a pension of £10,000, something he could ill-afford.[66] Yet secretly, she brought with her the pride of the Romanovs' jewel collections that had been hidden in her Saint Petersburg home. She then hid this fantastic hoard of treasure for a decade. In October 1928, the box was finally opened to everyone's astonishment. Some of the prize items made their way into the collections of George's wife, Queen Mary, their total value being about £10 million at current prices.[67]

In Britain, the royals went to huge lengths to suppress the story of George and the Romanovs. Buchanan, Britain's embattled ambassador in Saint Petersburg, wrote his memoir, but was threatened with prosecution under the Official Secrets Act and the stoppage of his pension if he revealed the truth. Even more remarkably, Lloyd George was required to drop an entire chapter of his memoirs. The main purpose was to quash any reference to the antimonarchical movements in the country that had so terrified George and his private secretary into inaction in 1917.[68] Maurice Hankey, the cabinet secretary, "thought that the chapter on the Tsar's future residence should be suppressed altogether."[69] Indeed, the king had urged the former prime minister to drop his memoirs entirely, but Lloyd George characteristically replied, "He can go to hell."[70]

By late 1918, tension between Lloyd George and the king increased. The prime minister made the idea of putting the kaiser on trial a key part of his election campaign, employing the slogan "Hang the Kaiser." This issue had bubbled along all the way through the war. The German execution of the British spy Edith Cavell had caused widespread anger, as had the sinking of the *Lusitania*. Both Lloyd George and his foreign secretary pressed the War Cabinet to charge the kaiser with crimes against humanity.[71] King George did not have the same affection for the kaiser as he felt for Nicholas, but he did not wish to see further relatives face an execution squad.

Bizarrely, at this very moment, and quite unknown to the king, his own uncle, Prince Arthur, duke of Connaught, had triggered a renegade effort to bring the kaiser to justice. On June 11, 1918, Arthur was in France inspecting a unique American regiment, the 114th Field Artillery, the only volunteer

American regiment in the war. As such, it had been singled out for a royal visit. The commander was Colonel Luke Lea, in civilian life the publisher of the *Nashville Tennessean* and, as a former senator, someone of firm opinions. In his view, victory was rendered incomplete by the knowledge that "the number one war criminal, Kaiser Wilhelm, had escaped to Holland and was living there in relative luxury."[72]

After the inspection was over, Lea sat politely having tea and making small talk with Arthur. He asked about the war settlement, and soon Arthur was holding forth and "boasted of his close blood relationship to the Kaiser of Germany." He added that he was uncle to the kings of both England and Germany. Lea was soon convinced that the British were engaged in successful efforts "to protect the Kaiser." He was also annoyed by the fact that Arthur was covered in medals but "had probably never been near enough the front line . . . to hear a shell shriek."[73]

Arthur had convinced Lea that the European establishment would secretly protect the kaiser and intended for him to live out his days in luxury. Lea had other ideas. In January 1919, he and a group of three officers and three sergeants commandeered a military vehicle and headed out along snow-covered roads and attempted to seize the kaiser and bring him to the Paris Peace Conference for a war crimes trial.[74]

At first the secret party was refused entry to the Netherlands. Later, they produced documents that they claimed had been signed by the Dutch queen, and so on their second attempt they were saluted on their way past the border. Using false civilian passports and carrying concealed weapons, they arrived at the castle where the kaiser lived in exile. Lea bluffed his way in by claiming to be local nobility. Soon they were inside, but wisely the kaiser refused to see them. After a long standoff, and with a hostile crowd gathering outside, they finally retreated to their cars and fled back to France.[75]

General John J. "Black Jack" Pershing, commander of the American Expeditionary Forces, ordered his inspector general to investigate the escapade quickly. But fearing an embarrassing diplomatic incident, he decided against a court martial and opted for a private disciplinary warning. Ironically, Lea was unaware that it was in fact American diplomats, led by the tough-minded secretary of state, Robert Lansing, and supported by President Wilson, who were the keenest to avoid the prosecution of the kaiser and probably saved his neck.

The amateur kidnapping plot had repercussions. Further rumors of missions to capture the kaiser were now taken very seriously. There were even reports that a unit of the Belgian air force had decided to bomb the castle. During winter, the ice on the moat of the castle was broken up regularly to keep people away. In autumn 1920, the guard was reinforced because of rumors that a band of British ex-servicemen were heading across the Channel in an airship to kidnap the kaiser.[76]

Perhaps to offset private shame at the fate of his Russian cousin, King George now showered MI6 with awards and medals for its exploits in Russia. Sidney Reilly was awarded the Military Cross, George Hill received a Distinguished Service Order, while Paul Dukes, the MI6 chief in Moscow, received a knighthood, and is still the only MI6 officer to be knighted for his services as a spy. Bruce Lockhart was invited to come and describe his dangerous mission to the king. Moreover, George knighted Mansfield Cumming, the chief of MI6, at Buckingham Palace on July 26, 1919. He wore a full dress uniform and his previous decorations, which notably included the Orders of Saint Stanislas and Saint Vladimir awarded to him by the tsar three years before.[77] The most remarkable recipient was Augustus Agar, who was awarded the Victoria Cross for agent-running in the Baltic with motor torpedo boats under the directions of Cumming.[78]

After the war, George nurtured a lifelong hatred of Bolsheviks. Impressively, and intelligently, this did not transfer into visible anxiety about British socialists. After updating him about domestic republicanism, his private network of correspondents persuaded him to undertake a more open reign, engaging more regularly with working people and even cultivating trade unionists and Labour Party members of Parliament.[79] As Labour gained ground, George pragmatically thought it a matter of survival. His son and heir, the future Edward VIII, praised his "propaganda"—although George preferred to see it as "duty."[80]

Perhaps because of the king's intense hatred of Lloyd George, Ramsey MacDonald shone by comparison, and the king developed a warm and supportive relationship with Britain's first socialist prime minister. It certainly helped that, by this time, republicanism was not Labour Party policy. In January 1924, on his first meeting with MacDonald, the big issue was a treaty with Russia, and he told his new prime minister that he did not even want to shake hands with "the murderers of his relatives."[81] Anxious diplomats in the Foreign Office were nervous about showing MacDonald Soviet decrypts and so they procrastinated. For this period, the king might have seen more sensitive intelligence material than the head of his government.[82]

MacDonald lost the general election later that year, an event overshadowed by the "Zinoviev letter"—a document published by the *Daily Mail* four days before the election. The letter purported to be a directive from Grigory Zinoviev, the head of the Communist International in Moscow, urging subversion and welcoming the opening of diplomatic relations as a gateway to revolution in Britain. Perhaps misinformed by his right-wing contacts, the king wrongly noted: "I suppose there is no doubt that Z's letter is genuine? I see the Communists say it is a forgery."[83] It was almost certainly a forgery.[84]

This did not prevent the king from creating both informal and formal organizations to keep Buckingham Palace better informed about communism and republicanism in Britain. Stamfordham continued to solicit information from his network of religious and military figures whom he thought had fingers on the pulse of working-class opinion.[85]

Neither did it prevent him from launching a covert campaign to counter Soviet propaganda against the Royal Family during the interwar years. At about the same time, George made contact with the legendary MI5 spymaster Maxwell Knight by offering him a highly secretive and personal mission. The greatest secret of Knight's career was embodied by his most treasured possession, a gold cigarette case with the royal cipher of King George V and the inscription "Maxwell Knight, 1931." He had performed some secret service for which the Royal Family was extremely grateful—but what it was remains a mystery.[86]

By the 1930s, the king's hatred of Moscow had somewhat subsided. On the evening of November 27, 1934, Buckingham Palace threw one of the grandest receptions in years. The event honored the forthcoming marriage of George's youngest son, the rather dissolute duke of York, to Princess Marina of Greece. Almost a thousand people attended, including many of Europe's royal families and even Kirill Vladimirovich Romanov, the deposed tsar's cousin and head of the exiled imperial family. One of his daughters, Kira, was a bridesmaid. Princess Marina's mother, Elena, was also a Russian princess. The event was attended by all the ambassadors in London.

It created a degree of awkwardness, since the Soviet ambassador, Ivan Maisky, was present and, for some, the murderous events of 1918 were still fresh in the memory. Most royals, led by the elderly King George, joined the line and politely shook hands with Maisky, but Marina's mother demonstratively walked past him and his wife without greeting them. "Two or three wizened old witches ugly as sins, came out of the corner room and hesitated, whispering secretively and glancing in our direction," Maisky recorded in his diary, and skipped the line-up altogether. The Russian emperor's retinue, decorated with ribbons and diadems, "stumbled at the sight of me and immediately backed off every which way." Maisky noted with quiet satisfaction that "the Soviet ambassador had given them a fright!"[87]

Even in 1934, the very mention of the Romanovs conjured up multiple horrors for the king. Their violent deaths formed a potential focal point of a world revolution that now threatened to sweep away empires and monarchies—indeed, the Bolsheviks had vowed to do just that. To make matters worse, Nicholas had "let the side down" and was now seen for what he was, a kindly but incompetent idiot who had managed the war against Germany badly. Far worse was Alicky, his wife, who had been German by birth and formed the center of lurid accusations of German plots, with scurrilous pamphlets and books circulating not only in Russia but also in Britain.

The German problem had plagued the last years of Victoria, had obsessed Edward VII, and had underpinned the secretive efforts of George V to save the Romanovs. The members of the British Royal Family understandably feared similar accusations of being "pro-Boch" and had done their best to escape this by rebranding themselves "the Windsors" in the summer of 1917. But now, by shaking hands with the amiable Russian ambassador Ivan Maisky in 1934, George gave a clear signal: Britain's future problems lay not with Moscow—but with Berlin.

8

Abdication

Spying on Edward VIII and Wallis Simpson

Under surveillance.
—Edward VIII, *A King's Story*

In May 1935, a secret message from Adolf Hitler made its way circuitously to King George V. It set out nothing less than Hitler's vision for a future world peace. Framed in predictably racist terms, it called for cooperation between Britain and Germany, "the two Germanic nations." Hitler offered a crude deal: if Britain gave Germany a free hand to pursue *Lebensraum* on the continent, he would leave Britain free to pursue its imperial ambitions elsewhere.[1]

George was horrified. Confirming all his worst fears, he interpreted it as Hitler warmongering and conspiring against the French. The palace sent an icy reply through the same backstairs channels, and rebuked Lord Rothermere, the pro-Nazi newspaper proprietor, for serving as its conduit. George urged the prime minister and the foreign secretary to take note.[2] The secretive exchange was important, for it not only illuminated Hitler's overarching world view but also underlined his outdated obsession with the British royal family as a means to realize it. This would not be, by any means, Hitler's last attempt to reach out to British royals.

George had followed the rise of Hitler and Mussolini with alarm. He diligently read the daily top-secret material sent from Whitehall with "exact attention." Ever higher piles of red boxes arrived and, despite his declining health, he read them all and was keen to demonstrate his command of their detail. He saw the prime minister each week, as was the custom, but topped this up with more frequent meetings with the foreign secretary and intelligence chiefs.[3]

The slaughter of the First World War had horrified George, but he squarely blamed the Germans and, not wanting to give an inch to Hitler, he monitored developments carefully. In 1933, the British ambassador in Berlin wrote directly to him, warning that the "atmosphere and mentality" in Germany were alarmingly similar to the moments before the previous war. The king responded that "we must not be blinded by the apparent sweet reasonableness of the Germans."

The next year, he spoke sternly and in person to the German ambassador, telling him that "at the present moment Germany was the peril of the World."[4]

The king enjoyed access to the latest intelligence. In February 1935, he read secret service reports on rapid German rearmament, which left him "gloomy."[5] But even he was not told everything. At about this time, he dined with Stewart Menzies, deputy chief of MI6. Mindful of previous MI6 escapades in Moscow, which he had followed closely, the king mischievously asked the name of the most senior British intelligence officer in Berlin. Menzies smiled and refused to answer. George asked whether the famous threat, "Off with your head," would change his mind. Menzies was adamant: "My head would roll with my lips still sealed."[6]

By December, rumors circulated that George was dangerously ill. He managed to broadcast a flawless Christmas message to the empire alleviating concerns, but then faded fast on Sunday, January 19, 1936. He died the following night, just two months before Hitler's adventure in the Rhineland. His eldest son David, taking the formal title of Edward VIII, now ascended the throne at the age of forty-two. Edward VIII, always ambivalent about his formal role, would reign for just less than a year. Presciently, George had predicted that his son would abdicate some ten years before.

The king's funeral took place on January 28. Such events, bringing together world leaders, offered the opportunity for discreet diplomacy in their shadows. The next day, Maxim Litvinov, Moscow's foreign minister, headed for Buckingham Palace to spend an obligatory 15 minutes with the new king, but at Edward's request he stayed rather longer. Edward was courteous and amiable, but bombarded Litvinov with questions, some of which were of "a very delicate nature." He asked "why and under what circumstances was Nicholas II killed. Was it not because the revolutionaries feared his reinstatement?" Bounding from one hot subject to another, he then fired off questions about Trotsky. Edward agreed with Litvinov on the importance of peace: "no one wants war."

The king added a curious qualification. "Germany and Italy have nothing at all. They are dissatisfied. Something should be done to improve their condition." The Russians seem to have overlooked this ominous interjection and came away "impressed" with Edward as someone who was "a lively and spirited man, with a keen interest in world affairs." In the evening, Ivan Maisky, the Soviet ambassador, took his boss to the cinema to see *Top Hat*, the iconic Fred Astaire and Ginger Rogers movie, which he dismissed as "a very silly comedy" that Litvinov "did not enjoy." Edward would doubtless have been in his element.[7]

Edward VIII was born in 1894 and spent his childhood with his great-grandmother Queen Victoria still on the throne. Yet he was the very antithesis of Victorian values and instead embraced a modern spirit. Like his father, he spent time in the Royal Navy as a boy, but then went to Oxford before serving in the First World War.

Much to his frustration, Edward was not allowed to serve on the front line for fear of his capture. His lowest point was being awarded a Military Cross that he did not deserve, but which preserved the fiction that he was fighting. However, Edward, like his father, was assiduous in visiting military hospitals and worrying about the privations of the troops. Although his French was modest, his German was good, and this opened the door to some useful work, including taking part in the interrogation of German prisoners. After a while, he moved on to matters concerning the supply of ammunition, which he rated as "so much better" than "the Intelligence branch where I was before."[8] In truth, Edward enjoyed neither. He wanted to be closer to the front.

German intelligence was, meanwhile, watching France for royal visitors. In July 1917, Edward had discreetly joined King George and Queen Mary at Vimy Ridge and Messines. Despite strict secrecy, German spies spotted them. Within hours of the royals leaving Messines, the town suffered its heaviest air raid of the entire war.[9]

Edward enjoyed the support of clever and thoughtful organizers, including Alan "Tommy" Lascelles, who would serve as secretary to four monarchs between 1920 and 1953. He was joined by Godfrey Thomas, who had previously run the Foreign Office cipher department and who had a special talent for secrecy. Edward failed to appreciate their skills—even though he often deployed them to get him out of scrapes. He preferred the company of his fun-loving favorite equerry, Captain Edward "Fruity" Metcalfe, an Irish officer initially employed to look after the horses. Although professing to hate formal duties, Edward loved travel and the relative freedom it brought, undertaking sixteen overseas tours before ascending the throne, often in the company of "Fruity."[10]

Edward was considered to be remarkably good-looking as a young man and flaunted a sense of style. Embracing the jazz age, fun, and "flappers," he loved everything American and would have been perfectly comfortable inside the Jeeves and Wooster novels of P. G. Wodehouse. He dressed flamboyantly, and the camera loved him; every photo looked like it had come from the latest pages of *Vogue* magazine.[11]

From the outset, he preferred elder married women with a domineering personality, perhaps, as one historian has observed, because he was "neurotic, self-pitying" even "neo-masochistic."[12] As a young officer in France, he enjoyed a long liaison with Marguerite Alibert, a high-class Parisian prostitute. Infatuated, Edward wrote to her constantly. She carefully preserved the letters, creating a blackmail opportunity in the process. Not long after the end of the war, she visited London with her husband, with whom she had a stormy relationship. Returning to the hotel after seeing the operetta *The Merry Widow*, they had one of their frequent arguments. Early in the morning, Alibert shot her husband repeatedly from behind with a .32 caliber Browning automatic. He was taken to Charing Cross Hospital but died within hours.[13]

The royal family were desperate to hide her connection to the prince. The next day, his entourage acted fast. They canceled a summer schedule and packed him off on a three-month tour of Canada. While she awaited trial in Holloway Prison, Special Branch opened all her correspondence. The best lawyer was hired to portray her wealthy Egyptian husband as a sexual monster and sadist. With strings pulled behind the scenes, she went free in a trial that lasted only days. Most importantly, Edward was not mentioned—but the episode pointed to future trouble.[14]

Although Edward's minders tried to keep him out of further scrapes, he did not like "protection." In the words of his official biographer, the presence of plain clothes policemen was irksome and "affronted his passionate desire for privacy." This attitude had serious consequences for his safety. In August 1922, a panic erupted over an Irish Republican Army murder plot in London. The primary target was Winston Churchill, who was then secretary of state of the colonies. "Winston is first on the list to be murdered," Edward wrote to his mistress of the moment, Freda Dudley Ward, adding "your poor little parpee is the second." The home secretary ordered extra security for him, but Edward would not have it and ordered them to back off: "I will not stand for having a car following me." He added: "So please don't worry any more. If anyone wanted to kill me all the CID [Criminal Investigation Department] in the world won't stop him."[15]

But Edward badly needed protection. By the mid-1920s, he was conceivably the first global celebrity, pursued by hordes of photographers. Perhaps the most eligible bachelor in the world, he did not hesitate to have fun, flirting his way through royal tours, even with the wives of local officials. He struggled to keep to a time schedule because he was not especially committed to his royal duties. They bored him.[16]

George V found the playboy prince increasingly infuriating, and worried about his suitability as the future king. He worked closely with Edward's endlessly patient private secretary, Clive Wigram, to try to manage his worst habits.[17] Edward received his own private residence, Fort Belvedere, on the edge of the Windsor estate, in the hope of keeping his more esoteric activities out of the public eye. He decorated it in the latest art deco style and added a swimming pool, where he could entertain his friends.[18] Nor was he the only one straining at the royal leash; his youngest brother, Prince George, later the duke of Kent, traveled an even more dissolute path, including drug use, something from which his elder brother eventually rescued him. All this was a stark contrast to his father's twin passions for shooting and stamp collecting.

In January 1935, George's concern turned to panic. Courtiers secretly told the king that Edward had given a mysterious new woman £110,000 worth of jewels, close to £8 million at current prices, together with a substantial allowance. The prince was known to be rather strange about money, spending freely on luxuries yet rarely paying his bills and showing a notable reluctance to tip waiters, but this was peculiar behavior even for him. George suspected foul play—perhaps even blackmail. The awkward episode with the many letters he had written to the dangerous and wily Marguerite Alibert in Paris was still a painful memory.

George took the remarkable step of putting his son and heir under Special Branch surveillance. This was facilitated by the fact that he got on rather well with his later prime ministers, especially the confident Stanley Baldwin, who had recently replaced the ailing Ramsey MacDonald. Together, they met the head of the Metropolitan Police, Philip Game. Game needed a top officer whom he could trust and who would treat the incredibly sensitive operation with the utmost discretion. He turned to a rising star, Albert Canning.

Canning was an outstanding policeman. The son of a prosperous Essex businessman, in 1906 he had joined the police, where his superior abilities quickly became apparent, and he transferred to Special Branch after only six months on the beat. Politically sensitive and astute, he spoke fluent French and was a capable surveillance manager able to run a substantial team. He also knew the Edward of old, as he had traveled with him as his personal detective to Le Touquet in the summer of 1924. By all accounts, on this visit, Edward was delighted by him.[19]

During George's last months, at his personal request, Special Branch began to probe the life of a certain "Mrs Simpson." Born Wallis Warfield in Pennsylvania in 1896, she had traveled extensively, including a period in Shanghai, making details hard to collect. They established that she had been divorced and was now married to Ernest Aldrich Simpson.

Police attention centered on Wallis Simpson's address at 5 Bryanston Court, a block of high-class flats just north of Hyde Park, where she lived alone. Surveillance teams noted that the prince "visits frequently," but, they added, so too did other men. In addition to tracing her movements, Special Branch gathered intelligence on her personal relationship with Edward. Anxious about blackmail, they analyzed the power relationship and even the most minute details of their everyday lives. They watched the couple as they visited an antiques shop in Pelham Street, South Kensington, making purchases for "The Fort." Afterward, they interrogated the poor antiques dealer, who explained "that they were on very affectionate terms and addressed each other as "darling." Most important, the dealer, who was good at sizing up his customers, suggested that the lady "seemed to have the Prince of Wales completely under her thumb."[20]

As Canning and his team dug deeper, they concluded that Wallis and Ernest Simpson were simply a pair of professional hustlers, preying on the prince for money. The police reported that Simpson, whom they described as "of the bounder type," made no secret of his wife's association with Edward and seemed to enjoy some reflected glory, clearly hoping that it would lead to some sort of sinecure or well-paid promotion. One source reported that Simpson expected to become a baron at the very least when Edward took the crown.[21] These intelligence reports confirmed the worst fears of both the king and Baldwin.[22]

The Special Branch watchers must have been considerable in number to be able to chart her movements in such detail. Some of their reports even suggest telephone monitoring and letter opening. The operation was becoming intrusive. The watchers—and listeners—soon discovered tensions between Wallis and her husband: "Mrs Simpson has said that her husband is now suspicious of her association with other men as he thinks this will eventually cause trouble with the Prince of Wales. Mrs Simpson has also alleged that her husband is having her watched for this reason and in consequence she is very careful for the double purpose of keeping both the Prince of Wales and her husband in ignorance of her surreptitious love affairs."[23]

Wallis was right about being followed, but wrong about the culprits. She thought it might be private eyes working for her husband or even for Edward. In fact, it was Canning's teams of detectives, keen to discover who else she was seeing. There was one especially alarming candidate: Hitler's ambassador to London, Count Joachim von Ribbentrop. He was a regular guest at Bryanston Court—sometimes visiting Wallis on his own. This created a dangerous security risk, with the foreign secretary anxious that Britain's secret diplomatic cyphers could be "compromised" because "Mrs S is said to be in the pocket of the German ambassador."[24] Indeed, in London, Ribbentrop was referred to by some as the "arch-Hitler spy of Europe."[25] The idea that the heir to the British throne's lover was also having intimate relations with a leading Nazi was too ghastly to contemplate. So, it was a considerable relief when Canning discovered more.[26]

Special Branch learned that Wallis Simpson's secret lover was Guy Marcus Trundle. A successful Ford car salesman, he was clearly a charmer. The police reported that he was "very good looking, well-bred and an excellent dancer. He is said to boast that every woman falls for him." The report continued, "he meets Mrs Simpson quite openly at informal social gatherings as a personal friend but secret meetings are made by appointment when intimate relations take place. He receives money from Mrs Simpson as well as expensive presents." Wallis was using her considerable allowance from Edward to fund this exotic lifestyle.[27] Meanwhile, she feared that Edward might be transferring his affections to a new woman he had met in Austria. To describe this as a love triangle would have been something of an oversimplification.

In early 1936, after the death of King George V, this espionage and intrigue took on a more serious tone. Special Branch was no longer watching the prince of Wales and Wallis Simpson on behalf of the king and the prime minister; they were watching the new monarch and the person he wished to marry. The intelligence dossiers they compiled have been the subject of endless speculation down the years, but the poet Osbert Sitwell got in early and asked Baldwin what they contained. Baldwin dismissed the idea that Wallis was a Nazi spy but did concede that her MI5 file showed that "she was a paid agent of the Hearst press."[28]

Albert Canning now presided over all Special Branch activity, including its surveillance of Britain's burgeoning fascist movements, and must have found this rather confusing. Was he watching the new king to protect the monarch from a pair of hustlers? Or was he watching both Edward and Wallis because they were mixing with some of Britain's extreme right? After all, Oswald Mosely, Britain's most prominent fascist, had recently become the brother-in-law of Edward's favorite equerry, "Fruity" Metcalfe, leading to open speculation about Edward's politics. Although Mosely deliberately cut down his meetings with Edward once he became king to avoid embarrassing him, they were firm friends and remained so into old age.[29] When Edward did meet Mosely during his brief reign, oddly, he was accompanied not only by Wallis but also her husband, Ernest. Years later, Edward told Mosely that he "should have been prime minister" and insisted that "it was the Jews that brought us into the war." Even Mosely was shocked.[30]

Edward's political views have long been a subject of speculation. He has been the victim of gossip, exaggeration, and innuendo, not least because so many of Britain's upper classes feared communism and saw the rise of the far right as an antidote, so loose talk on this subject was common. Despite this, we cannot escape the fact that Edward expressed profound admiration for the Nazis in Germany and for fascism more generally, especially as a social system. As early as July 1933, he told former Kaiser Wilhelm II's grandson, Prince Louis Ferdinand, that it was "no business of ours to interfere in Germany's internal affairs either re Jews or re anything else." "Dictators are very popular these days," Edward had added. "We might want one in England before long."[31]

Special Branch officers, as Canning knew from his own experience, specialized in personal protection. They spied on Edward but also had to keep him safe.

This seemed easy, for he was one of the most popular personalities in the world and had a natural gift for connecting with the crowd. He was mostly hounded by harmless lovesick women and nuisance paparazzi rather than anarchist assassins or dangerous lunatics. Nonetheless, the biggest threat to royals in the early twentieth century remained assassination, and, with politics increasingly febrile, the king needed protection.

At midday on July 16, 1936, only a few months into his reign, Edward, resplendent in full-dress scarlet tunic and bearskin, rode back toward Buckingham Palace. He had been attending a military ceremony in Hyde Park, and the crowds were lining Constitution Hill for a glimpse of their glitzy monarch. Suddenly, a mysterious figure in a brown suit stepped forward from the front of the crowd. He dropped a newspaper to reveal a revolver, which he aimed squarely at the king.

A woman standing next to him, a Mrs. Alice Lawrence, cried out in alarm and immediately grabbed his arm. Noticing the commotion, a special constable punched the man's arm, sending the gun flying into the parade. Other policemen scooped it up and muscled the assailant away.

The mysterious figure was George Andrew McMahon. Arrested and bundled into a car, he was immediately escorted to the Hyde Park police station, where he was cautioned. McMahon insisted that it was merely "a protest" and he had no intention of harming anyone. However, when searched, he was found to have a picture of the king and two rounds of live ammunition. Closer inspection revealed that the newspaper he had used to hide the gun had the words, "May, I Love You" written on the back page.[32]

When brought to trial at the Old Bailey, McMahon insisted that a foreign power had paid him to shoot the king, but he had merely pocketed the money and then deliberately bungled the mission. The court did not believe him, and instead chose to regard him as an unhinged solo eccentric, perhaps with an Irish republican connection.[33] The episode had strong echoes of the many attempts against Edward's great-grandmother, and McMahon was lucky not to be placed in Broadmoor. Instead, he merely received twelve months for possession of firearms, which was distinctly odd. Even at the time, leads suggested that this was part of a wider plot. Before the attack, Alice Lawrence had seen McMahon talking intently to a tall, well-dressed man with a moustache and hat. Perhaps he was not acting alone.[34]

McMahon was a hard drinker and a petty criminal, but most importantly he had been a gunrunner during the Italian invasion of Abyssinia in early 1935. The efficient Italian military intelligence service paid him for information about weapons and clearly regarded him as an agent. Recently, McMahon's memoir has been discovered by the historian Alex Larman. It claims that the Italians had paid him to assassinate Edward, but that he was in fact a double agent working for MI5—and MI5 had ignored his warnings. Strikingly, declassified MI5 documents corroborate the memoir, including records of MI5 conversations with him before the attack.[35] McMahon was a long-term paid MI5 informant whose job was to convince the Italians that he was a willing recruit, but secretly to spy for the British. He was also seen selling copies of the fascist *Blackshirt* newspaper and may have had connections with the German or Austrian embassies. All this was covered up at the trial, where McMahon came across as a lone fanatic.[36]

This has presented historians with more questions than answers. Some have even wondered if MI5 and Special Branch were aware of McMahon's planned attempt and allowed him to go ahead. It would have removed a monarch whom some thought had Nazi sympathies.[37] Confusion is more likely than conspiracy. MI5 probably just wanted to cover up the fact that it had previous contact with McMahon, but had no idea about his intentions. The most intriguing part of the story is that McMahon's lost memoir finally turned up in the papers of Walter Monckton, Edward's close confidant and legal adviser. Monckton most likely informed Edward of its contents and even perhaps allowed him to read it. Historians will never know what Edward made of the story himself, or who he thought was lurking behind "The Man in the Brown Suit."[38]

With fascism booming and royal protection requiring ever more resources, Special Branch swelled to a strength of 180.[39] There was no shortage of work for Canning, who was now head of all these activities, and would keep this position all the way through until the end of the Second World War, working closely with MI5.[40]

Oswald Mosely had a great deal of working-class support. He was also popular among the nobility; so, too, were a miasma of other right-wing and pro-German organizations that operated alongside him. Edward and Wallis moved in some of these circles, but also mingled with a new rising class of the global super-rich whose pacifism seemed well intentioned but was in fact designed to protect their business interests. These included a number of Swedish, French, and American industrialists.[41]

Security and society overlapped. Clive Wigram, the king's private secretary, became especially disturbed by his social habits: his subservience to Mrs. Simpson's wishes, his extravagance, and his bad treatment of the staff at Buckingham Palace. Wigram believed that Edward was mentally unbalanced and once, after a particularly trying encounter, announced that "we shall have to lock him up."[42] Wigram's greatest anxiety was official security, and Edward's cavalier treatment of classified documents. Top-secret cabinet papers were carried in red boxes from Downing Street to Buckingham Palace for the king's eyes only, and that is where they were meant to stay.

Edward, who still spent much of his time relaxing at his unofficial residence, Fort Belvedere, had other ideas. The famous red boxes lay open there—a cocktail of cabinet papers, intelligence reports, and telegrams from top diplomatic posts. Wigram worried about who might be reading their sensitive contents. They were often not returned for weeks, and some of these red boxes were actually lost. This was more than Wigram could take, so in August 1936, horrified by these proceedings, he resigned and was replaced by Alec Hardinge. Baldwin, for the first time in British history, urged that the monarch should only be sent material requiring his signature.[43]

Odd things happened with the sensitive papers. One of the periodic guests at Fort Belvedere was Mike Scanlon, the air attaché at the American Embassy. As he left after a night of revelry, he was rather surprised to be passed some official red boxes with a request to drop them off at Buckingham Palace on his way back into London. He noted: "I had a feeling that Hardinge did not approve of the practice of confiding state papers to the care of an American intelligence officer."[44]

Clive Wigram did not disappear; instead, he remained in the shadows of Windsor Castle, and he continued to exert influence. Passionate about the security of documents, he retained a role as keeper of the Royal Archives, Britain's most exclusive and secret repository. More importantly, the next month, he joined a secret meeting in Scotland to discuss "up and down the problem of His Majesty." The gathering consisted of Wigram, together with his successor as private secretary, Alec Hardinge, and the archbishop of Canterbury, Cosmo Lang, a man of outspoken views on the crown, constitution, and royal consorts. This was prelude to an even more important meeting a month later.[45]

In September, Lang and Baldwin held a rather private conversation. Baldwin's views were already firm. He told his closest advisers: "I have grown to hate that woman," adding that he considered Wallis a "hard-hearted bitch." Having consulted government lawyers, he set out his options. "If he marries her," they warned, "she is automatically queen of England." Lang was of even firmer opinions. Over the next few weeks, he and Baldwin met in secret seven times, spoke on the telephone, exchanged letters, and shared their correspondence about the king. Lang provided Baldwin with theological arguments to use in his audiences with Edward as they moved him toward a shared objective: either dropping Mrs Simpson or abdication, preferably the latter.[46]

On November 16, Edward summoned Baldwin to Buckingham Palace. The king announced he would marry Mrs. Simpson despite the prime minister's opposition. He already knew the cabinet was against him, since Sam Hoare, first lord of the Admiralty and one-time MI6 officer, had been secretly briefing him on their ruminations.[47] Two weeks later, the British press, which, unlike the world's media, had been gagged, finally broke the story. Wallis received credible death threats and had already fled to France, where she lay under siege at the Villa Lou Viei, near Cannes, home of her close friends Herman and Katherine Rogers. Two Special Branch men accompanied her—they were now both her protectors and her watchers, reporting directly to Scotland Yard's chief, Philip Game, in London.

Baldwin and Lang wanted to force Edward to abdicate. They believed the British public and the Commonwealth would never accept an American divorcée as the king-emperor's wife. Edward's affection for German and Italian fascism lurked in the background, quietly shaping the debate. Some even feared that he might dismiss the government, triggering a right-wing coup by what some called the "King's Party." This was no mere fiction, and Britain's most senior civil servants weighed the possibility in their private journals, talking of Winston Churchill, Lloyd George, and Max Beaverbrook—the millionaire publisher of the widely read *Daily Express*, an arrogant political schemer, and the wartime minister of information—as conspirators.[48]

If a "King's Party" existed, then Beaverbrook was probably the most active conspirator. His main reason for supporting Edward was, as he admitted in his own words, to "bugger Baldwin" and keep the king on the throne.[49] Rather than being an ardent monarchist, Beaverbrook had harbored a grudge against Baldwin for over a decade, after the prime minister had called a general election against his advice and then, worse still, ignored his policy requests. Beaverbrook, the press baron, was not used to being sidelined.[50] By 1936, he had hoped to persuade Edward to drop Wallis, or at least abandon his intention to marry her, and thus remain on the throne. Although Churchill was coy about his own role in the affair, even when discussing it with friends, he later admitted that Beaverbrook was behind some of the threats made to Wallis Simpson in late 1936 that persuaded her to leave the country. This even included bricks "thrown through her windows" and letters threatening acid attacks.[51] Beaverbrook hoped that once she had departed for France, the king would be more malleable and might even give her up.[52] Meanwhile, Baldwin, who wanted abdication, described himself as being "like a dog in a sheep-dog trial who has to induce a single sheep into a narrow gate." He needed every shred of intelligence possible to outmaneuver the king. For this reason, he cranked up the surveillance operation yet again.[53]

Downing Street now turned to MI5. Horace Wilson, a key adviser to Baldwin, asked its director, Vernon Kell, to tap the phones of Edward, of his younger brother and the future King George VI, and of Wallis Simpson in France. Kell, a rather proper civil servant, was horrified. He did not see Edward and Wallis as a national security issue and so thought it entirely inappropriate to rummage through the knicker drawers of the aristocracy. To Kell, it was

clearly a political, even social, issue more about hedonistic lifestyles and trans-
gressions of social norms.[54]

Wilson was particularly influential during the abdication crisis, stoking up
fears of mob riots and violence. He and Baldwin's private secretary, Tommy
Dugdale, "did much delving into the gangster side of this affair; the seamy side
not politic for the Prime Minister to know about." Dugdale's wife thought Baldwin was "very suspicious" of their activity.[55] Baldwin was more worried about a
constitutional revolution—the first since 1688—which itself would have caused
much upheaval during these febrile years.[56]

Remarkably, the top-secret MI5 internal history, written by one of its senior
officers, John Curry, reveals that Kell's objections were overridden. The MI5
board considered Number 10's arguments that this was not just about politics;
it was also about national security. Eventually, they advised Kell to do what the
prime minister requested. As the abdication crisis accelerated in November, MI5
went ahead with telephone tapping. The final authority was given by Horace
Wilson, conveying the authority of the home secretary, John Simon: "Most
Secret. The Home Secretary asked me to confirm the information conveyed to
you orally with his authority by Sir Horace Wilson that you will arrange for the
interception of telephone communications between Fort Belvedere and Buckingham Palace on the one hand and the continent of Europe and various addresses
in London on the other." A normal telephone tap was too prone to leaks, and
MI5 could not count on the loyalty of those who staffed the royal exchange at
Windsor. MI5 therefore required an especially secret alternative plan.[57]

Kell turned to one of MI5's most distinguished officers, Thomas Argyll
Robertson, known as "TAR" Robertson. A very efficient intelligence officer,
Robertson was also a personal friend of Kell and had served in the same elite
Highland regiment as his son. Robertson would later rise to prominence as the
strategic mastermind behind Britain's brilliant wartime "Double Cross" decep-
tion operations, but for now he had a more tactical mission.

In early December, Robertson entered Green Park in the dead of night. By
placing a wiretap inside the telephone junction box, he and his colleagues could
eavesdrop on phone calls between Wallis Simpson, the king, and his brother,
circumventing the royal exchange at Windsor. Listening in on a conversation
between Edward and the future George VI, Robertson apparently picked up
some earth-shattering news: the king now intended to abdicate and hand over
his reign to his brother George.[58]

Wallis Simpson had hoped to be queen of England. Edward, on the other hand,
could not take the pressure and finally threw in the towel. On December 10,

Baldwin announced this to a packed chamber in Parliament. After Baldwin's parliamentary statement, Leo Amery, the Conservative politician, found Churchill in the smoking room of the House of Commons "completely in a rampage," insisting that he was totally for the king and was "not going to have him strangled in the dark by ministers." Privately, Amery, who knew Churchill very well, reflected that "Winston" only got this worked up when he had a secret scheme under way "for his own private ends." [59]

Baldwin feared conspirators of the "King's Party," such as Churchill, with good reason, but he did not fear the king. He thought Edward quite nice on a personal basis, but possibly insane, and entirely unsuitable to be king. [60]

It also turned out that Edward had secretly installed "five private telephone lines, one direct to Lord Beaverbrook." The rest of the Royal Family did not know this until after the abdication; eventually, Queen Mary discovered this rather surprising fact while "poking about upstairs." Given Beaverbrook's understandable caution on the phone, it is unlikely that MI5 managed to capture the full story. [61]

Others watched the maneuverings of Lloyd George. One of his associates concluded that "like Winston," in this matter, Lloyd George was only concerned with his personal advancement and "had no thought but for himself." But, by announcing the abdication, Baldwin had thwarted the "King's Party." [62]

On the same morning as Baldwin made the dramatic announcement, Edward signed his abdication papers at Fort Belvedere. [63] That night, Scotland Yard moved all available policemen into central London. Five hundred fascists joined the crowd outside Buckingham Palace, shouting "One two three four five! We want Baldwin dead or alive!" before making their way to Downing Street. [64]

The next day, Edward made his fateful speech to the nation: "I have found it impossible to carry the heavy burden of responsibility and to discharge my duties as King as I would wish to do, without the help and support of the woman I love." [65] Rather typically, he then retired to his bedroom and sat drinking whisky and sodas while having his toenails trimmed by a servant. [66] The very next day, he headed for the continent, perhaps not knowing that hereafter his return visits to his home country would be short and infrequent.

How much difference did the bugging make? Edward and Wallis clearly knew that they were being bugged. During the days leading up to the abdication, Wallis insisted that she had known less than anybody, because "it had been impossible to talk freely" with Edward on the telephone "as the wires were constantly tapped." [67] But like all those who know they are bugged, it is still hard to resist the medium of immediate communication, and much later she confessed that "I spent a long time over a very bad telephone line from France begging him not to abdicate. I went so far as to say if he abdicated I would not marry him![68] Did these unguarded moments make an impact on the last-minute negotiations? Edward had tried to persuade Baldwin to "let the matter of his marriage hang fire" until after the coronation, but the prime minister clearly scented future trouble and wanted them both gone.[69]

It was not just MI5. In fact, a world of spies was listening in, including the French police. A detective later confirmed that his job had been to "review the recorded telephone conversations between King Edward and Wally Simpson." When the king had called to tell her that he had definitely decided to abdicate and was about to announce this on the radio, her prompt response had been a curt "You God-damned fool!"[70] Lord Brownlow, Edward's loyal equerry, who had escorted Wallis to France, was especially sensitive to surveillance, and whenever he had left written messages for Beaverbrook from Edward they had been in code.[71] Months later, he confronted Kell and complained vehemently about the tapping of the king's phone by MI5, who "couldn't deny it." But the strange clicks and hissings on the line that he had heard most recently may have been the work of the French.[72]

The surveillance had been helpful to Baldwin, but even more important was the effect of the mere idea of surveillance. Those who were intent on working against him—especially Beaverbrook, with whom he had a long-running feud—were frightened by the idea that they might be overheard. Beaverbrook had already figured out this possibility and recalled a disturbing conversation with Edward on the phone at 2 a.m. at the height of the crisis. Beaverbrook had been "embarrassed" and "alarmed" because Edward had been speaking with "such freedom" while Beaverbrook was painfully conscious that there were others lurking on the line. Edward, he noted, was increasingly impatient, because of the "guarded nature of my replies."[73]

The government has always maintained that it does not intercept or tap royal communications. But this episode turns history on its head. Moreover, in late December 1936, as Edward departed for his new life on the continent, with the prospect of marriage and exile ahead, he probably thought he was now free from surveillance. Nothing could have been further from the truth. Incredibly, the surveillance became part of a far greater operation involving hundreds of spies across four continents, which would continue for at least a decade.

On December 11, 1936, an uncertain King George VI, with no idea that MI5 had eavesdropped on him, stepped up to replace his brother. Alarmingly, he was the third British king in just over a year. A series of official meetings and state occasions lay ahead before the coronation at Westminster Abbey in May 1937. One of his pressing duties was to meet all the ambassadors to the Court of Saint James's—in other words, all the top foreign diplomats in London. On the morning of March 4, they lined up together once more in order of seniority to present their credentials in the Bow Room of Buckingham Palace. Although this was something they had done recently for George's brother, things were slightly different this time. The Russian ambassador, Ivan Maisky, noted that Anthony Eden was there to help George with the conversation, as the king was "taciturn and easily embarrassed," adding "he also stammers."[74]

The ceremony seemed to be passing off relatively smoothly. Then suddenly, Ribbentrop, Hitler's ambassador, greeted the king not with the customary bow but with a Nazi salute, something that "offended the English deeply." Maisky was secretly delighted, since the two ambassadors were compared widely in the press and people observed that, by contrast, the nice Russian revolutionary had managed to greet the king properly, without "raising a clenched first above his head." To Maisky's disbelief, things only got better, for at five o'clock the same afternoon, the king and queen hosted an informal tea party for the ambassadors and their wives. Even in this more relaxed setting, among the canapés and cucumber sandwiches, Ribbentrop repeated his gaffe and gave another Nazi salute. The two young princesses, Elizabeth and Margaret Rose, began to giggle, and then misbehave, much to the "considerable embarrassment" of the queen.[75]

The press and public enjoyed mocking Ribbentrop's multiple faux pas. In private, however, it is unclear whether the Royal Family knew that he was a friend of Wallis Simpson and had enjoyed private meetings with Edward. Even if they did not know, their anxieties could hardly have been higher. Across the Channel, at Château de Candé in the Loire Valley, preparations were under way for a rather unusual royal wedding. Once again, Special Branch kept a close eye on the comings and goings.

Meanwhile, Edward, now duke of Windsor, had headed for Austria to stay with his friends the Rothschilds at Schloss Enzesfeldt. The visit was arranged by the security-conscious Lord Brownlow in the greatest secrecy, since half the newspapers in Europe were on his trail. Having accompanied Wallis on her flight to southern France the previous year, Brownlow now used coded language to prevent phone calls from being leaked to the press. He asked Baroness Rothschild if he might come to stay and also bring his "brother David" who was recovering from a cold. Rothschild hoped that this would "hoodwink the telephone tappers and journalists who were tracking the exiled King."[76]

The most important watcher was already there. London had arranged for Edward to be protected by a Special Branch officer named David Storrier. Just before the First World War, Storrier had left Angus, north of Dundee, with his brother, to join the police. The elder brother rose to be assistant chief constable of Glasgow; the younger brother, David, had an even more fascinating career. For eighteen years, he served as one of the few direct links between Edward and the government.[77]

As early as 1932, Storrier had served as King George V's bodyguard, earning the trust of the Royal Family.[78] Amid mounting concern about Edward's activities, Storrier's duties changed and he was assigned to the prince of Wales.[79] Working with Edward would be difficult. Knowing that any protection officer would need to keep up with irregular hours and esoteric behavior, the prince's equerry asked for a man of "about thirty" who was single. Sensitive to Edward's feelings about his diminutive size, they also wanted an officer who was "not a very big man."[80]

The police usually filled these posts with "good, keen ambitious detectives" and expected them to last about four years, or "else the appointment will be regarded by men of this type as a dead end."[81] Curiously, Storrier stayed rather longer: almost two decades. He was delighted to find that he was treated in an extremely courteous and friendly way by the duchess and was told privately that she described him to others as "one of the family." He repaid the compliment by describing her in his reports to London as "HRH," a title that the Windsors worked tirelessly to deny her.[82]

Storrier's role was to protect his royal charge but also to watch him closely. An honest policeman from rural Scotland, he clearly struggled with being asked to spy on his master. During early 1937, Storrier nurtured growing anxieties about his dual role. Writing from Schloss Enzesfeldt near Vienna, he told his superiors in London, "I shall communicate with you again, Sir. . . . I trust, Sir, you will not regard the foregoing as a breach of confidence on my part so far as HRH is concerned as I know you understand the already difficult position and I feel it my duty to report to you."[83]

Edward and Wallis borrowed their beautiful wedding venue from Charles Bedaux, one of the wealthiest men in France. Bedaux had purchased the sixteenth-century château in 1927, and lived there with his American second wife, the former Fern Lombard from Michigan. Bedaux had made his fortune pioneering efficiency studies for major manufacturers around Europe, and his companies were some of the first management consultancies. His work had the added benefit of creating high-level contacts across Europe, including in Germany and Sweden.

On June 3, 1937, Storrier was among a select group of guests gathering for the royal wedding. Even some of the couple's closest friends had boycotted the nuptials, for fear of censure by Buckingham Palace and, despite the conspicuous displays of flowers, the château felt curiously empty. No royals were present, not even Edward's closest brother, and all royal staff were warned that if they attended, they would be dismissed. The guests did include significant figures—including Walter Monckton, Baron and Baroness Rothschild, and Winston Churchill's son Randolph.[84] "Fruity" Metcalfe was best man. The guests were almost outnumbered by the world's press, for the Windsors were more famous than ever, already achieving cult status. Back in Britain, on the outskirts of Windsor Castle, the caretaker of Fort Belvedere, Walter Willis, cashed in on their prolonged absence. For a hefty fee, he took hardcore Windsor fanatics on private tours of the "closed" house and gardens. The crown estates office eventually caught him in the act and he was fired.[85]

After the wedding, the couple headed off on their honeymoon to the mountain resort of Schloss Wasserleonburg in Austria. His ever-present shadow, David Storrier, reported to London: "I must confess Sir, that never before have I seen HRH so obviously touched as at the conclusion . . . and HRH seems so far extremely happy with his bride and surroundings."[86] He found the south Austrian police efficient, comparing them favorably with the indolent French gendarmerie. "Apart from shopping expeditions to the neighbouring towns, HRH and The Duchess seldom leave the Castle."[87]

Storrier also noted boredom was slowly setting in. Edward, who had often complained about his official duties both as prince of Wales, and then briefly as king, now rather missed them. His friend and attentive law officer, Walter Monckton, came and went at weekends dealing with "business," but Edward longed for the buzz of London society. The astute Storrier noticed this, and as August turned to September, reported: "I personally feel that he is now experiencing greater difficulty in agreeably occupying his time and I notice also that HRH is now more easily irritated by minor details such as the non-arrival on time of things he may have ordered or a temporary breakdown of the weather."[88] Edward's friend Duff Cooper had warned him about possible tedium the previous year, but the duke had replied breezily: "Oh you know me, Duff, I'm always busy. I shall find plenty to do." He was now restless.[89]

Boredom offered opportunities for dubious characters; one already waited in the wings, in the form of Charles Bedaux. He and the Windsors shared the same political world outlook, believing that Western European democracies had grown weak and vulnerable to the Bolshevik threat. They saw fascism as an attractive alternative, an expression of modernism allowing society to move forward and perhaps offer full employment. Although, philosophically, Bedaux's ideas might have been closer to Italian syndicalism, British diplomats record that he "held pro-fascist views." The American authorities reached the same conclusion, but neither country yet had all the details. More spies and surveillance were required.[90]

Above all, Bedaux was an entrepreneur and opportunist. Exploiting Edward's ennui, he decided to arrange more vigorous activities for the duke. Reporting on the last day of August from the Schloss Wasserleonburg near the Italian border, Storrier explained to London that they would leave on September 7, 1937, "for Hungary for a few days shooting with Mr Bedaux," then to Paris, arriving about September 28, then onward to Germany in mid-October. Shock and horror reverberated across London. Storrier's report was the first that the British knew about Edward's intention to visit Nazi Germany.[91]

The political establishment had blundered badly. Having cut Edward off, and shunned his wife, they now had a royal who was out of control—a veritable loose cannon. The downside of cutting an ex-king loose was that you could not manage him. The British government could do nothing to stop Edward from being friendly with the Nazi enemy. Neville Chamberlain, who had replaced Baldwin as prime minister the previous spring, took the view that it was "not possible to stop the Duke of Windsor going to Germany."[92] Britain's embassy in Berlin was ordered to have nothing to do with the duke, but to watch his every move closely.

Bedaux was clearly a key orchestrator. He came to Germany about a fortnight before Edward, staying at the Adlon Hotel, to help arrange everything.[93] He planned the visit with Dr. Robert Ley, head of the German labor organization, who would later hang himself at Nuremberg before he was tried for war crimes. Though the details are murky, there are strong suggestions that Bedaux's own business dealings in the Reich benefited from arranging this special visit.[94]

Days later, drawing on local sources, London heard that the duchess herself admitted "that when in Germany they would be entertained by Herr Hitler."[95] Ribbentrop, until recently Germany's flat-footed ambassador in London, arrived and played a leading part in entertaining the Windsors. Having then met Herman Göring, commander of the Luftwaffe, and Joseph Goebbels, minister of propaganda, by September 27, they were on their way to meet Hitler in Munich.[96]

Oddly, while Storrier continued to be managed by Special Branch during this period, there is no indication of whether he traveled to Germany with them. It appears not.[97] The duke was accompanied by his loyal equerry, Dudley Forwood, but it is not clear who was watching them while they were there, nor whether any record of their meeting with Hitler survived. For some unknown reason, Churchill's son Randolph also accompanied the tour.[98]

During 1937, Edward and Wallis were lavishly funded by the shadowy Bedaux couple, their French-American millionaire hosts. After the successful visit to Nazi Germany, they suggested that the Windsors visit the United States the next year. Bedaux had clearly been "running" Edward and Wallis and paying many expenses. Bedaux also told Edward that after the United States they should visit Italy and Sweden, where he would be put in contact with a Swedish millionaire, Axel Wenner-Gren, who was also interested in "world peace." Bedaux advised him to take this world peace line in public, too, and even went so far as to express the opinion that by taking this line he might in due course be the "savior" of the British monarchy. Edward took this to heart and publicly emphasized his pacifist desire to avoid the horrors of the Western Front, rather than his admiration for the Third Reich, two views that he found entirely compatible within his somewhat elastic conceptual universe.[99]

At the end of 1937, the Windsors once more headed down to Cannes. They spent Christmas in the same villa where Wallis had taken refuge a year earlier. Others came to join them, including Winston Churchill and Lloyd George. Billed as a light-hearted, festive gathering, it was nothing less than a reassembling of the "King's Party," and it is hard to resist the conclusion that the duke briefed them on his recent talks in Germany. Once again, Storrier noticed that the duke had "great difficulty" in "filling in" the hours there, adding that "time hangs heavy."[100]

The "King's Party" had not been inactive. The avid supporters of the Windsors were a curious amalgam of public figures. One of their more colorful individuals was Compton Mackenzie, the energetic MI6 officer who had run the Athens station during the First World War and helped to push the pro-German king toward abdication. In the early 1930s, he had published several volumes of memoirs, recounting his intelligence exploits in Greece, and was prosecuted under the Official Secrets Act for his pains. Because of the royal aspect, Mackenzie believed that George V had "encouraged" the decision to take legal action against him.[101] He first responded with a comic novel about MI6 called *Water on the Brain*.[102] But the abdication offered him a bigger opportunity to fire back at the authorities. Already an established royal biographer, he quickly researched *The Windsor Tapestry*, a study of the "life, heritage and abdication of HRH The Duke of Windsor." He wrote so fast that at one point he collapsed. Nursed back to health, he finished the book, which was serialized in the *Sunday Dispatch*.

"What the European secret services were doing about King Edward's friendship with Mrs Simpson—that is what Mr. Compton Mackenzie tells us in the next instalment of the *Windsor Tapestry*," boasted the paper on July 17, 1938.[103] There were in fact six episodes, and the *Dispatch* had paid £5,000 for the serialization, almost half a million pounds at current prices, and it was worth it— the paper's circulation grew by 100,000 overnight.[104] The book attacked Stanley

Baldwin and Geoffrey Dawson, editor of *The Times*. It made assertions of multiple instances of "conspiracy."[105]

There followed a vicious spat between the various newspapers, which even resorted to putting pamphlets about the abdication through letter boxes in the more expensive parts of London. MI5 gathered examples of the pamphlets for their files.[106] Indeed, Mackenzie's suspicions would surely have been confirmed if he had known how closely he was being watched by the authorities and that a large MI5 dossier was being compiled, noting his associations with figures like Oswald Mosely. Mackenzie was a fervent Scottish nationalist, and MI5 agents had seen the two "in close and friendly conversation" after speaking together at London events.[107] One of the last secret servants to contribute material to his bulging files was a figure named Anthony Blunt.[108]

Mackenzie's book caused a sensation and went through many editions. But the literary enemies of the Windsors were also busy. Osbert Sitwell, another well-known author and former guards officer, had privately circulated a racy poem about the abdication, called "Rat Week." Sitwell was a close friend of Edward's brother George, now the king, and the poem criticized not only the Windsors but also their friends who had deserted them so quickly after the abdication. This poem was leaked to the press, leading to court actions over copyright and discussions of libel.[109] There was much debate about who exactly was a "rat." The newspapers loved it, but all this discomforted the authorities and kept the story in the public eye.

Edward had been in correspondence with Mackenzie about his book, and his mail was being opened by MI5.[110] Mackenzie also worked with Walter Monckton, Edward's solicitor. In the end, Edward decided not to officially endorse *The Windsor Tapestry*, because of its "violent" language, although he clearly enjoyed it.[111] Alongside all this propaganda and public bickering, the Windsors spent 1938 house-hunting in Paris, and Storrier found himself promoted for his diligent surveillance efforts.[112] Back in London, various government departments were still arguing over who should pay the eye-watering bills from Harvey Nichols for furniture removal from Fort Belvedere a year before.[113]

As for Bedaux, his attempt to cultivate Edward and Wallis ended in disaster. His plan for the promised royal visit to the United States ran up against serious opposition, not least from the British Embassy. The British ambassador, Ronald Lindsay, was "staggered" by the strict instructions to cold-shoulder the Windsors, but when he visited Balmoral in 1938, the matter became clear: the Royal Family stated plainly that they feared Edward might be "trying to stage a come-back."[114] This was little short of paranoia, but it explains the continued close surveillance. The trip was canceled. Bedaux found that raising his American profile led to serious tax demands on his subsidiaries that he could not pay and, by late 1938, he concluded that the Windsors were a losing proposition.

Meanwhile, Edward's shy and stammering brother George, a rather improbable publicist, scooped the pool with an enormously popular royal visit to North America the next year. In 1939, as the Windsors sat things out in Paris, the ever-patient Inspector Storrier watched and waited.[115] Walter Monckton, who knew more than almost anyone about Edward, and was a true friend, nevertheless confided to the head of the Metropolitan Police that staying close to the exasperating Windsors was hard work—and so Storrier was remarkable: "It would really take a saint to hold that job indefinitely without some deterioration."[116] Little did they know that international events were about to offer all of them a change of scene.

PART III

Royals and Spies
at War

9

The Outbreak of the
Second World War

The Duke expressed himself very freely. . . .
He was surrounded by agents.
—The German ambassador to Spain, July 1940

Alongside "Munich" and "Chamberlain," "appeasement" has long been a dirty
word. But this was not always the case; in the 1930s, many people, kings
included, gave it far more positive connotations. Some advocated appeasement as a means of addressing genuine German grievances in order to deliver
long-term peace. Others promoted it as the only rational response to a situation in which Germany had strong allies, in the form of Italy and Japan, while
Britain only had the friendship of a fractured and internally divided France.
Even those distrustful of Germany viewed it as a necessary way of buying time
while Britain tried to catch up in a race for rearmament. Only in the wake of
Germany's invasion of Czechoslovakia in the spring of 1939 did appeasement
start to become a byword for a policy of craven submission.

Neville Chamberlain, who became prime minister in 1937, is the British
leader most infamously intertwined with appeasement. But he was not alone.
Although now remembered as a victorious wartime king, George VI was an
equal—if not more ardent—fan of appeasement. In 1938, he actually vied
with Chamberlain to establish closer relations with Hitler, even drafting his
own personal letter to the German leader. Trying to find common ground, he
wrote: "This is a letter to Hitler, not as one statesman to another, but one ex-
serviceman to another," exhorting him to spare the youth of Europe another
disastrous conflict.[1] George was desperate to send it, and had to be restrained
not only by Lord Halifax, the foreign secretary, but also by Chamberlain himself. The prime minister explained that he feared Hitler might send "an insulting
reply," but perhaps he also privately wished to retain the plaudits of any peace
deal for himself.[2] Restless for appeasement, George then wanted to send similar missives to the Japanese. Most members of the Royal Family took a similar
line, especially the king's youngest brother, the duke of Kent.[3]

George was effusive when Chamberlain returned from meeting Hitler at his Berchtesgaden retreat in mid-September 1938. "How I admire your courage and wisdom," he told the prime minister, "in going to see Hitler in person."[4] He then sent him a haunch of venison from Balmoral as a gift, although, in a perhaps fitting metaphor, by the time the meat arrived in London it was so bad that Chamberlain had to destroy it.[5]

On September 27, Chamberlain took to the airwaves, lamenting the fact that Britain might go to war for Czechoslovakia—"a people of whom we know nothing." He even seemed to be evincing sympathy for Germany's position. Immediately afterward, the king sent him a message of praise.[6] A couple of weeks later, when Chamberlain returned from Munich loftily waving his agreement with Hitler, the king's aides had to stop him from rushing to the airport like an adoring fan. Instead, he sent a congratulatory letter, delivered as soon as Chamberlain landed, inviting him to "come straight to Buckingham Palace, so that I can express to you personally my heartfelt congratulations on the success of your visit to Munich."[7] George then engineered a photo-shoot on the palace balcony, where he publicly and visibly aligned himself with appeasement, a move that some thought imprudent and perhaps bordering on the unconstitutional.[8]

Just before Christmas 1938, the king started to change his mind. On December 18, he complained at length to the Czech ambassador, Jan Masaryk, about the difficulties of implementing appeasement when faced with "people such as Hitler and Mussolini." He had once seen them as inspiring their troubled nations with courage and confidence, perhaps seeking to address genuine grievances. "But," he added, "the useful mission of Hitler and Mussolini is over. Everything they do now is directed against us and against civilization."[9]

However, the king had not yet abandoned hopes of an agreement. In January 1939, he praised Chamberlain for developing "personal contact" with Mussolini in Rome. He then blamed Spain for being "the bugbear to any kind of appeasement in Europe."[10] Two months later, George acknowledged that Hitler's invasion of Czechoslovakia was a "blow," but he comforted Chamberlain: "Your labours have been anything but wasted, for they have left no doubt in the minds of ordinary people all over the world of our love of peace and of our readiness to discuss with any nation whatever grievances they think they have."[11]

By the summer of 1939, even Chamberlain had accepted the need to threaten Hitler with force. On July 3, George offered to talk with Philipp of Hesse, a German great-grandson of Queen Victoria and son-in-law of the Italian king. Hesse had been a member of the Nazi Party for a decade and enjoyed easy access to both Hitler and Mussolini. The go-between would be George's youngest son, the duke of Kent, who was often in Italy.[12] George wanted to use this royal channel to "convey to Hitler that we really are in earnest." Chamberlain turned him down, saying that Hitler already knew "we mean business this time."[13]

Chamberlain was wrong yet again. Hitler did not believe Britain would go to war for Poland, so he pushed ahead with his invasion. Britain declared war on Germany on September 3, 1939, and when Hitler received the news, he turned to Ribbentrop with a look of complete puzzlement and asked, "What do we do now?" Soon afterward, George's wife, Queen Elizabeth, thought she needed to learn a little more about what they were facing and decided to read *Mein Kampf*. On October 15, she sent a copy to Halifax, warning him: "I don't advise you to read it through, or you might go mad, and that would be a great pity." She suggested "a skip through" would reveal much about Hitler's extreme mentality.[14] Chamberlain resigned the next year, in May 1940.

Perhaps because of the king's multiple contacts with Germany and his earlier enthusiasm for appeasement, the intelligence services remained wary of the royals even after war began. Officials agreed to special arrangements to supply confidential information to George on a daily basis. Scarred by the experience with his elder brother, these came with a big caveat. Because the palace had lost a few red boxes recently, a duty officer from the Cabinet Office would now deliver the papers, stand outside as the king read them, and then return them to the government. The intelligence services, or perhaps his private secretary, Alec Hardinge, did not trust George enough to leave them unattended. Other sensitive documents went to Hardinge, but had to be returned to the secretary to the committee of imperial defense personally and by name.[15]

Britain's wartime intelligence and security agencies were now expanding fast. Many of the codebreakers moved to bigger premises at Bletchley Park in the countryside north of London. MI6 found its sabotage department taken away and developed into a whole new organization, called the Special Operations Executive. MI5 moved to a bigger location at Wormwood Scrubs Prison. A fortnight after the outbreak of war, Vernon Kell, the director of MI5, sent two of his officers to the duke of Windsor's former residence, Fort Belvedere, to consider whether he could requisition it as the headquarters for an MI5 section. It now looked rather different. Having stood empty for a year, the flags were rusting in the miniature golf course, dead leaves clogged the surface of the swimming pool, and weeds had sprouted everywhere. Kell doubtless enjoyed the idea of a section of MI5 being based at "the Fort," but he eventually rejected it as "too small" for his purposes.[16]

Buckingham Palace began to develop its own security organization. George soon boasted his own private army, called the Coats Mission, named after its commander, Major James Coats of the Coldstream Guards. This was a handpicked body of 5 officers and 124 men from the Brigade of Guards and

Household Cavalry, equipped with armored cars, on 24-hour call to take the king, queen, and young princesses to a safe house in the country if the German threat of invasion were to materialize.

In an emergency, Rolls-Royce armored cars would pull out of the Royal Mews; military police with special racing motorbikes would control traffic as Coats escorted the royal family to one of four country houses in remote locations, and, if necessary, on to Liverpool and eventually Canada. On Vancouver Island, Hatley Castle, a forty-room mansion built at the turn of the century in the Tudor revival style was purchased in 1940 as part of the plan.[17] Margaret Rhodes, Princess Elizabeth's cousin who lived at Buckingham Palace for part of the war, was initially comforted by this arrangement, until she realized that while the royal corgis were on the list of evacuees, "it did not include me."[18]

The threat felt real enough. Lord Hailsham, the lord chancellor, warned the new prime minister, Winston Churchill, that the Nazis were obsessed with royal families. "I observe that the Nazis both in Norway and in Holland made a desperate attempt to capture the Royal Family; no doubt they will do so the same in this country if they can." He advised Churchill that the two princesses should be sent away to safety but thought that the king was determined to stay and fight.[19]

Hailsham was right. The Germans had successfully captured the king of Belgium. In the Netherlands, Otto Begus, a former military police officer, had led the effort to capture Queen Wilhelmina. She escaped his clutches by only half an hour and eventually arrived on a train at Liverpool Street Station. The king rushed to greet her on the platform and found her wearing a tin hat and clutching nothing more than a shopping bag. Wilhelmina stayed in London to help organize the Dutch resistance, but the rest of her family soon fled to Canada.[20] Hailsham, Churchill, and the king wondered whether Begus would now lead a plot to kidnap the British Royal Family, perhaps 24 hours before the invasion.

Begus and his unit moved to a villa in Boulogne, just across the Channel from Dover, where a scrambler phone connected them to the Abwehr, the German secret service. He later claimed, perhaps somewhat extravagantly, that from here, he had presided over a Nazi plan to capture the royals. A crack "Royal Unit" of several hundred Nazi commandos would parachute into the palace grounds, kidnapping the family within just 10 minutes.[21] Although Begus was a real figure and did belong to an elite unit—indeed, both MI5 and US counterintelligence had files on him—it appears he may have exaggerated his role, the stage of preparations, and the dramatic speed with which he could "take" the Royal Family.[22]

Regardless of the reality, George exploited the perceived threat for propaganda purposes. He defiantly and publicly insisted that the family would stay and fight—even as the converted armored cars of the Coats Mission stood secretly by. Far from being evacuated to Canada, Princess Elizabeth soon donned a service uniform and joined the war effort with the Auxiliary Territorial Service.

Fears of invasion accelerated in late May 1940 with the Dunkirk evacuation. King George summoned Hugh Dalton, the politician in charge of the Special Operations Executive, to Buckingham Palace to talk about covert warfare and propaganda. The conversation then turned to Dunkirk, where a flotilla of hastily assembled small ships was dramatically rescuing stranded British soldiers from French beaches. The king asserted firmly that Hitler "wants to come here," suggesting that the invasion date had been fixed by the Germans for August 1. He became increasingly excited, insisting that Hitler planned "to exterminate us and plant Germans in the island. What will he do next? He will stop at nothing, neither raining gas from the sky nor poisoning our water." Dalton was a little unnerved by the royal outburst and tried to reassure the king that Britain had scientists working behind the scenes on preventive measures.[23]

In August 1940, with the invasion seemingly on the horizon, the king resolutely declared: "I want to get my German. I want to kill at least one of the invaders, and we will all fight to the last." "Well," Churchill responded, "you need to be able to kill more than one German." Shortly afterward, out of the blue, a specially gift-wrapped package arrived at Buckingham Palace. Churchill had sent the king a Tommy Gun. George, his family, and his equerries eagerly began shooting practice with pistols, rifles, and his new Tommy Gun.[24] This was a whole family activity.[25] Queen Elizabeth enjoyed firing in the garden of Buckingham Palace, where huge numbers of rats ran free because of the bombing raids. They formed moving targets to practice on.[26] The queen took instruction on her revolver every day, insisting, "Yes, I shall not go down like the others."[27]

Gift-wrapped Tommy Guns aside, George's relationship with Churchill was complex. Once an avid supporter of Chamberlain and appeasing Hitler, now George was king of a nation at war and partnered with the most outspoken opponent of appeasement. There is no doubt that the king would have much preferred Halifax as Chamberlain's successor and that he bent constitutional precedent to try to secure this outcome.[28] Temperamentally, the two men were very different: Churchill was charismatic and bullish; George was shy and reticent. More importantly, for the last four years, they had been on opposite sides over Edward VIII. George could hardly forget that Churchill had joined Beaverbrook, Lloyd George, and other renegade figures in forming the "King's Party" and had been one of the few prominent figures to visit the Windsors in 1937 on the French Riviera. Nor had he forgotten that his brother was still in France, a problem that he and his new prime minister would soon need to confront.

In May 1940, the Germans had attacked France. The Phony War was over. By the end of the month, they had reached the gates of Paris. The speed with which one of Europe's great powers collapsed astonished the world and led to much talk of a covert Nazi "Fifth Column" that had undermined the Allied war effort. Fears quickly spread about a similar fifth column lurking in Britain. Taking no chances, Churchill ordered the security agencies to "collar the lot," so large numbers of "enemy aliens" and expatriates, especially those of German descent, even Jewish refugees, were rounded up and sent off to detention camps in places like the Isle of Man.[29] The new home secretary personally briefed George on the security swoop that rounded up some of Churchill's relatives.[30]

There was one notable British expatriate still living in France who was of special concern: the duke of Windsor. Edward and Wallis had been at their luxury villa in Antibes, in the South of France, when war was declared. George offered to put his plane at their disposal to rush them back to London, but instead they opted to return at a more leisurely pace, taking a naval destroyer from Cherbourg, accompanied by Admiral Mountbatten.[31] A week after the outbreak of war, Edward and George had met; what words passed between them remain unknown, but it was reportedly a frosty exchange. Beneath the surface was the queen's lingering distaste for Wallis, whom she refused to see at this tense moment. Shortly afterward, she told Queen Mary: "I haven't heard a word about Mrs Simpson—I trust she will soon return to France and STAY THERE. I am sure she hates this dear country, & therefore she should not be here in wartime." Her views on Edward were no more charitable, now characterizing him as "exactly like Hitler" in thinking that anyone who disagreed with him was wrong.[32]

George changed his mind about what his brother might do in terms of the war effort. A special post was created for Edward with the Military Mission in Paris as a liaison officer to the French high command, but this did not keep him very busy, since everyone had been told he was a security risk and ordered to show him as few documents as possible. Indeed, he was even forbidden from entering the British sector. Chamberlain had remarked that "France can never keep a secret for more than half an hour," and so this seemed the perfect job for him since here neither he nor Wallis could do much harm, so they were left to bumble around Paris.[33]

Edward's liaison work during the Phony War has often been dismissed as pointless. In fact, he proved rather useful to his new commander, General Howard-Vyse, whose mission was based close to the French headquarters at Vincennes. Their task was to report on the robustness of the French war effort, but their allies were suspicious and secretive, refusing to allow anyone near the

Maginot Line. Edward had a background in intelligence work from the previous war, and the mission now saw his arrival as "a heaven-sent opportunity" to take a close look at the French front. Edward was restricted in visiting British troops, but the French gave him a free pass. He was soon sending perceptive and critical reports back to London, suggesting that the French officers were obsessed with the "excellence" and "impregnability" of the Maginot Line.[34]

As France fell in May 1940, the Windsors were still renting a gorgeous and impeccably stylish house at 24 Boulevard Souchet on the outskirts of Paris. Edward had been naively contemplating another vacation; but in London, the palace and Philip Game, head of the Metropolitan Police, began to panic about how to keep a Special Branch officer with him as the situation in Europe deteriorated.[35] With the Nazis advancing on Paris, the duke's staff stopped thinking about vacations and suddenly pleaded for better protection. On May 27, with the evacuation toward Dunkirk in full swing, Game wrote to the duke's equerry, Gray Phillips, about the tricky business of providing continuing police protection. Because British forces had been depleted, some six hundred police who were military reservists had now been called up, leaving Game stretched to the limit.[36] The duke promised to write personally, but, with all eyes on the beaches at Dunkirk, communications were interrupted.[37]

Suddenly, the Windsors fled Paris, perhaps tipped off by officers from the local MI6 station.[38] The party abandoned the flamboyant "Fruity" Metcalfe, Edward's long-serving unofficial assistant and best man. Poor Metcalfe rang in the morning to ask for his daily instructions from the duke, only to be told by a servant that they had fled at 6:30 a.m.[39] Edward's close friend was much aggrieved and later reflected that "his plans must have been made twenty-four hours before," yet he left without saying a word, he took all the cars, and, with the Germans closing on Paris, he ungallantly left Metcalfe and his wife with "not so much as a bicycle."[40]

Instead of escaping to Britain, Edward escorted Wallis south along crowded roads to Biarritz near the border with Spain. The town was choked with Rolls-Royces carrying their elegant owners and expensive luggage south toward safety.[41] MI6 seem to have played a role in keeping them away from their German friends. Noting the extreme secrecy involved, the American FBI later reported that "British Secret Servicemen covered the move."[42] MI6 not only traveled with them to Biarritz but also watched their every move and communication. "The British Secret Service," according to the FBI, "ascertained that the Duchess of Windsor had informed Ribbentrop of her itinerary, schedule, etc., prior to her departure."[43] Although the FBI was probably wrong to conclude that "the Duchess of Windsor had an affair with Ribbentrop" during his time as ambassador in England in 1936, she and Ribbentrop were clearly friends and do seem to have been in contact during this difficult period.[44]

By June 5, 1940, the remnants of British forces had completed their week-long evacuation from Dunkirk, rescuing most of their troops. A fortnight later, the battle for France was effectively over. Many felt Britain would be the next European country to fall. In some confusion, the royal couple moved backward and forward around France and then sped over the border into Spain, where London inexplicably lost track of them. Urgent telegrams arrived at the British consulates in Nice, Marseilles, and Bordeaux: "Please send me any information you have or can get from consular offices under your supervision regarding the Duke of Windsor's whereabouts and do anything you can to facilitate his return to this country."[45]

The Windsors finally surfaced in Barcelona, then moved to the luxurious Ritz Hotel in Madrid. Although Spain was neutral, it had close ties to Nazi Germany, which now dominated the European continent. Edward arrived just in time to meet up with the new British ambassador, his old friend and former MI6 officer Sam Hoare, also known in Whitehall as "Slippery Sam," whose main mission would be bribing the Franco government, paying millions to secure its continued neutrality.[46]

Hoare was regarded as an arch appeaser and a defeatist by many in Whitehall. Therefore Alexander Cadogan, the senior official at the Foreign Office, worried about what he would get up to with Edward. Walking through the gardens of Buckingham Palace with Halifax and his wife, Cadogan exclaimed hopefully that with any luck an Axis agent might assassinate him. He said "there was one bright spot—there were lots of Germans and Italians in Madrid and therefore a good chance of S. H. [Sam Hoare] being murdered." Halifax looked pained, but Dorothy Halifax "agreed heartily."[47] The next day Halifax asked why Hoare was in such a hurry to get to Spain. Cadogan replied "because he's frightened," adding "he's the first rat to leave the ship."[48]

In Spain, Hoare outwardly showed no fear and welcomed his old friend with gusto. There now followed a wave of lavish entertainment to win over the Windsors. Hoare put on the biggest Madrid cocktail party in living memory to influence which way they would jump.[49] He wanted them to board a flying boat for England, while the Spanish press, bribed by the Germans, warned loudly that they would be arrested as soon as they set foot in Britain.[50]

In their tempestuous flight south, the Windsors had not only abandoned "Fruity" Metcalfe; they had also left behind their closest French collaborator, Charles Bedaux. During the battle of France, he had "personally welcomed the German General Staff to his house near Tours." Bedaux then spent most of this time in a Parisian office controlling a large German staff organizing Jewish industries that the Nazis had taken over and ensuring maximum production.[51] Later, he worked with the sabotage branch of the Abwehr to command a covert mission to Persia to capture the British refinery at Abadan from his former client, the Anglo-Persian Oil Company.[52] A few years later, he would commit suicide in a Miami jail while charged with being a Nazi collaborator.[53]

Despite the blatant pro-Nazi behavior of their closest friends, the Windsors felt ideologically vindicated. In Spain, and encouraged by Hoare, the royal couple now professed their admiration for fascism more explicitly than ever. They clearly respected Hitler and believed in the modernity of fascism, which would herald economic progress and a new order. More than that, they now gloated that they had accurately predicted the future. Speaking with a US diplomat, Edward elucidated the dramatic military events they had just witnessed by asserting that "in the past ten years, Germany has totally reorganized the order of its society in preparation for this war." He added: "countries that were unwilling to accept such a reorganization and concomitant sacrifices should direct their policies accordingly and thereby avoid dangerous adventures." The duchess said much the same thing, but in darkly Darwinist language, observing: "France had lost because it was internally diseased and that a country that was not in a condition to fight a war should never have declared war."[54]

These provocative statements had personal consequences. They placed the Windsors at loggerheads with one of their friends and most powerful supporters, Winston Churchill. The tricky Windsor problem now landed on his desk at Number 10. He had gone out of his way to support them during the abdication crisis and had remained closer to them than any other leading British politician during the late 1930s. Despite the awkwardness, Churchill now sternly ordered Edward to return home, reminding him that he held military rank and with that came inescapable duties. The language was unambiguous, and, as the historian Deborah Cadbury has observed, perhaps even threatening: "Your Royal Highness has taken active military rank and refusal to obey direct orders of competent military authority would create a serious situation."[55]

Edward stood his ground, perhaps believing that defeat for Britain was only weeks away. He then bargained, demanding a suitable official post in Britain before pursuing his dearest ambition, securing "HRH" status for Wallis. The latter proved the deal breaker—King George would not hear of it. Moreover, politicians and the palace disagreed about where the Windsors should go. Churchill wanted to bring them home; but George and Elizabeth, who watched them closely, wanted to keep them as far away from England as possible. On July 3, the king exhorted Churchill about this, exclaiming: "I did not see what job he could have in this country and that she would not be safe here."[56]

While London weighed options, the Windsors were on the move again. They followed the advice of their friend Sam Hoare to travel to Lisbon, a more neutral but nonetheless dangerously spy-infested capital. They had to pause before departing, because Edward's younger brother, the duke of Kent, was visiting Portugal and nobody wanted two royals in the country at the same time.

The duke of Kent's visit in July 1940 is mysterious. Cadogan noted in his diary that there was now a "Funny pause" in the war: "Hitler doesn't like the look of invasion and is trying to tempt us to parley." Indeed, Hitler had said publicly that he saw no reason "why this war should go on" and appealed "once more to reason and common sense in Britain." Cadogan noted cryptically that approaches had been made through countries such as Sweden, the Vatican, and the United States. Was this another of the many feelers? Three weeks after Dunkirk, and with the skies thick with German fighters, it is unlikely that the duke of Kent was in Portugal simply to celebrate a national anniversary or play a round of golf.[57]

Edward's younger brother had been enlisted as a source of valuable information by British intelligence as early as July 1939. The king had suggested that he act as an emissary to Hitler via his cousin Prince Philip of Hesse, who was then the go-between for Hitler and Mussolini. Halifax and Chamberlain were lukewarm. and the project was eventually shelved. But in June 1940, the duke of Kent stepped up to carry out a "series of delicate and important missions." Some high-level German secret service agents were trying to pressure the neutral Portuguese dictator António de Oliveira Salazar into openly committing to Hitler. The duke was sent to find out what Salazar was really thinking and also to gain his confidence. A "perfect cover was found," in that he was selected to lead a delegation to attend the seven-day celebrations of Portugal's eight hundred years of independence. The duke spoke good Portuguese, and his presence was symbolic of the long-standing alliance between the two countries. He flew home on July 2, 1940, the same day that Wallis and Edward set out by car from Madrid to Lisbon.[58]

The duke of Kent's visit also underlined that air travel was still possible from Lisbon, even if it was hazardous with the Battle of Britain raging. Britain was not sure that it wanted Edward; and for his part, Edward hesitated to fly to what he regarded as an almost-defeated nation. He held out for a better offer from elsewhere. Perhaps he knew that, even before the invasion of France, German diplomats had sought an opportunity to reach out. As early as January 27, 1940, Julius Count von Zech-Burkersroda, the German ambassador to the Netherlands, confided to his superiors: "Through personal relationships I might have the opportunity to establish certain lines leading to the Duke of Windsor."[59]

Hitler misunderstood many things in world politics, including the role of the Royal Family in Britain. Assuming that the king played a role more like the kaiser in 1914, he saw monarchical politics as central to manipulating Britain. When Edward had abdicated, Ribbentrop had pandered to this bizarre view, reporting that it was all an anti-German plot. He suggested that "the abdication of King Edward is the result of the machinations of dark Bolshevik powers against the Fuhrer-will of the young King." He promised even more sensitive details about the royals would soon be reported to Hitler by word of mouth.[60] Hitler interpreted the abdication as driven by Edward's desire for Anglo-German rapprochement. There was now, he believed, "no other person in England who is ready to play with us." A depressed Hitler lamented that if only Edward had remained on the throne, "there would have been no differences—and no war—between England and Germany."[61]

Edward and Wallis arrived in Lisbon in early July. Looking out across the Atlantic Ocean, they still faced a moment of decision—whether to follow Churchill's order and return or stay in Lisbon hoping for a better offer from the Nazis. Meanwhile, MI6 gathered intelligence on the assiduous way in which the Germans were courting them.

The duke and duchess were addicted to luxury and conspicuous consumption. They worried about their property in France and especially the fate of their very expensive bed linen. Exploiting this, the Nazis back in Paris attended to their every whim. Gray Phillips, one of Edward's closest aides, told the chief of MI6, Stewart Menzies, about the "exceptional care" with which the Germans have fulfilled all of Edward's desires regarding his and Wallis's personal effects in France: "Special camions were sent to and fro, and a detailed inventory list was made of all the furniture and personal property of Duke and Duchess of Windsor, which was shown to the Duchess for approval."[62]

The top British secret service man on the ground in Lisbon was David Eccles. Rather than belonging to MI6, he was a member of Churchill's new sabotage service, the Special Operations Executive. A future Tory member of Parliament and later a viscount, he had royal connections, being married to the daughter of the royal physician. Comfortable moving in the upper echelons of society, Eccles met Edward frequently in Lisbon. He told his masters that he was determined "to watch him at breakfast, lunch and dinner with a critical eye."[63]

Eccles soon reported back to London. Once again, Edward and Wallis were spouting their defeatist views. "I had some conversation today with Duke and Duchess. . . . They are very clearly 5th column; at least they reckon we pushed France into a war she didn't want." Asked by Eccles if he thought the Germans would keep the terms of their deal with France, the duke simply replied: "Why not?"[64] This intelligence quickly found its way to the eyes of Britain's most senior diplomat, Alec Cadogan, and the foreign secretary.[65]

Eccles oversaw a team of willing assistants. They included Tommy Burns from Spain and a number of key figures involved in the dark arts of propaganda and economic warfare. Their best intelligence came from the garrulous

Nicholas Franco, the Spanish dictator's brother and ambassador to Portugal. He revealed to Eccles that a secret mission to get the Windsors back to Spain and hold them there was gathering pace. Spain, he explained, had sent Ángel Alcázar de Velasco, a bullfighter turned assassin, to assist the Germans. The border would be key to the plan's success: Germany had paid off the Spanish secret police, but Britain had paid off the Portuguese secret police. Everyone was warning the Windsors of the possibility of their assassination.[66]

Always professional spongers, Edward and Wallis had now found another new host with deep pockets: Ricardo Espírito Santo Silva. A banker and one of Lisbon's most respected residents, Silva had hosted members of the royal family before the war, but his allegiances were suspect. MI6 reported: "It appears that the Duke of Windsor is now occupying the house of a certain . . . Santo Silva . . . and is seeing a good deal of his landlord. We have learned from a reliable and well-placed source in Lisbon that Silva and his wife are in close touch with the German Embassy and that Silva had a three-hour interview with the German Minister." Again, Cadogan and Halifax, the foreign secretary, read the intelligence closely.[67]

Desmond Morton, a veteran MI6 officer who had been Churchill's most trusted aide for the last decade, was now the go-between for Downing Street and the intelligence agencies. His latest mission was to gather more intelligence on the Windsors' new host. MI6 reported: "Senor Espirito Santo is very pro-German and a centre of peace propaganda. . . . Politically he is a crook. . . . He is handling very large sums in bank notes and securities from Germany. . . . These monies are almost certainly German loot from captive countries."[68]

MI5 confirmed this shortly afterward. His bank was "an agency for the transmission of funds to German agents" in both Spain and Portugal.[69] For years Churchill had defended the duke publicly and privately, but his patience now wore thin. Multiple intelligence sources showed that Edward was effectively consorting with the enemy. It was time for action.

On July 4, British newspapers announced that Edward would be taking up a new post as governor of the Bahamas, a small collection of islands close to Florida, separated from the European war by thousands of miles of ocean. A few hours after the press was told, Edward also received the news of his new posting—a fait accompli. As a military officer, he was being given his marching orders. "I have done my best in a grievous situation," Churchill told him, putting it politely but firmly.[70]

Six days later, Churchill arrived at Buckingham Palace for his weekly meeting with the king and found they were in full agreement. They knew they had both sent Edward into exile on a desert island and were understandably anxious about it. George recorded in his diary: "It was better that he should not come here," adding: "What I had done, had had to be done for the country's sake."[71] Given the increasing volume of alarming intelligence, this was quite an understatement.

More warnings arrived on the desk of Stewart Menzies, the chief of MI6. Edward had not yet left for the Bahamas. The Germans thought that Britain was losing the war and that Edward and Wallis had switched sides. They were determined to seize what they saw as a fantastic opportunity. "A new source . . . has reported as follows: Germans expect assistance from Duke and Duchess of Windsor, latter desiring at any price to become Queen. . . . Germans have been negotiating with her since June 27th. Germans propose to form opposition government under Duke of Windsor." Halifax urged that this intelligence be shown to Churchill at once.[72] But by the middle of the month, Churchill did not need to depend on MI6 for this sort of information; it was being reported openly in the world press.[73]

Edward may not, at this point, have settled on the Germans, but the Germans had settled on him. They now began one of the most bizarre plots of the entire war. Code-named Operation Willi, the SS placed its top agent, Walter Schellenberg, in charge. Schellenberg's plan was for a Spanish friend of the duke to lure him to Spain on the pretext of a hunting trip. He could then either be kept in Spain, perhaps as the head of a rival British government in exile, or even taken to Germany.[74]

Above all, Edward wanted to be perceived as a peacemaker, and so was reportedly delighted and flattered by what he saw as a German peace initiative. According to German accounts, "the Duke paid tribute to the Fuhrer's desire for peace," admitting that it was, "in complete agreement with his own," because he "was firmly convinced that if he had been King it would never have come to war." He now asked Santo Silva to relay "an expression of admiration and sympathy for the Fuhrer."[75]

Remarkably, with the Battle of Britain raging but tempted by a Spanish offer of asylum, Edward even considered a public declaration disassociating himself from Churchill's policy of carrying on the war. He told Berlin that he would "postpone his journey to the Bahamas for as long as possible," hoping for an "early change in his favour." The German ambassador relayed Santo Silva's assessment that Edward was "a firm supporter of peaceful compromise with Germany." He added that Edward believed "with certainty that continued heavy bombing will make England ready for peace."[76]

Then, British flying boats tasked with bringing Edward back to Britain came and went without their royal passengers. A sense of crisis developed in London. All telegrams dealing with his arrangements were marked for immediate action.[77] The critical turning point had arrived. Alcázar de Velasco, the Spanish agent of the Abwehr, was pressing them to come to Spain for "a hunting trip." Edward hesitated, realizing the historical magnitude of his decision.[78]

Churchill now played his trump card. He sent one of Edward's most trusted friends, Walter Monckton, one of the few to break the 1937 social embargo on his wedding. Edward countered with a trump card of his own by responding to fears of a German plot with accusations of a British plot. Monckton told Churchill that Edward claimed to have "received from various sources, which he was not at liberty to disclose, though he regarded them as reliable, a report that he would be in danger if he went to Bahamas." Edward dramatically added "that there was a plot afoot against his security and that British influences, including probably some members of the Government, were implicated."[79]

Monckton, one of the few men Edward trusted, managed to persuade Edward that any assassination plot was a German fabrication to keep him in Lisbon: "I said that . . . what was wanted was some concrete evidence of the existence of such a plot."[80] Either way, the deliberations again delayed their departure.[81] With orders to move Edward and Wallis out of Lisbon as soon as possible, Monckton finally booked them onto the American liner *Excalibur*, bound for the Caribbean, on August 1. The Windsors reluctantly agreed to go.

Willing to do anything to prevent Edward's final departure, Schellenberg sabotaged the car carrying his luggage to the ship. He knew how important expensive clothes and personal effects were to the couple.[82] He also sent "bouquets of flowers to the Duchess warning her that the offer of an appointment in the Bahamas was merely a plot by the British to do away with him."[83] In the meantime, he "was empowered to offer to deposit fifty million Swiss francs in a Spanish bank account" if Edward was to cooperate and make statements distancing himself from London.[84] Schellenberg's charm offensive, warnings, and sabotage all failed. He watched among the crowds as the ship sailed off.

The Windsors had hesitated and then departed mostly for reasons of their personal safety. But they had not finished scheming, so, even as they departed, they still contrived to keep their options open. MI5's deputy director, Guy Liddell, recorded that even as Edward left, he fixed up "some kind of code with Espirito Santo Silva in order that he might fly back to Portugal from Florida if his intervention was required." Shockingly, as early as mid-August, at the height of the Battle of Britain, when Hitler hoped to overwhelm his adversary, the duke dispatched a coded telegram asking his pro-Nazi friend if that moment had now arrived. Liddell's diary, kept secret for so many years, now clearly reveals which way Edward was leaning.[85] Santo Silva alerted the German ambassador in Lisbon, who asked Berlin: "Should anything be sent in reply?"[86]

The Nazis now tried other—more ambitious—royal avenues. Just before the Windsors sailed for the Bahamas, King Gustav V of Sweden approached King

George, offering to act as a back channel for peace with Germany. Churchill helped the king draft a stern rejection, detailing Hitler's crimes and pointing to Swedish complicity. Churchill's language was so strong that diplomats had to tone it down before it reached the palace.[87]

Hitler's Scandinavian overtures gave Britain further insight into the racial nature of his thinking—and the odd role of British royalty within it. Hitler believed that "the white race" now consisted of two economic units: Germany, on the Continent; and the British Empire, together with America, as an ocean-based economy. Their mission was to work together to resist Russia as "a potential enemy" and above all to "resist the encroachment of the yellow race."[88] Once again, there was a sense that Hitler found the realities of world politics out of step with his bizarre racial vision, and he wished to use discreet royal diplomacy—whether from Edward or even George—as a means to correct this. The palace, government, and secret intelligence had to work closely together to counter it. In a curious way, royal peace feelers contributed to Hitler's hesitation on Operation Sealion—the invasion of Britain—and perhaps worked to Churchill's advantage.[89]

There is no doubt that the summer of 1940 still contains Britain's greatest secrets and mysteries. Some relate to the Royal Family, and members of their household were as keen to unravel them as anyone. Perhaps best placed to do this was Tommy Lascelles, the king's private secretary, who had relatives in MI5. Late at night, over dinner at the Travellers Club, his cousin, Cecil Liddell, revealed a successful intelligence operation that involved bugging senior German officers who were held as prisoners of war in a country house on the northern edge of London called Trent House—harvesting what the Germans thought were private conversations. They repeatedly referred to Hitler as "the carpet-biter," confirming his tempestuous moments of intoxicating rage, and expressed frustration about his interference in the final day of Dunkirk when he ordered the Wehrmacht to hold back. Lascelles learned that they complained that "but for Hitler's contrary orders, they could have concentrated enough artillery to make our embarkation impossible." Instead of destruction, Hitler wanted peace with Britain, ideally facilitated through emissaries to figures like Edward in Portugal, and he clearly thought it was possible.[90]

In this respect, Edward's temporizing in Lisbon perhaps makes him an accidental hero. The tantalizing possibilities he offered Hitler provided a moment of fascinating distraction at a critical point in the war, and they may have saved many British lives at Dunkirk. Hitler had obsessed about Edward for years, scheming to marry him to a minor German royal as early as 1934. Hitler had always displayed a habit of hesitation, and Edward's own behavior in June and July exacerbated it. As Michael Bloch has persuasively argued, it is no coincidence that, on August 1, the very day the Windsors sailed westward from

Lisbon, Hitler, after weeks keeping his generals waiting, finally issued his Directive No. 17, accelerating the air war against England.[91]

Whatever the Windsors' collective inner thoughts or allegiances, the German plots to use them for the purposes of the Third Reich were real. What would Churchill have done if they had not embarked on the *Excalibur* and set sail in early August? What if they had headed back to Spain, or even to Berlin? Against the backdrop of the Battle of Britain, these were desperate times.

10

War in the Americas

Might be kidnapped.
—The Duke of Windsor, 1941

In the summer and autumn of 1940, Britain was fighting for its life. France, the Netherlands, and Belgium had already fallen to the Nazis, leaving the southeast coastline vulnerable to attack. The German Luftwaffe filled the skies overhead, designed to force Churchill's surrender or, failing that, soften Britain up for an invasion across the Channel. Bombs hit Buckingham Palace, narrowly missing King George VI and Queen Elizabeth. The Royal Air Force famously won the battle but, for the next year, the empire and Commonwealth fought on alone against the odds, holding out only because of a vital but vulnerable chain of supply crossing the Atlantic.

This support from President Franklin D. Roosevelt, often in the face of domestic criticism, was essential. The United States was not yet in the war, and American public opinion tilted toward isolationism; many did not want to get dragged into a bloody conflict on the other side of a vast ocean. Churchill was therefore fighting on two fronts: a military campaign in Europe, to hold off a Nazi invasion; and a deeper political struggle, often conducted by covert means, to maintain American material support.

The first shot in this clandestine contest was fired back in the early summer of 1939, before war was even declared. George and Elizabeth set out on a long tour of Canada, initiated by Governor General Lord Tweedsmuir—better known as John Buchan the spy novelist and author of *The 39 Steps*, who had worked on British propaganda during the First World War.[1] The royal couple spent their final week in the United States hoping to generate support for the coming war.[2] They visited Mount Vernon, once George Washington's estate, on June 9 and the New York World Fair the next day. They then dined at Roosevelt's estate at Hyde Park in New York State, during which a smiling and relaxed Roosevelt served hotdogs, smoked turkey, and strawberry shortcake.[3]

The British worried that the royal couple would be poorly received. George and Elizabeth were accompanied everywhere by their two detectives as well as the US Secret Service, and they potentially faced "unfriendly demonstrations" caused by those who were "suspicions that Britain is continually scheming to involve the United States in its European troubles."[4]

But such protests failed to materialize. The visit was instead a massive triumph and had huge psychological significance for the king and queen, who were new to large-scale public engagements. For the first time, they far outshone their glitzier celebrity rivals, the duke and duchess of Windsor. Queen Elizabeth later observed emphatically, "That tour made us."[5]

In May 1940, the British covert psychological campaign in North America stepped up a gear. In New York, a Canadian MI6 officer named William Stephenson established a secret organization, British Security Coordination (BSC). A secret service department store providing a home for the burgeoning undercover organizations inside the United States, BSC operated from the thirty-fifth and thirty-sixth floors of Rockefeller Center throughout the Second World War. This prime real estate was only the tip of the iceberg, since some three thousand people were engaged in its operations across the continent. Notable secret operatives and collaborators included Noël Coward, Roald Dahl, Ian Fleming, and the philosophers Freddie Ayer and Isaiah Berlin.[6]

Ernest Cuneo, a newspaper editor and enthusiastic Anglophile, summed up BSC activities perfectly. "Throughout the neutral Americas, and especially in the US," he admitted, "it ran espionage agents, tampered with the mails, tapped telephones, smuggled propaganda into the country, disrupted public gatherings, covertly subsidized newspapers, radios and organizations, perpetrated forgeries—even palming one off on the President of the United States—violated the alien registration act, shanghaied sailors numerous times, and possibly murdered one or two persons in this country."[7]

On top of all this, BSC helped to create the forerunner of the Central Intelligence Agency. In 1940, America had no centralized foreign intelligence service. Stephenson worked closely with Roosevelt's friend, Colonel William J. Donovan, to create the Office of Strategic Services, which undertook both human espionage and sabotage, modeling itself closely on British activities.[8] The diminutive Stephenson was dubbed "Little Bill" while the larger Donovan was "Big Bill," and they became firm friends. Donovan, like Stephenson, was staunchly anti-Nazi, and his conviction that Britain would hold out against Germany, underpinned by repeat visits to London to tour secret service headquarters and meet the king, strongly influenced Roosevelt's thinking.[9]

Within hours of his first arrival in the summer of 1940, Donovan went to Buckingham Palace. After a hearty welcome from George, the conversation quickly turned to secret intelligence. The king showed Donovan a single flimsy sheet—a deciphered message from Hitler to his field commanders about the invasion of Britain—explaining it had come from "most secret sources." George knew not to share the precise secret of Bletchley Park with Donovan, but the American quickly worked out that Britain had so much inside information on the German high command that they must have had some success intercepting its communications. Although the source was left unspoken, Hitler's message revealed both his disappointment at the failure of his many peace overtures and his intention to invade and "eliminate England as a base for the prosecution of war against Germany."[10]

Discussing this intelligence, George assured Donovan that Britain would hold out in the air, making Hitler hesitate, adding that Buckingham Palace was now a target for bomber raids. Equally importantly, Donovan concluded that the Royal Family had no plans to run away.[11] He reported all this back to President Roosevelt, countering the more defeatist assessments of US isolationists.

British intelligence work in America was awkward, complicated, and dangerous. On one hand, BSC used disinformation and covert political warfare against American isolationists.[12] On the other hand, MI6 had to work closely with the FBI to battle Nazi agents in Latin America and the Caribbean.[13]

A vast mail-opening operation located in New York and Bermuda proved particularly valuable. The American authorities grumbled about it at first, but eagerly cooperated once they saw the fantastic haul of intelligence it generated.[14] Bermuda and neighboring islands in the Caribbean were a vast communications nexus, with real intelligence opportunities. Starting in 1940, some twelve hundred staff operated the main censorship center from a sprawling pink building, the Hamilton Princess Hotel, on the Bermudan shoreline.[15] The Pan-American Clipper Service ran from New York via Bermuda to Lisbon, carrying most air mail passing from the United States to Germany. Other islands carried German mail to South America. Secretly opening it uncovered Axis spies operating in the Western Hemisphere and also allowed MI6 to keep its finger on the pulse of public opinion in neutral America.[16]

The MI6 chief in the region was the formidable Harford Montgomery Hyde. He had begun his intelligence career as a mail opener, learning the trade from his boss, "Steam Kettle Bill," in the censor's office in Liverpool during the First World War. Now he presided over a vast operation. His censors processed 100 mailbags a day containing some 200,000 letters, of which they checked 15,000 daily for microdots or secret ink. In late July 1940, MI6 transferred a crack unit from Gibraltar commanded by Hyde's friend, Humphrey Cotton Minchin, which used special equipment to open and reseal mail without a trace.[17] The machinery did not always work perfectly. On one occasion, the team opened a letter sent from a German woman to her lover in Argentina enclosing a lock of pubic hair. They lost the hair and replaced it with bristles from a broom![18]

As the effort gathered pace, the colonial secretary told governors to expect an influx of intelligence officers to the region. They included Lieutenant Commander J. C. D. Harington, who, based in Jamaica, also covered British Honduras and the Bahamas.[19] Years later, he told his family over dinner that his most important wartime task was covering two particular new arrivals in the Bahamas: the duke and duchess of Windsor.[20]

Edward and Wallis set out across the Atlantic in early August 1940 on the American liner *Excalibur*. They were now out of sight, but not out of mind. They had expected to call in on New York en route, the ship's normal destination, and do some shopping, but the Foreign Office had other ideas. London offered to pay the shipping company the full costs of diverting the ship to the Caribbean, estimated at somewhere over $15,000. The Windsors did not go straight to the Bahamas, but first visited the island of Bermuda, which was fast becoming Britain's regional intelligence center. They stayed with the governor, Denis Bernard, and soon became "something of an embarrassment at Government House."[21] According to Hyde, they brought with them fifty-eight pieces of luggage (and three dogs), but Wallis still moaned that she did not have enough clothes. Hyde later met them in Nassau, where their baggage had been reinforced by fourteen additional pieces, including a trailer. "Every refugee has a trailer" was Wallis's sage comment.[22]

Habitual big spenders, they quickly made trouble from their far-flung outpost.[23] With the British population at home plunged into wartime rationing and austerity, the Windsors demanded huge sums to refurbish their own Government House in the Bahamas, which they considered distinctly unfashionable.[24] British officials were shocked at the extravagance.[25] But back in London, Churchill arranged for Hugh Dalton, minister for economic warfare, to suspend wartime currency regulations so that Wallis could send 10,000 francs back to German-occupied France to settle their affairs. Dalton noted that Churchill "always had a soft spot for the Duke."[26]

Within days of their arrival, Lord Lothian, Britain's ambassador in Washington, sounded a warning note. Support from the United States was on a knife edge and, he argued, it was "most important" to avoid the view that Edward was "not taking his duties in the Bahamas entirely seriously." The Americans rightly associated Edward and Wallis with "frivolity and extravagance," something that was likely to provoke "sharp criticism and disillusionment" with the British cause. Unfortunately, no one in London had much traction with the bitter and arrogant Windsors—not the foreign secretary, not Churchill, not even Edward's old friend Walter Monckton.[27] Any warning would go unheeded.

The Caribbean was far from the idyllic and trouble-free destination for which some had hoped. The whole region became a playground for agents, gunrunners, and neutralist millionaires on the make.[28] Indeed, the Windsors' ship the *Excalibur* was at the center of just such a scandal on its very next run through Bermuda and the Bahamas. In October, it was found to be carrying a huge haul of 500 contraband French impressionist paintings, including 270 by Renoir, 30 by Cezanne and 12 by Gauguin. Hyde took a strong interest, since the cargo was intended to raise much needed dollar currency for the Nazis. When the captain refused to open the ship's strong room, Hyde and a British naval team burned through the bulkhead with blowtorches and recovered the treasures. MI6 later turned the whole lot over to the National Gallery in Canada.[29]

Hyde now faced multiple kinds of Windsor trouble. Although countries like Brazil and Mexico swarmed with smugglers and Nazi spies, his main problem lay in the United States. Only 50 miles away, the Florida coast was a magnet for the rich and famous, just the sort of people with whom the loose-lipped Windsors loved to mingle. MI6 worried about who they would meet, what they would say, and whether they would encourage American isolationism.

As long as Britain appeared to be doggedly resisting the Nazis, Roosevelt would support them with money and supplies. If Britain wavered, or looked as if it would fall, Roosevelt, under strong pressure from isolationists, might withdraw his support. This is precisely why the king had met Colonel Donovan, Roosevelt's fact-finder, only months before, to bolster the idea of stalwart British resistance. The secret battle for the president's mind was intensifying. Needless to say, the Germans were keen for Edward to speak defeatism with Roosevelt. Alarmingly, Roosevelt was also keen to speak with Edward.

In September 1940, Churchill was incensed to learn that his chief diplomat in Washington, Lord Lothian, had raised the possibility of Edward meeting Roosevelt. He feared that Edward would indulge the president—and anyone else who would listen—in neutralist and pacifist talk, with potentially disastrous consequences. Sternly, the foreign secretary, Lord Halifax, told Lothian that any meeting "should be avoided for as long as possible."[30] Lothian insisted that Roosevelt was keen to meet Edward, and that it was a mere social call.[31] The American press, however, knew it was far more than that. One report put it bluntly: "President Roosevelt will try to bring about peace negotiations between great British and the axis powers; . . . the duke of Windsor may also play a part in this attempt." It ominously added that "the government sent him to the Bahamas to get him out of the way, but he accepted the appointment so that he could be within easy reach of the USA."[32]

Things went from bad to worse. In November, Downing Street was disconcerted to discover that Roosevelt was planning a tour of the Caribbean the next month and positively yearned for a royal audience. British officials plotted to keep the two men apart, asking Lothian to tell Roosevelt that we "discourage" any meeting and ensuring that Edward was deliberately "left in ignorance of the suggestion."[33]

Working with figures inside Edward's household, they contrived to fill the duke's diary by packing him off to Miami. Edward was told that it was supremely important that the governor of the Bahamas go there to present a cup at the local horse races.[34] Only after the trip was arranged, they hoped, would he realize that he would miss Roosevelt. The British ruse failed, since Roosevelt managed to catch up with the Windsors by using a ruse of his own.[35] He fooled the British by telling them their schedules now seemed out of line. "I am very sorry," Roosevelt added, "that I shall probably miss him."[36] In fact, he was so keen to meet Edward that he secretly sent a US naval aircraft to fly him out to join him.[37]

Roosevelt viewed appeasers as his political enemies. After winning a historic third term in the White House, he told King George that "there is absolutely no question that the appeasement element, the pro-Germans, the communists and the total isolationists did their very best for my defeat." He promised that he would now send every bit of spare military equipment to Britain, adding that "I have what we call a 'hunch'—not necessarily based on cold figures, that you have turned the corner" and that "luck will be more and more with you."[38] Despite this, he remained keen to hear the alternative point of view from George's older brother.

Roosevelt and Edward exchanged more than social pleasantries. What the president did not tell the duke was that, at that very moment, he was pondering the possibility of another deposed king, his brother George, arriving in the Western Hemisphere in the event of a successful cross-Channel invasion. Roosevelt knew about the plan to evacuate the Royal Family to Canada. He did not like it at all, and instead wanted George to be made governor of Bermuda, an even more remote outpost than the Bahamas. Roosevelt perhaps thought that the idea of two former British kings—each with his own little Atlantic island—was rather amusing.[39]

Predictably, Edward and Wallis were soon spending time with the wealthiest resident of the Bahamas: the Swedish multimillionaire Axel Wenner-Gren, the owner of Electrolux, then the leading brand in both vacuum cleaners and refrigerator technology. They had camped out with him for two months during the expensive refurbishment of Government House.[40] In December, he had ferried them to Miami on his magnificent yacht.

Wenner-Gren was an appeaser—a self-styled peacemaker. He was friendly with Hermann Göring, whose first wife was a Swede, and had acted as an intermediary between Göring and the British and American governments. Edward's predecessor as governor had told MI5 that Wenner-Gren had held "extremely confidential" conversations with Neville Chamberlain and was a friend of Roosevelt. He was also closely connected to the Windsors' previous sponsor, Charles Bedaux, and, like him, was soon added to the "trading with the enemy" blacklist. Yet his peace efforts had proved unsuccessful, with all parties regarding him as a self-promoting nuisance.[41]

By late 1940, Wenner-Gren's recent visits to Rome and Berlin convinced Guy Liddell, deputy director of MI5, that he "may be playing the German game."[42] Liddell was alarmed but knew that Edward and Wallis would ignore any warning about their wealthy new friend if it came from London. Instead, he approached the American ambassador to Sweden and arranged for a warning to reach Edward from the Americans.[43] MI6 was also suspicious. Stephenson reported that Wenner-Gren was "friendly to Nazis, and associated with appeasement circles." What bothered London most was that it simply looked bad in the American press and risked undermining the British cause. On December 11, the colonial secretary warned Edward that the press was saying that he had traveled to Miami in the yacht of "Goering's pal."[44] If anything, American suspicions of Wenner-Gren were even more intense, though exactly what he had done to make the whiskers of the FBI twitch so vigorously is still not clear.[45]

Edward simply did not care. In London, this triggered an anxious debate over whether to show him classified intelligence to back up warnings about his new friend. On December 14, Alec Hardinge, George's private secretary, received the security file on Wenner-Gren and duly showed it to the king. They were so alarmed that Hardinge thought the government should warn Edward formally "against this man." Revealing his view of Edward as a slippery customer, he added that if there was ever any scandal in the future, the duke might claim he knew nothing about Wenner-Gren, "whether it was true or not."[46]

Edward needed proof. Remarkably, given the duke's past record, Stewart Menzies, the chief of MI6, finally agreed to send him this classified material. Alec Cadogan, the head of the Foreign Office, noted "he may not be impressed by it, but he will at least have been warned."[47] Churchill repeatedly ordered the duke to stay away from Wenner-Gren, who was "in communication with the enemy."[48]

Bizarrely, the Windsors were now both targets of surveillance and also customers of the same sort of intelligence material. They read intercepted material on Wenner-Gren, while British intelligence intercepted material on their own conversations. American guests who visited the Windsors loved to brag to their friends about having met royalty and so reported every detail—every conversation—to them in letters. The massive MI6 mail censorship operation ensured that these details fell straight into the hands of British intelligence.[49] The Windsors also knew this, since hundreds of people were employed in the operation. Indeed, with the near cessation of tourism, the arrival of a veritable army of stealthy letter-openers in the region, complete with their steam kettles, had boosted the economy. But once again, Edward and Wallis did not seem to care.[50]

Perhaps the Windsors thought the only way to preserve their sanity was to see surveillance as a huge joke. The FBI had now begun to monitor the Windsors as well, and one FBI source emphasized that Edward was well aware that his staff was reporting back to London:

> He said that on one occasion when they were at a dinner party the Duke had joined in singing "There'll Always Be an England" and then in an aside had asked if there would always be a Scotland Yard. . . . He also stated that at a dinner at Government House where the Duke and Duchess were piped in, after being seated the Duchess made some remark to a dinner guest and then turned to the piper and made the statement, "You can also report that to Downing Street," which indicated to everyone present that they thought the piper was some kind of spy for England.[51]

Strangely, this did not cause them to moderate what they said to their dinner guests; indeed, rather the reverse. One of their more powerful visitors was the wealthy American Frazier Jelke, who seems to have known Edward quite well, and met him repeatedly. In March 1941, at dinner, Edward said it would be "very ill-advised of America to enter the war against Germany as Europe was finished anyway." Several nights later, Wallis told Jelke that if the US entered the war, this country would go down in history as "the greatest sucker of all time." Jelke came away with the impression that they both admired Hitler. MI6 read it all.[52]

Between April 18 and 23, 1941, Edward and Wallis spent five days in Palm Beach, a wealthy town on the East Coast of Florida known for its glitzy estates and white sandy beaches. Roosevelt seems to have ordered a veritable orgy of surveillance on the Windsors as they mingled with the ultrarich over chic cocktails.

Roosevelt chose Adolf Berle, a close confidant and assistant secretary at the State Department, to manage the surveillance.[53] He, like the FBI head J. Edgar Hoover, had been a staunch opponent of British intelligence activities against

US isolationism, fearing that BSC had tried to smear him. Now, in a strange turn of events, Berle found himself overseeing an intelligence operation targeting a key advocate of defeatism and isolationism. He confirmed that an FBI agent was to "exercise discreet observation" when Edward visited Miami, and that "a Special Agent to the Department of State" was acting "as personal guard." It was not enough, for Berle added that "a wider and less obvious coverage is desirable."[54]

The FBI took the operation seriously. It recorded that it had "issued instructions for an agent to be assigned to assist in the watch of Duke of Windsor on his visit to Palm beach. . . . Mr Tamm was handling the matter personally."[55] Tamm was one of two deputies to J. Edgar Hoover.

The FBI was keen to secure more intelligence on the Windsors, but ironically their biggest impediment was the British Special Branch. On the ground, the operation was run by the special agent in charge, Percy Wyly, a crack shot who had been personal assistant to Hoover. He explained that the Special Branch bodyguards were proving a problem. They made "it impossible to get within 100 yards of the Duke for surveillance purposes." Perhaps because of lingering tensions with BSC, the FBI was under strict instructions not to notify Scotland Yard "of our activities."[56]

Unable to get physically close enough to the duke, Wyly ensured that he had "all communications covered." This particular phrase, part of professional espionage parlance, suggests the use of microphones as well as telephone taps.[57] This is doubly interesting since Congress had recently restricted the FBI's use of such intrusive surveillance methods. Clearly, the Windsors were a special case. The FBI also interviewed their known friends and associates.[58]

The FBI's extensive intelligence operation proved unnecessary. The views of the Windsors, which British intelligence had gone to great lengths to keep quiet, were soon in plain sight. In early May, on returning from Miami, Edward gave a remarkable interview on the world situation to *Liberty* magazine, a popular American weekly, in which he advocated a peace deal with Germany. He suggested that there was no real substance to Anglo-American friendship and that the haughty British looked down on Americans as "colonial and provincials." He added that Britain would probably never repay its American loans and that the US would be better abstaining from the conflict and instead stepping in to mediate at some later point.[59]

The reaction in London was incandescent. In staggeringly undiplomatic tones, Foreign Office officials ranted to their new secretary of state, Anthony Eden, that "the Duke of Windsor is a notoriously pro-Nazi. He is also a heavy drinker, and what few wits he had have wilted." "He should," one diplomat continued without pausing for breath, "of course never have received a post like this, where, despite his intellectual insignificance, he is capable of much harm, as is now clear." Eden agreed that the interview could hardly have been worse.[60] More minders were clearly needed.[61]

MI6 knew that while the Windsors had eluded the Nazis' clutches in Spain and Portugal, German agents remained active in Latin America. British intelligence teams in the Caribbean doubled and redoubled to ensure that there could be no further plots to "liberate" Edward and Wallis from the island. It was for this reason that Hyde, the MI6 regional chief, made his way to the Bahamas in May 1941, where he intriguingly managed to solicit information from Edward's private secretary, Major Gray Phillips, "whom I have known personally for some years."[62] On his arrival, Hyde discovered that the Windsors were conducting much government business from their private residence. Secret files on Axel Wenner-Gren, Göring's friend, and other "individuals of security interest" were lying about in their accommodation for all to see. So much for London's decision to share MI6 intelligence with Edward.[63]

Hyde also spotted suspicious signs of Edward taking personal counter-surveillance a bit too seriously. He learned that "certain files," including ones on Wenner-Gren, were not to be shown to anyone without the duke's permission, and that Edward kept all the code and cypher books in his personal residence.[64] He was extremely concerned that his own correspondence should not be opened, and local officials insisted they had received "a direct order from HRH that his mail and that of his staff must not be censored."

But the net was tightening. Hyde decided to crank up the surveillance further and ordered his friend, Humphrey Cotton Minchin, the crack specialist in secret mail opening, away from Bermuda to take up the post of censor at Nassau.[65]

Hyde's main concern was not the files but personal security. He warned the duke that a German U-boat could "carry off Your Royal Highness and the Duchess and the rest of the occupants of Government House, before the Bahamians realised the island was being attacked." He followed this up with a warning to London about the severe danger of Edward being captured and used "as a puppet sovereign." He recommended more troops on the island, and even "an electrified fence around Government House." This dramatic request made its way through MI6 headquarters in New York and eventually ended up on Churchill's desk.[66] Edward was not keen on the suggestions, and protested that "local drunks would undoubtedly blunder into the fence and electrocute themselves."[67]

Meanwhile, Hyde had discovered that Wenner-Gren's yacht was secretly "heavily armed with bofors machine guns." He also received reports that the Swede was building an aerodrome and submarine base on his private island. In the mind of MI6, Wenner-Gren was taking on the character of a future Bond villain, with corporate interests in the globalized nebulae of the Caribbean and organized crime.[68] Hyde was concerned enough to send out two more operatives in quick succession. One began an "undercover" investigation into the millionaire's new crayfish canning plant at the west end of the island. The other overflew the island to look for signs of submarine base construction and then probed Wenner-Gren's staff, although they found nothing.[69]

Playing the victim, Edward dramatically told Hyde that he was "apprehensive that he might be kidnapped" from the Bahamas.[70] Apparently, his main fear was not being used as a puppet but instead "being traded for the release of Rudolf Hess," Hitler's deputy, who was being held after an ill-fated solo flight to Scotland.[71] MI6 was perhaps more worried that Edward would have been a willing target, voluntarily stepping onto a U-boat, maybe even from Wenner-Gren's mythical submarine base, after sending a coded message to his friends in Portugal.

In the early morning of Sunday, December 7, 1941, Japanese aircraft launched a surprise attack on Pearl Harbor, the US naval base in Hawaii. At a stroke, the subsequent US entry into the war ended the hopes of those on both sides of the Atlantic who had sought a compromise with Hitler. Dreams of appeasement became a distant shadow as rhetoric everywhere, even in America, turned to fighting on until total victory. That night, Churchill recalled how he "slept the sleep of the saved and thankful."[72]

Back in London, one-time appeaser King George VI was busily winning back the trust of the intelligence services. In a curious way, however, he did not always need access. George now had his own secret service, allowing the monarch, like Queen Victoria, King Edward VII, and King George V before him, to resort to a do-it-yourself approach. Through the royal families of Europe to whom he was related, he boasted a remarkable intelligence network of his own. Many of them were now refugees in London and were at the heart of governments in exile that powered the growing European network. These ersatz nations—most visibly the Dutch, the Norwegians, the Poles, and the French—were often run from slightly shabby hotels in Bayswater and Kensington, but their contacts were extraordinary.

George's use of his own private network could cause momentary surprises. One intelligence officer recorded that the king received a couple of bottles of 1941 burgundy, one of which he served to Churchill at one of their regular Tuesday luncheons "a deux." Churchill asked sharply how he had got hold of it, and was much put out to be told that "kings have their secrets too." Churchill had no idea that George was able to secure the wartime vintage from occupied France because his royal pilot, "Mouse" Fielden, also happened to fly missions for the Special Operations Executive, which Churchill had created—in his own words—"to set Europe ablaze." Fielden was dropping off secret agents in France but was wise enough not to return to the palace with an entirely empty aircraft.[73]

The members of the Royal Family were now flashing their military credentials. The young Princess Elizabeth would eventually be allowed to join the Auxiliary Territorial Service, spending time servicing military vehicles. Her cousin, Margaret Rhodes, living at Buckingham Palace for part of the war, chose a rather more exotic career. Initially joining the Women's Royal Naval Service, she quickly found herself mysteriously transferred to MI6. Each day she was, in her own words, "a small cog in the shadowy world of espionage," and by night she returned to sleep in the palace. Initially, she worked in the department controlling all MI6 personnel in the Middle East before moving to a more central role. "One of my daily tasks," she recalled, "was to read every single message transmitted by our spies all over the world." At just eighteen years of age, she enjoyed a ringside seat on the "above top secret" war; for example, she knew "all about Germany's wartime race for nuclear weapons and the planned raid on the heavy water plant in Norway."[74]

Rhodes was also aware of MI6 intelligence supplied by brave agents from plants on the Baltic coast, where the Germans developed their long-range missiles. Later in the war, one such rocket would miss MI6 headquarters by only 100 yards. Margaret dived to the floor as it whizzed past, killing 121 people in the nearby Guards Chapel in Wellington Barracks. Although living at Buckingham Palace was very convenient for MI6 headquarters, being "just a short walk across the park," it was also a more dangerous place than MI6—the palace was bombed nine times during the war.[75]

Increasingly, George summoned Hugh Dalton, ministerial chief of covert action, to Buckingham Palace to brief him on escapades of the Special Operations Executive.[76] One of his favorites was Operation Rubble. In 1940, the Nazis hoped to cripple the British war effort by blockading Swedish cargo ships containing ball bearings, steel, and tools vital for making arms and equipment. Dalton's newly formed Special Operations Executive was asked to rescue these badly needed supplies and so set about creating a secret team to steal the ships. This was a dangerous mission, and George followed it in real time knowing that the operatives might not return. The aged transport ships outran the Luftwaffe and German navy; George gloried in its success.[77] Hugh Dalton, a Labour minister in Churchill's coalition government, loved his trips to the palace and confessed himself a republican and antimonarchist "in every country but my own."[78]

The king was increasingly fascinated by the secret war. It offered glimpses of success at a dark time during the war, and so he demanded increasingly frequent updates, even when away from London. Accordingly, engineers installed the latest scrambler phones at Balmoral and Sandringham so that his staff could provide updates—they noted that this was "a remarkable invention, and is said to be perfectly secure."[79]

George did not always need to turn to ministers for stories of secret success against the Axis. One member of the Royal Family closest to the secret world worked at the cutting edge of covert warfare: David Bowes-Lyon. He was the queen's brother and a member of the Political Warfare Executive, an organization so new that he had actually named it. Based at Woburn Abbey, a large country house in Bedfordshire, and known colloquially as "Pee-Wee," this organization engaged in black propaganda, psychological warfare, and political subversion under the control of Dalton.

In late 1941, Bowes-Lyon invited his sister, the queen, and George to visit him and inspect the work of the new department for themselves. On November 19, they arrived at Woburn Abbey and listened to a remarkable presentation that was recorded and can still be heard today. The Political Warfare Executive humbly presents, the king and queen were told, "the free voices of Europe, a picture in sound of the use of a new force in your majesties' service." Bowes-Lyon then recounted the latest secret service ideas to his royal relatives:

> I am here to introduce one of Britain's secret armies. An army which strikes from within the enemy's lines. You are going to hear the voices of this army— the voices of the black radio stations of Europe. At all hours of the day and all hours of the night they are transmitting messages of defiance, encouragement and hope to the victims of Hitler. The first of these voices was heard a year ago in Germany. A patriotic German calling on true Germans to defy Hitler. This was followed immediately by a group of German socialists who were calling other German socialists to join with them in their fight for the socialist revolution. Today there are nineteen different stations.[80]

To their delight, the king and queen were then treated to recordings of German subversives denouncing Hitler by radio.

David Bowes-Lyon worked closely with Dalton and was heavily involved in the political struggles over the control of sabotage and political warfare. Dalton had his own royal connections, because his father had been a chaplain to Queen Victoria and tutor to King George V. In 1941, he had noted that while the king knew a little about economic warfare, he knew next to nothing about sabotage and secret agents. By the next year, George had found out about these more exciting activities—and wanted to know more, especially "what sort of people they are whom we use." He had also just discovered that Bowes-Lyon was being sent to Washington to work with Donovan's embryonic Office of Strategic Services.[81]

On Tuesday, November 3, 1942, Churchill was late for lunch at Buckingham Palace. The prime minister visited the monarch every Tuesday at lunchtime, but on this particular day Churchill did not appear, and as the minutes turned into hours, eventually his limousine arrived and he scurried in, carrying a battered red dispatch box. Confronting the king and queen together, he blurted out the words "I bring you victory." The queen recalled that they looked at each other and thought "Is he going mad?" because they had not heard those words since the war began—everything had been retrenchment, retreat, or complete disaster.[82]

Churchill was quite correct. His authority was Bletchley Park, and he produced two top-secret decrypts of messages from Rommel to Hitler. These were especially doleful and told of Rommel's defeat in the battle for Egypt and forecast the German retreat from North Africa. He had run out of gasoline, supplies, transportation, tanks, everything—and disaster loomed. The king was radiant, and all of them sat basking in glory. They realized that the Battle of El Alamein, fought to prevent the Axis from venturing into Egypt, was not just the turning of the tide in the desert war but also the beginning of the end for Hitler. The king noted in his diary: "What rejoicing there will be."[83]

Having once been arch-appeasers, the king and the queen now shared the innermost secrets of the war—even Bletchley Park. They also shared the inevitable paranoia that they brought. The king worried about becoming ill and accidentally blurting out secrets that might jeopardize the war. The queen was later asked if she was allowed to know the king's secrets. She replied that "he told me everything." This was partly about the loneliness of command. "There was only us there." The burden of secrecy they shared together was heavy, and years later she recalled how "even now I feel nervous sometimes, about talking about such things." One of the effects of being on the inside track and receiving a constant newsfeed from Bletchley Park was knowing what was really going on. People in the palace were "talking nonsense," but you "couldn't say a word about it."[84]

King George was gradually learning about new aspects of his secret service: black radios, deception, even the beginnings of electronic warfare. Now, with members of the royal household and even his family involved in the secret fight, he wanted to know more—and perhaps even join in a little of the action himself. His family connections provided the perfect opportunity and now, with the tide of war beginning to turn, he headed for the battlefront.

11

The End of the
Second World War

Thank the boys in the backroom.
—King George VI, 1943

On June 7, 1943, a month before the invasion of Sicily, General Lion stepped down from a Royal Air Force (RAF) York transportation aircraft onto the dusty tarmac in Algiers, a busy hub in the accelerating war against the Axis. His flights, first from Britain to Gibraltar and then onward to the Mediterranean, had been shrouded in secrecy and necessitated extremely elaborate protection plans. Indeed, the visit even warranted its own deception plan, called Operation Loader, with the British authorities spreading false stories that a secretary of state was en route to visit General Eisenhower in order to mask the real identity of this shadowy yet high-value passenger.

Even the aircraft was special. It was Churchill's personal, and specially adapted, airplane. Named *Ascalon*, after the sword Saint George used to slay the dragon, it boasted extra cabin space, a telephone for talking with the flight crew, a table with an ashtray, the latest newspapers, and a bar. Designers even added an electrically heated toilet seat, although Churchill found it too hot and so it was eventually disconnected.[1]

The mysterious General Lion was none other than King George VI. And even Buckingham Palace had taken part in the deception by making a false announcement that the king had gone away to visit the fleet at Portsmouth.[2] His trip was so secret that the real secretaries of state had no idea about it until he safely arrived in North Africa.[3]

And with good reason. Churchill had made the same journey shortly before George. Ever the showman, his own secrecy was quickly blown, and German pilots swarmed over the Bay of Biscay waiting for his return leg. Taking no chances, they shot down everything in the area while Churchill was in the vicinity, including a passenger plane operating a regular service from neutral Lisbon.[4] On this aircraft were Leslie Howard, perhaps Britain's most famous wartime actor, and his accountant, Alfred Chenhalls, who—bald, rotund, and rather fond of cigars—bore more than a passing resemblance to Churchill.[5]

Churchill knew his own visit had stirred up a hornet's nest; and the king's trip, only five days later, using the same precarious route, was highly risky. The most senior civil servants in the land insisted that all necessary precautions had been taken "to avoid identification of the principal passenger."[6] Privately, Churchill feared the worst and even discussed what the pilot should do if enemy fighters successfully hit the king's plane: whether it was better for him to ditch in the sea, or for the plane to crash-land in neutral Spain or Portugal.[7] As the war climaxed, the prime minister and king played a ludicrous game of competitive battlefield tourism, all while rebuking the other for being too important to engage in such foolhardy ventures. Churchill would even write to George in dramatic prose about what to do "in case of my death in this journey I am about to undertake."[8]

The deception worked, and King George landed safely. He was met personally by General Eisenhower, the commander of Allied operations in North Africa, with whom he had already established a strong friendship. They drove from the airport at Maison Blanche, southeast of the city, to Eisenhower's beautiful villa that his forces had requisitioned from the Vichy French after a major Allied victory the previous year. For all the intense secrecy and worry about George's personal safety, the visit was a great success.

Once there, the biggest frustrations came from within his own party. George's private secretary, Alec Hardinge, whom he had inherited from his brother after the abdication, continually fussed and fretted. He offered George ridiculous advice not to visit the Americans and plunged into detailed discussions with Harold Macmillan, the British minister in Algiers, about the politics of the French Resistance and the possibilities of deals with Italian "quislings"—whom George visibly despised. Macmillan dismissed Hardinge as "idle and supercilious"; and George, growing in confidence by the day, ignored his advice and visited all the Allied troops.[9]

Although it was Hardinge who had first tipped off George about the possibility of the abdication back in 1936, tensions between the king and his private secretary had been growing for years. Hardinge had thought him ignorant about public affairs and had not forgiven him for his love of appeasement. Meanwhile, George was now more assertive and, to Hardinge's shock, he fired him shortly after they returned home. His replacement was his deputy, Alan "Tommy" Lascelles.[10]

One of the king's top priorities was to visit Massingham, the headquarters of the Special Operations Executive (SOE) in North Africa. Created at a former French luxury pleasure resort called "Club de Pins" some 15 miles outside Algiers, Massingham was one of the first and most successful forward bases for dirty warfare. It served as a command center and training base for most clandestine operations across the western Mediterranean and south-western Europe, including in France and Italy. It played a major role in the liberation of Corsica and facilitated the secret armistice negotiations that led to the Italian surrender in September 1943. Later, officers based there instigated several large uprisings deep behind enemy lines during the Allied invasion of southern France. Throughout the war, Massingham dispatched 400 agents and 14,000 crates of arms to the French Resistance.[11]

Given the secrecy and deception surrounding the trip, George arrived at short notice. Douglas Dodds-Parker, a senior SOE officer at Massingham, assigned him the only spare room available in his own villa, which also served as the officers' mess; it was a remarkable structure set on a remote beach and projected out into the sea on a series of piles.[12] Affable, yet highly astute, Dodds-Parker was enjoying a distinguished—if secret—career with SOE. He had found himself involved in the planning to assassinate Reinhard Heydrich, acting Reich protector of Bohemia and Moravia, and later issued a pistol to one of SOE's French instructors, who would kill Admiral Darlan, a senior Vichy figure and the highest-ranking officer in Algeria before the Allies arrived, on Christmas Eve 1942.[13]

Now Dodds-Parker found himself in the company of the king. After a refreshing swim, during which they were guarded by some of SOE's toughest operatives, they sat alone together for a while as George opened up about the strains of the last few years and how much he had valued the support of his family. This risky trip to Algeria was his first solo mission overseas since 1940. Over four sunny afternoons at Massingham, George toured the station and its extensive training grounds, meeting Britain's experts in sabotage and irregular warfare. He watched fighting with daggers, parachute training, and even the detonation of improvised bombs. SOE staff members received strict instructions to carry out all their duties as normal when in the presence of the king so that he could get a detailed sense of ordinary life in a most unordinary field station—and he loved every minute of it.[14]

As much as he was enjoying himself, George had business to do. His main purpose for being there was to present a medal to Paulin Colonna d'Istria honoring his daring missions launched from a British submarine, HMS *Trident*, into enemy-occupied Corsica to reorganize the resistance.[15] A former police chief on Corsica and the son of a leading noble family, he had single-handedly transformed the local government into a secret underground network, paving the way for further successful networks in southern France and Italy.[16] Among the motley ranks of the resistance fighters were Poles, Italians, elderly Spanish communists, and plenty of American special operatives, including the film star

Douglas Fairbanks Jr. On the last day of George's visit, this curious international underground army turned out to cheer his departure.[17]

A week after arriving in Massingham, King George personally insisted on visiting Malta.[18] He knew that the civilian population on the small Mediterranean island had suffered horribly during a brutal siege that had lasted two years. He also understood that their bravery had proven critical in putting the squeeze on Field Marshal Rommel's Nazi supply lines, enabling only a few ships to reach Tripoli during the last months of 1942.

Here the work of Bletchley Park was especially crucial. With decrypts of German communications revealing that the Axis was running out of supplies in North Africa, Axis forces became trapped in a pincer movement during the spring of 1943, between British advances from Egypt and the Americans who had landed further west.[19] German forces were already in a "dire condition" by early April and, as the Allies closed in, Rommel fled, leaving 250,000 troops to surrender in Tunisia on May 12. Church bells rang out across Britain. Together with the Battle of Stalingrad, which had ended two months earlier, this marked the turning of the tide in the Second World War. George personally wanted to thank the Maltese people for playing a valiant part in this victory.[20]

Still subject to air attacks and occasional commando raids, Malta was a dangerous place to visit. Nevertheless, on June 20, George sailed under the cover of darkness aboard HMS *Aurora*, accompanied by Harold Macmillan and the chief of the naval staff, Admiral Andrew Cunningham. Arriving in Malta the following morning, the *Aurora* had to weave its way into the harbor through a graveyard of sunken ships. Wildly cheering crowds greeted George as he waved from a special platform constructed on the ship's bridge. "You have made the people of Malta very happy today, Sir," observed the governor gratefully as the day drew to a close. The king replied, "But I have been the happiest man in Malta today!"[21]

At the end of June, with George safely back in Britain, MI5 deliberately leaked news of his successful morale-raising tour to the Germans. They used Agent Cheese as the channel. An Italian of Jewish parentage, Cheese was a double agent who served as one of Britain's top deception operatives in wartime Cairo. He, and his fictional subagent created by MI5, had been cleverly feeding a mixture of false information and so-called chicken feed, information that is true but not damaging, to the Nazis since 1941.[22] Cheese's "intelligence" about the king's secret visit was classic chicken feed. It bolstered his credibility with the Nazis while doing no damage itself; but it also tormented them with the knowledge that two of their most prized assassination targets had visited the region and escaped unscathed.[23] The Mediterranean was no longer an Axis sea; it now belonged to the Allies.

George's sojourn in an SOE headquarters was not the only secret aspect of his Mediterranean tour. His meetings with planners covered the forthcoming invasion of Sicily and the elaborate deception schemes, which included the famous Operation Mincemeat, later portrayed by Hollywood as *The Man Who Never Was*. This imaginatively involved dropping a dead body carrying false plans off the shores of Spain, in the hope that it would wash up on a beach, reach the Germans, and disinform them that the main Allied thrust would come through Greece. Remarkably, it worked. After the successful invasion of Sicily in July 1943, the king wasted little time in thanking the "boys in the backroom" for the elaborate schemes, to which he attributed such little loss of life on the Allied side.[24]

More than anything, it was his four days with Dodds-Parker and SOE at Massingham that had fired the king's imagination, so much so that he wanted his whole family to see something of their extraordinary activities. Accordingly, the next autumn, the king and queen, accompanied by the two young princesses, took a short train ride north from London into the Bedfordshire countryside. Alighting at a quiet station in the quaint market town of Sandy, the Royal Family transferred into an unmarked saloon car to take them the last few miles to a small RAF station at nearby Tempsford. Unbeknown to the locals, the aerodrome here housed the special duties squadrons that flew MI6 and SOE agents into Europe and was superintended by "Mouse" Fielden, who also doubled as head of the royal flight and thus was a member of the king's household.[25]

Nearby Gaynes Hall, a handsome Georgian mansion, served as the holding station for these agents. It was a secret service hotel of sorts, where foreign nationals waited nervously for weather conditions suitable for Mouse and his team to drop them into occupied Europe. One of those working there recalled how much the queen loved the gadgets and agent toys. She was fascinated by the camouflaged exploding devices disguised to look like wine bottles, rocks, and logs—even stuffed rats and mice—that the resistance used to ambush the enemy. Her favorite gizmo was the exploding horse droppings that could be left innocently on a road but were powerful enough to destroy a vehicle; she was so excited by this that she rushed over to George persuading him to come and have a look. The details of agent clothing were no less fascinating; they were shown lipsticks, buttons, corks, and shaving brushes all made with hidden compartments for pills or microfilm. Shoelaces contained "giglis," or flexible saws, so agents could cut their way through wood or metal if imprisoned, while heels and soles contained compasses and silk maps. Most sinister were the tiny drills for implanting a cyanide capsule inside the back tooth of an agent if required.[26]

With Sicily secured, the Italian campaign now lay ahead. This had been a highly contested matter, with Churchill wanting to invade Italy, which he saw as the soft underbelly of Europe, but the Americans had prioritized France. Italy eventually won out; and, shortly after the invasion in the autumn of 1943, the king spotted an opportunity. Far from being a passive observer of grand strategy, he wrote to Churchill expressing his desire to now see Greece and Yugoslavia liberated quickly. He had his own wartime priorities focused on the preservation of European royal houses in countries as far apart as Greece and Sweden. The possibility that Russia might sweep across the continent, eliminating the crowned heads of Europe, was already causing anxiety—a worry that Churchill, as an ardent monarchist, also shared.[27]

The turning point for the king's secret war occurred in July 1943 and was something of an accident. When he replaced his long-serving and rather stuffy private secretary Hardinge with Tommy Lascelles, little did he know that he was taking on a former secret service officer. Lascelles had spent the early part of the war working part-time for MI(R), a sabotage organization that was eventually incorporated in SOE, along with elements of MI6.[28] More importantly, Lascelles was close to two of his cousins, Guy and Cecil Liddell. The former was deputy head of MI5 and the latter was head of MI5's Irish section. Cecil was an excellent cello player, and all three got together for musical sessions, where they exchanged the latest secret service gossip. Lascelles was a massive intelligence fan. When the queen asked for his recommendations for evening reading to while away the Blitz, he sent her one of Eric Ambler's thrillers, *Epitaph for a Spy*.[29]

By 1943, every secret establishment and wonder weapon was on the royal tourist trail. The king and queen visited the "Dambusters." RAF 617 squadron was in training at Scampton in Lincolnshire ready for its famous mission, since immortalized in film, to attack German dams. They were briefed by none other than Guy Gibson and Barnes Wallis, who designed the purpose-built bouncing bomb and explained how it could skip across water and bounce into dams. After the raid, the king presented Gibson with the Victoria Cross, before he was killed in action in September 1944 during a raid on Germany.[30]

Even more secret things were to come. In October 1943, King George was briefed on one of the biggest secrets of all: the emerging plans for D-Day, known as Operation Overlord, and the liberation of France. The presentation did not go as expected, for George reacted uneasily and feared disaster. His

opinions clearly mattered; and, early the next year, Eisenhower discussed Overlord with him personally in an attempt to reassure the nervous monarch about
possible casualties.[31]

Perhaps because of these concerns, the authorities now chose to give
George an operational role in the highly sensitive deception plans that would
screen the D-Day landings and reduce risk. On March 2, 1944, two MI5 men
turned up at Buckingham Palace. Sitting in the office of the king's private secretary, Tommy Lascelles, they quietly explained "how the King's visits in the
next few months could assist in the elaborate cover scheme whereby we are
endeavouring to bamboozle the German Intelligence regarding the time and
place for 'Overlord.'"[32] As king, George had clearly come a long way from his
early days as an appeasement sympathizer and, over the course of the war, had
won the trust of the security establishment.

George was already broadly aware that Britain was running something
called the Double Cross, or XX, System. This was a deception operation led by
MI5, in which German agents in Britain were captured and turned, then fed
dummy information to their Abwehr controllers. The brains behind the operation were provided by John Masterman, ably assisted by people like Jonny
Bevan and T. A. R. Robertson, who had earlier spied on King Edward VIII.
Under their command, scores of people worked on this deception and were
effectively the conductors of a vast orchestra.[33] Another was Dennis Wheatley,
one of the go-betweens who linked the palace and the Cabinet Office. Wheatley was also the king's favorite thriller writer, and George insisted on reading
all his planning papers. Indeed, George was surprised by how often his favorite writers and entertainers suddenly appeared in a secret wartime role. Noël
Coward, the king and queen's favorite entertainer, had also enjoyed a secret
wartime role in Paris.[34]

MI5 now deployed this vast deception mechanism to cover D-Day. As
Churchill said, sometimes the truth is so precious that it must be covered "by
a bodyguard of lies." The bodyguard was provided by Operation Fortitude,
designed to deceive the Germans about the location of the Normandy landings
in France. The idea was to reinforce German assumptions that the attack would
occur at Calais. Simply using double agents to hand over false plans would have
created suspicion. Instead, the Germans had to be allowed to piece the puzzle
together themselves, fragment by fragment. Agents gave the Germans minu-
tiae, such as inspections, unit numbers, and details of exercises. In the east of
Britain, George Patton, a well-known US general, was involved in building up
an entire fake army pointing to Pas de Calais. Deception planners even used
inflatable tanks to trick German aerial surveillance.[35]

The king provided puzzle pieces of his own after MI5 began to work with
Buckingham Palace starting in May 1944. George visited numerous fake

installations to bolster the fictitious narrative that the Allies would invade Calais. With the press reporting it near and far, deception planners coordinated
further royal visits, including to inspect troops in carefully selected locations, in
order to maintain the ruse.[36] MI5's planners painstakingly coordinated George's
movements, with the material being fed back to the Germans via double agents.
When he visited troops on the south coast, a double agent fed disinformation
back to the Germans that traffic in the Isle of Wight had been stopped to clear
the roads for troop movements.

This was a team effort and, for the first time, the queen and the heir apparent, Princess Elizabeth, were enlisted in the ruse. The members of the Royal
Family went north on the royal train to visit airborne and glider formations in
Lincolnshire and Yorkshire. They were very obviously and visibly attack formations. It was the seventh such inspection by the king in recent weeks, but
it was the first time the princess had made a full-length tour with her parents,
so it garnered wide publicity.

Double Cross agents again sent corresponding material back to the Germans to increase the credibility of assumptions drawn from the king's movements. When George visited troops in Hampshire, one agent sent a well-timed
report warning of an imminent invasion from the region, and another warned
of military activity in the Channel that may or may not have been a rehearsal
or a diversionary attack. The most famous was Agent Garbo, who was awarded
the Iron Cross by the Germans for his excellent intelligence work and then decorated by King George himself for his Double Cross activities.[37]

George was a wonderful tool with which the Double Cross team could highlight certain troops and locations to which they wanted to draw German attention.[38] As a small cog in the elaborate deception, he naturally wondered if his role
was having an effect. Using incredibly sensitive intercepts of German communications processed at Bletchley Park, the intelligence services kept him informed
about how far the Germans had bought it. On April 18, Johnny Bevan, one of
the leading strategic deception specialists, briefed Lascelles and explained that
"the elaborate 'cover scheme,' intended to bamboozle the Germans, . . . seems to
have succeeded." Lascelles was satisfied the plans were going well.[39]

The royal deception operation was elaborate, complex, and not limited to
the British mainland. In May 1944, George embarked on his most dangerous
mission—to the sheltered waters of Scapa Flow in the Orkney Islands, home of
a large UK naval base. The newspapers omitted George's destination, but one
clue made it very clear to the Nazis where the monarch was. The front page
of the *Daily Mail*, starting on May 15, reported that the king was in cold and
lonely northern waters under the headline "The King Takes Leave of His Fleet."
It stated: "The King has taken leave of his captains in the Home Fleet, and has
bidden them, their ships' companies and their ships God Speed before battle."[40]

Here the king was playing his part in a further deception plan, Fortitude North, suggesting that the Allies were preparing a full-scale invasion of Nazi-occupied Norway. George's visit to the Orkneys was hazardous. The islands are farther away from London than they are from Norway, and the area was fiercely patrolled by aggressive German U-boats. He took quite a significant risk to give credence to Fortitude North. A few days after his visit, double agent Garbo warned Berlin that an Allied invasion of Norway was imminent and that it might be the first attack in the invasion of Europe.[41]

The next month, George joined Eisenhower and Churchill at a mammoth final, five-hour briefing on Overlord held at Saint Paul's School in Kensington.[42] On June 6, everyone held their breath as thousands of troops crossed the Channel heading for the Normandy beaches. Two days later, George and Churchill lunched together at Buckingham Palace before traveling to Eisenhower's headquarters at Bushey to be shown the progress of the battle. From George's side, Lascelles could sense the relief that the invasion was finally under way. "All those who have been entrusted with the secret," he remarked, now "look 10 years younger."[43]

As the battle progressed, George and Churchill dined together and had Stewart Menzies, chief of MI6, read them a sheaf of intelligence telegrams about D-Day. All seemed "decidedly encouraging." Armed with the latest intelligence, the two men stayed up late talking with the chief of the General Staff. At one o'clock in the morning, the king asked the prime minister: "Well aren't you going to bed tonight?" "No sir," Churchill responded, before carrying on the discussion into the wee hours.[44]

D-Day reignited King George and Churchill's competitive battlefield tourism. Both wanted to be on board HMS *Belfast* to watch it unfold close to the action. Unsure of exactly who was in charge of whom, each gave the other strict orders explaining that they were not expendable and, in the event, successfully persuaded each other not to take the risk.

Churchill did not impede the king for long. In late July, under the new cover name "General Collingwood," George set off to Italy to visit Allied Force Headquarters.[45] Churchill acquiesced and again lent the king his own customized aircraft for the trip.[46] Known as Operation Trigger, this was no less hazardous than his earlier Mediterranean escapade, and he was soon visiting troops on the front line and inspecting the mountainous monastery of Monte Cassino, 80 miles southeast of Rome, which had provided the Germans with a natural fortress.[47]

Anthony Eden, the foreign secretary, was alarmed. He thought Rome was a political snake-pit and, in no uncertain terms, he instructed the king to stay away from any meetings with the king of Italy, which he deemed would be "highly embarrassing," or with the pope, in view of his war record and letters "sympathizing" with Germans. Ever the worrier, Eden was also extremely anxious about the king's personal security in a country replete with guerrillas—and which, he reminded Churchill, had only recently been an enemy state.[48] Churchill had concerns of his own: that the visit of a king would prejudice the delicate discussion of whether postwar Italy should be a monarchy or a republic.[49]

For all his fretting and micromanagement, Eden was a perceptive politician. He was right to suspect that George's visit would prove to be rather more than ceremonial. The king wanted to know about the progress of the war and to boost morale, but he was also deeply interested in the subterranean world of royal politics across the Mediterranean. Much of this involved SOE, another of the king's passions, because it often took the lead on policy toward the resistance in occupied countries. The enthusiasm for minor princes seemed to be reciprocated; SOE's first wartime chief was baffled by the fact that his officials displayed what he called "a Servants' Hall" mentality and so "always seem to be glamoured and bamboozled by local Kings." [50]

A month before D-Day, Fitzroy Maclean, a redoubtable adventurer and Britain's special representative to Josip Tito's partisans in Yugoslavia, had briefed the king. He told George about SOE assistance to the resistance there and the implications of this irregular warfare for the royal families in the Balkans. Leading a motley band of SOE fighters that included the author Evelyn Waugh and Churchill's own hard-drinking, aggressive, and courageous son Randolph, Maclean had first-hand knowledge of the vicious politics of Balkan resistance.[51]

George had taken a rather paternal approach to the young King Peter of Yugoslavia since the assassination of his father during a visit to Marseilles back in 1934. In April 1941, while still prince regent, he had cooperated with a British coup organized by SOE, but his regime was soon swept aside by the German invasion of the Balkans a few weeks later. Peter joined the many exiled in London, and no one knew quite what to do with him. He drifted, and eventually British officials were "shocked" to find him at a cottage owned by the Queen Mother in Bedfordshire playing darts alone in a shed at the back of the house. Eventually he joined the RAF and inevitably became involved in resistance politics.[52] Dalton saw him periodically in connection with SOE business and thought him "a funny little creature."[53]

However, Maclean now told the king frankly that Peter was not playing his hand well. He had lost any chance of holding his throne by not serving with the guerrillas and instead aligning with pro-German factions. Peter was to be cut adrift; Britain now supported Tito's partisans. George seems to have taken this well; after the meeting, Lascelles noted that Maclean was "a most impressive young man, of whom we shall hear more."[54]

The successful invasion of Europe presented George with other problems of royal politics. One of the most urgent was deciding what to do about Leopold III, king of the Belgians. His country, which had declared itself neutral in 1936, had been invaded without warning by Hitler in May 1940 and had desperately appealed for help. Anglo-French forces took up defensive positions but were soon pushed back by the Nazi advance. Although urged to flee to Britain and join the other governments-in-exile, Leopold unwisely opted to stay under German rule, despite his entire civil government decamping to London. He met Hitler but failed to persuade him to restore Belgian neutrality and instead remained a prisoner in his own country.

In June 1944, after the Allied invasion, Heinrich Himmler ordered Leopold's transfer to Germany and then Austria under armed guard. Meanwhile, in London, secret plans to replace him with his brother Charles were afoot. SOE even prepared to exfiltrate him out of the country. Although the ambitious attempt to rescue him failed, Charles did manage to escape to the countryside, where, living under a fake name, he hid until the liberation of Belgium.[55] On September 27, George sent a personal message to Charles telling him to prepare to act as regent in cooperation with advancing Allied forces.[56] The king's intervention was too late and unnecessary; Charles had taken the oath a week earlier, and Leopold, who never recovered from his decision to stay in Belgium, eventually abdicated after a period of exile.

Similar issues arose in Denmark. Since 1943, Flemming Muus, head of the Danish resistance, had been visiting London to deliver messages from King Christian of Denmark to George, often returning to his home country by parachute drop from a special duties flight. In September 1944, worried that the Germans knew about the Danish Royal Family's proresistance activities and fearing that they were planning on kidnapping the king and taking him to Germany, SOE considered a mission "of high secrecy" to smuggle him out to neutral Sweden.[57] Eden, long wary of SOE shenanigans, unsurprisingly had reservations. He did not think it was in King Christian's long-term interest for him to "make a bolt to a neutral country" but conceded that if he decided to flee, then SOE should help him.[58]

In the event, the Danish king was unmoved by the risk of kidnapping and opted to stay on and work with the resistance as the Allies gained more and more ground. In January 1945, George received Muus once again, this time decorating him. Under his command, sabotage operations against the Germans had increased dramatically, and he had played a central role in coordinating the Danish resistance and organizing receipts of arms and ammunition. He regaled Lascelles with tales of espionage and parachute drops, including detail about how a four-page letter could be reduced photographically to the size of a pin-head.[59] Muus had undergone plastic surgery to disguise himself; but, by 1945, as Buckingham Palace put it, "the Gestapo had identified him, circulated his photograph and placed a price of 500,000 Kroner on his head."[60] Shortly after-ward, Muus's colleague, Ole Lippmann, was sent back to Denmark to replace him as head of the resistance forces. He carried a message from George in a tube in his rectum.[61]

The story of the Greek Royal Family was another SOE success for Buck-ingham Palace. Churchill and George were united in supporting the monar-chists, and SOE provided them with the perfect secret conduit to do so. King George II of Greece, who had fled into exile after the German invasion in 1941, eventually settled in London. However, by 1944 the concerns of Buckingham Palace were less about combating the Nazis and more about which entity would replace them in Athens as the Germans retreated, since King George II and the Greek government-in-exile were not especially popular back home. This was hardly surprising, because George II was ineffectual and his younger brother, Prince Paul, even worse. Churchill lamented that the latter, who worked with the Political Warfare Executive in Cairo, was completely incapable of any public role and was "fit only for a life of luxurious seclusion."[62]

Meanwhile, the highly fragmented Greek resistance initiated a civil war between royalist and communist factions. British support for the royalists reflected fears that a Soviet dictatorship might be forced on Greece with the demise of yet another royal family.

Remarkably, in January 1945, as these events reached their dramatic height, George and Lascelles poured over intercepts from Bletchley Park that gave them the inside track on negotiations between King George II and the Greek cabinet about British policy and the future of Greece.[63] From the United States, Pres-ident Roosevelt expressed his horror at British efforts to restore the monar-chists. George II was a poorly regarded extreme conservative who converged with Edward VIII in his affection for Adolf Hitler. Nonetheless, he returned to the throne after a referendum marred by allegations of electoral fraud. Roosevelt was privately incensed. "How the British can dare such things!" he ranted, "the lengths they will go to hang onto the past!" The Greek monarchy survived, with George II being succeeded by his unpopular brother Paul in 1947.[64]

King George continued to visit field commanders and the front line. October 1944 saw Operation Partridge, a carefully managed royal expedition in which he, disguised as a General Chester, traveled to meet Montgomery in France and inspect his forces.[65] Churchill, worrying as ever about the king's proclivity for battlefield tourism, asked Montgomery if George would really be safe from enemy action. Montgomery was not concerned about the threat from the Luft-waffe, which had almost been eliminated by then, but worried about the king's constitution, knowing this could be fragile. "The only real danger might be to the visitor's health. I live in a caravan; . . . it is very cold. I seldom wear less than 4 woolies and a fur flying jacket. The change from a house to this is great and the visitor will need to be careful about chills and so on."[66] Before meeting him, the king asked Field Marshal Alan Brooke what sort of man the blunt, arrogant, and ambitious Montgomery was. Brooke said: "He is a very good soldier, but I think he is after my job." George replied: "What relief! I thought he was after mine!"[67]

On June 16, George crossed the Channel and made his way to the beach. Monty showed off his famous caravan, but it was now parked on the lawn of a luxurious château at Creullet where the commander mostly resided. They enjoyed a lunch with Camembert cheese, which had not been seen in London since 1940. George was keen to visit soldiers on the front line about 6 miles away, but Monty would not hear of it because the intervening countryside was "still full of stray snipers." He revealed that, in the garden of his château, they had just discovered a German soldier who had been hiding there for four or five days, who could easily have shot Monty, or indeed anyone else. The "sniper" was just a teenage boy, typical of the last desperate conscripts thrown into the German army, and when he was found, he had simply burst into tears. Press coverage of the royal visit accidentally revealed the location of Monty's bucolic headquarters, and he was "greatly upset" by the hurried evacuation to a less attractive alternative.[68]

Threats from German planes and snipers—or the French weather—were not uppermost in the king's mind. As the end of the war slowly came into view, his main worry was relations with Stalin and the Soviet Union. Knowing that Churchill had developed a rapport with the Soviet leader, bonding in particular over one "savage" late night drinking session in 1942, when a senior Foreign Office official found them "merry as a marriage bell" at three in the morning,[69] George personally urged Churchill to use all his famous powers of persuasion to secure a favorable settlement in Europe.[70] He and Churchill consulted again in considerable detail before Yalta in February 1945, perhaps the formative conference of the postwar era and still the most controversial.

As the war moved into its final chapter, King George grew progressively more optimistic about the prospects of the West in its developing war of nerves with Stalin. Although Britain was numerically the weaker of the Big Three, George was increasingly aware of the importance of science and technology for the future of warfare—an area where he knew Britain was well ahead. He was aware of Churchill's enthusiasm for "radio-location" and other "black magical war-wining devices."[71] The previous summer, he had visited the Telecommunications Research Establishment housed at Malvern College in Worcestershire to see the latest developments in radar technology. He and Lascelles were enthralled by the "astonishing" inventions without which, they learned, "we should never have overcome the U-boats, nor the German bombers' and would probably have lost the war.[72] In fact, George was so taken with these inventions that he was still talking fluently about radar long after the war had ended.[73]

George loved visiting all sorts of "hush-hush" places—but his favorite subject was still SOE.[74] Toward the end of the war, he and the queen were thrilled to tour a curious private museum exhibit: a startling display of SOE's secret gadgets and gizmos hidden deep inside the Natural History Museum in South Kensington.[75] Taking advantage of the museum's wartime closure, SOE's section XV took over six rooms and put on a display of weapons for VIPs only. XV equated most closely to James Bond's famous "Q" branch, the fictional research and development wing of MI6 responsible for a range of improbable gadgets, from invisible cars to bagpipe flamethrowers.

In reality, XV was based at an unlikely headquarters on the Barnet bypass just north of London, a former hotel called the Thatched Barn.[76] Constructed as residence for film stars working at the emerging Elstree Studios, it was requisitioned at the start of the war and was soon producing silent guns and exploding briefcases destined for real life. Other parts of the exhibition were put together by SOE's camouflage and makeup section, based more locally at 2–3 Trevor Square in more fashionable Kensington in west London.[77] The king and queen adored the exhibition. Scheduled to last only 45 minutes, they stayed for one and a half hours and viewed "a great diversity of death dealing devices," together with some very ingenious methods of communications.[78]

The most important secret science project was the atomic bomb. The first to brief Buckingham Palace about this deadly secret was the chief of MI6, Sir Stewart Menzies. On May 4, 1944, he related "hair-raising stories about the effects of bombs of the future," adding that their realization was not far away.[79]

On February 7 of the next year, Sir Edward Appleton, who ran the government's scientific research department, arrived at the palace. He updated Lascelles on the "rapid development" of the bomb and explained how the whole project had moved to America because of the Blitz. He briefed on the latest MI6 intelligence, which indicated that the Germans did not have an atom bomb but told how the Allies might have one in time to use against Japan. This pricked Lascelles's interest, and he asked what the result would be. "Oh," Appleton answered matter-of-factly, "a couple of them would end the war overnight— there is no doubt about that."[80]

Both George and Churchill were elated upon learning that this new and devastating weapon would soon be tested, and they again turned their attention to the postwar Soviet threat. By April, George demanded increasingly regular bulletins about relations with Stalin. He began to feel out of the loop, causing Lascelles to convey a mild rebuke to the prime minister. Lascelles assured Hastings Ismay, a key adviser to Churchill, that the king "reads carefully (under lock and key of course) all the weekly summaries you send him." So, he was a "little disturbed" not to have been informed of the increasing military tensions between Churchill and Stalin. George had hoped that Churchill would have "come over to Windsor on Easter Sunday" to brief him, and was disappointed that he had not done so.[81] The king had become accustomed to his excellent access to secrets and now felt it sharply whenever his government was less than forthcoming. Inducting a monarch into the subterranean world brings certain expectations; once the black box is opened, it is difficult to close.

On May 8, 1945, King George VI and Queen Elizabeth appeared on the balcony of Buckingham Palace to greet ecstatic crowds on V–E Day. With Winston Churchill between them, and the two princesses on either side, and with Princess Elizabeth wearing her auxiliary territorial service uniform, they waved to the thousands of people who had amassed outside to revel in a cathartic release of joy and relief. Such was the fervor that George and Elizabeth even allowed the young princesses, only nineteen and fourteen years of age, to venture into town, "swept along," Elizabeth remembers, "by tides of happiness and relief."[82]

At the end of the war, Churchill, accompanied by Stewart Menzies, the chief of MI6, reaffirmed the importance of Ultra intelligence to the king. Bletchley Park was one of the few secret places George had not visited during the last five years. "It is thanks to the secret weapon of General Menzies, put into use on all the fronts, that we won the war!"[83] Menzies happily basked in the praise lavished on Bletchley Park; his reputation was never higher, but perhaps the most important figure in the codebreaking effort was the shy and reclusive Alan Turing, the early leader of Hut 8, who, at the start of the war, was one of the few who believed that the Enigma code used by the Germans could actually be broken. George awarded Turing an OBE the next year, although the reason was kept carefully obscure from the public. With the Ultra secret highly classified for almost thirty years, Turing, much to the amusement of his friends, kept his award in a tin box filed with screws, nails, nuts, and bolts.[84]

Although he did not visit Bletchley Park, George enjoyed a detailed and strategic understanding of the unraveling of Enigma, including the dramatic capture of codebooks from a U-boat off Iceland in October 1942, which had altered the course of the entire war. The recovery of secret German coding material from U-110, at the cost of the lives of two of HMS *Petard*'s crew, enabled Bletchley Park's codebreakers to crack the new Enigma system, which had been introduced to cover the U-boat offensive. After ten critical months with no U-boat signals intelligence available, this breakthrough was the crucial factor in defeating Hitler's Atlantic wolf packs. Awarding Captain Baker-Cresswell his DSO, the king told him that this engagement was one of the most significant events of the war at sea—and he was probably right.[85]

Public celebration and private congratulations were accompanied by a more serious business: the scramble for secret wonder weapons. Since D-Day, in a race against the Russians, special teams had been hunting down everything they could find, including rockets, jet fighters, the latest U-boats, nerve gas samples, and, of course, nuclear weapons.[86]

On July 25, 1945, Churchill, at almost his last meeting with the king as prime minister, casually mentioned that the US would drop atomic bombs on Japan the "next week."[87] The king was fascinated by the emerging landscape of nuclear war. Almost a year after Hiroshima and Nagasaki, he was one of very few outside the Cabinet Office to be allowed to see the mythical "Revised Tizard Report." Prepared by Sir Henry Tizard, the government's senior defense scientist, it brought together all that Britain had learned from recent events and from the plundering of Nazi secret science in Germany, including V weapons, jet fighters, and nerve gas. Presciently, it predicted an age of mutually assured destruction and the emergence of nuclear deterrence as the major dynamic of the Cold War era. Much more sinisterly, it recognized that it might be ten years before Britain would acquire its own nuclear weapons and urged the production of nerve gas and biological weapons to fill the gap.[88] Tizard was right on the time scales at least; Britain did not acquire its own bomb until the reign of Elizabeth II. By now, however, George was no longer a wartime king. He had clearly come a long way from his early days as an appeasement sympathizer and, over the course of the war, had won the trust of the security establishment.

PART IV

Royal Secrets

12

Queen Elizabeth II

Coronation and Cold War

*I find that I can often put things out
of my mind which are disagreeable.*
—The Queen, on Anthony Blunt

On the morning of February 6, 1952, Tommy Lascelles, private secretary to the king, was at Sandringham. He called his deputy in London, Edward Ford, and said: "Edward, Hyde Park Corner. Go and tell the Prime Minister and Queen Mary"; he then abruptly hung up. King George VI's closest advisers had a series of secret code words to signal special eventualities. "Hyde Park Corner" was Buckingham Palace speak for "the King has died." The use of these code words belied the increasing use of scrambler phones at royal residences—there were some things that were just too secret to be spoken.[1]

George had died peacefully in his sleep just four months after an operation on his right lung. The somber news quickly reverberated around the government. Parliament suspended debate. The weekly meeting of the Joint Intelligence Committee was in full swing when the announcement came at 11:30 a.m. The most senior intelligence body in the land halted its discussion of the Cold War, Egyptian riots, and the expansion of NATO; its chairman solemnly asked all present to stand silently and adjourned the meeting.[2] Flags across London were at half-mast by noon—with one exception. Queen Mary refused to lower hers. The octogenarian wife of George V made it staunchly clear that, for her, the crown never dies.

With the crown still very much alive, the government's attention soon turned to welcoming the new monarch, twenty-five-year-old Elizabeth, back from a visit to Kenya and then how best to ensure a smooth succession.

Seemingly, there was little threat to the queen or the crown. Mass observation surveys, used to track popular opinion, revealed scant appetite for republicanism among a population still suffering the effects of the war. For many, King George VI had been a superb symbol of national unity and resilience: he left the monarchy in good health. As for his daughter, the young queen was particularly popular, epitomizing what many hoped would be a new era of optimism and peace.

The only shadowy maneuverings came from inside the upper classes themselves. Kenneth de Courcy—a right-wing politician, a prewar go-between for Germany, and one-time head of a private intelligence network—tried to stir controversy. Alongside Winston Churchill, de Courcy was one of the Windsors' oldest friends and had stayed close to them throughout the late 1940s, often visiting or writing to them in France and facilitating their visits to New York.[3] Back in 1949, he had suggested to Churchill that Elizabeth form closer relations with his friend and confidant, the duke of Windsor.[4]

With the king's health failing, de Courcy had conspired for the exiled duke to return to England as regent for the inexperienced Elizabeth. Desperate for any formal position and adulation he once enjoyed, Edward was inevitably keen to return, and he found support among those fearing the influence of the ambitious Lord Louis Mountbatten, Prince Philip's uncle, on the impressionable young princess.

Intriguingly, de Courcy chose to make his pitch to the more ambitious Wallis. Rather well informed, he explained that the king was in fact "gravely ill" and effectively already "out of circulation." He warned that the Royal Family now faced a crisis in which the influence of the Mountbattens "might be fatal" and urged Edward and Wallis to head this off. "All these dangers could be averted . . . if the duke were to return to live in England," where he would be a discreet but "decisive influence . . . upon the Regency." De Courcy chose his words carefully, but added that with "extremely careful and painstaking work," Edward might succeed in "laying entirely fresh foundation stones upon which the monarchy in the latter part of the 20th and 21st century might be built."[5] Edward decided to stay in Paris, but these conversations with Churchill and others triggered an ugly reaction.

In 1951, the crown launched a propaganda counteroffensive against the Duke and Duchess of Windsor. It was precisely at this point, de Courcy recalls, that "the authorities repeatedly and widely asserted that the Secret Services had prepared a dossier about Mrs Simpson." This was the infamous "China Dossier," and was said to contain details of her private life in China while married to Earl Spencer. "The alleged details were wholly sexual and the authorities said she became expert at deviationist sexual activity which she learned in China and that was one reason why she had a hold over Edward VIII." The individual chosen to brief about this was Jack Coke, Queen Mary's equerry, and later gentleman usher to King George VI and finally extra gentleman usher to Queen Elizabeth. Both Churchill and de Courcy were told that this dossier was the main issue that "was held against the duchess." De Courcy was probably right in asserting that the dossier was "totally false" but was nevertheless a "winning story."[6]

The royals were firing their propaganda in the wrong direction. Edward had briefly returned to Britain at the end of the war, before taking up life as a quasi-exile in Paris. He had, as Lascelles put it, "certain disagreeable personal skeletons in his cupboard," but, even as palace officials desperately tried to hunt down and suppress incriminating letters between him and the Nazis, Edward remained typically oblivious. At one point, he breezily attempted to return to his beloved Germany. Officials could hardly believe their ears, and swiftly forbade it. By the time George died, Edward was drifting among the overfed and idle rich in France and Florida, resigned to life as a mere café society royal. He was no longer a security threat.

Suspicions about the intentions of Prince Philip's power-hungry uncle had more substance. A sense of intrigue now swept the palace again. Many saw "Uncle Dickie," as Mountbatten was affectionately known, as an arch-manipulator who, over a decade, had engineered his nephew's improbable rise to the heart of the British Royal Family. When Edward briefly returned home for his brother's funeral, he noted of Mountbatten that "one can't pin much on him but he's very bossy and never stops talking. All are suspicious and watching his influence on Philip." Rumors even circulated that Mountbatten plotted to make Philip the king consort.[7]

An article warning of Mountbatten's leftist influence was the source of much of the gossip. It appeared in the freelance "Bulletin of the International Services of Information," which was run by a former American intelligence officer, Ulius Amoss. Specifically, it warned that Peter Murphy, a longtime confidant of Mountbatten, was a member of the Communist Party. Although the FBI rated Amoss an eccentric, MI5 conducted its own investigation and sent the deputy director of naval intelligence to raise their concerns with Mountbatten personally.[8]

Mountbatten was furious at being accused of wielding subversive leftist influence inside palace circles, but he accepted that suggestions about his sway with the queen were inevitable. He reeled off a long list of his staff members for MI5, emphasizing that each one was beyond reproach. Unfortunately, the intelligence services forgot to make a note of their names.[9] A few days later, MI5 received information that Mountbatten and his entourage were "looking at" not only Murphy but also a known communist named Pavitt.[10]

Less than three weeks after George had died, Elizabeth's grandmother, Queen Mary, who was highly attuned to politics where they affected the crown, angrily summoned Jock Colville from Number 10. She trusted Colville, who had once been Elizabeth's private secretary and had provided discreet advice on Philip before he married into the family. Still an influential member of the establishment, he now performed the same role for Winston Churchill. Mary had been keeping a close eye on Mountbatten and, as perennial matriarch of the House of Windsor, had long enjoyed an informal surveillance network across the British aristocracy.

News quickly reached her from Prince Ernst of Hanover that Dickie was boasting of victory. At a dinner party of royal guests held at his house at Broadlands, he had announced: "The House of Mountbatten now reigned." She "spent a sleepless night" and passed on the reports to Colville, who, in turn, informed the prime minister. Philip, whom Elizabeth had married in 1947, had even written a document protesting against the royals remaining as the House of Windsor. This had "annoyed" Churchill, and indeed the whole cabinet.[11] To the anger of Mountbatten and Philip, and to the resigned frustration of Elizabeth, Churchill insisted on the queen taking the name Windsor—rather than Mountbatten. The aging prime minister, perhaps influenced by the gossip, saw Mountbatten as a subversive rival.[12] Despite the intrigue and meddling, the succession passed smoothly, and the House of Windsor still reigned.

The coronation itself, taking place in June 1953, proved a vast undertaking. It was the first to be broadcast on television—and an utter headache for security. Westminster Abbey was closed for an entire year as additional seating was added to expand the capacity from 2,000 to 8,000 guests, allowing minor royals and dignitaries from around the world to attend. Behind the scenes, courtiers and government officials tussled over the guest list. The Maltese prime minister struggled to secure an invitation, despite Elizabeth's long associations with the island, and then complained about being "lumped in" with the Africans. Some African leaders were not welcome at all, and officials went to considerable lengths to deter the leftist Kwame Nkrumah, prime minister of the Gold Coast (later Ghana), from turning up. There was also the problem of pretenders. Guests included the "Princess of the Pitcairn Islands," a self-styled title adopted by a resident of Tahiti who had never set foot on Pitcairn.[13]

Physical security was important. A successful attack on the coronation might have rendered upper-class spats about Elizabeth's surname utterly immaterial. By this time, three months after Stalin's death, MI5 did not expect the Communists to pose much danger. Instead, the threat came from a more unexpected quarter. Scottish nationalists had earlier stolen the Stone of Scone, an ancient symbol of the Scottish monarchy, from Westminster Abbey. Ever since the death of George VI, they had made what Colville described as "an absurd fuss about the Queen being Elizabeth II rather than Elizabeth I," on the grounds that Elizabeth I had never ruled Scotland.[14]

This culminated in a so-called pillar box war. Angry young Scots sabotaged—and even blew up—Scottish postal boxes marked with the new "EIIR" ensign just six weeks before the coronation.[15] Quietly, the decision was made to replace them with a new design that carried the crown of Scotland. Guy Liddell, of MI5, noted that this was causing "some concern," especially given that police thought republicans—"equivalent to the IRA in Ireland"—were to blame.[16] A couple of weeks before the coronation, Liddell warned of "extreme irresponsible splinter groups within the Scottish Nationalist Party, who are quite capable of student pranks or something worse."[17]

On Coronation Day itself, the Metropolitan Police, reinforced by units from across the country, battled the abnormally miserable weather to maintain a close watch over the crowds. They paid particular attention to unoccupied premises, foreigners and, as the police put it, "suspected mental cases."[18]

Pavements were packed with people braving the rain; thousands more watched for the first time on brand-new television sets. Celebrations rang out, and the coronation passed smoothly. A string of formal dinners followed, with the banquet thrown by the Foreign Office presenting potential hazards. Nehru, the Indian prime minister, went out of his way to talk about his imprisonment by the British. Meanwhile, the young queen struggled with minor royals, finding them "impatient and difficult to deal with."[19]

With the coronation out of the way, Queen Elizabeth was able to devote more time to her constitutional duties. She enjoyed access to top-secret intelligence and, like her fastidious father, took her reading seriously. Every evening at around seven o'clock, except for Easter and Christmas, she received a red leather dispatch box stuffed full of important matters of state. Its contents included Foreign Office cables, budget documents, cabinet papers, and highly classified secret intelligence, including MI6 reporting on international crises.[20] Copy number one of the government's weekly summary of current intelligence went to the queen.[21] If war broke out, she would have had access to highly classified daily situation reports alongside all the intelligence, no matter how secret, on future operations. This was on one condition: that she burn them after reading.[22]

In stark contrast to King Edward VIII's sloppy practice, which risked secrets falling into Nazi hands, tight security surrounded the box. Elizabeth was orderly and well drilled, perhaps by the likes of Martin Charteris, who had served with military intelligence in Palestine before joining the queen's staff as assistant private secretary. Only four keys existed: Elizabeth held one, and her private secretaries kept the others.[23] By eight o'clock the next morning, she had returned her box, having ticked off each document and underlined interesting bits in red pencil. Rarely did she write comments.[24]

Elizabeth was not the only member of her family reading classified material. In July 1954, the Queen Mother began receiving her own daily box of Foreign Office telegrams and practically all the material sent to the cabinet. She deliberately stopped short of asking for "anything of a very secret nature," but she appreciated access to classified state papers.[25] Moreover, mother and daughter spoke with each other on the telephone every day, providing the monarch with a sounding board for difficult issues.

Strikingly, the Queen Mother wanted the state papers in a personal capacity—out of nosiness rather than duty. She had been used to knowing everything during the war, when George would confide the most sensitive business—from secret intelligence to military deception—to his wife. Frustrated with now being out of the loop, she told Churchill that "one can read the newspapers with much greater interest and less suspicion, if one knows a little of the true background of the news."[26]

Anthony Eden, the foreign secretary, was hesitant. He insisted that, regardless of her previous access and influence, nothing top secret should now reach her.[27] This was hardly a "need to know" scenario, yet, perhaps influenced by their close relationship during the war, Churchill quickly agreed to her request. He justified it on the grounds that when Elizabeth was away, her mother became the senior member of the Council of State.[28]

Not wanting to freeze Philip out, for the prince could be touchy about such things, Churchill extended the offer to him as well. Palace staff assumed that the queen privately showed her husband papers of interest anyway,[29] but Philip, ever desperate for recognition in his own right, jumped at the offer.[30] This was partly because the queen never shared the contents of her own red boxes with him—but now he had his own green boxes.

Her Tuesday afternoon audiences with prime ministers, themselves deeply interested in intelligence after the war, were particularly fruitful. For Elizabeth, this was a time when her prime ministers could "unburden themselves or they tell me what's going on if they have got any problems." "Sometimes," she added, "one can help."[31]

Sitting across from the prime minister, she would put forward her own point of view. "Perhaps," she later noted, "they hadn't seen it from that angle." More often, she asked questions in a Socratic manner, subtly arching an eyebrow, to indicate her concerns. Although initially skeptical about the inexperienced monarch, Winston Churchill, a veteran of many an audience with her father, soon found her conscientious, well informed, and serious minded. Their meetings grew in length, and the queen was one of the very few whom he informed about his strokes, a secret he kept even from his cabinet colleagues.[32]

When Churchill finally retired in 1955, she thanked him for his leadership during the Cold War. Its "threats and dangers," she told him, were "more awe inspiring than any which you have had to contend with before, in war or peace."[33]

By now, the Cold War had been under way for a decade. Amid growing tensions between East and West, the queen adopted a quasi-political role. According

Elizabeth I's "Rainbow Portrait," which glorifies the place of surveillance in royal statecraft. Note the eyes on her garments. *Source:* Wikimedia Commons, from the Collection of the Marquess of Salisbury, Hatfield House.

From early in her reign, Queen Victoria was subjected to numerous assassination attempts. This led to the birth of Britain's modern security services. *Source:* Wikimedia Commons.

Alexandra of Denmark (top) became princess of Wales when she married Queen Victoria's son Edward, the prince of Wales and future Edward VII (bottom). When Prussia invaded Denmark in 1864, Edward asked his mother for access to secret Foreign Office documents about the situation in Denmark; but she refused, fearing that Edward and Alexandra would send intelligence to the Danish king. *Source:* Library of Congress.

Princess Vicky, shown here in 1884, was Queen Victoria's eldest daughter and became crown princess of Prussia through her marriage to the crown prince, the future Frederick III of Germany. Vicky became a key informant for Britain about German affairs through ongoing correspondence with her mother. *Source:* Wikimedia Commons.

Cousins Tsar Nicholas II of Russia (left) and King George V of Great Britain (right) at the wedding of the kaiser's daughter in Berlin in 1913. The wedding was one of the last great social events of European royalty before the First World War began fourteen months later. The Germans had hoped—and British officials feared—that George might be coaxed into discussions on naval arms control. But he deftly avoided foreign policy issues, and instead asked endless questions about shooting and the management of the Prussian royal stables. *Source:* Wikimedia Commons.

The police arrest the would-be assassin George McMahon, after he pointed a revolver at Edward VIII. This was on July 16, 1936. *Source:* Classic Image / Alamy Stock Photo.

Edward and Wallis, the duke and duchess of Windsor, became the subjects of surveillance by British intelligence after they made a grand tour of Nazi Germany. Here they are pictured meeting with Hitler and senior Nazi officials at the Berghof, Hitler's retreat near Berchtesgaden, Bavaria, on October 22, 1937. *Source:* Shawshots/Alamy.

George VI, Britain's monarch during the Second World War. *Source:* Library of Congress.

Ian Fleming (left) with Sean Connery on the set of the first James Bond film, *Dr. No* (1962). Fleming preferred writing Bond novels to royal speeches. *Source:* PictureLux / The Hollywood Archive / Alamy Stock Photo.

While a student at Cambridge, Prince Charles was almost kidnapped by a group of women students from Manchester University. *Source:* Trinity Mirror / Mirrorpix / Alamy Stock Photo.

Lord Mountbatten of Burma, the queen's uncle, was assassinated by the Irish Republican Army in 1979. A bomb was placed on his fishing charter boat while he was on vacation in Mullaghmore, Ireland. *Source:* Wikimedia Commons.

Queen Elizabeth II with the art historian Anthony Blunt, surveyor of the queen's pictures and the Kremlin's man in the palace. This photograph was taken in November 1979 during the queen's visit to the Courtauld Institute of Art. *Source:* PA Images / Alamy Stock Photo.

Queen Elizabeth II meets the James Bond actor Daniel Craig at the world premiere of the Bond film *Casino Royale* on November 14, 2006, at Leicester Square in London. The queen and Daniel Craig collaborated to create a memorable opening television sketch for the 2012 London Olympics. *Source:* PA Images / Alamy Stock Photo / Michael Dunlea.

In 2019, Queen Elizabeth II and the director Jeremy Fleming unveiled a plaque in London to mark the centenary of GCHQ, the British signals and cybersecurity intelligence agency. *Source:* PA Images / Alamy Stock Photo.

Prince William spent a week in 2019 attached to MI6, mainly in its ziggurat-style headquarters building, pictured here, to learn about Britain's foreign intelligence capabilities. *Source:* Wikimedia Commons / Fred Romero.

to one royal biographer, she "was deployed as a lure to defuse the Cold War between Britain and Russia."[34] Soviet leaders Nikita Khrushchev and Nikolai Bulganin arrived for a historic, high-profile state visit to Britain in April 1956. It included a controversial meeting with Queen Elizabeth and Prince Philip.

Intrigue and espionage were endemic. The Soviet delegation included Ivan Serov, officially serving as chief of their security. In fact, he was head of the KGB, and later became head of Soviet military intelligence, the GRU. Famously oppressive of Russian minorities in areas like the Ukraine, he was hated by exiles from the "captive nations" inside the USSR and became a walking target for terrorists. Prime Minister Anthony Eden had banned offensive intelligence operations for the duration of the visit. He feared that a potential spy scandal would undo his presummit hard work, but Britain's propagandists could not resist a small operation of their own. They discreetly tipped off journalists about Serov's real job and the brutality it involved. As a result, reporters hounded him up and down the country, giving him unflattering nicknames, including Ivan the Terrible and Ivan the Butcher.[35]

Predictably, Special Branch, which was guarding the Soviet party, was unhappy about the propaganda effort. Partly because of Serov's presence, officers worried about assassination attempts by dissident nationalists. These concerns were redoubled when the Foreign Office accidently released a detailed program of the visit, complete with places and times a week beforehand: "These were supposed to be secret for security purposes." There were many receptions with much vodka; but at each event, guests had to enter single file to be scrutinized by "obvious Special Branch men."[36] Most events went well, other than a dinner for the Soviets held by the Labour Party. The shadow foreign secretary, George Brown, heckled Khrushchev during his speech and attacked him over the Nazi–Soviet pact of 1939. Khrushchev was in "a furious temper," and he replied tartly that if he lived in Britain, he would vote Conservative.[37]

Like Eden, Khrushchev and Bulganin also hoped intelligence activities would not mar the occasion.[38] Guy Burgess and Donald Maclean, two Soviet agents inside the Foreign Office, had defected to Moscow five years earlier, as British intelligence closed in on their double lives. A couple of months before the state visit, the Kremlin had permitted them to hold a press conference from Moscow. It was the first proof of life since their defection and inevitably caused a furor back home.

For all the drama, the Soviets intended to put their one-time prize agents to good use and instructed Burgess to share political intelligence in advance of the visit. He provided insight into the places Khrushchev and Bulganin would visit, and the people they would meet. These included Queen Elizabeth herself. Burgess assessed that "in line with the family tradition, to say nothing of political considerations, the Royal Family harboured hostile feelings for Soviet leaders, because they have not forgotten what happened to the last Tsar and his family." He recommended that when visiting Windsor, they ask to see portraits of great statesmen, including Alexander I, to remind both sides of when Britain and Russia had been allies against a European tyrant.[39]

Shortly after their arrival, Khrushchev and Bulganin were escorted to Buckingham Palace, accompanied by William Hayter, the ambassador to Moscow, and Thomas Barker, a specialist from the Foreign Office who would later become head of its propaganda unit.[40] A few days later, armed with Burgess's intelligence—"B&K," as the press dubbed them—arrived at Windsor Castle.

Elizabeth, dressed in a plain white outfit, with Philip and their children at her side, met the Russians at the door. Eden had told Khrushchev that the queen was a simple, pleasant person, and Khrushchev thought her "the sort of young woman you'd be likely to meet walking along Gorky Street on a balmy summer afternoon."[41] She offered them a tour of the castle, perhaps taking in the portraits recommended by Burgess, and now curated by his friend Anthony Blunt, before sitting down to tea. Philip had thought the idea of tea with the Russians "bloody silly," but soon warmed to his guests.[42]

An encrypted Russian telegram sent back to Moscow recorded that Philip praised the hospitality received by British naval officers during a visit to Leningrad in 1955. He joked that he would like to visit the city incognito.[43] Elizabeth asked polite questions about the plane that delivered the Russians' mail to them while in England. Khrushchev, desperate to show it off as one of the first passenger jets in the world, was delighted.[44]

He was less keen to receive questions about his other mode of transportation, the Soviet cruiser on which he had arrived, currently docked in Portsmouth's large natural harbor. Three days earlier, an MI6 diver, Buster Crabb, had embarked upon an unauthorized mission to inspect its hull—but never returned. As MI6 scrambled, Khrushchev made a cryptic reference over dinner to the ship and lost property.

It is unlikely that the queen had advance knowledge of the Crabb dive; but if she did, it would have come via Mountbatten. Despite his denials, Uncle Dickie seems to have known all about the controversial operation—and tried to hush the story up. A keen diver with close links to MI6, he had known Crabb in Gibraltar during the war and afterward, when Crabb was supposedly doing "some type of secret work" at a research lab in Bushey Park, northeast of London. There are even accounts of Mountbatten meeting Crabb shortly before the fateful dive.[45]

Either way, Khrushchev left the castle "very impressed" by the queen. "She had," he recalled, "such a gentle, calm voice. She was completely unpretentious, completely without the haughtiness that you'd expect of royalty." He downplayed her role, portraying her more as a mother and wife than as the queen.[46]

But the royals maintained discreet influence. The Queen Mother later had a quiet talk with President Eisenhower, whom she had known since the war. "We must be firm" in dealing with the Soviets, she stressed, before catching herself and adding that this was her own private opinion rather than the government line. Either way, it had an impact. During talks with the British cabinet the very next day, Eisenhower repeated what the Queen Mother had told him after ministers complained of the weak hand they held. The foreign secretary tempered the Queen Mother's line: "We have to be firm on essentials."[47]

The Americans exploited royal influence in other ways, too. The CIA watched Bulganin and Khrushchev's visit to the UK closely, using it as part of a large psychological warfare operation targeting East Germany. Code-named LCCASSOCK, the CIA was disseminating 20,000 copies at a time of material made to closely resemble official East German publications. The operation aimed to "exploit special events" in order to "promote the spirit of resistance." One CIA publication mimicking an East German weekly newspaper criticized the state visit to Britain, reporting "statements of Khrushchev which aroused the indignation of the British." Another article, the CIA explained, told readers that Queen Elizabeth would not wear a fur coat presented to her by the Soviets on the grounds that British officials feared that Moscow "would make propaganda of this matter if she appeared in the coat." Ironically, in doing so, the CIA was secretly making propaganda of the queen themselves.[48]

Khrushchev's compatriots were not so dismissive of the monarchy. Six months after the state visit, a spontaneous uprising erupted in Hungary, taking MI6 by surprise. Rebels, some of whom were armed only with kitchen knives, scored a string of improbable successes before Soviet tanks rolled in. Over two thousand Hungarians died as the Russians put a brutal end to the revolution; hundreds of thousands fled. It was one of the darkest episodes of the Cold War.

Shortly afterward, in the face of mounting pressure, the Soviets tried to use the queen as a pawn in the propaganda war. Buckingham Palace received an odd telegram from Marshal Voroshilov, the Soviet head of state. He asked that the queen "correctly" understand Soviet action in Hungary. Diplomats in the Foreign Office thought it an outrageously hypocritical and sanctimonious move.[49]

More cynically still, the Russian Embassy in London quickly telephoned the Foreign Office to ask if it could publish the letter alongside the queen's reply. This really ruffled the mandarins, because Elizabeth had not sent any letter to the Soviets, and the Foreign Office's staff members had no intention of allowing her to send one now. They worried that the Soviets were fishing for anything they could publish to give the impression that the queen tacitly accepted the Soviet version of events. Criticizing the ploy as "cynical hypocrisy," senior diplomats refused even to allow Elizabeth to have anything to do with the letter at all.

They were particularly nervous because just ten days earlier, Moscow had released a letter from Bulganin to Eisenhower to the local press before Eisenhower had even received it.[50] Voroshilov's letter to the queen was, according to one diplomat, a "serious and most displeasing incident" that warranted summons of the Soviet ambassador to the Foreign Office.[51]

Diplomats called the Soviets' bluff. The next day, a Russian official admitted that there was in fact no message from the queen. Moscow recognized their letter was a "serious mistake," apologized profusely, and agreed to withdraw it.[52] This humiliating climb-down took senior diplomats by surprise. Patrick Reilly, the British ambassador in Moscow, was amazed that the Russians had behaved "almost humanely" over the withdrawal. It was, he thought, a "very queer affair."[53]

Oleg Penkovsky was another Russian who did not doubt the queen's importance. He was a dynamic and aggressive colonel in Soviet military intelligence. Penkovsky was also an MI6/CIA agent, passing much secret material, mostly on missiles, but also delicious Kremlin political gossip, to the West. He was undoubtedly one of the top agents of the Cold War. When offering to defect, he wrote a letter addressed to Queen Elizabeth, among others. It read: "I ask you to consider me as your soldier. Henceforth the ranks of your armed forces are increased by one man." Instead of defecting, he was kept as a spy in place—both more valuable but also more dangerous. Therefore, meetings with Penkovsky were infrequent to protect his security.

An opportunity arose in the autumn of 1961. Penkovsky was sent to London on official business and was able to meet secretly with both MI6 and CIA, including Harry Shergold, one of MI6's most experienced agent handlers. Penkovsky had an intriguing request. He pointed out that when the Soviet cosmonaut Yuri Gagarin visited London recently, he had met the queen, so Penkovsky asked: "Why can't I meet the Queen?"

The CIA recalls that this was where Shergold really "sweated crocodile drops." Penkovsky hoped to swear his loyalty to the queen personally. He was a star agent, providing bundles of useful intelligence to MI6 and the CIA—including, as we shall see, on the Cuban missile crisis. All the while, he wondered why he had not yet met the queen.[54] In the event, he had to settle for a message from Mountbatten delivered by Dick White, the chief of MI6. White assured him that the queen's cousin would tell her all about his important work. White sensed his disappointment, and later recalled: "He wanted to be praised personally by the Queen for his monumental contribution and to have a medal pinned on his chest. There was no possibility of this."[55]

Penkovsky was a fantastic asset for MI6, but the Russians had recruited spies of their own. They were buried surprisingly deep in the heart of the British establishment. Both the KGB and its military counterpart, the GRU, were keen to gather intelligence not just on the government but also on the upper eche-lons of society for blackmail and subversive purposes. A series of spy scandals punctuated the first decade of the queen's reign.[56]

Some inside government and the palace worried about Prince Philip's behav-ior. At one point in 1956, the palace was forced to put out an unprecedented denial that the royal marriage was on the rocks, after Philip's lengthy solo tour to Melbourne, where he had opened the Olympic Games. Behind the scenes, offi-cials grew concerned because, according to one royal biographer, they knew from intelligence reports that Philip and his equerry, Mike Parker, gallivanted flirta-tiously around London's clubs and risked causing embarrassment to the queen.[57]

This was more than about marriage. Philip risked opening himself up to Soviet blackmail. He was a member of the notorious Thursday Club, which met in Soho every week for boozy lunches, which sometimes stretched long into the night. Members included controversial spy-turned-writer Compton Mackenzie, the witty actor David Niven, and Stephen Ward, the infamous society osteopath at the heart of the Profumo affair.[58]

Even Kim Philby, the MI6 officer and Soviet spy, once attended Philip's club and yet, for all his famed charm and charisma, he was apparently deemed too boring to be invited back.[59] "The dullest man in the place," as Mike Parker counterintuitively recalled.[60] Philby was already under intense suspicion at the time for being a Soviet agent. Perhaps someone received a quiet warning about the guest list.

Prince Philip has always denied rumors that he was unfaithful to Elizabeth during these early years of marriage, pointing out that his protection officers would have prevented him from indulging in clandestine assignations. What-ever the reality, this is a fairly weak defense: protection officers protect their charges. They do not cast moral judgment or prevent them from doing some-thing that would not otherwise imperil their safety.[61]

Protection officers can—and did—report behavior that compromised secu-rity and made their charges vulnerable to blackmail. King Edward VIII's po-licemen, as we have seen, had him under surveillance during and after the abdication crisis. Whatever the truth and source, Philip's behavior was enough to concern the prime minister, Winston Churchill. He summoned the prince, deliberately kept him waiting, and then growled: "Is your objective the destruc-tion of the whole Royal Family?"[62]

When Philip was invited to tour the US, Whitehall officials conspired to keep him away from public or social engagements. The British ambassador in Washington suggested keeping his time in the capital and New York as short as possible, with the prince instead touring Ohio, Omaha, and Colorado Springs. Even Churchill insisted that the visit be "as military as possible." Philip, it seemed, had to be kept away from temptation and trouble.[63]

The Thursday Club brought the Royal Family dangerously close to the toxic Profumo scandal in 1963. John Profumo, the secretary of state for war, denied having sexual relations with a nineteen-year-old model, Christine Keeler. In March 1963, as rumors swirled, he defiantly stood up in the House of Commons to threaten writs for libel and slander against anyone making scandalous allegations of impropriety. That very afternoon, he attended horse racing in Surrey with the Queen Mother. Labour politicians angrily derided what they saw as a public show of support from the royals.[64]

Prime Minister Harold Macmillan privately worried that "the tide of gossip might even lap around the Royal Family."[65] As well as having plenty of mutual friends, Philip had known Ward personally for quite some time. He had attended parties thrown by Ward back in the late 1940s and had stayed in touch through the 1950s. Ward was also an accomplished portrait painter, and Philip sat for by him in the spring of 1961, followed by Princess Margaret, the queen's younger sister. In June 1963, the FBI reported that Philip was involved in the Profumo affair but did not say exactly how.[66]

Ward was a complex character. He mixed with the highest in society and revealed to Christine Keeler that he, Prince Philip, and his cousin, the marquess of Milford Haven, had visited "all the nightclubs together" in the period before the prince was married: "They were quite wild times, and it was thought a little delicate for Prince Philip when Elizabeth became Queen."[67]

Publicly, Ward was a determined social climber. His mostly female friends were amazed that his patients included Winston Churchill, Frank Sinatra, and a significant section of the nobility: "His main weapon was his connections." But privately, he disdained them. Christine Keeler recalled that he had "no time for Prince Phillip and was always putting him down in conversation" because he hated the establishment. Becoming quite animated, Ward ranted: "They marry their cousins and land up retarded and deformed with the interbreeding."[68]

At this time, within Soviet intelligence, the GRU took the lead on targeting the Royal Family, rather than the KGB.[69] Captain Eugene Ivanov was a GRU military intelligence officer under cover as an assistant naval attaché at the embassy in London. He was friends with Ward, but also enjoyed sexual relations with Christine Keeler. Ivanov's involvement turned a society sex scandal into a security affair. Keeler explained the chain of events precisely: "If I hadn't gone to bed with Yevgeny Ivanov that night, it is very likely that none of it would ever have happened. My love affair with John Profumo, the Minister of War, would never have developed overtones of treason. Harold Macmillan's government might not have been rocked to its socks. Stephen Ward would never have killed himself."[70]

Given the security paranoia that the Profumo affair eventually triggered, it is truly remarkable how smoothly Ivanov swam in the higher echelons of British society in the early 1960s. Whizzing round London, sometimes at the wheel of a Rolls-Royce owned by his friend Paul Richey, the famous fighter pilot, or weekending at Cliveden, home of the rich and influential US-born Astor family and location of many a high society party, his rise was irresistible—yet intensely puzzling.

Ivanov's entrance into British society came via a chance meeting at an embassy party with Sir Colin Coote, managing director of the *Telegraph* and a close friend of Churchill. They bonded over their mutual suspicions of West German rearmament, and later Coote introduced Ivanov to Stephen Ward at the Garrick Club. Ward was trying to get a visa for Russia to sketch members of the Politburo, and Coote thought Ivanov could help—the friendship between the two quickly took off. Ivanov was being watched, and so Ward was approached by MI5.[71] Some have suggested that this was all arranged by MI5 as an entrapment, but whether this was true or not, Ward provided Ivanov with some royal opportunities. On July 21, 1960, Ivanov attended his first garden party at Buckingham Palace.[72]

Ivanov was deeply interested in the royals, especially Philip, and believed that the connection between Ward and the Royal Family was valuable. He first contrived to meet Philip by acting as an interpreter for a famous Soviet polar explorer, Mikhail Somov, who was visiting London. The location was a reception at the Royal Geographical Society. Ivanov engaged the prince in conversation, and "the subject of physical geography soon gave way to political geography." He tried to engage Philip on topics such as the German question, the nuclear arms race, and the Common Market, but "he cautiously evaded my bait."[73]

Ivanov concluded that his "head-on attack" had failed, so he resolved to try "more subtle means." He returned to his trusted friend Ward and plied him for more background information on Philip. "Remember that photo album?" Ward helpfully responded. Ivanov had forgotten about it. "Look at the photographs again and you'll understand," he added significantly. Ivanov looked again and saw Philip and his cousin David at a club together with Antony Beauchamp, son-in-law of Churchill; Arthur Christiansen, editor of the *Daily Express*; and a number of girls—including "Nicole" and "Maggie." Ward drifted away toward the kitchen to make coffee, and Ivanov momentarily thought about stealing the photos—but thinking better of it, he produced his Minox camera and "photographed five or six of the snapshots." Ward returned and talked about Philip's life in parties and clubs. Ivanov reciprocated with gossip about high life in Moscow. Later he recalled, "I sent the photographs and my report to Moscow Centre."[74]

All this was part of a wider Russian operation targeting the whole Royal Family called Operation House.[75] MI5 knew that the Russians were spying on the royals and that Ivanov had sent various society tidbits, supposedly including photographs, back to his headquarters in Russia. Neither Ivanov nor his colleagues ever used the compromising information to try to blackmail the Royal Family, however. This, according to one senior MI5 officer, was because the GRU thought it was fake.[76] Either way, it caused enough consternation to be taken seriously by the inquiry into the Profumo affair—and for the relevant files to remain locked away from historians' eyes.

How did MI5 know all this? It appears that the security service had an agent at the very center of Ward's flamboyant social circle. This was Mariella Novotny, aka "Miss Kinky"; Keeler believed she was "an informant" for both the police and MI5.[77] Lord Denning, a senior judge appointed by the government to conduct an inquiry into the affair, interviewed her at length. Intriguingly, and perhaps for this reason, she was airbrushed from the final report, which was devoured with voyeuristic relish by the public.[78] The other reason that Novotny vanished is that she most likely had a relationship with John F. Kennedy. The Kennedy connection set the nerves of the White House jangling, and waves of FBI officers were dispatched to London and New York to uncover any stories of espionage or scandal.[79] They were ordered to keep it close to their chests and only "personally advise the president" of anything they found.[80] Novotny continued to work for the authorities for two decades and died in curious circumstances in 1983, shortly before the scheduled publishing of a personal memoir. The book has never been published.[81]

Profumo was obviously Ivanov's top target. Second were the Astors, a high society family of politicians and business leaders, who opened amazing doors for him into the establishment. "Third on my list were Princess Margaret and Antony Armstrong-Jones." Again, he recalled that he was introduced to them by Ward, "who also equipped me with certain details about their life" which were available to him because "he loved gossip and had known the royal family for years." This connection, he added darkly, "held out the possibility of getting information through provocation and blackmail."[82]

Ivanov targeted Princess Margaret, the queen's sister, quite successfully. He met her on numerous occasions, hoping to elicit scandalous information. He even attended the reception after her wedding to Antony Armstrong-Jones and then spent time with them at Ascot and at the Henley Regatta. They never missed a regatta, and afterward "they usually invited me into their boat." After chatting with Margaret on a voyage along the Thames, he then returned to Ward and traded royal gossip.[83]

Unfortunately for Ivanov, blackmail was hardly possible, since he soon found himself in hopeless competition with the newspapers; rumors detailing Margaret's personal life were rarely out of the press.[84] Ivanov was apparently not the only one targeting Margaret; an unnamed senior officer from Soviet military intelligence later claimed that one of her butlers, Thomas Cronin, was actually a Russian agent—code-named Rab. He apparently fed maps of state rooms and royal gossip back to Moscow.[85]

In April 1963, the Profumo scandal broke. Ivanov fled back to Moscow, escaping what was possibly a honey-trap operation that was about to envelop him.[86] Meanwhile, investigative reporters from the *Sunday Times* stumbled on the royal dimension. They were interviewing an expressionist painter, Feliks Topolski, who hosted Ward's circle in his studios, when Philip's name came up. Four years earlier, Philip had commissioned Topolski to paint a huge, ninety-five-foot-long mural commemorating Elizabeth's coronation. It was to be hung in the state apartments at Buckingham Palace. Now, after mentioning Philip's name in relation to the Profumo affair, Topolski quickly dried up.

Soon afterward, a certain "Mr. Shaw," from MI5, telephoned one of the reporters and asked if he, along with two colleagues, could meet him in a hotel near Saint James's Park tube station. Shaw, in his mid-fifties, appeared with two younger men. They had known about pretty much every person the journalists had interviewed, but specifically wanted to know what Topolski had said about Prince Philip. The journalists explained that they were investigating political coverups and the consequences for Macmillan's faltering government. The Philip angle, tantalizing as it might have been, was irrelevant. Shaw and his colleagues seemed relieved, leaving the journalists suspicious that MI5 had a special team to protect the Royal Family's interests.[87]

And maybe it did. Three years earlier, Princess Margaret had privately alluded to MI5 making special arrangements for her partner Antony Armstrong-Jones to meet the queen and ask permission to marry. Officers had escorted him across muddy fields of the Sandringham estate to avoid any watching photographers. Margaret told a friend shortly after the engagement that "it's wonderful no one guessed the reason of his visit and I only wish you had been in on the MI5 arrangements by which he was whisked into the Queen's room to ask the vital permission."[88]

Profumo resigned in disgrace in early June 1963; he begged to be excused the customary valedictory audience with the queen.[89] Labour politicians were disappointed. They hoped that any such meeting would highlight the closeness between the royals and Profumo, doing immense damage to the establishment and helping to create the conditions for a Labour government.[90]

Meanwhile, Macmillan, ill and fading from office, wrote personally to the queen to apologize after this latest sorry episode in the series of spy scandals that had dogged his administration. He apologized for mishandling the crisis—which, with its mixture of sex, spies, and the establishment—had damaged the fabric of society. Macmillan explained that he had had no idea "of the strange underworld in which other people, alas beside Mr Profumo have allowed themselves to become entrapped."[91] This was all the more humiliating for Macmillan because his wife, Dorothy, was having a decades-long affair with Robert Boothby, the bisexual politician—and the Royal Family knew all about it.[92] The queen consoled Macmillan, saying how difficult it was for people with high standards to suspect others of lacking them.[93]

Elizabeth—via her dispatch boxes, the press, and her connections—learned about the Profumo affair as it unfolded. She refused to blame the beleaguered minister and remained on good terms with him as he publicly devoted his later life to charity work. However, it appears his private life remained unreformed, and he rather enjoyed his notoriety. At a dinner party thrown in his honor by the Queen Mother, he took the opportunity to proposition a teenage girl, using the most direct language.[94] The Queen Mother still lunched with Profumo as late as 2000.[95]

The queen also knew all about Anthony Blunt. Blunt, a close friend of Queen Mary, had worked illustriously for MI5 during the war, and accepted the position of surveyor of the king's pictures, effectively the royal art historian, when it ended in 1945. If being a spy and an art historian were not enough, Blunt also had a third life, as a talent spotter for Soviet intelligence, starting in 1937.

In 1945, the KGB was delighted with Blunt's position in the palace, hoping that his royal connections would give him access to the king—and the king's secrets. Sadly for Moscow, this turned out not to be the case.[96] He avoided royal social events and, starting in the early 1950s, when Queen Elizabeth inherited him, he delegated much of this work to his deputy, Oliver Millar.[97] Before the war, Blunt was a charismatic socialite, but his secret life took its toll. Outwardly appearing the composed and elegant academic, he suffered from exhaustion and turned to drink in the 1950s. He gradually became more introverted and colder, concentrating on his academic work.[98] Nonetheless, MI5 intercepted mail from Guy Burgess in which the Soviet spy, now living in Moscow, played upon "his knowledge of the association between BLUNT and the British Royal Family."[99]

What is now clear is that the Royal Family knew that Blunt was a KGB agent as early as 1948. Tommy Lascelles even referred to him as "our Russian spy." Blunt's treachery was tightly held in MI5 but was the subject of common or garden tea-time gossip in the palace. The next year, Mark Milbank, master of the royal household, made exactly the same quip to Oliver Millar when he arrived as Blunt's deputy.[100]

Blunt had undertaken discreet business on behalf of the royals in the past. He had visited Europe twice in 1945 and twice again in 1946 to recover sensitive documents and other materials for the Royal Family. Nearly two decades later, as the Profumo scandal broke, Blunt had apparently conducted another discreet mission, purchasing an embarrassing portrait of Prince Philip drawn by Stephen Ward.[101] A teenage assistant to Ward, who later became a Labour-member of Parliament, recalls only that "a member of the royal household" bought the picture for cash, "no questions asked."[102]

Although he no longer had direct access to classified material, Blunt did keep in touch with Soviet intelligence while working at the palace, passing on gossip or tidbits that came his way. And he certainly came into enough contact with royal life for the palace to raise concerns about him as early as 1951. The dramatic defection of Guy Burgess and Donald Maclean in May of that year provoked questions about Blunt, who was a known friend of Burgess. King George VI had pressed Lascelles for details on the case soon after the pair went missing. Guy Liddell, Lascelles's cousin and deputy director of MI5, replied that he had no more news beyond what the newspapers had reported.

This was not the whole truth. After the Foreign Office put out a bland statement that two diplomats, one of whom had suffered a mental breakdown a year before, were missing from their homes, the press reveled in wild speculation. Journalists asked embarrassing questions about widespread sexual perversion in the Foreign Office. Behind the scenes, the government launched an urgent inquiry into security, and the net began to close in on the most famous traitor of all, Kim Philby.[103]

Liddell held back on the truth about the treachery of Burgess and Maclean, but the king was more concerned about Blunt. The art historian had barricaded himself in his apartment, away from the legions of hungry journalists outside on the street. Blunt and Burgess had actually shared an apartment during the war; the two were close. Liddell reassured him that "no mention was made of Anthony and his association with Burgess, which had been referred to by at least one paper."[104]

A month later, Lascelles was on the phone again. The palace was still concerned about Blunt. Liddell again reassured him that he was "convinced" that Blunt, whom he knew well, had "never been a communist in the full political sense, even during his days at Cambridge." Lascelles was "very glad to hear this, since it was quite possible that the story might get around to the Royal Family." He worried that the king or queen would raise the topic with him and was glad to be able to reassure them.[105]

Lascelles then told Liddell how "Blunt had on one occasion intimated to the Queen that he was an atheist, . . . and that the Queen had been a little shaken by his remarks. He was certain that if he now went up and told her that Anthony was a communist, her immediate reaction would be "I always told you so.""[106]

Liddell was wrong; the king was right to be worried. While working at the palace, Blunt had acted as a courier for Burgess between 1945 and 1947, and had occasional meetings with Russian intelligence. He later confessed that

Burgess had warned him about the net closing in on Maclean and that, using his Russian contacts, he had facilitated their arrangements to defect.[107] Afterward, still working at the palace, he also assisted Philby's contact with the KGB on one occasion. Later, he insisted that he had had no contact with Russian intelligence after 1956.[108]

Yuri Modin, the key KGB handler for the Cambridge Five, recalled just how important Blunt was at this time: "Blunt, in effect, served as Burgess's permanent liaison with me. I would also seek him out whenever I needed information about MI5, where he still had plenty of friends. Sometimes I even asked him to procure up-to-date data on individual agents in the British counterespionage service. . . . I was to continue seeing Blunt until 1951."[109]

Blunt was a Soviet spy in the palace. He maintained his position in the royal household after the Burgess and Maclean scandal, and even after the writer Goronwy Rees made what turned out to be accurate allegations about him to MI5 shortly afterward. Rees offered no evidence, but the allegation generated eleven interviews between MI5 and Blunt. He remained composed and appeared in control. As part of the royal household, he received a knighthood in 1956.

In April 1964, armed with new intelligence, MI5 was ready to try interview number twelve. On April 13, its director general, Roger Hollis, informed the most senior official in the Home Office, Charles Cunningham, that MI5 intended to interrogate Blunt the next week. Given their previous failures in getting anything to stick, intelligence officers now wanted to offer Blunt immunity from prosecution in return for a confession. Three days later, the attorney general agreed.

The deal—if Blunt accepted—had clear implications for the Royal Family, given that he still worked for the palace. Hollis and Cunningham briefed Michael Adeane, Queen Elizabeth's private secretary, immediately afterward.[110] They told him that Blunt was suspected of having been a Russian agent, but that, provided he confessed and cooperated with MI5's inquiries, he would be granted immunity.[111]

Adeane listened intently, before asking what action the queen should take if Blunt did indeed confess. None, Hollis responded, because any action, such as firing him, would alert Russian intelligence and any other potential moles under investigation.[112]

On April 23, Blunt confessed. "Give me five minutes while I wrestle with my conscience," he responded, before admitting to MI5 of having been a Russian intelligence agent during the 1930s and that he had been privy to the defection of Burgess and Maclean in 1951.[113]

Shortly afterward, Adeane apparently called Peter Wright, a senior MI5 officer investigating Soviet moles, to the palace. Adeane was "punctilious and correct," assuring Wright that "the Palace was willing to co-operate in any inquiries the Service thought fit." He spoke, Wright recalled, "in the detached manner of someone who wishes not to know very much more about the matter." The queen, Adeane continued measuredly, "has been fully informed about Sir Anthony, and is quite content for him to be dealt with in any way which gets at the truth." But he did insist on one stipulation: "You may find Blunt referring to an assignment he undertook on behalf of the Palace—a visit to Germany at the end of the war. Please do not pursue this matter. Strictly speaking, it is not relevant to considerations of national security."[114] The palace duly followed the MI5 advice and allowed Blunt to remain in his post.[115]

Wright's account is not the most reliable, but other evidence corroborates that the queen did know. Prime Minister Edward Heath offered the queen a detailed report about Blunt's spying in the early 1970s.[116] It was the first time the government had formally told her, although successive prime ministers and cabinet secretaries professed not to know how much Adeane had informally passed on back in 1964. Such conversations were sacrosanct.[117] Heath was surprised to learn that she had already been told in general terms a decade earlier.[118]

Historians will likely never know her reaction. Perhaps a remark made by her mother could act as a guide. When talking about Burgess and Maclean, the Queen Mother once declared, in a comment relayed back to Blunt: "The one person I cannot stand is a traitor."[119]

Importantly, Queen Elizabeth knew far more about the case than the prime minister of the time, Alec Douglas-Home. Indeed, even Michael Adeane knew more about it than the prime minister.[120] Douglas-Home was not told about Blunt's activities, in his words, "before the knowledge was public property" in November 1979. This was surprising given the seriousness of the matter and the queen's involvement, but Douglas-Home insisted he would have remembered being told—even only orally.[121]

Perhaps it was precisely because it affected the queen that Douglas-Home was frozen out. Hollis apparently advised against briefing him. The aristocratic prime minister got on well with the queen. When he visited Balmoral, he did so as a friend as much as a prime minister. Hollis feared that Douglas-Home might refuse to compromise the queen by allowing Blunt to stay in the role. Doing so would have fatally undermined Blunt's cooperation.[122]

This seems unlikely. The secret was bound to come out at some point, embarrassing both Douglas-Home and the queen. When later digging into the affair, Margaret Thatcher's government deemed it far more likely that "in order to avoid the risk of compromising Blunt's co-operation, knowledge of his confession should be strictly confined to those who really needed to know, and that did not include Ministers." The failure to tell Douglas-Home was more misjudgment or negligence than conspiracy.[123]

Either way, the secret created a constitutional quandary. If the queen did know—and the prime minister did not—then it is striking that she did not raise the issue with him during their weekly audience. The unmasking of a Soviet spy was, after all, an extraordinary development.[124] Perhaps she was warned against it. The queen would have been unable to conduct her constitutional duties of advising and warning—this time for the unusual reason of knowing more secret information than a prime minister.

If Blunt now thought he could quietly stick to his scholarly day job and put his murky past behind him, he was sorely mistaken. The immunity deal did not spell the end of his association with intelligence—even as he continued his career at the palace.

Starting in 1964, he agreed to collaborate with MI5. He provided information about Russian intelligence activities and his association with Burgess, Maclean, and Philby. On top of this, and more intriguingly, he "collaborated with the Security Service in counterespionage operations, some of which are continuing."[125]

It is not clear how extensive these operations were. Hypothetically, they could have been rather active and involved him passing information, carefully curated by MI5, back to the Russians in order to mislead them. MI5 certainly wanted Russian intelligence to be "left in uncertainty about the extent of his disclosures to us."[126]

More likely, Blunt provided information to the British security services. MI5 acknowledged that, for years after his confession, he "provided information about his own activity in the service of the Russians during wartime, when he passed a great deal of material to them, and about others whom he knew or believed to have worked for the KGB or GRU before or during the war."[127] He also provided information about his role as a talent spotter in the 1930s. MI5 used Blunt's information to establish a "research team" to investigate the alleged ring of moles inside British intelligence. He helped it to achieve "considerable success" in uncovering both individuals and activities, including the removal of a senior Admiralty scientist from a sensitive post.[128]

An MI5 "special unit" also spent six years investigating communist involvement in student politics between 1929 and 1945, covering not just Cambridge University but also Oxford, London, Bristol, Leeds, Liverpool, Southampton, Sheffield, and other universities. Blunt would have been a key source, and the investigation ultimately examined eight thousand cases.[129] One thing is certain: Blunt's confession was not a one-time occurrence. He continued to discreetly collaborate with MI5 for a decade—all while still working for the queen.

At the same time, MI5 did not trust him. Intelligence officers assumed that he was still holding information back: "He may still be protecting friends." More than a decade after his confession, they wondered whether he still had some loyalty to the Russians or was even under a degree of Russian control—but after twenty years of investigation, they could not prove it.[130]

MI5 therefore put Blunt under surveillance. Every home secretary, from 1964 onward, signed "interception warrants on Blunt."[131] They clearly watched him—and listened to him—closely, wondering whether he was still double-crossing them. This raises the intriguing possibility that his communications with the royal household were tapped as part of the broader surveillance operation.

All the while, Elizabeth continued to see her royal art historian at various official events, including at the opening of the new Courtauld Gallery in 1968. In general, however, he avoided the queen in daily court life. When he had to go to the palace—for example, when offering tours to distinguished guests from the art world—he would creep around, desperately trying to avoid bumping into her.[132] On another occasion, he stood silently next to Prince Philip as the duke and Hugh Casson, the architect and designer, picked out paintings for the guest wing at Windsor Castle. Blunt, disdainful of their modernist choices, said nothing.[133] He did, however, maintain a good relationship with the Queen Mother. She thoroughly appreciated her own tour of the Courtauld Gallery, and the two very occasionally shared a box at the opera.[134] It is highly unlikely that she knew about his treachery.

Queen Elizabeth personally congratulated him on his eventual retirement in 1972. At long last, Blunt would leave the royal household, and the government could draw a line under his complex and sensitive career. Unfortunately, the retirement degenerated into a classic Whitehall farce. Martin Charteris remembers how he nearly fell off his chair when the lord chancellor, who did not know about Blunt's treachery, offered Blunt the honorary post of adviser on the queen's pictures, thereby continuing his association with the palace for a further six years.[135]

Blunt had few qualms about remaining in the royal household. He had no idea that MI5 had told Adeane back in 1964, and he did not accept any suggestion that he should have resigned: "I was there to do a job, and I still thought it was important to do and I was still doing it. I don't see why a confession in 1964 made any difference."[136]

By mid-1977, however, a super sleuth was on his trail. This was Peter Hennessy, Whitehall correspondent for the *Times*, who was adored but also feared by civil servants. He had just written a KGB "fourth man" story about Donald Beves, a don at Kings College, and other suspected communist trainers at Cambridge in the 1930s. In September, over a quiet dinner at Odin's Restaurant, he confided in Prime Minister Jim Callaghan's senior policy adviser, Bernard Donoughue, that he had other suspects: "One possible line had led to Sir Anthony Blunt, keeper of the Queen's pictures. Another pointed toward a former head of MI5." Donoughue concluded that there was "a time bomb in there somewhere," adding "as usual a lot of public school homosexuality. . . . All very messy."[137]

But for some strange reason, Hennessy's editor, William Rees-Mogg, was trying to "put him off the story."[138] Donoughue began watching the situation for Downing Street. Two months later, he discovered that Hennessy's source for the story about Beves was none other than Dick White, former head of MI6. He concluded that "this was clearly a delicate plant, to mislead Peter" and keep him away from a bigger story. The blameless Beves had been dead for years and so was ideal distraction material. The security agencies were worried about something with a royal aspect emerging. Donoughue noted in his diary: "Blunt?"[139]

Still under surveillance, Blunt resigned his final honorary consultancy in November 1978, after learning that his identity was about to be revealed.[140] He was overseeing a Holbein exhibition when, nervous and depressed, he asked to see an MI5 officer. They talked about Blunt's "residual connection" to the palace—a connection that was severed almost immediately afterward.[141] Remarkably, Blunt's association with the palace lasted until the very end.

The scandal started to emerge at the start of 1979, when it became clear that a revelatory book would indicate that the so-called fourth man was Anthony Blunt. Callaghan was troubled by the developments, even though he knew the story well and, as home secretary, had signed warrants for the intelligence services to intercept Blunt's communications long after his confession.[142] As prime minister, he now asked why Blunt should retain his knighthood, why the problem had not been dealt with earlier, and why it had taken the publication of a history book to prompt the government's disclosure.[143]

When the secret was about to be spilled, the cabinet secretary, Robert Armstrong, warned him that he "would have to consider very carefully how he had acquiesced in the continuing secrecy." Armstrong helpfully suggested that Callaghan might simply state that he did not want to embarrass the queen. This provided Callaghan, and others, with a premade get-out-of-jail-free card.[144] Sometimes the royals—and the secrecy surrounding them—provided a useful excuse for governmental obfuscation.[145]

With Blunt's identity about to be revealed, Callaghan needed a line to take on Blunt's palace connection. John Hunt, Armstrong's predecessor, had come up with this: the prime minister was not responsible for appointments in the royal household; "by 1964 he had his appointment for nearly 20 years, during which time he had no access to classified information"; and "although he had confessed, he had been given immunity from prosecution." Blunt was also, the government thought it prescient to point out, "undoubtedly a most distinguished art historian."[146] Hunt followed up with a detailed briefing on the royal dimension to the scandal, much of which remains classified.[147]

This was a fair defense. However, the relationship was more complex than the government wanted to admit. There are rumors that while working for the Royal Family, Blunt traveled to Beirut to tip off Kim Philby about his impending interrogation in the early 1960s. Blunt may well have had access to the inside story through his friendships with Dick White and Victor Rothschild, and he lied about supposedly visiting Lebanon in search of the frog orchid—a flower that did not grow there. The ambassador there was an old friend and, upon finding out about Blunt's guilt, was furious at the thought that Blunt might have used him as an excuse to make two trips to see Philby.[148]

Even if those rumors are false, documents show that Blunt continued to collaborate in counterespionage operations and remained under MI5's surveillance—a reality far removed from the anodyne government line that Blunt had no association with the secret world while a member of the royal household.

By the time the scandal finally broke in November 1979, Margaret Thatcher had just replaced James Callaghan in Downing Street. With the heady mix of royals, security, and spies, Robert Armstrong knew this was a "minefield." He warned Thatcher's team that "if you are not thoroughly familiar with it, it is both easy and dangerous inadvertently to put a foot wrong."[149]

So delicate was the question of the queen that successive private secretaries had to give their express permission for Thatcher to reveal publicly that Adeane "had been kept fully in the picture throughout the episode."[150] There was no question of revealing whether he had told the queen.

We are unlikely to ever know the full truth about Blunt and the royals. In November 1979, as the Blunt bombshell burst in public, Thatcher privately gave Armstrong the mission of exploring the affair on her behalf and finding out just what deals had actually been struck down the decades. First, he carefully read all the top-secret material, and then he contacted the key participants. He later recalled: "I wrote to Michael Adeane, who had been Private Secretary to the Queen, and to Sir Charles Cunningham, who had been Permanent Secretary at the Home Office. Cunningham and Adeane both had totally different recollections from the account that was in our official files."[151]

Meanwhile, others scrambled over lurid stories emerging in the press. The *Sunday Times* reported a garbled story that accused Jock Colville of having lunch with John Cairncross while the former was Princess Elizabeth's private secretary. Cairncross had worked on the Enigma decrypts at Bletchley Park during the war, but had secretly shared the material with Soviet intelligence. He had since been outed as a Soviet spy. Colville panicked and quickly telephoned the prime minister's office to set the record straight. They had actually lunched in 1939—long before Cairncross had passed intelligence to the Soviets, and long before Colville worked at the palace.[152] Anything mixing the queen and Soviet espionage, however wrongly or tangentially, was dynamite.

Thatcher barely commented on the palace dimension, merely pointing out that Blunt's knighthood, conferred in 1956, was "the queen's personal gift" and that he forfeited it not on the government's recommendation but on that of the palace.[153] Blunt, trying to save face, claimed that when he found out the queen was going to strip him of his knighthood, he immediately wrote "to the proper authority offering to resign it, but presumably the letter did not arrive before the announcement was made."[154] Shortly afterward, friends asked the Queen Mother for her opinion. "Lovely day, isn't it," she replied, keeping a fixed smile.[155] It was not for nothing that Tommy Lascelles dubbed her "the imperial ostrich."[156]

Opinion about Blunt divided the establishment. In some ways, this mirrored his own schizophrenia as both a professional snob and longtime secret servant of the Soviet Union. He offered a self-serving and dishonest account at a press conference stage-managed by the *Times*, where he was served with white wine and smoked trout.[157] About this event, Roy Strong, director of the Victoria and Albert Museum and an intimate of the royal family, challenged William Rees-Mogg, the paper's editor—who then rather sheepishly conceded that Blunt was indeed vile. In Strong's opinion, Blunt had emerged into the spotlight with "suave condescending deviousness," expressing not a word of regret for the embarrassment he had caused the queen; everything was "blurred by deceit and deviousness."[158]

Thereafter, as Strong probed his friends in the art world, he was "amazed by how many people seem to have known about it." Though many shared his "revulsion" for Blunt, this did not extend to the royals.[159] In November 1981, Strong attended a private dinner given by Princess Margaret for about twenty people at Kensington Palace, which he noted was now rather "grubby and run-down." The princess was "straight onto the whisky and cigarettes." Strong did not enjoy himself and "escaped" early, noting that "it was awful to hear HRH droning on about how wonderful Anthony Blunt was."[160]

Elizabeth was a young queen at the height of the Cold War. She soon found herself dragged into international intrigue and spy scandals. Through it all, she was, as Harold Macmillan put it, "incredibly well informed."[161] She knew all about Profumo and Blunt. She once abruptly shut down the Labour politician Richard Crossman when he tried to ask her about Kim Philby.[162]

She also knew about some of the most sensitive aspects of international politics. Macmillan briefed her, for example, on the CIA's secret army in Laos.[163]

He took full advantage of her total discretion, and found her a great support.[164] He once confessed to the queen that he had fallen asleep as the West German chancellor, Konrad Adenauer, delivered a postlunch speech about how to counter communism.[165] Macmillan was enthusiastic about royalty and a loyal defender of the establishment, but perhaps the royals did not enjoy his company as much as they pretended. Behind his back, they enjoyed calling him "the Horse," and were inclined to laugh at him. In fact, they rather preferred his less stuffy Labour opponent, Harold Wilson.[166]

Wilson, who came to power in 1964, also treated the queen as a confidante. He attached great importance to his weekly audiences, which became longer and longer. One lasted for two hours; another finished with an invitation to stay for drinks. He never divulged what was said in those meetings, but he returned to Number 10 in a euphoric mood and sometimes seemed to have modified his opinions as a consequence of talking with the queen.[167]

The feelings were reciprocated, and Wilson was probably the queen's all-time favorite prime minister. Shortly before, the Americans had expressed worries about Wilson's loyalty amid swirling rumors about his relations with Soviet intelligence. Did his Conservative predecessors brief the queen about these worries? The CIA had indeed asked Macmillan directly about Wilson, but he considered this quite "absurd," adding, "I don't suppose in the history of this country—at least in modern history—a PM has had such an extraordinary question asked by an ally about the Leader of the Opposition."[168] MI5 had taken an interest in him for some time because of his frequent trips to Russia while in the opposition during the 1950s. Like many other politicians, the KGB had assigned him a code name, "Olding," but they did not recruit him.[169]

For all the intrigue, espionage, and discreet diplomacy of the Cold War, Britain was also facing a more immediate threat: the decline of what remained of its Empire. So, along with battling the Kremlin, the crown also fought the insidious forces of decline, and a key battleground was the queen's relations with the royal families of the Middle East.

13

Queen Elizabeth's Empire

Intrigue in the Middle East

Queen Elizabeth was "surprised nobody had
found means of putting something in his coffee."
—Evelyn Shuckburgh's diary

During Queen Victoria's reign, the British Empire ruled the world. It had
expanded to become the biggest in human history, covering a quarter of the
world's land surface. It stretched from the white sands of the Caribbean in the
west to the dense jungles of Malaya in the east. Although its economic power was
declining even in the nineteenth century, its geographical vastness peaked shortly
after King Edward VII's death in 1910; after the two world wars that followed,
the British Empire was visibly faltering. George VI was the last king-emperor of
India, for so long the jewel in the imperial crown. India achieved independence
in 1947. Burma, Palestine, and Ceylon followed suit soon afterward. Many of the
transitions from empire to Commonwealth were presided over by Lord Mountbatten in grand and colorful ceremonies; he was the royal undertaker of empire
"who never wore black."[1]

By the time Queen Elizabeth ascended the throne, the empire had dwindled
to parts of southern and eastern Africa, Aden, British Guiana and some small
Caribbean islands, Malaya, and Singapore. Fervent nationalism, emboldened by
success after success, swept from one moribund colony to the next. The young
Elizabeth inherited a communist insurrection in Malaya that had broken out
in 1948. One of the very first documents that bore the now-familiar line "Her
Majesty's Government" was a blueprint for winning it. Another insurgency was
beginning in Kenya even as she became queen in 1952.

Elizabeth's reign oversaw colossal change: the decline of Britain and the
death of its empire. The Commonwealth, of which she was head, was to be the
future. Supporters have lauded her role in steadfastly guiding this transition as
the defining achievement of her reign. In truth, the Commonwealth was little
more than a myth; for though it played a significant development and education
role, its global significance was ever decreasing.[2] The Middle East underwent
an especially messy transition; by 1952, much of the formal empire was gone

in that region, but the British presence remained provocatively strong, taking the form of military bases, businesses, co-dominions, and close advisory relationships with pliant sultans.[3]

Accordingly, the Middle East became a flashpoint of rising nationalism and declining imperialism in the early years of Elizabeth's reign. It was a region of vital strategic importance. Aden, one of the few remaining real colonies, allowed Britain to project force into the Far East, which was essential, given that Conservative Party leaders intended for the country to remain a global power; the Suez Canal, running through Egypt, formed the core artery for transporting goods and oil between east and west; and oil fields in the region, especially in Iran and Iraq, were of immense importance for Britain's faltering postwar economy. British influence was such that historians often describe the region as an "informal empire." Managing this was a ticklish business: Britain had to balance the security of oil and imperial communications with the retention of Arab and Iranian tolerance by showing some recognition of nationalist aspirations.[4]

By the 1950s, the scales tilted in the nationalists' favor. As the British desperately tried to cling on to their influence, the communists—and the Americans—sought their own foothold and emboldened nationalists pressed for more autonomy. The Middle East became a hotbed of subversion and intrigue, coups, and countercoups. Given the importance—and constant turbulence—in the region, it is unsurprising that Elizabeth took a keen interest in intelligence and shadowy goings on. Harold Macmillan, as foreign secretary in the mid-1950s, repeatedly praised her "uncanny knowledge" of Middle Eastern politics and its leaders.[5]

Iran was particularly rife with intrigue and espionage. It had been a theater of Anglo-Russian competition during the Great Game, and, more recently, Britain had quietly supported an Iranian coup in 1921 to counter Soviet designs on the country, something that had brought the shah to power. But in September 1940, during the Second World War, German intrigue began to bubble up in the region, so the British and the Soviets invaded Iran, removed the suspect shah, and replaced him with his son, Mohammad Reza Pahlavi. The new shah never forgot that British intrigue had been responsible for both the rise and the fall of his father, who died a British prisoner in South Africa in 1944.[6]

In late July 1948, the young shah, still only in his late twenties, visited Buckingham Palace. The focus was military power, and the shah, himself a qualified Spitfire pilot, was taken to the Royal Air Force and naval flying displays.[7] Later, he asked King George VI, constitutional monarch to constitutional monarch, for an alliance between their two countries. George snubbed him with an "extremely noncommittal" response. Diplomats sitting across Saint James's Park in the Foreign Office breathed a collective sigh of relief. They worried that any such alliance would create unnecessary trouble by upsetting the Soviets for little material benefit. After George dismissed the request, the young shah had better sense than to raise it again.[8]

In 1951, Iran's popular and nationalist prime minister, Mohammad Mossadeq, nationalized Iranian oil. At a stroke, he wiped out about £170 million—about £3 billion in today's terms—of British revenue each year. In London, cabinet ministers described the move as "dynamite."[9] Through the Anglo-Iranian Oil Company, Britain had come to enjoy the lion's share of Iranian oil profits, upon which politicians heavily depended as they struggled with the brutal financial consequences of the Second World War. America's war loans now had to be repaid, so Iran's oil nationalization was financially disastrous for Britain.

By early 1953, the situation had deteriorated even further. For Britain, with Queen Elizabeth now on the throne, Iran was a priority, indeed a crisis. The shah was still in power, but he endured a tempestuous relationship with his prime minister. Meanwhile, Mossadeq's dramatic move rang alarm bells about the spread of nationalism elsewhere, notably in Iraq, where the UK managed the Iraq Petroleum Company, and Egypt, where it controlled the Suez Canal. The government quickly instigated a campaign of subversion, propaganda, and bribery, hoping to remove Mossadeq from serving as prime minister. Plans centerd on discrediting the prime minister and ultimately convincing the wavering shah to replace him with a more amenable candidate.[10]

In February 1953, it looked as if the shah, whom the lead MI6 officer described as "a kind of Hamlet," was on the verge of leaving Iran—potentially forever.[11] His departure would have fatally undermined plans for a coup. Without him, the Iranian opposition would have had no rallying point; Mossadeq would be the uncontested leader of Iran.

On February 14, Mossadeq lashed out at British subversion. He had already expelled Britain's diplomats and intelligence officers from the country. Now he told the US ambassador, Loy Henderson, that the "British, whilst pretending that they desired settlement, were using their numerous Iranian contacts to overthrow him through alliances of forces."[12] He had a point: in the very same week, the chief of MI6 was in Washington trying to persuade the CIA to join it in engineering a coup.[13]

Meanwhile, diplomats in the Foreign Office got cold feet; and, a week later, they decided to gradually "taper off" the monthly sum of £10,000 that they had been giving local agents to buy politicians and column inches for the past year and a half. This reflected the sentiments of Britain's foreign secretary, Anthony Eden, who had doubts about covert action.[14]

Against the background of all this uncertainty, rumors began to circulate about the shah's imminent departure. Alarmed, American and British officials knew that the shah was their main asset and that his absence would provide a golden opportunity for communists and other domestic opponents to smear him. The shah would have no means to defend himself once in hiding.[15]

On February 27, Queen Elizabeth, who had been on the throne for almost exactly a year, appeared to discreetly meddle in Iranian affairs herself. Naturally sympathetic to the plight of another constitutional monarch, she shared the growing concerns that the shah's departure would have a disastrous impact on Iran. With the shah due to leave the following day, Elizabeth seemingly urged Eden to find "some means of dissuading him from leaving."[16]

Back in Iran, Henderson, the US ambassador, was himself desperately try-ing to dissuade the shah from departing. With the British Embassy closed, he was the main conduit for messages not only from Washington but also from London. Suddenly, he received an encoded telegram "from Anthony Eden from Queen Elizabeth" exhorting the shah to stay in place. At once, he leapt on the message, ensuring that it reached the shah personally. It indicated, Henderson told one of the shah's aides, that a "very important personage" for whom the shah "had most friendly feelings had also expressed sincere hope that Shah could be dissuaded from leaving country."[17]

The shah was about to flee. But ever the prevaricator, the message piqued his interest enough for him to speak with Henderson directly. The stakes were high and the risks were real. Henderson knew full well that Mossadeq might have tapped the telephone line between the embassy and the palace; but, given the circumstances, thought it was a risk worth taking. He implored the shah not to leave and, worrying about eavesdroppers, told him as indirectly as possible that Queen Elizabeth wanted him to stay. The shah expressed appreciation, but insisted that he must go anyway.[18]

Elizabeth's supposed message was particularly sensitive because Mossadeq still accused "British agents" of "trying to stir up dissension" in the country. Any hint that the queen herself was personally involved in interfering in the internal affairs of Iran would have been explosive.[19]

Remarkably, there had been a colossal misunderstanding. The message had come from a different Queen Elizabeth—the boat, not the monarch. Anthony Eden had been on board the SS *Queen Elizabeth* en route to a conference in Canada when he had urged the shah to stay.[20]

The US Embassy in London hastily sent an embarrassed follow-up and cor-rection: "Queen Elizabeth refers of course to vessel and not—repeat not—to monarch." The garbled original message was badly drafted and open to misin-terpretation. By this time, however, the damage had been done. Henderson had alluded to the queen's intervention in error. He was aghast, and he confessed that he would never have dared do all the things he had done in the last twenty-four hours unless he had thought he was under direction from Buckingham Palace.

And so began an American cover-up. Knowing that Britain—and the monarch—would have been furious, the US diplomats quietly agreed among each other not to inform their British counterparts. They also kept it from the shah. He had listened to the message "from the queen" in good faith. If the US told the truth now, he would have felt misinformed—or even intentionally duped. This could have had terrible implications for the already fragile relationship between the shah, Britain, and the United States. He had been persuaded to take a big risk in staying; and had thought that—monarch to monarch—the queen had provided advice. It was a false premise.[21]

News of the shah's impending departure leaked to two of Mossadeq's most implacable enemies: Ahmad Qavam and the family of Fazlollah Zahedi (who had been arrested shortly before). Qavam, with the secret encouragement of Britain, had briefly served as prime minister in 1952 before protests forced him out.[22] Zahedi, a general and former police chief, would become the MI6/CIA choice to head the eventual coup.

Qavam quickly called Ayatollah Behbahani, a friend of the beleaguered shah and widely believed to be under British influence. Foreign Office diplomats had rated him as "quite unscrupulous and corrupt, ready to sell his influence on the bazaars to the highest bidder."[23] Meanwhile, Zahedi's family called Ayatollah Kashani, a one-time ally of Mossadeq who now derided him as a communist puppet. Both Behbahani and Kashani successfully rallied a crowd of a few thousand to protest against Mossadeq. Other pro-British political organizations, military personnel, and paid thugs soon joined in. The mob besieged the prime minister's house a few hundred yards from the palace. At 3 p.m., the shah informed his supporters that he would not, after all, leave the country.[24]

Just over a fortnight later, in mid-March, the CIA delivered the news for which MI6 had long been hoping: the US was finally ready to discuss tactics for a coup against Mossadeq. Under pressure from Prime Minister Winston Churchill, and reassured by the offer of a joint covert operation, the Foreign Office finally approved it a month later.[25] Conveniently, the ever-anxious Eden was in the hospital awaiting an operation, leaving the bullish Churchill in full control of foreign affairs.

The shah remained nervous about the British because he had a notably exaggerated view of the capabilities of the British Empire and its secret service. In mid-May, he confided in Henderson that they could "keep him in power or remove him as they saw fit." Despite believing he had received a message from the queen asking him to stay, he was very anxious to know what London was thinking and was full of wild fears. He asked: "Did the British wish to substitute another Shah for himself or abolish the monarchy? Were the British behind the present efforts to deprive him of his power and prestige?"[26] On May 22, 1953, Churchill sent him a message, again asking him to stay, adding that he would "be very sorry to see the Shah leave his current post or be driven out," and he asked Henderson to assure the shah that "it comes personally from me."[27]

In August, amid a blizzard of protests and propaganda, the shah replaced Mossadeq with Zahedi as prime minister. The move almost unraveled when Mossadeq evaded arrest, and his supporters took to the streets. The shah hid, never quite trusting the British. Back in London, Churchill was furious with the lack of updates.[28] In the end, as mob violence eventually turned the tables against Mossadeq, the plan succeeded.

Norman Darbyshire, the MI6 officer who worked most closely with the CIA, recalled: "My brief was very simple; . . . use the intelligence service for any money you might need to secure the overthrow of Mossadegh by legal or quasi-legal means." In creating rent-a-mobs and buying newspapers, he spent "vast sums of money, well over a million-and-a-half pounds." Together with CIA officers, he was personally "directing the street uprising."[29]

The similarities between the August coup and the events of late February, when the queen "intervened," are striking. It formed a prelude for the eventual overthrow of Mossadeq; the shah demanded a secret message from London proving that Britain was on board before launching the crucial order, while the CIA and MI6 resurrected many of the propaganda lines used back in February, especially those accusing Mossadeq of forcing the shah to abdicate and instigating a regime change of his own.[30]

In the aftermath of the coup, Loy Henderson, the US ambassador in Tehran, was in a celebratory mood. He suggested that "it might be useful for Queen Elizabeth II or Prime Minister Churchill to send an oral message of congratulations to the Shah through American channels."[31] Eisenhower had already sent a missive praising the shah and, with no evident sense of irony, he urged strong leadership to "eliminate foreign-inspired subversion."[32] With words like "subversion" in the air, officials in London mused: "I don't think there can be any question of the Queen sending a message."[33] They did not need to worry, for the very next day, Churchill, enamored by the covert operation, insisted on sending the message himself: "I salute and congratulate Your Majesty on your safe return to your country."[34]

Privately, animosity and suspicion remained. In January 1954, Eden, now returned from the hospital, warned his officials that "the shah is a miserable and despicable character."[35] Much of the tension surrounded the fact that the oil nationalization issue remained unresolved and difficult.

With the British Embassy in Tehran now reopened, opportunities presented themselves for more secret work. One British diplomat there, Charles

Wiggin, was at a function when he found himself in the company of Eva Karl, the mother of the Iranian queen, whom he described uncharitably as "a pretty hefty German blonde." Explaining that she had married the Iranian ambassador to West Germany in the 1950s, she was now stuck in Tehran, where she was kept short of money by her new family. Wishing to escape and retire to Switzerland, she made the British an unusual offer: "She would fix the oil dispute for us for cash; there need be no formalities about it; she had influence and, if we gave her the money, she would soon get the government to sign; was I influential enough to see that our side played their part in the deal?"

Wiggin was less worried about "the Queen's mother soliciting a bribe" and more worried about the fact that, having been drinking, she had spoken rather too loudly. He reflected that top society in Tehran held "dangers" for the inexperienced. In London, officials found the report rather amusing, and noted: "Strongly recommended reading. Ought we to send . . . to the Palace?"[36]

In February the next year, with the vexed oil issue finally settled, the shah himself visited Buckingham Palace to meet the queen.[37] He was a demanding guest, but Churchill was especially keen that it go well.[38] He was very clear that he owed his position to British intelligence and, when back at home, now insisted on meeting with the MI6 station chief weekly.[39] Even in the 1960s, he continued to meet both the MI6 and CIA station chiefs once a fortnight.[40] What exactly he said to the queen in Buckingham Palace is lost to history, but the lessons of the uncertain dynasties around her must have been clear; nothing could be taken for granted.

Because of oil, the shah and his dynasty remained a key intelligence target. A month after his visit, Britain received royal medical intelligence from the CIA. Medical intelligence on leaders was a new field and, in some cases, it even involved competition by field agents to collect urine samples from foreign leaders in the hope of gauging their health and longevity.[41] In this case, in 1955, Kermit Roosevelt of the CIA informed Britain that the shah and his wife had undergone medical tests to explore why they were having difficulty producing children. Sadly, and partly for these reasons, the shah and his wife, Queen Soraya, whom he loved deeply, eventually divorced.[42]

This provided a remarkable intelligence opportunity. The shah was now in search of his third wife, and he particularly desired a European princess. He was rejected by Princess Maria Gabriella of Savoy, a daughter of the deposed Italian king, and then turned his attention to Princess Alexandra, the daughter of the duke of Kent and Princess Marina—and the cousin of Queen Elizabeth. Belatedly, he realized that marriage to a Christian princess would raise too many difficulties at home and was now "resigned" to marrying an Iranian girl. Very privately, he told Geoffrey Harrison, the British ambassador, that "there are three girls in the running," and he was likely to choose quickly. He badly wanted a "British court official of advanced years and proven discretion to coach the bride-to be in Court etiquette." The shah felt the British court "was far more experienced and wise in court procedure than any other." London could not believe its luck.[43]

Securing intelligence from within Iranian inner court circles was hard. Now they had an extraordinary opportunity to insert a secret listener, plucked from British royal circles and placed in the heart of the Iranian court. But they worried that an elderly courtier, a Hardinge or even a Lascelles, would arouse "hostility." Better to go for a discreet ex-lady in waiting to Princess Margaret, who "could be represented in Teheran as a private secretary or English tutor . . . and would be less likely to give offence or arouse suspicion."[44] The British court remained quietly useful on these most sensitive of missions.

The subterranean court battle for intelligence on the shah was constant. Some years later, with a heavy heart, MI6 had to warn the head of the shah's entourage that the palace housekeeper, a British woman named "Florence," again engaged for her expertise in royal protocol and procedure, was in fact "having an affair with the chief of the KGB at the Soviet embassy." The minister of the court was horrified, but the shah seemed unsurprised and simply sent her on her way.[45]

In 1955, Queen Elizabeth grew concerned about developments in Jordan. The country had been a close ally since the First World War, and its rulers allowed Britain to retain air bases and a military force inside their territory. In return, Britain provided support to the Arab Legion, headed by British officers, which had become the nucleus of the Jordanian Army. Communist influence was negligible, but Egyptian and Saudi subversion was rife. The Egyptians tarred King Hussein of Jordan as an imperialist puppet; the Saudis bribed Jordanians, including members of the Royal Family, to weaken the king's influence.[46]

British intelligence soon warned of nefarious influences on young Hussein. Groomed for power by his grandfather, King Abdullah, from an early age, he had studied at Harrow School in northwest London, where, incidentally, he befriended Faisal, the future king of Iraq. Hussein was at his grandfather's side when an assassin murdered him. Just thirteen months later, in 1953, Hussein took the throne himself after his schizophrenic father abdicated. He was woefully inexperienced and only seventeen years old.

Hussein looked to his uncle, Sharif Nasser bin Jamil, for support and guidance. Britain feared that Nasser was turning the impressionable king against the British officers running the Arab Legion, including its British commander, Lieutenant General John Bagot Glubb. Small and courageous, "Glubb Pasha," as he was known, had led the legion for over twenty years, building it into one of the most formidable forces in the region. Out-surviving the British Empire, he still enjoyed unparalleled influence and respect in the country. Some saw him as a second Lawrence of Arabia or an uncrowned king of Jordan. He became a symbol of British influence and a target for anticolonial sentiment. Nasser's hostility toward Glubb stemmed partly from understandable nationalist rancor, but also from the more pragmatic fact that he saw Glubb as an obstacle to his business smuggling hashish and arms.

When diplomats in the Foreign Office found out that he sought to remove Glubb and his British colleagues from Jordan, they decided to "get rid of Nasser." They planned covert political action to discredit and smear him. They had to do so discreetly; if an operation was too obvious, then it would simply have turned Nasser into a martyr and consolidated the king's anti-British stance. Therefore, they subtly tried to implant doubts in Hussein's mind about Nasser's loyalty, thereby engineering his removal.[47]

Queen Elizabeth discussed the situation with Evelyn Shuckburgh, the diplomat in charge of Middle Eastern affairs, in a bright room sporting orange and gold pillars inside Buckingham Palace. Shuckburgh briefed her on the "machinations of the wicked uncle, Nasser." She responded by criticizing the impressionable young king: "She didn't really think it a good idea to send Arabs to English public schools. She had seen poor little Hussein fresh from Harrow a year or two ago, and all he could do was stand stiffly to attention, saying 'Your Majesty' and not another word."[48]

"As for Uncle Nasser," Shuckburgh remembered Elizabeth saying, "she was surprised nobody had found means of putting something in his coffee." This may have been a lighthearted comment, but it was not too far off the mark. MI6 would begin various plots to assassinate the other Nasser—the president of Egypt—the next year, and British covert operations were spreading like wildfire across the region. In the middle of the 1950s, MI6 officers were plotting regime change in Yemen, Saudi Arabia, Syria, and Egypt. Wittingly or not, Elizabeth was helping to legitimize covert action from inside Buckingham Palace.

Distracted by a cigarette steadily burning his fingertips behind his back, Shuckburgh replied that assassinating him "was a good idea which ought to be applied to a number of people in the Middle East." He "promised to send her the gossip we have heard about Hussein."[49]

Elizabeth's quip played on Shuckburgh's mind: "It was not until afterwards that I thought of what I ought to have said to this—that it was dangerously like a remark made on a famous occasion by her predecessor King Henry II."[50] Here, he was alluding to Henry's exhortation: "Will no one rid me of this troublesome priest?" leading to the death of Thomas Becket, archbishop of Canterbury, in

1170. The analogy points to the expression of a royal wish that may be interpreted as a command by subordinates.

British covert operations to discredit—rather than assassinate—the Jordanian Nasser failed. King Hussein expelled General Glubb less than a year later, in March 1956. He felt the need to publicly distance himself from the British because, throughout the region, political opponents commonly accused each other of being agents of a foreign power.[51] Hussein, equally keen to shake off his playboy prince reputation and prove himself a serious king, was therefore susceptible to his uncle's whispers.[52]

Glubb was given just two hours to leave the country. The stunned general refused: "I have lived here for twenty-six years. Almost all my worldly possessions are here, to say nothing of my wife and children." As a compromise, he agreed to leave the next morning. It was a personal tragedy for Glubb and another blow to Britain's position in the region.[53] The United States replaced Britain as the main country training its officers and supplying arms, while King Hussein soon became a paid agent of the CIA.[54]

This underlined the curious relationship between the CIA and MI6 in the region, simultaneously cooperating against Russia, but also competing for influence, especially with the various royal dynasties. A couple of weeks later, the queen learned of a new British covert action planned for neighboring Syria. Communism posed a far greater threat in this unreliable and unstable country than it did to the south in Jordan; so, too, did pan-Arab nationalism. With echoes of Iran, Britain had been trying for months to bring the reluctant CIA on board for a joint operation to overthrow the Syrian government. Together, a CIA–MI6 working group eventually drew up a plan, complete with the names of those they would assassinate.[55]

In March 1956, Anthony Eden approved regime change in Syria. His cabinet instructed the Foreign Office and MI6 to "establish in Syria a Government more friendly to the West."[56] This striking line—an incredibly rare allusion to covert action in a cabinet document—would surely have come up during his weekly audience with the queen. Shortly afterward, officials assured the foreign secretary that "covert action to diminish" Egyptian influence across the region was "being actively prepared."[57] Unfortunately for Eden, Britain's secret attempts to overthrow the Syrian regime collapsed in October 1956, not least because of concurrent events in Egypt—the infamous Suez Crisis was now unfolding.

A different Nasser now caused Britain a far greater headache than Hussein's "wicked" uncle. Gamal Abdel Nasser, president of Egypt and bête noire of

Prime Minister Anthony Eden, spearheaded a wave of Arab nationalism in the middle of the 1950s. It was this Nasser whose influence from Jordan to Syria and elsewhere really alarmed the British. MI6 officers, spurred on by Eden, really did consider slipping something into *his* coffee.

In July 1956, Nasser nationalized the Suez Canal after months of growing tension with Britain and France. Eden, suffering from ill health and increasingly unstable, reacted violently. Secretly colluding with Israel and France, he launched an ill-fated invasion. This precipitated a crisis that destroyed Eden's reputation, damaged relations with President Eisenhower, and offered a visible symbol of British imperial decline. Behind the scenes, it ignited decades of speculation about how much Queen Elizabeth knew—and whether she approved.

Nasser dramatically announced his decision about the canal on Thursday, July 26, 1956. The next weekend, Elizabeth and Philip were staying with Mountbatten at Broadlands, his country estate in Hampshire. An urgent phone call from Jean Chauvel, the French ambassador in London, interrupted Mountbatten as he entertained the royal couple. On the phone, Mountbatten learned that his French counterpart, the chief of the naval staff, had just arrived in London to convey the sense of urgency in Paris about the Suez Crisis. He wanted to make it abundantly clear that France would use military force to remove Nasser once and for all.[58]

Mountbatten apologized to his nephew and the queen before rushing to London on Sunday morning. The French offered Mountbatten and the defense secretary the full support of their armed forces to defeat Nasser.[59]

Elizabeth knew what was unfolding during the tense summer of 1956. She received intelligence reports, including the Joint Intelligence Committee's highly sensitive weekly summary of current intelligence, which gave a clear impression of growing Soviet influence in Egypt and across the region more broadly. She received intelligence warnings that the threat of force alone would not reverse Nasser's position, and that any military intervention had to be quick and decisive. Anything less would risk extreme international embarrassment. This turned out to be rather prescient; and international embarrassment was something about which the queen cared deeply.[60]

She also received papers from the cabinet's unwieldy Egypt Committee, which had been established to undertake both the military preparations and the diplomatic efforts to resolve the crisis.[61] Although Eden increasingly sidelined the committee as the planning became more secret, even cutting out the Joint Intelligence Committee, the queen remained informed through personal contacts, including Mountbatten. In August, he spent four days with her at Balmoral and, by autumn, was a regular at Windsor and Buckingham Palace.[62]

Uncle Dickie was critical of plans for an invasion and, as first sea lord, he exercised much influence during the crisis. With the chair of the Chiefs of Staff committee away ill, Eden treated him as the key figure when asking for service advice. Mountbatten, never lacking in self-confidence, was often willing to stray into political territory—much to the irritation of the Foreign Office. At the same time, Eden was sensitive to concerns that Mountbatten, whether directly or through his nephew Philip, had an unhealthy influence on the queen.[63]

Starting in early August, Mountbatten urged restraint and even considered resigning. It is inconceivable that he, never known for discretion, did not share his reservations with the queen. According to Martin Charteris, the queen's assistant private secretary, Mountbatten told Elizabeth that Eden's plans were "absolutely lunatic," hoping that she would then pass this message on to Eden, but representing it as her own warning. Charteris even claimed that the queen shared Mountbatten's concerns—much to Eden's anger.[64]

Elizabeth, of course, had more sources than just Mountbatten. She knew from Foreign Office papers that diplomats were becoming increasingly uncertain about Eden's policy.[65] On October 24, after three days of intensely secret negotiations outside Paris, Eden agreed to collude with Israel and France. The plan involved Israel invading Egypt, paving the way for Britain and France, feigning surprise, to intervene and separate the combatants. Foolishly, Eden hoped that this would provide a pretext to justify British military action.

That night, Patrick Dean, a senior diplomat, returned from the secret meeting in France to brief Eden and the inner circle. The only chief of staff present was none other than Mountbatten. Uncle Dickie was almost certainly one of the very few people to see a copy of the notorious "collusion" agreement before it was burnt.[66]

The next day, with collusion in place, Eden told the cabinet—and the queen—that the Israelis were "after all, advancing their military preparations with a view to making an attack on Egypt." He continued: if British forces went in, "we must face the risk that we should be accused of collusion with Israel." Cabinet "agreed in principle that, in the event of an Israeli attack on Egypt, the Government should join with the French Government in calling on the two belligerents to stop hostilities." If they failed to do so, "British and French forces would intervene to enforce compliance." Eden gave a clear—and deceitful—impression that all this was a mere contingency plan to be executed if, rather than when, Israel invaded.[67]

The eminent historian Peter Hennessy thinks that cabinet ministers, in claiming not to know about the collusion plot, were deluding themselves: "They did not need a background at GCHQ—the British signals and cybersecurity intelligence agency—to decode the import of those messages given in the Cabinet Room." They should have subjected the prime minister to "the heat of questioning."[68]

Unlike the cabinet, the queen had probably cracked the code. After all, Mountbatten had done so, and it would have been outrageous for a constitutional monarch to be kept in the dark about such an important development, preventing her from exercising her duty to advise, encourage, and consult the prime minister. An anonymous source told the respected biographer Ben Pimlott that "she knew the inside story." Elizabeth "knew about the secret deals beforehand."[69] Eden, furious about any suggestions that he had misled the queen, later insisted that she "understood what we were doing very well."[70]

It is telling that, after the invasion, Norman Brook, the cabinet secretary, anxiously asked the palace to return papers from those crucial cabinet meetings held in the run-up to Suez. He reminded Michael Adeane, the queen's private secretary, that "some of the points" discussed were "of a particularly sensitive nature." This is an understatement, given the hints of collusion they contained. More surprising, and demonstrating the enormous significance of these papers, is Brook's nervousness that they would not have been safe locked away inside Windsor Castle.[71]

It is likely that Eden or Brook kept the queen broadly—if informally—aware of the crucial developments unfolding outside Paris; but given the lengths Eden went to keep it secret, it is highly unlikely that any of the documents sent to the palace explicitly mentioned the collusion. Given Eden's growing desperation and mental instability, it is difficult to know exactly how much he told her about specific details and timings.[72]

Even if she did not know, Elizabeth would still have been in a position to submit Eden to her own "heat of questioning" during her two audiences with the prime minister in the run-up to Suez. According to Charteris, she "in some ways was better informed in advance of the operation than many members in the cabinet."[73] After all, she received a range of sensitive intelligence and papers; she had Mountbatten whispering in her ear; and two of her assistant private secretaries, both experienced in Middle Eastern politics, opposed Eden's approach to Egypt. Courtiers remember tense conversations and Eden fidgeting edgily around the palace.[74] He was extremely agitated at his weekly audience with the queen, and, according to Charteris, she thought "Eden was mad."[75]

However, she was a young and inexperienced monarch. By contrast, Eden was a man whom she had recently knighted precisely for his mastery of foreign affairs.[76] Almost as much as Churchill, he retained the reputation of having resisted wartime fascism. Therefore, he represented this episode as a further effort to resist a dictator. Michael Adeane, Elizabeth's most senior adviser, unlike his assistants, supported the invasion of Suez.[77]

It seems that Adeane and Eden failed to persuade Elizabeth. Anecdotal evidence strongly suggests that she did not support the Suez invasion, and she may well have had strong reservations about it. Charteris later recalled that "the basic dishonesty of the whole thing" left her worried, as did the effect it would have on the Commonwealth, where Australia was broadly supportive but India opposed the invasion. This put Elizabeth, as head of the Commonwealth, in a difficult position. She was torn between leaking secrets to Commonwealth prime ministers or withholding information and deceiving them about British plans.[78]

The queen had influence but not power. Perhaps she arched an eyebrow and asked Eden her trademark question: "Are you sure you are being wise?"[79] Not doing so, with all the information at her disposal, would have been as self-deluding as the cabinet—a dereliction of her duties as a constitutional monarch.

On October 29, as planned, Israeli troops invaded the Sinai Peninsula and made their way toward the Suez Canal. Feigning surprise, Britain and France issued their ultimatum, which, also as planned, Israel promptly ignored. Two days later, Britain and France began bombing Egyptian positions to force the reopening of the canal. In response, Nasser sank forty ships, blocking the waterway. The next day, the queen received the first of her daily bulletins, many of which contained top-secret intelligence. It informed her about the progress of the Israeli attack and where forces had met Egyptian resistance.[80] On November 5, British and French paratroopers landed at Port Said, near the entrance to the canal.

Eisenhower was angry about Suez. He was cross that American intelligence received warning of the conspiracy but did not act on it, and furious that Eden had not kept him informed. He felt that Anglo-French aggression in the Middle East undermined his own criticisms of simultaneous Russian aggression against the uprising in Hungary. These twin crises, Hungary and Suez, had both hit him during an election campaign, so the timing was especially unwelcome. He phoned Downing Street to protest, and an official picked up the phone. Thinking he was speaking directly with Eden, Eisenhower barked: "I can only presume that you have gone out of your mind."[81]

The president responded by putting economic pressure on the pound sterling. Facing overwhelming American opposition, Britain and France agreed to a cease-fire two days later. The next evening, Buckingham Palace hosted a reception. In the margins of the palace, Rab Butler, the lord privy seal, took the American ambassador to one side and "deplored the existence of what he termed mutual misunderstandings of policy" between the two governments. He was clearly "greatly disturbed" by the actions of the cabinet—although he stopped short of actually saying so.[82] As for the queen, she told Churchill that she hoped "the present feeling that this country and America are not seeing eye-to-eye will soon be speedily replaced by even stronger ties between us."[83] The language was different from that of Eisenhower, but the meaning was clear. This was a classic understated rebuke.

Elizabeth's bulletins continued during the final two days of fighting. They covered photographic intelligence from British planes on Egyptian and Israeli positions, as well as intelligence on Egyptian subversion: "Underground resistance is . . . increasing and the populace is being incited to take up arms against the British."[84] She had access to even the most sensitive intelligence acquired by GCHQ—code-named EIDER—which officials candidly told her came from "signals intelligence sources."[85] It monitored possible Soviet preparations for war and whether any other states were preparing to intervene in the conflict. Despite ominous reports of Russian aircraft flying toward the theater, this intelligence was generally reassuring throughout the crisis.[86]

On November 22, the day after the first United Nations troops landed in Egypt, Elizabeth received her final bulletin: "Port Said remains quiet and there has been less curfew breaking."[87] She thanked all those who had been involved in preparing them and recognized the trouble taken to keep her "supplied with the latest information."[88]

America had applied immense economic might and began to sell the pound heavily, so the outcome was inevitable. Toward the end of the month, Britain reluctantly started withdrawing troops from the theater. Eden, ill and under immense stress but determined to continue as prime minister, left for Ian Fleming's Goldeneye estate in Jamaica to recover. Back in London, the cabinet agreed on a common line to take. The spin was nothing short of outrageous: "We have stopped a small war and prevented a larger one"; the UK had "unmasked Soviet plots in the Middle East and have done something to awaken the United Nations to the dangers there"; and the cabinet was "united and firm." The queen read and returned it without comment to the Foreign Office.[89]

The pressure was too much; and the outcome was too humiliating. Eden resigned in early January the next year. Elizabeth wrote to him: "You know how very deeply I felt your resignation last week and how much I sympathize in the tragic turn of fate which laid you low at the moment when our country is beginning to see the possibility of some brightening in the international sky."[90]

She consoled him that "there is no doubt that you took the only possible course, after the doctors had given you their verdict, but one can only guess at what it must have cost you to do it." And she thanked him "for the loyal and distinguished service you have given to me, first as Foreign Secretary and then as Prime Minister, but for the many years' work, both in and out of office, which you have devoted to the greatness and prosperity of our country."[91] Eden promptly lost the letter.

Many in the palace were quietly relieved by Eden's resignation. The royals had never liked Eden, and the personal relationship between monarch and prime minister had been much more forced than during Churchill's day. One former courtier recalled that Eden "didn't give you the feeling he trusted you with sensitive information."[92] Despite this, the queen seemed to bear Eden no ill will over the collusion at Suez. Eden later recalled that she had never indicated "anger or humiliation" toward him: "On the contrary." The two stayed in touch, and she even took the rare step of accepting private hospitality from him.[93]

Privately, Elizabeth had thought the open invasion of Egypt, inadequately hidden by the hopeless "collusion" with Israel, was stupid. Now she was confronted with consequences for her own empire: a dramatic decline in British prestige and grotesque embarrassment at the hand of Nasser. Why had Eden not followed the simpler approach of just slipping something into his coffee? Prince Bernhard of the Netherlands, who followed the invasion closely, told British insiders "that you should not have mounted a military operation at all, instead you should have offered £5,000 for Nasser's head." British ministers pretended to be "very shocked," but many were doubtless thinking the same thing.[94]

Bizarrely, at the very moment when assassination was in the air, the real worlds of 007 and the queen actually crossed. In 1956, Martin Charteris sought to recruit Ian Fleming, the creator of James Bond, as a speechwriter for the queen. Fleming had written a speech for Elizabeth back in 1949, although in the end Charteris did not use it.[95] As is so often the case in the upper echelons of British society, connections existed between the Charteris and Fleming families. Charteris was the cousin of Ann Fleming, Ian's wife, so they saw each other socially. Although Fleming had published his first Bond novel, *Casino Royale*, a few years before and was rising in celebrity, he still had a day job working for the *Sunday Times*, managing its network of foreign correspondents. Charteris wondered if a little "007" magic would not help to lift the queen's oratory. There were other connections, because both Fleming and Charteris enjoyed a background in intelligence work in the 1940s.

But there was also a problem. Fleming did not like the idea of regular dealings with one Commander Richard Colville, the queen's press secretary. Colville was a famously negative figure, described as "stiff, irascible, and something of a snob." For years, the royal press office had been under the command of this notorious figure, an old Harrovian of fabulously gloomy temperament. He was entirely unsuitable and had only secured the post through his cousin, Jock Colville, who had been a predecessor to Charteris.[96] Some have called him an "anti–press secretary," and his approach to press management was simple: allow as little access as possible and avoid all excitement. Because his demeanor was so dour and miserable, his nickname within the royal household was "Sunshine."[97]

Famous for refusing every reasonable request, Colville had a different nickname among the press of Fleet Street: "the Abominable No Man." In 1957, after some hesitation, Fleming "found the prospect of dealing with Colville hard to take, and retired gracefully to Goldeneye," his vacation retreat in Jamaica, where Eden had recently convalesced. There, under the Caribbean sun, "the talent that might have worked wonders for the royal word" was instead poured into writing *Dr. No*.

This new Bond book was a rather more salacious work than his previous adventures.[98] The character of Dr. No was loosely based on Fu Manchu, but where did the name come from? It is well known that Fleming was something of a naval magpie when choosing names for his characters. Typically, the name of "Drax," the villain in *Moonraker*, was borrowed from an admiral.[99] Perhaps Commander Colville, the queen's press secretary and the Abominable No Man, was the inspiration. Either way, when his novel hit the silver screen a few years later as the first "007" film, it was a runaway success.[100]

In the wake of the political and economic humiliation that was Suez, the monarchy arguably became yet more important. The queen, working through the vehicle of the Commonwealth, tried to rescue the remnants of great power, offering the narrative of a liberal democracy engaged in a willing retreat from empire and seeking a new partnership with the Global South. But this was a hard sell set against the awkward aftermath of the Suez misadventure, which rendered British decline more apparent than ever. Nationalism continued to spread across the Middle East, threatening Britain's position elsewhere. Behind the scenes, the secret services worked frantically to stop the rot.

Iraq, another state with a young constitutional monarch, was Britain's closest ally in the region. Britain was a leading member of the Baghdad Pact, a military alliance founded in 1955 to contain Soviet ambitions in the region. The next year, Iraq worked closely with MI6 in the ill-fated covert operation to overthrow the Syrian government—and shouldered the blame when it unraveled. King Faisal II paid a state visit to London that summer; Queen Elizabeth, dressed in a summer floral flock and straw hat, greeted him in all his green and gold military finery on the platform at Victoria Station. Accompanying him to the palace, she described Iraq as "the model of a modern state, built on ancient and famous foundations and confidently facing towards the future."[101]

This confidence was misplaced. Many Iraqis resented the Baghdad Pact as a means of Western meddling. Egyptian propaganda was quick to whip up further discontent, especially in the aftermath of the Suez debacle, when Iraqi association with Britain became particularly toxic.

More and more Iraqis, including military officers, found themselves sympathetic to Nasser's nationalist line. In February 1958, the joining of Egypt and Syria to form the United Arab Republic bolstered pan-Arab nationalism further still. A group of Iraqi officers now vowed to put the ruling regime on trial as collaborators with the British imperialists.[102] Faisal's uncle, the crown prince of Iraq, became worried about growing anti-British feelings among the Iraq establishment. Faisal's beautiful fiancée, Princess Fadhila, was a particular concern. She was descended from Ottoman and Egyptian royalty but, with wedding plans and a palace refurbishment under way in Baghdad, she made some unfortunate remarks about Britain.

In April, with nationalist disturbances on the rise, the crown prince had a private word with the British ambassador to Iraq, Michael Wright. He explained "how anxious" he was "that Princess Fadhila should come to feel the same affection for Britain as the King and himself." He wondered whether Queen Elizabeth might discreetly intervene to win her over. Fadhila was currently at school at Heathfield College, near Ascot. Might Elizabeth "feel able to pay her some attention, and enable her to make the acquaintance of the younger members of the Royal Family?"[103]

Wright thought this was a good idea: "When Princess Fadhila becomes Queen, she will be in a position to exercise great influence in the background. Whatever can be done while she is in England to befriend her may be of considerable importance for the future."[104]

Britain's most senior diplomat, Frederick Hoyer Millar, passed the message on to Michael Adeane at Buckingham Palace. "Princess Fadhila's family background," he explained, emphasizing the necessity of the queen's task, "has on the whole been anti-British. It is therefore all the more important that her stay here should be a success and she should take away a happy memory of this country. She is only 16½ and at an impressionable age. I am sure that any attention paid her would be worthwhile." Hoyer Millar, whose own daughter went to the same school and spoke well of the princess, added some briefing notes to help the queen influence her: the princess was "very keen on music and the ballet."[105]

Queen Elizabeth agreed. She thought it was a "good plan" to invite her to Windsor Castle during the forthcoming race meeting at Ascot in the middle of June.[106] As Elizabeth and the Foreign Office planned to cultivate Fadhila as a long-term person of influence, other plans were afoot back in Iraq. British intelligence was oblivious to plotting by a secret military group, the Free Officers, to emulate Nasser's achievements in Egypt and overthrow the Iraqi monarchy.

MI6 had excellent sources among pro-British and royal factions but had been unable to penetrate the nationalists. The Iraqi prime minister maintained that the military was apolitical and, despite four foiled plots so far in 1958 alone, would remain loyal to the monarchy. One of the problems was that MI5's attempts to liaise with the Iraqi security authorities severely impeded the scope for covert intelligence operations run by MI6.[107] As a result, with coup plotting at an advanced stage, the Foreign Office received skewed intelligence and the queen continued to plan a charm offensive to win over Fadhila.

The revolutionary Iraqi officers struck in the early hours of July 14, 1958, just ten weeks after the Foreign Office request to the palace and four weeks after Ascot. At 5:30 a.m. the palace was attacked with machine guns. The queen, the crown prince, and his sisters were killed outright. The king died later of his wounds. The house of the prime minister, Nuri al-Said, was also attacked; and although he escaped, a price of 10,000 dinars was put on his head and he was soon hunted down. The body of the crown prince was given to the mob, mutilated, publicly hanged, and "dragged by the crowd through the streets." A body alleged to be that of Nuri was either handed to the crowd on July 16 or 17 or was dug up by them after burial, then "dismembered." A howling mob then lynched visiting Jordanian ministers, three American citizens, and a German.[108]

British intelligence maintained a close liaison with the ill-fated regime until the end—one former intelligence officer lamented how British agents were hanged in the square after the coup—but was unable to predict or prevent the revolution.[109] Princess Fadhila was not in Baghdad on the night of the attack, because she was preparing for her wedding to Faisal the next day, so she escaped with her life. However, her long-term utility to the British died amid the gunfire.

Even so, the British remained loyal to the exiled minor royals of Iraq. Diplomats used the secret intelligence fund to pay off one prince on the grounds that he had been deprived of his inheritance. After a while, a senior diplomat met him in an upmarket Washington hotel to deliver the unwelcome news that he would no longer receive any more payments. The prince later turned up at the Foreign Office with his family and threatened to camp out on the premises until he was paid. Britain's soft spot for royalty—and use of intelligence to support them—only stretched so far.[110]

Arab regimes gradually turned to America, and in particular the CIA, to escape the taint of British imperialism. Unbeknownst to them, however, the CIA was heading in an opposite direction. The 1958 coup in Iraq represented a turning point in Anglo-American relations, and the CIA and MI6 began to secretly work together, not only against Soviet influence but also to contain Arab nationalism and bolster the last pro-Western monarchs in the region. Despite the reverse situation in Iraq, the CIA was increasingly a fan of the queen, the Commonwealth, constitutionalism, and corgis.[111]

The Egyptian and Iraqi monarchies had fallen in the space of a few years, while the Jordanian monarchy had publicly distanced itself from the British, turning to America. Saudi Arabia also looked to Washington, and only the minor sultans of the Gulf remained resolutely loyal to Britain. Each of these events was a considerable blow for Britain's position in the Middle East, but also for Queen Elizabeth, the Commonwealth—which had little traction in the region—and the British brand of constitutional monarchy. She had maintained a close interest in the intrigue and turbulence of the Middle East in the years after her coronation, and she had even been prepared to intervene personally to discreetly influence events. Yet as British power collapsed alongside friendly potentates, she must have wondered whether it had all been in vain. In a bid to maintain Britain's self-perceived global role, she turned her attentions more widely and became a quasi, if discreet, diplomat.

14

Discreet Diplomacy

The Global Queen

The Queen is personally interested.
—Foreign and Commonwealth Office, January 1980

Like her great-grandfather, King Edward VII, Queen Elizabeth recognized the value of royal diplomacy. She recognized it so much that after thirteen years on the throne, it dawned on her that she was running out of friendly countries to visit. This became a worry: traveling outside her Commonwealth comfort zone would create difficulties for the intelligence services and diplomats alike.

Some places remained off limits. Despite hosting the Soviet leaders Khrushchev and Bulganin back in 1956, Elizabeth made it known to the Foreign Office a decade later that she still had no intention of visiting Russia. Michael Adeane, her private secretary, warned the UK's most senior diplomat that the assassination of her relatives after the 1917 Revolution was not yet consigned to the glass case of history.[1]

Adeane offered a more guarded assessment to Tony Benn, the Labour politician, during a state banquet at Hampton Court Palace: "The memory of the massacres at Ekaterinburg would certainly have prevented George V or VI from going" and a state visit to the Soviet Union "still might be difficult." Benn, always happy to needle the monarchy, asked why there had been no embarrassment about Elizabeth's German relatives who had fought against us in two world wars. Adeane replied, "Oh but the German royalty are all very decent chaps."[2]

When the queen visited Germany in May 1965, Anthony Eden wrote to her from his retirement. Still in touch with her almost a decade after the humiliating Suez collusion, he now drew comparison with Edward VII's personal diplomacy in the run-up to the First World War. Eden told the queen that the Germans lacked political sense and, as a result, were too easily led and lacked standards: "Their fervour and loyalty can be misplaced." The impact of Elizabeth's visit would be similar to how Edward's "diplomacy and personality thawed the more sophisticated French," leading to the Entente Cordiale.[3]

Prince Philip made a private visit to Germany the next year and raised eye-brows in the British Embassy. On the guest list for lunch at a yacht club was one Alfred Krupp von Bohlen. He was a keen yachtsman, but he was also a prominent industrialist who had supplied weapons to the Nazis. After the war, he was convicted of crimes against humanity for using slave labor in his facto-ries and served three years in prison.[4] Now, the duke of Edinburgh was inviting him—effectively a convicted Nazi war criminal—for lunch.

British diplomats in Bonn did not know what to do. Frank Roberts, the ambassador, worried that "it would clearly be very difficult and could cause serious misunderstandings if we were to try to get Krupp 'disinvited' or even to use such behind-the-scenes influence as we have to suggest that Krupp should not come." Unable, or unwilling, to meddle in private royal affairs, he simply hoped that the press would not be looking too closely and that no one would notice Philip's dodgy company.

Watching from the sidelines, he suggested that "we should take no action and let matters take their course, which I hope will not be an embarrassing one." The diplomats essentially crossed their fingers and hoped. Von Bohlen was certainly less toxic than he used to be, but Roberts feared public "preju-dices, however irrational, where the Royal Family are concerned." There was clearly a sensitivity to the connection, however distant or unfair, between the Windsors and Nazi Germany. The Foreign Office duly told Philip about the predicament—but did not actively intervene.[5] When a revised guest list reached Bonn two weeks later, von Bohlen's name had mysteriously disappeared.[6] Per-haps Philip had got the hint.

The Foreign Office raised the prospect of Japan, another wartime enemy, as a "difficult" country for the queen to visit. She was more amenable, profess-ing to "be prepared to contemplate a visit one day." She suggested that if the Japanese emperor visited the UK, then he might arrive in Windsor rather than in the capital. Feelings about Japan's treatment of wartime prisoners of war still ran high in Britain.[7] Conscious of security, she thought this would "avoid the possibility of any untoward happening during a carriage drive in London."[8]

Queen Elizabeth was reluctant to visit Latin America. This was not because of any historical animosity, personal conflicts of interest, or even the distances involved; she simply feared being upstaged by Charles de Gaulle's extensive trip undertaken in the autumn of 1964. The French president had taken in ten countries, from Guadeloupe to Venezuela, regaling cheering crowds with an impressive message of noninterventionism, respect for the developing world, and self-determination. Watching from London, Elizabeth worried that she could not compete.[9] She only acquiesced four years later, once local memories had faded, to a Foreign Office request to visit Chile and Brazil.

British diplomats had paid close attention to Latin America since the start of the decade. Regional growth combined with the perceived decline of the US after the CIA's disastrous attempt to overthrow Fidel Castro in 1961 created a golden opportunity to capture a new economic market.[10] British policy cynically centered on "making the Latin Americans feel that they are being taken seriously."[11] A royal visit was one way of doing this; another, as officials recognized, was a massive increase in covert action and propaganda in the region.[12] Royal diplomacy and covert operations were not mutually exclusive.

As early as 1961, the Foreign Office supported a visit by Philip to the region. Diplomats hoped a trip might deter "further defections on the Cuban model."[13] Royal diplomacy was one tool in the state arsenal complementing a wide variety of others—overt and otherwise. An information campaign, including distributing 9,500 booklets on the British monarchy, accompanied the queen's visit in the autumn of 1968.[14] On top of this, the Foreign Office commissioned specially written feature articles on "royal themes" to be used by the local press.[15]

Meanwhile, more covert attempts were under way to ensure that the queen's visit was a success. Nigel Clive was a specialist in the dark arts of statecraft. He had earlier headed MI6's special political action unit, tasked with covert influence operations. He now ran the Foreign Office's propaganda arm, the Information Research Department (IRD).

Ahead of the queen's trip, Clive visited the embassy in Chile to discuss "ways and means of getting the maximum advantage from the State Visit." The bulk of these were open and obvious, such as exhibiting replicas of the crown jewels, but the IRD had recently bolstered its covert effort in Chile, and its local representative in Santiago found himself very busy during the state visit.[16] He was so preoccupied that he had been unable to visit any other cities and had fallen behind in his efforts to interfere in forthcoming Chilean elections. Both British intelligence and the CIA were keen to retard the efforts of the hard left.[17]

Since the 1964 US-backed coup in Brazil, the IRD had sought to covertly manipulate *Ultima Hora*, a leftist newspaper that had opposed the coup and the ensuing dictatorship. By the time of the queen's visit, British officials boasted of having "assiduously cultivated" its founder and editor, Samuel Wainer.[18] The influence proved successful: *Ultima Hora* published remarkably positive coverage of the royal visit. In fact, it was so positive that the US assumed Britain had simply paid off the newspaper. "Not a penny," came the IRD's proud response.[19] Over the period 1964 to 1974, the CIA had, by comparison, spent a total of $10 million on covert action in Chile, mostly on propaganda projects to support President Eduardo Frei.[20]

Meanwhile, in Chile, British propagandists had busily tried to provoke a split among the socialists between the "hotheads" who believed in violence and others who were "at heart 'drawing-room revolutionaries.'" They did so by disseminating pamphlets to the Chilean security services, trade unions, and student leaders, and by placing IRD articles in local newspapers using pseudonyms.[21]

Shortly after arriving in Chile, Elizabeth and Philip met one of the main propaganda targets: Salvador Allende, the socialist politician who later became president. He used the opportunity of a royal visit to criticize Western treatment of underdeveloped countries, accusing the rich of getting richer by sucking raw materials from poorer nations. He boldly turned up to meet the royal couple in improper attire of "street clothes" rather than formal dinner wear. According to US diplomats present, Allende "stuck out like a sore thumb amongst the tails, trains and tiaras."[22]

Philip, not one, according to the US diplomats, to be "intimidated by such plebeian airs of superiority," could not resist a swipe at his dress sense. Their exchange heated up when Philip mocked him for failing to win three presidential elections. Allende told Philip that the people were dissatisfied with Chilean politics and that he, as the representative of those people, would change things for the better. Philip retorted that he quite understood Allende's dissatisfaction as a representative of the people, given that he had been rejected by them three times in a row.[23]

This dig was particularly acerbic because, four years earlier, British propagandists and MI6 had attempted to influence the Chilean presidential election—precisely to keep Allende out of power. "Once in power," the local ambassador had warned, "the chances are that Allende would be maneuvered by the communists, either willingly or otherwise, and that the end-product might well be a Government on the Cuban pattern."[24] Although British operations were dwarfed by those of the CIA, covert action continued and, by the year of the state visit, IRD expressed its secret goal with unusual directness: "Because there is a very real danger that the Communists might gain control of this country by constitutional means, we are concentrating on covert operations which we think could influence the result of the next election."[25]

The palace's briefing pack included the line that Chile was a "Parliamentary Democracy and there is a very strong tradition of democratic government and respect for the rule of law. President Frei was elected in September 1964 (for a term of six years) as the head of the first Christian Democrat Government in Latin America."[26] No mention, of course, of the covert action to put him there.

After Elizabeth and Philip had left, the British ambassador rated the visit a triumphant success. He predicted an increase in trade, but also noted the political impact. The tour had "probably brought a welcome boost to President

Frei's Government" at a "time when he badly needed it." Frei had also told him with satisfaction that "the fractious Opposition leader, Allende, so closely and warmly associated himself with the visit that the entire Chilean people seemed for one week to be united in agreement at least on one subject."[27] This was short-lived, but it aligned with the simultaneous intelligence operations designed to split Allende from the "hot-heads." The royal trip to Chile and Brazil demonstrates the different arms of British influence—royal, diplomatic, and secret—working together in harmony.

With détente in the air, Downing Street now resurrected discussions about a potential royal visit to the Soviet Union. As early as July 1965, Prime Minister Harold Wilson had suggested an exchange of visits between the two heads of state, Queen Elizabeth and the Soviet president, Anastas Mikoyan. But the problem was not only the liquidation of the Romanovs in 1918; Mikoyan hated the British, as he had been a prisoner of British forces during the Russian civil war.[28]

Wilson did not give up, and in February 1967, just a year after the queen had ruled it out on the grounds of bloody family history, he told Alexei Kosygin, the Soviet premier, over lunch at Number 10 that the queen would now like to visit Russia after all. He added that it would be necessary to break the ice by first sending a more junior member of her family. Kosygin excitedly interjected that he knew all this already; Elizabeth had told him personally over dinner the previous evening.[29] She also told him, slightly dismissively, that Princess Margaret was "for some reason anxious to go."[30]

Kosygin would have been disappointed to learn that Elizabeth had not told him the whole truth. As their conversation had become more awkward, moving into personal and diplomatic territory that made the queen unconformable, Elizabeth flailed and had to be rescued by the prime minister. An urgent message reached Wilson as he was drinking coffee nearby; he gallantly strode over to the queen and steered the conversation away.[31] It was too late.

Personally, she liked Kosygin, so much so that she had lent him the royal train for a visit to Edinburgh on February 10. Yet in private, she was actually rather anxious to avoid Russia—at least for the time being. According to senior diplomats, she and Philip both wanted to "avoid identification with the 50th anniversary of the Communist Revolution and its attendant family tragedy."[32]

A year later, the Soviets raised the question more formally. This time, Wilson rebuffed them with the standard line that the queen was unavailable due to unspecified "other commitments"; but he did say that she might be willing to send Princess Margaret in her place.[33] In truth, there was no prospect of Elizabeth visiting Russia "for some time to come."[34] Aside from the queen's lingering familial animosity, another sticking point involving Cold War espionage made any visit politically problematic. But it also provided an opportunity.

In April 1965, the KGB had arrested a young British lecturer, Gerald Brooke, as he led a group of student-teachers in Moscow. The Soviets found him guilty of passing propaganda leaflets to dissidents and jailed him for subversion. He was sentenced to five years' detention, and later admitted to distributing documents on behalf of an anti-Soviet organization but claimed not to know their contents. Brooke had in fact been under MI6 control and had been engaged on a fairly worthless operation that, once discovered, annoyed Downing Street [35]

With Brooke laboring in grueling camps and British public opinion clamoring for his release, the Kremlin tried to use him in an old-fashioned spy swap for Helen and Peter Kroger. The Krogers, a husband-and-wife duo of spies, were in prison for gathering classified intelligence on Britain's underwater warfare technologies. Wilson rejected the Soviet offer as tantamount to blackmail.[36] Instead of a spy swap, he wondered whether the dangle of a royal visit could convince the Soviets to release Brooke—or at least ease his harsh treatment.

Queen Elizabeth did not object to playing a discreet role in an unprecedented spy/royal swap, but she wanted these issues to be linked only "very obliquely."[37] It had to be deniable; Elizabeth, for good reason, did not want to be used too obviously as a pawn in a Cold War espionage game.[38] After consulting the palace, Wilson chose his words carefully: without any "helpful gestures" on the Brooke case, he told Moscow that "there might be certain difficulties about a Royal visit." He left it at that, and Elizabeth expressed her gratitude.[39]

The royal visit did not happen, and not simply because the dangle was too oblique. The Soviet invasion of Czechoslovakia in the summer further dislocated diplomatic relations, effectively making a royal visit impossible. The Soviets unsuccessfully continued to press for an exchange with the Krogers regardless. As stalemate ensued, they blackmailed Britain even more outlandishly by threatening to increase Brooke's sentence if the government did not hand the couple over. This time, Wilson reluctantly agreed, and in the summer of 1969, Gerald Brooke, pale and thin, stepped off a plane at Heathrow Airport into a scrum of journalists.[40] Meanwhile, the Krogers headed home, having received what one British diplomat called "a royal pardon."[41]

Princess Margaret enjoyed fewer constraints and a greater sense of adventure than her older sister. She did get her visit behind the Iron Curtain—albeit to Yugoslavia—in June 1970. The visit, which the Foreign Office inevitably dubbed a resounding success, began with a curious security incident.

Shortly before she left, Princess Margaret's private secretary, Francis Leigh, received some worrying intelligence from the queen's detective. An Air Commodore Panton—whom Leigh did not know—had apparently warned that the Russians planned to plant a bomb on Margaret's aircraft. It would not go off but rather be "discovered" as part of a KGB operation to "make bad blood between the UK and Yugoslavia." The tipoff was suitably alarming and mysterious to work Leigh up into quite a state. The Foreign Office's protocol department did not have a clue who Panton was either, but cautiously warned that "we cannot afford to ignore any story of this nature, however fantastic."[42]

It turned out that the enigmatic Air Commodore Panton was a credible source: the Ministry of Defence officer responsible for the security of the Royal Air Force. As this was the first time the Queen's Flight was due to venture behind the Iron Curtain, he had grown particularly anxious. Panton warned the palace not to leave Margaret's luggage unsupervised lest "anyone who might wish to embarrass Anglo-Yugoslav relations by planting an explosive device would have an opportunity to do so." Officials were already nervous about sending a senior member of the Royal Family to Eastern Europe. Their paranoia transformed Panton's advice into a stark intelligence warning of KGB mendacity.[43] After investigation, the Foreign Office reassured Leigh that there was "no specific threat of any such action."[44]

In 1972, discussions about royal trips to the Soviet Union resurfaced. The Soviets remained eager; the British reluctant. Aside from the usual historical and political sticking points, the British Embassy in Moscow worried that the visiting royals would simply not enjoy themselves: they would rather be taking in the beautiful tourist sites of Moscow and Saint Petersburg than required to show an "appropriate amount of interest" in the staid achievements of communism.[45]

Despite the reluctance, Britain's propagandists covertly used the Royal Family to shape Eastern European understanding of Britain. The Information Research Department busily planted articles about the royals in Soviet magazines. They published two about Princess Anne's equestrian activities between 1972 and the spring of 1973. When the European three-day event championship was due to be hosted in Kiev, the IRD included, with palace approval, a line about the princess "perhaps defending her title in Kiev."[46] Meanwhile, her father and chairman of the International Federation for Equestrian Sports, Prince Philip, was keen to take advantage of the opportunity to "see something of their home-world."[47] A royal visit was finally becoming possible.

The Soviets attempted some propaganda of their own. Victor Louis, a KGB agent masquerading as a journalist and specializing in peddling disinformation, publicly hinted about a royal visit to the Soviet Union in an article for the *Evening News*.[48] Louis had a track record of spreading stories that the leadership would not want to acknowledge openly, and this time they hoped unattributable press coverage would put pressure on the palace to send Philip to Kiev.[49]

British diplomats were well aware of Louis's connections and quickly realized that the Kremlin was discreetly trying to sound out British public opinion. This, they assumed, "would be greeted with incredulity by the British press in general" as a result of the poor state of Anglo-Soviet relations.[50]

Incredulity would not have rendered the operation a failure. It was a clever move by the Soviets because, whatever the reaction, "it would almost certainly prompt press enquiries which would oblige the Palace to confirm that the Duke of Edinburgh has received an invitation."[51] When later challenged by a Soviet specialist from the Foreign Office over another story written by Louis, this time intimating that the queen herself would visit, Russian diplomats denied all knowledge of having briefed Louis. These denials, however, were "belied" by a "knowing grin."[52]

British diplomats did not oppose Philip visiting Kiev, but they did warn of Russia trying to make political capital out of it. This was less than two years after Britain had dramatically expelled 105 Soviet intelligence officers from the country in Operation Foot. The unprecedented mass expulsion left the Soviets reluctant to do business with the Conservative government. They instead sought to use Philip to bypass "reactionary Conservative ruling circles" and improve their image with the British people by dealing with Philip directly. Diplomats warned that he could not be used as a pawn in a Russian Cold War public relations campaign.[53]

That said, the Foreign Office knew that a visit by Philip could improve Anglo-Soviet relations in the longer term and could provide a way out of the impasse since Operation Foot.[54] The royals were a valuable tool: "We should not underestimate the impact of the Royal mystique on the Russian mind."[55]

Philip told Denis Greenhill, the most senior official at the Foreign Office, that both he and Anne "very much" wanted to go to Kiev.[56] As the prince pestered diplomats for a response, his private secretary, William Willett, worried about security aspects.[57] He imagined that the duke and his party would "have to be very cagey about social contacts" and assumed that "we cannot put it past the hosts to 'bug' the hotel rooms."[58] He also wanted Philip's police officer to have a voice in the local security arrangements.[59] The ambassador reassured the palace that, although "security arrangements will be largely out of our hands," they would be "very effective."[60] The KGB did not mess around.

With the palace reassured, Philip accepted the invitation. Detailed planning could now begin. Planning for overseas trips was always detailed, combining byzantine protocols about dress codes and seating plans with meticulous security assessments. The legacy of Operation Foot gave this particular trip an added complication. The British learned that one of the Russian officials involved on the Kiev side was a man named A. A. Gresko. His name was familiar; he was one of the 105 intelligence officers expelled from London back in

1971. He had since supposedly taken up a post at the state committee for sport and was due to accompany Philip throughout the visit. Over the next ten years, he would become the key interface between the KGB and Olympic sport. The embassy in Moscow was suspicious, assuming that the Russians "clearly seemed to be testing the water."[61] In effect, they were taunting the British by putting a known intelligence officer—who had been expelled from London—alongside Prince Philip.

Diplomats in the Foreign Office's protocol department whirred into action. In normal circumstances, the advice would have been to "maintain a dignified silence," "however distasteful it might be," and avoid contact with Gresko as far as possible. But the royal dimension upped the stakes. If journalists found out, they might interpret it as a deliberate snub of Philip. The Foreign Office would be criticized for allowing a KGB man to get close to the duke.[62]

What if Philip found out? The Foreign Office could hardly ask him whether he minded being accompanied by "one of the 105." He could not be involved in such a political matter and, if he did mind but the Soviets refused to budge, then the Royal Family would have been "officially snubbed."[63]

Roderic Lyne, a young British diplomat in the Moscow Embassy, received prompt instructions to "stifle this at birth." He caught up with Gresko and warned him off. It would not be appropriate, he insisted, for Gresko to "appear in public with the Duke." Instead, he should "stay entirely behind the scenes." Gresko listened carefully before railing against the unjustness of Operation Foot. He passively accepted what Lyne had said and then promptly disappeared. Mysteriously, he failed to turn up for a final meeting three days later.[64] Back home, the sticklers in the protocol department were relieved to learn that "he had been moved to other duties."[65]

This came at a price. The Foreign Office had planned to use Tony Bishop as an interpreter for Philip.[66] Bishop had been expelled from the Moscow Embassy in 1965 as part of the Gerald Brooke spy case—a mutual friend had advised Brooke to pass his subversive material to Bishop if he was unable to deliver it to his contact himself. This was enough for the Kremlin to declare Bishop persona non grata.[67]

Diplomats had privately accepted that the trip did not require a formal interpreter, but wanted to use the opportunity to slip Bishop back inside the Soviet Union "under the Duke's wing." The Gresko démarche derailed the plan and there was now little chance of getting Bishop into the country without a row.[68] The Foreign Office refused to draw parallels between Gresko and Bishop. They assumed that the Russians had "no real evidence of any illicit activities by Bishop" and that the 105 expelled in Operation Foot were an "entirely different kettle of fish."[69] Nonetheless, it was not worth pressing the point. The Soviets would provide their own interpreter for Philip.[70]

After the Gresko and Bishop tangles, diplomats warned Philip to avoid any conversation about Soviet spies. The gaffe-prone duke was also warned off talking about the fate of the Russian Royal Family—especially conspiracy theories about their survival—and internal Soviet politics. Nationalism inside the Soviet Union was also off limits, even though Philip was briefed that nationalist feelings were "still very much alive in non-Russian areas, especially in the Ukraine and the Baltic republics," and that the Soviets had launched propaganda to quash it. Philip, unsurprisingly, was not told that British intelligence operations sought to foster and exploit this very nationalism in order to undermine the Soviet Union. Instead, he was allowed to talk about sport, youth exchanges, environmental protection, and Anglo-Soviet cooperation during the Second World War.[71]

Philip visited Kiev, via Moscow, in September 1973. The KGB assessed that it was a major political, rather than sporting, event for the British. As predicted, Russian intelligence did put the buildings where Philip and his staff were staying under surveillance; the KGB was especially suspicious of diplomats traveling down from the British Embassy in Moscow, some of whom the Russians were convinced were intelligence officers. The KGB also covered the journalists, competitors, and spectators—but stopped short of active intelligence operations targeting the British and Philip.[72]

The British ambassador informed the queen that the visit, despite being unofficial, was "of very great importance and an undoubted success." He was particularly struck by the role of the KGB. Russian intelligence had intervened at the last minute and revised the program "in direct contradiction of Prince Philip's wishes, which we had been invited to express and which, we were told, would be paramount." The KGB's eleventh-hour intervention confined Philip "far too much in the straitjacket reserved for high-level official visitors to the USSR, from which he had great difficulty in escaping." But he did manage to once give his minders the slip, nipping "smartly out of his lunch tent at the cross-country," chased by "hordes of leaden-armpitted KGB" in pursuit.[73]

The KGB impressed and frustrated in equal measure. The British ambassador confessed that "it was a bizarre experience to be working in close cooperation with that part of the KGB which concerns itself legitimately and properly with security in the Soviet Union. Those of its personnel involved were indeed of a type whom I should not care to run into if I myself were on illegitimate business on a dark night. But their performance in our service on this occasion was irreproachable."[74]

Although constrained to "antiseptic VIP meals, with virtually identical and unbelievably boring guest lists and menus," Philip played his part stoically and scrupulously adhered to his equestrian role—much to the disappointed surprise of the Russians who hoped to politicize the visit. The agent Victor

Louis suspiciously appeared during the three-day equestrian event in Kiev "in the highly unlikely role of equestrian correspondent." Once again, he did the Kremlin's bidding, this time by floating the idea of a visit by the queen herself.[75]

The KGB was suspicious of the British journalists who were ostensibly there to watch Philip. Intelligence officers noted the journalists' wide array of cameras and sound recording equipment—although this can hardly have come as a surprise. They also noted, with slightly more alarm, that the journalists paid rather too much attention to ordinary Soviet citizens, accusing some of trying to secretly record conversations. They thought one worked for MI6; others were merely rude. The KGB managed to acquire the reflections of a sympathetic *Daily Mirror* photographer. They recorded with interest his description of Princess Anne, the queen's daughter, as "capricious, arrogant and not very bright." He seems to have told the KGB that "I would like the princess to fall from a horse or something similar would happen to her. Then my mission would be justified, and I would be able to take great shots." Soviet intelligence assessed Anne as "leading a modest lifestyle" and sinisterly added that she always traveled with her personal bodyguard, who would be staying in the hotel room next door.[76]

Despite all the intrigue, Philip clearly enjoyed his visit to Russia, as he returned in the winter of 1979, this time to Moscow, to plan for a future Olympics. What the embassy loved about the tour was that things had now relaxed somewhat; unusually, Philip got to meet real everyday Russians, something the KGB normally conspired to prevent. He met Russians who "bred horses, rode horses, owned horses, raced horses, photographed horses, wrote about horses, legislated for horses; in short the equestrian society of the Soviet Union." These people were not "the cardboard cut-out" Soviet figures with whom British diplomats normally did business. Soviet security officials decided to borrow a British Embassy Range Rover because they thought it would cope better with heavy snow than their own military vehicles. However, the KGB was rather taken aback when Prince Philip provocatively suggested that "Soviet security arrangements for the competitors were inadequate."[77]

In November 1975, the governor-general of Australia, John Kerr, dramatically sacked the Labour prime minister, Gough Whitlam. The move came after a series of scandals and a decisive Conservative by-election victory, which the opposition used to block money from reaching the government. It created a constitutional crisis and risked dragging the queen into the internal politics of a country almost ten thousand miles away.

Rumors quickly circulated about various hidden hands. The Australian press wondered whether the CIA had been involved. After all, spy fever was mounting in Washington as eager senators investigated and uncovered spiraling CIA operations, including its activities in Australia. Kerr told Queen Elizabeth herself that any such claims were "absurdly tenuous."[78]

The potential hidden hand of Buckingham Palace proved far more controversial—and difficult to dismiss. In July 2020, after a lengthy legal battle, the Australian archives finally declassified the secret letters between the palace and Kerr. They had initially been classified as "personal," and so lay beyond the prying eyes of historians for the best part of half a century.

Kerr floated the idea of sacking Whitlam with Martin Charteris, the queen's private secretary. They had been discussing the possibility of dismissal and the powers of the governor-general since the summer of 1975.[79] In October, Kerr confided in Prince Charles—the heir apparent, then in his late twenties—about the possibility of Whitlam racing to the queen first and asking her to sack Kerr instead, replacing him with someone more amenable to Whitlam's cause. If he hoped that Charles would relay this fear back to his mother, then he was correct. Charteris comforted Kerr that the queen would "take most unkindly" to such a move; but he ultimately conceded that, if requested to do so, she would have to agree.[80]

The secret conversations continued as the crisis reached its climax. A week before the dismissal, Charteris agreed that Kerr had "the powers" to sack Whitlam and could use them "in the last resort and then only for constitutional and not political reasons."[81] This was not far short of a green light from Buckingham Palace.

On November 11, Kerr did just that. Significantly, he did so without informing the palace in advance, telling Charteris that "it was better for Her Majesty not to know in advance." Charteris was delighted that the queen effectively had plausible deniability: "If I may say with the greatest respect, I believe that in *not* informing the Queen what you intended to do before doing it, you acted not only with perfect constitutional propriety but also with admirable consideration for Her Majesty's position."[82]

Nobody knew about the palace's role, but the sacking sparked widespread demonstrations against Kerr and his interference. On Commonwealth Day the next June, Kerr and his wife were guests of honor at a reception in Melbourne. About four hundred demonstrators arrived and, as Kerr told Charteris, "the scene was pretty nasty." In a "highly organised affair," protesters smashed the front window of his car, leaving one of his aides requiring medical attention.[83] The queen was "extremely sorry to hear of this unfortunate business," and Charteris added that he hoped any response would be "robust."[84]

Kerr stayed in close touch with the palace, passing on Australian intelligence about subversive and extreme organizations on both sides of an increasingly angry debate. He shared the usual warnings about anti-governor-general

demonstrations by local communists, but also passed on a report by the Australian Security Intelligence Organisation into what he called a "very right wing"
organization: the Australian League of Rights. A promonarchy group, it publicly supported him with pamphlets and advertisements. Kerr told the palace
that "the sort of things it is saying are accurate enough." Australian intelligence
was more cautious, warning that the group was racist and anti-Semitic as well
as being promonarchy and pro-empire. Beyond its "respectable stated objec-
tives," its policies were "extreme" and its aims "radical." The report made its way
to the palace. The queen's reaction to support from such unsavory bedfellows
remains unknown.[85]

Whitlam would doubtless have been fascinated to follow the inside story of
a simultaneous and somewhat smoother transfer of power in London. During
1975, Prime Minister Harold Wilson had become increasingly tired and, in the
words of one of his closest advisers, Bernard Donoughue, had "lost the appetite
for power and the will to govern."[86] By the autumn, he had concluded that he
should resign and hand over to his successor, Jim Callaghan. The queen was
the first to know. In September, while they were visiting Balmoral, she drove the
prime minister and his wife to a small chalet on the estate. To ensure complete
secrecy, they left their detectives behind. When they arrived, the queen filled
the kettle while Wilson imparted his unusual announcement.[87]

Privately, the queen was "very concerned" about the departure of her favorite prime minister. She did not want him to step down, even though she knew
his mental health was not good.[88] "She does not want him to do it and there has
been discussion of trying to get him to change his mind," noted Donoughue.
Once again, Martin Charteris loomed in the shadows, and in January 1976 he
told senior political figures that the palace "was concerned about the succession." But by March, after he held private discussions with the cabinet secretary,
John Hunt, he was "quite properly dissuaded from taking such an approach,"
not only because of "constitutional proprieties" but also because everyone knew
it would be unsuccessful—Wilson was determined to go.[89] Indeed, the prime
minister had become increasingly anxious about bugging and even prone to
conspiracy theories.[90] There may have been "dark forces" trying to destabilize
him during his two administrations, but perhaps he was reassured to know that
the most senior member of the establishment was desperate for him to stay on.

Joe Haines, Wilson's press secretary, recalls that there was "still one moment
of pure, if black, comedy to come." In the short period before Wilson's departure was publicly revealed, the weekly meetings between the prime minister
and the queen focused on another forthcoming announcement: Princess Margaret and Lord Snowdon would soon divorce. The queen was anxious about all
the fuss in the press that was bound to follow. Helpfully, Wilson offered a plan
to mitigate this. He suggested that the palace should reveal the divorce on the

same day that he announced his resignation, adding "my going will blanket it." But Wilson's scheme was not a complete success, as the royal-hungry tabloids still featured Margaret on the front page and pushed Wilson's news into "second place."[91]

The Commonwealth continued to create problems for the government and palace. Courtiers and officials had successfully protected the queen from embarrassment over the sacking of Whitlam, but two years later the government turned to covert operations to protect her from diplomatic embarrassment closer to home.

In the early 1970s, Idi Amin, the Ugandan president, had grabbed power in a military coup orchestrated by the Israelis and swiftly become a brutal dictator. Initially, he seemed an improvement on his predecessor, Milton Obote. But soon he turned nasty, murdered political opponents, seized the property of Uganda's Asian and Jewish communities, forced swathes of people into exile, and terrorized intellectuals, destroying books and locking up journalists. Public order evaporated, leading to widespread looting, rape, and murder. Amin declared himself president for life.

British politicians—and likely the palace—reacted with horror at this prospect. They had advised the queen against traveling to Ottawa for a Commonwealth meeting in 1973 simply to prevent her from having to shake his hand, but the queen insisted on going.[92] She quipped to the foreign secretary that it "would not have been the first time" she "had met murderers" at such a meeting.[93] But her courtiers were still anxious to curtail any incident.

Fortunately, Amin nurtured well-founded fears about overseas conferences. He had himself seized power when his predecessor had been abroad at a Commonwealth conference in Singapore. Accordingly, in 1973, to "great hilarity" at Buckingham Palace, a message arrived from Kampala. Idi Amin said he had the greatest respect for the queen and looked forward to meeting her in Ottawa but was anxious about his security. He therefore asked whether "Her Majesty" would "kindly send a regiment of her 'Scotch' Guards to protect him." The queen sent a notably "deadpan reply" and Amin decided not to attend, to everyone's considerable delight.[94]

In 1975, the queen was deployed in a last-ditch attempt to control Amin. A rather esoteric British citizen living in Uganda, Denis Hills, had written a book about Amin called *The White Pumpkin*. The fearsome security authorities had secured a copy before it was published and duly presented it to Amin. He ordered Hills to be arrested on a charge of treason, which carried the death penalty. The Foreign Office protested in vain.

Elizabeth sent a delegation carrying her personal message, asking that Hills
be released. When they arrived, Amin kept them waiting for three days, eventually receiving them in a large thatched hut miles away in the countryside. The
entrance was so low that they had to enter on their hands and knees. Amin had
carefully arranged for photographers to take pictures of the queen's emissaries
crawling on their knees as they entered. Having humiliated them, Amin sent
them back empty-handed. Hills was only liberated when the foreign secretary,
Jim Callaghan, turned up and pleaded for his life. This, of course, was what
Amin had wanted all along. He took Callaghan for a spin around Kampala in
his Maserati, and then Hills was finally released.[95]

Unfortunately, in 1977 the issue of the Commonwealth Heads of Government Meeting returned. Uganda was still in the Commonwealth; its leaders
would therefore be invited to London for the 1977 meeting. To make matters
worse, the meeting would coincide with the queen's Silver Jubilee. Idi Amin,
the mass murderer, would meet Elizabeth.

By 1977, Amin had only become more authoritarian and more widely
reviled in Britain. He had murdered thousands of people in repeated security
purges. It was also now known that he had divorced and then killed one of his
four wives, whom he suspected of adultery, and had personally mutilated her
body, cutting off her legs and arms.[96] Backbenchers lobbied the government
to prevent him from coming to London. Parliament passed a motion that he
would be unwelcome, and Prime Minister Callaghan secretly planned to use
special forces to bundle him back out of the country if he attempted to land
at a British airport. The elaborate operation was code-named "BOTTLE" and
served as a dramatic last resort. It would have had serious consequences not
only for the impending Commonwealth meeting but also for the safety of about
250 British nationals living in Uganda who would likely have suffered violent
reprisals.[97]

It was a delicate situation: Britain had no veto over who could and who
could not attend the meeting, while trying to dissuade Amin from attending
would offend other African delegates and risk a continent-wide boycott altogether. London could not openly appear to be interfering in the affairs of what
were once imperial territories. They were, after all, now equals. When British
diplomats used Saudi Arabia as a discreet emissary to pass on a confidential
warning not to come, Ugandan radio publicly accused Britain of inappropri-
ately neocolonial heavy handedness.[98]

The Foreign Office turned to covert action to deter Amin and to protect the
queen from embarrassment. Officials plotted to spread disinformation inside
Uganda warning of an impending coup if Amin dared to leave the country.
It was a plausible line, given the circumstances in which Amin himself had
assumed power—and Britain had a long track record of using Black propaganda

in postimperial Africa to maintain influence, spread fear, and attack adversaries. The secret capabilities were in place.

The historian Spencer Mawby discovered that, shortly before his death, Foreign Secretary Anthony Crosland recommended using what he called "private deterrents" to convince Amin that he would lose power if he left the country or, worse, he might be assassinated on the streets of Britain. Prime Minister Callaghan was initially reluctant but, as opposition grew and it became increasingly likely that Amin would attend, he returned to the idea of spreading "misinformation about a possible coup during his absence" and spreading "misinformation about a possible attempt on his life in this country." Another option, to be conducted by MI6, remains classified.[99]

British intelligence launched its covert action to prevent Idi Amin from shaking the queen's hand. Although the archival trail dries up, there is enough evidence to show that the UK did indeed successfully run operations to deter him. In June 1977, coinciding with the meeting, local newspapers suddenly reported turmoil and assassination plots. Amin went missing. One South African magazine reported that his disappearance was a consequence of a well-organized assassination attempt that had very nearly succeeded. At the same time, the foreign secretary, David Owen, discussed plots against Amin with his Kenyan counterpart.[100]

The moment of high drama—whether Amin would turn up—occurred at Saint Paul's Cathedral during a service of thanksgiving for the Silver Jubilee with all Commonwealth leaders in attendance. Mountbatten noticed that the queen was not her normal self and asked why she looked "cross and worried." She laughed and replied: "I was just thinking how awful it would be if Amin were to gatecrash the party." Mountbatten then asked her what she would have done if he showed up. The queen responded that the lord mayor's pearl sword had been placed before her as part of the ceremony, and so she would seize it and "hit him hard over the head" with it.[101]

Elizabeth did not have to draw her sword; Amin did not show up in London for the start of the Commonwealth conference. But, being Idi Amin, he launched an influence campaign of his own: his mysterious absence stole the show, as delegates and officials speculated where the mercurial leader might be. Amin deliberately confused onlookers by putting decoys onto various airplanes and hinting he was aboard. One false rumor suggested he was circling Dublin Airport. Callaghan insisted to reporters that Amin was still in Uganda. When he did eventually reappear, he dramatically announced that imperialist agents had tried to kill him.[102]

Amid all this discreet diplomacy, subterfuge, and countersubterfuge, one thing was clear. Amin was nowhere near the queen—much to the government's relief. But Amin could not be evaded forever. Prince Charles found himself just a couple of seats away from the bloody dictator at the funeral of Kenyan president Jomo Kenyatta in Nairobi in August 1978. They eyed each other rather warily.

Repeatedly discomforting multiple royals has its price. David Owen, Britain's foreign secretary, recalls that "Amin was a menace and I got rid of him." On his return to Uganda, Amin went to war with Tanzania, and its president, Julius Nyerere, came to Britain for help. Owen privately increased Nyerere's aid budget "to buy ammunition." Owen mused that he might go to jail now for using aid money to buy ammunition. "But there was nothing on paper." Idi Amin lost the battle and was soon in exile, never to return.[103]

One aspect of the queen's global itinerary caused constant tension: Iran and its despotic ruler the shah. The Foreign Office prioritized Iran as the second-biggest export market in the Middle East "and expanding." It was the source of about 20 percent of Britain's oil, and it provided military stability. Arms sales were voluminous and effectively subsidized the British military. GCHQ also had hidden ground stations there for listening to the Soviets. Diplomats noted that relations were "extremely close and friendly." They continually begged for more royal visits, as they knew the shah and all his family loved to visit Britain.[104]

But the shah's visits to Britain were increasingly a security nightmare. His regime was blood-thirsty and repressive, and in 1972, when he arrived on one trip, about a hundred students back home in Tehran were on trial; seventy were expected to be shot. Iranian students abroad therefore tended to riot when he arrived in a European city, as had happened recently in Munich and Geneva. The Swiss regarded the threat as so high that they moved him only by helicopter.[105] There were also tensions with other Arab states, especially Libya, which meant that he might be shot at by any number of rebel groups. Accordingly, he brought his own security team of ten men, all with their own weapons.[106] They also had plenty of machine guns in the embassy and were disappointed when Special Branch refused to allow them onto the streets.[107]

The shah was determined to ride to Ascot alongside the queen in an open-topped carriage, and he thus "totally rejected" the idea of a bulletproof limousine.[108] Special Branch was horrified, and thought it "extremely unwise," as did the shah's own security detail, and indeed the matter went all the way up to the prime minister, Ted Heath.[109] In his weekly meeting with the queen, he implored her not to do this, as it was "high risk."[110] But the queen said she had little choice and went ahead. As if to torment British security officials further, the shah also hoped that some of his intelligence officers might go to Northern Ireland to study MI5's techniques for dealing with "subversives."[111]

Security was not the only problem. The queen considered the shah a crush-
ing bore and hated his company, as he only talked about administrative matters. When she was finally persuaded to make a return visit to Iran in October
1973, diplomats noted privately: "the poor Queen," adding "she didn't want
to do this at all."[112] In the Middle East, the October War between Israel and a
coalition of Arab states was now in progress, and the security of royal flights
became an extreme concern. Although perilous, she clearly thought the gamble
was worth taking, not least because her contact time with the shah was now
limited to just a few hours.

Remarkably, the Royal Air Force found that the best way to make the flight
safe was to notify the Russians of the queen's route and then fly her to Tehran along the northern border of Iran, "going into the Soviet Union." Because
of Philip's recent successful visit, they thought Moscow would be helpful and
that the Soviet Air Force were less likely to shoot down the queen's plane than
anyone else.[113]

Predictably, on arrival, the shah treated the queen to a dull monologue on
steel production in his country.[114] She tried to lighten the mood by voicing her
dislike of the Sydney Opera House.[115] Later, the October War caused the can-
celation of visits by Princess Margaret and the Kents to Egypt and Jordan. MI5
was deeply worried about their security in both countries.[116]

The diplomats pressed for yet more royal visits, ideally with the shah coming to Britain again. The queen was completely horrified. The palace stalled and
said she "would be pleased to do something for the Royal children."[117] Accordingly, in 1974, a tour of Scotland for the shah's three children was arranged.
The eldest son, Crown Prince Reza, was "fascinated by all things tartan" and
was a manic Rangers fan. So the highlight was a match at Edinburgh's Easter Road Stadium between the Rangers and Hibernian on July 31, 1974. The
crown prince fortified himself beforehand by having two helpings of hamburg-
ers, chips, beans, and peas at the nearby Epicure Snack Bar. He then spent the
match "cheering wildly" at each of the Rangers' three goals. The only moment
of anxiety for the British security team was when he insisted on shaking hands
with many Rangers fans after the third goal.[118]

Privately, British diplomats hated these visits as much as the queen, but
they were essential to grease the wheels of the special relationship with Iran.
In public, they were professional; but in private, they occasionally vented their
feelings. In May 1975, Anthony Parsons, Britain's ambassador in Tehran, was
compelled to devote much time to the details of a visit to London, via Paris,
for the shah's elder sister, Princess Shams, whom he regarded as "neurotic." The
princess would not go anywhere without her dogs, and thus demanded to circumvent Britain's quarantine regulations. Parsons complained bitterly to London: "She has a large number of revolting little brutes, each about the size of an

average rat: and she herself is not much bigger, but looks more like a Pekinese than a Yorkshire terrier which her dogs are, I think." He told the Iranians that it was no good, and quarantine meant that she would have to leave her beloved pooches in Paris.[119]

Iranian matters became much more complicated toward the end of the decade. Serious unrest broke out in 1978. The queen was due to visit Iran in February the next year as part of another tour to generate goodwill and encourage trade.[120]

As late as mid-December, amid growing violence, Elizabeth's visit to Tehran was still scheduled to take place. Finally, David Owen, the foreign secretary, now declared it impossible, due to the "staggering numbers of demonstrators" on the streets.[121] As domestic opposition to the shah mounted, Prime Minister Callaghan canceled the Iranian leg of the trip altogether. It was now too dangerous. He even explored the possibility of cultivating alternative leaders in case a coup became necessary.[122] Hard-line Iranian clerics had other ideas—and launched a revolution of their own.

After months of disorder, martial law finally broke down on Wednesday December 27, 1978. There was terrible violence and general anarchy. Police and army headquarters were attacked. and the buildings used by the shah's feared secret police, Savak, came in for special attention. The homes of Savak officials were targeted, and even their families were killed. In early January 1979, one of the shah's military aides spoke to him with unusual frankness and said that if he stayed, he risked meeting the fate of Nicholas II of Russia. Queen Farah said that if her husband departed, she would stay and lead the resistance, but the aide scoffed and asked if she wanted to be Marie Antoinette. They both expressed shock and sent him away, but hours later they began to pack their bags.[123]

Elizabeth and Philip were on board the royal yacht in the Gulf when the revolution broke out. George Walden, the principal private secretary at the Foreign Office, was with them as he received a flurry of telegrams. Carrying crucial updates about events in Tehran, they arrived on a silver tray in his cabin. Prince Philip jokingly asked if they were Dead Sea Scrolls.[124]

Back in Iran, the British ambassador, Anthony Parsons, deliberately kept his distance from the shah during the turmoil. With memories of 1953 looming large, he did not want to give the impression of foreign interference. After the shah had decided to leave, Parsons called on him to say goodbye and agreed that it was the right move if the monarchy was to stand a chance of surviving.[125] Meanwhile, Elizabeth and Philip's tour of the Gulf continued regardless, with the revised aim of steadying the nerves of local rulers and encouraging them to respond to internal and external problems efficiently.

By February, the shah had fled to Morocco but was causing trouble for his hosts. Threats against the Moroccan Embassy in Tehran had recently forced its evacuation. Complicating matters further, Palestinian and Arab leaders refused to visit the country as long as the shah was there. The embarrassed Moroccan king wanted him gone.[126]

This created a diplomatic problem—where would he end up? President Sadat repeatedly invited him to Egypt, but the shah did not want to go there. He ended up temporarily in the Bahamas; he was not the first exiled monarch to wash up there.[127]

Meanwhile, the shah made it clear that he wanted a permanent move to Britain, the country that had supported him back in 1953 and ever since. The prime minister, Jim Callaghan, had doubts. Just like David Lloyd George after the Russian Revolution, he worried that allowing the shah into Britain would damage relations with the new Iranian regime. His foreign and home secretaries agreed, citing security and domestic public order issues. The shah's presence on British soil would also have given rise to plots and—just as bad—rumors of plots. David Owen worried that an Iranian royal court would soon assemble around him, inevitably leading to conspiracies that would taint London. To make matters worse, the shah might even be assassinated on British soil.[128]

Indeed, assassination was Owen's main worry, since, for a decade, London's streets had seen several professional "hits" by Middle East terror groups. He warned: "Most important of all, the security problem would be very difficult and continuing. The extremist groups—Fedayeen and mujahidin—are tough and devoted people with a long and impressive record of political assassination. They and others will never give up trying to assassinate the shah and, given the vast number of Iranians in Britain at any one time, we would have to deploy a very large security force indeed to give the shah any kind of guarantee of protection." Owen thought they should try to give the shah an intimation, "of an informal but fairly clear nature, that his coming would not be welcome to us."[129]

In May 1979, Margaret Thatcher replaced Callaghan as prime minister. She initially wanted to offer the shah a home in Britain but was persuaded to change her mind. Ever sensitive to issues of export and business, it would clearly be the end of any dealing with the new regime. Moreover, Anthony Parsons warned that over a thousand Britons living in Iran would be taken prisoner or even shot.[130] With sadness, she secretly sent Sir Denis Wright, a former ambassador to Iran, to explain to the shah personally why he was not allowed in.[131]

Despite all the risks, Queen Elizabeth still wanted to offer the shah asylum. She passed a message through royal networks to let him know that she would have liked "to have the Shah come" but that her government was "reticent."[132]

She also brought up "the fate of the shah" when sending her new ambassador to Washington.[133] She was angry about letting the shah down and, unusually, let this be known. It was the beginning of a frosty relationship with her new prime minister.[134]

Meanwhile, the shah traveled to New York for cancer treatment. His stay validated many of the British government's concerns: it attracted great criticism from the revolutionary regime in Iran and necessitated intense security on the ground. President Jimmy Carter's brief and reluctant hospitality even exacerbated the Iranian hostage crisis, when revolutionaries held fifty-two US diplomats and intelligence officers hostage in Tehran for over a year.[135] There was no way he could come to Britain now.

Blocked from his initial destination of choice, and despite the queen's earlier wishes, the shah traveled to Panama in December 1979. He lived under virtual house—or hospital—arrest. The next month, ambiguous intelligence reached the Foreign Office that he had been arrested and faced extradition back to Iran. In the confusion, the queen left diplomats in little doubt that she expected updates about his fate. "The Queen," one ominously wrote to colleagues on the spot, "is personally interested."[136]

Back in Tehran, the Iranian hostage crisis rumbled on, putting pressure on President Carter. Meanwhile, and adding yet more pressure on the US, the Soviets invaded neighboring Afghanistan. The Soviet occupation sparked one of the largest Western covert action campaigns of the Cold War, in which the CIA and others supported local resistance fighters with money and weapons. Thatcher told Princess Margaret how Iran and the hostages had "dominated every conversation" she had on a recent trip to the US. She lamented that "the events in Afghanistan have cast a shadow over the whole world." "If only Iran had never taken those hostages, or would now release them," she continued, "we should be in a far better position to tackle the Russians in that part of the world."[137] Margaret complained that she found "it quite impossible to find out *what* is happening in Afghanistan." She asked the prime minister: "are they about to wheel into Iran and get all the oil?"[138]

The shah, who had reluctantly moved to Egypt, finally died in July 1980. Attention turned to whether his family would be allowed to visit, or even live, in the UK. Remarkably, Prince Charles asked the Foreign Office to consider exfiltrating a minor member of the Iranian Royal Family out of the country. Given the state of diplomatic relations between the UK and Iran, he must have known such a request would have entailed a daring MI6 covert operation. British diplomats dutifully followed up the royal request but soon grew puzzled. They had never heard of the target, and their "discreet enquiries" among Iranian exiles in London had "drawn a blank." In a bizarre twist, Charles had got the wrong name.

Diplomats told the prince that overt exfiltration—once they had worked out who he meant—would be impossible after the Iranians had seized American hostages. As for covert exfiltration, they told Charles that several clandestine organizations did exist to get people out of Iran, but that it was dangerous, expensive, and that the government was not involved. It was, however, fairly easy to access these channels through Iranian exiles in London—especially with enough money.[139]

The efforts of Charles to get people out were rather urgent. The Khomeini regime was conducting a vicious purge of those associated with the shah, many of whom were personally known to the British royal family. Almost the only royal courtier to evade the firing squad was Hossein Fardust, the shah's friend since childhood and trusted aide. He did this by quickly writing a memoir that accused the shah of corruption, torture, sexual perversion, and espionage for foreign governments. He focused on the historic theme of MI6's influence in Tehran and explained that the "secret brains behind Savak's special intelligence branch was actually the 'satanic' Queen Elizabeth II." He insisted that the shah met the MI6 head of station every day to receive his instructions like a puppet.[140] This, of course, was not true, but, almost uniquely for a foreign leader, the shah had met the MI6 and CIA heads of station regularly throughout his reign; albeit more out of fear than affection.[141]

Royal diplomacy was not over yet. In August, the queen used an audience with Thatcher to ask about the possibility of the shah's widow coming to the UK. Royal networks were in full swing, for she had received the message via ex-king Constantine of Greece, who had been holidaying in Cowes. The Cowes Regatta had hosted the tsar, the kaiser, and a hundred less distinguished royals down the years. The idea put the government back into a spin, fearing that allowing the former empress's entry could lead to demonstrations, domestic terrorism, and diplomatic rows.[142]

Constantine continued to engage in intrigue on behalf of the Iranians. He advised the deposed royals to "form some sort of committee—not a government in exile—which would form a focus for the Iranian exiles," presumably for opposition and counterrevolution.[143] Meanwhile, supporters of the shah talked of quietly sounding out the UK about the possibility of a potential coup. The British ambassador in Dubai urgently warned that his counterpart in London "was cooking up a plot of some kind."[144]

Remarkably, in October 1980, the empress asked the British to use their influence, working alongside Arab monarchies, to restore the Iranian throne. She had assumed that Britain would be predisposed to help because of close ties between both royal families. Diplomats reacted with surprise and alarm. It was out of the question.[145]

At the same time, however, the likes of Julian Amery, an operative of the Special Operations Executive turned politician who had been involved in many covert operations since the Second World War, maintained contact with the shah's supporters and unsuccessfully lobbied for a countercoup.[146] All the while, Queen Elizabeth watched closely, asking about the empress's fate and receiving letters from her via the embassy in Cairo.[147]

A year later, Amery, who was still in contact with the exiled Royal Family, asked the foreign secretary if the shah's son could visit the UK. Once again, diplomats refused, on security grounds. MI5 added that the risk of assassination was simply too high.[148]

Royal diplomacy was a tricky business, intertwining discreet influence and security. Relations with Iran catapulted the queen—often reluctantly—into a quasi-diplomatic actor. Her influence and the importance of royal networks were clear; but Iran also showed the limitations of monarchy, given that neither Elizabeth nor Charles succeeded in helping their royal counterparts.

The queen worked hard to transform the empire into the Commonwealth and old enemies into friends. All the royals offered insights of their own from their contacts and conversations. They could even play a more active role, such as being dangled as an incentive to release an imprisoned spy, as in the Brooke case. On more than one occasion, the world of royalty and espionage collided, as the aftermath of Operation Foot demonstrated.

Most importantly, royal activity was an important means of projecting British influence. In the case of Chile, it perfectly complemented Britain's covert action. Two arms of the British state—both secretive and misunderstood in their own ways—were working together in harmony. But there were limits. The queen remained reluctant to visit the Soviet Union. Right up until 1989, she continued to pointedly call Leningrad "Saint Petersburg."[149]

Intelligence also kept the royals safe as they traveled to dangerous places, and it protected them from political embarrassment at home. But as the turbulent last years of the shah underlined, the royals were now, more than ever, not just vulnerable to protest and political turmoil but were also inviting targets for terrorists everywhere.

PART V

Protecting the Realm
and the Royals

15

Terrorists and Lunatics, 1969–1977

Your greatest danger is still the lone nutcase . . .
—Princess Anne, 1980

The queen's royal diplomacy placed her in some dangerous situations. Politicians, journalists, and the broader public worried about her safety—especially when she was visiting countries in the midst of upheaval. But the new danger in the 1960s and 1970s was the growth of international terrorism, often targeting heads of state. These fresh worries put serious pressure on her governments, which feared putting the queen in harm's way. Prime ministers Harold Wilson and then Edward Heath both endured sleepless nights fretting not just about the queen's welfare overseas but also about opposition members of Parliament exploiting it to make trouble for the government about "royal risk"—and there were certainly a few narrow squeaks.

On other occasions, the government cynically played the security card to prevent a royal from doing something that could be politically embarrassing. The prime minister even lied to the queen to spare her blushes. In 1967, Prince Philip was due to take a vacation in the Indian city of Jaipur, famous for its romantic dusty pink hues and historic buildings, as a guest of the maharajah. The local political situation was in turmoil: the state government had broken down and, from the Jaipur Palace, the maharajah's wife led intense political agitation against Indira Gandhi's premiership. Some twenty-one people died in riots before Gandhi imposed direct rule and a twenty-four-hour curfew.

Despite this turmoil, Philip faced little personal threat. The emergency powers removed any serious risk to his personal safety; and Mountbatten, who was already in Jaipur, offered a sanguine assessment from the ground. Back in London, the British government accepted this intelligence but remained deeply concerned about the trip. To have Philip staying with a prominent antigovernment figure would lead to some "pretty wild allegations" about royal meddling in Indian affairs. It would create a highly embarrassing impression—however unfair—of Philip subverting the elected government. Prime Minister Harold

Wilson canceled the visit entirely. He did not let on the real reason, preferring instead to hide behind the security explanation, telling the queen simply that "there was a risk to life."[1]

Queen Elizabeth sensed that the institution of royalty would wither and die if its current placeholders locked themselves away in a tower or hid behind lines of armor and shields. She was quite fatalistic about the prospect of assassination, perhaps inheriting some of Queen Victoria's divine faith in God's protection. Royal protection officers were not allowed to hurl the queen to the floor to protect her—as their US equivalent could do to presidents. Instead, they could simply advise—strongly if necessary—to change course. She did not always agree.

The royalty protection group was small. Recruitment was opaque and lacked proper vetting procedures. Like the intelligence services, it relied on tapping "good chaps" on the shoulder. The queen typically had full-time protection, as did her immediate family, to preserve the line of succession. Each had an allocated plainclothes police officer. The individuals were doggedly loyal, but the overall organization was fragmented, poorly coordinated, and asking for trouble. Underpinning this was a belief that the British Royal Family was wonderful and no one could possibly want to attack its members—and this proved to be wrong.[2]

The role of intelligence became crucial if the queen could not be locked away behind a ring of steel. Forewarned is forearmed, as intelligence officers say. Accurate and timely information would need to identify trouble before it arose, allowing the queen to see and be seen, as she put it. Intelligence allowed the Royal Family to maintain an illusion of accessibility and to make their legend—chosen by God to lead loyal subjects and affirm the authority of the state—a reality.[3]

This was easier said than done. Fears increased after the assassination of President John F. Kennedy in 1963 and his brother Robert in 1968. By the end of the decade, the rise of international terrorism had drastically complicated royal security planning. Prince Philip had vetoed the use of armed protection—calling it unbecoming and unnecessary—and was only persuaded to alter his opposition once Prince Charles and Princess Anne entered their teens.[4] Even then, royal security remained flimsy.

In the 1960s, Prince Charles went to Trinity College at Cambridge University accompanied by his loyal security guard, Michael Varney. Charles was a naturally active and enthusiastic person who threw himself into university life, especially amateur dramatics, and was adored by his fellow students. He appeared in many productions including the Joe Orton play *Erpingham Camp*.[5] Although his tutors banned him from joining a number of student societies, everything from the Buddhist Society to the Conservative Association, for fear of seeming political, university life allowed him some scope for social and philosophical exploration.[6]

His minder recalls that he also "had a talent for getting himself into situations that were potentially embarrassing or even physically dangerous." He enjoyed performing in plays at the Pitt Club, which, as his bodyguard noted, was rather unlike the Athenaeum and brought the prince into close proximity with a range of unconventional characters, including belly dancers. But the most alarming situations occurred when he was the "victim of other people's machinations."[7]

Providing discreet protection for Charles at Cambridge was tricky. His Special Branch guards did not want to embarrass him by sticking close behind him "like a police dog." Charles preferred to cycle around Cambridge. and his security guards followed in a rather beat-up old Land Rover at a respectful distance. Everyone was trying to preserve the pretense that he was just any student out on his own. Their biggest worry was young women, especially during Rag Week, a notoriously debauched week in the British student calendar, when various activities took place for charity and in which, in their words, "licence became almost anarchy."[8]

Rag Week in the famous year of 1968 "came within a hairsbreadth" of disaster. Varney learned, through police intelligence, that a group of female Manchester University students, "all Women's Libbers of the most strident kind," planned to raid Trinity and kidnap Charles and hold him for ransom. Worse still, "a fifth column" existed inside Cambridge since the team from Manchester had eager and willing accomplices from the women of Girton College. Together, they were keen to pull off "their coup" without "any male assistance whatsoever."[9]

"It was a well-planned operation almost worthy of professional kidnappers." The Manchester team had not only hired a getaway car but had also arranged a safe house for their victim. The snatch was assigned to what the police called a "squad of Amazons" who were ready for a fight and who "prepared to cart Prince Charles off bodily." His loyal guard had a sneaking suspicion that Charles might have enjoyed the whole escapade and was perhaps politically sympathetic, but at the same time he was "painfully aware" that if the kidnapping was successful, "it would be my head that rolled in the basket." Varney was, in his own words, "totally unamused."[10]

Varney engineered a face-to-face meeting with the leader of the kidnappers. He warned her that they already had all the details of the plan and that if it went ahead, it would cause a great deal of legal trouble for all those involved.

The year 1968 was not one of political correctness, so he also offered a stark warning that "if you do go ahead and try to pull it off, I will personally see that you won't sit down for a fortnight." The leader of the kidnapping plot gave as good as she got, calling him by "all the four-letter names I'd ever heard"—in a posh Cheltenham accent. Either way, the Manchester kidnapping was off.[11]

More serious dangers awaited him in Wales. Prince Charles had been prince of Wales since boyhood. In July 1969, Charles interrupted his studies at Cambridge for the formal ceremony of investiture. During his second year, he undertook a short period of study at Aberystwyth University, on the Welsh coast, before being formally bestowed with a bejeweled crown, ring, mantle, sword, and gold rod, at Caernarfon Castle in front of a televised audience of millions. About two hundred thousand people lined the streets to catch a glimpse as the archaic pageant of pomp and circumstance rolled through the ancient town, an antidote to the swinging 1960s.

Not everyone was excited. Violent Welsh nationalism was on the rise, and Britain's intelligence services worried about the threat terrorists could pose to the ceremony. The nationalists interpreted royalty as an English institution imposed from across the border and the title of prince of Wales as an insult, especially since Charles's own links with Wales were rather thin. The ceremony was a mock medieval charade, an exercise in regional tokenism that nationalists believed masked historic English oppression of the Welsh.

The location, a medieval castle in remote northwestern Wales, a long way from the well-protected streets of London, caused particular concern. In the years running up to the ceremony, Welsh nationalists had attacked reservoirs and water pipelines between Liverpool and Birmingham. A bomb exploded in the nonreligious Temple of Peace in Cardiff hours before the first meeting to organize the investiture took place inside. Another bomb at the Welsh Office deliberately coincided with a visit of Princess Margaret. This campaign, carried out by the shadowy Mudiad Amddiffyn Cymru (MAC; Movement for the Defence of Wales), culminated with an attempted bombing of four different locations.[12] One of the leaders of MAC was a former British soldier, Brian Jenkins, who had seen service in Berlin and Cyprus. His time in the latter posting had offered him insights into the nationalist Cypriot movement EOKA, and he recalls how he was influenced by seeing first-hand how a small but organized group of revolutionaries could free a country in the grip of colonialism.[13]

Burke Trend, the cabinet secretary, told Harold Wilson that MI5 and Special Branch had increased efforts to gather intelligence against Welsh extremists and were working closely together.[14] Special Branch established a unit in

Shrewsbury to focus specifically on the threat to Charles. Demonstrating a lack of confidence in the Welsh police, it coordinated all incoming intelligence sources before passing details on to the Welsh chief constables.[15]

MI5 tried to reassure Wilson that though extremist propaganda was increasing, the threat of violence was in decline. An explosion at the tax office in Chester and at the new police headquarters in Cardiff, both in April 1969, suggested that this intelligence was rather optimistic. MI5 wondered whether the attack was linked to the forthcoming trial of nine Welsh nationalists, which would take place when Charles was due to be in Aberystwyth. More violence might be expected.

The trial spotlighted the worst weakness of the Welsh nationalists: their addiction to publicity. One militant boasted that he had fitted a harness to his dog that he said would be used to carry sticks of explosive gelignite toward the royal family. He claimed he had dozens more dogs all trained to carry magnetic devices under security vehicles. The story about these "kamikaze dogs" duly appeared in newspapers and prompted hundreds of angry letters from dog lovers. It was as a result of this revulsion among Welsh public opinion that the nine members had been arrested in the first place. They were charged with a number of offenses, including possession of firearms, explosives, and public order offenses. The trial, in Swansea, lasted fifty-three days, ending on the day of the investiture. Self-proclaimed leader Cayo Evans, his second-in-command Dennis Coslett, and four other members were convicted. Evans and Coslett spent fifteen months in jail.[16] The arrests prevented the group from carrying out other bizarre plans, including flying a radio-controlled helicopter carrying manure over the castle and dropping its fetid cargo on the prince's head.

As the ceremony neared, intelligence still assessed that the risk to Charles was "more a matter of personal embarrassment than of physical harm, although it is never possible to rule out the activities of a determined fanatic."[17] The home secretary, Jim Callaghan, found it all rather "disturbing";[18] Wilson considered canceling the Aberystwyth prelude to the trip altogether.[19] In the end, Charles made it to Aberystwyth to study the Welsh language and history for a few weeks—a sop to the principality and a red rag to nationalists—but found his student accommodation cell-like, his fellow scholars rather hostile, and his existence lonely. This was a far cry from his idyllic existence in Cambridge.[20]

Harold Wilson took royal security very seriously. He was keen to emphasize to the royal household that this was a priority, so he developed a decidedly hands-on approach.[21] Prime ministerial meddling frustrated Callaghan, the cabinet minister actually responsible for Charles's safety. Wilson's staff warned the prime minister to back off before Callaghan found out that Wilson was receiving his own private intelligence updates outside Callaghan's reach. Callaghan would have exploded. More cynically, Wilson was also told not to meddle too much because "if anything were to go wrong," Callaghan "might possibly take the line that you had in fact assumed the responsibility." Downing Street wanted Callaghan to be the minister for disaster if the worst happened.[22]

Nevertheless, Wilson did feel a sense of personal responsibility, not least because it was he, as an ardent monarchist, who had originally pressed for this expensive and constitutionally unnecessary expression of formidable pageantry. Moreover, the rise of Welsh nationalism was challenging Labour's electoral support across Wales, and Wilson's government hoped the ceremony would promote dual British and Welsh identity.[23] Egged on by the Welsh Labour Party, he pushed hard for it to go ahead, despite some reluctance from the palace.[24]

Elizabeth was personally worried. With the BBC prerecording obituary tributes in case of Charles's assassination, she told Wilson that she feared for her son's safety.[25] This unsurprisingly sent Wilson into another spin. He even suggested canceling the entire ceremony after a live bomb was found near a pier at Holyhead, where the royal yacht *Britannia* was due to dock, just days before Charles was to be crowned.[26] Another was planted near the castle but failed to go off. It was found by a ten-year-old boy on vacation from the home counties. Believing it to be a football, he kicked it and it exploded. He was seriously injured and spent weeks in the hospital and remains disabled.[27]

As the investiture approached, the actor Richard Burton, who was providing the television commentary for ITV, noticed that this was a rather risky outing. He was staying with Princess Margaret and her husband, Lord Snowdon, and remarked to them that his own role on the day was all fairly straightforward, "unless some shambling, drivel mouthed, sideways moving, sly-boots of a North Wales imitation of an Irishman might decide to blow everybody to bits."[28]

Wilson was particularly worried about the security of the royal train. It was the biggest of its kind in living memory—with some fifteen coaches—and was packed with dignitaries. Mountbatten was thrilled to be on board, and noted happily that he had his own large bedroom and bathroom. But this mobile entourage of royals presented a dream target for terrorists.[29] Drawing on the latest intelligence, Callaghan had earlier warned Wilson that "certain extremists are said to be considering plans to disorganise selected railway junctions on or before the day of the Investiture by derailing trains."[30] Wilson pressed for a "pilot train" to travel ahead of the royal party to test the tracks and prevent what he euphemistically called "any untoward incident."[31] The royal train was bulletproof and had two diesel engines, a specification dating back to 1937, when one had failed and the train got stuck.[32] Neither would have prevented it from derailing.

Wilson also demanded special precautions, including troops if necessary, at all vulnerable points before and during the ceremony. Officials in the Home Office had to tell him that this was impossible but reassured him that MI5 had identified the most vulnerable locations throughout Wales and the border counties and had advised the local police forces about suitable precautions. "All of the most important points," officials insisted, "are being watched or frequently visited by police."[33] The army provided three surveillance helicopters to help out.[34] "Everything possible is being done," the prime minister was told, "but one must not underestimate the difficulties."[35]

Amid all the focus on Welsh extremism, nobody noticed a secret Soviet plot to disrupt the preparations, embarrass British intelligence, and stir up tensions between the government and the Welsh. Operation Edding involved blowing up a small bridge on the road from Porthmadog to Caernarfon using British-manufactured gelignite. On the eve of the explosion, a letter was to be sent to a Plaid Cymru member of Partliament, Gwynfor Evans, warning him that MI5 planned a "provocation" to discredit the nationalists and provide a pretext for a major security clampdown in Wales. The Soviets hoped that when the bridge exploded, Evans would accuse the British government of a false flag attack designed to undermine the nationalist cause. The Soviet leadership eventually canceled Operation Edding on the grounds that KGB involvement would come to light and fatally undermine the deception.[36]

Ultimately, it was the Welsh nationalists who almost got through. One extremist group tried to plant a bomb at a government office in Abergele, where, just as Wilson had feared, the royal train would shortly be passing through. Their device exploded prematurely, killing two members of MAC, Alwyn Jones and George Taylor.[37]

One the evening before the investiture, a vast royal party boarded the train. In an attempt to relieve the tension, there was much "joshing and horseplay." Members of the BBC were also on board and showed a rerun of its film of the rather chaotic 1911 investiture of the future Edward VIII. Charles arrived in the middle of this showing to be told by his grandmother that, because of the worsening security situation, and his likely liquidation, they had decided to go ahead with the ceremony but to replace him using a stunt double.[38]

Despite the jokes, one member of the royal household later recalled that "there was a fairly tense atmosphere the night before with bombs going off as we were on the Royal Train." At one point, a bomb hoax stopped the train altogether.[39] Although it "looked like a time bomb," it was in fact just a packet of clay with an alarm clock attached—most royals slept through the alert.[40] On the day itself, some devices failed to detonate, apart from one small explosion close to the castle, which was drowned out by the twenty-one-gun salute.[41]

The investiture was a qualified success; albeit one in which the police outnumbered the crowd in places.[42] In the courtyard of the medieval castle, the queen draped her eldest son in a purple velvet robe, trimmed with ermine. With a crown on his head and scepter in his hand, Charles delivered his speech. Lord Snowdon later recalled that the young prince was "shit scared."[43] As for his mother, afterward Elizabeth retired to bed for six days with nervous exhaustion.[44]

How close had Prince Charles come to meeting his end? The answer is, quite close. MAC supremo John Jenkins was arrested in November 1969. Incredibly, he had been in Caernarfon on the day of the investiture while still serving as a sergeant in the British Army. He has claimed that he could have taken a rifle and shot the prince during the ceremony. Convicted of offenses involving explosives, Jenkins was sentenced to ten years' imprisonment in April 1970.[45]

The most dramatic royal security breach of the Windsor era targeted Charles's younger sister, on March 20, 1974. A lone gunman, Ian Ball, attempted to kidnap Princess Anne and hold her for ransom. He had been planning the kidnapping for a long time, selecting Anne because she was the only young woman in the family and, in Ball's own words, "would have been the easiest."[46]

At about 7:45 p.m., the princess, then in her mid-twenties, and her husband, Mark Phillips, were being driven down the Mall toward Buckingham Palace. Ball's white Ford Escort, following them across town, quickly overtook the royal car and forced it to stop suddenly. Anne was thrown to the floor. Ball got out and marched toward Anne's car. From the front passenger seat, Anne's protection officer, James Beaton, assumed that Ball was approaching to argue about some imagined traffic incident. Beaton climbed out of the door ready to diffuse the situation.

Out of nowhere, Ball whipped out a pistol and shot Beaton in the shoulder. Wounded, Beaton drew his own weapon and tried to return fire but missed and hit the back of the car. Bleeding from his shoulder, he tried again, this time steadying his gun with both hands. It failed to fire, jamming at the worst possible moment.[47]

Anne's driver, Alex Callender, bravely rushed from the car to disarm Ball, grabbing his arm. "I'll shoot you," Ball shouted back at him, before firing from point blank range at his chest.[48] On the floor, Beaton fiddled with his gun, trying to fix the jam. "Put your gun down or I'll shoot her," Ball instructed. Beaton obediently placed his useless gun down on the road.[49]

Ball turned his attention to the princess, trying to persuade her to get out of the car. "I want you to come with me for a day or two, because I want £2 million," he said politely. "Will you get out of the car?"

Anne replied: "Not bloody likely; and I haven't got £2 million."

"I only want you for two days," he responded, surprisingly courteously. "I don't want to hurt you." He then managed to open the door and tried to drag

Anne out by the forearm. She tried to stay calm, repeating again and again that she did not want to get out of the car. "Come out or I'll have to shoot you," he insisted.

"I nearly lost my temper with him," Anne later recalled, "but I knew that if I did, I should hit him and he would shoot me."[50] Her husband, Mark Phillips, grabbed her other arm to prevent Ball from pulling her out. Ball shot Beaton again in the melee, this time in the right hand. A glass window behind him shattered.[51] The tussle over the princess continued, splitting her dress and ripping the shoulders; this, she recalled, was "his most dangerous moment," as "I lost my rag at this stage." Another police officer, Michael Hills, wandered onto the scene but did not notice that Ball was armed or that two people had already been shot, so when he tapped Ball on the shoulder, he also quickly received a bullet.[52]

As the surreal negotiations between Anne and her assailant continued, a number of pedestrians came past. Anne recalled that the first one came quite close to get a good view of the struggle. "He came all the way across the road, looked in through the window, and then went 'Hmm, so it is,' and turned and he walked all the way back, wandering off down the Mall."

Eventually more passersby turned up and tried to help. The first was a journalist, Brian McConnell, who was also shot for his pains. The second was Ron "The Geezer" Russell, a former heavyweight boxer, who punched Ball twice in the back of the head. As he did this, more police arrived on the scene.[53]

Ball then fled into Saint James's Park but was quickly rugby-tackled to the ground. He had fired eleven shots in all, hitting four people. Anne thought he must be running out of bullets. Remarkably, she was unscathed; but Beaton was shot three times.[54] Sir Robert Mark, the Metropolitan Police commissioner, concluded: "It was a miracle no-one was killed." The queen decorated both Beaton and her daughter for bravery.[55] She also awarded Ron Russell the George Medal, and as she presented it told him: "The medal is from the Queen, but I want to thank you as Anne's mother."[56]

Prime Minister Harold Wilson enjoyed reading a classified report of the incident. "A very good story," he noted in the margins. "Pity the Palace can't let it come out."[57] He praised Anne for behaving with "quite extraordinary courage and presence of mind."[58] Prince Charles, serving in the navy on HMS *Jupiter* some eight thousand miles away, echoed these sentiments and recorded in his diary: "Imagine seeing four people shot in cold blood in front of you and still refusing to get out. . . . My admiration for such an incredible sister knows no bounds!"[59]

Queen Elizabeth was half a world away in Indonesia. Number 10 moved to reassure the royal party, telling Charteris that it was just the work of an "isolated nutcase." Although it could inspire copycat attacks, "perhaps it is less worrying than it would be if it seemed that there was something more behind it."[60]

The police quickly recovered Ball's ransom letter, which was addressed to the queen. It demanded £3 million to be paid in used, unmarked £5 notes and delivered in an "unlocked thirty-inch suitcase." Ball also sought immunity from prosecution, not just for the kidnapping but also sinisterly for any crimes committed earlier, "from parking offences to murder."[61]

Ball's plan was byzantine and bizarre in equal measure. He had sought to take Anne to Heathrow Airport, where, under police escort, they would board a plane. The queen would arrive to offer the pardons in person. She would first be "asked questions and required to give a sample signature to ascertain that she is in fact the queen." Ball would then take Anne to Zurich to deposit the money in a Swiss bank, before flying back with her to London, where Ball would release her. "The above instructions are quite clear," Ball wrote "and are not capable of any ambiguity. Unless they are carried out to the letter ANNE WILL BE SHOT DEAD. If the police make any attempts to find the hideout or if they try to storm the hideout ANNE WILL AUTOMATICALLY BE SHOT DEAD."[62]

This was clearly the work of a dangerous lunatic. Ball was working alone and was not known to Special Branch.[63] Anne later stated that "perhaps the greatest danger seems to be the lone nutter who had just enough to pull it together. That said, if anyone was seriously intent on wiping one out, it would be very easy to do."[64] Queen Victoria would have agreed with this analysis.

The ill-fated kidnapping spurred a speedy review of royal security. Special Branch and the intelligence services assessed that the Royal Family faced a threat from "madmen and exhibitionists" on one hand and "groups of criminals or political extremists on the other." Violence in Northern Ireland and the assassination of President Kennedy and his brother risked inspiring people who wanted to attack the queen. On the plus side, Britain lacked a tradition of assassination, allowing officials to hope that public revulsion would provide enough deterrence—at least against domestic terrorists, if not madmen. Kidnapping provided a far greater threat, not least because developments in mass media, especially the growth of television, would ensure publicity for the kidnappers.[65]

The Princess Anne kidnapping attempt was also a classic case of Whitehall departments not talking with each other. Over the previous four years, several British diplomats and officials had been kidnapped and held for ransom. In 1971, the ambassador to Peru was captured and eventually freed after Ted Heath had approved the payment of £100,000. President Allende of Chile had chaired the negotiations personally between British officials and the kidnapper in a darkened room to hide his identity.[66] The Foreign Office had already begun to use the Special Air Service (SAS) to check on the security of overseas embassies. Kidnapping had also happened in Northern Ireland, but

Whitehall thought it could not happen in London, and a royal attack was just unthinkable.

These events now had an impact on planned royal visits. Weeks before the attack on Princess Anne, British diplomats had been thrilled to receive the "splendid news" that the queen and the duke of Edinburgh might make a royal visit to Mexico in March 1975. "No news could be more welcome," they gushed. Keen for the royal visit to go ahead, they wanted to offer London reassurance about the "security situation here" but perhaps offered too much detail.

They gave an enthusiastic account of the Mexican government's success in battling the rise of political kidnapping. Although admitting that there had recently been an increase in kidnappings, bank robberies, and murders, they added that the government was now "cracking one group after another." The Mexicans had decided to get tough rather than giving in to ransom demands after the kidnapping of the British consul in Guadalajara. One official enthused: "Lately various known ring-leaders have mysteriously been 'found dead' after what the authorities described as inter-gang fights. I suspect that one of the 'gangs' is frequently security forces." Therefore, they assured London, things were totally "within the grip" of the local authorities.[67] Predictably perhaps, the royals had seen enough of kidnapping, and the visit did not go ahead.

Despite the mounting danger, as late as 1974, the royals were not subject to regular threat assessments.[68] Royal security was still surprisingly lax. The royal protection group consisted of just twelve men. Anne—along with the queen, Philip, the Queen Mother, Charles, and Margaret—had full-time protection. Her younger siblings, Andrew and Edward, had limited protection, while minor royals such as the duke and duchess of Kent had protection only when required. Some of the wider family flapped after the kidnapping attempt. The queen's cousin, Princess Alexandra, on the "C" list, requested further protection of her children, but this was not granted.[69]

Even full-time protection for key royals was underwhelming. It simply involved a single "protection officer" accompanying their royal charge from the moment they left their residence to the time of return. Each of the police officers had undertaken limited weapons training and carried—at their own discretion—a Walther self-loading pistol.[70] Often they chose not to carry weapons. Princess Anne had a single protection officer; Charles had two.[71]

The protection officer sat in the front passenger seat of each car. Only the queen had a second following behind—backup that Princess Anne would surely have craved during the kidnapping attempt. Royal cars lacked decent radio communications, bulletproof glass, and armor plating. None of the Royal Family had a motorcycle escort—something despised by the queen as an indicator of despots and dictatorship. The sight of police outriders, with sirens wailing, would have been too "militaristic in appearance."[72] James Beaton, who later became the superintendent in charge of royal protection, explained that their vehicles were still not fitted with radios, as "it was deemed on a royal car that it would spoil the look of it."[73]

The government scrambled to bolster royal security in the days after the incident. But armor plating remained too heavy; and bulletproof glass was too obtrusive. The queen did agree to increasing the size of the royal protection team and to installing radio sets and mirrors, despite her concerns that radio calls would destroy the solitude of her car journeys. Beaton's jammed gun became the main scapegoat, and within days protection officers switched to a better pistol and more expensive bullets.[74] Again, the main impediment was Philip, who was adamant that they should not have a "tremendous increase in security" that would have an impact on their lifestyle.[75]

Nevertheless, behind the scenes, certain members of the royal household were discreetly dispatched to undertake training to deal with hostage situations.[76] Early the next year, the queen's protection officer, Michael Trestrail, visited the SAS's new specialist facility for training in hostage rescue.[77]

The SAS had acquired an elite counterterrorist mandate in the early 1970s and had been practicing bodyguard duties for some years. Its officers traveled the world to train the bodyguards of friendly heads of state—Britain became the defensive shield of the world's remaining sovereigns. To perform its newfound hostage rescue function, the SAS began training in a specially constructed six-room house in Hereford known colloquially as the "Killing House."

Designed on a single piece of graph paper and built by a local builder for £30,000, the house included a number of rooms, joined by corridors, full of furniture and other obstacles. The SAS could hone skills in entering a building, distinguishing terrorists from hostages, and deciding when—and when not—to shoot.[78] Here it shot hundreds of live rounds into "Carlos the Jackal" targets "almost daily." Trestrail attended a three-day course, including the use of live ammunition, that exposed him to the latest developments in hostage release operations. He was the first of many royal protection officers to tread this path.

Prince Philip's protection officer followed suit, but returned to the palace unimpressed and resistant to the Hereford commando style, which was a million miles from the low-profile approach long favored by the Royal Family.[79] The courses were also intended to give royal protection officers a better idea of what the SAS could do. Although the police maintained primacy, the SAS could be called on by the home secretary if a member of the Royal Family was kidnapped.[80]

Within eight years, the protection force had grown from twelve officers to forty-three, largely as a result of the failure to protect Anne.[81] The main issue was the imbalance between armed personal protection and static duty. Over a hundred officers were patrolling royal residences, but only fifteen persons were providing personal protection with their elegant Bond-style Walther PPK auto-matics.[82] The royal squad at least had better firearms, while those protecting Britain's cabinet ministers had to put up with clunky, old-fashioned Smith & Wesson revolvers until the mid-1990s.[83]

What of Ian Ball, Princess Anne's would-be kidnapper? During his interrogation after being arrested, the then–twenty-six-year-old told the police that he had intended to draw attention to the plight of the mentally ill, adding sadly: "I suppose I'll be locked up for the rest of my life." Ball was right, and he remains detained in Broadmoor, despite frequent attempts to secure a review of his case and a period on hunger strike. His solicitor insists that had he done this to anyone other than a member of the Royal Family, he would have been quietly freed long ago, so now he is effectively "a political prisoner."[84]

Royal protection would face its biggest challenge yet in 1977. The queen and the duke of Edinburgh paid a tense visit to Northern Ireland that August as part of the lengthy Silver Jubilee celebrations that saw her criss-cross the country. But Northern Ireland was not like the rest of the country. The sectarian violence between Irish nationalist paramilitaries and those loyal to the crown ensured that the short trip became the biggest royal security operation in history. Some thirty-two thousand troops and police were deployed in Belfast alone.[85] All eleven battalions of the controversial, mostly Protestant, Ulster Defence Regiment were called upon to contain the IRA threat in the run-up.[86]

Royal trips to Ireland were not commonplace. Shortly before the outbreak of the Troubles in 1969, the Irish government quietly blocked Princess Margaret from traveling to County Offaly in the heart of Ireland on a family vacation to visit her mother-in-law. Margaret was furious, but security authorities warned that the threat posed by extremists "to create trouble" was too great.[87] When Princess Alexandra, the queen's younger cousin, was due to visit Northern Ireland on an icebreaking trip a few years later, Elizabeth questioned whether Belfast was safe enough.[88]

Visiting Northern Ireland in 1977, at the height of the Protestant marching season, would be politically sensitive and personally risky. The schedule was inevitably confined to Protestant areas to minimize the threat and reduce adverse publicity, but this did nothing to reassure the Catholic minority that the crown was not above politics.

The problem was the timing. The queen's Silver Jubilee coincided with sensitive dates, including the anniversary of internment. Back in August 1971, amid much controversy, the Stormont government introduced detention of suspects without trial under the Special Powers Act. The army swept in and quickly arrested hundreds of Catholics and nationalists. When John Hume, the moderate deputy leader of the Social Democratic Labour Party, eventually heard about it, he was incredulous at the folly of the queen's advisers for planning her visit on what he called "the most emotive days possible."[89] Therefore, when those in charge of planning the jubilee tour started to consider just what would be possible in any Northern Ireland leg, they did not dare ask for security advice. So tense was the situation on the ground that they feared the security authorities would simply advise against any trip at all. Instead, they worked out a tentative plan with the palace first.[90]

This put the queen in a bind: any suggestion that she was unable to visit part of her own country would have gifted the IRA with a propaganda coup. Yet the physical risk was real and dangerous. At Elizabeth and Philip's request, Martin Charteris, now the queen's private secretary, asked directly about the latest intelligence on the IRA threat and whether the trip could be canceled if necessary—even at the last minute.[91]

The Whitehall response hardly filled the palace with confidence. Charteris learned that the threat was more "oblique than direct"; that the "normal bubblings of discontent" would be inevitable; and that intelligence could not identify an "individual fanatic" as a threat. The best they could do was identify a "positive collective threat"—and even then, the chances of doing so were only "fair to good." On the plus side, the trip could be canceled at any time.[92]

Officials in the Home Office asked Charteris bluntly: "Does she want to go or not?" They discreetly offered to "get her out of it" if necessary. Charteris duly put the question to Elizabeth. Typically, she responded that since the visit had already been announced, she had better follow through with it.[93] Northern Ireland could not be seen as a no-go area for the crown. And, if she was going to go, then, as ever, she had to be visible and accessible. She insisted on "seeing and being seen."[94] This phrase haunted the planners; everyone knew it would increase the risk further.

Military intelligence and the local police took the lead in assessing the threat. Planning was conducted on a strictly need-to-know basis, and palace officials were involved throughout. The list of potential threats reeled off by the army was terrifying: a mortar attack on the royal yacht; a shooting from a nearby vessel; an underwater mine on the hull of the royal yacht; and there was even a remote possibility of a personal attack on board by a terrorist carrying a concealed weapon. On land, the queen faced more threats from mortar attacks, remotely detonated bombs, hoax bombs, and ultimately assassination.[95]

Overall, the actual physical risk to the queen herself was slight, especially with rigorous security precautions in place.[96] The royal yacht *Britannia* was to be moored beyond the range of land-based missiles and fitted with special sonar able to identify metal on the seabed. Naval divers would hunt for bombs planted below the water line.[97] Those in charge of security wondered how much counterterrorism and hostage release training the royal protection officers had undertaken with the SAS. "Had they done the course?"[98] Many of them, including Trestrail, were successful alumni.

Amid all this morbid thinking, a local policeman made a throwaway remark trying to reassure Trestrail: "We expect no serious trouble. Just, maybe a wee demonstration somewhere." Trestrail asked what sort of a wee demonstration. "Well now," came the response, "they might just blow up the oil refinery."[99] Military intelligence told Charteris that the security forces would probably be able to contain this, but warned that "some spectacular incident, such as the bombing of a prominent building, is possible."[100]

The IRA certainly did demonstrate in the weeks before Elizabeth and Philip arrived. Terrorists mounted a campaign of violence, including arson attacks on Protestant shops in Belfast, hoping to force the government to cancel the trip on safety grounds. When that failed, they promised to give the queen "a visit to remember."[101] As tensions rose, their loyalist counterparts threatened to retaliate against any disruption of the visit.[102]

Charteris, a veteran of military intelligence and many a risky royal trip, was on board; others were less keen. Royal jitters reverberated from the palace. Ronald Allison, the queen's press secretary, went off script and raised security fears with the man tasked by the government to ensure positive press coverage. Charteris was furious. He insisted on the culprit's correspondence being hunted down and "abolished." Given the sensitivities surrounding any official announcement about the visit and the constant need to steady nerves, both the government and palace piled pressure on Allison to be more positive.[103]

The visit would go ahead as planned. Outside the security realm, the palace pondered what the queen might say publicly during the visit. Charteris offered some ideas, which were so astonishingly out of touch with the politics of Northern Ireland that they horrified civil servants and would have inflamed the security situation in their own right.

Delicate language was at a premium. He suggested that the queen acknowledge that "some of my ancestors behaved less than well in this part of the world in centuries gone by" but added the provocative qualification that their thinking was "understandable enough." "Implanting a British garrison," on the island of Ireland, "made a certain sense." If that was not enough of a red flag to nationalist opinion, Elizabeth would go on to say: "What happened three, four hundred years ago is not our fault. It is our business but not our fault." One alarmed civil servant scribbled "phew!" after reading it.[104]

On the morning of August 10, *Britannia* arrived in Belfast Lough. Elizabeth, alongside Trestrail, then nervously and reluctantly boarded a helicopter—something she had always steadfastly avoided.[105] The terrorist threat on the ground precluded her from traveling by car. Even hoax roadside bombs would have disrupted the carefully arranged program. Marchers descended on the republican Falls Road in Belfast behind a black banner declaring "ER Queen of Death." Riots followed. The IRA even managed to set up a brief roadblock. The royal helicopter was "undignified, uncomfortable, and noisy," but Elizabeth flew successfully if anxiously over the divided city to the relative safety of Hillsborough Castle.[106]

The next day, she opened the New University of Ulster at Coleraine, on County Londonderry's scenic north coast. Derry itself was off limits, and even though Coleraine was in loyalist territory, this function was the riskiest part of the brief visit. The new university's buildings could never be as secure as Hillsborough Castle or *Britannia*. The queen arrived once again by helicopter before taking a cautious, two-minute drive to the campus, where she and Philip spent most of the day.

Intelligence focused on the bomb threat but did not rule out the possibility of an assassination attempt.[107] Security services had kept the campus under close surveillance before the royal visit, but despite extensive electronic sweeps, they had found nothing and received no tip-offs until the end of July, when a routine search uncovered a small bomb hidden in a campus restroom. The army quickly defused it, and Charteris was quietly informed.[108]

Forty-eight hours before Elizabeth and Philip arrived, another bomb exploded on university grounds. Roy Mason, the Northern Ireland secretary, now thought the queen showed "none of the excitement and interest that had been so evident the day before." Still, calling the visit off would have given the IRA a propaganda victory over the British crown. The opening went ahead, but with a level of security that, in the words of one historian, "practically created conditions for martial law."[109]

Soldiers and bomb disposal experts watched nervously as the queen undertook her formalities.[110] She toured the library, unveiled a plaque, and attended a function for 2,000 carefully screened guests. Merlyn Rees, the home secretary, fretted terribly and tried to prevent the queen from doing all manner of things.[111] She was, according to one British minister, "terribly, terribly tense."[112] Elizabeth made her speech—a greatly toned-down version of the inflammatory remarks the palace had initially suggested—in front of television cameras after lunch. "There is no place for old fears and attitudes born of history," she said, "nor for the attribution of blame for the past."[113]

She and Philip left by helicopter at 5 p.m. All had passed smoothly until five hours later, when a third bomb exploded on the campus. It caused little damage. The IRA had mistimed the detonator; it was supposed to go off at 10 a.m. By now, the queen was long gone.[114] Prince Philip patted Elizabeth's hand and comforted her: "There now, it's over. Unless they sink the *Britannia* we're safe."[115]

A relieved Charteris, who retired afterward to become provost of Eton, recalled that it "felt wonderful sailing away."[116] The queen did not return until 1993.

This jubilee visit to Ireland, amid rioting and sectarianism, had particularly important consequences for the Royal Family. The tight security cordon and static locations prevented the crown from performing its traditional function of *affirming* the authority of the state by greeting jubilant subjects. Instead, the queen performed a rather more constitutionally dubious *assertion* of state authority—an assertion carried out with the help of armored troops. The brief visit aimed to reassure loyalists, but it inevitably associated the monarchy with the unionists. It inadvertently helped to politicize the monarchy and, in the eyes of violent republicanism, to legitimize the royals as a target for attack.[117] Although it was to have lethal consequences, this somber thought was far from Charteris's mind as he sailed off into retirement.

The Royal Family went on to face increasing threats from violent nationalists and lone fanatics. But its members simply ignored the politics and adjusted to being targets with a certain sangfroid. As she grew more experienced, the queen remained famously stoic but reassuringly nervous. By the mid-1970s, terrorist incidents were occurring across Europe and the Middle East almost daily.

In 1976, the Queen Mother visited Paris to open a new British cultural center. Her escort was the famously flamboyant British ambassador "Nico" Henderson. She arrived at Le Bourget airport "dressed in her usual powder blue Norman Hartnell attire" and wearing her familiar "beaming smile." She embodied the French word *rayonnement*, for which there is no exact English equivalent.

She boarded the ambassadorial Rolls-Royce, and a footman placed a tartan rug over her knees. As they sped across Paris, Henderson explained that her visit coincided with that of King Juan Carlos of Spain, who was under dire threat from Basque terrorists, a group that was desperate to kill him. The two royal motorcades frequently crossed each other's paths, and he quipped to the Queen Mother: "It would be such a pity if our car was mistaken for his and she found herself dying for Spain." The Queen Mother laughed and enjoyed "the bad taste joke," but the detective sitting in the front of the limousine failed to see the funny side.[118] It would not be long before terrorists successfully killed a senior British royal.

16

Terrorists and Lunatics, 1979–1984

*A mixture of desperate emotions swept over me—agony, disbelief,
a kind of wretched numbness, closely followed by a fierce and violent
determination to see something was done about the IRA.*
—Charles, on the death of Mountbatten, 1979

In the summer of 1979, Queen Elizabeth was due to be catapulted into the long-running bush war on the border between Zambia and Rhodesia. Guerrilla violence had broken out after Rhodesia's unilateral declaration of independence fifteen years earlier. Back then, the queen had resisted royal involvement as both sides tried to drag her into the political quagmire.

Now, she was supposed to travel to Zambia to undertake a nine-day tour of the region and open the Commonwealth's Heads of Government meeting. Not for the first time, fears for her personal safety threatened to derail planning an overseas visit. Guerrilla rebels used sanctuaries inside Zambia to attack targets across the border. The Rhodesian air force responded by frequently bombing their bases, including sites near Lusaka where the queen was scheduled to arrive.

Prime Minister Margaret Thatcher worried about a missile attack on the queen's aircraft. This was not out of the question, especially after Zambian antiaircraft guns had accidentally fired on their own helicopters in the chaotic aftermath of one Rhodesian raid on rebel intelligence headquarters in a suburb of Lusaka.[1] Thatcher also worried that she herself might be physically attacked as she stepped off the plane at night, and indeed she wore sunglasses for fear of an acid attack.[2]

The Joint Intelligence Committee, Britain's most senior intelligence assessment body, issued a stark warning: "The concentration of air-defence equipment at Lusaka International Airport and the proximity of trigger-happy" guerrillas forces "whom the Zambian authorities are unable to control will continue to make the use of the airport hazardous." There is, the intelligence continued, "a considerable risk of further mistaken attacks" on aircraft. The cabinet secretary, John Hunt, warned that "we may have to give rather careful thought to The Queen going to Lusaka."[3]

Two Rhodesian civilian airliners had recently been destroyed in exactly this manner. One disintegrated midair as the missile struck, killing all on board, while the other crashed. Eighteen people survived from the second aircraft, but the majority were executed by guerrillas as they escaped the wreckage.[4]

Julian Amery, a right-wing Conservative member of Parliament with links to the intelligence world, and Britain's longtime unofficial minister for covert action, offered a more outlandish threat assessment. He told Thatcher about a Cuban-sponsored plot to murder the queen. Amery's conspiracy theory involved an assassination, which would then be blamed on the Rhodesians.[5]

The risk of an accidental attack on the queen's plane seems far more plausible than an assassination plot. Thatcher was keen to exploit it for political gain. She was reluctant to attend the Commonwealth meeting herself, knowing that both apartheid in South Africa and the status of Rhodesia would dominate discussions. She knew full well that other leaders would criticize her for not doing enough to end the two conflicts.

Thatcher was reluctant for Elizabeth to go either. The whole meeting undermined British policy and threatened to embroil the queen in a Commonwealth row.[6] If the queen was to go, then Thatcher thought the visit might as well be used for political leverage. It offered a "strong card" that could put pressure on the Zambian president to remove ground-to-air missiles from the rebels, whom she called terrorists, in his territory. There was no point in sending the queen without receiving anything in return.[7]

Thatcher's zealous and political use of the security card irritated the queen. Elizabeth also had access to the intelligence assessments, and, as a great supporter of the Commonwealth, did not see anything inside them to put her off. The two had a frosty relationship at the best of times, and now the queen objected to being used as a pawn in the government's Rhodesia policy, and the palace made it clear that she intended to go. Thatcher backed down, and both attended.[8]

As it happened, Elizabeth's role was a great success—it is a rare documented example of the monarch directly involving herself in international politics. Sitting alongside the Zambian president in the back of his motor car, she persuaded him, after Thatcher had failed to do so, to drop offending passages from a speech likely referring to the rebels as freedom fighters. The summit paved the way for the settlement of the long-standing Rhodesia problem.[9]

Sadly, shortly after Elizabeth returned from Africa, assassination from a somewhat more predictable source struck closer to home.

On August 27, 1979, at about 11:30 a.m., Louis Mountbatten, now an old man of seventy-nine, climbed into his fishing boat, *Shadow V*. The boat was docked, unguarded, in the small harbor at Mullaghmore on the northwest coast of the Republic of Ireland near Sligo. Mountbatten had been vacationing in the area for the best part of thirty years at Classiebawn Castle, a country house built for Viscount Palmerston and inherited by his wife Edwina.

A decade earlier, when terrorist violence broke out in the north, the intelligence services had advised him that the risk of vacationing in County Sligo was "one that can reasonably be taken."[10] But there were always precautions, and as early as 1971, he reassured the queen that twelve policemen were on duty during his time at the castle. The next year, he sought the Cabinet Office's advice before setting out; the main anxiety was that he might be taken hostage. By 1974, the twelve-man guard had become twenty-eight. The "castle" was more like a small picturesque eighteenth-century folly, so this was almost one policeman for each room.[11]

All across Europe. the terrorist threat was growing. In May 1978, Mountbatten's distant cousin, Prince Moritz of Hesse Kassel, had been kidnapped and injured in Germany. Moritz reported that his captors had also expressed a strong interest in Mountbatten, adding "we have been going into his case very carefully." As a result, the commissioner of the Met, Sir David McNee, had dispatched one of his most senior officers and a member of MI5 to find out more. It was assumed that kidnappers were connected to the leftist Baader-Meinhof Gang; but when asked about this, they were indignant, insisting that they were entrepreneurs and "were only out to make money by way of ransom." Mountbatten listened to the police advice carefully, and thereafter always went to bed with a loaded shotgun.[12]

As the bitter war against the IRA dragged on, the security advice grew dangerously outdated. A raid on an IRA safe house in Southampton, 10 miles from his Broadlands estate, confirmed that Mountbatten was an IRA target and that there had been a plan to attack him in the early 1970s. The IRA had called it off due to the risk of civilian casualties. In August 1978, the IRA aborted a plot to shoot him aboard his boat only because choppy waters made it impossible for the sniper to take aim. That same summer, someone tried to sabotage the boat by loosening a rubber bung and letting in water. All this pointed to trouble.[13]

Given these serious threats, the police advised Mountbatten against taking his annual Irish vacation in 1979.[14] Maurice Oldfield, until recently the head of MI6, personally advised him not to travel because of an intelligence warning that the IRA planned to target the Royal Family.[15] They had the capabilities: terrorists had recently assassinated the Conservative member of Parliament Airey Neave and had come close to assassinating the head of NATO. "But the Irish are my friends," Mountbatten protested. "Not all of them," came the reply.[16]

The IRA watched him all summer. Its intelligence units reported that Mountbatten's Monday trip around the lobster pots might be the last chance to kill him that season. The only drawback was that the other passengers on the boat could also be killed. The IRA weighed it up and, on balance, ruthlessly decided that the chance to assassinate a royal target—a world-famous imperial figure whom they thought personified British arrogance—was too good to miss. IRA volunteers arrived in Mullaghmore especially for the operation.[17]

A young corporal, who had been trained by the Special Air Service (SAS) and was involved in Mountbatten's protection, was suspicious. He warned that *Shadow V*, moored in a public harbor and easily boarded unseen at night, was a soft target. He also reported that a car with a Belfast number plate kept returning to the quayside; the driver watched the boat through binoculars. The army and police recognized the car as being used for transporting IRA bombs. Remarkably, it had apparently been bugged for months by army intelligence tracking its movements. The warnings came to nothing.[18] The IRA volunteers managed to smuggle a bomb, rigged to a radio-controlled detonator, directly beneath Mountbatten's seat.[19]

The circle of people who knew there was trouble ahead was truly remarkable. The earl of Durham later recounted that, for weeks before it happened, Mountbatten had problems getting any local boatmen to take him out: "They must have heard that something was being plotted against him." He considered Mountbatten "foolhardy" for refusing to take precautions.[20]

The local police prepared to follow the boat from the costal road in case of trouble. They watched as it left the harbor walls and sped up toward the lobster pots. The bomb then exploded. It killed Mountbatten instantly, along with his teenage grandson and a young boatman. Another passenger, Dowager Lady Brabourne, was fatally injured. Mountbatten's body was found floating face downward a few yards away.[21] On the same day, a roadside bomb killed eighteen soldiers at Warrenpoint.

The IRA quickly accepted responsibility. The successful "execution" was designed to "bring emotionally home" the costs of imperialist occupation "to the English ruling class and its working-class slaves."[22]

The queen was having lunch in Balmoral when her assistant private secretary delivered the somber news. This was a terrible blow to the Royal Family. Mountbatten was not only a family member whom she saw regularly but also an important adviser and troubleshooter. For all his faults, he had never been afraid of telling Elizabeth what she did not want to hear, and he had long provided an important link with Whitehall, especially the military and intelligence establishment.[23]

Prince Charles was particularly devastated. He confided in his diary that Mountbatten was "a combination of grandfather, great-uncle, father, brother, and friend," adding, "life will *never* be the same now that he has gone."[24] "I fear," he wrote angrily, "it will take me a very long time to forgive these people."[25]

Princess Margaret was also bitter, referring to the Irish as "pigs" when she visited Chicago shortly afterward. She then traveled to Los Angeles, where local police received intelligence from London of an IRA plot to assassinate her. The US authorities immediately doubled her Secret Service protection, added snipers to her entourage, and upgraded her limousine to one equipped with bulletproof armor. The FBI raided a room where the gunman, known as "the Jackal," was believed to be staying. It was empty.[26] A later visit by Margaret to Washington was canceled on account of security threats. "Serves 'em right" was her typically forthright response.[27]

The assassination of Mountbatten and the attack at Warrenpoint prompted a rethink about personal protection and much else. Thatcher set up a new secret security directorate under Maurice Oldfield. Two days after the attack, she visited County Armagh against the advice of the Northern Ireland Office.[28]

Mountbatten's death brutally highlighted the vulnerability of the Royal Family. Despite this, just six months later, the queen was riding with her cousin, Margaret Rhodes, through heavy mist on the Sandringham estate. She turned and remarked: "I've been informed that the IRA have a new sort of sniper that sees through the mist." They rode on.[29]

For all the famed stoicism of the Royal Family, something had to change. Immediately after the murder of Mountbatten, and still only five years after the attempted kidnapping of Princess Anne, the commissioner of the Metropolitan Police instigated a much-needed review of royal protection. The main difficulty, as ever, came in the management of risk. The members of the Royal Family were in what they liked to call "the happiness business," and to be popular they had to be accessible.[30]

It was a paradox that made protection difficult and placed a premium on intelligence. Timely and accurate intelligence minimized the need for visible protection. In turn, discreet security perpetuated legitimacy and a sense of popularity. This was the theory. In practice, senior civil servants were scathing about the poor quality of protection. Security was discreet, not because of timely and accurate intelligence but because it was practically nonexistent.

They reeled off an embarrassingly long list of failures: "Many of the Royal protection officers are inadequately trained; some of them are not physically fit; and there are doubts about the techniques they use and the effectiveness of their weapons." Royal vehicles "were frequently left unattended and not properly checked" and "some of the Royal residences, including Buckingham Palace, are very vulnerable to intruders." The whole setup was "distinctly amateur."[31] It was grossly inadequate in an era of rising terrorism.

For all the shocked indignation at the Home Office, Scotland Yard handled the Royal Family more diplomatically. David McNee, the Met commissioner, glossed over the Mountbatten and Anne incidents when informing the queen's private secretary, Philip Moore, that "over the past years the system of protection has worked, by and large, reasonably well." By and large.

He then warned: "We are now however in an era where terrorism is carried out nationally and internationally by intelligent and dedicated persons capable of highly effective tactics and sophisticated weapons. Faced with these developments, it is essential that those responsible for the security of Her Majesty and others are better organised, equipped, and trained than their adversaries."[32]

All police officers providing royal protection would now come under one command, headed by a new supremo, and run from a permanently manned headquarters inside Scotland Yard. More efficient communications would also be necessary. Royal safety was the responsibility of more than one government department, including MI5.[33]

Those beleaguered civil servants used to dealing with palace intransigence knew all this would be controversial. "The greatest possible tact," they advised, "was needed in handling the Royal aspect," especially when it came to the "new overlord post." The royal household much preferred the existing decentralized system, in which separate units—led by the queen's protection officer, Michael Trestrail—were assigned to individual family members. Sensitive to their feelings and scared to push too far, McNee was at pains to point out that the new coordinator would complement rather than dismantle the traditional system.[34]

Another key change created backup units to assist the individual protection officers. Each would include a specially equipped vehicle and nine specially trained sergeants. Something similar was proposed after the attempted kidnapping of Princess Anne, but it had amounted to little. Even now, royal intransigence blunted the idea: individual royal preferences would still decide how active each unit would be.[35]

The government publicly initiated a program to "install security devices" at royal residences. In total, ministers spent about £2 million on improving royal security in the two years after Mountbatten's death.[36] This resulted in little real change.

Athough the monarchy and government bickered over policing levels, the IRA did not let up. In the spring of 1981, the security services managed to intercept and defuse a letter bomb addressed to Prince Charles.[37] At about the same time, Elizabeth and Philip, accompanied by King Olav of Norway, visited the Shetland Islands for the opening of a new BP oil terminal, the largest in Europe. The police had undertaken little advance preparation. Dense fog had prevented many officers from leaving the mainland in time to complete security checks and "sterilize" the area.

As the national anthems played, a bomb exploded in a nearby power station just 500 yards from the queen. It was a damp squib: few people even noticed; no injuries were inflicted; and the queen was decidedly unruffled, not least because she had no idea that a bomb had even exploded until later.[38]

The IRA were disappointed by the anticlimax. They had hoped to disrupt the ceremony at the very least, but still boasted afterward that they had successfully breached the queen's security. They added that the queen would have been assassinated if the bomb had been closer.[39] This was a stretch, but the IRA did have a point.

It was yet another royal security failure, although this time MI5 deflected the blame onto BP. An intelligence officer from MI5's C Branch, which oversaw security at key economic sites, had visited the remote location several times in the run-up to the queen's visit. He made specific recommendations about protecting the facilities, but BP had balked at the seven-figure cost. Discussions were still ongoing when the IRA struck in May.[40]

There was a further narrow squeak the next month. A fame-hungry teenager fired six blanks at Elizabeth during the annual Trooping the Colour ceremony. Marcus Sarjeant stepped out of the crowd and, unable to get hold of a real gun, shot a starting pistol at close range as the queen rode side saddle from Buckingham Palace to Horse Guards Parade. It was nothing more than a fantasy assassination, but for a moment it appeared very real.

For a split second, the queen had stared down the barrel of Sarjeant's gun. The Household Cavalry immediately turned toward her, causing her horse to rear up. Elizabeth famously controlled the startled horse calmly and expertly, continuing on to Horse Guards Parade. Sarjeant, a loner obsessed with the attempted assassinations of Ronald Reagan and Pope John Paul II, was taken to Canon Row Police Station, the established repository for many such assailants down the years, and was charged. Ian Blair, the young detective inspector on the case, expected to have about five weeks to take statements and prepare the necessary paperwork before the case was committed to the Crown Court. But then, he recalls, something odd happened:

> A week after the events, an Assistant Commissioner came unannounced into my office, a much more senior figure than anyone I had ever met or thought about meeting. He told me, not as a suggestion but as an unassailable fact, that he had just come from a meeting with the Private Secretary to the Queen, who he had assured that the committal would take place by the end of the coming week. With that and without seeking any response, he walked out.[41]

Sarjeant was indeed committed for trial within days, and was sentenced to jail under the Treason Act dating back to 1842 and similar attacks on Queen

Victoria.[42] He became the first person since 1966 to be prosecuted under this act, and he spent five years in Grendon Psychiatric Prison in Buckinghamshire.

Later the same year, while touring New Zealand, Elizabeth came closer to being assassinated. Again, it was not the IRA but, as Princess Anne had predicted, another disturbed lone gunman. As the queen stepped out of her Rolls-Royce, Christopher Lewis, another teenage would-be assassin, fired a rifle toward her from a deserted toilet cubicle five storys above. The bullet missed.

The toilet cubicle had not been Lewis's first choice of location. A police search had forced him to delay his plans a few days earlier. His original choice of shooting position was far better—and he would likely have hit the queen.

Local authorities, embarrassed by the failure of royal protection, played down the incident. They told the British press that the loud bang was caused by a traffic sign falling over, then fumbling with the cover-up, changed their story to firecrackers. Rather than trying Lewis for treason or attempted assassination, prosecutors downgraded the charges to discharging a firearm in a public place on the tenuous grounds that he had not been able to find a suitable vantage point from which to kill the queen. Although local intelligence discreetly investigated the assassination attempt, the authorities never revealed Lewis's true intent, perhaps fearing that the queen would not return to the country.[43]

Once more, Elizabeth was unruffled. This was more through ignorance than stoicism. She had no idea what was going on, and it remains unclear when—or even whether—she was later told. The British security authorities did not learn that anything had happened at all until Lewis was jailed.[44]

Despite these growing incidents, the royal family remained fearless in the face of danger. In 1982, Princess Anne decided to visit Lebanon, one of the world's most dangerous locations. Initially scheduled to embark on a tour of Africa for the Save the Children charity, she suddenly announced that she wanted to finish up in Beirut. This was in the middle of the Lebanese civil war, and Oliver Miles, the diplomat superintending the Middle East and North Africa, recalls understandably that there was a lot of "sucking of teeth in the Foreign Office."

They asked: "Was it sensible for her to go in the middle of a civil war?" But they were also impressed by her bravado, so nobody wanted to make the decision. The awkward question weaved its way up through the Whitehall hierarchy and eventually reached the prime minister. Risk-averse mandarins were confident that "if we put a piece up to Mrs Thatcher, she will blow it out of the water," and that would be the end of the matter. Hostages were already big business in Beirut, and Thatcher "had very strong views about the Royal Family not getting involved in anything which was too risky, so we thought we knew her mind."[45]

The queen stepped in. The diplomats had forgotten that it would come up during one of the Tuesday meetings between Thatcher and the queen. Thatcher emerged from the palace with a change of heart: she saw no reason why Anne should not travel to Beirut, provided the security assessments pointed in the right direction. Diplomats confessed they would have loved to have been "a fly on the wall" during that particular exchange between monarch and prime minister.

Unsurprisingly, David Roberts, the ambassador in Beirut, was especially keen for the princess to visit. He sent back a breezy security assessment saying that everything was fine. He had personally walked down the city's main thoroughfare, Rue Hamra, "where Her Royal Highness will go," and he was glad to report that the security situation was better than it had been for months: "There is scarcely any heavy shelling to be heard and machine guns can hardly be seen, except in the side streets." Eventually, a Special Branch reconnaissance team agreed. The visit went ahead, and Roberts did walk down Rue Hamra with Princess Anne, accompanied by machine guns to the left and right. Later, he gleefully reported that his French diplomatic colleague was green with envy.[46]

In the space of eighteen months, the queen had faced assassination in her own backyard, the outermost reaches of the UK, and the other side of the world. Yet remarkably, very little had changed since Mountbatten's death.

The Royal Family remained deeply resistant to improvements. For the queen, protection officers were not simply responsible for discreetly keeping her safe but also for providing a screen between her family and the more militant arms of VIP protection whom she called the "Thugs." She had seen presidential personal protection up close on five continents and was repulsed by it. Rivalry between security authorities and protection officers also hindered progress, with the former deriding the latter as "protocol officers."[47] Two more security breaches the next summer, both involving the queen, jolted the ancient wheels of royal bureaucracy into action.

The first was the most dramatic, an almost unbelievable lapse. At about 6:45 in the morning of July 9, 1982, Michael Fagan, a scruffy unemployed laborer, climbed barefoot over the railing near the Ambassadors' Courtyard of Buckingham Palace and entered the ground floor through an unlocked window. The doors were locked.

Undeterred, he climbed back out the window and shimmied up a drainpipe onto a flat roof before entering the main palace building through another unlocked window. He walked, unchallenged, through palace hallways for about 15 minutes, managing to find his way toward the queen's private apartments.

He entered an anteroom and smashed a glass ashtray, later claiming he wanted to slash his wrists in front of the queen. With a shard of glass in his hand, he entered Elizabeth's bedroom at about 7:15 a.m. and opened the curtains close to her bed. She quickly pressed the alarm.

Nothing happened. The footman was outside walking the dogs; the maid was cleaning in another room; and the policeman had clocked off over an hour earlier when the day staff arrived. She phoned for the police, but they were slow to arrive. The queen found herself alone with an unknown intruder.

"I got out of bed," she later told a courtier, "put on my dressing gown and slippers, drew myself up to my full regal height, pointed to the door, and said 'Get Out!' and he didn't."

Elizabeth managed to usher the intruder into a nearby pantry on the pretext of offering him a cigarette, as he talked about his personal troubles. She, and her footman who had now returned, managed to keep him there until help belatedly arrived. According to the queen, "he just talked the usual sort of bilge that people talk to me on a walkabout, I can handle that." She was angry, though, excoriating the police after Fagan had been led away.[48] Famously, when the palace chambermaid first saw Fagan in the queen's apartments, she uttered the words, "Bloody hell ma'am, what's he doing here?"[49]

The news of the Fagan break-in bounced around the world. In Washington, President Reagan told the British ambassador that he was greatly impressed by the queen's "sang-froid," but could not help adding that it had produced a "snide" reaction from the US security authorities. Reagan had visited the queen only a month before, and British security officials had been "dismissive" of the elaborate security precautions that their American counterparts had wanted to take against the possibility of an assassination attempt. "Such things don't happen here" had been their attitude. Reagan knew the score, having survived a serious assassination attempt only the previous year.[50]

Days later, in an unconnected incident, the queen's long-standing and trusted police officer, Michael Trestrail, was forced to resign after a blackmail attempt. After the Fagan story broke, a man got in touch with the *Sun* hoping to make money with a classic tabloid sex-and-royals story. He claimed to be a male prostitute employed over a period of years by Trestrail.

Editors refused to publish the story but informed the palace, sparking an immediate police investigation. The same prostitute had earlier tried to blackmail Trestrail for £2,000, claiming to have had a compromising photograph of the two of them together. Trestrail, knowing his career would be over, failed to report it. A subsequent inquiry found that "in behaving as he did, Trestrail clearly laid himself open to blackmail." There was "no actual breach of security," but he had to resign because "the risks he took and the indiscretions he committed, no matter how compulsive the urge which drove him to act as he did, must be seen as raising serious doubt as to the soundness of his judgement."[51]

Trestrail's relationship with the male prostitute raised questions about the reliability of those close to the queen. No formal method of selecting royalty protection officers had existed at all before 1969.[52] Protection officers did not have to undertake positive vetting until early 1982 with the acknowledgment that some, like Trestrail, needed access to secret intelligence.[53] He duly received clearance in April, successfully hiding his secret double life in the process.[54]

In a kneejerk reaction after the scandal, Sir David McNee, the Met commissioner, quickly insisted that all forty-three officers involved in royal protection should be subject to positive vetting clearance, even though this had achieved little in the case of Trestrail.[55] As of late 1982, just eight members of the royal household, likely including the queen's private secretaries, had clearance.[56]

Sadly, Trestrail resigned, having served the Royal Family for almost two decades. McNee thought that "his record of service had been outstanding," displaying an eye-catching personality and "an impeccable demeanour." All those who served with him had "extremely high regard for him" and thought it was a tragic end to a distinguished career in public service. Lord Bridge of Harwich, who was appointed to report on the affair, noted: "I share those sentiments."[57]

Fagan's cavalier trespassing was by far the bigger incident of the two. "It was a disgraceful sequence of events," observed McNee, that included a mixture of technical failures and lazy policing. The media clamor for "heads to roll" made McNee feel vulnerable, rightly concluding that it was "the higher the person whose head rolled the better." It looked as if either his head or that of the home secretary, William Whitelaw, was on the chopping block.[58]

On July 13, McNee was sitting in his office at Scotland Yard. He received an unannounced visit from Sir Brian Cubbon, the permanent secretary at the Home Office, "never a man readily at ease." Focusing on Fagan, he suggested "out of the blue" that it should be McNee who resigned. McNee refused and pointed out that the Home Office and the stubborn royal household had resisted his efforts at security reform, dragging their feet. Cubbon then essentially admitted that the visit was his own private "mission" to protect his boss, Whitelaw, and that he had kept it from the home secretary.[59]

In the end, William Whitelaw brassed it out. He defended the system by pinning the blame on "human error rather than any defect in the arrangements themselves." He insisted that the main problem was "a failure by the police to respond efficiently and urgently," and he tried to reassure colleagues that those responsible had either resigned, been transferred to other duties, or faced disciplinary action.[60] Secretly, the Home Office began a review of the law of trespassing, which they noted was in response to "public pressure" to give more protection to the Royal Family after "the Michael Fagan incident."[61]

Others were unconvinced. Prince Philip was predictably volatile and wanted to hand all royal protection duties over to the army.[62] Opposition politicians accused the government of squandering the £2 million pledged in the aftermath of Mountbatten's murder. Whitelaw maintained that he had doubled the number of uniformed police at the palace and installed new devices at various residences—on top of the money spent since 1979.[63] He also instigated a separate review of the risk to the Royal Family posed by psychiatric patients. The results remain classified.[64]

After the dust had settled, and security had been tightened up, a team from the SAS made five attempts to enter Buckingham Palace covertly. This had been arranged by the greatest government admirer of the SAS, Margaret Thatcher herself. Apparently, each of the five attempts succeeded, and in the final raid they managed to lift a small silver "trophy." Efforts to return the trophy failed, since the palace "denied all knowledge."[65]

The shock of these various intrusions, in the most private part of the palace, necessitated deeper change. Royal reticence could no longer halt reform. Whitelaw informed the cabinet that "the division of responsibility for the security of the Royal Family, which had existed for many years with the approval of the Palace authorities, would have to be ended." A new royalty protection department led by a senior police officer, Deputy Assistant Commissioner Colin Smith, would take its place. Smith would oversee the security arrangements for all members of the Royal Family. Whitelaw also created a new permanent group, which reported to him personally, to examine the effectiveness of security arrangements. Pointedly, he told Parliament that the queen's staff had now "promised their full co-operation."[66] This had not always been the case.

The IRA soon struck again. In the same month as the Fagan break-in and the Trestrail resignation, terrorists detonated a nail bomb in Hyde Park. It targeted the Household Cavalry Blues and Royals, the queen's official bodyguard regiment. Four soldiers and seven horses died. Two hours later, another bomb exploded, this time targeting soldiers in Regent's Park. Six died instantly and another was fatally wounded. That night the queen lamented over and over again: "The horses, the poor horses."[67] She described it as "the most ghastly day of my life."[68]

A year later, the IRA tried to assassinate Prince Charles and Princess Diana during a royal gala to raise money for the Prince's Trust charity. Duran Duran and Dire Straits were headlining the event at the Dominion Theatre in central London. Terrorist leaders, desperate for revenge after the death of ten hunger strikers in 1981, instructed Sean O'Callaghan to plant a bomb close to the royal box. Fortunately for Charles and Diana, O'Callaghan was an informant working for the Irish police.

Echoing the plots against Queen Victoria, the Irish police were unsure about how far to let the planning develop before stepping in to make arrests. Going in too early would deprive them of evidence; going in too late would risk royal lives. To make matters worse, the Irish police feared losing control of the plot and so refused to tell their British colleagues. They hoped to make the arrests before O'Callaghan set foot in England by raiding an IRA meeting in Dublin, finding incriminating evidence, and convicting everyone present of IRA membership.

Unfortunately, the police bungled the arrests by making so much noise outside the door that the targets had ample time to burn incriminating documents. Without sufficient evidence, all but one received bail. Remarkably, O'Callaghan still had the opportunity to travel to England to assassinate Charles and Diana.

He reached London with a false passport, fake driving license, and £2,000 in cash. He even got as far as the flimsy royal box inside the old theater. The plan was to plant a bomb in the men's restroom directly behind the box, preferably behind the wall tiles, as would happen in the successful Brighton bombing of the Conservative Party conference the next year. O'Callaghan knew that such a bomb would certainly kill the prince and princess—and many others too. He needed to find a way out without making the IRA suspicious. The explosives were due to arrive in Highgate, north London, in five days.

The Irish police had little choice but to brief Scotland Yard, which, in turn, leaked a story to the press that an IRA assassination team, headed by a man again nicknamed "the Jackal," had arrived in England. The revelation prevented O'Callaghan from going ahead and allowed him to quietly leave England with his cover still intact.[69] Duran Duran only found out about the plot years later. Its drummer, Roger Taylor, described being told as the "scariest moment" of his life.[70]

In the 1970s, many of the police who served as royal protection officers were still unarmed. Their American opposite numbers, the US Secret Service, found this laughable. But by the 1980s this had changed, and the police officers who provided royal protection were required to make their way to the SAS headquarters at Hereford for specialist training in firearms. Triggered by the Fagan incident, their numbers markedly increased, and a new police station was built inside the grounds of Buckingham Palace behind the queen's gallery at a substantial cost. More like a military bunker, it was artfully hidden from public view and was screened by a mound of earth and a row of trees. This not only had state-of-the-art communications but also a direct line to SAS headquarters, including a series of code words to indicate the seriousness of any incident when they called for help.[71]

For decades, the SAS has trained for an incident that might involve a royal kidnapping or, worse, a hostage situation. After the Fagan incident, it undertook a target mapping of the whole network of royal palaces. Each and every room in every palace was photographed from multiple directions, and the pictures were curated carefully at SAS headquarters. This was to ensure that if the SAS ever needed to storm Sandringham, or abseil down the front of Buckingham Palace, the troopers would know the precise layout of each room and exact position of each chair or sofa.[72]

The royals also needed direct reassurance. The queen visited the SAS headquarters at Hereford and viewed the infamous "Killing House" herself. Most members of the Royal Family would eventually follow suit to watch demonstrations of rescue operations. Security authorities hoped to give them the confidence that professional help would quickly be at hand if they were ever kidnapped.[73]

The queen watched and waited. All of a sudden, an explosion rang out across the room and an assault team burst inside, springing, diving, and rolling across the floor, firing bullets inches from her nose. She was apparently "absolutely unperturbed." A second demonstration followed in pitch black, where the hostage—and the queen—could see nothing but the flashes of gunfire. Using night vision goggles, SAS officers watched her look nervously toward the exits, but "her stiff upper lip never quivered."

The final demonstration involved a helicopter rescue. This time the hostage wore a Margaret Thatcher mask. One soldier recalls: "As we rose into the sky, dangling beneath the heli with our imitation Maggie, I thought I detected a slight change in the queen's expression. For a moment I could have sworn that there was a twinkle in her eye."[74] Perhaps Thatcher's apathy towards the Commonwealth still rankled.[75]

With the terror threat increasing in the early 1980s, there was an endless stream of royal visitors to the Killing House. In late 1982, Prince Charles and Princess Diana made their way to Hereford for a full demonstration. Their guide was a salty senior noncommissioned officer, Rusty Firmin, who had taken part in the Iranian Embassy siege in 1980. Since then, he had been honing his skills by spending "endless hours" on the close quarter battle target ranges. Their VIP visitors were not just there to view the capability; they were also present as "prime kidnapping targets," so the SAS wanted to familiarize them with exactly what would happen if they needed to be rescued. In other words, this was in part SAS training for the royals.[76]

The operation that the SAS chose to show Charles and Diana was an assault on a building containing hostages. They used three Range Rovers that carried ladders. Firmin explained that they would quickly exit the vehicles; scale the ladders; and throw special stun grenades, charges that had loud bangs and flashes but no harmful blast—before freeing the hostages and killing the terrorists.

Diana, delighted and entering into the spirit of things, volunteered to drive one of the Range Rovers herself. The exercise started, and Diana roared up to the building, accompanied by other vehicles. Firmin recalls: "Unfortunately, Princess Di hadn't fully closed her driver's side window, and when the flash-bangs started to go off, one of the little pellets—which we called screamers—came back through the window and stuck in her hair. Now these things are hot and as I watched, I could see her hair was catching fire."[77]

Firmin quickly brushed it away and started patting the princess's hair to stop it burning. "Prince Charles and his entourage were laughing their heads off," not the most sympathetic response. Nevertheless, the SAS was now firmly on the royal tourist trail, and Princess Anne followed her brother the next year.[78]

Responsibilities of the new royalty protection group extended beyond the queen's domestic trips. Overseas travel formed a trickier proposition, given the propensity for even more turf wars. The group had to liaise with local police, British embassies, and British intelligence. Concerned about the potential for fatal confusion, the Foreign Office reminded the palace to keep diplomats informed of all royal visits overseas, including private ones, so that posts abroad and the intelligence agencies could consider proper security measures.[79]

In March 1984, the queen was due to pay a state visit to Jordan. Thatcher asked Peter de la Billière, until recently the director of the SAS, to fly to Amman, the capital, and conduct a personal risk assessment.[80]

Terrorist activity in the Middle East was high. There had been 6 attacks in Amman alone during the previous year, and close to 500 in the wider region.[81] On Wednesday, March 21, five days before the queen was due to arrive, de la Billière delivered his verdict to Thatcher; Philip Moore, the queen's private secretary; and Colin Smith, the new royal protection supremo. The Jordanians would be able to protect the queen despite the high level of terrorism. With the queen keen to go, the meeting lasted only an hour.[82] Thatcher promptly advised her to travel as planned and thanked King Hussein for accommodating the "rather unusual request" of sending a former director of the SAS.[83]

Days later, on the Saturday, a small bomb exploded in an Amman hotel being used by journalists ahead of the trip. Three people suffered minor wounds. Jordanian officials blamed the Black June terrorist organization for trying to force the cancellation of the trip. According to the CIA, Black June targeted the queen's visit in retaliation for British imprisonment of its members responsible for attempting to murder the Israeli ambassador in London in 1982.

The CIA predicted that "further attacks are likely during the Queen's visit in an attempt to embarrass the Jordanians."[84] British intelligence probably concurred.

Senior figures debated the issue all Saturday at Chequers. The assembled team included Michael Heseltine, the secretary for defense; Richard Luce, minister of state; Robert Armstrong, the cabinet secretary; Philip Moore, the queen's private secretary; Tony Duff, the chairman of the Joint Intelligence Committee; and John Leahy, one of the most senior officials in the Foreign Office. Thatcher explained that she would take it upon herself to make the final decision, but first she wanted to hear what each one of them had to say. The cabinet ministers were worried, and they said that the government would never be forgiven if anything happened to the queen. Thatcher cut them off and said that if anything happened, "she would resign within the hour." Philip Moore quietly explained that the queen wanted to go, so if she was to be dissuaded, the argument "would have to be a very strong one." Thatcher heard this but then spoke to King Hussein on the telephone before deciding the visit should go ahead.[85]

The debate then dragged on as more important intelligence came in. Thatcher summoned de la Billière to Downing Street for an emergency meeting of the inner cabinet. Philip Moore returned from the palace. Discussions started at 6 p.m. and dragged on over dinner until 10:15 that night.[86]

It was a risky trip given the high terrorist threat, but it was important in terms of arms sales, both to Jordan itself and as a discreet funnel of arms to Iraq. Thatcher knew as early as 1981 that military equipment supplied to Jordan quietly found its way there, in contravention of the ban on selling lethal equipment to either side in its conflict with Iran. As a moderate Arab leader, King Hussein was also important in the Middle East peace process.[87] It was important to keep him on their side. After a lengthy debate, Thatcher agreed the benefits outweighed the risks; the queen could still go.[88]

Queen Elizabeth arrived amid incredibly tight security. Sharpshooters kept watch from the rooftops, police were stationed every few hundred yards, and a ring of soldiers hugged the runway. Brand-new antimissile devices were clearly visible under the wings of her airplane.[89] On the same day she arrived, the Jordanian authorities discovered and defused three bombs, two of which were directed against British targets.[90]

The visit passed off peacefully, with the queen declaring it a "lifelong ambition" to visit Jordan. She praised King Hussein for having made Jordan a "beacon of stability" in the region.[91] Hussein interpreted the visit as "a striking gesture of confidence in Jordan."[92] Once the queen had safely returned, Thatcher wrote to the head of GCHQ, Peter Marychurch, to thank the staff for their success in intercepting related terrorist communications and monitoring the threat.[93]

In October, just five months after the queen's trip, Michael Heseltine visited King Hussein to clinch a deal selling defense equipment worth £300 million to Jordan. A month later, defense intelligence warned that Hussein was diverting arms to Iraq.[94]

Elizabeth's visit was controversial for another reason. The press accused her of wading into the Arab–Israeli conflict by disapproving of the Israeli occupation of the West Bank. She had told her hosts that no country had been more affected than them by "the tragedy which has befallen the Palestinian people"; described a map showing Israeli activity on the West Bank, which was captured from Jordan in 1967, as "depressing"; and dubbed Israeli planes flying over occupied territory "frightening."[95]

It was a theme President Reagan picked up during a visit to the UK a few weeks later. The Middle East, and Jordanian entry into talks with Israel, was a designated talking point for his meeting with the queen.[96] A few years earlier, US diplomats had hoped that Elizabeth, whom they thought enjoyed "high prestige in much of the Arab world and in Israel," would personally sponsor activities that might create an environment for useful contact between the Arabs and Israelis.[97] What Reagan and the queen spoke about remains unknown, but both her own government and that of the US clearly appreciated her regal connections to King Hussein.

Sadly, there was a cost to the queen's visit. Unable to attack Elizabeth because of the incredibly tight security, terrorists decided to strike in Greece. On the third day of the queen's visit to Jordan, an unidentified Arab gunman murdered British diplomat Ken Whitty, a first secretary at the Athens embassy, in his car in downtown Athens and also killed a Greek woman riding with him. The gunman flagged down Whitty's car as it came to an intersection two blocks from the embassy and cruelly shot him three times in the head when he rolled down his window to speak.[98] The British ambassador in Athens recalls: "It was a political murder. It was done because the Queen was in Jordan at the time and they didn't like that. . . . They wanted a British victim."[99] The perpetrators were the Abu Nidal group, one of the most dangerous terrorist organizations that had been especially active in Jordan.[100]

Queen Elizabeth ruled by common consent and refused to hide behind armed guards. Improvements to her protection therefore moved at a glacial pace. It was not until 1986 that Thatcher finally announced palace acceptance of the various security changes. An additional £1 million would be spent on electronic surveillance at royal homes. The queen was still not happy and pushed back against a proposal to erect barriers around Buckingham Palace, including the

Queen Victoria memorial, which security authorities warned could be used as an excellent sniper position. She refused to be hidden from the public.[101] Elizabeth, like Queen Victoria before her, maintained a rather fatalistic attitude toward assassination. Both were unwilling to limit their interactions with the public.[102] When credible intelligence warned of an IRA mortar attack on Windsor Castle in the early 1990s, she refused to leave.[103]

For a long time, the Royal Family formed an impressively stubborn counterforce against trends toward more firepower and tougher security. Queen Victoria had no intention of hiding like a fugitive inside Buckingham Palace; neither did Queen Elizabeth.[104]

Elizabeth could not hold back the tide forever. Just a single personal security officer protected her at her first Trooping the Colour ceremony in 1952. By 1986, about 3,500 policemen were on duty, including armed detectives undercover in the crowds.[105]

Once the tide finally broke, it led to a flood of enhanced security. After the terrorist attacks on the United States on September 11, 2001, MI5 insisted on installing an extensive new alarm and camera system both outside and inside Buckingham Palace and strengthening the palace's perimeter. Three years later, the new security arrangements allowed police to quickly assess the threat when protesters climbed on top of the palace's roof. The commissioner of the Met Police, John Stevens, confirmed that the intruder would have been shot before entering the building if assessed as a threat.[106] This was a stark contrast to the Fagan intrusion.

Intelligence kept the queen and her family safe. But it was more than that. The security of the monarch was political. The queen needed to appear visible and accessible for the institution to survive. She was fond of saying, "I have to be seen to be believed."[107] Intelligence allowed her to be seen safely. It kept the legend of the monarchy alive, perpetuating an illusion of power, popularity, and divine protection.

17

The Diana Conspiracy

I think he was bumped off.
—Princess Diana, 1987

"I do things differently," Princess Diana once commented, "because I don't go by a rule book; . . . albeit that's got me into trouble." "Some don't like that," she added defiantly, "but that's the way I am."[1]

This was perhaps her most profound self-reflection. Her independent spirit, which grew over the years, was one of her most attractive qualities, bringing originality and freshness to everything she did. But it also made her marriage to Prince Charles, her protocol-ridden life within the Royal Family, and above all her own royal duties onerous. She found the intersection of the public and private especially oppressive; and she responded by disregarding the impediment of ever-present security.

Diana was the youngest daughter of John Spencer, an earl who had once been equerry to the young Queen Elizabeth, and Frances Shand Kydd, herself born on the royal estate in Sandringham. In 1967, when Diana was only seven years old, her parents divorced, and her relationship with her new stepmother was turbulent. After attending a number of fee-paying schools, and then a finishing school in Switzerland, she moved to London, where she lived with friends and worked in a kindergarten. Happily, she became what was then called a "Sloane Ranger"—indeed, to some extent, she epitomized the phenomenon and its fashions, yet at the same time she enjoyed a degree of invisibility.[2]

In 1981, she shot into the public eye. Aged twenty-one, she became engaged to Prince Charles, the heir to the throne, after a brief and secretive courtship. Their wedding in July of the same year was a fairy-tale event. The public lapped it up, bringing the monarchy an extraordinary new level of popularity, approval, and international press interest. Diana, now princess of Wales, seemed to have achieved the impossible, providing the Royal Family with not only freshness and modernity but also a sense of old-style romance and magic. For those obsessed with dynasties, she followed this with further success, quickly producing two sons, Prince William in 1982 and Prince Harry in 1984. Much had happened in just a few short years.

However, the behavior of the press was already bad and deteriorating. Back in the 1970s, the media had mostly remained quite respectful of the Royal Family. Indeed, it was perhaps one of the last areas of journalistic self-restraint. But that did not mean the press were happy. For decades, the royal press office had been under the command of the notorious Commander Richard Colville, who thought the best place for energetic journalists was "a dungeon in the tower."[3]

By the 1980s, even with the more accommodating Michael Shea as the palace press secretary, reporters and a new breed of paparazzi were increasingly prepared to break the rules. And there was now an additional factor giving this activity more purpose and resource—the rise of Rupert Murdoch. An Australian and a republican who loathed the Royal Family, he had a personal interest in bad behavior toward the royals. Almost from the moment of Diana's wedding to Charles, he unleashed the hounds. Press attention was not the same as being spied on by government security agencies, but the techniques were increasingly similar, and sometimes these worlds merged.

Charles and Diana are often perceived as having a certain honeymoon period, but by early 1984 things had already fallen apart. In April, Roy Strong, a discerning keeper of national art collections and an even more diligent diary keeper, noted with some delight that Princess Michael of Kent had come to an event at the V&A Museum and was "wildly indiscreet." She explained that the marriage was a catastrophe, droves of the household were leaving, and Charles "had bought Highgrove to be near his former girlfriends." Princess Michael added that the Royal Family often regarded her as their highest risk factor, but she insisted that "the time bomb is Diana."[4]

Sadly, Diana's marriage to Charles was doomed because the couple was fundamentally incompatible: Diana found the reflective and serious Charles stuffy and uncool; Charles found Diana superficial, mercurial, moody, and uncommitted to the life of monarchy, which involves countless hours of dutiful drudgery. Both had several extramarital affairs. Charles maintained a lingering attachment to an old flame, Camilla Parker Bowles. Diana later had a number of affairs, including a long liaison with the army officer James Hewitt, who served in the same regiment as Camilla's husband. The British prime minister, John Major, announced Diana and Charles's separation in 1992.

As the couple's relations became more publicly acrimonious, Diana required protection from the press. She had long found royal security shocking and difficult to deal with. On the night of her wedding, the Special Branch officer guarding her warned ominously: "I just want you to know that this is your last night of freedom ever in the rest of life, so make the most of it."[5]

Tired of being muzzled by the palace's distinctly uncooperative approach, a new brand of paparazzi was now prepared to break the rules. The members of press who followed Diana were known as the "royal rat-pack" and were a self-confessed nasty bunch. As Ken Wharfe, Diana's loyal and long-serving protection officer, has observed, they were organized, well-funded, and increasingly equipped with electronic scanners and other devices that would not have disgraced the average spy. A motley crew, often sunburnt from many hours on stakeouts, their ample bellies festooned with binoculars, they were an elite force of sorts. Wharfe recalls that Prince Charles once vehemently told veteran *Sun* reporter Harry Arnold that they were all "scum." Arnold replied, politely and respectfully: "We may be scum, sir, but we are la crème de la scum."[6]

In terms of tradecraft and surveillance expertise, this was actually a rather astute observation. At this time, MI6 boasted several crack units that provided special skills on covert operations. One was the so-called increment, a force of Special Air Service (SAS) and Special Boat Service veterans who assisted with paramilitary activities and provided protection when operating in dangerous areas like Eritrea. The other was UKN, an elite group of pilots, safe-crackers, scientists, and other specialists who could be called on at a moment's notice to perform exotic tasks. UKN boasted the world's top long-range photographer, and, predictably perhaps, his day job was working as a royal paparazzo.[7]

Diana took more and more risks to evade them. Of course, the queen and other members of her family also took startling security risks, indeed perhaps were even literally in the line of fire, in the course of their duties. But this was done in a calculated way, and with great consultation and planning, working together with security teams behind the scenes. Perhaps the only person who was as cavalier with their security as Diana was Mountbatten, and that also did not end well.

After her separation, Diana, still the princess of Wales, remained a royal and continued to live in an apartment on the north side of Kensington Palace. She still wore jewelry that she had received during her marriage and could still use the air transportation of the British Royal Family and government. But in late 1993, very much against advice, she dropped most of her police protection, hoping for more privacy.[8] Hitherto, the Met's specialist SO14 unit had provided protection around the clock. Now, she was given protection only when on an official visit or on a trip where her sons accompanied her.[9]

There were also changes in Diana's private life. For over a year, between early 1996 and June 1997, she dated the British-Pakistani heart surgeon Hasnat Khan, often described as "the love of her life" by her confidants. In the summer of 1996, she visited Lahore, where, in secret, she met his family. Khan was intensely private, and their relationship was conducted in great secrecy, with Diana lying to members of the press who questioned her about it. They broke up the following summer, partly because Khan found the press intrusion impossible to deal with—but also because Diana's family disapproved of a relationship with a Muslim man. Diana stopped talking to her mother for a while as a result.[10]

On the rebound, in July 1997, Diana began a relationship with Dodi Fayed, son of the Egyptian tycoon and flamboyant owner of Harrods, Mohamed Al-Fayed. That summer, security and intrusion again became important forces in her life. She had considered taking her sons on a holiday to the Hamptons on Long Island, New York, but security officials advised against it. After deciding against a trip to Thailand as too risky, she accepted Fayed's invitation to join his family in the Mediterranean, where his compound, yacht, and large security detail would keep her safe from prying eyes.

On August 31, two months after beginning their liaison, they died together in Paris. The couple had decided, at short notice, to make the trip to France. Previously, Diana had spent some time on vacation with her close friend Rosa Monckton.[11] Then, on August 30, she and Dodi flew from Sardinia, arriving at Villa Windsor, Edward VIII's old house in the Bois de Boulogne now rented by Al-Fayed. At 4:30 in the afternoon, Diana, Dodi and their security guard, Trevor Rees-Jones, an ex-soldier who was employed by Al-Fayed's team, were driven to the Ritz Hotel. They tried to go out for dinner but eventually retreated to their suite because of the attentions of the paparazzi—the French press being especially notorious and persistent. Just after midnight, they decided to move again, this time to Dodi's own apartment not far away in Rue Arsène Houssaye, close to the Arc de Triomphe.[12] Pursued once more by merciless paparazzi, their car collided with a pillar in the Pont de l'Alma tunnel while traveling at speeds of up to a hundred miles an hour. Only Rees-Jones survived.

This shattering event, which was over in seconds, triggered three painstaking inquiries or inquests that lasted for over a decade. In September 1997, the French appointed an examining magistrate, Judge Hervé Stéphan, to look into the case. Taking two years, he eventually found that there was insufficient evidence against the paparazzi, who were being investigated for involuntary manslaughter, or indeed against anyone else. He declared that Diana's death was a simple accident. But not everyone agreed. Mohamed Al-Fayed in particular loudly asserted foul play by the British government.

For this reason, in January 2004, John Stevens, previously commissioner of the Metropolitan Police, began a more thorough investigation known as Operation Paget, drawing on many of the leads opened by the French. Stevens was perhaps Britain's most experienced and independent senior police investigator, so he was the ideal person to conduct such an inquiry. His conclusions were more sophisticated, asserting that a combination of factors caused the fatal accident, including the condition of her driver, his speeding, the pursuit by the paparazzi, and the fact that the passengers were not wearing seatbelts.

Although explicitly ruling out any conspiracy theories, accusations of the hidden hand continued to swirl. Therefore, in an unprecedented decision, a third major inquiry was ordered under Justice Scott Baker, which reached broadly the same conclusion. But in the course of all this digging, the inquiries uncovered many fascinating facts about the interaction of spies, security, and royals.

More than a third of British people believe that Diana's death was "not an accident"—in other words, it was an assassination plot. Despite the exhaustive inquiries that took evidence from hundreds of people, including the then chiefs of MI6 and GCHQ, many still point the finger at "dark forces": a conspiracy between the Royal Family, supposedly spearheaded by Prince Philip, and his friends in British intelligence.[13]

The primary reason behind this is simple human psychology. Unexpected and catastrophic events cause panic in the public mind. They challenge people's desire for clear, rational, and ordered explanations. As Diana's favored biographer, Andrew Morton, neatly put it, people need big explanations for big events.[14] The messy and sporadic reality of a globalized world is disquieting and feeds these tendencies.

Moreover, the exhaustive inquiries, designed to reduce public anxiety, inevitably turned up a bewildering number of puzzling, idiosyncratic, and even suspicious-looking "facts." These mostly occurred because governments are unwieldy bureaucracies and make mistakes. As any police officer will confirm, eyewitnesses rarely agree on a single account of any event, and so there are bound to be curious discrepancies in the narrative. But this seeming lack of congruity only feeds the public's appetite for a "hidden hand" explanation. Fundamentally, human beings often prefer a dark conspiratorial account that offers an image of strong central control to the option of accepting that history is often the result of coincidences, mistakes, and accidents. In the world of conspiracy, at least someone, however malevolent, is holding the metaphorical steering wheel.

Yet, at a higher level, the secret state does have something to answer for. Governments—and even the Royal Family—have engaged in real plots in the past. Given that MI6 and other secret units almost certainly participated in the assassination of Rasputin; considered the assassination of Hitler; and discussed, attempted, or encouraged others to kill Rommel, Mussolini, President Nasser of Egypt, and Prime Minister Lumumba of Congo—then why not others? Even the urbane David Owen, foreign secretary in Jim Callaghan's Labour government, speaking on Radio 4's *PM* program, admitted that he had proposed assassinating Idi Amin. Knowledge of some genuine covert actions, however embryonic, spawns the reasonable assumption that there have been others.[15]

In other words, real conspiracies have an additional cost; a sort of postmodern blowback that often takes the form of public paranoia.[16] This is most visible in the Middle East and Asia, which for centuries were the stages of imperial meddling and intrigue, and where every British consulate, however minor, had its own secret service funds. Anxiety about the Western hidden hand became so great that in India during the 1970s, even natural events like monsoons and crop failures were attributed to MI6, the CIA, or the KGB. It is no surprise that the first people to assert that Diana was killed by MI6 were Gaddafi's Libya and Saddam Hussein's Iraq. An account of MI6 and the Diana conspiracy, written by Al-Fayed, became a sensational overnight bestseller in Egypt.[17]

Al-Fayed made matters far worse. Grief-stricken, he offered $20 million for information about the "killing" of Dodi and Diana and attracted precisely the wrong sort of attention. Oswald Le Winter stepped forward, claiming to be a former CIA operative with access to key documents on the events in Paris, and offering to hand them over in return for the full reward. He claimed that these American messages showed that MI6 had contacted the CIA for help with the "assassination." Although shying away from carrying out the deed themselves, the CIA then supposedly put MI6 in touch with an Israeli Mossad-affiliated hit squad operating out of Switzerland.[18] Le Winter was a well-known fabricator who had already done time in jail for drug-related crimes. He frequently tried to make money from intelligence-related sensations and would end up imprisoned for fraud by a Swiss judge.[19]

Nevertheless, Al-Fayed continued to insist that his son and Diana were assassinated by MI6 on the orders of Prince Philip. He believed that she was pregnant with Dodi's child and that the Royal Family "could not accept that an Egyptian Muslim could eventually be the stepfather of the future King of England." Therefore, he continued, the British intelligence and security services "covertly obtained the information concerning pregnancy and engagement, with or without the co-operation of overseas agencies, precipitating the need to put into operation a plan to murder them." An establishment cover-up then prevented the conspiracy from coming to light.[20]

Al-Fayed leapt to this conclusion within days—even hours—of the fatal crash. Conducting his own inquiries, he asked his head of security, John McNamara, a former detective chief inspector at the Met, to arrange meetings with some of the leading paparazzi, including Darryn Lyons, who was often considered to be one of the leading exponents of this arcane art. Lyons met Fayed on the top floor of Harrods. As he entered the office, the tycoon rose and greeted him warmly, before asking straight out: "Do you think those bastards killed my son? Because I think those bastards killed my son." Lyons, knowing he meant the Royal Family and MI6, tried to be both sympathetic and noncommittal, but he recalls: "I was with him for forty-five minutes and most of the conversation seemed to be him convincing himself that something had been done to the couple; . . . it was very hard to get a word in."[21]

Yet not all the accusers who supported the Al-Fayed view are fraudsters, fantasists, or writers of dubious footnote-free "true crime." McNamara, admittedly an employee of Al-Fayed, but also a senior ex-policeman, agreed that it "was an assassination" and that the paparazzi were used to cover it up.[22] Michael Mansfield QC, who represented Al-Fayed in the Scott Baker inquest, is a most distinguished barrister and perhaps Britain's best-known human rights lawyer, having represented the Birmingham Six and the family of Charles de Menezes. From the outset, he "felt very strongly there was more to this case than a mere accident."[23] But what was the substance of their case?

The prosecution's star witness was Richard Tomlinson, an MI6 officer who had served during the 1990s. A New Zealander, he had grown up in Britain and, showing an early talent for science, won a scholarship to Cambridge University to study mathematics and physics in 1981. Affable, widely liked by his peers, and seeming to fit the profile for an intelligence officer, he nevertheless failed MI6 selection after university and worked for a consultancy in London. Finding his desk job financially rewarding but unsatisfying, he joined the Territorial Army in September 1989 and, after passing selection, served as a reservist with the SAS in the Artists Rifles, and then 23 SAS, qualifying as a military parachutist and radio operator. Ten years after his first efforts, entering through a side door, he finally arrived in his desired profession as an intelligence officer in MI6 on September 23, 1991.

If Tomlinson is to be believed, he was the best recruit in his batch, sailing through the "Iconic" course at MI6's quirky training establishment, Fort Monckton near Portsmouth. He quickly took up a position in the "Soviet" department, at an exciting time, when the former Soviet Union was hemorrhaging secrets. From March 1992 until September 1993, he then worked in the Eastern European department, before being posted to Sarajevo for six months as the MI6 representative during the breakup of Yugoslavia. He was a targeting officer, with a mission to identify potential informants and gather intelligence. Moving again, from 1994 to 1995, Tomlinson worked in the counterproliferation department, supposedly infiltrating a network of arms dealers.[24]

On May 22, 1995, Tomlinson was suddenly dismissed. This should not have been entirely a surprise to him, because his probationary period had been extended again and again beyond the standard six-month duration, due to a line manager's doubts about his personality. Tomlinson claimed that he had become depressed after the death of his long-term girlfriend from cancer and that he had suffered from post-traumatic stress after witnessing violence in Sarajevo. Admittedly, MI6 was famously poor at supporting its own officers with either physical or mental health problems, displaying "a sink or swim" mentality toward troubled officers.[25]

Tomlinson tried to challenge the decision, but his efforts were quickly quashed by the foreign secretary. Angry and disillusioned, he then went abroad to write a tell-all book detailing his five years at MI6. Panicking, the service initially tried to buy him off by arranging interesting jobs, including a desirable position with a Formula One team. But this did not work, and, in 1997, MI6 lost patience. Tomlinson was imprisoned under the Official Secrets Act; the authorities seized his manuscript. He served six months before leaving the country once more, finally in 2001 publishing his book, which focused on MI6's supposed "licence to kill."[26]

After the death of Diana, Tomlinson quickly stepped forward. He dramatically claimed that MI6 had considered assassinating Slobodan Milošević, the president of Serbia, by staging a car crash in a tunnel using a powerful strobe light to blind the driver, later adding that this was a mainstream assassination technique and had even been covered as part of his training. The similarities to Diana's death were striking and, Tomlinson suggested, MI6 may have killed her in the same way.

Tomlinson claimed that when a friend showed him the assassination plan for Milošević, he first "checked the date on the top left-hand corner" to establish that it was not April Fools' Day. He then read the two-page memo. The first page was a justification for the assassination, citing Milošević's secret support for Radovan Karadžić and his genocidal plans for the Albanian population of Kosovo. The second page outlined the possibilities of an actual assassination.

According to Tomlinson, MI6 proposed three alternative plans for implementation and considered the advantages of each. The first was to use a joint MI6/special forces unit to train and equip a dissident local paramilitary faction to assassinate Milošević in Serbia. The advantage of this plan was its deniability; but, on the downside, proxies were notoriously difficult to control. The second plan was to use a UK special forces team to infiltrate Serbia and kill the president themselves with a bomb or a sniper ambush. This option came with a higher chance of success but would not have been deniable if it went wrong. The third was to arrange a car accident to kill him, possibly while he was attending peace talks in Geneva. MI6 supposedly proposed using a bright flashing strobe gun to disorient Milošević's chauffeur while the cavalcade passed through a tunnel.[27]

Shocked by the "audacity and ruthlessness" of the plan, Tomlinson responded: "You're off your trolley." He advised his colleague that the very mention of such a plan would damage his career and have an impact on his reputation with senior officers. But his friend replied confidently, "What do you know?" as if Tomlinson was an innocent schoolboy "learning for the first time the facts of life."[28]

Despite senior MI6 officers pleading implausibly poor memories, documents and witnesses finally surfaced during the various Diana inquiries to show that an assassination was indeed discussed. An MI6 officer working on the Balkans had frustratedly argued that Cold War "spy games" were a million miles from this "bloody civil war in the centre of Europe, where tens of thousands of innocent people are being killed." He suggested using either dissidents or special forces to assassinate a radical Serbian leader, albeit not Milošević. The MI6 officer in charge of the region rejected the plan outright. "The whole idea of SIS [Secret Intelligence Service] being involved in targeted assassination," he spluttered, "is repugnant to the ethos of the service and certainly repugnant to me personally."[29] The Diana inquiry heard that, while the plan existed, it was eventually "deleted and shredded."[30]

At first glance, Tomlinson's testimony seems compelling. It bore an uncanny resemblance to events in Paris; and an MI6 officer did propose an assassination in the Balkans, partly corroborating him. There were problems, however, including his assertion that this was some sort of mainstream assassination technique, but these left him shocked when actually proposed. The biggest problem was that Tomlinson seemed to have changed his story. In the version of his memoir seized by police before the death of Diana, he offered only the first assassination option; but in the versions and testimony after her assassination, there were suddenly three.[31] Over the years, he added that he thought MI6 was monitoring Diana before her death and that her driver on the night she died, Henri Paul, might have been an MI6 informant.[32] But Tomlinson undermined his testimony by making other errors, misidentifying Sherard Cowper-Coles, the embassy's political counselor, as head of the Secret Intelligence Service's Paris station.[33] Whatever the nature of his allegations, the investigative work of John Stevens had effectively busted Tomlinson as a reliable witness.[34]

Sherard Cowper-Coles recalls that the conspiracy theorists "crawled out of the swamp" after Diana's death. In fact, the timeline began rather earlier.[35] The most remarkable star witness affirming the assassination conspiracy was Diana herself. Since 1987, she had repeatedly claimed that people in the "Establishment" were out to kill her. During the mid-1980s, she had become rather close to one of her police protection officers, Barry Mannakee; and for this reason, in 1986, he was moved to diplomatic rather than royal protection. Shortly afterward, he died in a motorcycle accident. Riding pillion with a friend, they collided with a car coming out of a junction.[36] Diana told several close friends that he had been "bumped off."[37]

Such paranoia was understandable. Both Charles and Diana lived for years with the constant threat of assassination and had adapted their life accordingly. When they traveled abroad, they were accompanied by three metal cases that contained extra supplies of their blood in case of an accident or "a terrorist outrage." They were marked with the label "Vital: Keep at Room Temperature," so one of the key jobs of the secretaries was to make sure the air conditioning did not malfunction and allow the royal blood to go off.[38] She was a regular on the police gun range at Lippins Hill in Loughton in Essex, where the police did their firearms training. On one occasion she brought William and Harry, who both reveled in firing a .38 Smith & Wesson revolver, under the close supervision of a police instructor.[39]

Suspicion gradually turned to paranoia after the 1992 "Squidgygate" episode, in which transcripts of Diana's private phone calls were published by the press. Her private secretary, Patrick Jephson, remembers that her anxiety about security had now "reached new heights." "She saw plots everywhere," he explained, and "was obsessed with the thought that she was being bugged." Still living in Kensington Palace, she received the full countersurveillance protection extended to other royals—yet she increasingly suspected that these very same people were the culprits. When asked about these allegations, Jephson expressed "polite mystification," adding that "exasperation would have been nearer the mark." After all, "none of these hidden microphones had actually been discovered."[40] The Conservative minister and friend of Prince Charles, Nicholas Soames, accused Diana of being in "the advanced stages of paranoia." A junior member of the royal household decoded this, remarking that my "super-sized friend" is "saying that she is completely mad."[41] Prime Minister John Major apparently had to slap him down for the remark.[42]

On one occasion, Diana pulled up a carpet in an upstairs room at Kensington Palace, to show Jephson what she believed was evidence of bugging: fresh sawdust and disturbed planks. "She pointed silently at the sawdust, and nodded significantly." Jephson tried to reassure her that this was simply the result of the safety work and rewiring of all the royal palaces, after the 1992 fire at Windsor Castle, but Diana, gesturing for him to be silent, was unconvinced.[43]

By 1995, Diana was voicing her fears with increasing frequency. Her solicitor, Lord Mishcon, recalled her predicting that "efforts would be made if not to get rid of her (be it by some accident in her car such as a pre-prepared brake failure or whatever) . . . at least to see that she was so injured or damaged as to be declared 'unbalanced.'"[44] This scenario was something she also discussed with her inner circle of friends. Typically, she told one confidant, Roberto Devorik:

> I am a threat in their eyes. They only use me when they need me for offi-
> cial functions and then they drop me again in the darkness; . . . they are
> not going to kill me by poisoning me or in a big plane where others will
> get hurt. They will either do it when I am on a small plane, in a car when
> I am driving or in a helicopter. The only time I really feel safe is when I am
> in the USA. Everybody in America likes me. I am very popular there. The
> "Establishment" doesn't like me and there is no "Establishment" there.[45]

Diana's butler, Paul Burrell, claimed she wrote a similar note in 1996, and, although the date is disputed, this is merely one among many examples.[46]

Diana believed that her fears reflected her real experience. In 1995, she was driving through London alone and without bodyguards in her distinctive green Audi A4 Cabriolet. As she made her way toward a junction, the traffic lights turned red, and she braked. Nothing happened. The car kept rolling forward, but mercifully there was no collision. When she finally came to a stop, she jumped out in a state of distress and flagged down a taxi. She returned to Kensington Palace and rang a close friend, insisting that someone had tampered with her brakes. Mechanics blamed the brake failure on normal wear and tear and lack of maintenance.[47]

This was supposedly not the only incident involving dodgy brakes. Rita Rogers, one of Diana's "psychics" and spiritual healers, warned the princess of a premonition that someone had tampered with her brakes. When Diana duly checked them, she indeed found a problem.[48] Whether Rogers really did have a premonition is immaterial; the important point is that Diana discussed her worries about her brakes with psychics and friends, but not her driver and security staff. She became increasingly suspicious of those who were designated to protect her.

These views were encouraged by the growing army of therapists, psychics, and astrologers, whom she had mustered by 1995. Jephson laments that some had become "highly influential and coloured her thinking with unpredictable results." They frequently predicted the death of Charles in a helicopter crash. This had "a destructive effect on the princess's own judgement," and even encouraged a "blind belief in her own intuition" that became a substitute for reasoned analysis or basic common sense. Meetings with these people took up a remarkable amount of her time. Although restrained and polite in his language, this astute observer was convinced that collectively they "fed the paranoia that never lurked far below the well-groomed surface."[49]

For much of this time, the policeman in charge of her security was the kind and long-suffering Ken Wharfe. He was gradually transforming from personal protection officer into a kind of pest control officer focused on the press, especially the foreign press; one of his main roles was to scout out vacation sanctuaries where the princess and her children could escape "prying eyes."[50]

Sadly, his superiors criticized him for this, insisting that his role was "not that of a press officer but a protection officer." But Wharfe was more sophisticated, and he understood that the boundary between security and other kinds of intrusion was increasingly fuzzy. He recalled that he and his three assistants were up against the "crack troops of the world's press," adding that even General Custer "had better odds" of success than them. On Diana's foreign travels, Wharfe struck deals to try to keep the hordes away, appreciating full well the extent to which the press posed an indirect threat to her safety and even her mental health.

In the winter of 1993, in Lech in Austria, Diana evaded her own protection team by making a night-time leap into deep snow off a first-floor balcony in her hotel and then going for a late night walk. Wharfe later asked her: "Ma'am, what were you thinking?" Their relationship of mutual trust was coming to an end. He left her service, and thereafter she dispensed with routine police protection, a dangerous strategy indeed.

Somewhat later, Diana had a frank conversation with David Meynell, a senior police officer who ran SO14, the Metropolitan Police unit presiding over all VIP protection in Britain. She explained that while "she had a lot of enemies," she also "had a lot of friends, some in places of knowledge." She had used these high-level contacts to probe what was really going on and to ask questions. According to Meynell, "She could not name them because they could lose their jobs, but she had been told that without any doubt five people from an organisation had been assigned full-time to 'oversee' her activities, including listening to her private phone conversations, and from the same source she knew that two people from the same organisation performed a similar function in respect of Parliament."

In other words, Diana suspected that a small, deep-state unit was engaged in political surveillance, probably unknown to routine members of MI5, MI6, or GCHQ. Meynell replied that this was a "very serious matter," but he insisted he had seen no evidence of it.[51]

The jump off the balcony into the snow in December signified Diana's desperate bid for freedom. At 11:20 on the morning of December 13, 1993, Meynell came to Kensington Palace for a formal meeting about Diana's security protection, already knowing her general intentions. He warned her that quite apart from the press, SO14 had "on record the details of some 3,000 individuals who have various fixations about the Royal Family" and who "would not be put off." It was a list of royal obsessives and maniacs long maintained by the police and the Home Office. But the princess was "very determined" that there be no interference with her plans.[52] Indeed, Meynell recalled that the princess "was quite gleeful about it."[53]

The police gradually—and reluctantly—withdrew Diana's protection over the next year. David Veness, one of the most senior officers in the Met, observed that it was "unwise." He later recalled that the police gave Diana "unequivocal" advice against seeking any changes at all to her security measures, both in person and through her own advisers. "She was, however, adamant, and insisted that her wishes prevail." The views of the Met were supported by MI5, which had "primary responsibility for assessment of threats to the Royal Family." Worried officials at MI5, the Met, and the Foreign Office met to discuss and indeed lament the implications of her request, but ultimately could do nothing about it.[54] In February 1994, the home secretary, Michael Howard, asked to be "absolved of all responsibility," and threatened to involve the prime minister. Thereafter, Diana received police protection only when on official duties or when traveling with her sons.[55]

Diana made this distinctly odd decision because she now associated everyone who was in an official role, no matter how kind and well meaning, with a gargantuan plot. She not only became the subject of conspiracy theories but also ultimately had succumbed to them herself. Family, friends, protectors, detractors, paparazzi, protection officers, private security, and secret service all overlapped, in what was an increasingly claustrophobic world. One cannot help feel that her fears of the secret service, however misplaced, had tipped her over the edge; and accordingly, when she arrived in Paris in August 1997, she had lacked the support of the Met's highly professional and kindly protection teams.

Patrick Jephson speaks eloquently of this bizarre decision. He admired her police protection officers working their weekly shifts. They were seasoned by years of policing in the capital and honed by periodic "training with the SAS." Jephson rated them as "loyal, discreet, wise, and brave," and he remains mystified by her decision to dispense with their protection and replace it with the "well-meaning amateurishness of hired substitutes."[56]

The BBC stoked her paranoia further before the bombshell *Panorama* interview in November 1995. Diana wanted to give her side of the story, and in a remarkably candid performance, she told her interviewer, Martin Bashir, about her self-harm and mental health struggles. She also uttered the infamous line: "There were three of us in this marriage." Twenty-three million people tuned in. Shortly afterward, the queen angrily called it a "frightful thing to do, frightful thing my daughter-in-law did."[57]

This landmark interview raised all sorts of questions about why Diana had agreed to be so open. In early 1995, Bashir had begun working on a story about the Royal Family. "Well-placed sources" suggested to him that Charles and Diana were being closely scrutinized—"possibly even bugged." He needed more information and access to Diana herself, eventually meeting the princess through her brother, Earl Spencer. Spencer later claimed that Bashir had intentionally duped him and Diana by playing on her fears of espionage. Bashir had allegedly created fake bank statements intended to suggest that senior courtiers and security staff were being paid to spy on her. The BBC later admitted that Bashir did ask a designer to mock up at least one of these documents, and the inquiry found it highly likely that he had fabricated others, but Bashir insisted that they had played no role in securing the interview.

Bashir told Diana explicitly that he was interested in the campaign against her; he made it clear that he wanted to discuss this in an interview. In response, she said she thought someone was bugging and following her.[58] The eventual interview evolved from this conspiratorial starting point, and his actions were highly unethical.

The BBC later acknowledged that Bashir had made notes on the subject of MI5's surveillance, but he had no documentary proof. Nonetheless, unsubstantiated rumors soon swirled in the press that she had given the interview because Bashir had evidence that MI5 was spying on her.[59] It all added to the princess's claustrophobic paranoia. She could trust very few people.

When Diana appeared in Paris, she was not entirely without cover. The Al-Fayeds had a large private security team numbering some forty people, often with guns. Indeed, it would not be an exaggeration to say that the Egyptian tycoon boasted a veritable private army. Because of his long-running feud with a business rival, Tiny Rowland, his teams reportedly had been engaged in the covert filming and recording of his own employees. Former policemen were employed by both sides in this famously bitter business battle. There also seem to have been extensive telephone monitoring operations in some of his key hotels, including the Ritz in Paris. Diana had perhaps stepped out of one panopticon into another.[60]

In Paris, Henri Paul, acting head of security at the Ritz, oversaw her safety and also served as her driver during the fateful pursuit through the tunnel. Accompanying them was the bodyguard and former soldier Trevor Rees-Jones. Paul himself moved in the world of intelligence and has been the subject of endless speculation.

Paul, a forty-one-year-old Frenchman who cultivated an action man reputation, was clearly known to several intelligence agencies. He was in regular contact with the Direction Général de la Sécurité Extérieure (DGSE), the French equivalent of MI6. He also had informal relations with the Direction de la Surveillance du Territoire (DST), which is the equivalent of MI5. His personal notebooks contained the names and telephone numbers of two people next to the letters "DST."[61] According to an American law enforcement official and an American intelligence agent, Paul spent the last several hours before the crash "with a security officer from the DGSE."[62] On this occasion, he was paid 12,560 francs, over £1,000, and still had the money on him when he died.[63]

Such arrangements were common, even routine, among security staffers at premier international hotels. Sometimes they had to manage delicate situations, such as weapons on the premises or incidents involving high-profile international guests. Indeed, earlier that year, he had dealt smoothly with the death of the elderly US ambassador in the hotel pool.[64] Less formally, he was perhaps a useful informant for French intelligence, given the number of influential guests, especially from the Arab world, who stayed at the hotel. Paul relished this work rather more than most and was a spy by any other name. His girlfriend recalled that for this reason he was unpopular with his colleagues but was able to provide "satisfaction to his superiors," namely, the hotel manager and Al-Fayed. He was nicknamed "the Ferret" by his colleagues because he was always "sticking his nose in everywhere."[65]

Meanwhile, Paul's passion was recreational flying, something hard to do on his salary of about £40,000 a year. But his freelance security work for both secret services and visiting VIPs brought him a healthy additional income. He had deposited about £43,000 into his accounts in the last eight months of his life. Some have attempted to dismiss these payments as mere "tips," but they perhaps point to rather more substantial spy work.[66]

Either way, Paul worked harder for himself than for his superiors and presided over a ramshackle security system. He was not a professional driver, and was supposed to use professional chauffeurs for VIPs, but he meekly complied when Dodi ordered him to drive on the fateful night. Worst of all, he was probably under the influence of both alcohol and prescription drugs when he drove the car.[67]

The manner of their departure from the hotel also broke with convention. One of the golden rules of convoy protection is to have a team of cars. But the party of several cars had not left the Ritz together; instead, Dodi hatched an ill-considered "decoy plan" that involved vehicles leaving from both the front and rear of the hotel. This left him and Diana exposed in a single vehicle without a backup car.[68] Rees-Jones, the bodyguard, had misgivings: "I was not happy, as Dodi was splitting the two security officers up, but I toed the line."[69]

More remarkably, neither John McNamara, the head of Al-Fayed's security organization in London, nor anyone on his team initially had any idea that Dodi and Diana had even gone to Paris.[70] By contrast, the paparazzi were expecting them. Unlike the security officials, they had paid sources inside air traffic control and so knew the celebrity couple were coming, even before they touched down in France.[71] In 1997, the voracious press even paid one unnamed bodyguard £30,000 just for revealing Diana's location.[72]

Diana was the source of a major media industry that generated unimaginable wealth for certain journalists and transformed the profession, but not for the better. Darryn Lyons confessed that after she died, "the paparazzi world went into meltdown." The leaders of the pack tried diversifying into extreme sports, animal shots, or "anything we could pull in just to keep the till ringing." Others simply panicked and wondered "what the hell they were going to do now." They had traveled the world in Diana's wake, often on lavish expenses. After her death, Lyons spoke the truth in rather cold words, observing that their "gravy train had just been derailed in a truly spectacular fashion."[73]

It was now the turn of the paparazzi themselves to come in for some unwelcome attention. Lyons received photographs of the crash scene on his computer just hours after Diana's death. Someone then burgled his offices at about 11 p.m. that night. The home of another photographer, Lionel Cherruault, was also broken into on the same night. Cherruault was informed by the crime investigation officer that it had been "no ordinary burglary": the intruders gained entry seamlessly.[74] They seemed to have knowledge of the premises and only took selected items. Cherruault asked him: "Do you mean the grey men, MI5, MI6, whatever?" The officer replied: "Well, you can call them what you wish; local henchmen," adding, "You would be surprised what kind of people they use." The policeman's main intent was to reassure him that because this was a professional government job, their lives had not been in danger.[75] The photographer felt that the clear implication by the police was that the burglary had been carried out by the security services.

Oddly, one of Diana's closer personal associations with the security services is rarely mentioned. One of her dearest and most loyal friends was Rosa Monckton; together, they often undertook charity work supporting vulnerable children. Monckton was in almost daily contact with Diana in the days before she set off for her last vacation on the Al-Fayed yacht before traveling to Paris. She was anxious about her friend's relationship with Dodi. In the week before her departure, Diana arranged for her mobile phone to be allocated a new number that "only a handful of people would know."[76] Monckton would have been one.

Monckton's youngest brother, Anthony, was a long-serving and distinguished MI6 officer who arrived in the former Yugoslavia in the early 1990s and had sometimes worked alongside Tomlinson. A decade later he was still there, based in the British Embassy in Belgrade and engaged in the tricky business of bringing war criminals before the tribunal in The Hague. In February 2004, he was horrified when he was "outed" in a memoir by Zoran Mijatovic, the former deputy chief of the Serbian intelligence service. Exposed, he feared that he might now be targeted by Milošević's supporters, so he grew a beard to change his appearance. He fled, never having netted his greatest prize, General Ratko Mladić.[77] Al-Fayed suggested that Rosa Monckton was reporting on Diana to MI6; indeed, he even asserted that she had befriended the princess precisely for this purpose, but there is no evidence to suggest this.[78]

Instead, it is more likely that the relationship was the other way around: perhaps Rosa and her brother were among the helpful friends in high places of whom Diana asked questions back in 1993, when she feared the activities of the supposed deep state. Wisely, Rosa had warned Diana to stay away from Al-Fayed, insisting that he was "the man who put lots of cash in 25 brown envelopes and bribed MPs."[79]

Fascinatingly, Rosa and Anthony were the grandchildren of Walter Monckton, the lawyer and later cabinet minister who had remained a loyal friend to Edward VIII throughout the abdication and beyond. Walter Monkton had often traveled to Paris to advise him, staying at what subsequently became Al-Fayed's home, the Villa Windsor in the Bois de Boulogne—Diana's first stop on her fateful visit of Paris in August 1997.[80]

Diana had asserted that she would be killed by the "men in grey suits." There was no doubt that during the early 1990s, many in the establishment believed she represented an existential threat to the British monarchy. Squidgygate and then the 1995 BBC *Panorama* interview with Martin Bashir were shocking. Prince Philip railed about this frequently, but then his temper was short, and he railed against a long list of people. In private, he was always kind to the princess. More importantly, these episodes took their toll on both Charles and Diana.

Diana's death in Paris was unlikely to have been an assassination for one simple reason. Diana and Dodi chose to go to Paris at short notice and on a whim. This makes the existence of a state plot highly unlikely, because secret services are ultimately government bureaucracies and a deliberate death takes months to arrange. Equally important, unlike the French, Russians, and Americans, British intelligence has no established track record of assassinations. It certainly has no "licence to kill." Covert actions are very rarely independent initiatives by spies known in the trade as "rogue elephants." The more serious the action, the more likely it is the decision makes its way circuitously and ponderously to the very top. Even if MI6 were in the assassination business, it would not have acted without prime ministerial approval; and Tony Blair—a new, young, and idealistic leader—would hardly have authorized the assassination of a popular princess only months into office.

In any country, once a "hit" is approved, teams of assassins, backed by further supporters are dispatched. After months of planning, the CIA sent a team of a dozen to simply kidnap one person from Italy in 2003. Similarly, when Israel killed a leading member of Hezbollah in Dubai in 2010, it sent no fewer than twenty assassins, some disguised as tennis players. A large British assassination team operating in Paris that night would not have stayed untraceable, let alone plausibly deniable, for long.

The fact that Lord Stevens was chosen to head the British police inquiry also lends confidence. He had previously led an investigation into collusion between British security forces and loyalist paramilitaries in Northern Ireland, and he believed that simple statements by the security services that "they have no involvement in illegal activities such as assassinations is not credible." In other words, Stevens, perhaps more than any other such figure, was likely to keep an open mind and probe the evidence. He was certain that she was not assassinated.[81]

Although Diana's fears of the secret state, expressed with increasing frankness in the years before she died, overlap with Al-Fayed's allegations in some respects, in other important ways they do not. Fayed insisted that Diana was effectively killed on the orders of the duke of Edinburgh. But Hasnat Khan—the quiet, kind, and intelligent doctor, who was perhaps closest to Diana in the year before she died—recalls, "although she did not like the Duke of Edinburgh, she never expressed any fear of him."[82] Though Diana was not the victim of a conspiracy, she was effectively the victim of *conspiracy theory*, and it was her fears of "dark forces" that persuaded her to withdraw her police protection, against even the pleading of the home secretary. If that protection had been in place in Paris, she would have been professionally cared for and would not have died on the last day of August 1997.

Patrick Jephson recalls with emotion her decision to "dispense with her bodyguards." Her team of police officers long afterward retained a deep emotional loyalty to their "wayward charge." Ever watchful and professional to the end, he met them after her death and encountered the profound distress that they expressed, noting that she had died in circumstances that they would never have allowed to develop given their years of careful training.[83]

Meanwhile, Michael Mansfield, who acted for Al-Fayed in the Scott Baker inquiry, and penned his own account in 2009 after all the inquiries had finished, presents us with almost nothing. Instead, his essay on the Diana episode, titled "Big Brother," is a rhetorical *tour d'horizon* of the British secret state from

George Orwell to omnipresent CCTV. Every historic skeleton in the cupboard of MI5 and MI6 is rattled, but he has surprisingly few things to say about the case itself. This notably laconic treatment of the key issues by a skilled advocate is all but a frank admission that he and his team had little to go on.[84]

More facts continue to emerge, and they do not reflect well on the case for the prosecution. In 2017, investigators showed that the car involved in the fatal crash enjoyed a remarkable "first life." It had been bought new and then stolen two years before the death of the princess by an escaped prisoner who took it on a joyride in the countryside near Paris. It was found destroyed in a field near Charles de Gaulle Airport after rolling over several times. As a result, it was subsequently classified as a total loss and the owner was reimbursed in full by the insurer. Yet a company, Etoile Limousine, which rented out cars with drivers and worked in part for the Ritz in Paris, bought the rebuilt car from a Mercedes dealer. It was soon clear that it had stability problems. A former driver complained that it was unpredictable if driven faster than 60 kilometres an hour.[85] As more details appear, from the car to allegations against Bashir, one thing is for certain: the controversial case continues to fascinate.

Conclusion

The Secret Royals

In the spring of 2019, a new recruit showed up for work at MI6. The thirty-six-year-old, balding father of three looked rather nondescript. Each day he passed through the "circlelock" security doors backlit with softly glowing aqua-blue glass. He ate in the canteen and, like many of his colleagues, was known only by his forename: "Will."

Prince William spent most of his time at MI6 based in its iconic "ziggurat" headquarters at Vauxhall Cross. Here, he learned about tradecraft: how intelligence officers recruit and nurture foreign agents. He noted how MI6 monitors risks to national security, to the economy, and, particularly close to his heart, to military effectiveness. He also gained a rare insight into covert action, learning about how intelligence can identify and exploit opportunities to shape events overseas.

The next week, William transferred across the river to MI5. He worked with covert counterterrorism teams as they conducted surveillance, potentially even including riding in undercover vehicles, and sitting alongside intelligence analysts.

He spent the third week at the impressive base of Government Communications Headquarters (GCHQ) in Cheltenham. Often described as "the Doughnut," it rather more resembles a vast silver flying saucer. Each day he commuted to work from Prince Charles's Highgrove estate a few miles to the south. Again, he saw a range of intelligence activities, including how cutting-edge technology monitors targets and, through online covert action, disrupts threats. GCHQ's head of counterterrorism operations praised William for comfortably holding his own among highly trained intelligence officers and analysts.

William attended security briefings with senior officials to discuss the threats facing Britain. Learning how intelligence agencies monitor the threat from extremists, especially those returning from Syria, he was exposed to the full range of counterterrorism operations, including those launched against the Islamic State, the far right, and the Real IRA. Some activities targeted Russia. He even got into the field during practice operations.

At the end of his intelligence assignment, William expressed a deep interest in security and defense and, like other royals before him, felt that intelligence gave him an insight into the threats to Britain and the British people. He said that "spending time inside our security and intelligence agencies, understanding more about the vital contribution they make to our national security, was a truly humbling experience."

"These agencies," he continued, "are full of people from everyday backgrounds doing the most extraordinary work to keep us safe. They work in secret, often not even able to tell their family and friends about the work they do or the stresses they face. They are driven by an unrivalled patriotism and dedication to upholding the values of this country. We all owe them deep gratitude for the difficult and dangerous work they do."[1]

William was too polite to say which service he preferred, but each royal has their favorite. Queen Elizabeth seemed to have a soft spot for GCHQ. For fifty years, the successors of Bletchley Park kept her "boxes" packed with the most remarkable secrets. In more recent years, GCHQ has taken on another role that is perhaps even more important—the defense of "cyberspace." Responsibility for the security of the Internet is a job that could have reasonably ended up in the in-tray of any one of a dozen government departments, but few had the depth of technical expertise. In the end, the GCHQ defensive team that had built the queen's scrambler phones in the 1980s then became responsible for the defense of banks and automated teller machines in the 1990s, and finally took over the defense of "everything" as Britain rushed toward e-government in the twenty-first century. GCHQ now has the tricky job of keeping the Internet flowing safely.

On February 17, 2017, the queen visited Britain's first "open" secret building. GCHQ's striking new National Cyber Security Centre in London's Victoria district is the first secret service headquarters that anyone can visit—at least the ground floor. She expounded the growing importance of the Internet not only for government but also for the everyday lives of her subjects. She was shown a book of secret cyphers used by her father, King George VI, to communicate during the war. Robert Hannigan, the director of GCHQ, responded warmly and recalled: "During the War, King George VI, who was a regular reader of Bletchley's intelligence reports, was told that our mathematicians and engineers were building Colossus, the world's first digital computer." He explained that this breakthrough was to have consequences well beyond the vital job of code-breaking, ushering in the era of digital information and computing power. He characterized the sixty-five years of the queen's reign as the "new Machine Age" and added that now she had a new branch of the secret services that was designed to defend it.[2]

The queen herself was a titan whose era spanned the most exciting decades of secret history. She was able to look back as well as forward, and so in 2019, she commemorated GCHQ's centenary by unveiling a green plaque at Water-gate House, near Charing Cross Station, the birthplace of the organization. The Government Code & Cypher School, as it was known at the time, was established on November 1, 1919, as a peacetime cryptanalytic unit made up from staff from the Admiralty's Room 40 and the War Office's MI1(b).

For generations, the Royal Family has shown a close interest in intelligence. As the secret world gradually becomes less secretive and more bureaucratic, its relationship with the monarchy is becoming more formal and public. The queen was at its center.

When Prince Philip died in 2021, the intelligence services were quick to pay tribute. The chief of MI6, Richard Moore, described Philip as a "true friend of the Service" and recalled that Philip had visited the agency on numerous occasions: "Always his sharp mind, experience gained from active service and knowledge of global affairs shone through." Philip "called it as he saw it with directness and wit. Visits were never dull."[3]

Philip had served as royal colonel of the Intelligence Corps. According to Tom Tugendhat, a soldier turned Conservative politician, Philip was both enter-taining and diligent in this role, "always astute in keeping an eye on what the Corps was up to." One colleague apparently asked him why the unit had never been made the Royal Intelligence Corps. His answer was simple: "Because you bastards aren't gentlemen."[4]

Like his father, Prince Charles, before becoming king, was the colonel in chief of the Parachute Regiment, and he has been particularly interested in action. In 2019, the heir to the throne followed in his mother's footsteps and met James Bond actor Daniel Craig on the set of the twenty-fifth *007* film. They "bonded" over a display of eight classic 1960s Aston Martin DB5s. Surrounded by stars, Charles joked: "The cars are the interesting thing here, much more interest-ing." He joined Naomie Harris, who plays Moneypenny, and Ralph Fiennes, who plays "M," along with director Cary Fukunaga in M's office. After watching some rushes from the film, Charles went to see the set of Q's workshop. But the media were not allowed to follow and see the gadgets because of the strict secrecy surrounding "Bond 25."

"Q" did not realize that Charles could have given them all a few tips. In the spy world, life often imitates art and vice versa.[5] As prince of Wales, he was the patron of the intelligence agencies and, as such, regularly engaged with real intelligence officers. On a visit to GCHQ in 2019, at which he received "top secret briefings," Charles praised their "utterly essential work." "Few people in this country," he told the intelligence officers, "will ever know just how great a debt we all owe you."[6] He has visited GCHQ headquarters at least three times, including shortly after the terrorist attacks on the United States on September 11, 2001; a secret GCHQ base in Scarborough; and has met the head of GCHQ in Clarence House, the prince's London residence.

The number of visits is remarkable. He has also visited MI5's Thames House at least three times, including the week after the attempted assassination of former Soviet spy Sergei Skripal in Salisbury and the day after Britain accused Russia of his attempted murder. Charles also met MI5 directors general Jonathan Evans and Andrew Parker at Clarence House. In July 2020, he received the new MI5 director general, Kenneth McCallum, the youngest in its history.

Charles has visited MI6 headquarters three times as well, most recently in October 2021. He has also met MI6 chiefs at Clarence House. In the late summer of 2014, he hosted John Sawers in the aftermath of an incredibly busy few weeks for MI6, with intelligence grappling with Russian covert operations in Ukraine, the Syrian civil war, Iranian nuclear negotiations, and the rise of the Islamic State of Iraq and Syria. They must have had plenty to discuss.

On top of these visits, Charles has hosted regular award ceremonies at Clarence House and Saint James's Palace. These ceremonies—perhaps the most exclusive in the UK—are where he has handed out secret commendations for intelligence officers known as the Prince of Wales's Intelligence Community Awards. These are the espionage equivalent of the Victoria Cross, the highest honor in the British system awarded for bravery, and are allocated for the most special kinds of service.

The arms trade is a shady and often unspoken area where royals, the secret services, and the Special Air Service (SAS) come together. The SAS's role in masterminding royal protection formed an important nexus with arms sales. Sultans and sheiks from Bahrain to Brunei queued up to have their bodyguards or special forces advised by the men in black balaclavas. Intelligence has long been used in support of British-based private commerce, providing intelligence on the negotiating positions of rival manufacturers. Britain's intelligence services are often presented to the public in terms of counterterrorism or warning mechanisms like the Joint Intelligence Committee. Lurking underneath are a range of parallel practices that are often informal. The royals interact with this more hidden world.[7]

The member of the Royal Family closest to this curious world was Prince Andrew. More than anyone else, he had enjoyed a serious and successful military career of twenty-two years, serving as a helicopter pilot in the Falklands War. This gave him an insight into the world of military technology, including both advanced naval ships and aviation. When he left the navy and became an ambassador for British trade, military technology was always high on his list of priorities for promotion.

In late October 2008, the American ambassador to Kyrgyzstan, Tatiana Gfoeller, was offered a surprising glimpse of this activity. Her British opposite number in Bishkek, the new nation's capital, invited her to a large business lunch at which she was the only participant from outside Britain or the Commonwealth. She reported back to Washington on Andrew's comments, which she found "astonishingly candid," adding that the discussion at times verged on "the rude." As Andrew fielded questions, he was reportedly "superengaged" and then, addressing the ambassador directly, stated frankly that Britain was "back in the thick of playing the Great Game." Now rather animated, he added cheekily: "and this time we aim to win!"[8]

Andrew next turned his fire on the Serious Fraud Office. He ripped into its investigators, who had had the "idiocy" of almost scuttling the al-Yamama arms deal with Saudi Arabia, reportedly worth some £40 billion. The ambassador explained to Washington that the prince "was referencing an investigation, subsequently closed, into alleged kickbacks a senior Saudi royal had received in exchange for the multiyear, lucrative BAE Systems contract to provide equipment and training to Saudi security forces." Andrew then went on to attack "those (expletive) journalists," especially from the *Guardian*, "who poke their noses everywhere" and made it harder for British businessmen to do business. "His mother's subjects seated around the table roared their approval."[9]

Andrew's salty comments surfaced shortly afterward when the ambassador's cable was released by WikiLeaks. But the security services' fears over him more recently shifted to blackmail vulnerabilities. Andrew's friendship with the late billionaire paedophile Jeffrey Epstein came under close scrutiny after a disastrous interview he gave to the BBC in 2019. He strenuously denies knowledge of, or involvement in, Epstein's activities. His friendship, however, created a potential counterintelligence risk.

MI6 apparently feared that Russia could link Andrew to the abuse, thereby creating a blackmail—or "leverage"—possibility. *The Times* reported that MI6 was concerned about a former Florida policeman who had access to the investigation, and claimed to have confidential documents, but who then moved to Russia, where he made contact with a senior Russian government official sometimes referred to as a mentor to President Vladimir Putin. According to a "Western intelligence source," this information on the Epstein case "would have been of great interest to Russian intelligence."[10] Security officials have since carefully reviewed the security of the prince's Internet and phone connections in case of bugging.[11]

Since then, Andrew's downfall has been swift and humiliating. The queen stripped him of his military titles and royal patronages in early 2022, and he reluctantly agreed to stop using the title His Royal Highness. Meanwhile, the security minister, Damian Hinds, refused to confirm whether Andrew would continue to receive taxpayer-funded security protection thought to cost up to £2 million a year.[12] Andrew was absent from the balcony during the Queen's Platinum Jubilee celebrations, and his career in public life is effectively over.

Perhaps the most ambiguous relationship has been with the silent sentinels of Special Branch, who protected the royals around the world for over a hundred years. The royals created problems for their bodyguards, but also feared that the police reported on them. King Edward VIII is the most notorious example, and there is no doubt that his secret policemen protected him but also spied on him—something he knew full well—making for a very special relationship.

The queen created all sorts of problems for her silent sentinels by insisting on being accessible and visible even in an era of rising international terrorism. Locking herself away would have caused the crown to wither and die. Secret intelligence and advance warning proved vital in achieving this.

Gradually, as times changed and threats increased, security became more oppressive. For Princess Diana, it was too much. Engulfed in a claustrophobic world and increasingly concerned, she first evaded her security and then shed it altogether.

Diana's youngest son, Prince Harry, tried to scale back his own royal duties in 2020. His wife is Meghan Markle, the duchess of Sussex, an articulate and outspoken American actor whom many hoped would bring new dynamism and diversity to the institution. Unfortunately, things soon deteriorated. The press persistently attacked her for the most bizarre things: eating avocados, opening car doors wrongly, and even caressing her pregnant stomach. Meghan told friends not to worry: the palace would protect her.

Soon, however, like Diana, she did not feel safe. She faced a constant barrage of press attention—along with issues of race and social media trolling with which Diana did not have to contend. She became lonely and depressed.

When pregnant, she learned that her child would not receive security. Amid all the clickbait and paparazzi, she found that particularly difficult to accept. She felt trapped.[13]

In late 2019, she and Harry left the UK and moved to Canada. They claim that the Royal Family quickly cut off their security. Harry felt neither secure nor safe, especially as the newspapers revealed their location. He protested that even though his status may have changed, the threat to his safety had not. London prevaricated before agreeing that the latest intelligence did in fact show that the threat had not changed. However, he was no longer a working member of the Royal Family, so his security would be cut. Harry was shocked: "I never thought that I would have my security removed, because I was born into this position. I inherited the risk."[14]

Meghan wrote letters to the palace pleading: "Please keep my husband safe. I see the death threats. I see the racist propaganda. Please keep him safe. Please don't pull his security and announce to the world when he and we are most vulnerable."[15]

The next March, days after the first coronavirus lockdown, Harry and Meghan moved to Los Angeles. They initially had to rely on private security provided by the media mogul Tyler Perry. As they settled in California, they claimed they then had to sign lucrative contracts with Netflix and Spotify simply to afford security.[16]

In autumn 2021, the British Home Office refused to provide police protection for Harry—and even refused him the right to pay for it himself. He was horrified and claimed that it was now too dangerous for him to visit the UK, the country he considers home. His legal team insisted that his private security team, which protected him in the US, lacked jurisdiction abroad and, more importantly, lacked access to UK intelligence necessary to protect him and his family. The next year, he launched a legal challenge against the decision.[17]

This was a remarkable situation: two of the most famous people on the planet, a target for a long list of terrorists and maniacs, denied security. It is also a stark contrast to many of Harry's relatives. Queen Victoria, King Edward VIII, Queen Elizabeth II, and even his own mother had resisted security. Harry wanted more. Times had certainly changed.

From the days of Victoria to the present day, the British monarch has long been an adviser and confidant to the prime minister, including on intelligence and national security matters. Monarchs require intelligence to perform these duties. They enjoy the constitutional right to offer comments, encouragement, and, most important, warning. In 1986, the queen's private secretary insisted that doing so actually constituted a duty rather than a mere right, thereby allowing the monarch a more active role. A 2011 Cabinet Office's manual extended these rights or duties to include advising and being informed. Although the monarch must remain above party politics or risk undermining confidence in the office, he or she can express opinions on policy to the prime minister in an entirely confidential manner.[18] Prime Minister David Cameron recalled that the queen asked "incredibly perceptive" questions—a view shared by senior intelligence officials.[19] She could only do this if she was well briefed and had a full picture of what is going on, including classified material. This is a classic example of intelligence as a form of power.[20]

The relationship between spies and royals raises a crucial question in liberal democracies: to whom are intelligence officers ultimately loyal? The government or the crown? After all, officially speaking, MI6 officers are not civil servants, they are "crown servants." The military historian Ian Beckett claims that, for many military officers, the crown represents a higher form of authority than the government of the day. Being servants, first and foremost, of the crown—albeit of the symbol rather than the individual monarch—allows the military to distance itself from the squalid nature of politics.[21] A similar idea extends to the intelligence services. This is not an abstract constitutional conundrum. It manifested itself most prominently and awkwardly in 1936, when the prime minister asked intelligence officers to spy on the king. It also manifested itself in 1974, when rumors emerged about intelligence officers, loyal to the crown, agitating against the prime minister, Harold Wilson, ironically the queen's favourite premier.

In this murky world, one thing is certain. Queen Elizabeth II knew more state secrets than anyone else alive; she acquired them over decades of reading classified intelligence. In fact, she probably knew more state secrets than anyone in history. Famously discreet, she took them to her grave. How she used that information—and how future monarchs will do so—raises important questions about the role of the crown in British politics. There is so much about the secret royals and their influence that we do not yet know.

One thing is for sure: the role of the monarch is more influential than many assume. There is far more to the crown than the pomp and pageantry for which it is famous around the world. The monarch is more than a gilded sponge, soaking up events as they unfold around them.

Queen Elizabeth and now Charles III obviously have far less influence than Victoria did; and even Victoria, as a constitutional monarch, wielded far less influence than did her predecessors. Victoria, and to a lesser extent Edward VII, exploited their own private networks of intelligence spanning Europe's interconnected royal houses. She used this to both support and compete with her prime ministers, depending on the issue at hand. When many of these royal houses collapsed after the First World War, George V and George VI had fewer opportunities to follow suit. Any desire to influence was further curtailed by the growth and formalization of the UK's intelligence services. That said, George V maintained an informal domestic network, while George VI provided a royal connection to support the Special Operations Executive's operations in occupied Europe during the Second World War.

Elizabeth followed in Victoria's footsteps as an astute consumer of intelligence, but not as a producer, analyst, and covert operator. Unlike Victoria, she did not maintain her own private networks to shape foreign policy in her favor. Nonetheless, it is reasonable to assume that she acted as a quasi-diplomat when dealing with other royal houses, especially in the Middle East. If she picked up the odd titbit of privileged information through royal sources, she lacked the ability—and probably the desire—to outmaneuver official channels. The global coverage of MI6 and GCHQ is incomparable to the amateurs operating in Victoria's day, thus minimizing any scope for royal leverage.

Domestically, it came to light in 2021 that the Royal Family vetted more than 1,000 laws during Elizabeth II's reign, before Parliament was allowed to debate them. Although the Royal Family claimed that this was just a formality, the family has managed to shape content.[22] Elizabeth may not have vetoed things in the world of intelligence and security policy, but she did draw on decades of classified information—and a long memory—to question, encourage, and warn.

It is almost impossible to judge the effect of this role, because such advice remains a closely kept secret. Even the most fabulously indiscreet minister is careful not to divulge conversations with the monarch when writing their memoirs. In principle, however, the monarch's advice amounts to a check on and a balance to the UK's constitution. Checks on an overbearing executive undermining democracy or on rampant populism is a good thing. In practice, however, and like most aspects of the British constitution, it depends on "good chaps" acting in good faith, as well as on the monarch having the physical ability to perform the check. In her last years, one can only speculate on how the nonagenarian queen's frailty, increasing isolation, and high-profile family problems made an impact on her ability to raise an eyebrow in the direction of the populist prime minister Boris Johnson.

The queen was hugely popular among the British public, and was widely regarded as a stabilizing force. Charles, conversely, has been less so and, at least while prince of Wales, had a reputation for political meddling. Although the public would be glad of the queen's backstage advice and role, the mood may now shift after her death. Many people might realize they are actually Elizabethans rather than hereditary monarchists. In June 1985, two of Britain's longest-serving members of Parliament, Julian Amery and Tony Benn, found themselves together after a meeting of the Commons Select Committee of Privileges. Amery had long been close to MI6 and was a lifelong enthusiast for covert action. Benn was one of Parliament's most avid observers of the secret state. Both had been denizens of Westminster for decades, and they chatted amiably for half an hour, with the conversation gradually turning to the underlying nature of power in Britain. Amery declared: "Oh, we're not a democracy. . . . We're a constitutional monarchy." He explained that it was a "collective monarchy," which consisted of officials and permanent secretaries, while elected ministers could only shift policy slightly, and "only if that is acceptable to the collective Crown." Benn was rather shocked and told him he should say it publicly. Amery replied that he did so and "often." Amery, expressing surprise, then asked his friend: "Surely, you knew it all along?"[23]

Appendix

Ruling the Past—A Note on Methods

Has sufficient time elapsed for part of the truth to be publicly told?
My answer is obviously an unequivocal "No."
—Tommy Lascelles, 1967

On January 2, 1984, Kenneth Rose, a superb writer and doyen of royal biographers, lunched with Princess Margaret. The princess told him "how busy she has been for the past week or two destroying much of the Queen Mother's old correspondence and the battered attaché cases in which it has been kept." Rose was quite aghast at this "terrible news," yet Margaret gushed on enthusiastically: "I have already filled two big sacks and the servants are so pleased at my cleaning up the mess." This was not a momentary whim, but an organized program of destruction; three years later, she was still at it. These included letters from Princess Diana to the Queen Mother.[1]

"Griffin," her chauffeur, was her accomplice in this historical crime. Overseen by the princess, who had pulled on an outsize pair of yellow rubber gloves, he had set up a royal incinerator in a dustbin outside the garage at Kensington Palace where Margaret had an apartment. "The smoke was so thick it made her eyes water and she had to leave," recalls Griffin. They returned repeatedly to Clarence House afterward to collect more letters and papers—and burned them all. He saw Diana's name on a few, and even her crest and handwriting, and there were lots of others, from decades earlier, addressed to the king and queen. "The Princess never said why she was doing it, but she was very determined that they should all be destroyed, thousands of them. I remember thinking we were putting a match to history."[2]

Margaret's behavior is symptomatic of a royal determination to rule not only the present but also the past. Anthony Blunt's famous "raiding expeditions" to the continent in the company of the Windsor librarian—in search of archives, paintings, and jewels—were in fact routine. There is even a prime ministerial file about this in the National Archives titled "Royal Family: Duke of Windsor's Papers: Allegations . . . That They Were Stolen by Secret Agents." Inevitably, the file is closed.[3]

Mountbatten was sent on a similar expedition to Paris and reportedly "stole some of the Duke of Windsor papers during a visit in his declining years."[4] This seems an absurd suggestion, but Rose's wonderful diaries again shine a brief but illuminating light. All of a sudden in 1972, as Edward faltered, there seems to have been a sudden charm offensive. Martin Charteris described "a rather macabre tea party" when the queen visited the duchess in Paris. There was happy conversation in the drawing room while the duke lay dying upstairs. Charteris added with satisfaction that "all his papers are now safely in England." There was a follow-up maneuver, at the duke's funeral at Windsor, when Mountbatten and Prince Philip persuaded the duchess "to part with the rest." Within a day of her return to Paris, a truck drew up in the Bois de Boulogne "and whisked them away."[5]

The removal of the Duke's papers was controversial, and the reverberations of this eventually reached Downing Street. Nick Sanders, Margaret Thatcher's private secretary, wrote forcefully to deny the allegations that the papers were stolen by "the Queen's Secret Agents from the House of the Duchess of Windsor" while she was in London "as the guest of Her Majesty at the Duke's funeral." He insisted that these papers were taken to Windsor "with the full knowledge and consent of the duchess of Windsor."[6] This explanation is most likely correct.

What documents are we missing here? Fortunately, one winsome figure, the writer and biographer James Pope-Hennessy, cast eyes on some of these documents in Paris in 1957. He recalls that after a hearty breakfast, he "settled down to 1936" and found the material "irresistible," adding that if this explosive material was ever published, it would offer a "complete picture of the Abdication chaos." They include "grave letters from ministers," "brilliant" material from Churchill, "screeches" from Lady Oxford, fascinating material from Diana Cooper, and "bleak letters from Queen Mary" all crowded together. This is the wonderful material that the history police have suppressed.[7]

It is not just the big fish that are caught in the net. Small fish are also hunted down. In 2007, William Talon, steward and member of the Queen Mother's staff at Clarence House, died in his Duchy of Cornwall apartment in Kennington, where his body lay undiscovered for some time. The "authorities" then quickly arrived and cleaned out his private papers, including "self-pitying letters from Prince Charles."[8]

All this material makes its way to the vast archive at Windsor Castle. This is clearly a special archive with peculiar rules, and even those who preside over it do not always know what lies inside. There are arcane levels of clearance and access. Tommy Lascelles was perhaps one of the most trusted royal servants, and so was put in charge of this historical treasure house. Yet even he recalls a moment of jealousy when Harold Nicolson, official biographer of George V, was "shown everything," adding that this included intimate letters, "which I, though Keeper of the Archives, had never seen."[9]

Even the loss of the smallest morsel is cause for panic. Prince Charles was not only bullied at Gordonstoun but also stolen from mercilessly by the other boys. Anything with his signature was valuable; even name tags that had been ripped from his vest and pants fetched half a crown with eager local dealers. Panic set in when his English-language exercise book was taken, in which he had expounded on all sort of things, including "theories on corrupt governments"—it had last been seen lying on the prince's desk. Although initially sold for only seven shillings and sixpence, it was soon in London changing hands for thousands of pounds. "Finally, by a clever trick of deception it was retrieved by Special Branch and returned to the parents of the rightful owner."[10]

The Royal Archives are also vast because they are fed by the government machine. Much goes in, but little comes out. Diplomats all around the world are encouraged to report to the royals about royals. Warwick Morris, a lowly third secretary at the British Embassy in Paris in the early 1970s, recalls that there was much to tell. Many French people were fascinated by the British Royal Family, having done away with their own in the revolution. Certain French newspapers and magazines like *France Dimanche* and *Paris Match*, as well as the more sensational ones, featured articles every week about the royals. "These included outrageous and fictitious ones, like the whole Everton football team having been in Princess Anne's bedroom at Buckingham Palace, or the Queen Mother being dead and having a living double." The British Embassy used to send a selection of "these scurrilous stories" to Buckingham Palace from time to time. Never having got any reaction, they eventually wrote proposing to stop. Suddenly a reply came: "No, please don't. The Family derives huge entertainment and amusement from what you send. Keep them coming!"[11]

As we have seen, in so many ways, the intelligence services and the Royal Family have much in common. They are small, secretive, and highly mythologized with a band of loyal devotees at their center. They both know many secrets and, through their various channels, thrive on the gathering of information—although they have not always shared it with each other. Both have even intervened secretly in the affairs of other states.

Both control and curate their own histories carefully; both are exempt from freedom-of-information requests. Historians have to wait a long time for intelligence files to make their way to the National Archives—but at least some do eventually arrive. The members of the Royal Family, by contrast, are the real enemies of history. There is no area where restrictions and redactions are so severe.

Like MI6, they are also engaged in positive information control. For more than half a century, Britain's secret intelligence service has not only assisted the right defectors to pen their memoirs but has also opened the door of its archives to favored historians.[12] The Royal Archives at Windsor, especially files covering more recent decades, operate in exactly the same way. Cameras are forbidden. Even then, historical supplicants obediently have to sign a form promising to let the palace see how they will use the material in advance of publication. They sometimes ask for quotes to be removed from a manuscript.[13] Favored historians are given access to more recent documents, such as King George VI's rather boring diaries, creating an incentive to write yet more syco-phantic biographies. The rest languish on ancient history or hunt for scraps.

Where is the scrap heap? In west London, alongside the Royal Botanic Gardens at Kew, the National Archives are a barren wasteland of royal history. What the historian most wants to see is the minutes of meetings between mon-archs and prime ministers, but they do not exist here—and even if they did, historians would not be allowed to read them. The "files" on Harold Macmillan's weekly audiences with the queen, for example, merely include dull correspon-dence about scheduling and whether the prime minister could wear a certain suit. Even so, many of these are closed.

The only record of these meetings depended on drink. No one else sits in on the prime minister's weekly audience with the queen, each Tuesday after-noon. Clearly, the queen's private secretary would like to attend. So, down the years, the gambit was to offer the various prime ministers a drink afterward and try to debrief them. Martin Charteris found Jim Callaghan very frustrat-ing because he would not play the game. Callaghan recalls that he wanted a drink but "deliberately refused to talk to Martin about our audiences, which I regarded as confidential between the queen and her PM." It was not all about spies and secrets—often, the queen would talk about family matters and clearly found the confidential setting therapeutic.[14] Where prime min-isters played the private secretaries' game, a partial record may exist in the Windsor archives.

On the rare occasion when a good file on the royals makes its way to the archives, it can be clawed back. In 2018, Philip Murphy, director of the Institute of Commonwealth Studies and one of Britain's most skillful royal researchers, found a file about the royal yacht. Murphy's discovery was a classic example of historical sleuthing, for instead of heading for the highlights of Cabinet Office files, he had doggedly pursued a trail into obscure Welsh Office material. Here he found a gem.

What he was able to demonstrate was that in the 1990s, when the queen was crying public tears for the retirement of the royal yacht *Britannia*, she was privately lobbying for a brand-new vessel. The file contained a delicately worded letter from her deputy private secretary, Kenneth Scott. He explained that she was "deeply interested in the subject" and would "naturally very much welcome" a replacement for the twenty-first century. The *Britannia* is now berthed in Edinburgh and is visited by hundreds of thousands of tourists each year. But Prince Philip wanted it broken up and the familiar fittings that he loved installed in a new vessel. When this story emerged in *The Times*, there was trouble. The palace rang the Cabinet Office and stamped its foot, so in no time at all the history police were on their way to Kew. The file has now been withdrawn, and the catalogue says: "This record is closed whilst access is under review."[15]

The relative absence of royal records even prompted one enterprising historian to create his own. Martin Allen wrote three books about the Nazis based partly on forged documents, including one titled *Hidden Agenda: How the Duke of Windsor Betrayed the Allies*. This triggered a police investigation, and the National Archives eventually uncovered the full scale of the deception. It unearthed some twenty-nine faked documents, planted in a dozen separate files at some point between 2000 and 2005, which were used to bolster Allen's specious arguments.[16] The journalist and historian Max Hastings observed that it was hard to conceive of actions "more damaging to the cause of preserving the nation's heritage than wilfully forging documents designed to alter our historical record."[17]

What about interviews? In writing this book, we have mostly tended to stay away from the temptations of oral evidence. All stories grow with the telling, but royal stories grow faster. Nevertheless, these testimonies are fascinating, and we are always interested in stories about "the files." With MI6, it is tales of jewelry thefts on behalf of the crown or top agents being smuggled into the palace to meet a monarch as a special treat. With MI5, it is normally stories about the surveillance of the royals themselves. A number of knowledgeable figures at MI5 have asserted that dossiers on the Windsors did exist and were kept out of the main registry because they were "too hot." Instead, they were kept in a separate safe in the director general's office. This was largely because Edward was thought to be too close to Ribbentrop. We are assured that these files, if they existed, are now long gone.[18]

The phenomenon of the "special" office safe is fascinating—every government department has one. Sherard Cowper-Coles, one of Britain's most distinguished diplomats, who served as ambassador in war-torn Kabul, offers us a rare glimpse of such a fascinating facility. When serving as private secretary in the office of the most senior diplomat in the Foreign Office, he recalls that in the corner sat "an ancient safe" that was "about the size of a washing machine." It did not contain big national secrets in the sense of material with eye-wateringly high classifications, or compartmentalized stuff from secret agents. Instead, it held material that was "too sensitive" to be placed in the main Foreign Office file registry. What did its "explosive contents" consist of? It was a selection of delicious scandal: mole-hunting in MI6, secret payments to foreign rulers, and, of course, complaints from ambassadors "about the behaviour of members of the Royal Family visiting their parish."[19] For decades, the misdeeds of Britain's royals and foreign monarchs alike were a rich source of dinner table stories in all government departments.[20]

Even fictitious files have their uses. The infamous "China Dossier" on Mrs. Simpson is a case in point. Our conclusions are that this almost certainly did not exist and that no one ever laid eyes on it. But by 1951, the Windsors' circle, including Churchill, were being told of the China Dossier. Kenneth de Courcy, a close friend of Edward, probably rightly, concludes that this "file" was used repeatedly to deflate continued supporters of Edward and Wallis. Jock Colville insisted that, despite his many years alternating between Downing Street and the palace, he had "never heard" of the dossier.[21]

No less than in the spy world, the story of the Windsors is often a wilderness of mirrors. Despite these impediments, we have painstakingly pieced together fragments scattered across thousands of files and personal accounts. Memoirs are a potentially useful source; people love to write about their encounters with royalty. Yet these too are censored. The queen's comment about assassinating a Middle Eastern leader was mysteriously airbrushed from Evelyn Shuckburgh's published diaries about the Suez Crisis. Alexander Cadogan's famous wartime published diaries are strangely thin on references to royals. Nomadic historians have to travel far and wide to forage in the hand-written originals.

Writing intelligence history is difficult; writing contemporary royal history, using primary source material, is more difficult still. Yet as the intelligence services have become more open, so too has their relationship with the Royal Family. But beyond the much-publicized royal tours of shiny new intelligence headquarters, a deeper and far more clandestine relationship binds these two powerful institutions together. Like the intelligence services, the crown has its secrets. Neither wants them to be told.

Are the members of the Royal Family the antichrists of history? Perhaps not entirely so. It is certainly reported that Elizabeth II did not like books about the Royal Family. She had often refused to say anything to official royal biographers; indeed, even figures as loyal as Philip Ziegler had been blanked. Yet there is one book about the Royal Family that Elizabeth liked—her own. Apparently, she kept a meticulous diary. Historians can only dream of the wonderful secrets it contains. One day, perhaps we will read it . . .

Acknowledgments

Writing about spies is challenging; writing about royals is more difficult; and writing about spies and royals has sometimes seemed impossible. But the intellectual journey has been fascinating, not least because of what it has taught us about efforts to control and shape the past. Research for this book began back in 2015 and took us well beyond our comfort zone. It was made more difficult by the COVID-19 "lockdown" in 2020–21, which even hampered access to books in our own university's offices. Every successful raid on a body of records depends on good intelligence, and so often we have benefited from the thorough reconnaissance of others. Therefore, more than with our previous books, we have depended on the kindness of friends and invaluable assistance from many people over many years, and we are very pleased to be able to thank them here. Any errors of fact or interpretation, of course, remain our own. Please do write to us with comments and corrections at r.j.aldrich@warwick.ac.uk or rory.cormac@nottingham.ac.uk.

A wide circle of friends and colleagues have encouraged, warned, advised, and consulted with us. We would particularly like to thank Christopher Andrew, Sally Bedell Smith, Huw Bennett, Gill Bennett, Piers Brendon, Jock Bruce, Ed Burke, Gordon Corera, Oliver Daddow, Philip Davies, Annabelle de Heus, Stephen Dorril, Rob Dover, Peter Dunn, Huw Dylan, Tom Eason, David Easter, John Ferris, Tom Frew, Jamie Gaskarth, Jules Gaspard, Liam Gearon, David Gioe, Anthony Glees, Susan Glen, Michael Goodman, Andrew Hammond, Jonathan Haslam, Max Hastings, Peter Hennessy, Michael Herman, Lewis Herrington, Davinia Hoggarth, Mark Hollingsworth, Gerry Hughes, Peter Jackson, Rhodri Jeffreys-Jones, Clive Jones, Matthew Jones, Athina Karatzogianni, John Kasuku, Sheila Kerr, Anthony King, Dan Larson, Paul Lashmar, Thomas Leahy, Magda Long, Andrew Lownie, W. Scott Lucas, Paul McGarr, Paul Maddrell, Victor Madeira, Tom Maguire, Peter Martland, Spencer Mawby, Paul Mercer, Chris Moran, Philip Murphy, David Omand, Mark Phythian, David Porter, Tilman Remme, Dina Rezk, Lee Richards, Daniela Richterova, Peter Rooke, David Schaefer, Ann Sebba, Zakia Shiraz, Michael Smith, David Stafford, Mark Stout, Phil Tinline, Karina Urbach, Damien Van Puyvelde, Kate Vigurs, Calder Walton, Wesley K. Wark, Michael Warner, Cees Wiebes, Simon Willmetts, Nikita Wolf, and John Young. In particular, Mike

Kenner and Philip Murphy both read sections of this book for us, providing helpful corrections and feedback.

Despite the unfortunate disruptions to travel in 2020–21, our research took us to fabulous places, from the Hoover Institution in Stanford to the Resistance Museum in Oslo. We are grateful to them all, but in particular to the help and support of archivists and librarians on both sides of the Atlantic. These include, in the UK, the National Archives, Churchill College Cambridge, the Bodleian Library, the British Library, Cambridge University Library, the Churchill Archives, the House of Lords Library, National Archives II, the Royal Archives, and King's College London. We are especially grateful to Anthea Boylston and Celia Catchpole for allowing us to quote from the Seabury Ashmead-Bartlett Papers. We are grateful to "the permission of Her Majesty the Queen" for allowing us to quote from the Royal Archives. In the US, we are grateful to staff at the National Archives and Records Administration, the presidential libraries, Library of Congress, Georgetown University, and the National Security Archive.

The universities of Warwick and Nottingham have provided stimulating environments for conducting this research over the years, including generous periods of study leave. Warwick's unique undergraduate research program provided us with two wonderful researchers, Bryan Hughes and Kiran Heer Kaur, who assisted our work at Kew. Nottingham kindly funded a fact-checker, and we are very grateful to Charley Ferris for carrying out this work. We are also grateful to Anastasia Zabludovskaya for translating documents. Colleagues have been incredibly supportive, including through times of personal difficulty (special thanks to George Christou, David Gill, Chris Moran, Nikki Muckle, and Andrew Mumford). Our wonderful postdoctoral researchers and postgraduate students at both universities have provided constant encouragement and criticism. Our respective secret intelligence modules provided tough but constructive testing grounds for many a royal anecdote.

A few individuals deserve special thanks, and some sadly are now longer with us. Matthew Aid, Julian Lewis, Bradley F. Smith, and David Stafford collectively and long ago pioneered the lateral research techniques we use today and that will be deployed by our research students tomorrow. Michael Herman developed the idea of "intelligence power" that informs this study. Oddly, one of the most helpful authors is someone we have never met. The wonderful works of Kenneth Rose were often our unseen companion; and his diaries, beautifully edited by D. R. Thorpe, illuminated our path.

This book would not have happened without Paul Elston, who spotted the potential in a couple of pages about King Edward VIII in our previous book *The Black Door*. A visionary director, he tenaciously turned it into a highly successful two-part television documentary on the Windsors for Channel 4. This then evolved into two further documentaries on royals and intelligence, and we are particularly grateful to Paul and his very professional team for continually pushing us on, and to Channel 4 for placing their faith in us and allowing us to showcase deep archival research. Helen Ford at the Warwick Modern Records Centre has generously provided us with the university equivalent of Pinewood Studios on the fringes of Coventry. We are grateful to our literary agents, Andrew Lownie in the UK, together with Martin Redfern and a tremendous group at Northbank Talent for North America. Likewise, we are grateful to Don Jacobs and his colleagues at Georgetown University Press, together with the editors of the Studies in Intelligence History Series, for their wonderful care and attention in developing and publishing the book.

Above all, once again, we owe an enormous debt to our families. Rory's family has doubled in size since this project began. Finlay and Genevieve have provided ample distractions, and a growing interest in inappropriate royal bedtime stories, especially the investiture of Prince Charles and the kidnapping of Princess Anne. This book, and indeed much else, would not be here without Joanne. Thank you. It should also be noted that Christy Cormac, who is fed up with Joanne receiving acknowledgments in book after book, is a "hero." Richard is grateful to Harrie, Tom, and Nick for enduring endless anecdotes about the antics of royal dogs of every shape and size, especially the royal Labrador who was taught "basic French" at Sandringham before being gifted from the French president. Libby has tolerated Richard's inexplicable passion for Princess Margaret with commendable good humor and quiet bemusement. As always, she has offered boundless love and encouragement despite the late nights, turning to the gray light of dawn, as the book drew to its conclusion.

Notes

INTRODUCTION

Epigraph: Fleming, *On Her Majesty's Secret Service.*
1. Hennessy, *Establishment*, 17.

CHAPTER 1. QUEEN VICTORIA

Epigraph: Hibbert, *Queen Victoria*, 424.
1. Porter, *Plots*, 83–84; Andrew, *Secret Service*, 5, 6.
2. Porter, *Plots*, 81.
3. St. Aubyn, *Queen Victoria*, 236; Marshal, *Victoria*, 103.
4. Queen Victoria's Journals, December 22, 1851.
5. Leopold to Victoria, July 24, 1837; Benson and Esher, *Letters*, vol. 1, 113.
6. Leopold to Victoria, October 9, 1837, Benson and Esher, 120.
7. Queen Victoria's Journals, March 5, 1839.
8. Weintraub, *Victoria*, 144, 156–57, 170.
9. Sinclair, *Other Victoria*, 75.
10. Sinclair, 20–21.
11. Hibbert, *Queen Victoria*, 196.
12. Queen Victoria's Journals, June 10, 1840.
13. Queen Victoria's Journals.
14. Murphy, *Shooting Victoria*, 55.
15. Queen Victoria's Journals, June 10, 1840; Hibbert, *Queen Victoria*, 421.
16. Murphy, *Shooting Victoria*, 59–60.
17. Queen Victoria's Journals, June 10, 11, and 12, 1840.
18. Queen Victoria's Journals, June 15, 1840.
19. Guizot, *Embassy*, 117.
20. Guizot, 5–6.
21. Guizot, 37.
22. Queen Victoria's Journals, June 12 and 15, 1840; July 11, 1840.
23. Murphy, *Shooting Victoria*, 4–5.
24. Griffin, "Detective Policing," 232.
25. St. Aubyn, *Queen Victoria*, 162.
26. Thomson, *Story*, 105.
27. St. Aubyn, *Queen Victoria*, 162.
28. Murphy, *Shooting Victoria*, 180.
29. Queen Victoria's Journals, July 1, 1842.
30. Murphy, *Shooting Victoria*, 54–64.
31. Lacey, *Royal*, 19.

32. Victoria to Leopold, May 31, 1842; Benson and Esher, *Letters of Queen Victoria*, vol. 1, 499.
33. Queen Victoria's Journals, May 30 and 31, 1842.
34. Moran, "Punitive Uses," 171.
35. Queen Victoria's Journals, July 1, 1842.
36. Queen Victoria's Journals, July 3, 1842.
37. Holmes, *Queen Victoria*, 58.
38. St. Aubyn, *Queen Victoria*, 163.
39. Griffin, "Detective Policing," 226, 292, 311.
40. Flanders, "Creation"; Worthington, *Rise*, 3–75.
41. Black, "Victorian Information Society," 53–90.
42. Lyon, *Electronic Eye*, 14.
43. Queen Victoria's Journals, January 20, 1843.
44. Queen Victoria's Journals, January 21, 1843.
45. Peel to Victoria, January 25, 1843; Benson and Esher, *Letters*, vol. 1, 572.
46. Chamberlain, "Charlton History."
47. Queen Victoria's Journals, March 5, 1843.
48. Rix, "Towards a More Just Insanity Defence," 44–52.
49. Murphy, *Shooting Victoria*, 225.
50. Peel to Victoria, March 27, 1843; Benson and Esher, *Letters*, vol. 1, 591–92.
51. Campbell, *Fenian Fire*, 10.
52. Murphy, *Shooting Victoria*, 275.
53. Queen Victoria's Journals, May 20, 1849.
54. Darryl, June 27, 1850.
55. St. Aubyn, *Queen Victoria*, 164.
56. Smith, "British Post Office," 189–99.
57. Porter, *Plots*, 77–78.
58. Moran, *Classified*, 27.
59. Vincent, "Surveillance," 1–3.
60. Queen Victoria's Journals, April 4 and May 11, 1838; January 1, 1839.
61. Queen Victoria's Journals, January 1, 1839; September 2, 1840; December 29, 1840.
62. Queen Victoria's Journals, January 3, 1839.
63. Queen Victoria's Journals, October 5, 1838.
64. Queen Victoria's Journals, October 6, 1838.
65. Queen Victoria's Journals, September 30, 1838.
66. Queen Victoria's Journals, November 11, 1838.
67. Queen Victoria's Journals, May 3, 1839.
68. Queen Victoria's Journals, June 25, 1844.
69. Vincent, "Surveillance," 1–3.
70. Porter, *Plots*, 77–78.
71. Cobain, *History Thieves*, 45.
72. Andrew, *Secret World*, 381–83.
73. Queen Victoria's Journals, March 1, 1845.
74. Queen Victoria's Journals, March 6, 1853.
75. Queen Victoria's Journals, December 1, 1855.
76. Porter, *Refugee Question*, 1–11, 201–28.
77. Kemp, *Bombs*, 51.
78. Griffin, "Detective Policing," 294–95.

79. Griffin, 299–300.
80. Griffin, 301; Porter, *Refugee Question*, 149–52.
81. Griffin, "Detective Policing," 304.
82. Queen Victoria's Journals, April 2 and 4, 1848.
83. Brown, *Palmerston*, 90.
84. Queen Victoria's Journals, January 22, 1849.
85. Queen Victoria's Journals, January 22, 1849.
86. Queen Victoria's Journals, January 22, 1849; Victoria to Russell, January 22, 1849; Benson and Esher, *Letters*, vol. 2, 251. See also Brown, *Palmerston*, 90.
87. Queen Victoria's Journals, January 24, 1849.
88. Chamberlain, *Pax Britannica?* 96.
89. Marshall, *Victoria*, 107.
90. Porter, *Plots*, 91.
91. Porter, 88.
92. Queen Victoria's Journals, May 1–2, 1851.
93. Queen Victoria's Journals, October 14 and 23, 1851.
94. Queen Victoria's Journals, October 28 and 31, 1851.
95. Queen Victoria's Journals, November 2, 1851.
96. Albert to Duke Ernst II, Duke of Saxe-Coburg-Gotha, December 29, 1851; Bolitho, *Prince Consort*, 126.
97. Queen Victoria's Journals, April 22, 1853.
98. Queen Victoria's Journals, May 26, 1850.
99. Leopold to Victoria, June 3, 1853; Benson and Esher, *Letters*, vol. 2, 544.
100. Queen Victoria's Journals, October 13, 1848; Marshall, *Victoria*, 107.
101. Queen Victoria's Journals, October 13, 1848.
102. Leopold to Victoria, June 3, 1853; Benson and Esher, *Letters*, vol. 2, 544.
103. Queen Victoria's Journals, February 26, 1853.
104. Marshall, *Victoria*, 104–6.
105. Queen Victoria's Journals, December 22, 1851.
106. Queen Victoria's Journals, March 3, 1852.
107. Queen Victoria's Journals, March 18, 1853.
108. Queen Victoria's Journals, January 15, 1858.
109. Porter, *Plots*, 91–92; St. Aubyn, *Queen Victoria*, 304.
110. Queen Victoria's Journals, February 20 and 28, 1858.
111. Queen Victoria's Journals, January 28, 1858.
112. Porter, *Plots*, 92.
113. Marshall, *Victoria*, 117.
114. Queen Victoria's Journals, February 20, 1858.
115. Queen Victoria's Journals, February 19, 1858.
116. Malmesbury to Victoria, March 7, 1858; Benson and Esher, *Letters*, vol. 3, 346.

CHAPTER 2. QUEEN VICTORIA'S SECRETS

Epigraph: Queen Victoria's Journals, April 28, 1866.
1. Queen Victoria's Journals, August 7, 1853.
2. Victoria to Clarendon, August 24, 1953; Benson and Esher, *Letters of Queen Victoria*, vol. 2, 549.
3. Weintraub, *Victoria*, 235–36.

4. Queen Victoria's Journals, October 9, 1853.

5. Andrew, *Secret Service*, 8–9; Wade, *Spies*, 69.

6. Hibbert, *Queen Victoria*, 222; Weintraub, *Victoria*, 232–34.

7. Queen Victoria's Journals, January 4, 1854.

8. Queen Victoria's Journals, January 9, 1854.

9. Weintraub, *Victoria*, 235.

10. Queen Victoria's Journals, January 21 and 23, 1854.

11. Weintraub, *Uncrowned King*, 296–98. See also Weintraub, *Victoria*, 232–34.

12. Hibbert, *Queen Victoria*, 223.

13. Weintraub, *Uncrowned King*, 6–18.

14. Andrew, *Secret World*, 402.

15. Quoted by Hibbert, *Queen Victoria*, 224.

16. Andrew, *Secret World*, 402.

17. Judd, *Crimean War*, 95.

18. Weintraub, *Victoria*, 242.

19. Queen Victoria's Journals, March 29, 1854.

20. Harris, *British Military Intelligence*, 234–58.

21. Queen Victoria's Journals, August 2, 1854.

22. ODNB: Cattley, Charles Robert.

23. Andrew, *Secret World*, 404–5; ODNB: Cattley, Charles Robert.

24. Queen Victoria's Journals, July 27, 1855; Harris, *British Military Intelligence*, 69.

25. Victoria to Panmure, July 30, 1855; Benson and Esher, *Letters*, vol. 3, 170.

26. Bartley, *Queen Victoria*, 145–75.

27. Hibbert, *Queen Victoria*, 225.

28. Queen Victoria's Journals, April 18, 1855.

29. Weintraub, *Victoria*, 246.

30. Panmure to Simpson, September 12, 1855; Benson and Esher, *Letters*, vol. 3, 181.

31. Queen Victoria's Journals, January 17, 1856.

32. Weintraub, *Victoria*, 255.

33. Queen Victoria's Journals, February 27, 1856.

34. Queen Victoria's Journals, March 30, 1856.

35. Queen Victoria's Journals, March 13, 1854.

36. Sinclair, *Other Victoria*, 50–52.

37. Pakula, *Uncommon Woman*, 106.

38. Pakula, 197.

39. Pakula, 354–55.

40. Kollander, "Empress Frederick," 53.

41. Sinclair, *Other Victoria*, 82–87.

42. Vicky to Victoria, June 8, 1863; Buckle, *Letters of Queen Victoria, 1862 to 1878*, vol. 1, 87.

43. Vicky to Victoria, June 21, 1863; Buckle, 92.

44. Hardie, *Political Influence*, 146; Victoria to Vicky, January 27, 1864; Buckle, *Letters of Queen Victoria, 1862 to 1878*, vol. 1, 153; Victoria to Granville, January 27, 1864; Bourne, *Foreign Policy*, 373.

45. Mosse, "Queen Victoria," 273.

46. E.g., see Queen Victoria's Journals, February 8 and 11, 1864.

47. Sinclair, *Other Victoria*, 93.

48. Vicky to Victoria, April 13, 1864; Buckle, *Letters of Queen Victoria, 1862 to 1878*, vol. 1, 170–71.

49. Victoria to Russell, April 19, 1864; Buckle, vol. 1, 174.
50. Vicky to Victoria, May 26, 1864; Ponsonby, *Letters*, 54–55.
51. Queen Victoria's Journals, June 20, 1864.
52. Mosse, "Queen Victoria," 263–77.
53. Mosse, 278–79.
54. Hardie, *Political Influence*, 152, 157.
55. Steinberg, *Bismarck*, 430.
56. Mosse, "Crown," 206.
57. Sinclair, *Other Victoria*, 106–7.
58. Mosse, "Crown," 214.
59. Duchess of Coburg to Victoria, March 28, 1866; Buckle, *Letters of Queen Victoria, 1862 to 1878*, vol. 1, 812.
60. Sinclair, *Other Victoria*, 106–7.
61. Sinclair, 107; Vicky to Victoria, March 20, 1866; Buckle, *Letters of Queen Victoria, 1862 to 1878*, vol. 1, 305.
62. Sinclair, *Other Victoria*, 106–7.
63. Queen Victoria's Journals, February 4, 1863.
64. Mosse, "Crown," 212.
65. Sinclair, *Other Victoria*, 108–9.
66. Queen Victoria's Journals, April 9, 1866.
67. Loftus to Grey, April 14, 1866; Buckle, *Letters of Queen Victoria, 1862 to 1878*, vol. 2, 318.
68. Queen Victoria's Journals, April 1–2, 18, and 23, 1866; Sinclair, *Other Victoria*, 108–9.
69. Queen Victoria's Journals, April 28, 1866.
70. Queen Victoria's Journals, April 23, 1866.
71. Queen Victoria's Journals, May 15, 1866.
72. Otte, *Foreign Office Mind*, 37.
73. Mosse, "Crown," 208–22.
74. Victoria to Stanley, August 7, 1866; Buckle, *Letters of Queen Victoria, 1862 to 1878*, vol. 2, 364.
75. Otte, *Foreign Office Mind*, 39.
76. Sinclair, *Other Victoria*, 129.
77. Howard, *Franco-Prussian War*, 50.
78. Vicky to Victoria, March 12, 1870; Buckle, *Letters of Queen Victoria, 1862 to 1878*, vol. 2, 10; Millman, *British Policy*, 170.
79. Pakula, *Uncommon Woman*, 266.
80. Memorandum by Crown Prince of Prussia (undated; July 1870); Buckle, *Letters of Queen Victoria, 1862 to 1878*, vol. 2, 10.
81. Queen Victoria's Journals, July 13, 1870.
82. Millman, *British Policy*, 190.
83. Sinclair, *Other Victoria*, 140–43; Howard, *Franco-Prussian War*, 53.
84. Pakula, *Uncommon Woman*, 269.
85. Bourne, *Foreign Policy*, 120.
86. Queen Victoria's Journals, July 15 and 10, 1870.
87. Clarendon to Victoria, March 31, 1866; Buckle, *Letters of Queen Victoria, 1862 to 1878*, vol. 1, 314.
88. Granville to Victoria, July 15, 1870; Buckle, vol. 2, 35.
89. Vicky to Victoria, July 18, 1870; Buckle, vol. 2, 43.

90. Millman, *British Policy*, 201.
91. Millman; Seton-Watson, *Britain*, 32.
92. Queen Victoria's Journals, July 26, 1870.
93. Millman, *British Policy*, 202.
94. Pakula, *Uncommon Woman*, 271.
95. Ponsonby to Victoria, October 12, 1870; Buckle, *Letters of Queen Victoria, 1862 to 1878*, vol. 2, 75; Hardie, *Political Influence*, 158.
96. Sinclair, *Other Victoria*, 147.
97. Queen Victoria's Journals, July 31, 1870.
98. Sinclair, *Other Victoria*, 150–51.
99. Evans, *Memoirs*, 169–98.
100. Queen Victoria's Journals, September 23, 1870.
101. Burgoyne to Ponsonby, September 15, 1870; Buckle, *Letters of Queen Victoria, 1862–1878*, vol. 2, 68–70; see also Evans, *Memoirs*.
102. Burgoyne to Ponsonby, September 15, 1870; Buckle, 68–70; Queen Victoria's Journals, September 23, 1870.
103. Burgoyne to Ponsonby, September 15, 1870; Buckle, *Letters of Queen Victoria, 1862–1878*, vol. 2, 68–70.
104. Queen Victoria's Journals, August 14, 1884.
105. Queen Victoria's Journals, January 30, 1890.
106. Sinclair, *Other Victoria*, 168.
107. St. Aubyn, *Queen Victoria*, 462.
108. Erickson, *Her Little Majesty*, 153.
109. Sinclair, *Other Victoria*, 202.
110. Pakula, *Uncommon Woman*, 398; see also 390–91.
111. Hibbert, *Queen Victoria*, 389.
112. Sinclair, *Other Victoria*, 220–21.
113. Pakula, *Uncommon Woman*, 599.
114. Vicky to Victoria, August 24, 1889; Ponsonby, *Letters of the Empress Frederick*, 384–85.
115. Cathcart, *Anne*, 88.
116. Clay, *King*, 79.

CHAPTER 3. QUEEN VICTORIA'S GREAT GAME

Epigraph: Queen Victoria's Journal, January 21, 1893.
1. Wade, *Spies*, 2–15.
2. Farwell, *Queen Victoria's Little Wars*, 1.
3. Andrew, *Secret Service*, 5.
4. Cowles, *Romanovs*; Van der Kiste, *John Alfred*; VIC/MAIN/H/41/131 Ponsonby to HM 19/1/74; Queen Victoria's Journals, March 13, 1881.
5. RA:VIC/MAIN/H/42/82, HM to Derby, June 11, 1877, and 83, Derby to HM, June 12, 1877.
6. Victoria to Romanian ambassador, March 3, 1879, www.raabcollection.com/queen -victoria-autograph/queen-victoria-signed-height-victorian-diplomacy-during -great-game-queen.
7. RA:VIC/MAIN/H/46/103, Sir Frank Lascelles to HM 30/1/95. His observations, addressed directly to the queen, can be found at FO800/17.

8. Andrew, *Secret Service*, 11.
9. See, e.g., Queen Victoria's Journals, December 15, 1891.
10. Barry, *War for the East*, 116.
11. Ferris, "Lord Salisbury," 25.
12. Ferris, 9.
13. Ferris, 24.
14. Burnaby, Frederick Gustavus, ODNB.
15. Hopkirk, *Great Game*, 376–77.
16. Hopkirk, 378–79.
17. Ponsonby, *Henry Ponsonby*, 170–71.
18. ODNB: Burnaby, Frederick.
19. Hibbert, *Queen Victoria*, 362.
20. Ponsonby, untitled memorandum, July 8, 1876; Disraeli to Victoria, July 14, 1876; Buckle, *Letters*, vol. 2, 470–72.
21. Victoria, untitled memorandum, September 7, 1877; Buckle, *Letters of Queen Victoria, 1862 to 1878*, vol. 2, 567; see also Hardie, *Political Influence*, 161.
22. Quoted by Hibbert, *Queen Victoria*, 362.
23. Weintraub, *Queen Victoria*, 422.
24. Isba, *Gladstone*, 171–73; see also Baylen, "Madame Olga," 255–71.
25. Weintraub, *Queen Victoria*, 424.
26. Hopkirk, *Great Game*, 378–79.
27. Ponsonby, August 30, 1877; Ponsonby, *Henry Ponsonby*, 165–66.
28. Hibbert, *Queen Victoria*, 36; Hopkirk, *Great Game*, 378–79.
29. Disraeli to Victoria, May 2, 1877; Buckle, *Letters of Queen Victoria, 1862 to 1878*, vol. 2, 535; Victoria to Derby, June 8, 1877, Derby to Victoria, June 11, 1877; Buckle, 539–41.
30. Prince of Wales to Victoria, August 1, 1877; Buckle, 559.
31. Wellesley to Victoria, August 30, 1877; Buckle, 565–66.
32. Hardie, *Political Influence*, 162.
33. Queen Victoria's Journals, August 8, 1877.
34. Queen Victoria's Journals, July 29 and 30, 1877.
35. Charmley and Davey, "Invisible Politician," 28.
36. Bourne, *Foreign Policy*, 131.
37. Weintraub, *Queen Victoria*, 428.
38. Charmley and Davey, "Invisible Politician," 30–32.
39. Ponsonby, August 16, 1877; Ponsonby, *Henry Ponsonby*, 164.
40. Charmley and Davey, "Invisible Politician," 30–32.
41. Hibbert, *Queen Victoria*, 363.
42. Thanks to Barbara Emerson for pointing this out.
43. Ferris, "Lord Salisbury," 24.
44. Barry, *War*, 114–17; Wellesley, *Recollections*, 133–47.
45. Ferris, "Lord Salisbury," 24.
46. Queen Victoria's Journals, February 12, 1878.
47. Queen Victoria's Journals, February 15, 1878.
48. Queen Victoria's Journals, February 20, 1878.
49. Queen Victoria's Journals, March 21, 1878.
50. Hopkirk, *Great Game*, 380.
51. Hopkirk, 380–81.

52. Queen Victoria's Journals, September 15 and 19, 1878; October 12 and 24, 1878.
53. Hopkirk, *Great Game.*
54. Johnson, *Spying,* 146.
55. Queen Victoria's Journals, August 19, 1878.
56. Queen Victoria's Journals, September 14, 1878.
57. Hopkirk, *Great Game,* 386.
58. Queen Victoria's Journals, September 6, 1879.
59. Victoria to Disraeli, September 6, 1879; Buckle, *Letters of Queen Victoria, 1862 to 1878,* vol. 3, 42.
60. Victoria to Ponsonby, May 30, 1882; Ponsonby, *Henry Ponsonby,* 301.
61. Northbrook to Victoria, July 3, 1882; Buckle, 304–5.
62. Weintraub, *Queen Victoria,* 453; Farwell, *Queen Victoria's Little Wars,* 254.
63. Queen Victoria's Journals, August 11, 1882.
64. Victoria to Granville, July 26, 1882; Buckle, *Letters of Queen Victoria, 1862 to 1878,* vol. 3, 313.
65. Farwell, *Queen Victoria's Little Wars,* 253–69.
66. ODNB: Wolseley, Garnet.
67. Alison, Sir Archibald, ODNB.
68. Queen Victoria's Journals, August 31, 1882; Buckle, *Letters of Queen Victoria, 1886 to 1901,* vol. 3, 322.
69. Childers to Victoria, August 6, 1882; Buckle, 322.
70. Ponsonby to Wolseley, August 25, 1882; Ponsonby, *Henry Ponsonby,* 224.
71. Queen Victoria's Journals, September 11, 1882; Farwell, *Queen Victoria's Little Wars,* 253–69.
72. Victoria to Gladstone, September 21, 1882; Buckle, *Letters of Queen Victoria, 1886 to 1901,* vol. 3, 338.
73. Fielding, "Major General Sir Alexander Bruce Tulloch."
74. Wade, *Spies,* 116–18.
75. Queen Victoria's Journals, December 11, 1882.
76. RA:VIC/MAIN/H/45/20, Ponsonby to Lord Granville and Lord Kimberley, March 17, 1885.
77. Farwell, *Queen Victoria's Little Wars,* 316.
78. RA:VIC/MAIN/Q/21/633, Ponsonby to Granville, June 15, 1882.
79. RA:VIC/MAIN/Q/21/633, Granville to HM, July 28, 1882.
80. Andrew, *Secret Service,* 5–6.
81. Frankland, *Witness,* 198–203; ODNB: Wolseley, Garnet.
82. Queen Victoria's Journals, August 22, 1886.
83. Queen Victoria's Journals, August 22–24, 1886.
84. Queen Victoria's Journals, August 27–September 1, 1886.
85. Queen Victoria's Journals, September 1, 1886.
86. Rekun, *How Russia Lost Bulgaria,* 117.
87. Queen Victoria's Journals, September 2, 1886. The government entered a secret agreement with Reuters in 1894, paying £500 for access to confidential reports. See West, *A–Z,* 447.
88. Queen Victoria's Journals, September 4, 1886.
89. Jelavich, *Tsarist Russia,* 233–56.
90. Basu, *Victoria and Abdul,* 57–59.
91. Hibbert, *Queen Victoria,* 447–48; Taylor, *Empress,* 254; Basu, *Victoria and Abdul,* 188.

92. Basu, *Victoria and Abdul*, 203, 284.
93. Hibbert, *Queen Victoria*, 447–48; Taylor, *Empress*, 254; Basu, *Victoria and Abdul*, 188.
94. Quoted by Hibbert, *Queen Victoria*, 449.
95. Basu, *Victoria and Abdul*, 191, 224–27.
96. Baird, *Victoria*, 454–55.
97. Miles, *Empress*, 253; Basu, *Victoria and Abdul*, 209–10.
98. Taylor, *Empress*, 253.
99. Taylor, 256–57.
100. Salisbury to Victoria, October 16, 1895; Buckle, *Letters of Queen Victoria, 1886 to 1901*, vol. 2, 567.
101. Baird, *Victoria*, 456.
102. Taylor, *Empress*, 256–57.
103. Reid, *Ask Sir James*, 151–55.
104. Hibbert, *Queen Victoria*, 451–53; Ray, "Queen and Karim."
105. Baird, *Victoria*, 455.
106. Basu, *Victoria and Abdul*, 228.
107. Taylor, *Empress*, 254.
108. Leach, "Lost Diary."

CHAPTER 4. QUEEN VICTORIA'S SECURITY

Epigraph: Salisbury to Victoria, October 20, 1898; Buckle, *Letters of Queen Victoria, 1886–1901*, vol. 3, 294–95.

1. Yarmolinsky, *Road*, 272–87; Radzinsky, *Alexander II*, 417–19.
2. Yarmolinsky, *Road*, 286–87, Radzinsky, *Alexander II*, 414-5.
3. Ponsonby, *Henry Ponsonby*, 389.
4. Hughes, "British Opinion," 261.
5. RA:VIC/MAIN/H/43/74, Duke of Edinburgh to HM, March 21, 1881.
6. RA:VIC/MAIN/H/44/7, translation of Grand Duke of Hesse to HM, April 4, 1881.
7. Queen Victoria's Journals, April 1, 1881.
8. RA:VIC/MAIN/H/44/23, Ponsonby to HM, April 11, 1881; 24, QV to Ponsonby April 11, 1881.
9. Porter, *Plots*, 102.
10. RA:VIC/MAIN/H/44/27, Ponsonby to Granville, April 12, 1881.
11. Queen Victoria's Journals, March 30, 1881.
12. Wilson and Adams, *Special Branch*, 40–41; see also RA:VIC/MAIN/H/43.
13. RA:VIC/MAIN/H/43/107, Ponsonby to Granville, March 27, 1881.
14. RA:VIC/MAIN/H/43/108, Granville to Ponsonby, March 30, 1881.
15. Murphy, *Shooting Victoria*, 463–67.
16. St. Aubyn, *Queen Victoria*, 373.
17. Queen Victoria's Journals, March 4, 1868.
18. Campbell, *Fenian Fire*, 11.
19. Andrew, *Secret Service*, 17.
20. Ponsonby to Victoria, March 16, 1883; Buckle, *Letters of Queen Victoria*, ser. 2, vol. 3, 416–47.
21. Harcourt to Victoria, March 17, 1883, Buckle, 417.
22. E.g., Queen Victoria's Journals, October 13, 1883.
23. Campbell, *Fenian Fire*, 11.

24. Queen Victoria's Journals, October 14, 1884.
25. Wilson and Adams, *Special Branch*, 74.
26. Harcourt to Ponsonby, June 18, 1882; Ponsonby, *Henry Ponsonby*, 270–71.
27. Campbell, *Fenian Fire*, 11.
28. Harcourt to Victoria, February 29, 1884; Buckle, *Letters of Queen Victoria*, ser. 2, vol. 3, 480–81.
29. Andrew, *Secret Service*, 18.
30. Harcourt to Victoria, February 29, 1884, Buckle, *Letters of Queen Victoria*, ser. 2, vol. 3, 481.
31. Porter, *Plots*, 108–9.
32. Victoria to Gladstone, May 4, 1882; Buckle, *Letters of Queen Victoria*, ser. 2, vol. 3, 281.
33. Victoria to Granville, May 7, 1882; Buckle, 285.
34. Wilson and Adams, *Special Branch*, 21–22; Queen Victoria's Journal, April 13, 1883.
35. Wilson and Adams, *Special Branch*, 22.
36. Owen McGee, "Francis Frederick McGee," *Dictionary of Irish Biography*.
37. Campbell, *Fenian Fire*, 176–77, 293.
38. Campbell, 234, 360, 378; Kenna, "Victorian War."
39. Victoria to Harcourt, February 18, 1883; Buckle, *Letters of Queen Victoria*, ser. 2, vol. 3, 411.
40. Hibbert, *Queen Victoria*, 380.
41. Murphy, *Shooting Victoria*, 495.
42. Andrew, *Secret Service*, 19; Wilson and Adams, *Special Branch*, 36.
43. Kenna, "Victorian War."
44. Campbell, *Fenian Fire*, 240–41.
45. Queen Victoria's Journals, June 21, 1887.
46. Murphy, *Shooting Victoria*, 499.
47. Campbell, *Fenian Fire*, 295, 300.
48. Wilson and Adams, *Special Branch*, 36.
49. Jensen, "International Campaign," 91–95.
50. Andrew, *Secret Service*, 19–20; Jensen, "International Campaign," 93.
51. Asquith to Victoria, February 22, 1884; Buckle, *Letters of Queen Victoria*, ser. 2, vol. 3, 360–61.
52. Queen Victoria's Journals, February 17, 1894.
53. Queen Victoria's Journals, June 25, 1894.
54. Victoria to Rosebery, July 13, 1894, and Rosebery to Victoria, July 13, 1894; Buckle, *Letters of Queen Victoria, 1886–1901*, vol. 2, 414–15; Collyer, "Secret Agents," 287.
55. Buckle.
56. Queen Victoria's Journals, September 11, 1898.
57. Queen Victoria's Journals, September 23, 1898.
58. Jensen, "International Anti-Anarchist Conference," 325–26.
59. Salisbury to Victoria, October 20, 1898; Buckle, *Letters of Queen Victoria, 1886–1901*, vol. 3, 294–95.
60. Jensen, "Battle," 151–52.
61. Jensen, "International Anti-Anarchist Conference," 327–28; Deflem, "Wild Beasts," 275–81.
62. Jensen, "International Campaign," 329; How, *Life*, 303–12.

63. Wilson and Adams, *Special Branch*, 55–73; Murphy, *Shooting Victoria*, 497.
64. Queen Victoria's Journals, February 6, 1886.

CHAPTER 5. EDWARD VII AND THE MODERNIZATION OF INTELLIGENCE

Epigraph: Quoted by Markovich, *British Perceptions*, 76.
1. Magnus, *King Edward*, 81.
2. Granville to Ponsonby, December 26, 1871; Ponsonby, *Henry Ponsonby*, 102.
3. Cave Brown, *"C,"* 15; Dorril, *MI6*, 3.
4. Hibbert, *Edward VII*, 235–36; Andrew, *Secret World*, 434.
5. Hibbert, *Edward VII*, 127.
6. St. Aubyn, *Edward VII*, 153–54.
7. St. Aubyn, 198.
8. Frankland, *Witness of a Century*, 185–86.
9. Ponsonby, *Henry Ponsonby*, 104; Magnus, *King Edward*, 167.
10. Magnus, *King Edward*, 177, 190; St. Aubyn, *Edward VII*, 204.
11. Ponsonby, *Henry Ponsonby*, 104.
12. Magnus, *King Edward*, 237; St. Aubyn, *Edward VII*, 204, 205.
13. McLean, *Royalty*, 182–83; Hibbert, *Edward VII*, 248; Ridley, *Bertie*, 474; Magnus, *King Edward*, 307; Sinclair, *Other Victoria*, 4, 247.
14. Lee, *King Edward VII*, 76–77, 81; Heffer, *Power*, 118–20.
15. Moran, *Classified*, 39.
16. Moran, 39.
17. Lee, *King Edward VII*, 88–89; see also Judd and Sturridge, *Boer War*, 269–80.
18. St. Aubyn, *Edward VII*, 459; ODNB: Brett, Reginald Baliol, Second Viscount Esher; Lee, *King Edward VII*, 92; Heffer, *Power*, 121.
19. Frankland, *Witness*, 229–31; ODNB: Brett, Reginald Baliol, Second Viscount Esher.
20. Esher to Edward, November 1, 1902; Esher, *Journals*, vol. 1, 360.
21. Esher to Edward, April 30, 1903; Esher, 399.
22. Esher to Edward, March 11, 1903, Esher, 387–88; Fergusson, *British Military Intelligence*, 118.
23. Black, "Victorian Information Society."
24. Fergusson, *British Military Intelligence*, 119–20; Davies, *Intelligence*, 77–78; Kennedy, "Great Britain Beyond 1914," 176.
25. Heffer, *Power*, 131; Magnus, *King Edward*, 277; Hibbert, *Edward VII*, 208–9; McLean, *Royalty*, 181.
26. Fromkin, *King*, 117; MacMillan, *War*, 114–15; St. Aubyn, *Edward VII*, 311; Hibbert, *Edward VII*, 207–8; Heffer, *Power*, 131.
27. St. Aubyn, *Edward VII*, 321–22; Ponsonby, *Recollections*, 154.
28. St. Aubyn, *Edward VII*, 321.
29. McLean, *Royalty*, 144; St. Aubyn, *Edward VII*, 321.
30. Ponsonby, *Recollections*, 169; McLean, *Royalty*, 145; Glencross, *State Visits*, 100.
31. Glencross, *State Visits*, 72.
32. See Glencross; Ridley, *Bertie*, 380.
33. St. Aubyn, *Edward VII*, 335.
34. McLean, *Royalty*, 150.
35. Verrier, *Through the Looking Glass*, 19; Hopkirk, *Great Game*, 507–17.

36. Soroka, *Britain*, 80.
37. Seligman, "Prince Louis," 168.
38. McLean, *Royalty*, 159–60.
39. Lee, *King Edward VII*, 355.
40. McLean, *Royalty*, 157; Heffer, *Power*, 241.
41. RA:VIC/MAIN/X/20, Rice to Knollys, October 31, 1905; Ridley, *Bertie*, 399.
42. ODNB: Wallace, Sir Donald Mackenzie.
43. St. Aubyn, *Edward VII*, 357.
44. Kaiser Wilhelm to Tsar Nicholas, August 22, 1905; Kaiser Wilhelm and Tsar Nicholas, *Between Two Emperors*, 219.
45. Kaiser Wilhelm and Tsar Nicholas.
46. Reynolds, *Summits*, 23.
47. FO800/103, Grey to Knollys, March 28, 1906.
48. MacMillan, *War*, 114–15.
49. Glencross, *State Visits*, 171.
50. Ponsonby, *Recollections*, 195.
51. McLean, *Royalty*, 167; Heffer, *Power*, 255.
52. McKee, "British Perceptions," 231; Andrew and Green, *Stars*, 166–67.
53. Andrew, *Secret Service*, 6.
54. Lee, *King Edward VII*, 235, 350.
55. Ridley, *Bertie*, 432.
56. Lee, *King Edward VII*, 321–25, 544; Salmon, *Scandinavia*, 61–69.
57. Lee, *King Edward VII*, 129–30.
58. RA:VIC/MAIN/X/21/35,37,38, Correspondence between Davidson and FO, September 22–23, 1906.
59. St. Aubyn, *Edward VII*, 437.
60. MacMillan, *War*, 113.
61. St Aubyn, *Edward VII*, 44; Heffer, *Power and Place*, 256.
62. Seligmann, *Spies in Uniform*, 223; Heffer, *Power and Place*, 256–57.
63. MacMillan, *War*, 111–12.
64. Andrew, *Secret Service*, 49.
65. St. Aubyn, *Edward VII*, 349; Ponsonby, *Recollections*, 248.
66. Ponsonby, *Recollections*, 248.
67. St. Aubyn, *Edward VII*, 349.
68. St. Aubyn, 343.
69. Lee, *King Edward VII*, 678.
70. Quoted by Heffer, *Power*, 270.
71. Lee, *King Edward VII*, 681.
72. Lee.
73. Ridley, *Bertie*, 432.
74. Heffer, *Power*, 271.
75. Kennedy, "Great Britain," 179–83.
76. Jeffery, *MI6*, 3–5; Andrew, *Defence*, 6–7.
77. Esher Journals, March 30, 2009; Brett, *Journals*, vol. 2, 379.
78. Andrew, *Defence*, 18–19.
79. St. Aubyn, *Edward VII*, 376.
80. McLean, *Royalty*, 174.
81. Humphries, "Perfectly Secret," 1156–79.

82. Higgins, "How Was Haldane?" 21; MacMillan, *War*, 114–15.
83. Jeffery, *MI6*, 6–7.
84. Magnus, *King Edward*, 277.
85. Ponsonby, *Recollections*, 127.
86. McLean, *Royalty*, 177.
87. McLean, 181–82.
88. FO800/103, Edward to Grey, September 1, 1909. See also RA:VIC/MAIN/X/23/9, Edward to Grey, August 28, 1909, 10; Ponsonby to Elliot, August 10, 1909, 15; Elliott to Davidson, October 2, 1909, 16; Edward to Elliot, October 5, 1909, 17; and Elliot to Ponsonby, October 19, 1909.
89. Geraghty, *Bullet-Catchers*, 53.
90. Porter, *Plots*, 128; Crowdy, *Enemy Within*, 202–3.

CHAPTER 6. KING GEORGE V AND THE FIRST WORLD WAR

Epigraph: Rose, *George V*, 165.
1. Sanabria, *Republicanism*, 101–22.
2. George V, diary, May 31, 1906, RA, quoted by Rose, *George V*, 68.
3. Sinclair, *Two Georges*, 67–71.
4. *Irish Times*, "When Dublin Did a Roaring Trade in Lions."
5. McLean, *Royalty*, 192.
6. Rose, *George V*, 167.
7. Navy List, RN College Greenwich; here he is listed by his previous name "Mansfield G. Smith," 311; Jeffery, *MI6*, 9.
8. Judd, *Quest for "C,"* 17–18.
9. Mensdorff to Aehrenthal, September 2, 1910, quoted by Rose, *George V*, 165.
10. *Irish Times*, "When Dublin Did a Roaring Trade in Lions."
11. Judd, *Quest for "C,"* 239.
12. McLean, *Royalty*, 192–94.
13. Lady Wigram diary 1926, quoted by Rose, *George V*, 166.
14. King George V to Nicky, January 24, 1910, cited by Maylunas and Mironenko, *Lifelong Passion*, 329.
15. King George V to Nicky, May 14, 1910, cited by Maylunas and Mironenko, 329.
16. King George V to Nicky, March 2, 1911, cited by Maylunas and Mironenko, 342.
17. Beckett, "November 1913."
18. Sulzberger, *Fall of Eagles*, 202–3.
19. Hastings, *Catastrophe*, xxix.
20. Otte, *Foreign Office Mind*, 461; Clay, *King*, 309.
21. RA: GV/PRIV/GVD/1914, August 1, 1914, quoted by Heffer, *Staring at God*, 61.
22. Nicholas to King George V (via Buchanan), August 2, 1914, cited by Maylunas and Mironenko, *Lifelong Passion*, 146–47.
23. Clay, *King*, 313.
24. Heffer, *Staring at God*, 68–69, 74–87.
25. Boghardt, *Spies*, 62–63; Andrew, *Defence*, 50–52.
26. Seymour, *Noble Endeavours*, 168–79; Clay, *King*, 307.
27. Lambton, *Mountbattens*, 215.
28. Asquith to Venetia Stanley, October 24, 1914; Brock and Brock, *Asquith Letters*, 285.
29. Heffer, *Staring at God*, 432.

30. Rose, *George V*, 174.
31. Bennett, *Churchill's Man*, 27.
32. ODNB: Wigram, Clive; Rose, *George V*, 227.
33. Douglas-Home and Kelly, *Dignified*, 40.
34. Douglas-Home and Kelly, 43.
35. Glencross, "Cause of Tension?" 160; Douglas-Home and Kelly, *Dignified*, 43.
36. Churchill, *In the Eye of the Storm*, 150–51.
37. Churchill, 52.
38. Glencross, "Cause of Tension?" in *Monarch*, ed. Glencross and Rowbotham, 160; Douglas-Home and Kelly, *Dignified*, 43.
39. Churchill, *In the Eye*, 140; Douglas-Home and Kelly, *Dignified*, 46.
40. Diary entries for March 14, 1916, and May 19, 1916. Seabury Ashmead-Bartlett Papers, privately held. We are grateful to Anthea Boylston and Celia Catchpole for permission to publish this and to Jock Bruce for sharing this information with us.
41. Churchill, *In the Eye*, 105–7, 181.
42. Churchill, 73–77, 181.
43. Churchill, 94–95.
44. Ferris, *Behind the Enigma*, 29–63; Stout, "World War I," 378–94; Warner, *Rise and Fall*, 79–130.
45. Georgie to Nicky, August 8, 1915, cited by Maylunas and Mironenko, *Lifelong Passion*, 432.
46. Georgie to Nicky, August 8, 1915.
47. Ania Vyrubova, memoirs, cited by Maylunas and Mironenko, *Lifelong Passion*, 513.
48. Buchanan, *My Mission*, 43–49.
49. RA:PS/GV/Q/1550/313 (draft), quoted by Clay, *King*, 328.
50. RA:PS/GV/Q/1550/314, quoted by Clay.
51. Mikhailovich, *Once a Grand Duke*, 185.
52. November 22, 1916; Stevenson, *Lloyd George*, 127.
53. Jeffery, *MI6*, 103–6.
54. Kington, "Recruited by MI5."
55. Milton, *Russian Roulette*, 14.
56. Cullen, *Rasputin*, 15; Hoare, *Fourth Seal*, 67–68.
57. Ruud and Stepanov, *Fontanka 16*, 293–94.
58. Grand Duchess Xenia, diary, January 25 and 26, 1912; Moscow State Archives, cited by Maylunas and Mironenko, *Lifelong Passion*, 329.
59. FO/371/2093, Buchanan to Grey, May 14, 1914.
60. Carter, *Three Emperors*, 411.
61. Ruud and Stepanov, *Fontanka 16*, 298–99.
62. Cook, *To Kill Rasputin*, 2–12; Smith, *Six*, 198–205.
63. Yusupov, memoirs, quoted by Maylunas and Mironenko, *Lifelong Passion*, 385.
64. Sebag Montefiore, *Romanovs*, 606.
65. Police Department Report, "Rasputin," February 18, 1913, Moscow State Archives, cited by Maylunas and Mironenko, *Lifelong Passion*, 353.
66. Milton, *Russian Roulette*, 17–18.
67. Ruud and Stepanov, *Fontanka 16*, 312.
68. Milton, *Russian Roulette*, 24–25.
69. Judd, *Quest for "C,"* 432–43.
70. Youssoupoff, *Rasputin*, passim; Cullen, *Rasputin*, 17.

71. Fuhrmann, *Rasputin*, 230–31. Also see Cook, *To Kill Rasputin*, 232; and Smith, *Six*, 201–3.
72. Fuhrmann, *Rasputin*, 606, 612; Smith, *Six*, 205.
73. Mikailovich, *Once a Grand Duke*, 279.
74. Buchanan, *My Mission*, 47–51.
75. Jeffery, *MI6*, 106–7.
76. Judd, *Quest for "C,"* 436; Smith, *Six*, 206.
77. Cullen, *Rasputin*, 165, 193, 199.
78. McKee, "British Perceptions," 282.
79. Jeffery, *MI6*, 106–7.
80. PS/PSO/GV/C/Q/722/37, Hanbury-Williams to Bigge, January 7, 1917.
81. Clay, *King*, 333.
82. Cambridge University Library, Hardinge Papers, vol. 23, Buchanan to Hardinge, January 20, 1917.
83. Le Queux, *Rasputin*, 69; Le Queux, *Minister of Evil*, 26.
84. Cook, *Murder*, 62.
85. Yusupov, memoirs, quoted by Maylunas and Mironenko, *Lifelong Passion*, 353.

CHAPTER 7. KING GEORGE V AND THE BOLSHEVIKS

Epigraph: RA:GV/GVD/1918, July 28, 1918, quoted by Clay, *King*, 345.
1. George, diary, February 28, 1917, quoted by Maylunas and Mironenko, *Lifelong Passion*, 541.
2. George, diary, March 2, 1917, quoted by Maylunas and Mironenko, 546.
3. Hall, *To Free the Romanovs*, 48–49.
4. "Journal No. 1 of the Sitting of the Provisional Government on the Deportation of the Tsar's Family and Member of the Imperial Family Abroad," March 2, 1917, Moscow State Archives, quoted by Maylunas and Mironenko, *Lifelong Passion*, 544.
5. FO/371/2998, March 19, 1917.
6. Hanbury-Williams, *Emperor Nicholas II*, 169–70.
7. McKee, "British Perceptions," 305.
8. Rappaport, *Race*, 55, 66.
9. Lord Stamfordham, meeting at Buckingham Palace, March 9, 1917 (March 22), quoted by Maylunas and Mironenko, *Lifelong Passion*, 559–60. Also see Rose, *George V*, 211.
10. FO/371/3008.
11. RA:22/4/17, PS/PSO/GV/C/1067/M/29, Heffer, *Staring at God*, 587.
12. RA:PS/PSO/GV/C/M/1067/29, Stamfordham, March 22, 1917.
13. Nicky, diary, March 23, 1917, Tsarkoe Selo, Moscow State Archives, cited by Maylunas and Mironenko, *Lifelong Passion*, 567.
14. Rappaport, *Race*, 81.
15. Prochaska, "George V and Republicanism," 32–33.
16. January 23, 1977; Thorpe, *Who's In*, 539; RA:PS/PSO/GV/C/1067/M/26, cited by Heffer, *Staring at God*, 588.
17. RA:PS/PSO/GV/C/M/1067/39, Stamfordham to Balfour (FS), March 30, 1917.
18. Prochaska, "George V and Republicanism," 33–37.
19. RA:PS/PSO/GV/C/M/1067/26, Verney to Stamfordham, March 21, 1917.
20. RA:PS/PSO/GV/C/M/1067/44, Balfour to Stamfordham, April 2, 1917.

21. RA:PS/PSO/GV/C/M/1067/51, Stamfordham to Balfour, April 6, 1917.
22. RA:PS/PSO/GV/C/M/1067/52, Stamfordham to Balfour, April 6, 1917.
23. Prochaska, "George V and Republicanism," 30.
24. RA:PS/PSO/GV/C/M/1067/61, Stamfordham minute, April 10, 1917.
25. Bennett, *Churchill's Man*, 27.
26. RA:PS/PSO/GV/C/M/1067/63, telegram from Buchanan, April 15, 1917.
27. Cook, *Murder*, 90.
28. FO/800/205, Balfour to Buchanan, April 18, 1917, Balfour Papers.
29. FO/800/78, Hardinge to Lascelles, April 17, 1917.
30. Mikailovich, *Grand Duke*, 334.
31. Kettle, *Russia, Vol. 1*, 168.
32. Heffer, *Staring at God*, 591–96.
33. Rappaport, *Four Sisters*, 329–38.
34. Day, *Trotsky's Favourite Spy*, 48; HO/144/2158, Chicherin file, 1917.
35. CAB/23/4/295, December 10, 1917.
36. Nansen, *Through Siberia*, 132–49; McKee, "British Perceptions," 315–16.
37. Hoare to Nansen, November 28, 1921, file 8, Russian refugees, Constantinople, 1920–24, Templewood papers, Cambridge University Library; Summers and Mangold, *File*, 249–52.
38. Rappaport, *Race*, 204–8.
39. Gilliard, *Thirteen Years*, 256.
40. Cook, *Murder*, 152.
41. Crossland, "British Spies."
42. Urbach, *Go-Betweens for Hitler*, 335.
43. FO/371/3329/93852.
44. Mohr, *Czech and Slovak Legion*, 65; Pipes, *Russian Revolution*, 640.
45. Lockhart, *Memoirs*, 317.
46. Smith, *Six*, 228–31.
47. Jeffery, *MI6*, 134–37.
48. Lockhart, *Memoirs*, 323.
49. Reilly, *Adventures*, 42–46.
50. Reilly.
51. Lockhart, *Memoirs*, 317.
52. West, *MI6*, 16–17.
53. Hall, *To Free the Romanovs*, 152–53.
54. Radzinsky, *Last Tsar*, 239–41.
55. Radzinsky, 341–43.
56. Baklitskaya, "Go East."
57. FO/800/205, FORSINT, the Intelligence Coordinator for All British Forces and Missions in Russia and Siberia, August 28, 1918.
58. Hall, *To Free the Romanovs*, 183–85.
59. PS/PSO/GV/C/M/1344A/31, Stamfordham to Milner, September 1, 1918.
60. Hall, *To Free the Romanovs*, 183–85.
61. Hall, 186–87.
62. FO/371/3977, Sir Basil Thomson, DI, July 3, 1920, file 983, 208702; also see PRO/30/26/144.
63. FO/800/205, Sir Arthur Balfour to Lord Stamfordham, July 23, 1918.
64. George, diary, July 25, 1918, cited by Maylunas and Mironenko, *Lifelong Passion*, 640.

65. Rappaport, *Race*, 268–69.

66. Rose, *King George V*, 243.

67. Day, *Trotsky's Favourite Spy*, 86.

68. Rappaport, *Race*, 272, 278.

69. Cook, *Murder*, 175.

70. Rose, *King George V*, 385.

71. Schabas, *Trial*, 13–56.

72. Lea and Alderson, "Attempt to Capture the Kaiser," 222–61.

73. Lea and Alderson.

74. Lea and Alderson.

75. Schabas, *Trial*, 223–32.

76. Schabas.

77. West, *MI6*, 18–19; Judd, *Quest for "C,"* 435.

78. Agar, *Baltic Episode*, 215.

79. Prochaska, "George V," 49.

80. Churchill, *In the Eye*, 225.

81. Rose, *King George V*, 334.

82. Andrew, *Defence*, 149.

83. Rose, *King George V*, 336.

84. Bennett, *Zinoviev Letter*, 1–4.

85. Prochaska, "George V," 42.

86. Hemming, *"M,"* 77.

87. November 27, 1934; Gorodetsky, *Maisky Diaries*, 18–21.

CHAPTER 8. ABDICATION

Epigraph: Edward VIII, *A King's Story*, 362.

1. RA:M.2472, quoted by Nicolson, *George V*, 668.

2. Nicolson, 668.

3. Nicolson, 661–63.

4. Nicolson, 665–66; Rose, *King George V*, 386–68.

5. Rose, *King George V*, 388.

6. Smith, "Brilliant History"; Cave Brown, *"C,"* 151–52.

7. January 29, 1936; Gorodetsky, *Maisky Diaries*, 64–65.

8. Ziegler, *King Edward VIII*, 54–55, 59.

9. Rose, *Prince*, 55–56.

10. Rose, 72–75, 129.

11. Lord Norfolk, interviewed for *Spying on the Royals*, Channel 4, April 2, 2017.

12. Rose, *Prince*, 312.

13. Bland, *Modern Women*, 142–43.

14. Rose, *Prince*, 172–84.

15. Ziegler, *King Edward VIII*, 165.

16. Sebba, *That Woman*, 75–96.

17. Lord Wigram, interviewed for *Spying on the Royals*.

18. "The Windsor Woods," *Illustrated London News*, March 18, 1933.

19. HO/38/151, Trotter to Carter, May 24 and June 10, 1924.

20. MEPO/10/35, Canning Report, n.d.

21. MEPO/10/35, Canning to Game, June 25. 1935.

22. MEPO/10/35, Canning Report.

23. MEPO/10/35, Canning Report.
24. Larman, *Crown in Crisis*, 46.
25. June 16, 1935, Heffer, *Henry "Chips" Channon*, 435.
26. Much is made of this, but it is unlikely; see, e.g., Morton, *17 Carnations*, 54–58.
27. MEPO/10/35, Canning to Game, July 3, 1935.
28. Ziegler, *King Edward VIII*, 269.
29. November 27, 1969; Thorpe, *Who's In*, 384.
30. November 26, 1969; Thorpe, 383; November 1, 1972; Thorpe, 466.
31. Young, *Diaries*, 263.
32. MEPO/3/1713, "George Andrew McMahon: Attempt on the Life of HM King Edward VIII at Constitution Hill."
33. Parris, *Man in the Brown Suit*, 129–30.
34. *Melbourne Age*, "Edward's Would-Be Killer."
35. Alberge, "British State 'Covered Up Plot.'"
36. Andrew Cook, *Guardian*, January 3, 2003.
37. The most cogent analysis is by Larman, *Crown in Crisis*, 50–71.
38. Alberge, British State 'Covered Up Plot.'"
39. Wilson and Adams, *Special Branch*, 70–71.
40. E.g., January 1, 1941; West, *Guy Liddell Diaries, Vol. 1*, 119.
41. April 13, 1935; Heffer, *Henry "Chips" Channon*, 413.
42. March 5, 1943; Hart-Davis, *King's Counsellor*, 108.
43. Thornton, *Royal Feud*, 93, 99; Milne, *Nicolson*, 86–87.
44. Ziegler, *King Edward VIII*, 273.
45. Beaken, *Cosmo Lang*, 87–109.
46. Beaken, "How to Topple a King." See also Beaken, *Cosmo Lang*.
47. Norwich, *Duff Cooper Diaries*, 230–31.
48. MSS., Cadogan diary, 1936, CCC.
49. Howarth, *George VI*, 61.
50. Aitken, William Maxwell, first Baton Beaverbrook, *ODNB*.
51. June 1953, Colville, *Fringes of Power*, 717.
52. Pope-Hennessy, *Quest for Queen Mary*, 200.
53. Beaken, "How to Topple a King."
54. *Spying on the Royals*, Channel 4.
55. Phillips, *King Who Had to Go*, 124–40.
56. Cannadine, *In Churchill's Shadow*, 64.
57. CAB/301/101, Memo to Gardiner, December 5, 1936.
58. Elliot, *Gentleman Spymaster*, 84–86.
59. Faber, *Speaking for England*, 275.
60. Faber.
61. Pope-Hennessy, *Quest for Queen Mary*, 200.
62. December 28, 1936; Ball, *Headlam Diaries*, 105.
63. Cadbury, *Princes at War*, 3–4.
64. Dorril, *Blackshirt*, 406.
65. Windsor, *King's Story*, 409–11.
66. January 26, 1977; Thorpe, *Who's In*, 540.
67. Spring 1937; Buckle, *Self-Portrait*, 52.
68. Ziegler, *Mountbatten*, 680.
69. Spring 1937; Buckle, *Self-Portrait*, 52.
70. Clark, "Diplomacy." See also Morton, *Wallis in Love*, 221.

71. "Abdication Crisis," 48–49, BBK/G/6/10, Beaverbrook papers.

72. Martin, *Woman He Loved*, 168–69. Martin spoke to Brownlow at length. We are indebted to Mark Hollingsworth for this reference.

73. Larman, *Crown in Crisis*, 151–52.

74. March 12, 1937; Gorodetsky, *Maisky Diaries*, 74–75.

75. Gorodetsky.

76. Roberts, *Sunshine and Shadow*, 378–79.

77. Strachan, "Museum to Shine a Light."

78. MEPO/3/558, memo "SD Inspector Storrier," November 22, 1933.

79. MEPO/3/558, memo by DAC1, "Royalty," 26/PTN/109, September 27, 1934. Edward's previous detective, Len Burt, had become ill.

80. MEPO/3/558, Aird to Laurie, January 17, 1934.

81. MEPO/3/558, Division A Memo, "Division Sub-Inspector Storrier," n.d. [1934].

82. MEPO/10/35, Storrier (Wasserleonburg) to Game, June 18, 1937.

83. MEPO/10/35, Storrier (Enzesfeld) to Game, June 18, 1937.

84. MEPO/10/35, "Admettre au Chateau Personnes Suivantes," 1937.

85. CRES/35/417, Savill, memo, "Fort Belverdere: Caretaker," September 22, 1937.

86. MEPO/10/35, Storrier to London, June 7, 1937.

87. MEPO/10/35, Storrier (Wasserleonburg) to Game, July 1, 1937.

88. MEPO/10/35, Storrier (Wasserleonburg) to Game, August 30, 1937.

89. Norwich, *Duff Cooper Diaries*, 231.

90. FO/1093/23, Appendix to Report 166, "Rogers, Herman."

91. MEPO/10/35, Storrier (Wasserleonburg) to Game, August 30, 1937.

92. FO/954/33, win/37/32.

93. FO/954/33, Forbes to London, "This letter which I have typed myself will not be put in the Chancellery archives."

94. Cadbury, *Princes at War*, 49–66. See also Morton, *Wallis in Love*, 251.

95. FO/954/33, Berlin to London, October 6, 1937.

96. FO/954/33, Embassy, Berlin, October 13, 1937; FO/954/33, FO tel. 178, October 6, 1937.

97. MEPO/10/35, Canning to Game, November 15, 1937.

98. Ziegler, *King Edward VIII*, 393.

99. FO/954/33, Embassy Berlin to SoS, October 17, 1937.

100. MEPO/10/35, Storrier to Game, December 19, 1937.

101. KV 2/1272, Prost to Anthony Blunt MI5.B1b, June 3, 1942.

102. Linklater, *Compton Mackenzie*, 253–54; Andrew, *Secret Service*, 351–52.

103. KV/2/1271, *Sunday Dispatch*, July 17, 1938.

104. Linklater, *Compton Mackenzie*, 280–81.

105. Mackenzie, *Windsor Tapestry*, 139, 160, 213–14, 459.

106. KV/2/1271, MI5 minute, August 10, 1938.

107. KV/2/1271, F.41196, "Compton Mackenzie," September 6, 1934.

108. KV/2/1272, Prost to Anthony Blunt, MI5.B1b, June 3, 1942.

109. Sitwell, *Rat Week*, 15–16, 37, 67.

110. See, e.g., KV/2/1271, F.41196 (Intercepted) Mackenzie to Pollitt (CPGB), November 17, 1936.

111. Linklater, *Compton Mackenzie*, 280–83.

112. MEPO/10/35, Storrier to Game, January 26, 1938.

113. CRES/35/417, Stock to Savill, April 5, 1938.

114. Bloch, *Secret File*, 116.

115. MEPO/3/567, Game to Monckton, April 4, 1939; MEPO/3/567, Monkton to Game, April 6, 1939.
116. MEPO/3/567, Monckton to Game, April 13, 1939.

CHAPTER 9. THE OUTBREAK OF THE SECOND WORLD WAR

Epigraph: Stohrer to Berlin, December 23, 1940, no. 211, *DGFP*, D, X, 276–77.
1. Howarth, *George VI*, 84.
2. Shawcross, *Queen Elizabeth the Queen Mother*, 440.
3. Weisbrode, *Churchill and the King*, 54.
4. CAD:NC/7/3/26-65, George to Chamberlain, September 16, 1938.
5. CAD:NC/7/3/26-65, PM to Palace, September 23, 1938.
6. Shawcross, *Queen Elizabeth the Queen Mother*, 441.
7. Howarth, *George VI*, 84; Chamberlain papers, De57, F.157, BUL.
8. Shawcross, *Queen Elizabeth the Queen Mother*, 443.
9. December 18, 1938; Gorodetsky, *Maisky Diaries*, 150–51.
10. CAD:NC/7/3/26-65, George to Chamberlain, January 19, 1939.
11. CAD:NC/7/3/26-65, George to Chamberlain, March 18, 1939.
12. Petropoulos, *Royals*, 200–221.
13. Chamberlain papers, De57, F.157, BUL.
14. Howarth, *George VI*, 104–5.
15. CAB/21/4552, Hastings to Hardinge, July 25, 1939.
16. CRES/35/417, Kell to Stokes, September 21, 1939.
17. Paget, *Second to None*, 488; Stewart, *King's Private Army*, 47–54.
18. Rhodes, *Final Curtsey*, 68.
19. Howarth, *George VI*, 112–13.
20. Shawcross, *Queen Elizabeth the Queen Mother*, 508–9.
21. McKinstry, *Operation Sealion*, 229–32.
22. For a skeptical critique, see Stewart, *King's Private Army*, 111–19.
23. April 31, 1940; Pimlott, *Second World Diary*, 31. Also, July 27, 1940; Dilks, *Cadogan Diaries*, 317.
24. August 6, 1940; Smith, *Hostage to Fortune*, 457. Also, Churchill to King, May 15, 1945; Langworth, *Churchill*, 84.
25. Manchester, *Last Lion*, 64.
26. Rhodes, *Final Curtsey*, 69.
27. July 10, 1940; Nicolson, *Nicolson Diaries*, 100.
28. Costello, *Ten Days*, 47–48.
29. Gillman and Gillman, *"Collar the Lot!"* 112.
30. Gillman and Gillman; CAB/67/6, WPG (40)131, Anderson memo.
31. Ziegler, *Edward VIII*, 402–3.
32. Shawcross, *Queen Elizabeth the Queen Mother*, 494–95.
33. March 21, 1971; Thorpe, *Who's In*, 456.
34. Bloch, *Secret File*, 147–49.
35. MEPO/3/567, Hardinge to Game, May 8, 1940. They rented this until 1949, then moved to 85 rue de la Faisanderie.
36. MEPO/3/567, Game to Phillips, May 27, 1940.
37. MEPO/3/567, Phillips to Game, June 5, 1940; Game to Phillips, June 8, 1940.
38. MEPO/3/567, Phillips to Game, June 5, 1940; Game to Phillips, June 8, 1940.

39. Thornton, *Royal Feud*, 201.
40. Ziegler, *King Edward VIII*, 417.
41. Morton, *Wallis*, 263.
42. FOI:FBI EDWARD VIII P1-5, Memo to Director of FBI, September 13, 1940.
43. FOI:FBI EDWARD VIII P1-5.
44. FOI:FBI EDWARD VIII P55, Memo to the Director, May 2, 1941.
45. FO/800/326/183, Halifax to Consulates, June 19, 1940.
46. Day, *Franco's Friends*, 171, 182.
47. May 20, 1940; Dilks, *Cadogan Diary*, 287.
48. May 21, 1940; Dilks, 288.
49. Burns, *Papa Spy*, 119–30.
50. FO/800/327, Hoare to FO, June 20, 1940.
51. Christy, *Price*, 235; Glass, *Americans*, 197–98.
52. RG/319/E134B/B14.X 8062007: CIC file, "Bedaux, Charles Eugene."
53. Thornton, *Royal Feud*, 142.
54. FRUS 1940, III, Weddell to SoS, 2/1240.
55. Cadbury, *Princes*, 174.
56. Cadbury.
57. Entry for July 26, 1940; Dilks, *Cadogan Diary*, 317.
58. Whiting, *Kents*, 96–99.
59. Von Burkersroda to Weizacker, January 27, 1940, *DGFP*, 1918–45: D, VIII, 713.
60. KV4/1, Curry, "The Security Service: The Problems and Organisational Adjustments, 1908–1945" (1946), part II: The Nazi Threat, 86.
61. Dorrill, *Blackshirt*, 406–7.
62. FO/1093/23, C/5023, MI6 to Cadogan 26/9/40, enclosing MI6 report from Lisbon. Three days later, Churchill noted "seen" on the document.
63. Bloch, *Operation Willi*.
64. FO/1093/23, Eccles to Jebb, July 4, 1940.
65. FO/1093/23, mins. by Cadogan, July 6, 1940, and Halifax, July 7, 1940.
66. Burns, *Papa Spy*, 119–30.
67. FO/1093/23, Menzies to Cadogan, July 19, 1940, C/4720, seen by Halifax.
68. FO/1093/23, Morton to Churchill, August 4, 1940.
69. West, *Cold War Spymaster*, 2–10; KV/4/446, August 24, 1945, Liddell Diary.
70. Cadbury, *Princes*, 174–76.
71. Cadbury, 174–77.
72. FO/1093/23, MI6 to Cadogan, July 7, 1940, C/4633, and Cadogan minute, July 7, 1940.
73. Cadbury, *Princes*, 199–215.
74. Bloch, *Operation Willi*, 171–98.
75. Huene to Ribbentrop, August 2, 1940, nos. 276–77, *DGFP*, D, X, 397–40. Also, Cadbury, *Princes*, 154–55; and Lownie, *Traitor King*, 94–108.
76. Lownie, *Traitor King*; Sweet, "Windsor File," 266.
77. FO/1093/23, Selby, Lisbon, July 22, 1940.
78. Costello, *Ten Days*, 370–71.
79. CO/967/122, extract of a letter from Monckton, July 8, 1940, to PM.
80. CO/967/122.
81. CO/967/122, Note for SoS FA, July 23, 1940.
82. Schellenberg, *Memoirs*, 139–46.

83. West, *Cold War Spymaster*, 5.
84. Ziegler, *King Edward VIII*, 431.
85. West, *Cold War Spymaster*, 1–12.
86. Hoyningen-Huene to Ribbentrop, August 15, 1940, no. 884, DGFP X.
87. FO/371/26542, C4216/324/16.
88. FO/371/24408, Mallet to Cadogan, September 7, 1940, C/1973.
89. Costello, *Ten Days*, 402–3.
90. Entry for December 28, 1942; Hart-Davis, *King's Counsellor*, 87–88.
91. Bloch, *Secret File*, 165.

CHAPTER 10. WAR IN THE AMERICAS

Epigraph: Hyde, *Secret Intelligence Agent*, 119–20.
1. Lownie, *John Buchan*, 186–212, 241–72.
2. Bousfield and Toffoli, *Royal Spring*, 12–36.
3. Fuller, "That Time FDR Served Hot Dogs to the King."
4. NARA/RG59, Counsellor (London) to SoS, June 18, 1939, P294/#41, Great Britain, June 1939.
5. Bradford, *George VI*, 281.
6. Jeffery, *MI6*, 441; Hyde, *Secret Intelligence Agent*, 135.
7. Undated memo, CIA file, box 107, Cuneo Papers, FDR Library.
8. Mahl, *Desperate Deception*, 21–22.
9. Mahl, 442–45; Stafford, *Station X*, 25–29.
10. Dunlop, *Donovan*, 209–10. Also see Soley, *Radio Warfare*, 50.
11. Dunlop, *Donovan*, 209–10.
12. Mahl, *Desperate Deception*; Cull, *Selling War*, 57–100.
13. Dahl, *Desperate Delusions*, 54–106.
14. Rankin, *Defending the Rock*, 89–102.
15. Hyde, *Secret Intelligence Agent*, 68.
16. D/L to B, July 12, 1940, enclosing section IX, sub-section D/L, Censorship, Montgomery Hyde papers, March 2011, CCC.
17. D/L to B.
18. Rankin, *Defending the Rock*, 89–102.
19. Hyde, *Secret Intelligence Agent*, 98–99, 108.
20. Private information.
21. Lloyd to Duke of Windsor, July 29, 1940, CHAR/20/9a/105, Churchill papers, CCC.
22. Hyde, *Secret Intelligence Agent*, 61–62.
23. CO/967/122, Edward to Lord Lloyd, October 12, 1940.
24. CO/967/122, Monckton to Thomas, November 11, 1940.
25. CO/967/122, Monckton to Churchill, August 8, 1940.
26. November 9, 1940; Pimlott, *Second World War Diary*, 98.
27. CO/967/122, Lothian to Cadogan, September 4, 1940, 4424.
28. Thomson to Montgomery Hyde, April 22, 1941, enclosing Halifax to Duke of Windsor, April 21, 1941, Montgomery Hyde papers, March 2011, CCC.
29. Hyde, *Secret Intelligence Agent*, 73–75.
30. FO/371/24249, Halifax to Lothian, September 1940: WSC min., October 3, 1940.
31. FO/371/24249, Lothian to Halifax, October 11, 1940.
32. FO/371/24249, NNNS, October 8, 1940 (intelligence).

33. FO/371/24263, FO to Lothian, November 29, 1940.
34. FO/371/24263, Butler to FO, November 22, 1940.
35. FO/371/26191, Jacksonville to London, December 20, 1940.
36. Roosevelt to Lothian, November 30, 1940, box 34, PSF files, FDR Library. See also Lothian to Roosevelt, November 29, 1940, box 34, PSF files, FDR Library.
37. Roosevelt, *FDR*, vol. 4, 1086.
38. Roosevelt to George VI, November 22, 1940, box 34, PSF Files, FDR Library.
39. Howarth, *George VI*, 113.
40. "Report on the Co-ordination of Security Intelligence in the West Indies and Caribbean Area," by Montgomery Hyde, April 3, 1941, HYDE 3/13, CCC.
41. FO/1093/24, Governor to Kell, October 18, 1939.
42. KV4/185, February 29, 1940, Liddell Diary.
43. January 17, 1941, Guy Liddell Diary, KV4/185.
44. FO/1093/24, Governor to Duke, December 11, 1940.
45. Hoover to Berle, March 8, 1940, FBI file Wenner-Gren, FBI:FOIA, no. 1485731-000.
46. FO/1093/24, Hardinge (Buckingham Palace) to Cadogan, December 14, 1940.
47. FO/1093/24, min. to Cadogan, January 1, 1941, Cadogan min., January 1, 1941; "C" to Hopkinson, January 3, 1941.
48. CO/967/125, PM to Duke of Windsor (deciphered by HRH's personal secretary), private and personal, March 17, 1941.
49. FO/371/26191, mail intercept, May 3, 1941, to CO/FO/MI5, Jelke to Baxter, private and personal, March 17, 1941. April 14, 1941, A3509/165/45.
50. Hyde, *Secret Intelligence Agent*, 63.
51. FBI:FOIA EDWARD VIII P28.
52. FO/1093/23, "C" to Hopkinson, enclosing censorship interception on Jelke, April 12, 1941.
53. Berle memo to SoS, 5/9/41, Berle papers, 0308, FDR Library.
54. FBI:EDWARD VIII P89, My Dear Attorney General, April 14, 1941.
55. FBI:EDWARD VIII P19, Memo to Foxworth, April 18, 1941.
56. FBI EDWARD VIII P18, April 19, 1941, time: 9:10 AM.
57. FBI EDWARD VIII P18.
58. Hyde, *Secret Intelligence Agent*, 83.
59. FO/371/26191, Interview with Oursler, May 16, 1941, *Liberty*, and *Sunday Dispatch*. Carried in the European press May 9. Berne to FO, May 12, 1941.
60. FO/371/26191, Minute to Scott, May 14, 1941; FO/371/26191, Eden minute, May 15, 1941.
61. CO/967/125, Moyne to Davidson, March 31, 1941.
62. "Report on the Co-ordination of Security Intelligence."
63. Hyde, *Secret Intelligence Agent*, 119–20.
64. "Report on the Co-ordination of Security Intelligence."
65. Memo Nassau BWI, August 10, 1941. This MI6 document was initially marked "closed until 2042, 'Withhold Sensitive HRH DOW.'"
66. Hyde, *Secret Intelligence Agent*, 119–20.
67. Ziegler, *King Edward VIII*, 478.
68. "Report on the Co-ordination of Security Intelligence."
69. "Report on the Co-ordination of Security Intelligence."
70. Hyde, *Secret Intelligence Agent*, 119–20.
71. Ziegler, *King Edward VIII*, 477.

72. Churchill, *Second World War*, vol. 3, 540–41.

73. Shawcross, *Queen Elizabeth the Queen Mother*, 794; Rose, *King*, 105.

74. Rhodes, *Final Curtsey*, 76–89.

75. Rhodes, 77–90.

76. February 7, 1941; Pimlott, *Second World War Diary*, 154.

77. Jackson, *SOE's Balls*, 179.

78. March 30, 1941; Pimlott, *Second World War Diary*, 179.

79. August 13, 1942; Hart-Davis, *King's Counsellor*, 45–46.

80. Bowes-Lyon, "WWII Secret Activities."

81. Howarth, *George VI*, 138; February 4 and March 4, 1942; Pimlott, *Second World War Diaries*, 361, 388.

82. Entry for QM, conversations with Eric Anderson, 1994–95, RA/QEQM/ADD/MISC, quoted by Shawcross, *Queen Elizabeth the Queen Mother*, 559.

83. King diary, November 3, 1942, RAG:VI/PRIV/DIARY, quoted by Shawcross, *Queen Elizabeth the Queen Mother*, 559.

84. Entry for QM, conversations with Eric Anderson, 1994–95, RA/QEQM/ADD/MISC, quoted by Shawcross, *Queen Elizabeth the Queen Mother*, 560.

CHAPTER 11. THE END OF THE SECOND WORLD WAR

Epigraph: CAB/127/30, Lascelles to Ismay, July 28, 1943.

1. Sterling, "Getting There."

2. AIR/8/775, Portal to Churchill, "Operation Loader," June 11, 1943; Bridges (Cabinet Secretary), "LOADER: Cover for General Lion's Absence from the UK," June 11, 1943, AIR/8/775.

3. PREM/3/497/3, Churchill to Bridges, June 8, 1943.

4. Entry for June 2–4, 1943; Diary of John Mitchell, MISC.59, CCC, 14–17.

5. Entry for June 2, 1943; Payn and Morley, *Diaries of Noël Coward*, 21.

6. AIR/8/775, Hollis to Macfarlane, "LOADER," June 11, 1943.

7. AIR/8/775, Portal to Churchill, "Operation Loader."

8. Churchill to George VI, June 16, 1942, AP/19/1, Avon Papers, BUL.

9. Bradford, *George VI*, 467–69; Macmillan, *War Diaries*, 120.

10. ODNB: Hardinge, Alexander.

11. Wales, "'Massingham' Mission," 42–65.

12. Wilkinson, *Foreign Fields*, 131.

13. Wilkinson.

14. Dodds-Parker, *Setting Europe Ablaze*, 130–31.

15. Brooks, *Secret Flotillas*, 276.

16. Richards Brooks, reel 9, Oral History Collection, Imperial War Museum.

17. Richard Brooks.

18. AIR/8/775, Portal to Churchill.

19. Bennett, *Intelligence Investigations*, 74–112.

20. Churchill to Alexander, April 11, 1943, CHAR 20/109/114, Churchill Papers, CCC.

21. Castillo, *Maltese Cross*, 211. See also Macmillan, *War Diaries*, 124.

22. Walton, *Empire of Secrets*, 41.

23. West, *Double Cross*, 104.

24. CAB/127/30, Lascelles to Ismay, July 28, 1943.

25. Major Kempholme, *The History of RAF Station Tempsford*; unpublished.

26. O'Conner, *Tempsford Academy*, 88–91.
27. Wheeler Bennett, *George VI*, 595.
28. March 1, 1945; Hart-Davis, *King's Counsellor*, 298.
29. Shawcross, *Queen Elizabeth the Queen Mother*, 555.
30. Shawcross, 571.
31. October 1943 and January 1944; Hart-Davis, *King's Counsellor*, 170, 194.
32. March 3, 1944, Hart-Davis, 204.
33. Howard, *British Intelligence, Volume 5*, 110–21.
34. Wheatley, *Time Has Come*, 670; Morley, *Noël Coward*, 73.
35. Hesketh, *Fortitude*, 261–67.
36. Rankin, *Genius*, 399.
37. Hesketh, *Fortitude*, 274; see also KV/4/194-5.
38. *The King Who Fooled Hitler*, Channel 4, broadcast May 5, 2019.
39. April 18, 1944; Hart-Davis, *King's Counsellor*, 214.
40. *Daily Mail*, "King Takes Leave."
41. *The King Who Fooled Hitler*.
42. Stafford, *Ten Days*, 123.
43. May 6, 1944; Hart-Davis, *King's Counsellor*, 230–31.
44. June 14, 1944, Hart-Davis, 233.
45. CAB/120/16, Lascelles to Wilson, July 20, 1944.
46. CAB/120/16, Churchill to George VI, July 24, 1944.
47. CAB/127/30, George VI to Maitland Wilson, August 4, 1944.
48. FO/954/14A/214, Eden to Churchill, July 12, 1944.
49. FO/954/14A/214, Churchill to Lascelles, July 2, 1944.
50. March 29, 1941; Pimlott, *Second World War Diary*, 179.
51. Foot, *Resistance*, 317–18.
52. December 4, 1941; Pimlott, *Second World War Diary*, 330.
53. September 30, 1942, Pimlott, 499.
54. May 4. 1944; Hart-Davis, *King's Counsellor*, 217.
55. See HS/6/216: "PATRON Mission: Proposed Exfiltration by Sea of Prince Charles, Brother of King Leopold."
56. FO/954/26B/467, Lascelles to Lawford, September 27, 1944.
57. HS/2/34, Whiteley to Mockler-Ferryman, "King of Denmark," September 18, 1944.
58. FO/371/43130, Min. by Warner of Conversation with Mockler-Ferryman, "Possible Evacuation from Denmark of King Christian," November 30, 1944. Also see FO/371/43130, Eden minute, June 16, 1944.
59. Annual Obituary, Roland Turner, Saint Martin's, 1982, 466. See also January 16, 1945; Hart-Davis, *King's Counsellor*, 289.
60. HS/2/34, Mieville to Wilson, January 8, 1945; see also Tillotson, *SOE*, 68.
61. Tillotson, *SOE*, 73.
62. Entry for March 30, 1941; Pimlott, *Second World Diary*, 179.
63. Hart-Davis, *King's Counsellor*, 286–87.
64. Iatrides, *Revolt*, 213–14.
65. PREM/3/339/8, Bridges to Rowan, October 10, 1944.
66. PREM/3/339/8, Montgomery to Churchill, October 6, 1944.
67. January 2, 1944; Pimlott, *Second World War Diary*, 693.
68. June 16–21, 1944; Hart-Davis, *King's Counsellor*, 235–38.

69. FO/1093/247, Cadogan to Halifax, August 1942.

70. PREM/3/339/8, King to Churchill, October 5, 1944.

71. September 26, 1943; Hart-Davis, *King's Counsellor*, 165.

72. July 19, 1944, Hart-Davis, 246.

73. Pincher, *Dangerous to Know*, 168.

74. February 7, 1945; Hart-Davis, *King's Counsellor*, 293.

75. Wilkinson and Astley, *Gubbins & SOE*, 192.

76. This episode is documented in HS 7/49.

77. Rigden, *How to Be a Spy*, 20–22.

78. March 1, 1945; Hart-Davis, *King's Counsellor*, 298.

79. May 4, 1944; Hart-Davis, 217.

80. February 7, 1945; Hart-Davis, 293.

81. CAB/127/40, Lascelles to Ismay, April 5, 1945.

82. Pimlott, *Queen*, 79.

83. Bertrand, *Enigma*, 256. See also Cave Brown, "*C,*" 671.

84. Turing, *Alan M. Turing*, 156.

85. Harper, *Capturing Enigma*, 26.

86. The importance of this report was first recognized by Lewis, *Changing Direction*, 310–32.

87. July 25, 1946; Hart-Davis, *King's Counsellor*, 341.

88. CAB/127/31, Zuletta minute, July 25, 1946, on Ismay to Lascelles, July 23, 1946. The paper was TWC (46)15 (Revise), "Future Developments in Weapons and Methods of War."

CHAPTER 12. QUEEN ELIZABETH II

Epigraph: Turner, "Real Elizabeth II."

1. Shawcross, *Queen and Country*, 15.

2. KV/4/474, Liddell diary, February 6, 1952.

3. E.g., Edward, Cap d'Antibes, to De Courcy, August 28, 1948, file 11, box 5, de Courcy papers, Hoover Institution.

4. Wilson, "Revealed."

5. de Courcy to Wallis, Ritz Hotel, Paris, May 13, 1949, file 11, box 5, de Courcy papers, Hoover Institution.

6. de Courcy to Blum, April 19, 1979, file 11, box 5, de Courcy papers, Hoover Institution.

7. Quoted by Lownie, *Mountbattens*, 257.

8. Lownie, 258.

9. KV/4/474, Liddell diary, February 28, 1952.

10. KV/4/474, March 5, 1952.

11. Colville, *Fringes of Power*, 640–41.

12. Pimlott, *Queen*, 184; Lownie, *Mountbattens*, 257.

13. Murphy, *Monarchy*, 54–59.

14. Colville, *Fringes of Power*, 327.

15. Colville.

16. KV/4/475, Liddell diary, March 15, 1953, and March 18, 1953.

17. KV/4/475.

18. MEPO/4/140, Commissioner's Office, "Coronation of Her Majesty Queen Elizabeth II," May 1953.

19. CAD: Shuckburgh Diary, MS191/1/2/2, June 5, 1953.

20. Bedell Smith, *Elizabeth the Queen*, 71–72.
21. Hennessy, *Secret State*, 5.
22. CAB/181/7, Precedent Book, Part V: Relations with Buckingham Palace," n.d.
23. Bedell Smith, *Elizabeth the Queen*, 71–72.
24. Hardman, *Her Majesty*, 156.
25. PREM/11/753, Kirkpatrick to Colville, May 25, 1954.
26. PREM/11/753, Queen Mother to Churchill, June 10, 1954.
27. PREM/11/753, Kirkpatrick to Colville, May 25, 1954.
28. PREM/11/753, Churchill to Queen Mother, June 4, 1954.
29. PREM/11/753, Colville to Churchill, June 2, 1954.
30. PREM/11/752, Colville to Kirkpatrick, June 4, 1954; Prince Philip to Churchill, June 10, 1954.
31. Hennessy, *Hidden Wiring*, 65.
32. Hennessy, 65, 69; Bedell Smith, *Elizabeth the Queen*, 67.
33. Bedell Smith, *Elizabeth the Queen*, 108.
34. Bradford, *Her Life in Our Times*, 66.
35. Aldrich and Cormac, *Black Door*, 188.
36. April 12 and 24, 1956; Thorpe, *Who's In*, 76, 80.
37. Thorpe, 83; Williams, *Diary of Hugh Gaitskell*, 509–15.
38. Davenport-Hines, *Enemies Within*, 484.
39. Kapitonova, "Visit of Soviet Leaders," 148–49.
40. FO/371/122824, "Decisions Taken at PM's Meeting on 28/3 on Arrangements for Soviet Leaders' Visit," March 29, 1956.
41. Khrushchev, *Khrushchev Remembers*, 406.
42. Bradford, *Her Life in Our Times*, 100.
43. Kapitonova, "Visit of Soviet Leaders," 143.
44. Khrushchev, *Khrushchev Remembers*, 406.
45. Lownie, *Mountbattens*, 275.
46. Khrushchev, *Khrushchev Remembers*, 407.
47. FRUS: President's Trip to Europe, August 29, 1959, Memorandum of Conversation, FRUS, 1958–1960, Western Europe, vol. vii, pt. 2, 856.
48. CREST:CIA, LCCASSOCK Review, October 19, 1956.
49. FO/371/122392, Brimelow, "Message from Marshal Voroshilov to the Queen about Hungary," November 15, 1956.
50. Békés, "President Kliment Voroshilov's Telegram to Queen Elizabeth," 128.
51. FO/371/122392, Brimelow, "Message from Marshal Voroshilov to the Queen about Hungary," November 15, 1956.
52. FO/371/122392, Hibbert, "Message about Hungary from Marshal Voroshilov to the Queen," November 15, 1956.
53. FO/371/122394, Reilly to Beith, November 19, 1956.
54. Corera, *Art of Betrayal*, 140, 153–54.
55. Duns, *Dead Drop*, 64.
56. Summers and Dorril, *Secret Worlds*, 290–92.
57. Davies, *Queen Elizabeth*, 129–30.
58. Davies.
59. Lacey, *Royal*, 208.
60. Quoted by Heald, *Duke*, 129.
61. Seward, *Queen and Di*, 92–93.
62. Seward, 93.

63. PREM/11/991, Millard to Stark, December 15, 1955; Stark to Millard, December 13, 1955.
64. Davenport-Hines, *English Affair*, 276.
65. Quoted by Pimlott, *Queen*, 320.
66. Summers and Dorril, *Secret Worlds*, xiv, 20, 103, 290.
67. Keeler, *Secrets and Lies*, 38.
68. Keeler.
69. Private information.
70. Keeler foreword to Ivanov, *Naked Spy*, 7.
71. Andrew, *Defence of the Realm*, 495–96.
72. Ivanov, *Naked Spy*, 29–32.
73. Ivanov, 92–93; Davenport-Hines, *English Affair*, 105–6.
74. Ivanov, *Naked Spy*, 92–93.
75. Ivanov.
76. Botham, *Margaret*, 75.
77. Keeler, *Secrets and Lies*, 40–41.
78. Summers and Dorril, *Secret Worlds*, 293.
79. FOI, Hoover to Legal Attaché, London, June 11, 1963.
80. FOI, Hoover to Attorney General, June 18, 1963.
81. Summers and Dorril, *Secret Worlds*, 329.
82. Ivanov, *Naked Spy*, 53.
83. Ivanov, 92–93.
84. Summers and Dorril, *Secret Worlds*, 329.
85. Lewis and Willsher, "KGB's Spy."
86. Davenport-Hines, *English Affair*, 262–63.
87. Irving, "What Netflix's *The Crown* Leaves Out."
88. The letter, dated March 5, 1960, was published by the *Mirror* in 1999 to the Royal Family's consternation. See North, "Elizabeth and Margaret Letters."
89. Bradford, *Elizabeth*, 307.
90. Crossman, cited by Davenport-Hines, *English Affair*, 294.
91. Aldrich and Cormac, *Black Door*, 230.
92. Bedell Smith, *Elizabeth the Queen*, 123.
93. Pimlott, *Queen*, 320.
94. Davenport-Hines, *English Affair*, 344.
95. Pincher, *Dangerous to Know*, 168.
96. Haslam, *Near and Distant Neighbours*, 151.
97. Carter, *Anthony Blunt*, 376.
98. ODNB: Blunt, Anthony Frederick.
99. KV/2/4115, Reed, notes on "I/L from Burgess to His Mother," April 30, 1956.
100. February 12, 2001; Thorpe, *Who Wins*, 350–51.
101. Carter, *Anthony Blunt*, 449.
102. *Ealing Today*, "Former Ealing MP Reveals Involvement."
103. Lownie, *Stalin's Englishman*, 247–50.
104. KV/4/474, Liddell diary, June 12, 1951.
105. KV/4/474, Liddell diary, July 13, 1951.
106. KV/4/474.
107. PREM/16/2230, "Sir Anthony Blunt," attached to Hunt to Thatcher, December 20, 1978; PREM/19/120, Note of Possible Supplementaries and Suggested Answers, 1979.

108. PREM/16/2230, "Sir Anthony Blunt," attached to Hunt to Thatcher, December 20, 1978.
109. Modin, *My Five Cambridge Friends*, 180.
110. PREM/19/120, untitled chronology of the Blunt case, undated, filed in inside cover.
111. Thatcher, Hansard, November 21, 1979, paras. 405–6.
112. Thatcher, Hansard.
113. PREM/16/2230, Hunt to Wilson, "Sir Anthony Blunt," July 3, 1974.
114. Wright, *Spycatcher*, 223. She also apparently told a friend of the investigative journalist Chapman Pincher that she had been well briefed of the affair while working her gundogs at a shoot lunch at Broadlands. See Pincher, *Treachery*, 515.
115. Thatcher, Hansard.
116. Andrew, *Defence of the Realm*, 706.
117. PREM/19/120, Armstrong to No. 10, "Blunt," November 20, 1979; notes for Thatcher's speech attached to Armstrong to Whitmore, November 18, 1979.
118. Andrew, *Defence of the Realm*, 706.
119. PREM/19/120, *Private Eye* no. 467, November 9, 1979.
120. Davenport-Hines, *Enemies Within*, 514; Moore, *Thatcher, Vol. 1*, 484.
121. PREM/19/120, Armstrong to Thatcher, November 20, 1979.
122. Bower, *Perfect English Spy*, 324–26.
123. PREM/19/120, notes for Thatcher's speech, Armstrong to Whitmore, November 18, 1979.
124. Pimlott, *Queen*, 337.
125. PREM/16/2230, Hunt to Wilson, "Sir Anthony Blunt," July 3, 1974.
126. PREM/16/2230.
127. PREM/19/120, MI5, "Investigation of Russian Penetration of the Secret Services," annexe to Hunt to Prime Minister, May 29, 1979.
128. PREM/16/2230, "Sir Anthony Blunt," attached to Hunt to Thatcher, December 20, 1978.
129. PREM/19/120, anon. "Background," undated.
130. PREM/16/2230, "Sir Anthony Blunt," attached to Hunt to Thatcher, December 20, 1978.
131. PREM/16/2230, John Hunt, "Sir Anthony Blunt," December 20, 1978.
132. Carter, *Anthony Blunt*, 449.
133. Heald, *Duke*, 108.
134. Carter, *Anthony Blunt*, 449.
135. Carter.
136. PREM/19/120, "Interview with Anthony Blunt by Christopher Morris," November 20, 1979.
137. September 21, 1977; Donoughue, *Downing Street Diary: Vol. 2*, 238. Donoughue renders the name "Beevers" in his diary.
138. Donoughue. See also Hitchens, "Crown and the Mole."
139. Entry for November 7, 1977, Donoughue, *Downing Street Diary: Vol. 2*, 259. See also Purvis, "When Spooks Pulled Strings," 62–67.
140. PREM/16/2230; "Note for the Record, June 21, 1977."
141. PREM/16/2230, John Hunt, "Sir Anthony Blunt," December 20, 1978; PREM/16/2230, Hunt to Cartledge, "Sir Anthony Blunt," December 17, 1978.
142. PREM/16/2230, John Hunt, "Sir Anthony Blunt," December 20, 1978.
143. PREM/16/2230, Hunt to Callaghan, January 16, 1979.
144. PREM 19/120, Armstrong to Whitmore, November 16, 1979.

145. PREM 19/120, Armstrong to Whitmore, November 16, 1979.
146. PREM/16/2230, Hunt to Callaghan, January 16, 1979.
147. November 16, 1979, John Hunt, "Blunt and the Palace," December 1978.
148. Carter, *Anthony Blunt*, 484; Carey, "Kim Philby."
149. PREM/19/120, Armstrong to Whitmore, November 14, 1979.
150. PREM/19/120, anon. "Blunt and the Palace," annexe to Hunt to PM, July 29, 1979.
151. November 14, 1989; Benn, *End of an Era*, 580–81.
152. PREM/19/120, Lankester to Whitmore, November 18, 1979.
153. PREM/19/3942, Thatcher to Leadbitter, December 11, 1979.
154. PREM/19/120, Anthony Blunt statement, November 1959.
155. Carter, *Anthony Blunt*, 486.
156. July 18, 1964; Jebb, *Diaries of Cynthia Gladwyn*, 309.
157. Moore, *Thatcher, Vol. 1*, 485.
158. November 28, 1979; Strong, *Splendours and Miseries*, 385.
159. November 8, 1983, Strong, 541.
160. November 6, 1981, Strong, 420–21.
161. February 8, 1957; Catterall, *Macmillan Diaries, Vol. II*, 3.
162. October 10, 1967; Crossman, *Crossman Diaries*, 342.
163. PREM/11/3280, Macmillan to Queen, "Laos," March 27, 1961.
164. Bedell Smith, *Elizabeth the Queen*, 122–23.
165. PREM/11/3480, Macmillan to Queen, December 23, 1959.
166. April 1968; Vickers, *Beaton in the Sixties*, 230–31.
167. Ziegler, *Wilson*, 215.
168. September 21, 1963; Catterall, *Macmillan Diaries, Vol. II*, 596–97.
169. Davenport-Hines, *English Affair*, 269–70.

CHAPTER 13. QUEEN ELIZABETH'S EMPIRE

Epigraph: CAD:MS 191/1/2/4, Shuckburgh Diary, July 7, 1955.
1. Cannadine, *Pleasures*, 67.
2. See Murphy, *Empire's New Clothes.*
3. Louis, *British Empire*, i–xx.
4. Balfour-Paul, "Britain's Informal Empire," 490–98.
5. Marr, *Diamond Queen*, 143.
6. Milani, *Shah*, 85.
7. FO/371/86726, Lascelles to Henniker, June 21, 1948; FO/371/68730, Flag Officer commanding, HMS *Tebbus* to C.in.C Home Fleet, July 27, 1948. See also Townsend, *Time and Chance*, 133–34.
8. FRUS: US ambassador to the UK to SoS, August 5, 1948 (1948, Near East, South Asia, and Africa v/1 doc.122).
9. FO/371/91522, minute by Bevin, January 19, 1951.
10. Cormac, *Disrupt and Deny*, 94–96.
11. LHCMA: Woodhouse 8/1, Woodhouse, "Iran 1950–3," August 16, 1976, 2.
12. Rahnema, *Behind the 1953 Coup*, xx.
13. Louis, "Britain and the Overthrow," 168.
14. Rahnema, *Behind the 1953 Coup*, xxi; Louis, "Britain and the Overthrow," 167.
15. FRUS: Telegram from the US Embassy in Iran to State Department, February 28, 1953 (1952–54, Iran, 1951–54, doc. 166).

16. NARA: US Embassy, London, to State Department, RG 59, Central Files 1950–54, 788.11/2–2753, tel. 4844 to Tehran, February 27, 1953.
17. FRUS: Telegram from the US Embassy in Iran to State Department, February 28, 1953.
18. FRUS: Telegram from the US Embassy in Iran.
19. FRUS: Telegram from the US Embassy in Iran.
20. *The Queen and the Coup*, Channel 4, broadcast June 14, 2020.
21. *The Queen and the Coup.*
22. Cormac, *Disrupt and Deny*, 95.
23. Rahnema, *Behind the 1953 Coup*, 39.
24. Bayandor, *Iran and the CIA*, 76–77; Rahnema, *Behind the 1953 Coup*, xxi, 50–51.
25. Rahnema, *Behind the 1953 Coup*, xxii; Louis, "Britain and the Overthrow," 168.
26. FO/371/104659, Makins to London, May 21, 1953.
27. FO/371/104659, Churchill to Strang, May 22, 1953.
28. Aldrich and Cormac, *Black Door*, 177.
29. Thorpe, "Documentary Reveals Evidence."
30. Bayandor, *Iran*, 78; Rahnema, *Behind the 1953 Coup*, 38.
31. NARA: US Embassy Iran to Department of State, RG59, Central Files 1950–54, 788.11/8-2353, tel. 462, August 23, 1953, quoted by FRUS: US ambassador UK to Department of State, August 25, 1953 (Iran, 1952–54, doc. 356).
32. FO/371/104659, Falla min. "Message to the Persian Government," August 21, 1953.
33. FO/371/104659, Montague Brown min., August 24, 1953.
34. FRUS: US ambassador to UK to Department of State, August 25, 1953 (Iran, 1952–54, doc. 356).
35. FO371/110092, Eden minute January 20, 1954, on Tehran to London, January 18, 1954.
36. FO371/110092, Wiggin to HE 19/3/54; Stewart minute, March 26, 1954.
37. February 18, 1955; Nicolson, *Later Years*, 276.
38. FO/371/110092, Churchill to Kirkpatrick, August 22, 1954.
39. Milani, *Shah*, 199–201, 363.
40. September 11, 1973; Alikhani, *Shah and I*, 316–17.
41. Aldrich and Cormac, *Black Door*, 268.
42. FO/371/114868, Bailey to Fry, March 3, 1955.
43. FO/371/140872, Harrison to London, "The Shah's Matrimonial Affairs," October 13, 1959, Personal and Very Confidential.
44. FO/371/140872, West memo, "The Shah's Prospective Fiancée," October 28, 1959.
45. June 15, 1974; Alikhani, *Shah and I*, 375–76.
46. Hashimoto, *Twilight*, 57.
47. Jevon, *Glubb Pasha*, 224–25.
48. CAD:MS 191/1/2/4, Shuckburgh Diary, July 7, 1955.
49. CAD:MS 191/1/2/4.
50. CAD:MS 191/1/2/4.
51. Hashimoto, *Twilight*, 155.
52. Ashton, *King Hussein*, 49–56.
53. Ashton, 52.
54. Ashton, 65–66.
55. Jones, "'Preferred Plan,'" 401–15.
56. CAB 128/30, Cabinet Minutes, CM24(56), March 21, 1956.

57. Quoted by Rathmell, *Secret War*, 118.
58. Kyle, *Suez*, 145.
59. Kyle, 145–46.
60. Hennessy, *Prime Minister*, 228, 231–22.
61. Pearson, *Sir Anthony Eden*, 156–57; Hennessy, *Prime Minister*, 221.
62. Smith, "Resignation," 115.
63. Smith, 108, 115.
64. Smith, 111–15; Murphy, *Monarchy*, 67.
65. Murphy, *Monarchy*, 67.
66. Smith, "Resignation," 124.
67. Hennessy, *Prime Minister*, 223–24.
68. Hennessy, 223.
69. Pimlott, *Queen*, 253.
70. Murphy, *Monarchy*, 68–69.
71. Hennessy, *Prime Minister*, 223.
72. Murphy, *Monarchy*, 68–69.
73. Pimlott, *Queen*, 253.
74. Pimlott, 255.
75. Pimlott, 253–55.
76. Moran, "Concealing Collusion," 364.
77. Murphy, *Monarchy*, 67.
78. Murphy, 67–68; Hennessy, *Prime Minister*, 218; Pimlott, *Queen*, 254.
79. Murphy, *Monarchy*, 69.
80. PREM/11/1163, "Bulletin for HM the Queen for the 24 Hours Ending 6 AM 1st November 1956."
81. Aldrich and Cormac, *Black Door*, 194–202; Aldrich, *GCHQ*, 149; William Clark, interviewed on BBC1's *An Ocean Apart*, Part 5, "If You Don't Like Our Peaches," 1988.
82. FRUS: US Embassy in the UK to the Department of State, November 12, 1956 (Suez Crisis, vol. XVI, doc. 571).
83. Bedell Smith, *Elizabeth the Queen*, 116.
84. PREM 11/1163, "Bulletin No. 20 for HM the Queen for the 24 Hours Ending 7 AM 21st November 1956."
85. PREM 11/1163, "Bulletin No. 16 for HM the Queen for the 24 Hours Ending 7 AM 15th November 1956."
86. PREM 11/1163, "Bulletin for HM the Queen for the 24 Hours Ending 7 AM 10 November 1956"; "Bulletin No. 19 for HM the Queen for the 24 Hours Ending 7 AM 20th November 1956."
87. PREM 11/1163, "Bulletin No. 21 for HM Majesty the Queen for the 24 Hours Ending 7 AM 22nd November 1956."
88. PREM/11/1163, Adeane to Gibbons, November 22, 1956; Gibbons to Richmond, November 23, 1956.
89. PREM 11/1163, Colonial Secretary to Jamaica, December 2, 1956.
90. CAD:AP23/2/18B, Elizabeth to Eden, January 16, 1957.
91. CAD:AP23/2/18B, Elizabeth to Eden, January 16, 1957.
92. Pimlott, *Queen*, 256.
93. Thorpe, *Eden*, 586, 589.
94. January 30, 1962; Thorpe, *Who's In*, 208–9.

95. Lycett, *Life of Ian Fleming*, 205.
96. Pearson, *Ultimate Family*, 144–45.
97. Lacey, *Monarchy*, 206.
98. Pearson, *Ultimate Family*, 182–83; see also Pearson, *Life of Ian Fleming*.
99. Macintyre, *For Your Eyes Only*, 88.
100. McCrisken and Moran, "James Bond," 804–10; Stillman, "Two of the MADdest Scientists," 487–94.
101. Pathé, "King Faisal Visits Britain, 1956," July 19, 1956.
102. Karam, "Missing Revolution," 693–709.
103. FO/371/134262, Wright to Hoyer Millar, April 21, 1958.
104. FO/371/134262.
105. FO/371/134262, Hoyer Millar to Adeane, April 30, 1958.
106. FO/371/134262, Adeane to Hoyer Millar, May 2, 1958.
107. Hashimoto, *Twilight*, 152–55; Karam, "Missing Revolution," 693–709.
108. FO/371/133139, 103//58, Baghdad to London, August 21, 1958.
109. Hashimoto, *Twilight*, 155.
110. Wright, *Behind Diplomatic Lines*, 4.
111. Ashton, "'Great New Venture?'" 59–89.

CHAPTER 14. DISCREET DIPLOMACY

Epigraph: FCO/8/3644; Miers, "Shah," February 8, 1980.
1. FO/372/8184, Adeane to Gore-Booth, May 23, 1966.
2. May 20, 1966; Benn, *Out of the Wilderness*, 414.
3. CAD:AP23/12/2, Eden to Queen, July 27, 1965.
4. Manchester, *Arms of Krupp*, 10–12.
5. FO/371/189311; Roberts to A. Campbell (FO), June 6, 1966.
6. FO/371/189311, Roberts to FO, "Duke of Edinburgh's Visit," June 20, 1966.
7. See FCO/21/923-5.
8. FO/372/8184, Gore-Booth to Adeane, May 20, 1966.
9. FO/372/8184.
10. FO/371/152126, PUSC, "Steering Committee: United Kingdom Policy in Latin America," SC (60)7(2nd Revise), May 20, 1960.
11. FO/371/152126.
12. FO/1110/1615, Glass, "Latin American Tour," May 6, 1963.
13. Hardman, *Queen of the World*, 508.
14. FCO/26/55, Minter to Shakespeare, "The British Monarchy Today: Latin American Portuguese Edition," August 13, 1968.
15. FCO/26/55, IPD, "Publicity for the State Visit to Brazil and Chile between 1 and 18 November 1968," undated.
16. FCO/7/1145, Mason to Diggins, cc. Charteris, "State Visit to Chile," October 15, 1968.
17. FCO/168/3069, Allott to Dyer, September 11, 1968.
18. FCO/168/3560, Allott, "Brief for Call by Sir David Hunt," September 3, 1969.
19. FCO/95/419, quoted by McEvoy and Hunt, "Britain."
20. Senate Select Committee on Intelligence Activities, staff report, "Covert Action in Chile, 1963–73," III: 10, Gerald Ford Library.
21. FCO/168/3069, IRD, "Chile: IRD Annual Report—April 1968," April 1968.

22. USDDO: State Department, "Queen Elizabeth's Visit to Chile Discussed," November 13, 1968.
23. USDDO: State Department, "Queen Elizabeth's Visit."
24. FCO/168/674, SPA in Chile.
25. FCO/168/3069, IRD, "Chile: IRD Annual Report—April 1968."
26. PREM/13/2358, FO, "State Visit to Brazil and Chile," September 13, 1968.
27. FCO/7/1145, Mason, "The State Visit of Her Majesty the Queen and His Royal Highness the Duke of Edinburgh to Chile, 11–18 November, 1968," December 3, 1968.
28. FO/371/1182764, Bridges to Wright, August 2, 1965.
29. PREM/13/2352, "Record of Conversation between the Prime Minister and Mr Kosygin Over Lunch at No. 10 Downing Street on 10 February 1967."
30. PREM/13/2352, Gore-Booth to Sutherland, February 10, 1967.
31. Wilson, *Labour Government*, 353.
32. PREM/13/2352, Gore-Booth to Sutherland, February 10, 1967; Adeane to Gore-Booth, February 6, 1967.
33. PREM/13/2352, Morphett to Palliser, January 12, 1968.
34. PREM/13/2352, Morphett to Palliser.
35. Bower, *Perfect English Spy*, 350.
36. Platt, "The Soviet Imprisonment of Gerald Brooke and Subsequent Exchange for the Krogers, 1965–1969," 193–212.
37. PREM/13/2352, handwritten note for PM, January 19, 1968.
38. PREM/13/2352, Adeane to Halls, February 2, 1968.
39. PREM/13/2352, Halls to Adeane, January 30. 1968; Adeane to Halls, February 2, 1968.
40. Platt, "Soviet Imprisonment," 193–212.
41. Walden, *Lucky George*, 142.
42. FCO/57/195, Mayall to Security Department, May 20, 1970.
43. FCO/57/195, Holmer to Mayall, May 21, 1970.
44. FCO/57/195, Mayall to Leigh, May 21, 1970.
45. FCO/28/2111, Waldon to Bullard, "Royal Visits to the USSR," May 17, 1972; Killick to Bullard, December 6, 1972.
46. FCO/28/2111, "Possible Visit to USSR by Princess Anne," December 11, 1972.
47. FCO/28/2111, Westwood, "Possible Visit of the Duke of Edinburgh to the USSR," October 16, 1972.
48. Cowan, *Spy's Wife*, 102.
49. FCO/28/2111, Walden to Bullard, "Royal Visits to Soviet Union," June 26, 1972.
50. FCO/28/2111, Walden to Scott, "Duke of Edinburgh's Visit to the Soviet Union," June 20, 1972.
51. FCO/28/2111.
52. FCO/57/539, Walden to Bullard, "Duke of Edinburgh's Visit to the Soviet Union," March 1, 1973.
53. FCO/28/2111, Walden, "Possible Visit by Prince Philip to the Soviet Union," May 17, 1972.
54. FCO/57/543, Mayall to Willett, July 19, 1972.
55. FCO/28/2111, Walden, "Possible Visit by Prince Philip to the Soviet Union," May 17, 1972.
56. FCO/57/539, handwritten note, Greenhill, January 22, 1973.

57. FCO/57/543, Willett to Mayall, July 5, 1972.
58. FCO/57/539, Willett to Curle, April 11, 1973.
59. FCO/57/540, Willett to Killick, July 31, 1973.
60. FCO/57/540, Killick to Willett, August 2, 1973.
61. FCO/57/542, Cartledge to Bullard, July 30, 1973.
62. FCO 57/540, Curle to Willett, July 17, 1973.
63. FCO 57/540, Westood, handwritten note, July 6, 1973; FCO/57/541, Bullard to Cartledge, July 22, 1973.
64. FCO 57/542, Cartledge to Bullard, July 30, 1973.
65. FCO/57/540, Curle, untitled note, July 31, 1973.
66. FCO/57/540, Killick to FCO, July 30, 1973.
67. Nicholson, *Activities Incompatible*, 55–56.
68. FCO/57/541, Douglas-Home to Killick, August 7, 1973; Killick to FCO, August 9, 1973.
69. FCO/57/541, Bullard to Cartledge, June 22, 1973.
70. FCO/57/541, Douglas-Home to Killick, August 7, 1973; Killick to FCO, August 9, 1973.
71. FCO/57/541, "Protocol and Conference Department," briefing pack, August 28. 1973.
72. Vice chairman of National Security Commission under Council of Ministers of the Ukrainian SSR, "National Security Commission Central Commission of the Ukrainian Communist Party: Announcement," August 31, 1973; KGB document found in the Ukrainian archives and shared on Twitter by @kgb_files, translated by Anastasia Zabludovskaya.
73. Travis, "Duke."
74. FCO/57/542, Killick, "Visit of HRH The Duke of Edinburgh to the Soviet Union," October 2, 1973.
75. FCO/57/542.
76. Vice chairman of National Security Commission, "Announcement."
77. BDOHP: Sir Curtis Keeble interview, 94.
78. NAA: AA1984/609 part II, "The CIA and Whitlam's Dismissal," *Australian Financial Review*, December 5, 1975; Kerr to Charteris, December 5, 1975.
79. NAA:AA1984/609, part I, Kerr to Charteris, September 12, 1975.
80. NAA:AA1984/609, part I, Charteris to Kerr, October 2, 1975.
81. NAA:AA1984/609, part II, Charteris to Kerr, November 4, 1975.
82. NAA:AA1984/609, part II, Kerr to Charteris, November 11, 1975, and Charteris to Kerr, November 17, 1975.
83. NAA:AA1984/609, part III, Kerr to Charteris, June 10, 1976.
84. NAA:AA1984/609, part III, Charteris to Kerr, October 16, 1976.
85. NAA:AA1984/609, part IV, Kerr to Charteris, June 10, 1976, including attachment: ASIO report, "Australian League of Rights," June 8, 1976.
86. March 15, 1976; Donoughue, *Downing Street Diary*, 697.
87. Pimlott, *Queen*, 430.
88. March 15, 1976; Donoughue, *Downing Street Diary*, 697.
89. Donoughue. See also January 19, 1976, 634.
90. Aldrich and Cormac, *Black Door*, 327–28.
91. Haines, *Glimmers*, 129.
92. Murphy, *Monarchy*, 132.

93. July 17, 1975; Thorpe, *Who's In*, 504.
94. BDOHP: Colin Munro interview, 8–9.
95. BDOHP: Sir James Hennessy interview, 8–15.
96. Kyemba, *State of Blood*, 77.
97. We are most grateful to Spencer Mawby for guidance on this. CAB 128/61, CM(77) 21st mtg., Confidential Annex, minute 2, May 26, 1977.
98. *The Times*, June 1, 1977; courtesy of Spencer Mawby; see also Murphy, *Monarchy*, 135.
99. FCO/68/714, Sinclair minute, March 17, 1977, Memo on CHOGM: President Amin's Attendance by Duff, March 25, 1977; FCO/31/2157, Rowlands to SoS (undated); FCO/31/2159, Memo on President Amin and the Commonwealth Heads of Government Meeting by Hunt (undated). Courtesy of Spencer Mawby.
100. FCO/73/358, Record of Private Conversation with Munyua Waiyaki by Owen, June 22, 1977. Courtesy of Spencer Mawby.
101. Hardman, *Queen of the World*, 83–85.
102. Charles Harrison, former editor of the *Uganda Argus*, provided the fullest account of these events in *The Times*. See *The Times*, June 21, 22, 23, 24, and 25, 1977. See also *Los Angeles Times*, June 21 and 26, 1977; *New York Times*, June 21, 1977. See also Reid, *History*, 61–62. Courtesy of Spencer Mawby.
103. Hardman, *Queen of the World*, 84–85.
104. FCO/8/2522, Parsons to London, October 6, 1975.
105. FCO/8/1887, Special Branch memo, "Visit of HM the Queen and the Shah to Ascot," June 15, 1972.
106. FCO/8/1886, Memo to Smith, "Shah's Visit," June 12, 1972.
107. FCO/8/1887, "Meeting at the Iranian Embassy to Consider the Security Plan for the Shah's Visit," June 19, 1972.
108. FCO/8/1887, Armstrong note, June 19, 1972.
109. FCO/8/1887, Charteris to Downing Street, June 21, 1972.
110. FCO/8/1887, Armstrong to Charteris, June 16, 1972.
111. FCO/8/1887, Memo to Smith, "Tehran Telegram 549: Shah's Visit," June 19, 1972.
112. BDOHP: Sir Peter Ramsbotham interview, 38.
113. FCO/8/2077, Grattan to MDR, "The Queen's Return Flight from Australia," October 11, 1973.
114. FCO/8/2077, "Some Points Made by the Shah in Private Meeting with the Queen on 23 October 1973 at Teheran."
115. October 23, 1973; Alikhani, *Shah and I*, 329.
116. FCO/8/2179, Craig minute, October 15, 1974.
117. FCO/8/2179, Wright to Campbell, attaching "Royal Visits between Iran and the UK," May 29, 1974.
118. FCO/8/2289, Thompson report, August 12, 1974.
119. FCO/8/2523, Parsons to Lucas, "Royal Visits," May 28, 1975.
120. FCO/8/2522, Parsons to Callaghan, April 30, 1975.
121. December 14, 1978; Radji, *In the Service*, 285.
122. Cormac, *Disrupt and Deny*, 216.
123. Cooper, *Fall of Heaven*, 468–79.
124. Walden, *Lucky George*, 182–83.
125. PREM/16/2131, Owen to Cartledge, January 8, 1979.
126. AAD: US Embassy Rabat to US SoS, "President Carter's Messages on His Middle East Trip," March 14, 1979, doc. 1979RABAT01698.

127. AAD: US Embassy Rabat to US SoS.

128. PREM/16/2131, Chilcot to Cartledge, February 14, 1979; Cartledge to Lever, February 15 and 19, 1979.

129. HO/287/2826, Owen quoted by Lever to Cartledge "the Shah of Iran," February 21, 1979.

130. Palmer, *Queen and Mrs Thatcher*, 76.

131. FCO/8/3392, Lever to Cartledge, May 21, 1979.

132. AAD: US Embassy Rabat to US SoS, "President Carter's Messages."

133. Henderson, *Mandarin*, 272.

134. Shawcross, *Shah's Last Ride*, 287.

135. Weiner, *Legacy of Ashes*, 274.

136. FCO/8/3644, Miers, "The Shah," February 8, 1980.

137. PREM/19/2577, Thatcher to Margaret, January 9, 1980.

138. PREM/19/2577, Margaret to Thatcher, February 7, 1980.

139. FCO8/3644, Walden to Adeane, July 18, 1980; Miers to Private Secretary, July 18, 1980.

140. Cooper, *Fall of Heaven*, 495.

141. Entry for January 30, 1973; Alikhani, *Shah and I*, 283. Entry for July 14, 1974, Alikhani, 380. See also August 8, 1978; Radji, *In the Service*, 213.

142. FCO/8/3644, Lever, "Ex King Constantine," August 6, 1980; Miers, "Admission," September 17, 1980.

143. FCO/8/3644, Humfrey to Miers, August 11, 1980.

144. FCO/8/3644, Roberts to FCO, August 19, 1980.

145. FCO/8/3644, Lamport to Beckett, October 20, 1980; Humfrey to Miers, October 15, 1980.

146. Cormac, *Disrupt and Deny*, 217.

147. FCO/8/3644: Miers to Weir, October 29, 1980; FCO/8/3645, Weir to Heseltine, December 29. 1980.

148. HO/287/2826, Amery to Carrington, December 22, 1981; Snuffbox to Home Office, January 1983.

149. National Security Archive, "Cold War: Politburo Discussion of MT-Gorbachev Meeting," April 13, 1989.

CHAPTER 15. TERRORISTS AND LUNATICS, 1969–1977

Epigraph: Princess Anne interview, *Parkinson*, BBC, 1980.

1. PREM/13/1772, Forster to Halls, March 10, 1967; FO to Bangkok, March 14, 1967; New Delhi to Commonwealth Office, March 14, 1967; note for the record, March 10, 1967.

2. PREM/19/916, Bridge Inquiry into the Activities of Commander Trestrail, November 24, 1982.

3. Geraghty, *Bullet-Catchers*, 56, 64.

4. Connor, *Ghost Force*, 153–54.

5. November 4, 1968; Vickers, *Beaton*, 275.

6. Dimbleby, *Prince of Wales*, 131.

7. Varney, *Bodyguard*, 124.

8. Varney, 126.

9. Varney, 127.

10. Varney, 128.

11. Varney.
12. Brooke, *Terrorism*, 49.
13. Thomas, *John Jenkins*, 10–24.
14. PREM13/2903, Trend to Wilson, February 28, 1968.
15. PREM13/2903, Callaghan to Wilson, "Wales: Security," February 12, 1969; Brooke, *Terrorism*, 49.
16. Crump, "Bizarre Plots"; *Independent*, "Dennis Coslett" (obituary).
17. PREM/13/2903, Callaghan to Wilson, April 14, 1969.
18. PREM/13/2903.
19. PREM/13/2903, No. 10 to Cubbon, April 16, 1969.
20. Bedell Smith, *Prince Charles*, 40.
21. PREM/13/2903, Callaghan to Wilson; PREM/13/2903, Cubbon to Wilson, "Investiture of the Prince of Wales," February 14, 1969.
22. PREM/13/2903, No. 10 to Wilson, March 1, 1968.
23. Kandiah et al., "Ultimate Windsor Ceremonials," 81.
24. Thomas, *Hands Off Wales*, 114–15.
25. Bradford, *Elizabeth*, 349–51; De Courcy, *Snowdon*, 191.
26. PREM/13/2903, Halls to Cubbon, June 25, 1967; Jagger, *Escorting the Monarch*, 43–45.
27. Crump, "Bizarre Plots."
28. April 6, 1969; Williams, *Richard Burton Diaries*, 272–73.
29. July 2, 1969; Ziegler, *From Shore to Shore*, 183.
30. PREM/13/2903, Callaghan to Wilson, April 14, 1969.
31. PREM/13/2903, Halls to Cubbon, June 27, 1969.
32. July 11, 1969; Benn, *Office Without Power*, 191.
33. PREM/13/2903, Cubbon to Halls, June 26, 1969.
34. PREM/13/2903, Maybe to Halls, June 27, 1969.
35. PREM/13/2903, Cubbon to Halls, June 26, 1969.
36. Andrew and Mitrokhin, *Mitrokhin Archive*, 491–92.
37. Brooke, *Terrorism*, 50.
38. Dimbleby, *Prince of Wales*, 162.
39. Hardman, *Her Majesty*, 58.
40. July 7, 1969; Ziegler, *From Shore to Shore*, 183.
41. Jagger, *Escorting the Monarch*, 43–45; Turner, "Meanwhile," 33.
42. Pimlott, *Queen*, 390.
43. Bedell Smith, *Prince Charles*, 40.
44. Hardman, *Her Majesty*, 59.
45. Crump, "Bizarre Plots."
46. DPP/2/5401, "Brief for the Prosecution," April 1974.
47. DPP/2/5403, "Statement of Witness: J. Beaton," March 28, 1974.
48. DPP/2/5403, "Statement of Witness: A. Callender," March 21, 1974.
49. DPP/2/5403, "Statement of Witness: J. Beaton."
50. PREM/16/268, Armstrong to Wilson, March 21, 1974.
51. DPP/2/5403, "Statement of Witness: J Beaton"; DPP/2/5402, "Collective Account of Princess Anne and Captain Mark Philips," March 21, 1974.
52. Princess Anne interview, *Parkinson*, BBC, 1980.
53. Princess Anne interview; Jagger, *Escorting the Monarch*, 54–55.
54. HO/287/2287/2, DAC, untitled report on the arrest of Ian Ball, March 21, 1974.

55. Mark, *In the Office*, 166.
56. *Guardian*, "Princess Anne Kidnap Medal."
57. Wilson scribbled note on PREM/16/268, Armstrong to Wilson, March 21, 1974.
58. PREM/16/268, Wilson to Miller, March 26, 1974.
59. Prince of Wales, Naval Journal, March 20, 1974; Dimbleby, *Prince of Wales*, 255.
60. PREM/16/268, Armstrong to Charteris, March 21, 1974.
61. HO/287/2287/2, "Random Demand for £3 Million Addressed to HM The Queen," n.d.
62. HO/287/2287/2.
63. HO/287/2287/2, DAC, untitled report on the arrest of Ian Ball, March 21, 1974.
64. Jagger, *Escorting the Monarch*, 54–56.
65. HO/287/2287/1, "Personal Protection," March 28, 1974.
66. Aldrich and Herrington, "Secrets, Hostages and Ransoms," 738–44.
67. PREM/16/640, to "state visit" Galsworthy to Carlisle, March 4, 1974 (Lord Bridges to see).
68. HO/287/2287/1, Gerrard to Hilary, April 5, 1974.
69. HO/287/2287/1, Met Police, "Royalty Protection," March 22, 1974.
70. HO/287/2287/1, Met Police, "Royalty Protection."
71. HO/287/2287/1, "Personal Protection," March 28, 1974.
72. HO/287/2287/1.
73. Jagger, *Escorting the Monarch*, 54–55.
74. HO/287/2287/1, "Personal Protection"; Geraghty, *Bullet-Catchers*, 81–83.
75. March 21, 1974; Ziegler, *From Shore to Shore*, 290.
76. HO/287/2287/1, "Personal Protection."
77. Geraghty, *Bullet-Catchers*, 83.
78. Fremont-Barnes and Winner, *Who Dares Wins*, 8–11; Asher, *Regiment*, 399.
79. Geraghty, *Bullet-Catchers*, 83–84.
80. Asher, *Regiment*, 423.
81. PREM/19/916, Bridge Inquiry into the Activities of Commander Trestrail.
82. HO/287/2287/1, memo, A-Department, Metropolitan Police, March 22, 1974.
83. Evans, *On Her Majesty's Service*, 48–49. Glocks came in 1994.
84. Hastings, "Crazed Gunman"; Dyer, "Hunger Strike."
85. Seward, *Queen's Speech*, 114.
86. CJ/4/1518, Stephens, "Call Out of UDR for 6–15 August," August 1, 1977.
87. See FCO/23/197, Carter to Vining, February 1968.
88. CJ/4/1527, Charteris to Cooper, November 12, 1975.
89. Apple, "Northern Ireland."
90. CJ/4/1519, Marsh to Waterfield, "Queen's Silver Jubilee: Visit to Northern Ireland 10/11 August 1977," October 11, 1976.
91. CJ/4/1519, Waterfield, "Jubilee—Queen's Visit to Northern Ireland—Meeting at Buckingham Palace 19 January: Note for File," January 19, 1977.
92. CJ/4/1519.
93. Pimlott, *Queen*, 449.
94. CJ/4/1521, Silver Jubilee—Operational and Planning Committee, "Appreciation of the Options for an Outline Programme for HM The Queen's Visit to NI in August 1977," February 1977.
95. CJ/4/1518, "A Military Assessment of the Threat and of Tasks for the Army during the Visit of HM The Queen to NI 10 and 11 Aug 77," July 11, 1977.

96. CJ/4/1518, "Op Inheritor—Threat Assessment," July 12, 1977.
97. Geraghty, *Bullet-Catchers*, 86.
98. CJ/4/1519, Waterfield, "Jubilee Visit Planning: Note for the File," December 23, 1976.
99. Geraghty, *Bullet-Catchers*, 84–88.
100. CJ/4/1518, Mason, "The Queen's Jubilee Visit to NI 10 and 11 August," July 19, 1977.
101. Seward, *Queen's Speech*, 114.
102. CJ/4/1518, Ramsay to Stowe, "The Queen's Jubilee Visit to NI," July 28, 1977.
103. CJ/4/1518, Waterfield, "Jubilee Visit-PR etc.," July 8, 1977.
104. CJ/4/1518, Charteris to Cubbon, July 13, 1977.
105. Hardman, *Her Majesty*, 62.
106. CJ/4/1521, Silver Jubilee—Operational and Planning Committee, "Appreciation."
107. CJ/4/1518, "Op Inheritor-Threat Assessment," July 12, 1977.
108. CJ/4/1518, Ramsay to Stowe, "Incident at the New University of Ulster," July 29, 1977.
109. Loughlin, *British Monarchy*, 370–71.
110. Geraghty, *Bullet-Catchers*, 84–88.
111. Hardman, *Her Majesty*, 57.
112. McKittrick, "Northern Ireland."
113. CJ/4/1518, Charteris to Cubbon, draft speech, July 28, 1977.
114. Geraghty, *Bullet-Catchers*, 84–88.
115. McKittrick, "Northern Ireland."
116. Pimlott, *Queen*, 449.
117. Loughlin, *British Monarchy*, 371–74.
118. Entry for October 25–28, 1976; Henderson, *Mandarin*, 129–31.

CHAPTER 16. TERRORISTS AND LUNATICS, 1979–1984

Epigraph: Prince Charles, diary, August 27, 1979, quoted by Dimbleby, *Prince of Wales*, 324.
1. Murphy, *Monarchy*, 140–41.
2. Carrington, *Reflect*, 295–96; Ingram, "Thatcher and Ramphal," 781–83.
3. Hardman, *Queen*, 315.
4. Hardman, 308–9.
5. Hardman, 331.
6. Pimlot, *Queen*, 467.
7. Murphy, *Monarchy*, 140–41.
8. Pimlott, *Queen*, 467.
9. Murphy, *Monarchy*, 141.
10. Taylor, *Brits*, 221.
11. Broadlands Archive, S19, Mountbatten to the Queen, August 25, 1971; Ziegler, *Mountbatten*, 697.
12. Entry for May 16, 1978; Ziegler, *From Shore to Shore*, 379–80.
13. Lownie, *Mountbattens*, 338.
14. Lownie, 340.
15. Pearce, *Spymaster*, 13.
16. Lownie, *Mountbattens*, 340.

17. Bowyer-Bell, *Secret Army*, 451.
18. Lownie, *Mountbattens*, 341.
19. Bowyer-Bell, *Secret Army*, 451.
20. December 28, 1987; Thorpe, *Who Wins*, 168.
21. Ziegler, *Mountbatten*, 699.
22. Ziegler.
23. Bradford, *Elizabeth*, 427; Bedell Smith, *Elizabeth the Queen*, 295–96.
24. Shawcross, *Queen Elizabeth, The Queen Mother*, 855; English, *Armed Struggle*, 220.
25. Bradford, *Elizabeth*, 427; Bedell Smith, *Elizabeth the Queen*, 295–96.
26. Warwick, *Princess Margaret*, 16.
27. July 4, 1981; Henderson, *Mandarin*, 404.
28. Moore, *Margaret Thatcher, Vol. 1*, 482.
29. Lacey, *Royal*, 260.
30. Hardman, *Her Majesty*, 60.
31. HO/287/2842, Andrew to Chilcot, "Protection of VIPs," September 12, 1979.
32. HO/287/2842, McNee to Moore, September 10, 1979.
33. HO/287/2842, McNee to Moore, September 10, 1979; Andrew to Chilcot, "Protection of VIPs," September 12, 1979; Dawson to Phillips, November 8, 1979.
34. HO/287/2842, Chilcot to Andrew, "Protection of VIPs," September 12, 1979; McNee to Moore, September 10, 1979.
35. DEFE/68/749, Home Office to Chief Officers of Police, "Protection of Members of the Royal Family, Ministers and Other Public Servants," July 7, 1981.
36. DEFE/68/749.
37. Erickson, *Lilibet*, 253.
38. Andrew, *Defence of the Realm*, 694.
39. Andrew, 695.
40. Andrew, 695–96.
41. Blair, *Policing Controversy*, 78–79.
42. Bedel Smith, *Elizabeth the Queen*; Pimlott, *Queen*, 476.
43. Roy, "'Damn . . . I Missed'"; McNeilly, "Declassified Intelligence Service Documents."
44. Geraghty, *Bullet-Catchers*, 99.
45. BDOHP: Oliver Miles interview, 68.
46. BDOHP, 68–69.
47. Geraghty, *Bullet-Catchers*, 62–63.
48. *New York Times*, "Text of Scotland Yard's Report"; Pimlott, *Queen*, 491.
49. Keay, *Royal Pursuit*, 199.
50. July 26, 1982; Henderson, *Mandarin*, 484.
51. PREM/19/916, "Bridge Inquiry into the Activities of Commander Trestrail," November 24, 1982.
52. PREM/19/916, "Briefing for Prime Minister's Questions on Thursday 25 November 1982."
53. PREM/19/916, "Question and Answer Brief for Responding to Enquiries on the Publication of Lord Bridge's Report," n.d. [1982].
54. PREM/19/916, "Bridge Inquiry."
55. PREM/19/916.
56. PREM/19/916.
57. McNee, *McNee's Law*, 220–21.
58. McNee, 215.

59. McNee, 216–17.
60. Whitelaw, "Buckingham Palace (Security)," July 21, 1982, Hansard column, 397–98.
61. HO/287/3110, meeting "The Law of Trespass," October 4, 1982.
62. Geraghty, *Bullet-Catchers*, 96.
63. Whitelaw, "Buckingham Palace (Security)."
64. HO/287/3216, "Royal Security: Assessments of Risk to the Royal Family from Psychiatric Patients 1982," January 1–December 31, 1983.
65. Keay, *Royal Pursuit*, 204.
66. CAB/128/74, Cabinet Conclusions, CC(82) 38th Conclusions, July 15, 1982; PREM 19/916, "Briefing for Prime Minister's Questions on Thursday 25 November 1982"; Whitelaw, "Buckingham Palace (Security)."
67. Seward, *Queen's Speech*, 127.
68. Helliker, "Queen Reveals."
69. O'Callaghan, *Informer*, 197–210.
70. Gallagher, "Duran Duran Drummer."
71. Hoey, *Not in Front of the Corgis*, 168–69.
72. Davies, *Queen Elizabeth II*, 314–15.
73. Connor, *Ghost Force*, 315–16.
74. Connor, 315–17.
75. Campbell, *Iron Lady*, 361.
76. Firmin, *Regiment*, 246–48.
77. Firmin.
78. Firmin; Newsinger, *Dangerous Men*; Vinen, *Thatcher's Britain*, 94; Rhodes, *Final Curtsey*, 110.
79. PREM/19/1698, Acland to du Boulay, "Protection of 19 British VIPs on Visits Abroad," December 1, 1981.
80. De la Billière, *Looking for Trouble*, 353.
81. Global Terrorism Database.
82. Thatcher Archives: THCR6/1/2/6, Thatcher Engagement Diary, March 21, 1984; De la Billière, *Looking for Trouble*, 353.
83. Thatcher Archives: THCR 3/1/36/f152, Thatcher to Hussein, March 23, 1984.
84. CIA, "National Intelligence Daily," March 26, 1984; CREST: CIA-RDP87T00970R 000200010059-6.
85. BDOHP: Sir John Leahy interview, 31–32.
86. Thatcher Archives: THCR 6/1/2/6, Thatcher's Engagement Diary, March 24, 1984; De la Billière, *Looking for Trouble*, 353–54.
87. Ashton, "Love's Labours Lost," 667.
88. Thatcher Archives: THCR6/1/2/6, Thatcher Engagement Diary, March 21, 1984; De la Billière, *Looking for Trouble*, 353–54.
89. *New York Times*, "Elizabeth."
90. CIA, "National Intelligence Daily."
91. *New York Times*, "Elizabeth."
92. Quoted by Ashton, "Love's Labours Lost," 654.
93. Moore, *Margaret Thatcher, Vol. 2*, 141.
94. Connett, "British Defence Equipment."
95. Apple, "Queen Embroiled."
96. "Background Information and Recommended Talking Points for President Ronald Reagan's 6/4–6/10 Visit to Great Britain," n.d., USDDO.

97. US Embassy in Doha to SoS, "US Support for Camp David," September 27, 1978, doc. 1978DOHA01309.
98. Anastasi, "British Diplomat Is Shot."
99. BDOHP: Sir Peregrine Rhodes interview, 40–45.
100. SoS to Algeria, "Abu Nidal Terrorist Group," December 6, 1985, https://wikileaks .org/plusd/cables/85STATE371963_a.html.
101. Geraghty, *Bullet-Catchers*, 104, 106.
102. Delffs, *Faith of Queen Elizabeth*, passim.
103. Hardman, *Queen*, 60.
104. Geraghty, *Bullet-Catchers*, 436.
105. Geraghty, 107.
106. David Blunkett, "Buckingham Palace (Security Breach)," September 13, 2004, Hansard column, 1089.
107. Hardman, *Queen*, 44.

CHAPTER 17. THE DIANA CONSPIRACY

Epigraph: Stevens, *Operation Paget Inquiry*, 132; and NBC broadcast.
1. Interview with Martin Bashir on *Panorama*, BBC, broadcast on November 20, 1995.
2. Bradford, *Diana*, 14–54.
3. Lacey, *Monarchy*, 206; Talbot, "Into the Nineties," 229.
4. Entry for April 24, 1984; Strong, *Splendours*, 556–57.
5. Peck, "Drawing Back the Curtain," 86.
6. Wharfe, *Guarding Diana*, 68.
7. Tomlinson, *Big Breach*, 51–53, 98.
8. Stevens, *Operation Paget Inquiry*, 6.
9. Stevens, 6–7.
10. Hasnat Ahmad Khan testimony, para. 85, lines 17–19, Morning, March 3, 2008, Scott Baker.
11. Clayton and Craig, *Diana*, 337.
12. Stevens, *Operation Paget Inquiry*, 7–8.
13. Jordan, "38% of Brits Think Princess Diana's Death 'NOT an Accident.'"
14. *Dewsbury Reporter*, "Dewsbury-Born Author."
15. "UK Considered Killing Idi Amin," BBC News, August 16, 2003.
16. See, e.g., Aldrich, "OSS."
17. Zonis and Joseph, "Conspiracy Thinking."
18. *Al-Fayed v. CIA US District Court, D. Columbia*, August 31, 2000, case 1:00CV 02092.
19. Loeb and Miller, "Tinker?"; *Al-Fayed v. CIA US District Court*.
20. Stevens, *Operation Paget Inquiry*, 5.
21. Lyons, *Mr Paparazzi*, 250–51.
22. McNamara interview by Stevens, *Operation Paget Inquiry*, 676.
23. Harding, "Diana Death."
24. Tomlinson, *Big Breach*, 81–174.
25. Temple, "Spy."
26. Barnett, "Jackie Stewart"; Tomlinson, *Big Breach*, 153–55, 207–10, 269–71.
27. Stevens, *Operation Paget Inquiry*, 759.

28. Stevens, 759–60.
29. Cormac, *Disrupt and Deny*, 246.
30. Testimony of "Witness F" (MI6), paras. 1–2, February 28, 2008, Scott Baker.
31. Stevens, *Operation Paget Inquiry*, 755.
32. Tomlinson affidavit to French judges' investigation, 1997.
33. Cowper-Coles, *Ever the Diplomat*, 184.
34. Stevens, *Operation Paget Inquiry*, 772.
35. Cowper-Coles, *Ever the Diplomat*, 184.
36. Langley, "Mannakee File."
37. Stevens, *Operation Paget Inquiry*, 130.
38. Goodall, *Palace Diaries*, 154.
39. Wharfe, *Diana*, 32–33.
40. Jephson, *Shadows*, 371.
41. Entry for November 1995; Goodall, *Palace Diaries*, 208–9.
42. Seldon, *John Major*, 619.
43. Seldon.
44. Inquest document INQ0006335, Scott Baker.
45. Stevens, *Operation Paget Inquiry*, 108.
46. Mansfield, *Memoirs*, 328–29.
47. Simmons, *Diana*, 244–46.
48. Stevens, *Operation Paget Inquiry*, 106.
49. Jephson, *Shadows*, 120, 423; see also Burrell, *Royal Duty*, xiii.
50. Wharfe, *Guarding Diana*, 23, 66–67, 218–19, 246.
51. Meynell memo, "Meeting with HRH Princess of Wales 10:45 am on 18 October 1994," October 18, 1994, INQ0058848, Scott Baker.
52. DAC Meynell memo, "Meeting on 13 December with Princess of Wales at Kensington Palace, 11:20 am," December 14, 2003, INQ0058863, Scott Baker.
53. DAC Meynell, evidence, para. 46, line 19, Morning March 4, 2008, Scott Baker.
54. Sir David Veness, former assistant commissioner, Metropolitan Police Service, Statement 227, cited by Stevens, *Operation Paget Inquiry*, 802.
55. RDPD (Met) memo, "Security of HRH Princess of Wales," February 1, 1994, INQ 0058850, Scott Baker.
56. Jephson, *Shadows*, 298.
57. Sir Richard Eyre, interview, in *Diana: The Interview That Shocked The World*, Channel 5, broadcast on October 11, 2020.
58. FOI: John Birt's Office (BBC), "Chronology," November 23, 1995; FOI: BBC "Statement to the Board of Governors," n.d.
59. FOI: Alison Jackson (BBC) to Richard Peel (BBC), "MI5," December 4, 1995.
60. Bower, *Fayed*, 192, 236, 262, 288, 332–37, 368–69, 408–9.
61. French Dossier, D975–D985 and D990–D1006, cited by Stevens, *Operation Paget Inquiry*, 160.
62. *Al-Fayed v. CIA US District Court*, paras. 61–68.
63. Stevens, *Operation Paget Inquiry*, 736.
64. Owen, "US Ambassador Pamela Harriman Dies."
65. French Dossier, D2208–D2213, cited by Stevens, *Operation Paget Inquiry*, 160.
66. Stevens, *Operation Paget Inquiry*, 774.
67. Interview with Hocquet, cited by Stevens, 159.

68. Interview with Moodie, cited by Stevens, 223.
69. Interview with Rees-Jones, cited by Stevens, 230.
70. Interview with McNamara, cited by Stevens, 623.
71. Stevens, *Operation Paget Inquiry*, 618.
72. Leveson Inquiry, afternoon, November 29, 2011, 73 (lines 2022), www.levesoninquiry .org.uk/wpcontent/uploads/2011/11/TranscriptofAfternoonHearing29November 2011.pdf.
73. Lyons, *Mr Paparazzi*, 266–67.
74. Stevens, *Operation Paget Inquiry*, 746.
75. Lionel Cherruault testimony, para. 23, lines 8–12, March 3, 2008, Scott Baker.
76. Burrell, *Royal Duty*, xi–xiii.
77. Traynor, "MI6"; Walker and Ivanovic, "Vengeful Serbs."
78. Evidence, para. 110, lines 19–25, afternoon, December 13, 2008, Scott Baker.
79. Testimony of Rosa Monckton, para. 111, lines 2–10, and para. 131, lines 24–25, December 13, 2007, Scott Baker.
80. Walker and Ivanovic, "Vengeful Serbs."
81. Stevens, *Operation Paget Inquiry*, 745.
82. Hasnat Ahmad Khan testimony, para. 86, lines 1–2, morning, March 3, 2008, Scott Baker.
83. Jephson, *Shadows*, 482.
84. Mansfield, *Memoirs*, 324–35.
85. Rodriguez, "Princess Diana"; Rostain, Mouron, and Caradech, *Qui a tué Lady Di?* 12–35.

CONCLUSION

1. Nikkah and Kerbaj, "MI6"; BBC News, "Prince William."
2. Hannigan, "GCHQ Director's Speech."
3. Moore, "Tribute."
4. Tugendhat, Hansard, cm. 60, April 12, 2021.
5. McCrisken and Moran, "James Bond"; Zegart, *Army*.
6. BBC News, "Prince Charles."
7. Dover, *For Queen*, 683.
8. US State Department, cable from Tatiana Gfoeller (Bishkek) to Washington, October 29, 2008, https://wikileaks.org/plusd/cables/08BISHKEK1095_a.html.
9. Leigh, Brooke, and Evans, "WikiLeaks."
10. Harper, "MI6."
11. Anon., *Private Eye*, no. 1527, July 31, 2020, 13.
12. *Guardian*, "Prince Andrew."
13. Oprah with Meghan and Harry." CBS, 2021.
14. Prince Harry, interviewed, "Oprah."
15. Meghan Markle, interviewed, "Oprah."
16. "Oprah."
17. *Guardian*, "Prince Harry."
18. Twomey, "From Bagehot to Brexit."
19. *The Times*, "Palace Anger Mounts."
20. Herman, *Intelligence Power*, passim.

21. Beckett, "Royalty," 110.
22. *Guardian*, "What Does the Queen's Legal Immunity Mean?" July 14, 2022; *Guardian*, "Revealed: How Prince Charles Pressured Ministers to Change Law to Benefit His Estate." June 28, 2022.
23. June 4, 1985; Benn, *End*, 410.

APPENDIX

Epigraph: Lascelles to Nigel Nicolson, January 1967, quoted by Hart-Davis, *Kings Counsellor*, 420–21.

1. Entry for January 2, 1984, Thorpe, *Who Wins*, 248; entry for May 3, 1887, Thorpe, 298.
2. Kay and Levy, "Mystery."
3. PREM 19/355, "Royal Family, Duke of Windsor's Papers: Allegations by Duc de Grantmesnil That They Were Stolen by Secret Agents, 1979 May 10–1980 Jun 18. Closed."
4. Entry for December 6, 1980; Thorpe, *Who Wins*, 29; entry for January 21, 1883, Thorpe, 68–69.
5. Entry for February 5, 1976, Thorpe, 516.
6. Sanders (Downing Street) to de Courcy, April 17, 1979, file 11, box 5, De Courcy papers, Hoover Institution.
7. Pope-Hennessy, *Quest*, 293.
8. Entry for December 1, 2007; Thorpe, *Who Wins*, 415.
9. Lascelles to Nigel Nicolson, January 1967; Hart-Davis, *King's Counsellor*, 420–21.
10. Bellisario, *To Tread*, 128.
11. BDOHP, Warwick Morris interview, 5.
12. Gordon Brook-Shepherd was one of many; see *Storm Petrels*, his account of early KGB defectors.
13. See, e.g., Heald, *Princess Margaret*, 318.
14. Entry for September 20, 1983; Thorpe, *Who Wins*, 84.
15. Low, "Queen's Request."
16. Lewis, "29 Fakes."
17. Fenton, "Himmler Forgeries."
18. Private information.
19. Cowper-Coles, *Ever the Diplomat*, 89–90.
20. See, e.g., DPP 2/10544, "(Prince Faisal of Saudi Arabia): Procuring the Execution of a Valuable Security by Deception and Conspiracy to Defraud between 22 April 1987 and 11 April 1989 in Various Locations; Convicted 1988 Jan 01–1994 Dec 31. Closed."
21. DPP 2/10544, Colville to de Courcy, January 4, 1999.

Bibliography

There are many books on British intelligence over the last hundred years and even more on the royals. We have only referenced those that we have used extensively or quoted. All references to primary documents in the notes are to the UK National Archives at Kew unless otherwise stated.

PRIVATE PAPERS

Max Beaverbrook papers, Houses of Parliament Archives
Adolf Berle papers, Franklin D. Roosevelt Library, New York
Alexander Cadogan papers, Churchill College, Cambridge
John Colville papers, Churchill College, Cambridge
Neville Chamberlain papers, Birmingham University Archives
Winston Churchill papers, Churchill College, Cambridge
Kenneth de Courcy papers, Hoover Institution, Stanford
Ernest Cuneo Papers, Franklin D. Roosevelt Library, New York
Oliver Harvey papers, British Museum, London
John Masterman papers, Worcester College, Oxford
John Mitchell papers, Churchill College, Cambridge
H. Montgomery Hyde papers, Churchill College, Cambridge
Lord Louis Mountbatten papers, Hartley Library, Southampton University
Harold Nicolson papers, Yale University Library
President Secretaries Files, Franklin D. Roosevelt Library, New York
President Secretaries Files, Lyndon B. Johnson Library, Austin
Queen Victoria's Journals, Royal Archives, Windsor
Templewood papers, University Library, Cambridge

ORAL HISTORY PROJECTS

British Diplomatic Oral History Project, Churchill Archives, Churchill College, Cambridge
Foreign Affairs Oral History Project, Special Collections, Lauinger Library, Georgetown University
Suez Oral History Project, Liddell Hart Centre for Military Archives, King's College London

INQUIRIES AND INQUESTS

Lord Justice Scott Baker Inquests into the deaths of Diana, Princess of Wales, and Dodi Fayed. https://webarchive.nationalarchives.gov.uk/20090607230333/http://www.scottbaker-inquests.gov.uk/index.htm.

Lord Chilcot: The Iraq Inquiry. https://webarchive.nationalarchives.gov.uk/2017112
3123237/http://www.iraqinquiry.org.uk/.

MEMOIRS, DIARIES, PUBLISHED DOCUMENTS, AND REPORTS

Agar, Augustus. *Baltic Episode.* Annapolis, MD: Naval Institute Press, 1963.
Alikhani, Alinaghi, ed. *The Shah and I: The Confidential Diary of Iran's Royal Court—Asadollah Alam.* New York: St Martin's Press, 1991.
Benn, Tony. *The Benn Diaries, 1940–1990.* London: Arrow, 1995.
———. *Out of the Wilderness: Diaries 1963–67.* London: Hutchinson, 1987.
———. *Office Without Power: Diaries 1968–72.* London: Hutchinson, 1988.
———. *Conflicts of Interest: Diaries 1977–80.* London: Hutchinson, 1990.
———. *The End of an Era: Diaries 1980–1990.* London: Hutchinson, 1992.
Benson, A. C., and Viscount Esher, eds. *The Letters of Queen Victoria, Vols. 1–3, 1854–1861.* London: John Murray, 1907.
Blair, Ian. *Policing Controversy.* London: Profile, 2009.
Bolitho, H., ed. *The Prince Consort to His Brother: Two Hundred New Letters.* London: Cobden-Sanderson, 1933.
Brett, Maurice V., ed. *Journals and Letters of Reginald Viscount Esher*, vols. 1–2. London: Ivor Nicholson and Watson, 1934.
Brock, M., and E. Brock, eds. *H. H. Asquith Letters to Venetia Stanley.* Oxford: Oxford University Press, 2014.
Buchanan, G. *My Mission to Russia and Other Diplomatic Memories*, 2 vols. Boston: Little, Brown, 1923.
Buckle, George, ed. *The Letters of Queen Victoria, 1862 to 1878, Vols. 1–3.* London: John Murray, 1926.
———, ed. *The Letters of Queen Victoria, 1886 to 1901, Vols. 1–3.* London: John Murray, 1932.
Buckle, Richard, ed. *Self Portrait with Friends: The Selected Diaries of Cecil Beaton, 1926–1974.* London: Weidenfeld & Nicolson, 1979.
Burgess, Colin. *Behind Palace Doors: My Service as the Queen Mother's Equerry.* London: Blake, 2007.
Burrell, Paul. *A Royal Duty.* London: Michael Joseph, 2003.
Campbell, Alastair. *The Alastair Campbell Diaries: Power and the People, 1997–99, Vol. 2.* London: Hutchinson, 2011.
Carrington, Lord. *Reflect on Things Past: The Memoirs of Lord Carrington.* London: Collins, 1988.
Catterall, Peter, ed. *The Macmillan Diaries, Vol. I: The Cabinet Years, 1950–1957.* London: Pan, 2004.
———, ed. *The Macmillan Diaries, Vol. II: Prime Minister and After, 1957–1966.* London: Pan, 2011.
Churchill, Winston S. *The Second World War: The Grand Alliance*, vol. 3. New York: Houghton Mifflin, 1950.
Clark, Lewis. "Diplomacy as a Career" (US Foreign Service Officer, 1926–58), ADST Oral History. https://adst.org/wp-content/uploads/2013/12/Clark-Lewis-memoir.pdf.
Colville, John. *The Fringes of Power: Downing Street Diaries Vol. 2, 1941–April 1955.* London: Sceptre, 1987.
Cowan, Janice. *A Spy's Wife: The Moscow Memoirs of a Canadian Who Witnessed the End of the Cold War.* Toronto: Lorimer, 2006.

Cowper-Coles, Sherard. *Ever the Diplomat: Confessions of a Foreign Office Mandarin.* London: Collins, 2012.

Crossman, Richard. *The Crossman Diaries: Selections from the Diaries of a Cabinet Minister, 1964–1970.* London: Jonathan Cape, 1979.

De la Billiere, Peter. *Looking for Trouble: SAS to Gulf Command.* London: HarperCollins, 1995.

Dodds-Parker, Douglas. *Setting Europe Ablaze: Some Account of Ungentlemanly Warfare.* London: Springwood Books, 1984.

Donoughue, Bernard. *Downing Street Diary: With James Callaghan in No. 10.* London: Cape, 2008.

Duke of Windsor. *A King's Story: The Memoirs of HRH the Duke of Windsor.* London: Cassell, 1951.

Evans, Ron. *On Her Majesty's Service: My Incredible Life in the World's Most Dangerous Close Protection Squad.* London: Blake, 2008.

Gilliard, Peter. *Thirteen Years at the Russian Court: A Personal Record of the Last Years and Death of the Czar Nicholas II and His Family.* London: Doran, 1923.

Goodall, Sarah. *The Palace Diaries: The True Story of Life at the Palace by Prince Charles' Secretary.* London: Dynasty, 2006.

Gorodetsky, Gabriel, ed. *The Maisky Diaries: Red Ambassador to the Court of St James's, 1932–1943.* New Haven, CT: Yale University Press, 2015.

Guizot, F. *An Embassy to the Court of St. James's in 1840.* London: Bentley, 1862.

Haines, Joe. *Glimmers of Twilight: Harold Wilson in Decline.* London: Politico's, 2003.

Hart-Davis, D. *In Royal Service.* London: Hamish Hamilton, 1979.

Hart-Davis, Duff, ed. *King's Counsellor: Abdication and War—The Diaries of Sir Alan Lascelles.* London: Weidenfeld & Nicolson, 2006.

Heffer, Simon, ed. *Henry "Chips" Channon: The Diaries, Vol. 1, 1918–38.* London: Hutchinson, 2001.

Henderson, Ian. *Man Hunt in Kenya.* New York: Doubleday, 1958.

Henderson, N. *Mandarin: The Diaries of an Ambassador, 1969–81.* London: Weidenfeld & Nicolson, 1994.

Hoare, S. *The Forth Seal: The End of a Russian Chapter.* London: Heinemann, 1930.

Hyde, H. Montgomery. *Secret Intelligence Agent.* London: Constable, 1982.

Ivanov, Yevgeny. *The Naked Spy.* London: Blake, 1994.

Jebb, M., ed. *The Diaries of Cynthia Gladwyn.* London: Constable, 1995.

Jephson, Patrick. *Shadows of a Princess: Diana, Princess of Wales 1987–1996.* London: Collins, 2000.

Kaiser Wilhelm and Tsar Nicholas. *Between Two Emperors: The Willy-Nicky Telegrams and Letters, 1894–1914.* London: A&F Reprints, 2017.

Keeler, Christinem, and Douglas Thompson. *Secrets and Lies.* London: John Blake, 2012.

Khrushchev, Nikita. *Khrushchev Remembers.* London: Book Club Associates, 1971.

Langworth, Richard. *Churchill by Himself: The Definitive Collection of Quotations by Winston Churchill.* New York: PublicAffairs, 2008.

Lockhart, R. B. *Memoirs of a British Agent.* London: Macmillan, 1932.

Lyons, Darryn. *Mr Paparazzi: My Life as the World's Most Outrageous Celebrity Photographer.* London: John Blake, 2010.

Macmillan, Harold. *Pointing the Way, 1959–61.* London: Macmillan, 1972.

———. *War Diaries.* London: Macmillan, 1984.

Mansfield, Michael. *Memoirs of a Radical Lawyer.* London: Bloomsbury, 2009.

Marcus, Leah, S. Janel Mueller, and Mary Beth Rose. *Elizabeth I: Collected Works*. Chicago: University of Chicago Press, 2000.

Mark, Sir Robert. *In the Office of Constable: An Autobiography*. London: Collins, 1978.

Markov, Sergei Vladimirovich, Frank Stuart Flint, and Dorothy Fraser Tait. *How We Tried to Save the Tsaritsa . . . Translated by F. S. Flint and D. F. Tait*. New York: G. P. Putnam's Sons, 1929.

Maylunas, Andrei, and Sergei Mironenko. *A Lifelong Passion: Nicholas and Alexandra—Their Own Story*. New York: Diane Publishing, 2005.

McNee, Sir David. *McNee's Law*. London: Collins, 1983.

Mikhailovich, Alexander. *Once a Grand Duke*. London: Cassell, 1932.

Modin, Yuri. *My Five Cambridge Friends*. London: Headline, 1994.

Nansen, Fridjtof. *Through Siberia the Land of the Future*. London: Stokes, 1914.

Nicholson, Martin. *Activities Incompatible: Memoirs of a Kremlinologist and a Family Man, 1963–1971*. Self-published, 2013.

Nicolson, Harold. *The Later Years: 1945–1962*. London: Atheneum, 1966.

Nicolson, Nigel, ed. *The Harold Nicolson Diaries: 1907–1963*. London: Weidenfeld & Nicolson, 2004.

O'Callaghan, Sean. *The Informer: The Real Life Story of One Man's War against Terrorism*. London: Bantam, 1999.

Payn, G., and S. Morley, eds. *The Diaries of Noël Coward*. London: Macmillan, 1982.

Pimlott, Ben, ed. *The Second World War Diary of Hugh Dalton*. London: Cape, 1986.

Pincher, Chapman. *Dangerous to Know: A Life*. London: Biteback, 2014.

Ponsonby, Arthur, ed. *Henry Ponsonby: Queen Victoria's Private Secretary, His Life in Letters*. London: Macmillan, 1942.

Ponsonby, Frederick, ed. *Letters of the Empress Frederick*. London: Macmillan, 1928.

———. *Recollections of Three Reigns*. London: Eyre and Spottiswoode, 1951.

Radji, Parviz. *In the Service of the Peacock Throne: The Diaries of the Shah's Last Ambassador to London*. London: Hamish Hamilton, 1983.

Reid, Michaela. *Ask Sir James: The Life of Sir James Reid, Personal Physician to Queen Victoria*. London: Eland, 1996.

Reilly, S. *The Adventures of Britain's Master Spy*. London: Elkins Mathews and Marrot, 1931.

Rhodes, Margaret. *The Final Curtsey: A Royal Memoir by the Queen's Cousin*. London: Birlinn, 2012.

Roberts, Cecil. *Sunshine and Shadow*. London: Hodder & Stoughton, 1972.

Roosevelt, Elliott. *FDR, His Personal Letters, Volume 4*. New York: Kraus, 1970.

Roy, Raj, and John Young, eds. *Ambassador to Sixties London: The Diaries of David Bruce, 1961–1969*. Dordrecht: Republic of Letters, 2009.

Sale, Lady. *A Journal of the Disasters in Afghanistan*. London: John Murray, 1843.

Schellenberg, Walter. *The Schellenberg Memoirs*. New York: Andre Deutch, 1956.

Smith, Amanda, ed. *Hostage to Fortune: The Letters of Joseph P. Kennedy*. New York: Viking, 2001.

Stevens, Lord. *The Operation Paget Inquiry Report into the Allegation of Conspiracy to Murder Diana, Princess of Wales and Emad El-Din Mohamed Abdel Moneim Fayed*. London: HMSO, 2007.

Stevenson, Frances. *Lloyd George: A Diary*. London: Hutchinson, 1971.

Strong, Roy. *Splendours and Miseries: The Roy Strong Diaries, 1967–1987*. London: Weidenfeld & Nicolson, 1997.

Thomson, Sir B. *The Scene Changes*. London: Collins, 1939.

Tomlinson, R. *The Big Breach: From Top Secret to Maximum Security*. London: Cutting Edge, 2001.

Thorpe, D. R., ed. *Who's In, Who's Out. The Journals of Kenneth Rose. Vol. 1, 1944–1979*. London: Weidenfeld & Nicolson, 2018.

———, ed. *Who Wins, Who Loses. The Journals of Kenneth Rose. Vol. 2, 1979–2014*. London: Weidenfeld & Nicolson, 2019.

Townsend, Peter. *Time and Chance: An Autobiography*. London: Collins, 1978.

Varney, Michael. *Bodyguard to Prince Charles*. London: Hale, 1989.

Vickers, Hugo, ed. *Beaton in the Sixties: More Unexpurgated Diaries*. London: Weidenfeld & Nicolson, 2003.

Waldegrave, William. *A Different Kind of Weather: A Memoir*. London: Constable, 2015.

Walden, George. *Lucky George: Memoirs of an Anti-Politician*. London: Allen Lane, 1999.

Wellesley, Frederick. *Recollections of a Soldier-Diplomat*. London: Hutchinson, 1948.

———. *With the Russians in Peace and War: Recollections of a Military Attaché*. London: Nash, 1905.

West, Nigel, ed. *The Guy Liddell Diaries, Vol. 1, 1938–1942*. London: Routledge, 2009.

———, ed. *The Guy Liddell Diaries, Vol. 2, 1942–1945*. London: Routledge, 2009.

Wharfe, Ken. *Diana: Closely Guarded Secret*. London: Michael O'Mara, 2002.

———. *Guarding Diana: Protecting the Princess Around the World*. London: John Blake, 2017.

Wheatley, Dennis. *The Time Has Come: An Autobiography*. London: Hutchinson, 1977.

Wilkinson, Peter. *Foreign Fields: The Story of an SOE Operative*. London: I. B. Tauris, 1997.

Williams, P. M., ed. *The Diary of Hugh Gaitskell, 1945–56*. London: Cape, 1983.

Williams, C., ed. *The Richard Burton Diaries*. New Haven, CT: Yale University Press, 2013.

Wilson, Harold. *The Labour Government, 1964–70: A Personal Record*. London: Weidenfeld & Nicolson, 1971.

Wright, Peter. *Spycatcher: The Candid Autobiography of a Senior Intelligence Officer*. London: William Heinemann, 1987.

Wright, Patrick. *Behind Diplomatic Lines: Relations with Ministers*. London: Biteback, 2018.

Young, Kenneth, ed. *The Diaries of Sir Robert Bruce Lockhart, 1915–1938*. London: Macmillan, 1973.

Youssoupoff, Prince. *Rasputin: His Malignant Influence and His Assassination*. Translated from the Russian by Oswald Rayner. London: Cape, 1934.

Ziegler, P., ed. *From Shore to Shore: The Final Years. The Diaries of Earl Mountbatten of Burma, 1953–1979*. London: Collins, 1989.

BOOKS

Aldrich, Richard J. *GCHQ: Centenary Edition*. London: Collins, 2019.

———. *Hidden Hand: Britain American and Cold War Secret Intelligence*. London: John Murray, 2001.

———. *Intelligence and the War Against Japan*. Cambridge: Cambridge University Press, 2000.

Aldrich, Richard J., and Rory Cormac. *The Black Door: Spies, Secrets and British Prime Ministers*. London: Collins, 2016.

Anand, Sushila. *Indian Sahib: Queen Victoria's Dear Abdul.* London: Duckworth, 1996.

Andrew, Christopher. *Defence of the Realm: The Authorised History of MI5.* London: Penguin, 2010.

———. *For the President's Eyes Only: Secret Intelligence and the American Presidency from Washington to Bush.* New York: Collins, 1996.

———. *Secret Service: The Making of the British Intelligence Community.* London: Heinemann, 1985.

———. *The Secret World: A History of Intelligence.* New Haven, CT: Yale University Press, 2018.

Andrew, Christopher, and Julius Green. *Stars and Spies: Intelligence Operations and the Entertainment Business.* London: Bodley Head, 2022.

Andrew, Christopher, and Vasili Mitrokhin. *The Mitrokhin Archive: The KGB in Europe and the West.* London: Penguin, 1999.

Archer, John M. *Sovereignty and Intelligence: Spying and Court Culture in the English Renaissance.* Stanford, CA: Stanford University Press, 1993.

Asher, Michael. *The Regiment: The Real Story of the SAS.* London: Penguin, 2008.

Ashton, Nigel. *King Hussein of Jordan: A Political Life.* New Haven, CT: Yale University Press, 2008.

Baird, Julia. *Victoria: The Queen: An Intimate Biography of the Woman Who Ruled an Empire.* New York: Random House, 2016.

Bartley, Paula. *Queen Victoria.* Abingdon, UK: Routledge, 2016.

Basu, Shrabani. *Victoria and Abdul: The Extraordinary True Story of the Queen's Closest Confidant.* Stroud, UK: History Press, 2017.

———. *Victoria and Abdul: The True Story of the Queen's Closest Confidant.* Stroud, UK: History Press, 2010.

Bayandor, Darioush. *Iran and the CIA: The Fall of Mosaddeq Revisited.* Basingstoke, UK: Palgrave Macmillan, 2010.

Beaken, Robert. *Cosmo Lang: Archbishop in War and Crisis.* London: I. B. Tauris, 2012.

Bedell Smith, Sally. *Elizabeth the Queen: The Woman, the Family, the Life.* New York: Penguin, 2012.

———. *Prince Charles: The Passions and Paradoxes of an Improbable Life.* New York: Random House, 2017.

Beesley, Ian. *The Official History of the Cabinet Secretaries.* Abingdon, UK: Routledge, 2018.

Bennett, Gill. *Churchill's Man of Mystery: Desmond Morton and the World of Intelligence.* Abingdon, UK: Routledge, 2006.

———. *The Zinoviev Letter: The Conspiracy that Never Dies.* Oxford: Oxford University Press, 2018.

Bennett, Ralph. *Intelligence Investigations: How Ultra Changed History.* London: Frank Cass, 1996.

Bland, Lucy. *Modern Women on Trial: Sexual Transgression in the Age of the Flapper.* Manchester: Manchester University Press, 2013.

Bloch, Michael. *Operation Willi: The Nazi Plot to Kidnap the Duke of Windsor, July 1940.* London: Weidenfeld & Nicolson, 1986.

———. *The Secret File of the Duke of Windsor.* New York: Bantam, 1988.

Boghardt, Thomas. *Spies of the Kaiser: German Covert Operations in Britain during the First World War Era.* London: Palgrave, 2004.

Botham, Noel. *Margaret: The Last Real Princess.* London: John Blake, 2002.

Bourne, Kenneth. *The Foreign Policy of Victorian England, 1830–1902.* Oxford: Clarendon Press, 1970.

Bousfield, Arthur, and Garry Toffoli. *Royal Spring: The Royal Tour of 1939 and the Queen Mother in Canada.* Toronto: Dundurn Press, 1989.

Bower, Tom. *Fayed: The Unauthorised Biography.* London: Macmillan, 1999.

———. *The Perfect English Spy: Sir Dick White and the Secret War, 1935–90.* New York: St. Martin's Press, 1995.

———. *The Rebel Prince: The Power, Passion, and Defiance of Prince Charles.* London: Collins, 2018.

Bowyer-Bell, J. *The Secret Army: The IRA.* London: Transaction, 1997.

Bradford, Sarah. *Diana.* London: Penguin, 2006.

———. *George VI: The Dutiful King.* London: Penguin, 2013.

———. *Queen Elizabeth: Her Life in Our Times.* London: Penguin, 2012.

Brewer, Susan. *To Win the Peace: British Propaganda in the United States during World War II.* Ithaca, NY: Cornell University Press, 1997.

Brooke, Nick. *Terrorism and Nationalism in the United Kingdom: The Absence of Noise.* London: Palgrave, 2018.

Brooks, Richards. *Secret Flotillas: Clandestine Sea Operations in the Mediterranean, Volume II.* London: Frank Cass, 2004.

Brook-Shepherd, Gordon. *Iron Maze: The Western Secret Services and the Bolsheviks.* London: Pan Macmillan, 1999.

———. *The Storm Petrels: The First Soviet Defectors, 1928–38.* London: Collins, 1977.

Brown, David. *Palmerston and the Politics of Foreign Policy, 1846–55.* Manchester: Manchester University Press, 2002.

Burns, Jimmy. *Papa Spy: A True Story of Love, Wartime Espionage.* London: Bloomsbury, 2009.

Cadbury, Deborah. *Princes at War: The British Royal Family's Private Battle in the Second World War.* London: Bloomsbury, 2016.

Campbell, Christy. *Fenian Fire: The British Government Plot to Assassinate Queen Victoria.* London: Collins, 2011.

Campbell, John. *Margaret Thatcher: The Iron Lady.* New York: Vintage, 2007.

Carter, Miranda. *Anthony Blunt: His Lives.* London: Pan, 2002.

———. *The Three Emperors: Three Cousins, Three Empires, and the Road to World War One.* London: Penguin, 2010.

Cannadine, David. *The Pleasures of the Past.* London: Fontana, 1990.

Casey, Bart. *The Double Life of Laurence Oliphant: Victorian Pilgrim and Prophet.* London: Post Hill Press, 2015.

Castillo, Dennis Angelo. *The Maltese Cross: A Strategic History of Malta.* Westport, CT: Greenwood Press, 2006.

Cathcart, Helen. *Anne and the Princesses Royal.* London: W. H. Allen, 1973.

Cave Brown, Anthony. *"C": The Secret Life of Sir Stuart Menzies, Spymaster to Winston Churchill.* New York: Macmillan, 1987.

Chamberlain, Muriel. *Pax Britannica? British Foreign Policy 1789–1914.* London: Routledge, 1989.

Christy, Jim. *The Price of Power: A Biography of Charles Eugène Bedaux.* Toronto: Doubleday, 1984.

Churchill, E. *In the Eye of the Storm: George V and the Great War.* London: Helion, 2018.

Clay, Catrine. *King, Kaiser, Tsar: Three Royal Cousins Who Led the World to War.* New York: Walker, 2007.

Clayton, Tim, and Phil Craig. *Diana: The Story of a Princess.* London: Hodder & Stoughton, 2001.

Cobain, Ian. *The History Thieves: Secrets, Lies and the Shaping of a Modern Nation.* London: Portobello, 2016.

Cohen, David. *Diana, Death of a Goddess.* London: Century, 2004.

Conant, Jennet. *The Irregulars: Roald Dahl and the British Spy Ring in Wartime Washington.* New York: Simon & Schuster, 2008.

Connor, Ken. *Ghost Force: The Secret History of the SAS.* London: Cassell, 1998.

Cook, Andrew. *To Kill Rasputin: The Life and Death of Grigori Rasputin.* New York: History Press, 2006.

———. *The Murder of the Romanovs.* London: Amberley, 2010.

Corera, Gordon. *The Art of Betrayal: Life and Death in the British Secret Service.* London: Weidenfeld & Nicolson, 2011.

Cormac, Rory. *Confronting the Colonies: British Intelligence and Counterinsurgency.* New York: Oxford University Press, 2013.

———. *Disrupt and Deny: Spies, Special Forces and the Secret Pursuit of British Foreign Policy.* Oxford: Oxford University Press, 2018.

Costello, John. *Ten Days to Destiny: The Secret Story of the Hess Peace Initiative and British Efforts to Strike a Deal with Hitler.* New York: Morrow, 1991.

Cowles, Virginia. *The Romanovs.* New York: Harper & Row, 1971.

Crockett, Peter. *Evatt: A Life.* Oxford: Oxford University Press, 1993.

Crowdy, Terry. *The Enemy Within: A History of Spies, Spymasters, and Espionage.* New York: Osprey, 2008.

Cull, N. *Selling War: The British Propaganda Campaign against American "Neutrality" in World War II.* Oxford: Oxford University Press, 1996.

Cullen, Richard. *Rasputin: The Role of Britain's Secret Service in His Torture and Murder.* New York: Dialogue, 2010.

Daily Mail. "The King Takes Leave of His Fleet." May 15, 1944.

Davenport-Hines, Richard. *Enemies Within: Communists, The Cambridge Spies, and the Making of Modern Britain.* London: Collins, 2018.

———. *An English Affair: Sex, Class, and Power in the Age of Profumo.* London: Collins, 2013.

Davies, Nicholas. *Queen Elizabeth II: A Woman Who Is Not Amused.* New York: Birch Lane, 1994.

Davies, Philip. *Intelligence and Government in Britain and the United States, Volume 2: Evolution of the UK Intelligence Community.* Santa Barbara, CA: Praeger, 2012.

———. *MI6 and the Machinery of Spying.* London: Frank Cass, 2004.

Day, Peter. *Franco's Friends: How British Intelligence Helped Bring Franco to Power in Spain.* London: Biteback, 2011.

———. *Trotsky's Favourite Spy: The Life of George Alexander Hill.* London: Biteback, 2017.

De Courcy, Anne. *Snowdon: The Biography.* London: Weidenfeld & Nicolson, 2008.

Delffs, Dudley. *The Faith of Queen Elizabeth: The Poise, Grace, and Quiet Strength behind the Crown.* Grand Rapids: Zondervan, 2019.

Dimbleby, J. *The Prince of Wales.* Boston: Little, Brown, 1994.

Docherty, Gerry, and James MacGregor. *Hidden History: The Secret Origins of the First World War.* Edinburgh: Mainstream, 2013.

Dorril, Stephen. *Blackshirt: Sir Oswald Mosley and British Fascism.* New York: Viking, 2006.

———. *MI6: Fifty Years of Special Operations.* New York: Fourth Estate, 2000.

———. *The Silent Conspiracy: Inside the Intelligence Service in the 1990s.* London: Heineman, 1993.

Douglas-Home, Charles, and Saul Kelly, eds. *Dignified and Efficient: The British Monarchy in the Twentieth Century.* London: Claridge, 2000.

Dukes, Paul. *Great Men in the Second World War: The Rise and Fall of the Big Three.* London: Bloomsbury, 2017.

Dunlop, Richard. *Donovan: America's Master Spy.* Wilmington, DE: Skyhorse, 2014.

Duns, Jeremy. *Dead Drop: The True Story of Oleg Penkovsky and the Cold War's Most Dangerous Operation.* New York: Simon & Schuster, 2013.

Eade, Philip. *Young Prince Philip: His Turbulent Early Life.* New York: HarperPress, 2012.

Elliott, Geoffrey. *Gentleman Spymaster: How Lt Col Tommy "Tar" Robertson Double-Crossed the Nazis.* London: Methuen, 2011.

———. *Policy and Police: The Enforcement of the Reformation in the Age of Thomas Cromwell.* Cambridge: Cambridge University Press, 1985.

English, Richard. *Armed Struggle: The History of the IRA.* London: Pan, 2004.

Erickson, Caroline. *Her Little Majesty: The Life of Queen Victoria.* New York: Simon & Schuster, 2002.

Erickson, Carolly. *Lilibet: An Intimate Portrait of Elizabeth II.* New York: St. Martin's Press, 2005.

Farwell, Bryan. *Queen Victoria's Little Wars.* New York: W. W. Norton, 1985.

Fergusson, Thomas. *British Military Intelligence 1870–1914: The Development of a Modern Intelligence Organization.* London: Arms and Armour Press, 1984.

Ferris, J. *Behind the Enigma: The Authorised History of GCHQ.* London: Bloomsbury, 2020.

———. *Intelligence and Strategy.* London: Routledge, 2015.

Ferro, Marc. *Nicholas II: Last of the Tsars.* Oxford: Oxford University Press, 1994.

Fleming, Ian. *On Her Majesty's Secret Service.* London: Jonathan Cape, 1963.

Foot, M. R. D. *Resistance: European Resistance to Nazism, 1940–1945* New York: McGraw-Hill, 1977.

Frankland, Noble. *Witness of a Century: Life and Times of Prince Arthur, Duke of Connaught.* London: Shepheard-Walwyn, 1993.

Fremont-Barnes, Gregory, and Pete Winner. *Who Dares Wins: The SAS and the Iranian Embassy Siege, 1980.* London: Osprey, 2009.

Fromkin, David. *The King and the Cowboy: Theodore Roosevelt and Edward VII, Secret Partners.* London: Penguin, 2008.

Fuhrmann, Joseph T. *Rasputin: The Untold Story.* New York: John Wiley, 2013.

Geraghty, Tony. *The Bullet-Catchers: Bodyguard and the World of Close Protections.* New York: Grafton, 1988.

Gillman, P. and L. *"Collar the Lot!": How Britain Interned and Expelled Its Wartime Refugees.* London: Quartet Books, 1980.

Glass, Charles. *Americans in Paris: Life and Death under Nazi Occupation, 1940–44.* London: Collins, 2009.

Glencross, Matthew. *The State Visits of Edward VII: Reinventing Royal Diplomacy for the Twentieth Century.* London: Palgrave Macmillan, 2015.

Glencross, Matthew, Judith Rowbotham, and Michael D. Kandiah, eds. *The Windsor Dynasty, 1910 to the Present: "Long to Reign Over Us"?* London: Palgrave, 2016.

Hall, Coryne. *Little Mother of Russia: A Biography of Empress Marie Feodorovna.* London: Shepheard-Walwyn, 2001.

———. *To Free the Romanovs: Royal Kinship and Betrayal in Europe, 1917–19.* London: Amberley, 2018.

Hanbury-Williams, Sir John. *Emperor Nicholas II as I Knew Him.* London: Humphreys, 1922.

Hardcastle-Taylor, Jeane D. *The Windsors I Knew: An American Private Secretary's Memoir of the Duke and Duchess of Windsor,* edited by Hugo Vickers. Privately published, 2018.

Hardie, Frank. *Political Influence of Queen Victoria, 1861–1901.* London: Frank Cass, 1938.

Hardman, Robert. *Her Majesty: Queen Elizabeth II and Her Court.* New York: Pegasus, 2012.

———. *Queen of the World.* London: Century, 2018.

Harris, Stephen. *British Military Intelligence in the Crimean War, 1854–56.* Abingdon, UK: Routledge, 2015.

Hashimoto, Chikara. *Twilight of the British Empire: British Intelligence and Counter-Subversion in the Middle East, 1948–63.* Edinburgh: Edinburgh University Press, 2018.

Haslam, Jonathan. *Near and Distant Neighbours: A New History of Soviet Intelligence.* Oxford: Oxford University Press, 2015.

Hastings, Max. *Catastrophe: Europe Goes to War, 1914.* London: Collins, 2014.

Hauner, Milan. *India in Axis Strategy.* Berlin: Klett-Cotta, 1982.

Heald, Tim. *The Duke: A Portrait of Prince Philip.* London: Hodder & Stoughton, 1991.

Heffer, Simon. *Power and Place: The Political Consequences of King Edward VII.* London: Phoenix, 1998.

———. *Staring at God: Britain in the Great War.* New York: Random House, 2019.

Hemming, Henry. *M: Maxwell Knight, MI5's Greatest Spymaster.* London: Penguin, 2017.

Hennessy, Peter, *The Hidden Wiring: Unearthing the British Constitution.* London: Indigo, 1996.

———. *The Prime Minister: The Office and Its Holders Since 1945.* London: Allen Lane, 2001.

———. *The Secret State: Whitehall and the Cold War.* London: Penguin, 2003.

Hesketh, R. *Fortitude: The D-Day Deception Campaign.* New York: Overlook, 2000.

Herman, Michael. *Intelligence Power in Peace and War.* Cambridge: Cambridge University Press, 1996.

Heuser, Beatrice. *Western "Containment" Policies in the Cold War: The Yugoslav Case, 1948–53.* London: Routledge, 1989.

Hibbert, Christopher. *Edward VII: A Portrait.* London: Allen Lane, 1976.

———. *Queen Victoria: A Personal History.* London: Collins, 2001.

Hodgson, Howard. *Charles: The Man Who Will Be King.* London: John Blake, 2007.

Holmes, Richard Rivington. *Queen Victoria.* London: Boussod, Valadon, 1897.

Hopkirk, Peter. *The Great Game: On Secret Service in High Asia.* London: John Murray, 2006.

Horne, Alistair. *Macmillan: The Official Biography, Volume 2, 1957–1986.* London: Macmillan, 1989.

Hoey, Brian. *Not in Front of the Corgis*. London: Biteback, 2011.

How, F. D. *The Life of Sir Howard Vincent*. London: Allen, 1912.

Howard, Michael. *British Intelligence in the Second World War, Volume 5, Strategic Deception*. London: H.M. Stationery Office, 1990.

———. *The Franco-Prussian War: The German Invasion of France, 1870–71*, 2nd ed. London: Routledge, 2001.

Howarth, Patrick. *George VI*. London: Hutchinson, 1987.

Iatrides, John O. *Revolt in Athens: The Greek Communist "Second Round," 1944–1945*. Princeton, NJ: Princeton University Press, 1972.

Iordanou, Ioanna. *Venice's Secret Service: Organizing Intelligence in the Renaissance*. Oxford: Oxford University Press, 2019.

Isba, Anne. *Gladstone and Women*. London: Continuum, 2006.

Jackson, Sophie. *SOE's Balls of Steel: Operation Rubble*. Cheltenham, UK: History Press, 2013.

Jagger, Chris. *Escorting the Monarch: We Lead, Others Follow*. London: Pen and Sword, 2017.

Jago, Michael. *Robin Butler: At the Heart of Power from Heath to Blair*. London: Biteback, 2017.

Jeffery, Keith. *The Secret History of MI6*. New York: Penguin, 2010.

Jelavich, Charles. *Tsarist Russia and Balkan Nationalism: Russian Influence in the Internal Affairs of Bulgaria and Serbia, 1879–1886*. Berkeley: University of California Press, 1958.

Jensen, Richard Bach. *The Battle Against Anarchist Terrorism: An International History, 1878–1934*. Cambridge: Cambridge University Press, 2014.

Jevon, Graham. *Glubb Pasha and the Arab Legion: Britain, Jordan, and the End of Empire in the Middle East*. Cambridge: Cambridge University Press, 2017.

Johnson, Robert. *Spying for Empire: The Great Game in Central and South Asia, 1757–1947*. London: Greenhill, 2006.

Judd, Alan. *The Quest for C: Sir Mansfield Cumming and the Founding of the British Secret Service*. London: Collins, 1999.

Judd, Denis. *The Crimean War, 1853–1856*. London: Hart-Davis & MacGibbon, 1975.

Judd, Denis, and Keith Sturridge. *The Boer War: A History*. New York: I. B. Tauris, 2013.

Junor, Penny. *Charles: Victim or Villain?* London: Collins, 1998.

Kahn, David. *The Codebreakers: The Story of Secret Writing*. New York: Scribner, 1996.

Kemp, Michael. *Bombs, Bullets and Bread: The Politics of Anarchist Terrorism Worldwide*. Jefferson, NC: McFarland, 2018.

Kettle, Michael. *The Allies and the Russian Collapse, March 1917–March 1918*. London: Deutsch, 1981.

———. *Russia and the Allies, 1917–1920: Volume 1, The Allies and the Russian Collapse, March 1917–March 1918*. Minneapolis: University of Minnesota Press, 1981.

Kyemba, Henry. *State of Blood: The Inside Story of Idi Amin*. New York: Putnam, 1977.

Kyle, Keith, *Suez: Britain's End of Empire in the Middle East*. London: Weidenfeld & Nicolson, 1991.

Lacey, Robert. *Royal: Her Majesty Queen Elizabeth II*. Boston: Little, Brown, 2002.

Lambton, Antony, *The Mountbattens: The Battenbergs and Young Mountbatten*. London: Constable, 1989.

Larman, Alexander. *The Crown in Crisis: Countdown to the Abdication*. London: Weidenfeld & Nicolson, 2020.

Loughlin, James. *The British Monarchy and Ireland: 1800 to the Present.* Cambridge: Cambridge University Press, 2007.

Le Queux, William. *The Minister of Evil: The Secret History of Rasputin's Betrayal of Russia.* London: Cassell, 1918.

———. *Rasputin, the Rascal Monk.* London: Hurst & Blackett, 1917.

Lee, Sidney. *King Edward VII: A Biography*, vol. 2. London: Macmillan, 1927.

Lees-Milne, James. *Harold Nicolson, 1930–1968.* London: Chatto & Windus, 1981.

Linklater, Andrew. *Compton Mackenzie.* London: Chatto & Windus, 1987.

Louis, William Roger. *The British Empire in the Middle East, 1945–1951: Arab Nationalism, the United States, and Postwar Imperialism.* Oxford: Oxford University Press, 1984.

Lownie, Andrew. *John Buchan: The Presbyterian Cavalier.* London: Constable, 1995.

———. *The Mountbattens: Their Lives and Loves.* London: Blink, 2019.

———. *Stalin's Englishman: The Lives of Guy Burgess.* London: Hodder & Stoughton, 2015.

———. *The Traitor King: Scandalous Exile of the Duke and Duchess of Windsor.* London: Blink, 2021.

Lycett, Andrew. *Ian Fleming.* New York: St. Martin's Press, 2013.

Lyon, David. *Electronic Eye: The Rise of the Surveillance Society.* Minneapolis: University of Minnesota Press, 1994.

Macintyre, Ben. *For Your Eyes Only.* London: Bloomsbury, 2008.

———. *The Spy and the Traitor: The Greatest Espionage Story of the Cold War.* New York: Viking, 2018.

Mackenzie, Compton. *The Windsor Tapestry Being a Study of the Life, Heritage, and Abdication of HRH The Duke of Windsor.* London: Rich & Cowan, 1938.

MacMillan, Margaret. *The War That Ended Peace: How Europe Abandoned Peace for the First World War.* London: Profile, 2013.

Magnus, Philip. *King Edward the Seventh.* London: John Murray, 1964.

Mahl, Thomas E. *Desperate Deception: British Covert Operations in the United States, 1939–44.* New York: Brassey's, 1999.

Manchester, William. *The Arms of Krupp: The Rise and Fall of the Industrial Dynasty That Armed Germany at War.* London: Michael Joseph, 1969.

———. *The Last Lion: Winston Spencer Churchill: Defender of the Realm, 1940–1965.* New York: Hachette, 2012.

Markovich, Slobodan G. *British Perceptions of Serbia and the Balkans, 1903–1906.* Paris: Dialogue, 2000.

Marr, Andrew. *The Diamond Queen: Elizabeth II and Her People.* London: Pan, 2012.

Marshall, Dorothy. *The Life and Times of Victoria.* London: Weidenfeld & Nicolson, 1972.

Martin, Ralph, G. *The Woman He Loved.* New York: Simon & Schuster, 1974.

Masterman, John. *Double-Cross System in the War of 1939 to 1945.* New Haven, CT: Yale University Press, 1972.

Mawby, Spencer. *The End of Empire in Uganda: Decolonization and Institutional Conflict 1945–1979.* London: Bloomsbury, 2020.

McGuire Mohr, Joan. *The Czech and Slovak Legion in Siberia, 1917–1922.* Toronto: McFarland, 2014.

McKinstry, Leo. *Operation Sealion: How Britain Crushed the German War Machine's Dreams of Invasion in 1940.* London: John Murray, 2015.

McLean, Roderick R. *Royalty and Diplomacy in Europe, 1890–1914.* Cambridge: Cambridge University Press, 2001.

Milani, Abbas. *The Shah.* London: Macmillan, 2011.

Millman, Richard. *British Policy and the Coming of the Franco-Prussian War.* Oxford: Clarendon Press, 1965.

Milton, Giles. *Russian Roulette: A Deadly Game—How British Spies Thwarted Lenin's Global Plot.* New York: Hachette, 2013.

Moon, Alan. *Alan Turing and Enigma Machine.* London: Lulu, 2014.

Moore, Charles. *Margaret Thatcher The Authorised Biography, Volume 1: Not for Turning.* London: Penguin, 2013.

———. *Margaret Thatcher The Authorised Biography, Volume 2: Everything She Wants.* London: Penguin, 2014.

Moran, Christopher. *Classified: Secrecy and the State in Modern Britain.* Cambridge: Cambridge University Press, 2013.

Morley, Sheridan. *Noël Coward.* London: Haus, 2005.

Morton, Andrew. *Diana: Her True Story.* London: O'Mara, 2017.

———. *17 Carnations: The Windsors, The Nazis and The Cover-Up.* London: O'Mara, 2015.

———. *Wallis in Love: The Untold Life of the Duchess of Windsor, the Woman Who Changed the Monarchy.* New York: Hachette, 2018.

Murphy, Paul. *Shooting Victoria: Madness, Mayhem, and Modernisation of the Monarchy.* London: Head of Zeus, 2013.

Murphy, Philip. *The Empire's New Clothes: The Myth of the Commonwealth.* Oxford: Oxford University Press, 2018.

———. *Monarchy and the End of Empire.* Oxford: Oxford University Press, 2013.

Newsinger, John, *Dangerous Men: The SAS and Popular Culture.* London: Pluto, 1997.

Nicolson, Harold. *George V.* London: Constable, 1952.

O'Conner, Bernard. *The Tempsford Academy.* Privately published, 2010.

Otte, Thomas. *The Foreign Office Mind: The Making of British Foreign Policy, 1865–1914.* Cambridge: Cambridge University Press, 2013.

Owen, David. *In Sickness and in Power: Illness in Heads of Government during the Last 100 Years.* New York: Praeger, 2008.

Paget, Julian. *Second to None: The History of the Coldstream Guards, 1650–2000.* London: Leo Cooper, 2000.

Pakula, Hannah. *An Uncommon Woman: The Empress Frederick—Daughter of Queen Victoria, Wife of the Crown Prince of Prussia, Mother of Kaiser Wilhelm.* New York: Touchstone, 1995.

Palmer, Dean. *The Queen and Mrs Thatcher: An Inconvenient Relationship.* London: History Press, 2015.

Parris, James. *The Man in the Brown Suit: MI5, Edward VIII, and an Irish Assassin.* London: History Press, 2019.

Pearce, Martin. *Spymaster: The Life of Britain's Most Decorated Cold War Spy and Head of MI6.* London: Transworld, 2017.

Pearson, John. *The Life of Ian Fleming.* London: Pan, 1967.

———. *The Ultimate Family: The Making of The Royal House of Windsor.* London: Bloomsbury, 2013.

Pearson, Jonathan. *Sir Anthony Eden and the Suez Crisis: Reluctant Gamble.* London: Palgrave Macmillan, 2003.

Petropoulos, Jonathan. *Royals and the Reich: The Princes von Hessen in Nazi Germany.* Oxford: Oxford University Press, 2009.

Pfennigwerth, Ian. *A Man of Intelligence: The Life of Captain Theodore Eric Nave, Australian Codebreaker Extraordinary.* Sydney: Rosenburg, 2006.

Phillips, Adrian. *The King Who Had to Go: Edward VIII, Mrs Simpson, and the Hidden Politics of the Abdication Crisis.* London: Biteback, 2016.

Pimlott, Ben. *The Queen: A Biography of Elizabeth II.* London: Collins, 1997.

Pincher, Chapman. *Treachery: Betrayals, Blunders, and Cover-Ups: Six Decades of Espionage.* London: Mainstream, 2012.

Pincus, Steven. *1688: The First Modern Revolution.* New Haven, CT: Yale University Press, 2009.

Pipes, R. *Russian Revolution.* New York: Alfred A. Knopf, 2011.

Poland, Perry. *The Queen, Her Lover, and the Most Notorious Spy in History.* London: Allen & Unwin, 2015.

Pope-Hennessy, James. *The Quest for Queen Mary*, edited by Hugo Vickers. London: Zuleika, 2018.

Porter, Bernard. *Plots and Paranoia: A History of Political Espionage in Britain, 1790–1988.* London: Unwin Hyman, 1989.

———. *The Refugee Question in Mid-Victorian Politics.* Cambridge: Cambridge University Press, 1979.

Quintin, Barry. *War in the East: A Military History of the Russo-Turkish War, 1877–78.* London: Helion, 2012.

Radzinsky, Edvard. *Alexander II: The Last Great Czar.* New York: Freepress, 2005.

———. *The Last Tsar: The Life and Death of Nicholas II.* New York: Anchor Books, 2011.

Rahnema, Ali, *Behind the 1953 Coup in Iran: Thugs, Turncoats, Soldiers, and Spooks.* Cambridge: Cambridge University Press, 2016.

Rankin, Nicholas. *Defending the Rock: How Gibraltar Defeated Hitler.* London: Faber & Faber, 2017.

———. *A Genius for Deception: How Cunning Helped the British Win Two World Wars.* New York: Oxford University Press, 2009.

Rappaport, Helen. *Four Sisters: The Lost Lives of the Daughters of Nicholas and Alexandra.* New York: Macmillan, 2004.

———. *The Race to Save the Romanovs: The Truth Behind the Secret Plans to Rescue the Russian Imperial Family.* New York: St. Martin's Press, 2018.

Rath, Andrew. *The Crimean War in Imperial Context, 1854–1856.* London: Palgrave, 2015.

Rathmell, Andrew. *Secret War in the Middle East: The Covert Struggle for Syria, 1949–1961.* London: I. B. Tauris, 1995.

Reid, Richard J. *A History of Modern Uganda.* Cambridge: Cambridge University Press, 2017.

Rekun, Mikhail. *How Russia Lost Bulgaria, 1878–1886: Empire Unguided.* Boston: Lexington, 2019.

Reynolds, David. *Summits: Six Meetings That Shaped the World.* New York: Basic Books, 2007.

Ridley, Jane. *Bertie: A Life of Edward VII.* New York: Vintage, 2012.

Rigden, Denis. *How to Be a Spy: The World War II SOE Training Manual.* Toronto: TNA / Dundurn Group, 2004.

Rose, Andrew. *The Prince, the Princess, and the Perfect Murder: An Untold History.* London: Coronet, 2013.

Rose, Kenneth. *King George V.* London: Weidenfeld & Nicolson, 2000.

———. *Kings, Queens, and Courtiers.* London: Weidenfeld & Nicolson, 1985.

Rostain, Pascal, Bruno Mouron, and Jean-Michel Caradec'h. *Qui a tué Lady Di?* Paris: Grasset, 2017.

Ruud, Charles A., and Sergei A. Stepanov. *Fontanka 16: The Tsars' Secret Police.* Toronto: McGill–Queen's University Press–MQ University Press, 1999.

Salmon, Patrick. *Scandinavia and the Great Powers, 1890–1940.* Cambridge: Cambridge University Press, 2002.

Sanabria, Enrique A. *Republicanism and Anticlerical Nationalism in Spain.* New York: Palgrave Macmillan, 2009.

Schabas, William A. *The Trial of the Kaiser.* Oxford: Oxford University Press, 2008.

Scott Cooper, Andrew. *The Fall of Heaven: The Pahlavis and the Final Days of Imperial Iran.* London: Picador, 2018.

Sebag Montefiore, Simon. *The Romanovs: An Intimate Chronicle of the Russian Royal Family.* London: Weidenfeld & Nicholson, 2014.

Sebba, Anne. *That Woman: The Life of Wallis Simpson, Duchess of Windsor.* London: Weidenfeld & Nicolson, 2011.

Seldon, Anthony. *John Major: A Political Life.* London: Weidenfeld & Nicolson, 1997.

Seligmann, Matthew. *Spies in Uniform: British Military and Naval Intelligence on the Eve of the First World War.* Oxford: Oxford University Press, 2006.

Service, Robert. *Spies and Commissars: Bolshevik Russia and the West.* London: Macmillan, 2011.

Seton-Watson, R. W. *Britain in Europe, 1789 to 1914: A Survey of Foreign Policy.* Cambridge: Cambridge University Press, 1955.

Seward, Ingrid. *The Queen and Di.* London: Collins, 2000.

Seward, Ingrid. *The Queen's Speech: An Intimate Portrait of the Queen in Her Own Words.* New York: Simon & Schuster, 2015.

Seymour, Miranda. *Noble Endeavours: The Life of Two Countries, England and Germany, in Many Stories.* New York: Simon & Schuster, 2013.

Shawcross, William. *Queen Elizabeth, The Queen Mother: The Official Biography.* London: Macmillan, 2009.

———. *Queen and Country.* London: BBC, 2002.

———. *The Shah's Last Ride: The Fate of an Ally.* New York: Simon & Schuster, 1997.

Simmons, Simone. *Diana: The Last Word.* New York: St. Martin's Press, 2005.

Sinclair, Andrew. *The Other Victoria: The Princess Royal and the Great Game of Europe.* London: Weidenfeld & Nicholson, 1981.

Sinclair, David, *Two Georges: The Making of the Modern Monarchy.* London: Hodder & Stoughton, 1988.

Sitwell, Osbert. *Rat Week: An Essay on the Abdication.* London: Michael Joseph, 1986.

Small, Hugh. *The Crimean War: Europe's Conflict with Russia.* London: History Press, 2018.

Smith, Douglas. *Rasputin.* New York: Macmillan, 2016.

Smith, Michael. *Six: The Real James Bonds, 1909–1939.* London: Biteback, 2011.

Soley, Lawrence C. *Radio Warfare: OSS and CIA Subversive Propaganda.* New York: Praeger, 1989.

Soroka, Marina. *Britain, Russia, and the Road to the First World War: The Fateful Embassy of Benckendorff, Count Aleksandr (1903–1916).* London: Routledge: 2011.

St. Aubyn, Giles. *Edward VII: Prince and King.* London: Collins, 1979.

———. *Queen Victoria: A Portrait.* London: Sinclair-Stevenson, 1991.

Stafford, David. *Camp X: SOE and the American Connection.* New York: Viking, 1986.

———. *Ten Days to D-Day.* Boston: Little, Brown, 2003.

Steinberg, Jonathan. *Bismarck: A Life.* Oxford: Oxford University Press, 2011.

Stewart, Andrew. *The King's Private Army: Protecting the British Royal Family during the Second World War.* Solihill, UK: Helion, 2015.

Sulzberger, C. L. *The Fall of Eagles.* New York: Crown, 1977.

Summers, Anthony, and Stephen Dorril. *The Secret Worlds of Stephen Ward: Sex, Scandal, and Deadly Secrets in the Profumo Affair.* New York: Headline, 2013.

Summers, Anthony, and Tom Mangold. *The File on the Tsar.* London: Gollancz, 1976.

Taylor, Miles. *Empress: Queen Victoria and India.* New Haven, CT: Yale University Press, 2018.

Taylor, Peter. *Brits: The War Against the IRA.* London: Bloomsbury, 2002.

Thomas, Wyn. *Hands off Wales: Nationhood and Militancy.* London: Gomer, 2013.

———. *John Jenkins: The Reluctant Revolutionary?* London: Lolfa, 2019.

Thomson, Basil. *The Story of Scotland Yard.* London: Grayson & Grayson, 1935.

Thornton, Michael. *Royal Feud: The Queen Mother and the Duchess of Windsor.* London: Michael Joseph, 1985.

Thorpe, D. R. *Eden: The Life and Times of Anthony Eden, First Earl of Avon, 1897–1977.* London: Pimlico, 2004.

Tillotson, Michael. *SOE and The Resistance: As Told in the Times Obituaries.* London: Continuum, 2001.

Twigge, Stephen. *Codebreakers: Images of the National Archives.* Barnsley, UK: Pen and Sword, 2020.

Urbach, Karina. *Go-Betweens for Hitler.* Oxford: Oxford University Press, 2015.

Van der Kiste, John. *Alfred: Queen Victoria's Second Son.* London: Fonthill, 2015.

———. *Queen Victoria and the European Empires.* London: Fonthill, 2016.

Vasey, C. *Nazi Intelligence Operations in Non-Occupied Territories: Espionage Efforts in the United States, Britain, South America, and Southern Africa.* New York: McFarland.

Verrier, Anthony. *Through the Looking Glass: British Foreign Policy in an Age of Illusions.* New York: W. W. Norton, 1983.

Vinen, Richard. *Thatcher's Britain: The Politics and Social Upheaval of the 1980s.* New York: Simon & Schuster, 2010.

Wade, Stephen. *Spies in the Empire: Victorian Military Intelligence.* New York: Anthem, 2007.

Walton, Calder. *Empire of Secrets: British Intelligence, the Cold War and the Twilight of Empire.* London: Collins, 2013.

Warner, Michael. *The Rise and Fall of Intelligence: An International Security History.* Washington, DC: Georgetown University Press, 2014.

Warwick, Christopher. *Princess Margaret: A Life in Contrasts.* London: Andre Deutsch, 2017.

Weiner, Tim. *Legacy of Ashes: The History of the CIA.* New York: Anchor, 2008.

Weintraub, Stanley. *Uncrowned King: The Life of Prince Albert.* New York: Free Press, 1997.

———. *Victoria.* London: John Murray, 1996.

Weisbrode, Kenneth. *Churchill and the King: The Wartime Alliance of Winston Churchill and George VI.* London: Penguin, 2015.

West, Nigel. *The A–Z of British Intelligence.* Plymouth, UK: Scarecrow Press, 2009.

———, ed. *British Security Coordination: The Secret History of British Intelligence in the Americas, 1940–1945*. New York: Fromm, 1999.

———. *Cold War Spymaster*. London: Pen and Sword, 2018.

———. *Double Cross in Cairo: The True Story of the Spy Who Turned the Tide of War*. London: Biteback, 2015.

Wheeler Bennett, John. *George VI*. London: Macmillan, 1958.

Whiting, Audrey. *The Kents: A Royal Family*. London: Hutchinson, 1985.

Wilkinson, Peter, and Joan Astley. *Gubbins & SOE*. Barnsley, UK: Pen and Sword, 1993.

Wilson, Ray, and Ian Adams. *Special Branch: A History, 1883–2006*. London: Biteback, 2015.

Worthington, Heather. *The Rise of the Detective in Early-Nineteenth-Century Popular Fiction*. Basingstoke, UK: Palgrave Macmillan, 2005.

Yarmolinsky, Avrahm, *Road to Revolution: A Century of Russian Radicalism*. Princeton: Princeton University Press, 2016.

Zegart, Amy. *Spies, Lies, and Algorithms: The History and Future of American Intelligence*. Princeton, NJ: Princeton University Press, 2022.

Ziegler, Philip. *Mountbatten: The Official Biography*. New York: HarperCollins, 1985.

———. *King Edward VIII: The Official Biography*. London: Collins, 1990.

———. *Wilson: The Authorized Life*. London: Weidenfeld & Nicolson, 1993.

ARTICLES AND CHAPTERS IN BOOKS

Alberge, Dalya. "British State 'Covered Up Plot to Assassinate King Edward VIII.'" *Guardian*, June 28, 2020.

Aldrich, Richard J. "OSS, CIA and European Unity: The American Committee on United Europe, 1948–60." *Diplomacy and Statecraft* 8, no. 1 (1997): 184–227.

Aldrich, Richard J., and Lewis Herrington. "Secrets, Hostages and Ransoms: British Kidnap Policy in Historical Perspective." *Review of International Studies* 44, no. 4 (2018): 738–59.

Anastasi, Paul. "British Diplomat Is Shot to Death in Athens." *New York Times*, March 29, 1984.

Apple, R. W., Jr., "Northern Ireland, Awaiting Jubilee Visit by the Queen, Erupts in Violence Fatal to Two." *New York Times*, August 10, 1977.

———. "Queen Embroiled in Mideast Dispute." *New York Times*, April 3, 1984.

Ashton, Nigel. "'Great New Venture'? Anglo-American Cooperation in the Middle East and the Response to the Iraqi Revolution, July 1958." *Diplomacy and Statecraft* 4, no. 1 (1993): 59–89.

———. "Love's Labours Lost: Margaret Thatcher, King Hussein, and Anglo-Jordanian Relations, 1979–1990." *Diplomacy and Statecraft* 22, no. 4 (2011): 651–77.

Baker, Helen. "Monarchy Discredited? Reactions to the Khodynka Coronation Catastrophe of 1896." *Revolutionary Russia* 16, no. 1 (2003): 1–46.

Baklitskaya, Kate. "Go East, Royal Dog Fled from Siberia into British Exile, Living in Shadow of Windsor Castle." *Siberian Times*, January 21, 2014.

Balfour-Paul, Glen. "Britain's Informal Empire in the Middle East." In *The Oxford History of the British Empire, Volume IV: The Twentieth Century*, edited by J. Brown and Wm Louis. Oxford: Oxford University Press, 1999.

Barnett, Antony. "Jackie Stewart Teamed Up with MI6 Renegade." *Observer*, August 27, 2020.

Baylen, Joseph O. "Madame Olga Novikov, Propagandist." *American Slavic and East European Review* 10, no. 4 (1951): 255–71.

BBC News. "Prince Charles Praises 'Utterly Essential' GCHQ Work." July 12, 2019. www .bbc.co.uk/news/uk-england-gloucestershire-48969333.

———. "Prince William Works with Security Agencies on Attachment." April 7, 2019. www.bbc.co.uk/news/uk-47842097.

Beaken, Robert. "How to Topple a King." *Church Times*, October 19, 1912.

Beckett, Ian F. W. "Royalty and the Army in the Twentieth Century." In *The Windsor Dynasty 1910 to the Present: "Long to Reign Over Us"?* edited by Matthew Glencross, Judith Rowbotham, and Michael D. Kandiah. London: Palgrave Macmillan, 2016.

Beckett, John. "November 1913: The Archduke, Nottingham and a Near Miss." Centre for Hidden Histories: Community, Commemoration, and the First World War. http:// hiddenhistorieswwi.ac.uk/uncategorized/2014/07/november-1913-the-archduke -nottingham-and-a-near-miss/.

Békés, Csaba. "President Kliment Voroshilov's Telegram to Queen Elizabeth of Great Britain on the Soviet Intervention in Hungary on 4 November 1956." *Slavonic and East European Review* 71, no. 1 (1993): 126–29.

Black, Alistair. "Information Management in the Intelligence Branch of Britain's War Office, 1873–1914: All Information Flows toward It, or Returns to It, in a Form Worked Up into Shape." *Open Information Science* 4, no. 1 (2020): 91–105.

———. "The Victorian Information Society: Surveillance, Bureaucracy, and Public Librarianship in the 19th Century." *Information Society* 17, no. 1 (2001): 53–90.

Bowes-Lyon, David. "WWII Secret Activities Around Milton Keynes." http://clutch .open.ac.uk/schools/emerson00/pwe_page2.html, n.d.

Carey, George. "Kim Philby: The Spy Who Went into the Cold." BBC, November 18, 2013. www.bbc.co.uk/news/uk-24803131.

Chamberlain, Darryl. "Charlton History: The Man Who Took a Bullet for the PM." *Charlton Champion*, August 16, 2001.

Charmley, John, and Jennifer Davey. "The Invisible Politician: Mary Derby and the Eastern Crisis." In *On the Fringes of Diplomacy: Influences on British Foreign Policy, 1800–1945*, edited by J. Fisher and A. Best. Farnham, UK: Ashgate, 2011.

Collyer, Michael. "Secret Agents: Anarchists, Islamists, and Responses to Politically Active Refugees in London." *Ethnic and Racial Studies* 28, no. 2 (2006): 278–303.

Connett, David. "British Defence Equipment 'Diverted to Iraq.'" *Independent*, June 22, 1993.

Crossland, John. "British Spies in Plot to Save the Tsar." *Sunday Times*, October 15, 2006.

Crump, Eryl. "The Bizarre Plots to Stop Prince Charles' Investiture Using 'Kamikaze Dogs' and Manure." *Daily Post*, July 1, 2019.

Cull, Nicholas. "The Munich Crisis and British Propaganda Policy in the United States." In *The Munich Crisis, Prelude to World War II*, edited by Igor Lukes and Erik Goldstein. London: Frank Cass, 1999.

Deflem, Mathieu. "'Wild Beasts Without Nationality': The Uncertain Origins of Interpol, 1898–1910." In *The Handbook of Transnational Crime and Justice*, edited by Philip Reichel. Thousand Oaks, CA: Sage, 2005.

Dewsbury Reporter. "Dewsbury-Born Author Andrew Morton Explores Royal Family Conspiracy Theory." May 3, 2015.

Dover, Robert. "For Queen and Company: The Role of Intelligence in the UK's Arms Trade." *Political Studies* 55, no. 4 (2007): 683–708.

Dyer, Clare. "Hunger Strike by Man Held for Bid to Kidnap Princess." *Guardian*, June 17, 2002.

Ealing Today. "Former Ealing MP Reveals Involvement in Profumo Affair." February 5, 2020. www.ealingtoday.co.uk/default.asp?section=info&page=eapoundprofumo001.htm.

Fenton, Ben. "Himmler Forgeries in National Archives Case Will Stay Unsolved." *Financial Times*, May 3, 2008.

Ferris, John. "Lord Salisbury, Secret Intelligence, and British Policy Toward Russia and Central Asia." In *Intelligence and Strategy, Selected Essays*, edited by John Ferris. New York: Taylor & Francis, 2005.

Fielding, Marcus. "Major General Sir Alexander Bruce Tulloch, K.C.B., C.M.G., Founder of the Royal United Service Institute of Victoria." Military History and Heritage Victoria, July 10, 2013. www.mhhv.org.au/?p=3495.

Flanders, Judith. "The Creation of the Police." British Library, April 15, 2014.

Fuller, Jaime. "That Time FDR Served Hot Dogs to the King." *Washington Post*, November 2, 2014.

Gallagher, Ian. "Duran Duran Drummer Tells How IRA Nearly Killed His Band." *Mail on Sunday*, July 26, 2015. www.dailymail.co.uk/news/article-3174722/Duran-Duran-drummer-tells-IRA-nearly-killed-band-Princess-Diana-Prince-Charles-gelignite-concert-bomb-plot.html.

Glencross, M. "A Cause of Tension? The Leadership of King George V—Visiting the Western Front." In *Monarchies and the Great War*, edited by M. Glencross and J. Rowbotham. London: Palgrave, 2018.

Guardian. "Prince Andrew Faces Calls to Pay for His Own Security." January 14, 2022.

———. "Prince Harry 'Does Not Feel Safe in UK,' Lawyers Tell High Court." February 18, 2022.

———. "Princess Anne Kidnap Medal Fetches £50,000 at Auction." March 4, 1974.

———. "Revealed: How Prince Charles Pressured Ministers to Change Law to Benefit His Estate." June 28, 2022.

———. "What Does the Queen's Legal Immunity Mean?" July 14, 2022.

Hamilton, Keith. "Addressing the Past." In *Britain in Global Politics, Volume 1: From Gladstone to Churchill*, edited by C. Baxter, M. Dockrill, and K. Hamilton. Berlin: Springer, 2013.

Hannigan, Robert. "GCHQ Director's Speech at the Launch of the NCSC." National Cyber Security Centre, February 13, 2017. www.ncsc.gov.uk/news/gchq-directors-speech-launch-ncsc-2.

Harding, Laura. "Diana Death 'Linked to Arms Trade' says QC." *Independent*, May 31, 2010.

Harper, Tom. "MI6 Fears Russia Can Link Prince Andrew to the Jeffrey Epstein Abuse Scandal." *The Times*, September 21, 2019.

Hastings, Chris. "Crazed Gunman Who Tried to Kidnap Princess Anne." *Daily Mail*, November 22, 2004.

Helliker, Adam. "The Queen Reveals the Worst Day of Her Life." *Express*, September 30, 2018. www.express.co.uk/news/royal/1024703/the-queen-news-queen-elizabeth-ira-bomb-hyde-park.

Hitchens, Christopher. "The Crown and the Mole." *Los Angeles Times*, April 21, 2002.

Hughes, Michael. "British Opinion and Russian Terrorism in the 1880s." *European History Quarterly* 41, no. 2 (2011): 255–77.

Humphries, Michael. "'Perfectly Secret and Perfectly Democratic': Lord Esher and the Society of Islanders, 1909–14." *English Historical Review* 127, no. 528 (2012): 1156–79.

Independent. "Dennis Coslett, Dashing Commandant of the Free Wales Army" (obituary). October 10, 2011.

Ingram, David. "Thatcher and Ramphal: A Long and Turbulent Relationship." *Round Table* 97, no. 398 (2008): 781–83.

Irish Times. "When Dublin Did a Roaring Trade in Lions." June 9, 2016.

Irving, Clive. "What Netflix's *The Crown* Leaves Out." *Daily Beast,* January 6, 2018.

Jensen, Richard Bach. "The International Anti-Anarchist Conference and the Origins of Interpol." *Journal of Contemporary History* 16 (1981): 323–47.

———. "The International Campaign Against Anarchist Terrorism, 1880–1930s." *Terrorism and Political Violence* 21, no. 1 (2009): 89–109.

Jones, Matthew. "The 'Preferred Plan': the Anglo-American Working Group Report on Covert Action in Syria, 1957." *Intelligence and National Security* 19, no. 3 (2004): 401–15.

Jordan, William. "38% of Brits Think Princess Diana's Death 'NOT an Accident.'" YouGov, September 17, 2013.

Kandiah, Michael, Judith Rowbotham, and Gillian Staerck. "The Ultimate Windsor Ceremonials: Coronations and Investitures." In *The Windsor Dynasty 1910 to the Present: "Long to Reign Over Us"?* edited by Matthew Glencross, Judith Rowbotham, and Michael D. Kandiah. London: Palgrave, 2016.

Kapitonova, Natalia. "Visit of Soviet Leaders Nikita Khrushchev and Nicholas Bulganin to Britain in April 1956." *Cold War History* 14, no. 1 (2014): 127–52.

Karam, Jeffrey. "Missing Revolution: The American Intelligence Failure in Iraq, 1958." *Intelligence and National Security* 32, no. 6 (2017): 693–709.

Kay, Richard, and Geoffrey Levy. "Mystery of Royal Love Letters Burnt by the Queen's Sister." *Daily Mail,* March 14, 2016.

Kenna, Shane. "The Victorian War on Terror." BBC History Extra, 2013.

Kennedy, Paul. "Great Britain Beyond 1914." In *Knowing One's Enemies,* edited by Ernest May. Princeton, NJ: Princeton University Press, 1986.

Kington, Tom. "Recruited by MI5: The Name's Mussolini, Benito Mussolini." *Guardian,* October 13, 2009.

Kollander, Patricia. "Empress Frederick: The Last Hope for a Liberal Germany?" *Historian* 62, no. 1 (1999): 47–62.

Langley, William. "The Mannakee File." *Telegraph,* December 12, 2004.

Lea, Luke, and William T. Alderson. "The Attempt to Capture the Kaiser." *Tennessee Historical Quarterly* 20, no. 3 (1961): 222–61.

Leach, Ben. "The Lost Diary of Queen Victoria's Final Companion." *Telegraph,* February 26, 2011.

Leigh, David, Heather Brooke, and Rob Evans. "WikiLeaks Cables: 'Rude' Prince Andrew Shocks US Ambassador." *Guardian,* November 29, 2010.

Lewis, Jason, and Kim Willsher. "The KGB's Spy at the Palace." *Mail on Sunday,* February 20, 2000.

Lewis, Paul. "The 29 Fakes Behind a Rewriting of History." *Guardian,* May 5, 2008.

Loeb, Vernon, and Bill Miller. "Tinker, Tailor, Poet, Spy?" *Washington Post,* February 15, 2001.

Louis, William Roger. "Britain and the Overthrow of the Mosaddeq Government." In
     Mohammad Mosaddeq and the 1953 Coup in Iran, edited by M. Gasiorowski and
     M. Byrne. Syracuse: Syracuse University Press, 2004.
Louis, William Roger, and Ronald Robinson. "The Imperialism of Decolonisation." In
     *Ends of British Imperialism: The Scramble for Empire, Suez, and Decolonization—
     Collected Essays*. London: I. B. Tauris, 2006.
Low, Valentine. "Queen's Request for New Royal Yacht *Britannia* Removed from Public
     Scrutiny." *The Times*, January 30, 2019.
Mawby, Spencer. "The Clandestine Defence of Empire: British Special Operations in
     Yemen, 1951–64." *Intelligence and National Security* 17, no. 3 (2002): 105–30.
McCrisken, Trevor, and Christopher Moran. "James Bond, Ian Fleming, and Intelligence:
     Breaking Down the Boundary between the 'Real' and the 'Imagined.'" *Intelligence
     and National Security* 33, no. 6 (2018): 804–21.
McEvoy, John, and Daniel Hunt. "Britain and Brazil's Dictatorship," *Brasilwire*, 2020.
     www.brasilwire.com/britain-brazil-dictatorship/.
McKittrick, David. "Northern Ireland: Memories of 1977 and a 'Terribly Tense' Royal
     Visitor." *Independent*, June 28, 2012. www.independent.co.uk/news/uk/home-news
     /northern-ireland-memories-of-1977-and-a-terribly-tense-royal-visitor-7893784
     .html.
McNeilly, Hamish. "Declassified Intelligence Service Documents Confirm New Zealand
     Assassination Attempt on Queen Elizabeth II." *Stuff*, March 1, 2018. www.stuff
     .co.nz/national/crime/101794948/the-snowman-and-the-queen-declassified-nz
     -intelligence-service-documents-confirm-assassination-attempt-on-queen.
Melbourne Age. "Edward's Would-Be Killer Leaves a Trail of Doubt." January 7, 2003.
Moore, Richard. "A Tribute to His Royal Highness The Duke of Edinburgh, 1921–2021."
     MI6 website, April 9, 2021.
Moran, Christopher. "Concealing Collusion: The Suez Crisis, Political Memoirs, and
     Official Secrecy." *English Historical Review* 134, no. 567 (2019): 358–89.
Moran, Richard. "The Origin of Insanity as a Special Verdict: The Trial for Treason of
     James Hadfield, 1800." *Law and Society Review* 19, no. 3 (1985): 487–519.
———. "The Punitive Uses of the Insanity Defense: The Trial for Treason of Edward
     Oxford (1840)." *International Journal of Law and Psychiatry* 9, no. 2 (1986): 171–90.
Mosse, W. E. "The Crown and Foreign Policy: Queen Victoria and the Austro-Prussian
     Conflict, March–May 1866." *Cambridge Historical Journal* 10, no. 2 (1951): 205–23.
———. "Queen Victoria and Her Ministers in the Schleswig-Holstein Crisis 1863–1864."
     English Historical Review 78, no. 307 (1963): 263–83.
New York Times. "Elizabeth in Jordan Under Tight Guard." March 27, 1984.
———. "Text of Scotland Yard's Report on July 9 Intrusion into Buckingham Palace."
     July 22, 1982.
Nikkah, Roya, and Richard Kerbaj. "MI6 Placement Gives Prince a Licence to Will."
     Sunday Times, April 7, 2019.
North, Nic. "The Elizabeth and Margaret Letters: Spies in Secret of Royal Lovers." *Daily
     Mirror*, January 20, 1999.
Owen, Elizabeth. "US Ambassador Pamela Harriman Dies." *Time Magazine*, February 5,
     1997.
Platt, Roger. "The Soviet Imprisonment of Gerald Brooke and Subsequent Exchange for
     the Krogers, 1965–1969." *Contemporary British History* 24, no. 2 (2010): 193–212.

Prochaska, Frank. "George V and Republicanism, 1917–1919." *Twentieth Century British History* 10, no. 1 (1999): 27–51.

Purvis, Stewart. "When Spooks Pulled Strings." *British Journalism Review* 27, no. 1 (2016): 62–67.

Ray, Datta. "Queen and Karim." *Open*, October 27, 2017. https://openthemagazine.com /essay/the-queen-karim/.

Rix, Keith. "Towards a More Just Insanity Defence: Recovering Moral Wrongfulness in the M'Naghten Rules." *BJPsych Advances* 22, no. 1 (2016): 44–52.

Rodriguez, Cecilia. "Princess Diana: Secrets That Never End About Her Death." *Forbes*, June 20, 2017.

Roy, Eleanor Ainge. "'Damn . . . I Missed': The Incredible Story of the Day the Queen Was Nearly Shot." *Guardian*, January 13, 2018.

Seligmann, Matthew. "Prince Louis of Battenberg." In *Royal Kinship: Anglo-German Family Networks 1815–1918*, edited by Karina Urbach. Amsterdam: De Gruyter, 2008.

Smith, Adrian. "Resignation of a First Sea Lord: Mountbatten and the 1956 Suez Crisis." *History* 98, no. 329 (2013): 105–34.

Smith, F. B. "British Post Office Espionage, 1844." *Historical Studies* 14, no. 54 (1970): 189–203.

Smith, Robert W. "A Brilliant History of the Ultimate Spy." *Chicago Sun-Times*, January 31, 1988.

Squiers, Carol. "Class Struggle: The Invention Paparazzi Photography and the Death of Diana, Princess of Wales." In *Overexposed: Essay in Contemporary Photography*, edited by Carol Squiers. New York: New Press, 1999.

Sterling, C. H. "Getting There: Churchill's Wartime Journeys." https://winstonchurchill .org/publications/finest-hour/finest-hour-148/getting-there-churchills-wartime -journeys/.

Stillman, Grant B. "Two of the MADdest Scientists: Where Strangelove Meets Dr. No; or, Unexpected Roots for Kubrick's Cold War Classic." *Film History* 20, no. 4 (2008): 487–500.

Stout, Mark. "World War I and the Birth of American Intelligence Culture." *Intelligence and National Security* 32, no. 3 (2017): 378–94.

Strachan, Graeme. "Museum to Shine a Light on the 'Guardian Shadow' of the King Who Signed Away the Crown." *The Courier*, September 6, 1918.

Sweet, Paul R. "The Windsor File." *Historian* 59, no. 2 (1997): 263–80.

Temple, Anthea. "The Spy Who Loved Me." *Guardian*, November 2, 2002.

Thorpe, Vanessa. "Documentary Reveals Evidence Confirming a British Spy's Role in Restoring the Shah in 1953." *Guardian*, August 2, 2020.

The Times. "Palace Anger Mounts as Cameron Spills Secrets." September 20, 2019.

Travis, Alan. "The Duke, the Spies, and the KGB: How Cold War Plotting Entangled Royal Visit." *Guardian*, April 26, 2004.

Traynor, Ian. "MI6 Involved in Spy Balkan Plot." *Guardian*, August 27, 2008.

Turner, Alwyn. "Meanwhile Back on Planet Earth." *BBC History Magazine*, August 2019.

Turner, Graham. "The Real Elizabeth II: Part Two." *Telegraph*, January 9, 2002.

Twomey, Anne. "From Bagehot to Brexit: The Monarch's Rights to Be Consulted, to Encourage and to Warn." *Round Table* 107, no. 4 (2018): 417–28.

Vincent, David. "Surveillance, Privacy and History." *History and Policy*, October 2013.

Wales, T. C. "The 'Massingham' Mission and the Secret Special Relationship." In *The Politics and Strategy of Clandestine War: Special Operations Executive*, edited by Neville Wylie. London: Routledge, 2005.

Walker, Tom, and Michael Ivanovic. "Vengeful Serbs Betray Top MI6 Man." *Sunday Times*, August 15, 2004.

Wilson, Christopher. "Revealed: The Duke and Duchess of Windsor's Secret Plot to Deny the Queen the Throne." *Daily Telegraph*, November 22, 2009.

Zonis, Marvin, and Craig M. Joseph. "Conspiracy Thinking in the Middle East." *Political Psychology* 15, no. 3 (1994): 443–59.

THESES

Griffin, Rachael. "Detective Policing and the State in Nineteenth-Century England: The Detective Department of the London Metropolitan Police." PhD thesis, University of Western Ontario, 2016.

Higgins, Simon. "How Was Haldane Able to Transform the Army? A Historical Assessment Using a Contemporary Change Management Model." PhD thesis, University of Birmingham, 2011.

McKee, C. T. "British Perceptions of Tsar Nicholas II and Empress Alexandra Fedorovna, 1894–1918." PhD thesis, University College London, 2014.

Peck, N. "Drawing Back the Curtain: A Post-Leveson Examination of Celebrity, Privacy, and Press Intrusion." PhD thesis, University of London, 2017.

TELEVISION PROGRAMS

D-Day: The King Who Fooled Hitler. C4 documentary, 2019.

Die Royals und die Nazis. ZDF Germany documentary, 2018.

Spying on the Royals: Part One. C4 documentary, 2017.

Spying on the Royals: Part Two. C4 documentary, 2017.

The Queen and the Coup. C4 documentary, 2020.

The Victorian War on Terror. BBC History Extra, 2013.

Index

About the Authors

Richard J. Aldrich is an award-winning spy writer, historian, and presenter of television documentaries. He is a Fellow of the Royal Historical Society, professor of international security at the University of Warwick, and the author of many books, including *GCHQ: Centenary Edition* (2019); and *The Black Door: Spies, Secret Intelligence and British Prime Ministers* (2016), with Rory Cormac. His writings have appeared in *International Affairs, Foreign Affairs*, and *Foreign Policy.*

Rory Cormac is a professor of international relations at the University of Nottingham, specializing in secret intelligence and covert operations. He is a Fellow of the Royal Historical Society; frequently appears on television, podcasts, and the radio; and is the author of many books. His most recent is *How to Stage a Coup and Ten Other Lessons from the World of Secret Statecraft* (2022).